KITCHEN

THE AUSTRALIAN
Women's Weekly

KITCHEN

FAVOURITE RECIPES AND ADVICE FROM THE AWW TEST KITCHEN

Contents

SPECIAL FEATURES

Kitchen is a companion to *Cook*, another fabulous cookbook with around 1000 recipes. The recipes, of course, have all been triple-tested by the staff (past and present) of the famous Australian Women's Weekly Test Kitchen.

Today's home-kitchens seem to fall broadly into two categories, they are either full-on working kitchens that have become the hub of the home, or they're minimalist, wonderful-looking kitchens that are rarely used. This book is all about the hub-of-the-home-kitchen, it's about preparing and cooking good food for all the right reasons – health, pleasure, sharing, satisfaction – all the things important to keep body, soul, family and friends together. It really doesn't matter what your kitchen looks like, as long as it's functional and a happy place to be. As well, a bit of order and cleanliness will make it pleasant and easy to work in.

We decided to split this book into chapters based on kitchen utensils, this gave us the opportunity to share lots of help and information on equipping your kitchen. We're not suggesting you rush out and buy everything we've talked about, instead, just accumulate things as the need arises. Buy carefully, it's not always the most expensive items that are the best. Within the chapters, like *Cook*, you'll find illustrated information about all types of things, ranging from what types of knives to buy through to how to deal with a lobster.

We hope you use this book over and over again, and learn how to get the best out of your kitchen.

Pamela Clark

Pamela Clark
Director,
The Australian Women's Weekly Test Kitchen

The Ideal Kitchen

This book is a guide to stocking your kitchen with the right utensils and tools. We take you through all the basic and useful items you might consider for your kitchen, each with its own chapter telling you what to look for when buying, how to care for and store it, and how to use it to its fullest advantage. You may not need all these items – our information will help you decide – but they add up to the basis of a well-rounded *batterie de cuisine* (kitchen utensils), a collection that would enable you to make almost any recipe.

Seasoned cooks will already have a number of these utensils; beginners may be able to afford only a few to start with. In either case, we suggest that you – we urge you to – add more pieces slowly. The stores are full of temptations, but train your eye for quality by looking in the stores that supply professionals and use the information in this book to help you choose.

THE KITCHEN

Most of us have an idea of the perfect kitchen – the one we'd love to have or, for some lucky ones, the one we've got.

The ideal kitchen is, of course, different from one cook to another. You may be a cooking devotee who wants a near-professional kitchen, a keen entertainer who needs one that can cope with food for a crowd, a family cook who wants to cook well but simply, a beginner with no more than a dream of something charming, or a "survival" cook who just wants efficiency to get you in and out of the kitchen fast.

You may cook solo or with a partner or other family members. You may be planning your first kitchen on a tight budget, or the dream kitchen you've wanted for years, or just a few modest improvements. You may not be planning anything, but could do with ideas about how to use your present kitchen better. For each of you, we hope, there is something useful in this chapter.

PLANNING A KITCHEN

Whether you're going to use a specialist kitchen planner or not, go and look at as many different kitchen showrooms and specialist storage shops as possible to get ideas. Make notes of anything you'd like to incorporate in your new kitchen, and of things that annoy you in the kitchen you have now, and those things you particularly like in it and want to have again.

Make notes of what you want your kitchen to be: an entertaining centre, a room for the family to eat in, an efficient busy place or a calm, cosy one, a home office, a space for children's homework, a place where you can work without interference yet not be cut off from everyone else. Use these notes to help you plan if you're doing it yourself, or pass them to your professional kitchen planner, draughtsman or builder.

THE FLOOR PLAN

Certain basics are the foundation of kitchen planning.

The ideal floor plan always starts with the "work triangle" – stove, sink and refrigerator arranged at the corners of an imaginary triangle, so that you don't have to walk past one to get to another. This set-up also makes the kitchen feel comfortable to work in, even if you don't consciously realise why.

The sink is best placed at a window so there is good light for washing-up, scrubbing vegetables and so on (and, with any luck, a view to cheer the worker).

If the sink or stove can only be fitted into a corner, it is better to place it across the corner rather than flush to a wall, so that there is access from both sides instead of only one.

The stove or cooktop should be against an outside wall if possible, so that it can have a rangehood or independent exhaust fan, vented to the outside, above it.

The stove and refrigerator should both have bench space adjoining so a pot from the cooktop or oven, or food from the refrigerator, can go straight down. Ideally, the bench space adjoining the stove should be made of material that can take a very hot pan.

If possible, there should be space enough to allow someone to walk past the refrigerator, oven or dishwasher (if there is one) when their doors are fully open.

LIGHTING

Every area of the kitchen should be well lit. Strip lighting mounted under overhead cupboards is good for benchtops. For benchtops with nothing above them, a board fitted with two or three little spotlights that can be angled where they are wanted can be mounted on the wall or ceiling.

It is especially important that the stove or cooktop should be well lit as poor lighting here can be dangerous. The ideal is good light from a rangehood but failing that, a lighting board such as that just mentioned, or even a strategically placed lamp, can do the job.

BENCH HEIGHTS

The standard height for benchtops, which suits most people, is about 90cm. Whatever your height, be sure to stand at the bench you are considering, lift a few heavy things on and off it, and also mime chopping and whisking on it, to check that it's going to be comfortable for you – neither low enough to make you stoop nor high enough to make you raise your upper arms.

If children are going to be helping with food preparation, they will need a stool to stand on. The small, light, cheap, moulded-in-one-piece plastic footstools that are available at major hardware stores and furniture chain stores are safer than stools with separate legs.

RUN-OF-BENCH SPACE

Ideally, at least one bench in the kitchen should be long enough, in one continuous run, to take a row of dinner plates plus a bit more for a serving pot or pan and perhaps a carving board so that you can serve dinner smoothly and easily. Try for at least space enough to take plates for all the household – more, for when you have guests, would be even better. This serving area should be adjacent to or at least close to the cooktop and oven – walking about with hot pans and dishes is asking for an accident.

MICROWAVE OVEN

The microwave oven is best accommodated in its own open-fronted box that forms the lower part of an overhead cupboard. The interior should be at eye-level and you shouldn't have to lift dishes above shoulder-level. Locate it near the main preparation area if possible.

MORE THAN ONE COOK

If two or more people will be working in the kitchen at times, it's a good idea to plan at least two well-separated "work stations", each with adequate benchtop space. A peninsula or island bench, or a bench at the other end of the kitchen from the main preparation area, can keep two workers happy and out of each other's way. If you have the space, wide walking spaces throughout the kitchen are a great help in maintaining harmony.

OPEN-PLAN KITCHENS

Many kitchens nowadays are open-plan, designed to face onto the dining area. In this case, it's important to have an exhaust fan with the power to expel cooking fumes fast. It's a good idea, too, to have a barrier (in kitchen showrooms, this is called a "rise"), 30cm or so high, along the counter adjoining the dining room so that diners don't have to look at any preparation mess or dirty pots and plates as they pile up. A shelf on top of the barrier can hold mats, napkins, flowers, a fruit bowl or attractive kitchenware, and can act as a serving counter on which you can put the salad bowl or bread-basket to go on to the table, or coffee cups ready for when the table is cleared.

RUBBISH DISPOSAL

How we dispose of our kitchen waste has become an important environmental issue. It is basic kitchen practice now to have multiple waste bins and to sort rubbish into food scraps, non-recyclables such as heavily soiled and plastic wrappings, and recyclables such as paper, glass and plastic. Allow space for these on the floor, standing in cupboards or mounted inside cupboard doors. If it's more convenient, install a pull-out rail – the kind usually used for hanging tea-towels – in a cupboard and hang several bags on it for the different kinds of waste.

EQUIPMENT

Every utensil and tool in your kitchen should be an excellent example of its kind, ready to do its job properly, thousands of times over. That often means serious expense – a good

saucepan or frying pan – but not always. A cheap, light wok from Chinatown is perfectly designed for its purpose and will actually do a better job than most fancier and expensive ones, while cheap chain-store potato peelers, lemon squeezers, measuring spoons and other such small essentials will do exactly the same job as their designer equivalent.

Good equipment lasts a lifetime, satisfies every time it's used, and helps you cook better. Second-rate equipment is not only a waste of money because it doesn't last, but frustrating to work with because it won't perform the way it should.

Be suspicious of sets of equipment such as saucepans: many look pretty but are of mediocre quality, and even if they're of good quality, there will probably be at least one in the set that you seldom use because it's not quite what you need.

STORAGE

EQUIPMENT STORAGE

Having invested in your *batterie de cuisine*, you want to keep it, orderly and protected, where you can get to the pieces you want quickly and easily.

If you are in the happy position of planning a new kitchen or renovating an existing one, you will be able to take advantage of the many new storage ideas that kitchen design specialists can show you – ideas that make cluttered cupboards and drawers a thing of the past. If you have an older kitchen, you can still improve things with simple, low-cost, do-it-yourself ideas and, when budget permits, by replacing old fittings with newer and better ideas for the same space.

The do-it-yourself approach could include:
- Taking advantage of the space immediately under overhead cupboards. Without encroaching on the working space of the benchtop, the underside of the cupboards could take a row of large hooks to hang cups, mugs and jugs, a light metal rail with metal pot hooks to hang larger utensils, a plate rack for small plates or a frame for wine glasses.
- Buying inexpensive plastic lazy Susans (a revolving tray or shelf) in sizes to fit the shelves of corner cupboards so that a twirl will bring any item to the front.
- Attaching narrow wire racks inside cupboard doors to hold paper towels, plastic wrap, foil, garbage bags and so on.
- Getting pots and pans out of cluttered cupboards and drawers by hanging them on hooks, as discussed in Pots and Pans on page 14.
- Clipping a PVC-coated wire grid to a wall above a benchtop to enable many utensils to be hung from hooks at varying heights (the grid is clipped, not attached, to the wall so that it can be removed for cleaning).

Replacing old storage arrangements with new ones in the same space could include:
- Replacing deep drawers and cupboards with glide-out shelves or roll-out units, as discussed under Pots and Pans and Appliances, both on page 14.
- Replacing ordinary shelves in hard-to-access cupboards with swing-out shelves.
- Installing pull-out wire baskets in the space under the sink to hold the cleaning items that usually live in a clutter, plus back-up supplies of dishcloths, rubber gloves etc.
- Having kickboards taken out and the space behind them utilised by fitting very shallow drawers to hold oven trays and platters, or items you seldom use.

POTS AND PANS You get out pots and pans every day, yet they're among the most difficult things to store conveniently because of their weight and awkward shapes. Many older kitchens have a couple of deep drawers or cupboards for pots and pans, which have the virtue of storing them out of sight. However, the drawback is that they have to be stacked and the lids piled up to get them all in, and this scratches the pans; it also means that any but the top or front pans are a pain to get out.

A more convenient arrangement, and a much better one for the pans, is to store pots and pans in a single layer on sturdy, shallow, glide-out shelves fitted with strong stoppers so they won't tilt, and with retaining strips to stop the contents from falling off. You can skimp on the space needed between the shelves by storing lids separately on racks fitted inside cupboard doors.

Or, it may suit you better to go for pull-out units on rollers, with narrow fronts and shelves at right angles to the front.

Another approach is to forget about trying to keep everything out of sight and display your pots and pans, either ranged along open shelves, hung on wall-mounted hooks, hung from hooks around a circular or rectangular metal rack suspended from the ceiling, or hung from hooks on a straight rail that goes from wall to wall near, but not above, the cooktop. Separate metal pot hooks are better than fixed hooks for these rails so you can adjust their positions.

Bear in mind that utensils on display get dirty if they're not used often; a practical compromise could be to put the occasionally used items away and keep the regularly used ones out.

KNIVES It is vital to store knives so they don't touch each other, so as to preserve their sharp edges. Also, store the steel close by so that it will be easy to keep your knives sharp by giving them a few strokes with the steel almost every time you use them (see Choosing & Caring for Knives, page 76 & 77). You can buy a wooden knife block with slots of various sizes and a hole for the steel, or a magnetic knife rack to mount on the wall; it may take two magnetic racks, one a little above the other, to hold heavy knives and the steel securely. If possible, store your knives within hand's reach of your main food preparation area.

PLATES, BOWLS, CUPS, SERVING DISHES ETC The ideal storage for the many items, large and small, that are used for serving food is a walk-in pantry with shallow shelves, a shallow cupboard, or open shelves, so you don't have to reach over one thing to get another. Even if there isn't room to store everything like this, relocating even some of the contents of the typical deep, cluttered cupboard can help. It's surprising where a few shelves (with retaining strips to hold things secure) can be fitted if they only have to be the width of one cup or bowl – the back of the cupboard door; the wall beneath an overhead cupboard; the side of a cupboard – there are spaces in most kitchens that could be utilised.

GLASSES AND CUTLERY Store glasses and cutlery close to where you eat, whether in the kitchen or elsewhere. Glasses should be stored in the same way as cups or bowls, and cutlery stored in specially divided drawers.

APPLIANCES Any appliances that you use from time to time, such as a deep-fryer, waffle-iron or ice-cream maker, can be stored on glide-out shelves or roll-out units, as discussed above in Pots and Pans. Appliances that you use every day, such as the toaster, electric kettle or juicer, and appliances that are too heavy to lift, such as a large stand mixer, are best kept

on the benchtop. If you prefer them out of sight, they can live in a little benchtop cupboard, preferably in a corner, with bi-fold doors or a flexible push-up shutter, like some roll-up garage doors, which disappears into the top of the cupboard when opened.

FOOD STORAGE

The golden rule of storing all food, whether in the cupboard, refrigerator or freezer, is to keep it rotating, using the longest-stored items first. It can be hard to keep this rule, but if your supplies are stored in an organised way where you can see what you have, you will at least be able to avoid the sad and wasteful experience of "losing" items and rediscovering them long after they were fit to consume.

PERISHABLE FOODS Seafood, all meats including chicken, dairy products, eggs, cooked food, anything you bought from the chilled cabinet, and most fruits and vegetables, should be stored in the refrigerator. The major exceptions are onions, garlic, tomatoes and potatoes. Potatoes can develop an unwanted sweet taste if they are refrigerated, so they should be stored in a cool, dry, dark place with good ventilation.

Have a good supply of inexpensive, re-usable, see-through plastic storage containers with covers (available at the supermarket) for storing perishable foods in the refrigerator or freezer. Get a variety of sizes but stick to square or rectangular shapes as these fit better on the shelves and stack better, with much less wasted space than bowls or round containers. However, don't overcrowd the fridge – the chilled air must be able to circulate to keep everything at the right, safe temperature. Also, to maintain the correct temperature, slightly cool hot food before putting it into the refrigerator. Most modern refrigerators can deal with moderately hot foods quite quickly.

For storing in the freezer, avoid having too many of your storage containers out of action for too long by lining a container or bowl with a freezer bag of appropriate size, allowing for some overhang; fill the food into the bag, fold the top over and put the container with the bag into the freezer until the food is frozen. Once frozen, remove the bag and secure it closed, then use a permanent marker to mark it with the date and contents and return it to the freezer. You can secure bags closed with the plastic or wire strips that come in the packaging, or use specially made zip lock bags.

If you decide to freeze something directly in a container, write the date and contents on one end of a small piece of paper and clamp the other end between the box and the lid when you put the lid on.

NON-PERISHABLE FOODS The standard deep cupboards in many kitchens will accommodate a lot of your food supplies, but items at the back are hard to find and it is difficult to keep the cupboard tidy.

A better way to store non-perishable foods is on fairly narrow shelves so that you can see everything at a glance, and you don't have to struggle to get out the back ones. In a new kitchen, these may be fitted into a walk-in pantry; or a wide, shallow cupboard; or a cupboard with shelves on the inside of the door and shelves inside the cupboard that are narrower than usual to allow space for the door shelves when the door is closed.

Other good ideas are shallow glide-out shelves and roll-out units with shelves at right-angles to a narrow front. These are discussed in the preceding section in relation to storing pots and pans, but they would work just as well for food.

In an existing kitchen you may be able to reduce clutter by fitting narrow open shelves to take at least some of your supplies. Other ideas, mentioned earlier and helpful for keeping your food supplies organised and accessible, are inexpensive plastic lazy Susans placed on the shelves of corner cupboards so that you can easily bring any item to the front, swing-out shelves for hard-to-access cupboards, and narrow wire shelves, to hold small store-cupboard items, fitted inside every cupboard door where they can be accommodated. It may also be possible to find room in or adjacent to the kitchen for stand-alone fitments such as a set of glide-out wire baskets.

However you store your non-perishable food supplies, try to place the items you use most often at approximately waist- or chest-level so that you can reach them effortlessly.

Although some non-perishable foods can be stored in their original packaging – cans, of course, and items sturdily packaged in heavy plastic or other impermeable material – this is not a good idea for grains such as rice or barley, or for grain-based foods such as flours, breakfast cereals, polenta, rolled oats and couscous, unless you are using them regularly and fairly quickly. Moths love to invade cupboards, find their way inside paper and cardboard packaging and lay eggs, which will turn into grubs. Cakes and confectionery are also susceptible. As a general rule, keep all food in plastic, metal or glass containers with tight-fitting lids. Biscuits should go into screw-top glass jars or into tins with tight-fitting lids to keep them crisp: plastic isn't quite airtight enough. You can buy plastic containers with snap-on lids cheaply at the supermarket and glass storage jars at kitchen shops, and you can accumulate screw-top jars for free by recycling pickle, peanut butter and mayonnaise jars.

THE CLEAN KITCHEN

It might sound obsessive, but keeping your kitchen orderly by putting things away and wiping up spills as you go is a lot more pleasant than having to face a scene of grot at the end of operations. Once you decide to try it, it soon becomes automatic.

Some useful strategies for keeping the kitchen clean without too much effort are:

- Even when you're busiest, at least fill dirty pots and pans with warm water as soon as they're empty, and stand spoons, spatulas etc., in the water to stop bits of food from drying on. If you can add a drop of detergent and give them a swish round and a rinse at any point, you've got the worst of the cleanup over.
- Keep cloths or sponges of one colour for wiping the floor and a different colour for wiping the stove, benchtops etc. Wash cloths and sponges often, adding them to a washing-machine load of towels with a little laundry disinfectant and dry in the sun if possible. Alternatively, you can add sponges to the load in the dishwasher, or even put them (damp) into the microwave oven for a quick blast to sterilise them.
- The nifty mopping devices with flat heads, onto which you secure a dry or damp cleaning cloth, do an effective, easy job of "sweeping" or damp-mopping the floor. They are available from large hardware stores – ask for dusting mops.
- No one else can tell you how often you need to carry out routine cleaning like wiping down the exteriors of cupboards and appliances – it depends on how your kitchen is used – but when they need it, a wipe with a cloth wrung out in warm water with a drop of detergent and a few drops of methylated spirits, followed by a clean damp cloth and then a dry one, will work as well as most expensive commercial products.

- For glass and chrome, methylated spirits followed by a rub with a clean, soft cloth will do the job.
- Keep all the instruction manuals for your appliances together in a strong, roomy plastic envelope (have a look at your local newsagent or stationer) on the shelf where you keep your cookbooks. Always check the manual before using any commercial product on your appliance, and also note the manufacturer's advice on routine maintenance such as how, and how often, to clean the filter of the rangehood.

Keep those three great, cheap cleaners and deodorisers – common salt, white vinegar and bicarbonate of soda (also known as sodium bicarbonate, carb soda or bicarb) – always at hand for the following jobs:

- Keep an open container of bicarbonate of soda in the refrigerator and another in the freezer to neutralise any odours. Replace every few months.
- Get rid of any "off" odour in the dishwasher by filling the detergent container with vinegar and running the machine through a short cycle.
- Deodorise a saucepan in which you have cooked curry, fish or anything garlicky by washing, then filling it with warm water with ¼ to ½ cup vinegar added and standing it for an hour or so.
- Rinse a wooden chopping board that you have used for onion, garlic, meat, chicken or fish with cold water, scrub with a handful of common salt to deodorise it and kill bacteria (this will deodorise your hands as well) and rinse again. If the board is really smelly, rinse then drizzle with vinegar, scrub with salt and stand for an hour or so before rinsing. Nylon chopping boards can also go into the dishwasher.
- Clean and deodorise a knife by rinsing, then rubbing with a wet cork dipped in salt, or putting a layer of salt on a damp cloth and drawing the knife firmly across it several times on both sides. Rinse and dry the knife immediately.
- Clean and deodorise the refrigerator every few months by wiping it out with a solution of 2 tablespoons bicarbonate of soda in a litre of water, then wiping with a clean damp cloth and drying with a tea-towel or disposable cloths. If the idea of emptying the whole fridge to do this is too daunting, do a couple of shelves at a time and wipe the interior at their level. Wipe shelves very well or, if necessary, take them out and wash them in the sink (glass ones in warm water only as hot water can crack them). Empty and wash up the crispers, and wipe under and around them with the bicarbonate of soda solution.
- If your drains seem a bit smelly, pour down ½ cup bicarbonate of soda, then ½ cup white vinegar, put the plug in and leave 5 minutes, then take out the plug and pour in a kettleful of boiling water.
- Keep an old toothbrush near the bicarbonate of soda and, if you need to clean an awkward spot, such as the bit behind a tap, sprinkle a little bicarbonate of soda on the damp brush and use it to get into the narrow space. Rinse with water and dry with a disposable cloth.

THE FRYING PAN

The Frying Pan

A medium-sized frying pan (20 to 22cm across the base) is the most useful. If you need greater capacity, a second medium pan provides more versatility and easier handling than having just one very large pan. The first thing to look for in a frying pan is not so much how it looks, but how it feels in your hand.

WEIGHT AND BASE

A good frying pan looks solid and feels heavy. Check the base is cast (shaped in a mould in one piece) and ground flat so that it never warps. It must be thick so that it will take up and hold the heat.

MATERIAL

In order to perform well, a pan must be made of material that is a good conductor – that is, it transmits heat rapidly and evenly to the whole cooking surface, and responds quickly when the heat is turned up or down.

A second consideration is whether the material will cause chemical reactions in foods, producing "off" flavours and odours, or discolouration.

COPPER is the best conductor of all and is beautiful, but its disadvantages – high cost and the need for constant cleaning – have caused it to lose favour. Copper readily stains, pits and develops a greenish coating that can be poisonous. To be safe, a copper pan must be lined with a non-reactive metal, usually tin.

ALUMINIUM is an excellent conductor but it must be thick. Its disadvantage is that it reacts with many foods, causing "off" flavours in fruit, tomatoes and spinach, intensifying the sulphurous odour of cabbage and broccoli, and giving pale sauces a greyish tinge.

STAINLESS STEEL is non-reactive but is a poor conductor. Manufacturers often bond a layer of aluminium or copper into or underneath the base in order to overcome this problem. Ask questions, however, about the thickness of the layer. Copper, being very expensive, is often applied only as a thin wash, which looks good but is almost useless.

BARE CAST-IRON is a good conductor, but can discolour pale foods and impart a metallic taste to food cooked in it for a long time. Its greatest disadvantage is its tendency to rust, stain and become pitted. This can be largely overcome by seasoning a new pan before use (see under Care, opposite) and re-seasoning as needed.

ENAMELLED CAST-IRON holds heat well and is handsome, non-reactive and easy to clean. However, it is very heavy and the porcelain enamel finish reduces conductivity, so these pans do not brown food well (though some now have a special black matt finish claimed to have improved the browning performance). Many cooks swear by them, others find them too heavy or say the non-stick performance doesn't always live up to manufacturers' claims.

TITANIUM cookware is one Danish company's attempt at the perfect cooking utensil. It is made by fusing a compound of titanium (a metallic element found in some clays) to a pressure-cast aluminium core. Non-reactive and easy to clean, titanium pans provide fast and even heat distribution and superior heat retention with no hot spots or warping. They are non-stick by virtue of their composition rather than a coating, so they brown food well and are not damaged by metal tools. Not surprisingly, they are expensive.

HANDLE AND LID

The handle should feel comfortable to your hand and well-balanced with the weight of the frying pan. A handle attached by screws can work loose and will need frequent retightening and, eventually, the thread may become too worn to tighten properly. Riveted or welded-on handles are better.

A handle that can go into the oven makes a frying pan more useful. A lid is also useful because browning is often only the first step in a recipe, to be followed by covered cooking. Both handle and lid knob should stay cool enough to pick up without a pot-holder during cooktop cooking (though remember that they will get too hot to handle in the oven).

FINISH

Many frying pans are available with a non-stick coating, but these reduce conductivity and so the pan's ability to brown well. These finishes don't usually last well in frying pans; they get worn and scratched during the speedy action that frying often calls for, and they also suffer from high heat. Manufacturers usually recommend using moderate temperatures only, but cooks know that high heat is needed to sear a steak or hamburger to a delicious brown crustiness on the outside without overcooking the interior.

In recent years, some doubt has developed about the safety of non-stick linings once they have become worn and scratched. It may be best to discard any utensil with a non-stick lining that has become badly abraded, scratched or lifted from the pan, as the material from which some linings are made can be toxic once the surface seal is broken.

CARE

Stainless steel, aluminium, enamelled cast iron and titanium frying pans need no more care than ordinary hand-washing.

Bare cast-iron needs seasoning before use and sometimes thereafter: wipe out with a paper towel dipped in a cooking oil such as peanut oil (not a polyunsaturated oil), and place in a moderate oven for 1 hour; let it cool in the oven. Repeat several times. Thereafter, wash with hot water only, no detergent. If necessary, remove any stuck-on food with a sponge or a non-metal brush and use coarse salt as an abrasive. Stand over a low heat for a few minutes to dry completely. With repeated use, the pan will gradually acquire an attractive, black, slightly slick surface, or patina, that will make it increasingly non-stick.

Caramelised chicken cutlets

PREPARATION TIME 20 MINUTES **COOKING TIME** 35 MINUTES **SERVES** 4

2 teaspoons vegetable oil

4 chicken thigh cutlets (800g), skin on

1 medium red onion (170g), sliced thinly

3 cloves garlic, sliced thinly

¼ cup (55g) brown sugar

1 tablespoon dark soy sauce

1 tablespoon fish sauce

⅓ cup coarsely chopped fresh coriander

1 Preheat oven to 200°C/180°C fan-forced.

2 Heat oil in large frying pan; cook chicken, both sides, until browned. Place chicken, in single layer, in baking dish. Roast chicken, uncovered, in oven, about 25 minutes or until cooked through.

3 Meanwhile, heat same pan; cook onion and garlic, stirring, until onion softens. Add sugar and sauces; cook, stirring, 3 minutes. Return chicken to pan with coriander; turn chicken to coat in mixture.

▢ **PER SERVING** 22.4g total fat (6.9g saturated fat); 1538kJ (368 cal); 16.3g carbohydrate; 24.8g protein; 1g fibre

A citrus-flavoured vermicelli salad marries well with the chicken cutlets: stand 250g rice vermicelli in boiling water until tender then drain. Combine the vermicelli in a large bowl with 2 segmented oranges, ½ cup loosely packed fresh mint leaves, 1 thinly sliced lebanese cucumber, 2 tablespoons lemon juice, 2 tablespoons orange marmalade and 2 teaspoons vegetable oil.

Veal with mustard and tarragon cream

PREPARATION TIME 10 MINUTES **COOKING TIME** 15 MINUTES **SERVES** 4

8 thin veal steaks (640g)

¼ cup (35g) plain flour

30g butter

2 shallots (50g), sliced thinly

1 clove garlic, crushed

½ cup (125ml) dry white wine

¼ cup (60ml) cream

2 teaspoons wholegrain mustard

2 teaspoons fresh tarragon leaves

1 Toss veal in flour; shake away excess flour.

2 Heat butter in large frying pan; cook veal, in batches, until browned on both sides. Remove from pan; cover to keep warm.

3 Add shallots and garlic to same pan; cook until soft. Add wine; bring to a boil. Add cream, mustard and tarragon; bring to a boil. Simmer, uncovered, until mixture thickens.

4 Serve veal drizzled with sauce; accompany with cooked pasta and radicchio leaves, if desired.

▢ **PER SERVING** 16.6g total fat (9.5g saturated fat); 1313kJ (314 cal); 1.2g carbohydrate; 35.1g protein; 0.3g fibre

Shallots, also called french shallots, golden shallots or eschalots, are small, elongated, brown-skinned members of the onion family; they grow in tight clusters similar to garlic. When a recipe calls for shallots, make sure not to use the often mistakenly-labelled green onion.

CARAMELISED CHICKEN CUTLETS

Moroccan chicken with pistachio couscous

PREPARATION TIME 20 MINUTES **COOKING TIME** 15 MINUTES **SERVES** 4

1 teaspoon ground cumin

1 teaspoon ground coriander

½ teaspoon sweet smoked paprika

¼ teaspoon ground turmeric

¼ teaspoon cayenne pepper

2 teaspoons finely grated lemon rind

600g chicken thigh fillets

1 medium red capsicum (200g), sliced thinly

1½ cups (300g) couscous

1⅓ cups (330ml) boiling water

⅓ cup (80ml) lemon juice

2 tablespoons olive oil

½ cup (70g) roasted pistachios, chopped coarsely

½ cup firmly packed fresh coriander leaves

1 Combine spices, rind and chicken in large bowl, rubbing spice mixture firmly onto chicken. Cook chicken, uncovered, in heated oiled large frying pan until cooked through. Remove chicken from pan; slice thickly.

2 Add capsicum to same cleaned heated pan; cook, stirring, 1 minute.

3 Meanwhile, combine couscous and the water in medium heatproof bowl. Cover, stand about 5 minutes or until liquid is absorbed, fluffing with fork occasionally. Stir in juice and oil. Add nuts and coriander; toss gently to combine.

4 Serve couscous topped with chicken and capsicum.

☐ **PER SERVING** 29.3g total fat (5.7g saturated fat); 2876kJ (688 cal); 62.4g carbohydrate; 41.9g protein; 3.2g fibre

---

Scotch fillet with pepper thyme sauce

PREPARATION TIME 10 MINUTES **COOKING TIME** 15 MINUTES **SERVES** 4

1 tablespoon olive oil

4 x 200g scotch fillet steaks

1 trimmed celery stalk (100g), chopped finely

1 medium brown onion (150g), chopped finely

½ cup (125ml) dry white wine

300ml cream

1 tablespoon mixed peppercorns, crushed

1 tablespoon coarsely chopped fresh thyme

1 Heat half of the oil in large frying pan; cook beef until cooked as desired. Remove from pan; cover to keep warm.

2 Heat remaining oil in same pan; cook celery and onion, stirring, until vegetables soften. Add wine; stir until liquid is reduced by half. Add cream and peppercorns; bring to a boil. Reduce heat, simmer, uncovered, stirring occasionally, about 5 minutes or until sauce thickens slightly. Remove from heat; stir in thyme.

3 Serve beef drizzled with sauce.

☐ **PER SERVING** 46.7g total fat (26.3g saturated fat); 2658kJ (636 cal); 5g carbohydrate; 44.2g protein; 1.4g fibre

Chicken and broad bean fricassee

PREPARATION TIME 25 MINUTES **COOKING TIME** 35 MINUTES **SERVES** 4

4 x 200g chicken breast fillets, halved

¼ cup (35g) plain flour

½ teaspoon salt

½ teaspoon cracked black pepper

2 teaspoons olive oil

20g butter

400g baby new potatoes, sliced thinly

200g baby carrots

2 cups (500ml) chicken stock

2 cups (300g) frozen broad beans, peeled

¼ cup (60ml) crème fraîche or sour cream

2 teaspoons fresh tarragon leaves

1 Toss chicken in combined flour, salt and pepper; shake away excess flour.

2 Heat oil and butter in large, deep frying pan; cook chicken until well browned all over and almost cooked through. Remove from pan.

3 Add potatoes and carrots to same pan; cook, stirring, 1 minute. Stir in stock, bring to a boil; simmer, covered, about 5 minutes or until vegetables are almost tender.

4 Return chicken to pan; simmer, covered, about 5 minutes or until cooked through. Add beans and crème fraîche; stir until heated through. Serve topped with tarragon.

PER SERVING 24.5g total fat (10.7g saturated fat); 2358kJ (564 cal); 28.8g carbohydrate; 53.6g protein; 6.8g fibre

For quick and easy chicken pies, divide the fricassee among small ovenproof dishes and top each with a disc of puff pastry. Bake in a moderate oven for about 15 minutes or until filling is warm and pastry is golden brown. If you don't have broad beans, frozen or fresh peas work just as well.

Crab cakes

PREPARATION TIME 30 MINUTES **COOKING TIME** 15 MINUTES **SERVES** 4

2 green onions, chopped finely

1 trimmed celery stalk (100g), chopped finely

500g crab meat

2 egg whites, beaten lightly

1 tablespoon finely chopped fresh dill

1 tablespoon worcestershire sauce

1 cup (70g) stale breadcrumbs

SOY AND HONEY SAUCE

½ cup (125ml) light soy sauce

2 tablespoons honey

1 Cook onion and celery in large heated oiled frying pan until onion is soft.

2 Combine onion mixture with remaining ingredients in large bowl. Using hands, shape mixture into 12 cakes.

3 Cook cakes, in batches, in same pan until browned both sides and cooked through.

4 Meanwhile, make soy and honey sauce.

5 Serve crab cakes with sauce and, if desired, a mixed green salad.

SOY AND HONEY SAUCE Combine ingredients in small bowl.

PER SERVING 1.4g total fat (0.2g saturated fat); 886kJ (212 cal); 27.3g carbohydrate; 21.2g protein; 1.3g fibre

Cocktail food needn't be a challenge, crab cakes are always a hit and best of all, they're a cinch to make. Instead of making 12 cakes as this recipe suggests, shape the mixture into tiny patties, say 36, and pan fry just before serving. You can even prepare the patties the morning of the party to save yourself from last-minute stress.

Not just a quick and
delicious main at dinner-
time, left-over schnitzel
makes a great lunchbox
meal, too. Cut open a
crusty bread roll, spread
liberally with mayonnaise,
fill with a handful of baby
rocket leaves and sliced
tomato then add some
strips of cold schnitzel.
Schnitzel is also a perfect
picnic partner; just cut into
bite-sized pieces and serve
with mayo mixed with finely
grated lemon rind.

Crumbed chicken schnitzel with mixed bean salad

PREPARATION TIME 25 MINUTES **COOKING TIME** 20 MINUTES **SERVES** 4

300g green beans

200g yellow beans

4 medium tomatoes (600g), seeded, sliced thickly

2 tablespoons olive oil

1 tablespoon red wine vinegar

2 teaspoons wholegrain mustard

2 tablespoons coarsely chopped fresh tarragon

2 tablespoons coarsely chopped fresh chervil

2 teaspoons drained green peppercorns, crushed

4 x 200g chicken breast fillets

¼ cup (35g) plain flour

2 eggs

1 tablespoon milk

2 teaspoons finely grated lemon rind

½ cup (50g) packaged breadcrumbs

½ cup (85g) polenta

vegetable oil, for shallow-frying

1 Boil, steam or microwave beans until tender. Rinse under cold water; drain. Place beans in large bowl with tomato, olive oil, vinegar, mustard, herbs and peppercorns; toss gently to combine. Cover; refrigerate until required.

2 Using meat mallet, gently pound chicken, one piece at a time, between sheets of plastic wrap until 1cm thick.

3 Whisk flour, egg, milk and rind together in shallow bowl; combine breadcrumbs and polenta in a second shallow bowl. Coat chicken pieces, first in egg mixture then in breadcrumb mixture.

4 Heat vegetable oil in large frying pan; shallow-fry chicken, in batches, until browned and cooked through. Drain on absorbent paper.

5 Serve schnitzel, sliced, with bean salad.

▭ **PER SERVING** 35.4g total fat (5.8g saturated fat); 2897kJ (693 cal); 33.5g carbohydrate; 57.1g protein; 5.8g fibre

---

Horseradish is a vegetable
having edible green leaves
but mainly grown for its
long, pungent white root.
It's most commonly
purchased in bottles at the
supermarket in two forms:
prepared horseradish and
horseradish cream. These
cannot be substituted one
for the other in cooking but
both can be used as table
condiments. Horseradish
cream is a commercially
prepared creamy paste
consisting of grated
horseradish, vinegar, oil
and sugar, while prepared
horseradish is the
preserved grated root.

Creamy horseradish chicken with garlic sauteed spinach

PREPARATION TIME 10 MINUTES **COOKING TIME** 20 MINUTES **SERVES** 4

1 tablespoon olive oil

4 x 200g chicken breast fillets

1 green onion, sliced thinly

2 tablespoons dry white wine

⅔ cup (160ml) cream

2 tablespoons prepared horseradish

2 teaspoons lemon juice

½ teaspoon dijon mustard

1 teaspoon finely chopped fresh dill

20g butter

2 cloves garlic, crushed

600g trimmed spinach, chopped coarsely

1 Heat half of the oil in large frying pan; cook chicken until cooked through. Remove from pan; cover to keep warm.

2 Heat remaining oil in same heated pan; cook onion, stirring, until soft. Add wine; bring to a boil. Reduce heat, simmer, uncovered, until liquid is reduced by half. Add cream; bring to a boil. Reduce heat, simmer, uncovered, about 2 minutes or until sauce thickens slightly. Add horseradish, juice, mustard and dill; stir over heat until heated through.

3 Meanwhile, melt butter in large saucepan; cook garlic, stirring, 2 minutes. Add spinach; cook over low heat, covered, about 2 minutes or until wilted.

4 Serve chicken with spinach drizzled with sauce.

▭ **PER SERVING** 38.6g total fat (18.8g saturated fat); 2366kJ (566 cal); 4g carbohydrate; 47.6g protein; 4.6g fibre

---

Cashew and parsley-crumbed chicken with rocket salad

PREPARATION TIME 20 MINUTES **COOKING TIME** 20 MINUTES **SERVES** 4

¾ cup (115g) roasted unsalted cashews

¾ cup finely chopped fresh flat-leaf parsley

1 cup (70g) stale breadcrumbs

2 eggs

4 x 200g chicken breast fillets

⅓ cup (50g) plain flour

2 tablespoons olive oil

250g rocket leaves, trimmed

250g yellow grape tomatoes, halved

1 medium red capsicum (200g), sliced thinly

MUSTARD VINAIGRETTE

1½ tablespoons olive oil

1 clove garlic, crushed

1 tablespoon white wine vinegar

2 teaspoons wholegrain mustard

If you like, substitute macadamias for the cashews in this recipe. This protein-rich nut has a delicate flavour to its crunchy texture, and tastes great with fresh herbs such as parsley. If you have macadamia oil handy, go ahead and use it in the salad dressing, instead of the olive oil, for a real flavour sensation.

1 Preheat oven to 180°C/160°C fan-forced.

2 Blend or process nuts until they resemble a coarse meal. Place nuts in medium shallow bowl with parsley and breadcrumbs; stir to combine. Beat eggs lightly in another medium shallow bowl.

3 Halve chicken pieces diagonally; slice through each piece horizontally. Coat pieces in flour; shake away excess. Dip chicken in egg then in breadcrumb mixture.

4 Heat oil in large frying pan; cook chicken, in batches, until browned both sides. Place chicken on oiled oven tray; cook in oven, uncovered, about 10 minutes or until cooked through.

5 Meanwhile, make mustard vinaigrette.

6 Place rocket, tomato and capsicum in large bowl with vinaigrette; toss gently to combine.

7 Serve chicken with rocket salad.

MUSTARD VINAIGRETTE Place ingredients in screw-top jar; shake well.

▭ **PER SERVING** 45.1g total fat (9g saturated fat); 3206kJ (767 cal); 30.1g carbohydrate; 57.7g protein; 6.1g fibre

Eggs ranchero-style

PREPARATION TIME 10 MINUTES **COOKING TIME** 30 MINUTES **SERVES** 4

1 small red onion (100g), chopped finely

4 medium tomatoes (600g), chopped coarsely

2 tablespoons water

1 tablespoon balsamic vinegar

1 medium red capsicum (200g), chopped finely

4 eggs

4 corn tortillas

1 Cook onion in oiled large frying pan, stirring, until softened. Add tomato, the water and vinegar; bring to a boil. Reduce heat, simmer, uncovered, 15 minutes, stirring occasionally. Add capsicum; cook, uncovered, 5 minutes.

2 Using large shallow mixing spoon, press four shallow depressions into tomato mixture. Working quickly, break eggs, one at a time, into cup, sliding each egg into one of the hollows in tomato mixture. Cover pan; cook over low heat, about 5 minutes or until eggs are just set.

3 Divide warmed tortillas among plates. Use egg slide to carefully lift egg and tomato mixture onto each tortilla.

☐ **PER SERVING** 6g total fat (1.7g saturated fat); 619kJ (148 cal); 13.1g carbohydrate; 10.1g protein; 3.4g fibre

---

Spanish tortilla

PREPARATION TIME 15 MINUTES **COOKING TIME** 30 MINUTES **SERVES** 4

800g potatoes, peeled, sliced thinly

1 tablespoon olive oil

1 large brown onion (200g), sliced thinly

200g chorizo sausage, sliced thinly

6 eggs

300ml cream

4 green onions, sliced thickly

¼ cup (25g) coarsely grated mozzarella cheese

¼ cup (30g) coarsely grated cheddar cheese

1 Boil, steam or microwave potato until just tender; drain.

2 Meanwhile, heat oil in medium frying pan; cook brown onion, stirring, until softened. Add chorizo; cook, stirring, until crisp. Drain chorizo mixture on absorbent paper.

3 Whisk eggs in large bowl with cream, green onion and cheeses; stir in potato and chorizo mixture.

4 Pour mixture into same heated oiled pan; cook, covered, over low heat 10 minutes or until tortilla is just set. Carefully invert tortilla onto plate, then slide back into pan; cook, uncovered, about 5 minutes or until cooked through.

☐ **PER SERVING** 64.1g total fat (32.5g saturated fat); 3390kJ (811 cal); 29.1g carbohydrate; 29.5g protein; 3.8g fibre

1 EGGS RANCHERO-STYLE **2** SPANISH TORTILLA
3 VEGETARIAN PAELLA [P 32] **4** ROSTI [P 32]

1

3 4

Vegetarian paella

PREPARATION TIME 25 MINUTES **COOKING TIME** 40 MINUTES **SERVES** 4

2 cups (500ml) vegetable stock

3 cups (750ml) water

1 tablespoon olive oil

1 medium red onion (170g), chopped finely

2 cloves garlic, crushed

2 medium tomatoes (300g), seeded, chopped finely

1 medium red capsicum (200g), chopped finely

¼ teaspoon ground turmeric

2 teaspoons smoked sweet paprika

1¾ cups (350g) arborio rice

1 cup (120g) frozen peas

100g frozen baby beans

¼ cup (40g) sliced black olives

⅓ cup finely chopped fresh flat-leaf parsley

1 Bring stock and the water to a boil in medium saucepan. Remove from heat.

2 Heat oil in large frying pan; cook onion, garlic, tomato, capsicum, turmeric and paprika, stirring, until vegetables soften. Add rice; stir to coat in spice mixture. Stir in stock mixture; bring to a boil. Reduce heat, simmer, uncovered, 20 minutes or until rice is almost tender.

3 Sprinkle peas and beans evenly over surface of paella; simmer, covered, 5 minutes or until rice is tender. Add olives and parsley; stand, covered, 5 minutes.

☐ **PER SERVING** 6g total fat (1g saturated fat); 1823kJ (437 cal); 80.3g carbohydrate; 11.6g protein; 5.7g fibre

Transport yourself to another continent by trying this recipe; pronounced pie-ay-ya and traditionally cooked in a caldero (paella pan), you can recreate this Spanish specialty in your own kitchen simply using a frying pan.

Rösti

PREPARATION TIME 5 MINUTES **COOKING TIME** 20 MINUTES **MAKES** 8

1kg potatoes, peeled

1 teaspoon salt

80g unsalted butter

2 tablespoons vegetable oil

1 Grate potatoes coarsely into large bowl; stir in salt, squeeze excess moisture from potatoes. Divide potato mixture into eight portions.

2 Heat 10g of the butter and 1 teaspoon of the oil in medium frying pan; spread one portion of the potato mixture over base of pan, flatten with spatula to form a firm pancake. Cook, uncovered, over medium heat, until golden brown on underside; shake pan to loosen rösti, then invert onto large plate. Gently slide rösti back into pan; cook, uncovered, until other side is golden brown and potato centre is tender. Drain on absorbent paper; cover to keep warm.

3 Repeat with the same amounts of remaining butter, oil and potato mixture.

☐ **PER ROSTI** 13g total fat (6.1g saturated fat); 777kJ (186 cal); 14g carbohydrate; 2.6g protein; 1.7g fibre

Rösti, the classic Swiss potato cakes, are best made from a starchy potato, such as spunta or russet burbank, which is grated raw, then immediately cooked fairly slowly in butter. Perfect rösti have a thick crunchy crust and are moist and buttery on the inside.

To avoid discolouring, grate the potato just before you are ready to cook the rösti.

Scrambled eggs with chorizo

PREPARATION TIME 5 MINUTES **COOKING TIME** 10 MINUTES **SERVES** 4

250g chorizo sausage, sliced thickly

8 eggs

¾ cup (180ml) cream

2 tablespoons coarsely chopped fresh chives

10g butter

1 Cook chorizo, in batches, in heated oiled medium frying pan until browned both sides; cover to keep warm.

2 Lightly whisk eggs in medium bowl; whisk in cream and half of the chives.

3 Melt butter in same cleaned pan over low heat; cook egg mixture, stirring gently but constantly, until egg mixture just begins to set.

4 Serve scrambled eggs, sprinkled with remaining chives, and chorizo on toast.

PER SERVING 50.8g total fat (24.2g saturated fat); 2378kJ (569 cal); 3.3g carbohydrate; 26.3g protein; 0.3g fibre

Creamy and decadent, scrambled eggs made with cream and chorizo is a treat that's a match made in heaven for Sunday brunch.

To achieve scrambled egg perfection, it's important that you cook your eggs over a low heat, stirring gently and constantly; the slower the egg mixture is cooked, the creamier the outcome.

Pumpkin, ricotta and parmesan frittata

PREPARATION TIME 10 MINUTES **COOKING TIME** 25 MINUTES **SERVES** 4

1 tablespoon olive oil

600g butternut pumpkin, peeled, cut into small cubes

1 medium red onion (170g), cut into thin wedges

1 clove garlic, crushed

6 eggs

2 tablespoons milk

¼ cup finely chopped fresh chives

200g ricotta cheese

¾ cup (60g) finely grated parmesan cheese

1 Heat oil in heavy-based frying pan (base measures 20cm, top measures 24cm); cook pumpkin and onion over medium heat, covered loosely and stirring occasionally, about 15 minutes or until tender. Add garlic; cook until fragrant.

2 Preheat grill.

3 Meanwhile, beat eggs in large jug or bowl, add milk and half of the chives; pour into pan over pumpkin mixture. Drop spoonfuls of ricotta over the top, sprinkle with parmesan. Cook, uncovered, over low heat, about 5 minutes or until edges are set.

4 Cover pan handle with foil; place pan under hot grill until lightly browned and just set. Sprinkle with remaining chives, serve with salad, if desired.

PER SERVING 23.9g total fat (10.4g saturated fat); 1513kJ (362 cal); 11.7g carbohydrate; 24.6g protein; 2.2g fibre

A rocket salad partners this frittata perfectly – the pepperiness of the rocket tastes great when teamed with the sweetness of the butternut pumpkin. Combine 100g baby rocket leaves, 2 tablespoons roasted pine nuts, 1 tablespoon balsamic vinegar and 1 tablespoon olive oil in a medium bowl for an easy accompaniment.

Seafood paella

PREPARATION TIME 20 MINUTES (PLUS STANDING TIME) **COOKING TIME** 1 HOUR 10 MINUTES **SERVES** 8

1kg clams

1 tablespoon coarse cooking salt

1kg uncooked medium prawns

1kg small mussels

⅓ cup (80ml) olive oil

1.5 litres (6 cups) chicken or fish stock

large pinch saffron threads

4 chicken thigh fillets (440g), chopped coarsely

400g chorizo sausage, sliced thickly ·

2 large red onions (600g), chopped finely

2 medium red capsicums (400g), chopped finely

4 cloves garlic, crushed

1 tablespoon sweet smoked paprika

4 medium tomatoes (600g), peeled, seeded, chopped finely

3 cups (600g) calasparra rice

2 cups (240g) frozen peas

¼ cup finely chopped fresh flat-leaf parsley

Calasparra rice is a short-grain rice available from Spanish delicatessens and gourmet-food stores. If you can't find calasparra, any short-grain rice can be substituted.

The traditional paella pan is shallow and wide. If you don't have a large enough pan, use two smaller frying pans; the mixture is about 4cm deep.

A good-quality marinara mix could replace the seafood.

1 Rinse clams under cold water, place in large bowl with salt, cover with cold water; stand 2 hours. Drain then rinse.

2 Shell and devein prawns, leaving tails intact. Reserve shells. Scrub mussels and remove beards.

3 Heat 1 tablespoon of the oil in large saucepan, add prawn shells, cook, stirring, until browned Add stock, bring to a boil; simmer, uncovered, 20 minutes. Strain through fine sieve into jug or bowl; add saffron to liquid.

4 Heat another 1 tablespoon of the oil in large frying pan (or a 45cm paella pan); cook chicken until browned all over. Remove from pan. Cook chorizo in same pan until browned all over; drain on absorbent paper.

5 Heat remaining oil in same frying pan; cook onion, capsicum, garlic, paprika and tomato, stirring, until soft. Add rice; stir to coat in mixture.

6 Add chicken, chorizo and stock to frying pan; stir until just combined. Do not stir again Bring mixture to a boil. Simmer, uncovered, about 15 minutes or until rice is almost tender.

7 Sprinkle peas over rice; place clams, prawns and mussels evenly over surface of paella. Cover frying pan with large sheets of foil; simmer about 5 minutes or until mussels and clams have opened (discard any that do not) and prawns are just cooked through. Sprinkle with parsley, serve immediately.

▭ **PER SERVING** 30.4g total fat (8.6g saturated fat); 3206kJ (767 cal); 72.3g carbohydrate; 51g protein; 4.7g fibre

Orange-glazed pork cutlets with spinach and pecan salad

PREPARATION TIME 20 MINUTES **COOKING TIME** 20 MINUTES **SERVES** 4

½ cup (125ml) orange juice

¼ cup (55g) white sugar

2 cloves garlic, crushed

4 pork cutlets (950g)

SPINACH AND PECAN SALAD

150g baby spinach leaves

¼ cup (35g) toasted pecans, chopped coarsely

150g snow peas, trimmed, halved

4 medium oranges (960g)

CITRUS DRESSING

2 tablespoons orange juice

1 tablespoon lemon juice

½ teaspoon dijon mustard

½ teaspoon white sugar

2 teaspoons olive oil

1 Bring juice, sugar and garlic to a boil in small saucepan. Reduce heat, simmer, without stirring, about 10 minutes or until glaze reduces to about ⅓ cup.

2 Brush cutlets both sides with glaze; cook, uncovered, in heated oiled large frying pan about 10 minutes or until cooked as desired, brushing frequently with remaining glaze. Cover to keep warm.

3 Meanwhile, make spinach and pecan salad.

4 Place ingredients for citrus dressing in screw-top jar; shake well. Pour dressing over salad; toss gently to combine. Serve cutlets with salad.

SPINACH AND PECAN SALAD Combine spinach, nuts and snow peas in large bowl. Segment peeled oranges over salad to catch juice; add segments to salad, toss gently to combine.

PER SERVING 17g total fat (3.8g saturated fat); 1935kJ (463 cal); 33.2g carbohydrate; 44.1g protein; 6.4g fibre

Mulled-wine pork and stone fruits

PREPARATION TIME 15 MINUTES **COOKING TIME** 15 MINUTES **SERVES** 4

2 cups (500ml) water

1 cup (250ml) dry white wine

½ cup (110g) sugar

2 cinnamon sticks

5 cloves

¼ cup (60ml) brandy

2 medium peaches (300g), seeded, quartered

4 medium plums (450g), seeded, quartered

2 medium nectarines (340g), seeded, quartered

4 medium apricots (200g), seeded, quartered

800g pork fillets, trimmed

1 fresh long red chilli, sliced thinly

1 long green chilli, sliced thinly

1 Combine the water, wine and sugar in large frying pan, stir constantly over heat, without boiling, until sugar dissolves; bring to a boil. Add cinnamon, cloves, brandy and fruit; reduce heat, simmer, uncovered, about 5 minutes or until fruit is just tender. Using slotted spoon, transfer fruit to large bowl; cover to keep warm.

2 Return poaching liquid to a boil; add pork. Reduce heat, simmer, covered, about 10 minutes or until pork is cooked as desired. Cool pork in liquid 10 minutes then slice thickly. Discard poaching liquid.

3 Combine chillies with fruit; divide fruit and any fruit juices among serving bowls, top with pork.

▭ **PER SERVING** 4.9g total fat (1.6g saturated fat); 2094kJ (501 cal); 46.5g carbohydrate; 46.2g protein; 5.3g fibre

---

Oyako donburi

PREPARATION TIME 30 MINUTES (PLUS STANDING TIME) **COOKING TIME** 45 MINUTES **SERVES** 4

4 dried shiitake mushrooms

2 teaspoons dashi powder

1 cup (250ml) boiling water

1 tablespoon peanut oil

3 large brown onions (600g), sliced thinly

1cm piece fresh ginger (5g), grated

1½ cups (300g) koshihikari rice

3 cups (750ml) cold water

¼ cup (60ml) japanese soy sauce

¼ cup (60ml) mirin

1 teaspoon white sugar

500g chicken breast fillets, sliced thinly

6 eggs, beaten lightly

2 green onions, sliced thinly

Donburi refers both to a particular shaped bowl as well as the rice-based main course that it is served in. Oyako translates to "parent and child" in Japanese, which, in this case, refers to the chicken and the egg. You can substitute medium-grain white rice if koshihikari is unavailable.

1 Place mushrooms in small heatproof bowl; cover with boiling water, stand 20 minutes, drain. Discard stems; chop caps coarsely. Combine dashi with the boiling water in small jug.

2 Meanwhile, heat oil in large frying pan; cook brown onion and ginger, stirring, over medium heat, about 10 minutes or until onion is slightly caramelised. Add half of the dashi mixture; reduce heat, simmer, about 5 minutes or until liquid evaporates. Transfer to medium bowl.

3 Bring rice and the cold water to a boil in large saucepan, uncovered, stirring occasionally. Reduce heat to as low as possible; cover with a tight-fitting lid, cook rice 12 minutes. (Do not remove lid or stir rice during cooking time.) Remove pan from heat; stand, covered, 10 minutes.

4 Meanwhile, bring sauce, mirin, sugar and remaining dashi mixture to a boil in same frying pan. Add chicken and mushrooms; cook, covered, about 5 minutes or until chicken is cooked through.

5 Combine egg with brown onion mixture in medium bowl, add to pan; cook, covered, over low heat, about 5 minutes or until egg just sets.

6 Divide rice among bowls; top with chicken mixture and green onion.

▭ **PER SERVING** 15.8g total fat (4.1g saturated fat); 2567kJ (614 cal); 67.6g carbohydrate; 46.2g protein; 2.7g fibre

Pepitas, dried pumpkin seeds, are available hulled or unhulled, raw or roasted. Most people here usually eat them as a snack or in a homemade muesli, but in many other countries (especially Latin American) they are ground into meal for use as a sauce thickener. Like nuts, pepitas go rancid easily, so are best kept, stored in an airtight container, in the refrigerator.

Steak with peppercorn and pepita rub

PREPARATION TIME 15 MINUTES **COOKING TIME** 15 MINUTES **SERVES** 4

1 clove garlic, quartered

1 tablespoon mixed peppercorns

½ teaspoon sea salt

1 tablespoon olive oil

⅓ cup (65g) roasted pepitas

4 x 200g scotch fillet steaks

25g butter

2 teaspoons red wine vinegar

1 tablespoon redcurrant jelly

400g can white beans, rinsed, drained

250g cherry tomatoes, halved

¼ cup fresh basil leaves

1 small radicchio (150g), trimmed

REDCURRANT DRESSING

¼ cup (60ml) olive oil

2 tablespoons red wine vinegar

1 tablespoon redcurrant jelly

1 Make redcurrant dressing.

2 Using mortar and pestle, crush garlic, peppercorns, salt, oil and 1 tablespoon of the pepitas to form a paste. Rub paste into beef.

3 Heat butter in large frying pan; cook beef until cooked as desired. Remove from pan; cover to keep warm. Add vinegar and jelly to pan; stir until combined.

4 Meanwhile, place remaining pepitas, beans, tomato, basil and radicchio in large bowl with dressing; toss gently to combine.

5 Serve beef, drizzled with pan juices, accompanied with salad.

REDCURRANT DRESSING Place ingredients in screw-top jar; shake well.

▭ **PER SERVING** 41.3g total fat (11.3g saturated fat); 2784kJ (666 cal); 20.1g carbohydrate; 50.1g protein; 7.3g fibre

It's not necessary to oil a frying pan when cooking bacon as the fat renders in the hot pan, creating its own frying medium.

Pancetta, an Italian unsmoked bacon, is pork belly cured in salt and spices then rolled into a sausage shape and dried for several weeks. It can be used in place of regular bacon for a more sophisticated mash; cook in the same way you would bacon.

Sausages with pea and bacon mash

PREPARATION TIME 5 MINUTES **COOKING TIME** 20 MINUTES **SERVES** 4

3 rindless bacon rashers (195g), chopped

1 tablespoon olive oil

2 medium brown onions (300g), sliced thinly

8 thick beef sausages (640g)

1kg potatoes, peeled, quartered

1 cup (250ml) milk, warmed

40g butter

½ cup (60g) frozen peas

1 Cook bacon in large heated frying pan until browned and crisp; remove.

2 Heat oil in same pan; cook onions and sausages until onions are soft and sausages are cooked through.

3 Meanwhile, boil, steam or microwave potatoes until soft; drain. Mash potatoes with milk and butter.

4 Boil, steam or microwave peas until just tender; drain. Add peas and bacon to mash.

5 Serve mash topped with sausages and onion.

▭ **PER SERVING** 60.8g total fat (28.9g saturated fat); 3649kJ (873 cal); 39.7g carbohydrate; 38.5g protein; 9.4g fibre

Saltimbocca

PREPARATION TIME 10 MINUTES **COOKING TIME** 25 MINUTES **SERVES** 4

8 veal steaks (680g)

4 slices prosciutto (60g), halved crossways

8 fresh sage leaves

½ cup (50g) finely grated pecorino cheese

40g butter

1 cup (250ml) dry white wine

1 tablespoon coarsely chopped fresh sage

1 Place steaks on board. Place one piece prosciutto, one sage leaf and one-eighth of the cheese on each steak; fold in half to secure filling, secure with a toothpick or small skewer.

2 Melt half of the butter in medium frying pan; cook saltimbocca, in batches, 5 minutes or until browned both sides and cooked through. Cover to keep warm.

3 Pour wine into same frying pan; bring to a boil. Boil, uncovered, until wine reduces by half. Stir in remaining butter, then chopped sage.

4 Serve saltimbocca drizzled with sauce. Serve with steamed green beans and risotto milanese (see page 168), if desired.

☐ **PER SERVING** 16.6g total fat (9.1g saturated fat); 1513kJ (362 cal); 0.3g carbohydrate; 43g protein; 0g fibre

Saltimbocca is a classic Italian veal dish that literally means "jump in the mouth" – just the sensation the wonderful flavours will produce with your first bite.

Steaks with red wine shallot sauce

PREPARATION TIME 20 MINUTES **COOKING TIME** 20 MINUTES **SERVES** 4

1 tablespoon olive oil

4 x 200g beef sirloin steaks

20g butter

12 shallots (300g), halved

¼ cup (60ml) dry red wine

1 teaspoon red wine vinegar

1 cup (250ml) beef stock

1 teaspoon worcestershire sauce

HERB MASH

1kg sebago potatoes, peeled, cut into 3cm pieces

40g butter

1 cup (250ml) hot milk

2 teaspoons finely chopped fresh flat-leaf parsley

2 teaspoons finely chopped fresh chives

1 Make herb mash.

2 Meanwhile, heat oil in large frying pan; cook steaks until cooked as desired. Remove from pan; cover to keep warm. Remove excess oil from pan.

3 Add butter to same pan; cook shallots, stirring, until soft. Stir in wine and vinegar; bring to a boil. Add stock and sauce; cook, stirring, until mixture boils and thickens.

4 Serve steaks with red wine sauce, herb mash and, if desired, steamed green beans.

HERB MASH Boil or steam potatoes until tender. Mash with butter and milk until smooth. Stir in herbs; cover to keep warm.

☐ **PER SERVING** 32.2g total fat (15.8g saturated fat); 2675kJ (640 cal); 33.6g carbohydrate; 49.9g protein; 4.1g fibre

Sebago potatoes are white-skinned and oval-shaped; they are particularly good fried, mashed and baked. If you can't buy sebago, try lasoda or desiree potatoes.

Kitchen implements

Some jobs require specific tools for the best results. Stay away from gadgetry and stick with the tried and true.

POTATO MASHER
Used vigorously, this tool produces perfect, lump-free mash. Also useful for mashing canned tomatoes as they cook for a pasta sauce, stewed fruit and sliced strawberries.

HEAT-SPREADING MAT
Also called a flame-tamer, this goes under a saucepan and is invaluable, especially if you cook on gas, for maintaining the low, even heat needed for simmering sauces and stews, steaming rice, making jam or cooking polenta.

FISH SLICE
The long, slightly flexible blade of a fish slice is set at an angle to enable it to be slid neatly under the cooked fish so that it does not break up as it is turned or lifted from the pan.

WHISKS
A flexible whisk (left) is good for emulsifying salad dressings and blending sauces and gravies. Balloon whisks blend ingredients and whisk egg whites and cream to a snow; choose one to fit your hand and bowl.

TONGS
Short tongs lift boiled eggs or vegetables from the water and do a hundred other lifting and turning jobs. Long tongs reach across a hot pan, into the oven or under the griller. Flat, wooden-handled ones can double as salad servers.

STRAINERS/SIEVES
Extremely useful for straining liquid from solids, sifting flour and turning pieces of food into a smooth puree by rubbing them through the mesh. They come in many sizes and degrees of coarseness/fineness.

EGG SLIDE

A spatula meant for lifting poached or fried eggs from the pan, with slots to drain away any cooking liquid or grease. A non-stick finish is an advantage.

LARGE METAL SPATULAS

A well-equipped kitchen has two large metal spatulas, one long (which could be a fish slice) and one medium for turning hamburgers or pikelets one at a time. A spatula in each hand is the best way to turn chopped onion.

SMALL METAL SPATULAS

A small, straight, flexible metal spatula will spread icing or slip between a cooked cake and the pan before turning out. A small "stepped" one will help fold an omelette out of the pan.

SLOTTED SPOON

For spooning out fried onions while leaving the fat behind, skimming the solidified fat from a chilled stock, lifting solids out of a liquid, removing a bouquet garni from a sauce and many other tasks.

CONICAL STRAINER

Also called a chinois for its fanciful resemblance to a Chinese pointed hat, this strainer/sieve goes down into the saucepan or bowl to deliver the liquid or sieved food without creating a mess.

SPATTER MAT

A wire-mesh spatter mat, placed over the frying pan, greatly reduces the number of fat specks that fly out on to the stove, while allowing steam to pass through so that the food still browns properly.

A classic Russian recipe known for at least two centuries, "Stroganov" was first brought to Europe by those fleeing the country after the fall of Imperial Russia. It became a popular dinner party dish, cooked at the table in a chafing dish. It remains a favourite in many families' weeknight repertoires and if cooked correctly is perfectly delicious.

Beef stroganoff

PREPARATION TIME 15 MINUTES **COOKING TIME** 15 MINUTES **SERVES** 4

600g piece rump steak, sliced thinly

1 tablespoon plain flour

1 teaspoon hot paprika

50g butter

1 medium brown onion (150g), chopped finely

2 cloves garlic, crushed

200g button mushrooms

2 teaspoons lemon juice

¼ cup (60ml) dry red wine

2 tablespoons tomato paste

300ml sour cream

2 tablespoons finely chopped fresh chives

1 Place steak into plastic bag with flour and paprika; shake until steak is well coated with flour mixture.

2 Melt butter in large frying pan; cook onion and garlic, stirring, over medium heat until onion is soft. Increase heat to high; cook steak, in batches, stirring constantly until steak is browned all over.

3 Return all steak to pan and add mushrooms, juice and wine; stir until combined. Reduce heat, simmer, covered, over low heat about 10 minutes or until steak is tender.

4 Add tomato paste and sour cream, stirring constantly over heat until heated through.

5 Serve sprinkled with chives and, if desired, with pasta.

☐ **PER SERVING** 28.5g total fat (17.7g saturated fat); 1555kJ (372 cal); 4.8g carbohydrate; 23.3g protein; 1.5g fibre

Leftover roast chicken can be used in place of the lamb in this recipe. Tarragon marries beautifully with chicken, so instead of using ground cumin, add 2 teaspoons finely chopped fresh tarragon to the batter for a result that's sure to please.

Lamb fritters with spicy yogurt

PREPARATION TIME 10 MINUTES **COOKING TIME** 20 MINUTES **SERVES** 4

2 teaspoons ground cumin

1 cup (280g) greek-style yogurt

1 egg

1¾ cups (260g) self-raising flour

1½ cups (375ml) buttermilk

150g piece pumpkin, grated finely

2 green onions, chopped finely

300g leftover roast lamb, chopped coarsely

vegetable oil, for shallow-frying

1 Dry-fry cumin in large frying pan, stirring, until fragrant.

2 Combine yogurt with half the cumin in small bowl.

3 Combine egg, flour and buttermilk in large bowl with pumpkin, onion, lamb and remaining cumin; mix well.

4 Heat oil in same pan; shallow-fry quarter cups of batter, in batches, until fritters are browned lightly. Drain on absorbent paper; serve with yogurt.

☐ **PER SERVING** 49.2g total fat (13.3g saturated fat); 3511kJ (840 cal); 60.3g carbohydrate; 37.6g protein; 3g fibre

Lamb with tomato radish salad

PREPARATION TIME 10 MINUTES **COOKING TIME** 15 MINUTES **SERVES** 4

2 tablespoons olive oil

2 cloves garlic, crushed

1 teaspoon dried oregano

1 teaspoon dried chilli flakes

800g lamb backstraps

500g baby new potatoes, halved

TOMATO RADISH SALAD

250g cherry tomatoes, halved

1 medium red onion (170g), sliced thinly

4 trimmed radishes (60g), sliced thinly

1 lebanese cucumber (130g), sliced thinly

1 cup loosely packed fresh flat-leaf parsley leaves

½ cup (80g) black olives

1 teaspoon sea salt flakes

¼ cup (60ml) white wine vinegar

1 Combine half of the oil with garlic, oregano and chilli in a small bowl; rub over lamb.

2 Cook lamb in large heated frying pan until cooked as desired. Transfer to a plate; cover, stand 5 minutes.

3 Meanwhile, boil, steam or microwave potatoes until just tender; drain. Using the back of a fork or potato masher, gently crush the potatoes. Drizzle potatoes with remaining oil.

4 Make tomato radish salad. Serve sliced lamb with potatoes and salad.

TOMATO RADISH SALAD Combine ingredients in large bowl; toss gently to combine.

PER SERVING 16.8g total fat (4.5g saturated fat); 1860kJ (445 cal); 24.8g carbohydrate; 45.7g protein; 5.8g fibre

To enjoy lamb at its succulent best, cook it medium-rare. After cooking, be sure to cover the lamb with foil and allow it to stand for at least 5 minutes before slicing it; by doing this, its delicious juices will settle, ensuring that the meat is tender and moist. Chop up a chunk of danish fetta cheese and toss it in the salad for a tasty addition.

Crumbed marinated lamb cutlets

PREPARATION TIME 25 MINUTES (PLUS REFRIGERATION TIME) **COOKING TIME** 30 MINUTES **SERVES** 2

6 lamb cutlets (450g)

2 tablespoons light soy sauce

1 clove garlic, crushed

¼ cup (35g) plain flour

1 egg

1 tablespoon milk

½ cup (35g) stale breadcrumbs

½ cup (50g) packaged breadcrumbs

1 tablespoon vegetable oil

1 Trim excess fat from cutlets. Using meat mallet, pound each cutlet between sheets of plastic wrap until cutlets are flattened slightly.

2 Combine cutlets with soy sauce and garlic in large dish. Cover; refrigerate 30 minutes, turning cutlets several times while marinating.

3 Place flour in plastic bag; add cutlets. Toss until cutlets are well coated with flour.

4 Dip cutlets in combined egg and milk, then coat with combined breadcrumbs.

5 Heat oil in large frying pan; cook cutlets, in batches, until cooked as desired.

PER SERVING 24.4g total fat (7.6g saturated fat); 2278kJ (545 cal); 41.8g carbohydrate; 37.9g protein; 2.7g fibre

For a low-fat version of this recipe, you can oven-bake the cutlets instead. Line an oven tray, coat with cooking-oil and place the cutlets on the tray. Bake in a moderate oven, uncovered, about 15 minutes each side or until cooked as desired.

Red emperor in thai-style coconut sauce

PREPARATION TIME 20 MINUTES **COOKING TIME** 25 MINUTES **SERVES** 4

1½ cups (300g) jasmine rice

3¼ cups (800ml) coconut milk

4 fresh kaffir lime leaves, sliced thinly

2 fresh small red thai chillies, sliced thinly

4cm piece fresh ginger (20g), chopped finely

1 tablespoon fish sauce

2 tablespoons lime juice

1 tablespoon finely chopped fresh coriander root

1 tablespoon finely chopped fresh lemon grass

1 tablespoon grated palm sugar

2 x 440g red emperor fillets, skinned

⅓ cup firmly packed fresh coriander leaves

1 Cook rice in large saucepan of boiling water, uncovered, until just tender; drain.

2 Meanwhile, combine coconut milk, lime leaves, chilli, ginger, sauce, juice, coriander root, lemon grass and sugar in large frying pan; bring to a boil. Reduce heat, simmer, uncovered, 10 minutes.

3 Add fish; simmer, covered, about 10 minutes or until fish is cooked through. Remove from heat; stir in coriander. Serve fish with coconut sauce on rice.

▭ **PER SERVING** 46.7g total fat (37.9g saturated fat); 3879kJ (928 cal); 71.4g carbohydrate; 54.4g protein; 4.4g fibre

Red emperor has a firm, flaky texture and a delicate, moist flavour. It's great pan-fried, barbecued, grilled, baked... a really delicious fish however you choose to cook it. Snapper or goldband snapper are acceptable substitutes if you can't get emperor.

Pork with celeriac and apple

PREPARATION TIME 15 MINUTES **COOKING TIME** 15 MINUTES **SERVES** 4

50g butter

1 tablespoon olive oil

750g pork fillets

1 small celeriac (550g), peeled, cut into thin wedges

1 small white onion (80g), sliced thinly

2 large apples (400g), quartered, sliced thinly

1 teaspoon yellow mustard seeds

½ cup (125ml) chicken stock

1 tablespoon fresh sage leaves

1 Heat half of the butter and half of the oil in large frying pan; cook pork until browned. Add celeriac; cook, covered, 10 minutes, turning occasionally, or until celeriac is tender.

2 Meanwhile, heat remaining butter and oil in medium frying pan; cook onion, apple and mustard seeds, stirring, until onion is soft. Add stock; cook, uncovered, stirring, 3 minutes or until apple is just tender. Remove from heat; stir in sage leaves.

3 Serve pork, sliced thickly, with celeriac and apple mixture.

▭ **PER SERVING** 19.6g total fat (9g saturated fat); 1768kJ (423 cal); 17g carbohydrate; 42.1g protein; 5.2g fibre

Pork and apple are a classic duo (think roast pork with apple sauce); by teaming this combination with sage, a pungent herb with a slightly bitter, musty mint aroma, you take out a perfect trifecta of flavours – sweet, salty and bitter.

RED EMPEROR IN THAI-STYLE COCONUT SAUCE

Lamb backstrap with celeriac mash

PREPARATION TIME 25 MINUTES **COOKING TIME** 20 MINUTES **SERVES** 4

1.5kg celeriac, trimmed, chopped coarsely

500g potatoes, chopped coarsely

40g butter

½ cup (125ml) cream

800g lamb backstrap

1 clove garlic, crushed

2 teaspoons coarsely chopped fresh rosemary

¼ cup (60ml) olive oil

2 tablespoons balsamic vinegar

1 Boil, steam or microwave celeriac and potato until tender; drain. Mash celeriac and potato in large bowl with butter and cream; cover to keep warm.

2 Meanwhile, combine lamb, garlic, rosemary and 1 tablespoon of the oil in large bowl. Cook lamb mixture in heated oiled large frying pan until browned both sides and cooked as desired. Cover lamb; stand 10 minutes then slice thickly.

3 Combine remaining oil and vinegar in small jug.

4 Serve lamb with mash; drizzle with dressing. Accompany with watercress, if desired.

▭ **PER SERVING** 51.6g total fat (22.9g saturated fat); 3198kJ (765 cal); 26.4g carbohydrate; 49.2g protein; 12.7g fibre

Celeriac makes up in flavour what it lacks in looks. A knobbly brown tuber with crisp white flesh, it tastes like a sharper version of its near relative celery, and can be eaten raw in a delightfully crunchy salad, or cooked and mashed with butter, like here, for a delicious, creamy mash.

Prosciutto-wrapped lamb with minted pea sauce

PREPARATION TIME 15 MINUTES **COOKING TIME** 20 MINUTES **SERVES** 4

4 slices prosciutto (60g)

4 x 200g lamb backstraps

2 teaspoons olive oil

20g butter

1 shallot (25g), chopped finely

1 clove garlic, crushed

1 rindless bacon rasher (65g), sliced thinly

2 teaspoons plain flour

¼ cup (60ml) dry white wine

⅓ cup (80ml) chicken stock

¼ cup (30g) frozen peas

2 tablespoons cream

1 tablespoon finely chopped fresh mint

1 Wrap one slice of prosciutto around each backstrap. Heat oil in large frying pan; cook lamb until cooked as desired. Cover; stand 5 minutes then slice thickly.

2 Meanwhile, melt butter in same pan; cook shallot, garlic and bacon until shallot softens. Add flour; cook, stirring, 1 minute.

3 Stir in wine; bring to a boil, stirring, until mixture boils and thickens. Stir in stock and peas; bring to a boil. Reduce heat, simmer, uncovered, until mixture reduces by half. Stir in cream.

4 Blend or process mixture until smooth; stir in mint. Serve lamb with minted pea sauce, and steamed broccolini, if desired.

▭ **PER SERVING** 20.3g total fat (9.9g saturated fat); 1651kJ (395 cal); 2.6g carbohydrate; 48g protein; 0.7g fibre

Prosciutto is a variety of unsmoked Italian ham, salted, air-cured and aged. It is usually eaten uncooked, however, in this recipe, the pan-frying crisps the prosciutto and adds moisture to the tender, juicy lamb that lies beneath.

Fajitas with guacamole and salsa cruda

PREPARATION TIME 25 MINUTES **COOKING TIME** 15 MINUTES **SERVES** 4

3 cloves garlic, crushed

¼ cup (60ml) lemon juice

2 teaspoons ground cumin

1 tablespoon olive oil

600g piece beef eye fillet, sliced thinly

1 large red capsicum (350g), sliced thinly

1 large green capsicum (350g), sliced thinly

1 medium yellow capsicum (200g), sliced thinly

1 large red onion (300g), sliced thinly

8 large flour tortillas

GUACAMOLE

1 large avocado (320g), mashed roughly

¼ cup finely chopped fresh coriander

1 tablespoon lime juice

1 small white onion (80g), chopped finely

SALSA CRUDA

2 medium tomatoes (300g), seeded, chopped finely

1 fresh long red chilli, chopped finely

½ cup coarsely chopped fresh coriander

1 small white onion (80g), chopped finely

1 tablespoon lime juice

Use a heavy-based frying pan to cook the fajita meat: a well-seasoned cast-iron pan or griddle plate is perfect, and the meat can go straight from stove to table sizzling in the pan.

Sour cream, mayonnaise or garlic don't belong anywhere near an authentic guacamole. The beauty of the "mole" (sauce) lies in its simplicity: a perfectly ripe avocado combined with fresh coriander, lime and onion is all you need to create a Mexican specialty. You can use white onion or red onion, the choice is yours.

1 Combine garlic, juice, cumin, oil and beef in large bowl, cover; refrigerate.

2 Make guacamole.

3 Make salsa cruda.

4 Cook beef, in batches, in heated oiled large frying pan until cooked as desired. Remove from pan; cover to keep warm.

5 Cook capsicums and onion in same pan until softened. Return beef to pan; stir until heated through.

6 Meanwhile, warm tortillas according to manufacturer's instructions.

7 Divide beef mixture among serving plates; serve with tortillas, guacamole and salsa.

GUACAMOLE Combine ingredients in small bowl.

SALSA CRUDA Combine ingredients in small bowl.

PER SERVING 31.5g total fat (7.6g saturated fat); 3089kJ (739 cal); 62.7g carbohydrate; 46.2g protein; 8.9g fibre

Bream fillets with lemon caper butter

PREPARATION TIME 10 MINUTES **COOKING TIME** 15 MINUTES **SERVES** 4

2 medium zucchini (240g)
2 medium carrots (240g)
80g butter
4 bream fillets (600g), skin on
2 tablespoons plain flour

¼ cup (60ml) lemon juice
2 teaspoons drained baby capers
2 tablespoons finely chopped fresh flat-leaf parsley

1 Using a vegetable peeler, peel strips from zucchini and carrots lengthways.
2 Melt 20g of the butter in large frying pan; cook zucchini and carrot, turning occasionally, until vegetables are just tender. Remove from pan; cover to keep warm.
3 Dust fish with flour; shake away excess flour.
4 Melt half of the remaining butter in same pan; cook fish, skin-side down, covered, until fish is just cooked through. Remove from pan; cover to keep warm.
5 Add remaining butter to pan; cook, over low heat, until butter browns. Add juice, capers and parsley; stir until combined.
6 Serve fish on vegetable strips with browned butter sauce.

⬜ **PER SERVING** 24.4g total fat (13.5g saturated fat); 1559kJ (373 cal); 6.3g carbohydrate; 31.1g protein; 2.7g fibre

Snapper or ocean perch can be substituted for bream in this recipe. White wine tastes great when used in a sauce with seafood; simply omit the lemon juice and capers in this recipe and replace with ¼ cup of a good-quality dry white wine.

Tuna and asparagus frittata

PREPARATION TIME 10 MINUTES **COOKING TIME** 30 MINUTES **SERVES** 4

5 medium potatoes (1kg), sliced thinly
1 medium brown onion (150g), sliced thinly
1 clove garlic, crushed
250g asparagus, trimmed, chopped coarsely

425g canned tuna, drained
8 eggs, beaten lightly
2 tablespoons finely chopped fresh flat-leaf parsley
cooking-oil spray

1 Boil, steam or microwave potato until almost tender.
2 Cook onion and garlic in small heated frying pan, stirring, until onion softens.
3 Combine potato and onion mixture in large bowl with asparagus, tuna, egg and parsley.
4 Preheat grill.
5 Reheat pan; remove from heat. Coat lightly with cooking-oil spray; return to heat. Spoon frittata mixture into pan; press down firmly. Cook, uncovered, over low heat until almost set; remove from heat. Place under heated grill until frittata sets and top is browned lightly.

⬜ **PER SERVING** 14.1g total fat (4.2g saturated fat); 1898kJ (454 cal); 35.8g carbohydrate; 42.3g protein; 6.4g fibre

The beauty of a frittata definitely lies in its versatility – it tastes good hot, cold or at room temperature; it's perfect at dinner time or for lunch and always a hit with kids and adults alike. For a splash of colour and extra flavour, throw in a handful of cherry tomatoes into the frittata mixture, if you like.

BREAM FILLETS WITH LEMON CAPER BUTTER

Cajun prawns

PREPARATION TIME 30 MINUTES **COOKING TIME** 15 MINUTES **SERVES** 4

1 tablespoon hot paprika

1 teaspoon chilli powder

1 teaspoon ground ginger

2 teaspoons ground cumin

1 teaspoon ground cardamom

1 teaspoon ground coriander

1 tablespoon vegetable oil

1 medium red onion (150g), chopped coarsely

1 clove garlic, crushed

24 uncooked medium king prawns (1kg)

1 teaspoon vegetable oil, extra

1 tablespoon lime juice

1 lime, cut into wedges

1 Blend or process spices, oil, onion and garlic until mixture forms a paste. Shell and devein prawns, leaving tails intact.

2 Heat extra oil in large frying pan; cook prawns, in batches, until just changed in colour.

3 Cook paste, stirring, in same pan about 2 minutes or until fragrant. Return prawns to pan with juice; cook until prawns are heated through.

4 Serve prawns with lime wedges and, if desired, bean and coriander salad (see page 409).

☐ **PER SERVING** 6.6g total fat (0.9g saturated fat); 740kJ (177 cal); 2.4 carbohydrate; 26.3g protein; 0.9g fibre

Different types of seafood, like fish and squid, as well as chicken, taste fantastic when cooked with the cajun spice paste made in this recipe. Make an extra large quantity of the paste to keep an on-hand flavour hit – it can be frozen for up to three months. Place tablespoons of paste in an ice-cube tray, wrap the tray tightly in plastic wrap and freeze the paste. Once frozen, remove the blocks of paste, then re-wrap them individually and return to the freezer until required.

Prawns saganaki

PREPARATION TIME 20 MINUTES **COOKING TIME** 25 MINUTES **SERVES** 8

2 tablespoons extra virgin olive oil

2 medium red onions (300g), chopped finely

2 cloves garlic, crushed

½ cup (125ml) dry white wine

400ml jar tomato pasta sauce

½ cup (125ml) water

1kg uncooked medium king prawns

150g fetta cheese, crumbled

1 teaspoon dried greek rigani (or dried oregano)

1 Heat oil in large frying pan; cook onion and garlic, stirring, until soft. Add wine; bring to a boil. Simmer, uncovered, until reduced by half.

2 Add tomato sauce and the water; simmer, uncovered, about 5 minutes or until thick.

3 Meanwhile, shell and devein prawns, leaving tails intact. Add prawns to pan; simmer, uncovered, about 5 minutes or until prawns are just cooked through.

4 Preheat grill to hot.

5 Transfer prawn mixture to an ovenproof dish; sprinkle top with fetta. Place under grill until cheese just begins to brown. Sprinkle with rigani.

☐ **PER SERVING** 9.4g total fat (3.6g saturated fat); 790kJ (189 cal); 5.3g carbohydrate; 17.5g protein; 1.6g fibre

Saganaki, despite sounding vaguely Japanese, is the traditional Greek name for a snack or entrée of floured, herbed then fried cheese (fetta, kasseri, haloumi or kefalograviera) which is sprinkled with lemon juice and eaten with bread. Today, it is commonly used to describe a dish that features cooked cheese as a main ingredient, as seen in this recipe.

Spiced salmon with yogurt

PREPARATION TIME 10 MINUTES **COOKING TIME** 15 MINUTES **SERVES** 4

1 clove garlic, crushed

1 tablespoon ground coriander

1 teaspoon ground cumin

1 teaspoon ground turmeric

2 tablespoons olive oil

4 x 200g salmon fillets

400g can white beans, rinsed, drained

½ cup lightly packed fresh coriander leaves

½ cup (140g) yogurt

This recipe calls for white beans, a generic term we use for canned or dried cannellini, haricot, navy or great northern beans which are all of the same family, phaseolus vulgaris, and are all interchangeable.

1 Combine garlic, spices and 1 tablespoon of the oil in small bowl. Rub flesh-side of the salmon with half of the spice mixture; reserve remaining spice mixture.
2 Heat remaining oil in large frying pan over medium heat; cook salmon, flesh-side down, until cooked as desired (salmon is best medium rare).
3 Meanwhile, heat half of the reserved spice mixture in small frying pan until fragrant; add beans, stir until heated through. Remove from heat; add coriander, toss gently.
4 Combine remaining reserved spice mixture with yogurt in small bowl.
5 Serve salmon on bean mixture, top with spiced yoghurt.

▭ **PER SERVING** 24.8g total fat (5.3g saturated fat); 1906kJ (456 cal); 11.1g carbohydrate; 45.1g protein; 4.4g fibre

---

Crêpes suzette

PREPARATION TIME 15 MINUTES (PLUS STANDING TIME) **COOKING TIME** 25 MINUTES **SERVES** 4

¾ cup (110g) plain flour

3 eggs

2 tablespoons vegetable oil

¾ cup (180ml) milk

ORANGE SAUCE

125g butter

½ cup (110g) caster sugar

1 ½ cups (375ml) orange juice

2 tablespoons lemon juice

⅓ cup (80ml) orange-flavoured liqueur

Perhaps the most famous "pancakes" in the world, crêpes suzette have a romantic history that evokes high society and midnight suppers. Restaurants can flame them at the table in a chafing dish for a spectacular finale, but we recommend you ignite them in the kitchen, with your exhaust fan off, then carry the crêpes to the table after the flame is extinguished.

1 Sift flour into medium bowl, make well in centre; add eggs and oil, gradually whisk in milk until smooth. Pour batter into large jug, cover; stand 1 hour.
2 Heat greased heavy-based crêpe pan or small frying pan; pour ¼ cup of the batter into pan, tilting pan to coat base. Cook over low heat until browned lightly, loosening around edge with spatula. Turn crêpe; brown other side. Remove crêpe from pan; cover to keep warm. Repeat with remaining batter to make a total of eight crêpes.
3 Make orange sauce. Fold crêpes in half then in half again, add to sauce; warm over low heat.
4 Divide crêpes among serving plates; pour hot sauce over crêpes.

ORANGE SAUCE Melt butter in large frying pan; cook sugar, stirring, until mixture begins to brown. Add strained orange juice and lemon juice; bring to a boil. Reduce heat, simmer, uncovered, about 3 minutes or until light golden. Add liqueur; remove from heat, ignite.

▭ **PER SERVING** 41g total fat (20.5g saturated fat); 3043kJ (728 cal); 66.9g carbohydrate; 10.3g protein; 1.3g fibre

These light and fluffy
pancakes taste just as
great with any berry of your
choice if you're not crazy
about strawberries. You can
also add unthawed frozen
blueberries or raspberries
to the batter if you like.

Buttermilk pancakes with glazed strawberries

PREPARATION TIME 15 MINUTES **COOKING TIME** 15 MINUTES **SERVES** 4

4 eggs

2 tablespoons caster sugar

1½ cups (375ml) buttermilk

100g butter, melted

1½ cups (225g) self-raising flour

GLAZED STRAWBERRIES

⅓ cup (80ml) water

½ cup (170g) marmalade

1 tablespoon caster sugar

2 tablespoons lemon juice

250g strawberries, quartered

1 Beat eggs and sugar in small bowl with electric mixer until thick; stir in buttermilk and half of the butter. Sift flour into large bowl; gradually whisk in egg mixture until smooth.

2 Heat heavy-based medium frying pan; brush pan with a little of the remaining butter. Pour ¼ cup of the batter into pan; cook, uncovered, until bubbles appear on surface of pancake. Turn pancake; cook until browned. Remove from pan; cover to keep warm. Repeat with remaining butter and batter.

3 Make glazed strawberries. Serve pancakes with strawberries.

GLAZED STRAWBERRIES Bring the water, marmalade, sugar and juice to a boil in small saucepan. Add strawberries, reduce heat; simmer, uncovered, 2 minutes or until hot.

☐ **PER SERVING** 28.5g total fat (16.5g saturated fat); 2867kJ (686 cal); 87.7g carbohydrate; 17.6g protein; 3.9g fibre

---

If you're looking for a
dessert to serve to guests
that will impress but won't
have you slaving in the
kitchen for hours, then
this recipe is the answer.
Mango also tastes great
married with coconut:
either use mango instead
of the banana or serve a
combination of the two for
a delightfully tropical dish.

Banana caramel pancakes

PREPARATION TIME 10 MINUTES **COOKING TIME** 15 MINUTES **SERVES** 6

1¼ cups (185g) self-raising flour

1½ tablespoons caster sugar

1 egg

1½ cups (375ml) milk

90g butter

¾ cup (165g) firmly packed
brown sugar

¾ cup (180ml) cream

½ cup (125g) sour cream

4 medium bananas (800g),
sliced thickly

2 tablespoons shredded
coconut, toasted

1 Sift flour and sugar into medium bowl, make well in centre; gradually stir in combined egg and milk until smooth. Cover; stand 30 minutes.

2 Pour 2 to 3 tablespoons of the batter into heated greased heavy-based frying pan; cook until lightly browned underneath. Turn pancake, brown on other side. Repeat with remaining batter to make a total of 6 pancakes.

3 Melt butter in medium frying pan, add brown sugar; stir over medium heat about 1 minute or until sugar is dissolved. Stir in creams. Add bananas and coconut; stir gently.

4 Serve pancakes with banana sauce.

☐ **PER SERVING** 47.6g total fat (31.1g saturated fat); 2809kJ (672 cal); 50.1g carbohydrate; 9.4g protein; 3.4g fibre

BUTTERMILK PANCAKES WITH GLAZED STRAWBERRIES

THE DEEP-FRYER

The Deep-fryer

Deep-frying means plunging pieces of food into hot oil deep enough for the food to float, so it is quickly crisped on the outside while steaming on the inside. It is vital that the oil stays at the correct temperature throughout the cooking process: not hot enough and the food will be soggy and greasy, too hot and the food will be burned on the outside by the time the centre is cooked or heated. Although the health-conscious may be horrified at the thought of deep-frying, it doesn't make the food itself greasy if it is carried out properly. As long as the oil is hot enough and the food is not immersed in it for too long, no oil will enter the interior, and the food will be light and digestible.

That said, no one can pretend you're not ingesting some oil when you're enjoying fish and chips or tempura vegetables – they're not something to indulge in everyday, but to savour from time to time.

Do you need a deep-fryer? If we're speaking of an electric one, the questions to ask yourself are whether you're happy to spend the money, whether you deep-fry often enough to justify it and whether you have room in your cupboard for yet another appliance. If we're speaking of deep-frying on top of the stove, you don't have to make a major decision because you probably have the main piece of equipment already, in the shape of a large, deep pan, and will need to add only a few accessories (see Tools, below). You can also deep-fry in a wok (see *The Wok*, page 212).

ELECTRIC OR COOKTOP? An electric fryer has the advantage of portability – it can be used on a deck or terrace as well as in the kitchen. It also has the major advantage of taking the worry out of keeping the oil at a steady heat, as it is thermostatically controlled.

However, deep-frying in an ordinary pan on top of the stove is perfectly efficient and controllable so long as you understand the safely rules and follow the instructions under Use, opposite.

TOOLS

THERMOMETER The best way to maintain the correct temperature for cooktop frying is to use a special deep-frying thermometer with a clamp on it so you can attach it to the side of the pan. Bring the oil slowly to the desired temperature and, during cooking, check constantly and adjust the heat as needed.

FRYING BASKET is used to add and remove all the food at the same time. A basket is supplied with an electric deep-fryer. For cooktop frying, use a wire basket with a long handle.

SKIMMERS AND TONGS are used to remove individual burned scraps of food or pieces that have cooked faster than the rest.

OVEN GLOVES for lifting out the frying basket.

SAFETY

All oils have a smoke point, a temperature at which they will start to smoke, begin to break down and eventually burst into flame. Hot oil will cause burns if it spatters, and will catch fire if it comes too close to a heat source. Always observe the following safety precautions:

- Ensure small children and pets are well out of the way.
- Have the kitchen fire blanket handy (yes, every kitchen should have one; they are available from hardware stores). If overheated oil should catch alight, clap lid on pan to smother the flames and use the fire blanket, if necessary.
- If frying on top of the stove, choose a pan that generously overlaps the burner, so that if any oil spills it will be less likely to catch fire. Many experienced cooks find a wide, deep metal casserole dish (known as a Dutch oven) is ideal for deep-frying.
- Never fill the pot more than barely half-full of oil, because it bubbles up when the food is added. Never lift or move the fryer until it and the oil are completely cooled.

USE

- Oils suitable for deep-frying include peanut, canola, safflower, sunflower and most blended oils. "Solid" oils, which have been processed to make them solid at room temperature, perform particularly well (though they are the most unhealthy of all oils).
- Change the oil after every few uses or if it darkens. Peanut and solid oil should last for 3 to 5 uses; polyunsaturated oils are less robust and will probably last for 1 or 2 fryings.
- To store used oil, filter by pouring very slowly into a jug through a sieve lined with a couple of layers of absorbent paper or disposable cloth, then store in tightly capped glass jars or bottles, away from light.
- Most foods need a protective coating of batter or egg and breadcrumbs, which form a crisp brown crust while the inside remains moist and tender. Food must be well dried before coating so that no moisture touches the oil, as this will make it spatter. Rest egg-and-breadcrumbed pieces for about 20 minutes before placing them in oil – this allows the egg to set so the coating will adhere better – then pat off excess breadcrumbs, before placing food in oil. Allow excess batter to drip off before placing food in oil.
- Potatoes and skin-on poultry do not need a coating, but must be well dried.
- Have the kitchen exhaust fan turned on high so that frying fumes won't settle on the kitchen walls and fixtures.
- Have pieces of food a uniform size so they will all be cooked at the same time.
- Fry in batches small enough for the pieces to float free without touching each other.
- Have an absorbent-paper-lined plate or oven tray ready to drain the food. If cooking in several batches, have a preheated slow oven ready to keep the early batches hot.
- Most foods are deep-fried at temperatures between 175°C and 190°C.

CARE

A deep-fryer needs a meticulous clean-up after every use. For an electric deep-fryer, follow manufacturer's directions. To clean a cooktop deep-fryer, empty it when cool and wipe out with absorbent paper or old disposable cloths to remove as much oil as possible before washing. Wash in very hot water with just a few drops of detergent; rinse, wipe dry immediately and then place over a stove burner turned very low to dry thoroughly. Wash skimmers, tongs and other tools in hot water with detergent in the usual way.

Seafood and vegetable tempura with lemon dipping sauce

PREPARATION TIME 35 MINUTES **COOKING TIME** 25 MINUTES **SERVES** 6

540g uncooked medium king prawns

1 medium brown onion (150g)

peanut oil, for deep-frying

450g ocean trout fillets, cut into 3cm pieces

1 large red capsicum (350g), cut into 3cm pieces

1 small kumara (250g), sliced thinly

8 baby zucchini with flowers attached (160g), stamens removed

plain flour, for dusting vegetables

1 lemon, cut into wedges

TEMPURA BATTER

1 egg

2 cups (500ml) cold soda water

1 cup (150g) plain flour

1 cup (150g) cornflour

LEMON DIPPING SAUCE

½ cup (125ml) rice vinegar

¼ cup (55g) caster sugar

1 teaspoon light soy sauce

¼ teaspoon finely grated lemon rind

1 green onion (green part only), chopped finely

1 Shell and devein prawns, leaving tails intact. Make three small cuts on the underside of each prawn, halfway through flesh, to prevent curling when cooked.

2 Halve onion from root end. Push four toothpicks, at regular intervals, through each onion half to hold rings together; cut in between toothpicks.

3 Make tempura batter. Make lemon dipping sauce.

4 Heat oil in deep-fryer. Dust prawns, onion, fish, capsicum, kumara and zucchini lightly in flour; shake off excess flour. Dip, piece by piece, in batter; deep-fry until crisp. Drain on absorbent paper.

5 Serve tempura with dipping sauce and lemon wedges.

TEMPURA BATTER Whisk egg and soda water in large bowl until combined. Add sifted flours whisking lightly until combined (batter will be lumpy).

LEMON DIPPING SAUCE Stir vinegar, sugar and sauce in small saucepan until sugar dissolves. Remove from heat, add rind; stand 10 minutes. Strain sauce into serving dish; discard rind. Sprinkle with onion.

▭ **PER SERVING** 17.2g total fat (3.3g saturated fat); 2140kJ (512 cal); 57.1g carbohydrate; 29.9g protein; 3.4g fibre

Potato chips

PREPARATION TIME 10 MINUTES (PLUS STANDING TIME) **COOKING TIME** 20 MINUTES **SERVES** 4

We use russet burbank (also known as an idaho potato in many cookbooks) for this recipe. Its floury texture and low moisture content makes the perfect chip, but you can also use bintje or spunta.

1kg potatoes, peeled
peanut oil, for deep-frying

1 Cut potatoes lengthways into 1cm slices; cut each slice lengthways into 1cm-wide pieces. Stand potato pieces in large bowl of cold water for 30 minutes to avoid discolouration. Drain; pat dry with absorbent paper.
2 Heat oil in deep-fryer; cook chips, in three batches, about 4 minutes each or until just tender but not browned. Drain on absorbent paper; stand 10 minutes.
3 Reheat oil; cook chips again, in three batches, separating any that stick together by shaking deep-fryer basket or with a slotted spoon, until crisp and golden brown. Drain on absorbent paper.

PER SERVING 10.9g total fat (1.9g saturated fat); 986kJ (236 cal); 27.8g carbohydrate; 5.1g protein; 3.4g fibre

Eggplant and haloumi skewers with roasted tomato sauce

PREPARATION TIME 35 MINUTES **COOKING TIME** 20 MINUTES (PLUS COOLING TIME) **MAKES** 36

Don't deep-fry these skewers until you want to serve them because haloumi cheese has a tendency to become hard and dry after it's cooled.

Use short or halved bamboo skewers or strong wooden toothpicks in this recipe.

1 medium eggplant (300g)
250g haloumi cheese
¼ cup (35g) plain flour
1 egg, beaten lightly
½ cup (35g) fresh breadcrumbs
½ cup (40g) finely grated parmesan cheese
36 medium fresh basil leaves
vegetable oil, for deep-frying

ROASTED TOMATO SAUCE
125g cherry tomatoes
cooking-oil spray
1 clove garlic, crushed
½ teaspoon white sugar
1 teaspoon red wine vinegar
1 tablespoon olive oil

1 Preheat oven to 180°C/160°C fan-forced; make roasted tomato sauce.
2 Meanwhile, cut eggplant into 36 squares. Cut haloumi into 36 squares.
3 Coat eggplant squares in flour, shake off excess; dip into egg then coat in combined breadcrumbs and parmesan.
4 Thread one piece of eggplant, one basil leaf and one piece of haloumi onto each skewer. Heat oil in deep-fryer, deep-fry skewers, in batches, about 30 seconds or until browned lightly; drain on absorbent paper.
5 Serve skewers with roasted tomato sauce.

ROASTED TOMATO SAUCE Place tomatoes on baking-paper-lined oven tray; coat with oil spray. Roast, uncovered, 15 minutes or until soft. Blend or process tomatoes with remaining ingredients until smooth. Cool to room temperature.

PER SKEWER 3.1g total fat (1.2g saturated fat); 192kJ (46 cal); 1.9g carbohydrate; 2.5g protein; 0.4g fibre

Chorizo and potato fritters

PREPARATION TIME 25 MINUTES (PLUS COOLING TIME) **COOKING TIME** 15 MINUTES

MAKES 40 FRITTERS & ½ CUP DIPPING SAUCE

2 teaspoons vegetable oil

1 chorizo sausage (200g), chopped finely

1 small brown onion (80g), chopped finely

2 fresh small red thai chillies, chopped finely

2 medium zucchini (240g), grated coarsely

450g potatoes, peeled, grated coarsely

1 small kumara (250g), peeled, grated coarsely

3 eggs, beaten lightly

1 cup (150g) plain flour

1 teaspoon sweet paprika

vegetable oil, for deep-frying

SWEET CHILLI DIPPING SAUCE

½ cup (120g) sour cream

2 tablespoons sweet chilli sauce

1 Heat oil in medium frying pan; cook chorizo, onion and chilli, stirring, until onion softens. Add zucchini; cook, stirring, 1 minute. Cool 10 minutes.

2 Meanwhile, make sweet chilli dipping sauce.

3 Combine chorizo mixture in large bowl with potato, kumara, eggs, flour and paprika.

4 Heat oil in deep-fryer; deep-fry level tablespoons of potato mixture, in batches, until fritters are browned lightly. Drain on absorbent paper.

5 Serve fritters with sweet chilli dipping sauce.

SWEET CHILLI DIPPING SAUCE Combine ingredients in small bowl.

▭ **PER FRITTER** 4g total fat (0.9g saturated fat); 276kJ (66 cal); 5.1g carbohydrate; 2.3g protein; 0.6g fibre
▭ **PER TABLESPOON DIPPING SAUCE** 1.2g total fat (0.8g saturated fat); 50kJ (12 cal); 0.3g carbohydrate; 0.8g protein; 0g fibre

A sausage of Spanish origin, made of coarsely ground pork and highly seasoned with garlic and chillies, chorizo is as good grilled and eaten on its own as it is used as an ingredient, as in these fritters. It is always part of an authentic paella.

Beer-battered fish with lemon mayonnaise

PREPARATION TIME 10 MINUTES **COOKING TIME** 20 MINUTES **SERVES** 4

⅔ cup (200g) mayonnaise

2 teaspoons finely grated lemon rind

¼ teaspoon cracked black pepper

1 teaspoon lemon juice

¾ cup (110g) self-raising flour

¾ cup (110g) plain flour

1 teaspoon five-spice powder

1 egg

1½ cups (375ml) beer

vegetable oil, for deep-frying

600g white fish fillets

1 Combine mayonnaise, rind, pepper and juice in small bowl.

2 Whisk flours, five-spice, egg and beer in medium bowl until smooth.

3 Heat oil in deep-fryer. Dip fish in batter; deep-fry fish, in batches, until cooked through.

4 Serve with mayonnaise mixture, and lemon wedges, if desired.

▭ **PER SERVING** 29.7g total fat (4.4g saturated fat); 2746kJ (657 cal); 51.2g carbohydrate; 38.7g protein; 2.4g fibre

Peanut and canola oils have very high flashpoints (the temperature at which an oil will ignite near a flame, considered to be around 325°C), so both are excellent for deep-frying. Peanut can impart flavour, however, so depending on what you want to cook, you might prefer to use canola.

Chilli salt squid

PREPARATION TIME 20 MINUTES **COOKING TIME** 10 MINUTES **SERVES** 4

1kg small whole squid

peanut oil, for deep-frying

2 fresh long red chillies, sliced thinly

1 cup lightly packed fresh coriander leaves

⅓ cup (50g) plain flour

2 fresh long red chillies, chopped finely, extra

2 teaspoons sea salt

1 teaspoon ground black pepper

1 Gently separate body and tentacles of squid by pulling on tentacles. Cut head from tentacles just below eyes; discard head. Trim long tentacle of each squid.

2 Remove clear quill from inside body and discard. Peel side flaps from body with salted fingers; peel away dark skin. Wash squid well; pat dry with absorbent paper.

3 Cut along one side of the body and open out. Score inside surface in a criss-cross pattern, using a small sharp knife. Cut body into pieces.

4 Heat oil in deep-fryer; deep-fry chillies in hot oil until softened. Drain on absorbent paper. Deep-fry coriander 10 seconds or until changed in colour; drain on absorbent paper.

5 Toss squid in combined flour, extra chilli, salt and pepper; shake away excess. Deep-fry squid, in batches, until just browned and tender; drain on absorbent paper. Sprinkle squid with deep-fried coriander and chilli. Serve immediately with lime wedges, if desired.

▭ **PER SERVING** 8.1g total fat (1.3g saturated fat); 807kJ (193 cal), 9.6g carbohydrate; 19.7g protein; 1.0g fibre

Take care when deep-frying chillies and coriander as the moisture in the vegetables will cause the oil to spit.

Felafel

PREPARATION TIME 45 MINUTES (PLUS STANDING TIME) **COOKING TIME** 20 MINUTES **MAKES** 50

2 cups (400g) dried chickpeas

1 medium brown onion (150g), chopped coarsely

2 cloves garlic, quartered

½ cup coarsely chopped fresh flat-leaf parsley

2 teaspoons ground coriander

1 teaspoon ground cumin

1 teaspoon bicarbonate of soda

2 tablespoons plain flour

1 teaspoon salt

vegetable oil, for deep-frying

1 Place chickpeas in large bowl, cover with cold water; stand overnight. Drain.

2 Combine chickpeas, onion, garlic, parsley and spices in large bowl. Blend or process, in two batches, until almost smooth; return mixture to bowl.

3 Add soda, flour and salt to chickpea mixture; knead on lightly floured surface 2 minutes. Stand 30 minutes.

4 Roll level tablespoons of mixture into balls; stand 10 minutes. Heat oil in deep-fryer; deep-fry balls, in batches, until golden brown. Serve felafel with separate bowls of dukkah and yogurt for dipping, if desired.

▭ **PER FELAFEL** 0.9g total fat (0.1g saturated fat); 79kJ (19 cal); 1.8g carbohydrate; 0.7g protein; 0.6g fibre

A snack eaten all through the Middle-East and North Africa, felafel are small croquette-like patties made of crushed dried chickpeas or beans and a variety of herbs and spices, the variety and proportions of which vary according to the individual cook. They are often eaten as a vegetarian alternative to lamb in sandwiches or as part of a mezze. Serve a batch of these moist and moreish bites with tabbouleh (page 399) for a satisfying and delicious vegetarian meal.

CHILLI SALT SQUID

Chorizo taquitos with chilli tomato salsa

PREPARATION TIME 40 MINUTES **COOKING TIME** 15 MINUTES **MAKES** 40

450g can refried beans

1 tablespoon water

400g chorizo sausage, chopped finely

½ medium red capsicum (100g), chopped finely

3 green onions, chopped finely

10 large flour tortillas, quartered

vegetable oil, for deep-frying

CHILLI TOMATO SALSA

425g can peeled tomatoes

2 fresh small red thai chillies, quartered

1 clove garlic, quartered

⅓ cup loosely packed fresh coriander leaves

1 small brown onion (80g), quartered

1 Heat beans with the water in small saucepan.

2 Meanwhile, cook chorizo in heated oiled large frying pan, stirring, until crisp; drain.

3 Combine bean mixture and chorizo in medium bowl with capsicum and onion. Divide filling among tortilla pieces; roll each taquito into cone shape, secure with toothpick.

4 Heat oil in deep-fryer; deep-fry taquitos, in batches, until browned lightly and crisp. Drain on absorbent paper. Remove toothpicks.

5 Meanwhile, make chilli tomato salsa. Serve hot taquitos with salsa.

CHILLI TOMATO SALSA Blend or process ingredients until just combined.

☐ **PER TAQUITO (INCL. SALSA)** 6g total fat (1.5g saturated fat); 435kJ (104 cal); 8.2g carbohydrate; 3.8g protein; 1.2g fibre

Deep-fried fontina bites

PREPARATION TIME 20 MINUTES **COOKING TIME** 10 MINUTES **MAKES** 32

500g piece fontina cheese

½ cup (75g) plain flour

½ cup (75g) cornflour

1 egg

¾ cup (180ml) water

1½ cups (150g) packaged breadcrumbs

1 tablespoon finely chopped fresh flat-leaf parsley

2 tablespoons finely chopped fresh oregano

½ teaspoon cayenne pepper

vegetable oil, for deep-frying

1 Cut cheese into 1.5cm x 4cm pieces.

2 Sift flour and cornflour into medium bowl; gradually stir in combined egg and water until batter is smooth. Combine breadcrumbs, herbs and pepper in another medium bowl.

3 Dip cheese pieces, one at a time, in batter then in breadcrumb mixture. Repeat process to double-coat each piece.

4 Heat oil in deep-fryer; deep-fry cheese pieces, in batches, until browned lightly. Drain on absorbent paper.

☐ **PER BITE** 19.9g total fat (9.6g saturated fat); 1346kJ (322 cal); 20.2g carbohydrate; 15.2g protein; 0.9g fibre

Pea pakoras with coriander raita

PREPARATION TIME 25 MINUTES **COOKING TIME** 15 MINUTES **MAKES** 24

1½ cups (225g) besan flour

½ teaspoon bicarbonate of soda

¾ cup (180ml) water

2 teaspoons vegetable oil

2 cloves garlic, crushed

½ teaspoon ground turmeric

½ teaspoon cumin seeds

1 teaspoon ground cumin

½ teaspoon dried chilli flakes

1 tablespoon coarsely chopped fresh coriander

1 cup (120g) frozen peas

2 green onions, chopped finely

40g baby spinach leaves, shredded coarsely

vegetable oil, for deep-frying, extra

CORIANDER RAITA

1 cup (280g) greek-style yogurt

1 cup coarsely chopped fresh coriander

½ teaspoon ground cumin

Besan, also known as gram flour, made from ground dried chickpeas, is a staple in the Indian kitchen, and is used to make roti, chapati and other breads. Pakoras are small Indian fritters usually served as snacks or appetisers that can be made with any number of different vegetables, meat or fish.

1 Sift flour and soda into medium bowl; whisk in the water to form a smooth batter.

2 Heat oil in small saucepan; cook garlic and spices, stirring, until fragrant. Add spice mixture to batter with coriander, peas, onion and spinach; mix well.

3 Heat extra oil in deep-fryer; deep-fry level tablespoons of the mixture, in batches, about 5 minutes or until browned lightly. Drain on absorbent paper.

4 Meanwhile, make coriander raita. Serve pakoras with raita.

CORIANDER RAITA Blend or process ingredients until smooth.

▭ **PER PAKORA (INCL. RAITA)** 3.2g total fat (0.8g saturated fat); 293kJ (70 cal); 7g carbohydrate; 3.1g protein; 1.5g fibre

---

Deep-fried whitebait

PREPARATION TIME 10 MINUTES **COOKING TIME** 15 MINUTES **SERVES** 4

500g whitebait

1 cup (150g) plain flour

¼ cup coarsely chopped fresh basil

1 teaspoon garlic salt

vegetable oil, for deep-frying

SPICED MAYONNAISE DIP

1 cup (300g) mayonnaise

2 cloves garlic, crushed

2 tablespoons lemon juice

1 tablespoon capers, drained, rinsed, chopped finely

1 tablespoon coarsely chopped fresh flat-leaf parsley

Don't crowd the fish in the basket when deep-frying; put only as many in each batch so that they can circulate freely in the oil.

1 Combine whitebait, flour, basil and garlic salt in large bowl.

2 Heat oil in deep-fryer; deep-fry whitebait, in batches, until browned and cooked through. Drain on absorbent paper.

3 Make spiced mayonnaise dip. Serve whitebait with dip.

SPICED MAYONNAISE DIP Combine ingredients in small serving bowl.

▭ **PER SERVING** 46.2g total fat (7.3g saturated fat); 2880kJ (689 cal); 40.9g carbohydrate; 27.2g protein; 2.2g fibre

Deep-fried prawn balls

PREPARATION TIME 25 MINUTES (PLUS STANDING TIME) **COOKING TIME** 10 MINUTES **SERVES** 4

1kg uncooked large king prawns

5 green onions, chopped finely

2 cloves garlic, crushed

4 fresh small red thai chillies, chopped finely

2cm piece fresh ginger (10g), grated

1 tablespoon cornflour

2 teaspoons fish sauce

¼ cup coarsely chopped fresh coriander

¼ cup (25g) packaged breadcrumbs

½ cup (35g) stale breadcrumbs

vegetable oil, for deep-frying

1 Shell and devein prawns; cut in half. Blend or process prawn halves, pulsing, until chopped coarsely. Place in large bowl with onion, garlic, chilli, ginger, cornflour, sauce and coriander; mix well.

2 Using hands, roll rounded tablespoons of prawn mixture into balls. Roll balls in combined breadcrumbs; place in single layer, on plastic-wrap-lined tray. Cover; refrigerate 30 minutes.

3 Heat oil in deep-fryer; deep-fry prawn balls, in batches, until lightly browned and cooked through. Serve with sweet chilli sauce; if desired.

PER SERVING 10.3g total fat (1.4g saturated fat); 1175kJ (281 cal); 17.4g carbohydrate; 28.5g protein; 2.3g fibre

Salt and pepper quail

PREPARATION TIME 30 MINUTES **COOKING TIME** 20 MINUTES **SERVES** 4

8 quails (1.3kg)

½ cup (75g) plain flour

1½ tablespoons sea salt flakes

2 teaspoons coarsely ground black pepper

vegetable oil, for deep-frying

LEMON PEPPER DIPPING SAUCE

¼ cup (60ml) vegetable oil

1 teaspoon finely grated lemon rind

⅓ cup (80ml) lemon juice

2 tablespoons grated palm sugar

1 teaspoon ground white pepper

1 Rinse quails under cold water; pat dry. Discard necks from quails. Using kitchen scissors, cut along sides of each quail's backbone; discard backbones. Halve each quail along breastbone.

2 Make lemon pepper dipping sauce.

3 Combine flour, salt and pepper in large bowl with quail; shake off any excess.

4 Heat oil in deep-fryer; deep-fry quail, in batches, about 6 minutes or until quail is cooked. Drain on absorbent paper.

5 Divide quail among serving plates; serve with dipping sauce.

LEMON PEPPER DIPPING SAUCE Place ingredients in screw-top jar; shake well.

PER SERVING 26.4g total fat (5.8g saturated fat); 1877kJ (449 cal); 20.4g carbohydrate; 32.4g protein; 0.8g fibre

Money bags

PREPARATION TIME 30 MINUTES **COOKING TIME** 20 MINUTES

MAKES 12 MONEY BAGS & 1 ½ CUPS DIPPING SAUCE

1 tablespoon peanut oil

1 small brown onion (80g), chopped finely

1 clove garlic, crushed

4cm piece fresh ginger (20g), grated

100g chicken mince

1 tablespoon grated palm sugar

1 tablespoon finely chopped roasted unsalted peanuts

2 teaspoons finely chopped fresh coriander

3 green onions

24 x 8cm-square wonton wrappers

vegetable oil, for deep-frying

PEANUT DIPPING SAUCE

1 tablespoon peanut oil

2 cloves garlic, crushed

1 small brown onion (80g), chopped finely

2 fresh small red thai chillies, chopped coarsely

10cm stick fresh lemon grass (20g), chopped finely

¾ cup (180ml) coconut milk

2 tablespoons fish sauce

¼ cup firmly packed dark brown sugar

½ cup (140g) crunchy peanut butter

½ teaspoon curry powder

1 tablespoon lime juice

Money bags, sometimes called "gold bags" on Thai restaurant menus, can also be a vegetarian appetiser: substitute mashed potato or kumara and finely chopped mushrooms for the chicken mince. They can also be made with dried bean curd skins or sheets ("yuba") instead of wonton wrappers. Prepared money bags can be frozen, covered, up to 1 month before you want to eat them. Place them on a metal rack on an oven tray and reheat in a moderate oven for about 15 minutes or until crisp and heated through.

1 Heat oil in wok; stir-fry brown onion, garlic and ginger until onion softens. Add chicken; stir-fry until chicken is changed in colour. Add sugar; stir-fry about 3 minutes or until sugar dissolves. Stir nuts and coriander into filling mixture.

2 Cut upper green half of each green onion into four long slices; discard remaining onion half. Submerge onion strips in hot water for a few seconds to make pliable.

3 Place 12 wrappers on board; cover each wrapper with another, placed on the diagonal to form star shape. Place rounded teaspoons of the filling mixture in centre of each star; gather corners to form pouch shape. Tie green onion slice around neck of each pouch to hold closed, secure with toothpick.

4 Make peanut dipping sauce.

5 Heat oil in deep fryer; deep-fry money bags, in batches, until crisp and browned lightly. Drain on absorbent paper.

6 Serve money bags with dipping sauce.

PEANUT DIPPING SAUCE Heat oil in small saucepan; cook garlic and onion until softened. Stir in remaining ingredients; bring to a boil. Reduce heat; simmer, stirring, about 2 minutes or until sauce thickens.

PER MONEY BAG (INCL. DIPPING SAUCE) 15.7g total fat (4.8g saturated fat); 1007kJ (241 cal); 16.5g carbohydrate; 8.8g protein; 2.4g fibre

Pork, peanut and kaffir lime spring rolls

PREPARATION TIME 50 MINUTES (PLUS STANDING TIME) **COOKING TIME** 20 MINUTES **MAKES** 20

4 dried shiitake mushrooms

½ cup (75g) roasted unsalted peanuts, chopped finely

2 green onions, chopped finely

1 medium red capsicum (200g), chopped finely

3 fresh kaffir lime leaves, shredded finely

2cm piece fresh ginger (10g), grated

500g pork mince

1 tablespoon light soy sauce

2 tablespoons oyster sauce

1 tablespoon chinese cooking wine

20 x 21.5cm square spring roll wrappers

peanut oil, for deep-frying

1 Cover mushrooms with boiling water in small heatproof bowl. Cover; stand 20 minutes, drain. Discard stems; chop caps finely.

2 Combine mushrooms in medium bowl with nuts, onion, capsicum, lime leaves, ginger, pork, sauces and wine.

3 Spoon rounded tablespoons of the pork filling onto a corner of one wrapper; roll once toward opposite corner to cover filling then fold in two remaining corners to enclose filling. Continue rolling; brush seam with a little water to seal spring roll. Repeat process with remaining wrappers and filling.

4 Heat oil in deep-fryer; deep-fry spring rolls, in batches, until golden brown and cooked through. Drain on absorbent paper.

▭ **PER SPRING ROLL** 6.6g total fat (1.4g saturated fat); 497kJ (119 cal); 7.3g carbohydrate; 7.3g protein; 0.8g fibre

---

Potato and parsley wafers

PREPARATION TIME 30 MINUTES **COOKING TIME** 5 MINUTES **SERVES** 4

500g potatoes, peeled

⅔ cup fresh flat-leaf parsley leaves

vegetable oil, for deep-frying

1 Using sharp knife, mandoline or v-slicer, cut potatoes into 2mm slices.

2 Top half of the potato slices with parsley leaves; top with remaining potato slices, press firmly to seal wafers.

3 Heat oil in deep-fryer; deep-fry wafers, in batches, until browned lightly and crisp. Drain on absorbent paper.

▭ **PER SERVING** 7.7g total fat (0.9g saturated fat); 610kJ (146 cal); 14.1g carbohydrate; 3.3g protein; 3.7g fibre

1 PORK, PEANUT AND KAFFIR LIME SPRING ROLLS **2** POTATO AND PARSLEY WAFERS
3 SALT AND PEPPER TOFU WITH CHILLI LIME DRESSING [P 70] **4** SPICY CARROT AND ZUCCHINI BHAJI [P 70]

1   2

3   4

Salt and pepper tofu with chilli lime dressing

PREPARATION TIME 25 MINUTES (PLUS STANDING TIME) **COOKING TIME** 10 MINUTES **SERVES** 4

Hot oil and water don't mix: make certain that the tofu has been thoroughly drained before deep-frying.

2 x 300g packets fresh firm tofu

1 small red capsicum (150g), sliced thinly

1 small yellow capsicum (150g), sliced thinly

100g snow peas, sliced thinly

1 small carrot (70g), sliced thinly

1 cup (80g) bean sprouts

½ cup loosely packed fresh coriander leaves

1 teaspoon coarsely ground black pepper

1 tablespoon sea salt

¼ teaspoon five-spice powder

⅓ cup (50g) plain flour

peanut oil, for deep-frying

CHILLI LIME DRESSING

2 tablespoons peanut oil

¼ cup (60ml) lime juice

2 tablespoons sweet chilli sauce

1 Dry tofu with absorbent paper. Cut each piece in half horizontally; cut each half into quarters (you will have 16 pieces). Place tofu pieces, in single layer, on absorbent paper. Cover with more absorbent paper; stand 15 minutes.

2 Meanwhile, combine capsicums, snow peas, carrot, sprouts and coriander in large bowl.

3 Whisk ingredients for chilli lime dressing in small bowl.

4 Combine pepper, salt, five-spice and flour in medium bowl; coat tofu in mixture, shake away excess. Heat oil in deep-fryer; deep-fry tofu, in batches, until browned lightly. Drain on absorbent paper.

5 Serve tofu topped with salad; drizzle with dressing.

▭ **PER SERVING** 28.2g total fat (4.7g saturated fat); 1772kJ (424 cal); 17.8g carbohydrate; 22g protein; 6.1g fibre

---

Spicy carrot and zucchini bhaji

PREPARATION TIME 15 MINUTES **COOKING TIME** 15 MINUTES **MAKES** 20

Some Indian cooks add about 2 to 3 tablespoons of the clean hot oil to the batter to make the bhajis crisp. If you want to try this, do so carefully as it will sizzle – carefully whisk it into the batter. Do not overcrowd batches of batter or it will stick together and form one big bhaji!

1 cup (150g) besan flour

2 teaspoons salt

½ cup (125ml) cold water

¼ teaspoon ground turmeric

1 teaspoon chilli powder

1 teaspoon garam masala

2 cloves garlic, crushed

2 small brown onions (160g), sliced thinly

1 medium carrot (120g), grated coarsely

1 medium zucchini (120g), grated coarsely

½ cup loosely packed fresh coriander leaves

vegetable oil, for deep-frying

1 cup (320g) mango chutney

1 Whisk besan, salt and the water in medium bowl until mixture forms a smooth thick batter. Stir in spices, garlic, onion, carrot, zucchini and coriander.

2 Heat oil in wok; deep-fry tablespoons of mixture, in batches, until vegetables are tender and bhaji are browned lightly. Drain on absorbent paper. Serve with chutney.

▭ **PER BHAJI** 2.3g total fat (0.3g saturated fat); 330kJ (79 cal); 12.1g carbohydrate; 2g protein; 1.6g fibre

Fish cakes

PREPARATION TIME 15 MINUTES **COOKING TIME** 10 MINUTES **MAKES** 16

500g firm white fish fillets, skinned and boned

2 tablespoons red curry paste

2 fresh kaffir lime leaves, torn

2 green onions, chopped coarsely

1 tablespoon fish sauce

1 tablespoon lime juice

2 tablespoons finely chopped fresh coriander

3 snake beans (30g), chopped finely

2 fresh small red thai chillies, chopped finely

peanut oil, for deep-frying

1 Cut fish into small pieces. Process fish with curry paste, lime leaves, onion, sauce and juice until mixture forms a smooth paste. Combine fish mixture in medium bowl with coriander, beans and chilli.

2 Roll a heaped tablespoon of the fish mixture into ball, then flatten into cake shape; repeat with remaining mixture.

3 Heat oil in deep-fryer; deep-fry fish cakes, in batches, until browned lightly and cooked through. Drain. Serve with fresh coriander leaves and lime wedges, if desired.

▭ **PER CAKE** 3.5g total fat (0.6g saturated fat); 255kJ (61 cal); 0.4g carbohydrate; 6.7g protein; 0.4g fibre

Called tod mun pla on Thai menus, these fish cakes are usually served with a cucumber dipping sauce drizzled over the top and a small mound of grated carrot on the side.

Prawns in wonton wrappers

PREPARATION TIME 20 MINUTES (PLUS REFRIGERATION TIME) **COOKING TIME** 15 MINUTES **MAKES** 24

24 uncooked medium king prawns (1kg)

1 teaspoon sesame oil

1 teaspoon peanut oil

2 cloves garlic, crushed

1 fresh long red chilli, chopped finely

2 green onions

12 wonton wrappers

vegetable oil, for deep-frying

CHILLI PLUM DIP

1/3 cup (110g) plum jam

1 fresh small red thai chilli, sliced thinly

1/4 cup (60ml) white vinegar

1 Shell and devein prawns, leaving tails intact. Combine prawns, oils, garlic and chilli in medium bowl. Cover; refrigerate 1 hour.

2 Meanwhile, cut green section of each onion into 3cm lengths. Slice each 3cm length in half lengthways; submerge onion strips in hot water briefly until just pliable.

3 Halve wonton wrappers. Top each wrapper half with an onion strip then a prawn. Brush edges of wrapper with a little water; fold wrapper over to enclose prawn and onion.

4 Heat oil in deep-fryer; deep-fry prawns, in batches, until brown. Drain.

5 Meanwhile, make chilli plum dip. Serve dip with prawns.

CHILLI PLUM DIP Stir ingredients in small saucepan over low heat until jam melts.

▭ **PER PRAWN (INCL. DIP)** 1.8g total fat (0.3g saturated fat); 238kJ (57 cal); 5.3g carbohydrate; 4.8g protein; 0.2g fibre

After you finish deep-frying, cool the oil until it's safe enough to handle. Strain it through absorbent paper, fine muslin or a coffee filter back into a glass jar or its original empty container (never mix it with unused oil). Store the oil, tightly sealed, in a cool dark place or the refrigerator. It may become opaque in the fridge but will become clear again when brought back to room temperature.

Suppli al telefono

PREPARATION TIME 15 MINUTES **COOKING TIME** 15 MINUTES **MAKES** 8

1 tablespoon olive oil

⅓ cup (40g) frozen peas

2 cloves garlic, crushed

1 cup cooked white medium-grain rice

⅓ cup (25g) finely grated parmesan cheese

1 egg, beaten lightly

1 tablespoon coarsely chopped fresh oregano

40g mozzarella cheese

½ cup (35g) stale breadcrumbs

vegetable oil, for deep-frying

1 Heat olive oil in large frying pan; cook peas and garlic until peas are just tender and garlic is fragrant.

2 Combine pea mixture in medium bowl with rice, parmesan, egg and oregano. Using hands, shape rice mixture into eight balls.

3 Cut mozzarella into eight cubes. Press a hole into the middle of each ball; insert one piece of the mozzarella, then re-mould rice to cover hole. Roll balls in breadcrumbs to coat.

4 Heat vegetable oil in deep-fryer; deep-fry balls, in batches, until lightly browned and heated through.

◻ **PER SUPPLI** 7.9g total fat (2.2g saturated fat); 548kJ (131 cal); 10g carbohydrate; 4.8g protein; 0.7g fibre

This popular Roman snack got its name from the stringy nature of the melted mozzarella cheese that resembles telephone wires when a suppli (rice croquette) is split open. You need to cook about ⅓ cup rice for this recipe but it's also a good way to use up yesterday's risotto.

Potato croquettes

PREPARATION TIME 20 MINUTES (PLUS REFRIGERATION TIME) **COOKING TIME** 25 MINUTES **MAKES** 24

1kg potatoes, peeled, chopped coarsely

2 egg yolks

20g butter

½ cup (75g) plain flour

½ cup (60g) finely grated cheddar cheese

⅓ cup (50g) plain flour, extra

2 eggs

2 tablespoons milk

1 cup (100g) packaged breadcrumbs

vegetable oil, for deep-frying

1 Boil, steam or microwave potato until tender; drain. Mash potato in large bowl with yolks, butter, flour and cheese. Cover; refrigerate 30 minutes.

2 Using floured hands, shape heaped tablespoons of the potato mixture into fairly flat fish-finger shapes, dust with extra flour; shake away excess. Dip croquettes, one at a time, in combined eggs and milk, then in breadcrumbs. Refrigerate 30 minutes.

3 Heat oil in deep-fryer; deep-fry croquettes, in batches, until browned lightly. Drain on absorbent paper.

◻ **PER CROQUETTE** 5.6g total fat (1.7g saturated fat); 464kJ (111 cal); 11.2g carbohydrate; 3.5g protein; 0.9g fibre

Croquettes can also be shaped into balls and either wrapped around a 5mm-square piece of mozzarella cheese or stuffed with a savoury filling.

SUPPLI AL TELEFONO

Knives

A selection of different knives for specific tasks is the starting point for everyone who's serious about cooking.

1 CHEF'S KNIFE

A chef's knife has a heavy, rigid blade for chopping. Blade lengths range from about 15cm to 32cm. Choose the heaviest one you can handle comfortably.

2 CARVING KNIFE

The long blade of a carving knife is meant for taking slices off a roast in one continuous action, so that each slice is clean-cut. The blade should be slightly flexible but firm enough to slice easily through soft rare meat.

3 PARING KNIFE

This small knife works like an extension of your hand for peeling, trimming and other close work. Hold it well towards the business end, with your thumb and forefinger on either side of the blade.

4 SANTOKU (EAST-WEST) KNIFE

Designed for the fine chopping, dicing and slicing often required when preparing Asian dishes, the santoku is like a shorter, thinner-bladed and straighter-edged chef's knife, often with an indented edge designed to keep food particles from sticking to the blade.

5 SERRATED KNIFE

A small serrated knife can slice through a ripe tomato or a cream bun without squashing either. A cheap one will do, but check that the blade is reasonably rigid so it will cut straight.

6 STEAK KNIFE

The correct knife for a table setting when steak, chops or bone-in chicken or other birds are to be served. The blade is thin but firm and usually serrated so diners can cut their meat without having to saw or struggle.

7 UTILITY KNIFE

Midway between a chef's knife and a paring knife, this is a useful extra for such jobs as julienning vegetables or dicing meat. It can also chop foods like onions and celery.

8 CHEESE KNIFE

This knife goes on the cheeseboard to cut a slice of cheese then pick it up on its forked tip to transfer it to a plate. You can also use it as a bar knife for cutting and spearing garnishes for drinks.

9 BONING KNIFE

Boning knives can range from large and rigid for meat with heavy bones to slim and flexible for small, delicate bones such as those of quail. A slightly flexible blade is a good all-purpose one.

10 BREAD KNIFE

A good bread knife has a long, sturdy, serrated blade that can cut through a heavy crust into a soft crumb without compressing it. Serrations are better than saw-teeth for this. This knife is also useful for cutting pies and cakes.

11 FILLETING KNIFE

Designed to separate the meat (fillets) on a fish from the skeleton, a filleting knife is thin and flexible and must be kept very sharp so it can slide between the bone and the delicate flesh without tearing it.

12 STEEL

A steel, used properly (see page 77), will keep your knives sharp. Being a precision instrument, it will be expensive. Don't bother with the cheap ones.

Choosing & caring for knives

After investing good money on quality knives, you should treat them with respect to maintain their cutting edge.

Good knives are all-important. Be prepared to spend what it takes for a top-quality chef's knife. A knife that is really good and also cheap is not a possibility, no matter what the ads may say. For a start, the blade has to be made of expensive high-carbon steel, usually *very* expensive high-carbon *stainless* steel which is unlike ordinary stainless in that it can be sharpened to a lasting razor-edge, and unlike ordinary carbon steel, food acids can't mark it and moisture can't rust it.

A good blade has to be forged to shape and strengthen it; tempered to harden it; ground to sharpen it; and, very importantly, aligned in such a way that the molecules of the metal gives strength to the thin, sharpened edge.

All these are some reasons why a quality knife is expensive. Then there are questions of balance – how it feels in your hand – and how securely the blade and handle are locked together so that the constant impact of chopping won't make it wobble.

A traditional sign of quality is for the tang, the metal that extends into the handle, to run the full length and be secured by rivets. Today, there are also excellent knives that have the blade and handle made from one piece of metal; these are harder to judge by looking, but the words to check for are "fully forged from high-carbon stainless steel".

CHEF'S OR COOK'S KNIFE

If you can afford only one good knife, make it this one. A chef's knife is the faithful workhorse of the kitchen: the one you reach for to chop a little parsley or a pan full of onions; to cut vegetables effortlessly and neatly into even-sized pieces; shred spinach or cabbage; divide a pumpkin into practical portions; reduce a chunk of ham to a fine mince; and a hundred other tasks.

Its blade is heavy and rigid, though there may be some flexibility at the tip. The professional way to chop is to rock the handle briskly up and down on to the board with one hand while the fingers of the other hand rest lightly on the tip of the blade. If greater impact is required, hold the knife with both hands, horizontal to, and a little above, the board, and chop up and down several times in rapid succession.

To choose a chef's knife, hold several different sizes to find the one that feels right for your hand. Remember that the heavier it is, the easier it makes chopping.

PARING KNIFE

Looking rather like a miniature chef's knife, this little knife fits the hand for peeling and close work. Hold it with your thumb on the side of the blade nearest to you and your index finger curled against the opposite side, while the heel of your hand and the other fingers grasp the handle. This grip lets you feel the food and turn your hand as needed, giving control over the entire blade. Judge a quality paring knife the same way you do a chef's knife.

LARGE SERRATED KNIFE (BREAD KNIFE)

Endlessly useful for cutting not only bread but cakes and pastries. A serrated edge is better than saw-teeth as it won't squash delicate sponges and hard-crust breads, plus it can be sharpened.

FRUIT AND VEGETABLE KNIFE (SERRATED KNIFE)

This has a small, serrated, pointed blade, which should be stainless so it won't stain or mark fruits and vegetables. It is meant for light work only. The feature that matters is its sharp teeth to cut soft fruits like tomatoes more cleanly than a straight blade.

CARVING KNIFE

Longer, thinner and more flexible than a chef's knife, it slices meat thin or thick with long, clean strokes. Judge it by the blade: the right metal, ideally high carbon stainless steel but at least good-quality stainless steel, properly forged and ground, is more important than a mirror finish.

OTHER SPECIALISED KNIVES

For pictures and information on other-purpose knives, see pages 74 & 75.

CARING FOR KNIVES

CLEANING AND STORING For advice about how to deodorise a knife, read page 19 of the section The Clean Kitchen. For advice about how to store your knives, please see page 14 under the section Equipment Storage.

WASHING Always wash and dry knives separately and return them promptly to their block or rack. Never put a good knife into the dishwasher. The strong detergent is bad for the blade and the repeated heating and cooling can damage the internal structure of the metal.

SHARPENING Knives are sharpened by drawing the edge at a 20° angle across the fine abrasive surfaces of a sharpening stone or wheel. This is a skilled job and usually best left to the professionals, many of whom can now be found at the farmers' markets that have become so popular. Your local butcher will also sharpen your knives for a small fee.

There are also little devices for drawing the knife through, against a couple of abrasive surfaces aligned to grind the edge. These have, traditionally, been regarded as a second-rate way to treat your knives, but there are now some made by respected knife manufacturers (and priced accordingly), which they consider good enough for their superior knives.

A steel is not meant for sharpening knives but for keeping them sharp. Store it next to your knives, pick it up almost every time you pick up a knife and just draw the edge of the blade from heel to tip, at a slight angle, down the front and then the back of the steel several times. One way to do this is to stand the steel on its point on the chopping board and "slice" down on one side, then the other, as if you were cutting a fine slice of ham. Most steels have magnetised points so that, as you draw the edge of the knife blade from heel to tip along the shaft, the correct alignment of molecules along the edge is reinforced

This sticky, nutty quenelle-like sweet from North India is traditionally served in an aromatic syrup flavoured with cardamom and rosewater; our syrup has had star anise and cinnamon added to it for a zestier spice hit. Do not overheat the oil or the gulab jamun balls will burn before they are cooked through.

Gulab jaman

PREPARATION TIME 20 MINUTES (PLUS STANDING TIME) **COOKING TIME** 15 MINUTES **MAKES** 12

2 cups (440g) caster sugar

8 cardamom pods, bruised

2 cinnamon sticks

3 star anise

2 cups (500ml) water

1 teaspoon rosewater

½ cup (75g) self-raising flour

¼ cup (25g) full-cream milk powder

125g spreadable cream cheese

12 raisins

vegetable oil, for deep-frying

1 Stir sugar, spices and the water in medium saucepan over heat, without boiling, until sugar dissolves. Bring to a boil; boil, uncovered, without stirring, 5 minutes. Remove from heat; stir in rosewater. Cool.

2 Combine flour, milk powder and cheese in medium bowl to a soft dough. Turn onto floured surface; knead 10 minutes or until smooth. Roll 1 heaped teaspoon of dough around each raisin.

3 Heat oil in deep-fryer; deep-fry balls, in batches, until golden brown. Drain on absorbent paper. Place gulab jaman in syrup; stand 1 hour before serving.

☐ **PER GULAB JAMAN** 5.1g total fat (2.7g saturated fat); 953kJ (228 cal); 42.8g carbohydrate; 2.1g protein; 0.3g fibre

---

Semolina is a coarsely ground durum wheat flour that's used to make the highest quality pasta, as well as couscous and various cereals, puddings and porridges. Many Middle Eastern and Indian sweets (halva in particular) are based on semolina rather than ordinary flour. It is also a good alternative to polenta when used on the underneath side of an uncooked pizza, to help it stick to the oven tray.

Semolina fritters with almond liqueur syrup

PREPARATION TIME 15 MINUTES **COOKING TIME** 10 MINUTES **SERVES** 8

75g butter, chopped

1 cup (250ml) water

½ cup (75g) plain flour

½ cup (90g) semolina

1 tablespoon caster sugar

4 eggs, beaten lightly

½ teaspoon almond essence

vegetable oil, for deep-frying

¼ cup (30g) almond meal

ALMOND LIQUEUR SYRUP

2 cups (440g) caster sugar

1¼ cups (310ml) water

1 tablespoon almond-flavoured liqueur

1 Make almond liqueur syrup.

2 Place butter and the water in medium saucepan, bring to a boil, stirring, until butter melts.

3 Add sifted flour and semolina all at once to pan; stir vigorously over heat until mixture leaves side of pan and forms a smooth ball. Transfer to small bowl of electric mixer. Add sugar then beat in eggs beating well after each addition. Stir in essence.

4 Heat oil in deep-fryer; deep-fry heaped teaspoons of mixture, in batches, until puffed and browned lightly. Drain. Dip in syrup, serve sprinkled with almond meal.

ALMOND LIQUEUR SYRUP Stir sugar and the water in medium saucepan over heat, without boiling, until sugar dissolves; bring to a boil. Reduce heat, simmer, uncovered, without stirring, 8 minutes. Remove from heat; stir in liqueur.

☐ **PER SERVING** 16.9g total fat (6.6g saturated fat); 1977kJ (473 cal); 71.7g carbohydrate; 6.1g protein; 1g fibre

GULAB JAMAN

Ricotta peach fritters

PREPARATION TIME 20 MINUTES **COOKING TIME** 20 MINUTES **MAKES** ABOUT 35

500g ricotta cheese

½ cup (75g) self-raising flour

⅓ cup (75g) caster sugar

3 eggs, beaten lightly

2 tablespoons flaked almonds

1 teaspoon finely grated lemon rind

½ cup (100g) finely chopped glacé peaches

extra light olive oil, for deep-frying

2 tablespoons icing sugar

1 Preheat oven to 150°C/130°C fan-forced.

2 Combine cheese, flour, caster sugar, eggs, almonds, rind and peaches in medium bowl.

3 Heat oil in deep-fryer; deep-fry level tablespoons of mixture, in batches, until browned and cooked through, turning regularly. Remove fritters with a slotted spoon; drain on crumpled absorbent paper on an oven tray. Place in oven to keep warm.

4 Serve fritters immediately, dusted with sifted icing sugar.

▭ **PER FRITTER** 3.7g total fat (1.4g saturated fat); 284kJ (68 cal); 6.4g carbohydrate; 2.4g protein; 0.1g fibre

---

Berlin doughnuts

PREPARATION TIME 20 MINUTES (PLUS STANDING TIME) **COOKING TIME** 15 MINUTES **MAKES** ABOUT 25

Also known as bismarcks, jam or jelly doughnuts, these are not your typical ring-shaped deep-fried sweet roll but are raised, cake-like rounds, usually filled with jam or preserves and sprinkled with sifted icing sugar. Originally from Germany, there is one version or another of the Berlin doughnuts in almost every country in the world.

2 x 7g sachets dried yeast

¼ cup (60ml) warm water

1 cup (250ml) warm milk

¼ cup (55g) caster sugar

60g butter, melted

2 eggs, beaten lightly

3¾ cups (560g) plain flour

1 teaspoon finely grated lemon rind

1 egg white, beaten lightly

½ cup (160g) raspberry jam, approximately

vegetable oil, for deep-frying

2 tablespoons caster sugar, extra

1 Combine yeast, water, milk and sugar in small bowl. Cover; stand in warm place about 10 minutes or until mixture is frothy.

2 Stir butter and eggs into yeast mixture. Sift flour into large bowl, stir in yeast mixture and rind; mix to a soft dough. Cover; stand in warm place about 45 minutes or until dough has doubled in size.

3 Turn dough onto lightly floured surface, knead about 5 minutes or until smooth. Roll dough until about 1cm thick; cut into 5cm rounds. Brush half the rounds with egg white. Drop about 1 teaspoon of the jam in centre of each round; top with remaining rounds, pinch edges together. Re-roll remaining dough, cut into rounds, repeat with remaining egg white and jam. Loosely cover rounds with oiled plastic wrap; stand in warm place about 10 minutes or until almost doubled in size.

4 Heat oil in deep-fryer; deep-fry doughnuts, in batches, until browned, turning once. Drain on absorbent paper; toss doughnuts immediately in extra sugar.

▭ **PER DOUGHNUT** 5.7g total fat (2.1g saturated fat); 656kJ (157 cal); 22.3g carbohydrate; 3.5g protein; 1g fibre

Banana fritters

PREPARATION TIME 15 MINUTES **COOKING TIME** 10 MINUTES **SERVES** 4

½ cup (75g) plain flour

½ cup (75g) self-raising flour

1 tablespoon caster sugar

2 eggs

½ cup (125ml) milk

1 teaspoon vegetable oil

1 teaspoon vanilla extract

vegetable oil, for deep-frying, extra

4 large bananas (920g), halved crossways

1 tablespoon caster sugar, extra

1 Sift flours and sugar into medium bowl; whisk in combined eggs, milk, oil and extract.

2 Heat oil in deep-fryer. Dip banana pieces in batter; deep-fry, in batches, until browned lightly. Drain on absorbent paper; toss in extra sugar.

3 Serve fritters with ice-cream and maple syrup, if desired.

PER SERVING 14.1g total fat (2.9g saturated fat); 1822kJ (436 cal); 63.5g carbohydrate; 10.9g protein; 4.8g fibre

Banana lumpia with brown sugar syrup

PREPARATION TIME 20 MINUTES (PLUS FREEZING TIME) **COOKING TIME** 15 MINUTES **MAKES** 12

¼ cup (55g) brown sugar

¼ cup (55g) caster sugar

1 vanilla bean, split lengthways

2 star anise

1 cup (250ml) water

2 tablespoons white sugar

2 teaspoons ground cinnamon

3 small ripe bananas (390g)

12 x 12.5cm square spring roll wrappers

1 tablespoon cornflour

1 tablespoon water, extra

vegetable oil, for deep-frying

¾ cup (35g) toasted flaked coconut

COCONUT ICE-CREAM

1 cup (75g) toasted shredded coconut

¼ cup (60ml) Malibu

1 litre vanilla ice-cream, softened

1 Make coconut ice-cream.

2 Stir brown sugar, caster sugar, vanilla bean, star anise and the water in small saucepan over heat, without boiling, until sugar dissolves. Bring to a boil; boil, uncovered, without stirring, about 15 minutes or until syrup thickens. Remove and discard solids.

3 Meanwhile, combine white sugar and cinnamon in small bowl.

4 Quarter each banana lengthways. Centre 1 piece of banana on each wrapper then sprinkle each with ½ teaspoon cinnamon sugar. Fold wrapper over banana ends then roll wrapper to enclose filling. Brush edges with blended cornflour and extra water to seal.

5 Heat oil in deep-fryer; deep-fry lumpia, in batches, until golden brown and crisp. Drain. Sprinkle with combined remaining cinnamon sugar and coconut, drizzle with syrup; serve with ice cream.

COCONUT ICE-CREAM Fold coconut and Malibu into ice-cream. Cover; freeze 3 hours or overnight.

PER LUMPIA & ⅓ CUP ICE-CREAM 9.9g total fat (6.9g saturated fat); 882kJ (211 cal); 24.8g carbohydrate; 2.4g protein; 1.5g fibre

How much oil to use depends on what and how much is to be deep-fried: the food being deep-fried must be submerged completely. Use care and do not overfill your pan or wok with oil because the level rises abruptly when the food is added. Slide rather than drop the food items into the hot oil to help prevent splattering. Add them in small batches so the pan is not overcrowded and the oil temperature isn't lowered. Remove food immediately it is cooked, using a wire basket, metal slotted spoon or metal tongs.

THE OMELETTE PAN

Omelettes, with their variety and ease in preparation, are wonderfully suited to today's busy lifestyle. They can be filled with just about any ingredient you have on hand, from avocado to zucchini, and can be the ultimate in comfort food or dazzlingly elegant. Basically, omelettes can be savoury or sweet, and just as suitable for dinner as for breakfast. They can be folded in half or in thirds, or left flat, either open-faced or turned. Perhaps the most well-known type of omelette is the filled one; this is the classic French omelette, still wet in the centre, the partially cooked eggs topped with the filling then folded and served. The flat omelette, similar to Italy's frittata and Spain's tortilla, is cooked longer and turned completely over in the pan midway through cooking. This is different from the open-faced version, which has the filling stirred in with the egg before it's added to the pan; it's not folded or turned but is usually finished by a brief flourish under a preheated griller.

Spanish omelette with tomato salsa

PREPARATION TIME 20 MINUTES **COOKING TIME** 55 MINUTES **SERVES** 6

2 large potatoes (600g), sliced thinly

2 medium brown onions (300g), sliced thinly

1 medium red capsicum (200g), chopped coarsely

150g green beans, trimmed, chopped coarsely

8 eggs

¼ cup (60ml) skim milk

¼ cup coarsely chopped fresh flat-leaf parsley

TOMATO SALSA

1 large tomato (220g), seeded, chopped finely

2 lebanese cucumbers (260g), seeded, chopped finely

1 small red onion (100g), chopped finely

2 long green chillies, chopped finely

¼ cup (60ml) lemon juice

2 tablespoons finely chopped fresh coriander

1 Heat oiled 26cm frying pan; cook potato and onion, stirring, 2 minutes. Reduce heat; cook, stirring occasionally, 15 minutes. Add capsicum and beans; cook about 5 minutes or until potato is tender. Remove from heat.

2 Whisk eggs, milk and parsley in large jug. Pour over potato mixture; stir gently.

3 Return pan to low heat; cook 20 minutes. Cover loosely with foil, cook 10 minutes or until omelette is cooked.

4 Meanwhile, make tomato salsa.

5 Serve omelette with salsa.

TOMATO SALSA Combine ingredients in small bowl.

▭ **PER SERVING** 7.4g total fat (2.2g saturated fat); 1672kJ (200 cal); 18.7g carbohydrate; 14.1g protein; 4.5g fibre

Bacon and corn soufflé omelettes

PREPARATION TIME 15 MINUTES **COOKING TIME** 10 MINUTES **SERVES** 2

Called a soufflé omelette because of the way it puffs and billows when cooked, since the whites have been separated from the yolks and beaten to soft peaks, its lighter-than-air appearance make this an impressive dish to serve for brunch. Serve it with a fresh chilli and tomato salsa, if you like. Cut the kernels from two cobs of fresh corn and cook them in the pan with the bacon mixture (instead of using canned corn) for an extra bit of crunch and flavour.

3 rindless bacon rashers (195g), chopped finely

1 clove garlic, crushed

½ medium red capsicum (100g), chopped finely

3 green onions, chopped finely

125g can corn kernels, drained

6 eggs, separated

1 tablespoon water

20g butter

½ cup (60g) finely grated gruyère cheese

1 Cook bacon in oiled omelette pan until crisp. Add garlic, capsicum, onion and corn; cook, stirring, until softened. Remove from heat; cover to keep warm.
2 Lightly beat egg yolks and the water in large bowl until combined. Beat egg whites in medium bowl with electric mixer until soft peaks form; fold into yolk mixture, in two batches.
3 Meanwhile, melt half of the butter in same pan. Pour half of the egg mixture into pan, smooth top. Cook over medium heat until browned underneath. If necessary, cover pan handle with foil, then place pan under preheated grill until top is just set.
4 Spoon half of the corn mixture over omelette, sprinkle with half of the cheese. Fold in half; slide onto serving plate. Repeat with remaining butter, egg, corn mixture and cheese.

▭ **PER SERVING** 41.7g total fat (19.2g saturated fat); 2483kJ (594 cal); 11.8g carbohydrate; 44g protein; 2.5g fibre

Chinese omelettes

PREPARATION TIME 15 MINUTES **COOKING TIME** 15 MINUTES **SERVES** 4

Chinese cooks traditionally use shao hsing (sometimes spelled shao xing or called chinese cooking or rice wine), having 13.5 per cent alcohol content and made from fermented rice, wheat, sugar and salt. It's not expensive and is easily obtained from Asian food shops, so if you do a lot of Chinese cooking, it's a good idea to keep a bottle of it in your pantry. If not, replace with mirin or use sherry as we have here.

1 cup (250ml) chicken stock

1 tablespoon oyster sauce

1 tablespoon dry sherry

1 tablespoon cornflour

¼ cup (60ml) water

10 eggs

4 cups (320g) bean sprouts, chopped coarsely

1 fresh small red thai chilli, chopped finely

2 baby eggplants (120g), chopped finely

4 green onions, sliced thinly

1 tablespoon peanut oil

1 Combine stock, sauce and sherry in small saucepan; bring to a boil. Stir in blended cornflour and the water; stir until sauce boils and thickens.
2 Combine eggs, sprouts, chilli, eggplant and three-quarters of the onion in large bowl.
3 Heat oil in omelette pan; add ½ cup of the egg mixture. Flatten egg mixture with spatula; cook, uncovered, until browned and set underneath. Turn, cook other side. Repeat with remaining egg mixture to make a total of eight omelettes.
4 Divide omelettes among serving dishes; drizzle with sauce, top with remaining onion.

▭ **PER SERVING** 18.2g total fat (5g saturated fat); 1154kJ (276 cal); 6.8g carbohydrate; 20.5g protein; 3.3g fibre

1 BACON AND CORN SOUFFLE OMELETTES **2** CHINESE OMELETTES **3** MUSHROOM, CAPSICUM AND CHEESE OMELETTES [P 92] **4** ZUCCHINI AND MUSHROOM OMELETTE [P 92]

1 2

3 4

An omelette is the ultimate fast food: it cooks in minutes, is nutritious and can be eaten at any hour of the day. Serve this omelette with toast made from a baguette or a loaf of ciabatta, or with a simple mixed leaf salad, and you have the makings of a great meal.

Mushroom, capsicum and cheese omelettes

PREPARATION TIME 15 MINUTES **COOKING TIME** 15 MINUTES **SERVES** 4

20g butter

1 small red capsicum (150g), sliced thinly

200g mushrooms, sliced thinly

2 tablespoons finely chopped fresh chives

8 eggs

1 tablespoon milk

4 green onions, sliced thinly

½ cup (60g) coarsely grated cheddar cheese

1 Melt butter in omelette pan; cook capsicum, mushrooms and chives, stirring occasionally, about 4 minutes or until vegetables soften. Drain vegetable mixture on absorbent paper; cover to keep warm.

2 Whisk eggs in large jug until frothy. Whisk in milk and onion.

3 Pour half of the egg mixture into pan; tilt pan to cover base with egg mixture. Cook over medium heat about 4 minutes or until omelette is just set. Spoon half of the vegetable mixture onto one half of the omelette; sprinkle mixture with half of the cheese. Fold omelette over to enclose filling. Slide omelette onto plate; cover with foil to keep warm. Repeat with remaining egg mixture, vegetable mixture and cheese to make a total of two omelettes.

4 To serve, cut each omelette in half; place one half on each serving plate.

PER SERVING 20.3g total fat (9.4g saturated fat); 1141 kJ (273 cal); 2.5g carbohydrate; 19.7g protein; 1.9g fibre

Drain the zucchini well before stirring into the pan by either squeezing it in your hands or in absorbent paper. This is a single serving omelette but you can increase the ingredients proportionately with no problem. If doubling it, the omelette can be cooked all at once but if you want the finished product to serve four, make two omelettes.

Zucchini and mushroom omelette

PREPARATION TIME 10 MINUTES **COOKING TIME** 10 MINUTES **SERVES** 1

10g butter

1 clove garlic, crushed

25g button mushrooms, sliced thinly

¼ cup (50g) coarsely grated zucchini

1 green onion, chopped finely

2 eggs

2 teaspoons water

¼ cup (30g) coarsely grated cheddar cheese

1 Heat half of the butter in omelette pan; cook garlic and mushrooms, stirring, over medium heat about 2 minutes or until mushrooms are lightly browned. Add zucchini and onion; cook, stirring, about 1 minute or until zucchini begins to soften. Remove vegetable mixture from pan; cover to keep warm.

2 Whisk eggs and the water in small bowl; whisk in cheese.

3 Heat remaining butter in same pan; swirl to cover base. Pour egg mixture into pan; tilt pan to cover base with egg mixture. Cook over medium heat until omelette is just set. Spoon vegetable mixture evenly over half of the omelette; fold omelette over to enclose filling. Slide omelette onto serving plate.

PER SERVING 29.5g total fat (15.3g saturated fat); 1526kJ (365 cal); 2g carbohydrate; 22.5g protein; 2.2g fibre

Fines herbes omelette

PREPARATION TIME 10 MINUTES **COOKING TIME** 10 MINUTES **SERVES** 4

12 eggs

2 tablespoons finely chopped fresh curly parsley

2 tablespoons finely chopped fresh chervil

2 tablespoons finely chopped fresh chives

1 tablespoon finely chopped fresh tarragon

¼ cup (60ml) water

20g butter

1 tablespoon olive oil

1 Lightly beat eggs, herbs and the water in large bowl.

2 Heat a quarter of the butter and 1 teaspoon of the oil in omelette pan. When butter is just bubbling, add a quarter of the egg mixture; tilt pan to cover base with egg mixture. Cook over medium heat until omelette is just set. Use a spatula to lift and fold omelette in half; cook further 30 seconds. Carefully slide omelette onto serving plate.

3 Repeat with remaining butter, oil and egg mixture to make a total of four omelettes.

◻ **PER SERVING** 24.4g total fat (8.2g saturated fat); 1254kJ (300 cal); 0.6g carbohydrate; 20.1g protein; 0.2g fibre

The French staple fines herbes (pronounced feen-erb) is traditionally a blend of chervil, chives, parsley and tarragon used to season omelettes, sauces and marinades. Dried fines herbes is widely available and is good to have on hand but, for the most delightful flavour, make your own using fresh herbs. Fresh fines herbes lose their effect if heated for too long: use the dried version for long-simmering stews and sauces.

Vietnamese omelette

PREPARATION TIME 15 MINUTES (PLUS STANDING TIME) **COOKING TIME** 30 MINUTES **SERVES** 4

5 dried shiitake mushrooms

8 eggs

½ cup (125ml) milk

1 tablespoon finely chopped vietnamese mint

1 tablespoon peanut oil

5 green onions, sliced thinly

2 cloves garlic, crushed

227g can sliced bamboo shoots, drained

1 medium carrot (120g), sliced thinly

1 large red capsicum (350g), sliced thinly

1 cup (80g) bean sprouts

1 tablespoon mild chilli sauce

2 tablespoons light soy sauce

1 tablespoon finely chopped fresh coriander

1 Place mushrooms in small heatproof bowl, cover with boiling water; stand 20 minutes, then drain. Discard stems; slice caps thinly.

2 Meanwhile, whisk eggs, milk and mint in medium bowl until combined.

3 Heat half of the oil in omelette pan; cook onion, garlic and bamboo shoots, stirring, until onion softens. Add carrot and capsicum; cook, stirring, until carrot is just tender. Add mushrooms, sprouts, sauces and coriander; cook, stirring, until hot. Remove from pan; keep warm.

4 Heat a quarter of the remaining oil in pan, add a quarter of the egg mixture; tilt pan to cover base. Cook over medium heat until omelette is almost set. Spoon a quarter of the vegetable mixture over half the omelette. Fold omelette over; slide onto serving plate. Repeat with remaining egg and vegetable mixture.

◻ **PER SERVING** 16.7g total fat (4.9g saturated fat); 1104kJ (264 cal); 9.1g carbohydrate; 17.8g protein; 5.9g fibre

Not a mint at all, but a pungent and peppery narrow-leafed member of the buckwheat family, vietnamese mint is also known by different names depending on each recipe's origins: in Thai cooking, it's called pak pai; the Indonesians refer to it as laksa leaf; and it's known as daun kesom in the food of Singapore. In Vietnamese cooking, it's called rau ram and is used as frequently as a Western kitchen uses onion. Eaten uncooked in rice-paper rolls and salads, it's always sprinkled over a bowl of steaming pho, stirred into an omelette or tossed in a stir-fry.

Preparing food decoratively

The addition of these finishing touches to your food instantly lifts the ordinary to the extraordinary.

MANGO CHEEKS
Lay fruit on narrow side and cut off each side close to the seed. Turn cheek, flesh-side up, cut into diamond shapes without piercing skin. Press underneath to open out.

NEAT LEMON WEDGE
Cut a lemon lengthwise into sixths, or eighths if large. Lay each wedge on cutting board and cut off the white rib cleanly. Remove any seeds. If preferred, cut out rib with slanting cuts on each side to give a notched effect.

DRIZZLING WITH SQUEEZE BOTTLE
Keep balsamic vinegar and/or olive oil in squeeze bottles and squeeze drops around the edge of plate, or squeeze zigzag trails across the food, being careful not to add too much.

SHREDDING GREEN ONIONS
For elegant shreds of green onion, trim onions and lay, two or three at a time, close together on a cutting board. Use a plain-edged, heavy knife, held at an acute diagonal to the stems, to cut very thin slices.

FLAKING PARMESAN CHEESE
For a Caesar or other salad, or a garnish for pasta, hold a block of parmesan in one hand and, with the other hand, draw a vegetable peeler or cheese plane down the narrow side to take off thin shavings.

LIME CHEEKS
To decorate Asian dishes and provide a refreshing dressing for diners to squeeze onto their food just before eating, cut limes lengthwise on each side of the centre to remove cheeks with none of the white core.

GRATING CHOCOLATE

For clean shreds of chocolate to decorate a cake or dessert, wrap tightly in plastic wrap and freeze until firm but not frozen, then grate or shave and refrigerate until required.

SERVING OYSTERS AND MUSSELS

To present oysters or mussels as an entrée or on a buffet table, make a bed of rock salt or crushed ice on individual plates or a serving platter and push opened shellfish into it in circles. Sauce can go in the centre.

GRATING OR SIFTING

Place cocoa, ground nutmeg and/or icing sugar in a sieve, hold over the plate and sift over by tapping the sieve. Whole nutmeg can be grated directly onto sweet or savoury dishes.

DEEP-FRYING HERBS

For a stylish and delicious garnish for seafood or meat, put washed and dried sprigs of parsley, other soft herbs or watercress, a few pieces at a time, into a metal sieve and plunge into a deep-sided pan containing very hot oil for about 3 seconds. Stand back, they will spatter.

ROASTING FLAKED ALMONDS

Roasted flaked almonds partner both sweet and savoury dishes perfectly. Fresh summer fruits, creamy ice-cream and delicate sponges taste even more glorious with a sprinkle of the roasted nut; throw a handful of roasted flaked almonds into a mixed green salad for a delicious crunch. To prepare, place the nuts in a heated frying pan and stir over heat until the nuts start to brown – be vigilant as they don't take long to brown and can burn in an instant.

SEGMENTING ORANGES

For skinless segments for a salad or dessert, cut a slice off the top and bottom of an orange; stand it upright and cut down all around, just inside the pith, to remove peel. Cut down each side of each membrane to remove segments.

The "tamagoyaki", a Japanese rolled omelette, is also known as a Japanese-style egg roll; it is usually served at breakfast or as part of a "bento", lunch box. In Japan, a tamagoyaki is made in a special small, rectangular pan, as the shape makes the final rolling easier. The addition of sweet mirin can tend to make the omelette scorch so it should be watched carefully. Mirin, along with soy sauce and dashi, is one of Japan's three essential condiments. Its subtle, natural sweetness and balanced flavour make it very versatile; it should not be confused with sake which is made of glutinous rice and alcohol expressly for cooking.

Japanese omelette

PREPARATION TIME 5 MINUTES **COOKING TIME** 10 MINUTES (PLUS COOLING TIME) **SERVES** 4

8 eggs

1 tablespoon water

2 teaspoons sugar

3 teaspoons mirin

2 teaspoons light soy sauce

2 tablespoons vegetable oil

⅓ cup (80ml) japanese soy sauce

¼ cup (60g) finely grated daikon, drained well

1 Stir eggs, the water, sugar, mirin and light soy sauce in large jug until sugar dissolves.

2 Heat lightly oiled omelette pan; pour in enough egg mixture to just cover base of pan. Cook, tilting pan to spread mixture evenly. Break any large air bubbles so omelette lies flat. When mixture is almost set, run chopsticks or spatula around edge of pan to loosen omelette.

3 Starting from back of the pan, fold omelette into three towards front of pan. Gently push folded omelette to back of pan.

4 Lightly oil pan again, repeat procedure, lifting up cooked omelette so egg mixture runs underneath it. When nearly cooked, fold in three, starting with the omelette already cooked and folded. Repeat this step until all mixture is used.

5 Tip omelette onto a bamboo mat and wrap firmly to form a compact rectangle. Cool omelette; cut into 1cm slices. Serve with japanese soy sauce and daikon.

▭ **PER SERVING** 19.7g total fat (4.4g saturated fat); 1045kJ (250 cal); 3.4g carbohydrate; 14.7g protein; 0.2g fibre

It's criminal to waste the 12 egg yolks here, especially when you can freeze them for another day. Drop a single yolk into each section of an ice block tray then cover the tray and freeze, popping out the yolks as your needs dictate. Some recipes that call for lots of egg yolks are hollandaise, aïoli, custard, lemon curd, crème brûlée, pots de crème, crème anglaise and zabaglione.

Egg-white omelette

PREPARATION TIME 25 MINUTES **COOKING TIME** 20 MINUTES **SERVES** 4

12 egg whites

4 green onions, chopped finely

½ cup finely chopped fresh flat-leaf parsley

¼ cup finely chopped fresh chives

¼ cup finely chopped fresh chervil

½ cup (60g) coarsely grated cheddar cheese

½ cup (50g) coarsely grated mozzarella cheese

1 Preheat grill.

2 Beat a quarter of the egg white in small bowl with electric mixer until soft peaks form; fold in a quarter of the combined onion and herbs.

3 Pour mixture into lightly oiled omelette pan; cook, uncovered, over low heat until omelette is just browned lightly on the bottom.

4 Sprinkle a quarter of the combined cheeses on half of the omelette. Place pan under preheated grill until cheese begins to melt and omelette sets; fold omelette over to completely cover cheese. Carefully slide onto serving plate; serve immediately.

5 Repeat with remaining egg white, onion mixture and cheese to make four omelettes.

▭ **PER SERVING** 8g total fat (5.1g saturated fat); 623kJ (149 cal); 1g carbohydrate; 18g protein; 0.7g fibre

Ratatouille omelette

PREPARATION TIME 15 MINUTES **COOKING TIME** 25 MINUTES **SERVES** 4

1 tablespoon oil	1 small red capsicum (150g), chopped
1 clove garlic, crushed	1 medium zucchini (120g), chopped
1 small red onion (100g), chopped finely	400g can chopped tomatoes
2 anchovy fillets, drained	6 eggs
1 small eggplant (230g), chopped	1 tablespoon water

1 Heat oil in frying pan; cook garlic and onion, stirring, until onion is soft. Stir in chopped anchovies, vegetables and undrained tomatoes; bring to a boil. Reduce heat, simmer, uncovered, about 10 minutes or until thickened.

2 Whisk eggs and the water in a medium bowl until just combined. Pour enough egg mixture into heated oiled omelette pan to just cover base of pan; cook until egg is almost set. Place about a quarter of the filling over half omelette. Fold omelette in half; slide onto serving plate. Repeat with remaining egg mixture and filling.

☐ **PER SERVING** 15.5g total fat (3.1g saturated fat); 915kJ (219 cal); 8g carbohydrate; 15g protein; 3.8g fibre

The ratatouille – or any soupy filling – should be cooked long enough so that it's fairly dry; if you add a really wet filling to an omelette it will ooze out the sides and can penetrate the omelette "package". The filling must be cooked completely because it won't cook any further once it meets the egg; similarly, the filling must remain hot so it doesn't cool the omelette. You can use almost anything for a filling but you still want to be able to taste the eggs.

Dessert omelette

PREPARATION TIME 15 MINUTES **COOKING TIME** 20 MINUTES **SERVES** 1

30g butter	2 eggs, separated
2 tablespoons brown sugar	2 tablespoons water
¼ cup fruit mince	1 tablespoon caster sugar
1 tablespoon dark rum	15g butter, extra
1 tablespoon finely grated lemon rind	

1 Melt butter in small frying pan, add brown sugar; cook, stirring, without boiling, until sugar is dissolved. Stir in fruit mince, rum and rind. Cover to keep warm.

2 Whisk egg yolks, the water and caster sugar in medium bowl. Beat egg whites in small bowl with electric mixer until soft peaks form; fold into yolk mixture, in two batches.

3 Preheat grill.

4 Heat omelette pan, add extra butter, swirl to cover base. Pour in egg mixture; cook over high heat about 20 seconds or until base of omelette begins to brown. Place pan under grill a further 20 seconds or until top is set. Use a spatula to fold omelette in half and slide onto serving plate. Serve immediately, topped with fruit mince mixture.

☐ **PER SERVING** 39.5g total fat (25.1g saturated fat); 3311kJ (792 cal); 85.6g carbohydrate; 13.2g protein; 3g fibre

This is a particularly good omelette to serve over the festive season as its flavours are reminiscent of a Christmas pudding – sprinkle it with a little sifted icing sugar just before serving. You can leave out the rum, if you prefer, and replace it with non-alcoholic vanilla or rum extract, or pineapple juice flavoured with almond extract.

THE GRILL PAN

The Grill Pan

The grill pan is used for cooking food in a way similar to barbecuing, but indoors on your kitchen cooktop. The French have cooked with ridged grill pans for generations, but it arrived here only in recent years. Most of us first encountered food cooked like this, with its distinctive dark-barred marking, in restaurants. It looked stylish and tasted marvellous, and when the grill pan became available for home cooks, it was a great success.

The food is charred where it has touched the very hot ridges, while the heat rising from the base of the pan cooks the parts in between. Char-grilling is a fast cooking method, best suited to small, tender items of food. It is a healthy way to cook because excess fat seeps off into the gutters between the ridges while the food is held above it. And, like the restaurant food that impressed us so much, it looks stylish and tastes marvellous. Grill pans are available in round, square and rectangular shapes, in various sizes.

MATERIALS

Grill pans are made from a number of different materials including enamelled cast iron, titanium and bare iron; read about the performance of these materials and how to care for them in *The Frying Pan* (see Material page 22 and Care page 23).

There also are grill pans made from aluminium, which has been "hard-anodised" to give it an extremely tough, naturally non-stick surface. Other grill pans made from aluminium have a trademarked finish called Calphalon, which is produced by an electrochemical process and is non-stick by virtue of its composition rather than a coating, so is extremely durable and safe. Both the hard-anodising and Calphalon processes change the behaviour of the aluminium so that it becomes non-reactive and has no adverse effect on the flavour, odour or colour of food cooked with it.

USE

Foods suitable for char-grilling include:

SEAFOOD thick meaty fish fillets and steaks (salmon, ling); prawns; scampi; crab; lobster

MEATS beef, veal, pork or lamb steaks, fillets, chops or cutlets; lamb backstrap; frankfurts, kransky or similar sausages (pre-poached); hamburgers; thickly sliced salami or similar

POULTRY skin-on chicken pieces; chicken thigh fillets; skinless chicken breast; butterflied quail, spatchcock or duckling; skin-on or skinless duck breast

VEGETABLES asparagus, zucchini, eggplant, corn on the cob, capsicum; halved or quartered onion; skin-on, thickly sliced, parboiled pumpkin, potato and sweet potato

FRUITS pineapple slices; peach, nectarine, apricot or fig halves; mango cheeks

BREADS thickly sliced sourdough or any other good bread; sandwiches; english muffins; pitta; halved brioches, bagels or hamburger buns (cut sides).

GRILL PAN TECHNIQUES

It is important to note that char-grilling creates smoky fumes and you need a good exhaust fan, preferably ducted to the outside, to avoid ending up with a smoke-filled kitchen.

Just before heating, brush or spray both food and grill pan with melted butter or oil (some manufacturers advise against using aerosol sprays on their cookware as it can impair the non-stick finish – in this case, you may wish to keep a plastic spray bottle of oil for the purpose). Also be aware that using an aerosol spray near a naked flame could cause flare-ups. Place food, spaced slightly apart, across the ridges of the grill. Immediately press each piece down lightly with tongs to ensure it has full contact with the ridges.

Allow the food to grill for a few minutes without moving it so that the char marks will be clearly defined; to get a criss-cross pattern, turn food at right angles to its original position once it is initially well marked. Lift one edge to check when food is done to your liking and turn to the other side, or remove if only one side is to be grilled. It's best not to turn food more than once, not only will you lose some of the char marks but it's not good for the food, particularly seafood and most meats.

GRILLING THIN OR DELICATE ITEMS seafood or thin steaks or cutlets may be all but cooked by the time they are well marked on the first side. If so, cook them on the second side for only a minute or less, then take them off whether the second side is marked or not. Serve with the well-marked side up, and the diner will neither know nor care what the underside looks like.

GRILLING LARGE ITEMS large or thick items, such as a chicken maryland, may not be cooked through even when they look well-grilled on the outside. Rather than continuing to grill the piece and risking scorching or drying it out, have an oven tray ready in a moderate oven and transfer the food to that to finish cooking, turning it once, if necessary.

GRILLING FISH dust fish with flour, if preferred, then coat in melted butter or spray with oil before cooking to protect it and help it colour quickly. All seafood should be removed from the grill pan while it is still a shade underdone, its own heat will finish cooking it by the time it is served. Tuna and salmon are often served barely seared.

CARE

Follow any directions from the manufacturer about seasoning or not seasoning your grill pan before use. Failing special instructions, season a bare iron grill pan as described in *The Frying Pan* (see Care on page 23).

Immediately cooking is finished, run very hot water over the grill or plunge it into a sink of very hot water (not cooler water as this may cause thermal shock to the very hot pan, weakening the inner structure of the metal, which could eventually cause it to crack). The water will boil up from the heat of the grill and loosen the food residues left on the pan. Brush with a stiff brush (not metal) to remove all residues. Dry with a cloth and place over very low heat for a few minutes to dry thoroughly.

Store where it won't get scratched. With repeated use, the pan will gradually acquire an attractive, black, slightly slick surface, or patina, that will make it increasingly non-stick.

Even non-vegetarians will enjoy this innovative way to eat tofu; firm silken tofu, made by straining soy milk through silk, makes a perfect burger patty when combined with spicy onions. The patties, served without the turkish bread, are an easy weeknight meal if accompanied with a watercress, pear and mint salad.

Tofu and vegie burger

PREPARATION TIME 20 MINUTES (PLUS STANDING TIME)
COOKING TIME 20 MINUTES (PLUS REFRIGERATION TIME) **SERVES** 4

300g firm silken tofu

1 tablespoon olive oil

1 medium brown onion (150g), chopped finely

2 cloves garlic, crushed

¼ teaspoon sweet paprika

1 teaspoon ground turmeric

2 teaspoons ground coriander

1 small zucchini (90g), grated coarsely

2 cups (140g) fresh breadcrumbs

¾ cup (190g) hummus

¼ cup (70g) greek-style yogurt

1 loaf turkish bread (430g)

⅓ cup coarsely chopped fresh mint

½ cup coarsely chopped fresh flat-leaf parsley

1 green onion, sliced thinly

30g snow pea sprouts, trimmed

1 Pat tofu dry with absorbent paper. Spread tofu, in single layer, on absorbent-paper-lined tray; cover tofu with more paper, stand 20 minutes.

2 Meanwhile, heat oil in medium frying pan; cook brown onion and garlic, stirring, until onion softens. Add spices; cook, stirring, until fragrant.

3 Combine onion mixture in large bowl with tofu, zucchini and breadcrumbs; shape into four patties. Cover; refrigerate 30 minutes.

4 Meanwhile, combine hummus and yogurt in small bowl.

5 Cut bread into four; split each in half horizontally. Toast cut sides on heated oiled grill pan.

6 Cook patties in same oiled grill pan until browned both sides and hot.

7 Spread bread with hummus mixture; sandwich combined mint, parsley and green onion, patties and sprouts between bread pieces.

☐ **PER SERVING** 24.1g total fat (4.6g saturated fat); 2880kJ (689 cal); 81.5g carbohydrate; 30.2g protein; 11.7g fibre

Add a finely chopped fresh red thai chilli or two to the mixture for a super hot and authentically Thai flavour.

Hot and spicy fish cutlets

PREPARATION TIME 10 MINUTES (PLUS REFRIGERATION TIME) **COOKING TIME** 10 MINUTES **SERVES** 4

1 tablespoon hot paprika

2 teaspoons ground ginger

1 teaspoon curry powder

¼ teaspoon chilli powder

¼ cup (60ml) malt vinegar

¼ cup (70g) tomato paste

1 cup (250ml) dry white wine

2 cloves garlic, crushed

4 firm white fish cutlets (1kg)

1 Combine ingredients in large bowl. Cover; refrigerate 3 hours or overnight.

2 Remove fish from marinade; discard marinade. Cook fish on heated oiled grill pan until cooked as desired. Serve with couscous and lemon, if desired.

☐ **PER SERVING** 4.6g total fat (1.4g saturated fat); 1091kJ (261 cal); 2.2g carbohydrate; 41.6g protein; 1.1g fibre

TOFU AND VEGIE BURGER

Grilled chicken with coriander and chilli

PREPARATION TIME 10 MINUTES (PLUS REFRIGERATION TIME) **COOKING TIME** 25 MINUTES **SERVES** 4

Red capsicum cooked on a grill pan has a beautiful smoky flavour; to make grilled capsicum, quarter two medium red capsicums then discard their seeds and membranes. Cook capsicum in the pan with the chicken, skin-side down, until the skin blisters and blackens. Cover capsicum pieces with plastic or paper for 5 minutes then peel away the skin. Serve the grilled capsicum, doused with a good squeeze of fresh lime, with the chicken cutlets.

8 chicken thigh cutlets (1.6kg)

CORIANDER AND CHILLI PASTE

2 teaspoons coriander seeds

4 fresh small red thai chillies, chopped coarsely

1 teaspoon ground cumin

2 cloves

2 cardamom pods, bruised

¼ teaspoon ground turmeric

10cm stick fresh lemon grass (20g), chopped coarsely

2 medium brown onions (300g), chopped coarsely

4 cloves garlic

⅓ cup (80ml) lime juice

2 teaspoons salt

2 tablespoons peanut oil

1 Make coriander and chilli paste.

2 Pierce chicken all over with sharp knife. Combine paste and chicken in large bowl, rubbing paste into cuts. Cover; refrigerate overnight.

3 Cook chicken, covered, in heated oiled grill pan 5 minutes. Uncover; cook, turning occasionally, about 20 minutes or until cooked.

CORIANDER AND CHILLI PASTE Blend or process ingredients until mixture forms a smooth paste.

PER SERVING 29.5g total fat (7.8g saturated fat); 2094kJ (501 cal); 5.2g carbohydrate; 53.5g protein; 1.7g fibre

---

Lamb kofta platter

PREPARATION TIME 20 MINUTES **COOKING TIME** 15 MINUTES **SERVES** 4

Pitta keeps well when frozen: simply pop it, piece by piece, in a microwave oven and zap it on HIGH for 30 seconds to make it warm, soft and almost as good as freshly baked to serve with this platter.

650g lamb mince

1 medium brown onion (150g), chopped finely

1 clove garlic, crushed

1 teaspoon ground cumin

1 teaspoon ground coriander

1 cup (70g) stale breadcrumbs

1 egg

4 pocket pitta

1 tablespoon olive oil

250g tabbouleh

1 medium tomato (150g), chopped finely

200g hummus

1 teaspoon olive oil, extra

¼ teaspoon hot paprika

200g beetroot dip

1 Combine lamb, onion, garlic, spices, breadcrumbs and egg in medium bowl.

2 Shape kofta mixture into 12 ovals; thread onto skewers. Cook skewers in heated oiled grill pan until cooked through.

3 Brush bread with oil; cook in same heated grill pan until browned.

4 Combine tabouleh and tomato in bowl. Drizzle hummus with extra oil, sprinkle with paprika.

5 Arrange kofta skewers, pitta, tabbouleh, hummus, beetroot dip and, if desired, lemon wedges, on a serving platter.

PER SERVING 38.3g total fat (9.7g saturated fat); 3612kJ (864 cal); 70g carbohydrate; 53.5g protein; 12.5g fibre

Italian-style mini meatloaves

PREPARATION TIME 15 MINUTES **COOKING TIME** 30 MINUTES **SERVES** 4

500g chicken mince

2 cloves garlic, crushed

1 fresh small red thai chilli, chopped finely

⅓ cup (35g) packaged breadcrumbs

1 egg

⅓ cup coarsely chopped fresh basil

⅓ cup (50g) finely chopped sun-dried tomatoes in oil

2 tablespoons roasted pine nuts, chopped coarsely

cooking-oil spray

4 slices prosciutto (60g)

Beef mince can be used in place of the chicken mince, if you like. While the meatloaves are cooking, add some sliced potato to the grill and cook until tender. Combine the cooked potato with olive oil, coarsely chopped fresh parsley, finely grated lemon rind and salt and pepper to taste, for a simple, yet delicious, accompaniment.

1 Combine mince, garlic, chilli, breadcrumbs, egg, basil, tomato and nuts in large bowl; shape mixture into four meatloaves.

2 Coat four 25cm pieces foil with cooking-oil spray. Wrap 1 slice prosciutto around each meatloaf; wrap meatloaves in foil.

3 Cook meatloaves in heated oiled grill pan, turning occasionally, about 25 minutes or until cooked through.

4 Remove foil from meatloaves; serve sliced with warm potato salad, if desired.

☐ **PER SERVING** 19.3g total fat (7.2g saturated fat); 1467kJ (351 cal); 10.8g carbohydrate; 32.1g protein; 2.9g fibre

Grilled thigh fillets with salsa verde and kipfler smash

PREPARATION TIME 15 MINUTES **COOKING TIME** 25 MINUTES **SERVES** 4

8 chicken thigh fillets (880g)

600g kipfler potatoes, unpeeled

50g butter, chopped

SALSA VERDE

½ cup coarsely chopped fresh flat-leaf parsley

¼ cup coarsely chopped fresh mint

⅓ cup (80ml) olive oil

½ cup (125ml) lemon juice

¼ cup (50g) capers, rinsed, drained, chopped coarsely

8 anchovy fillets, drained, chopped finely

2 cloves garlic, crushed

While we generally associate the word "salsa" with Mexican salads, sauces or dips, this zesty fresh herb sauce is, in fact, an Italian classic, that adds tang to poached or steamed fish dishes, and is a part of a traditional Italian bollito misto, the famous Piedmontese version of a boiled dinner. The herbs used in salsa verde can vary, with the single common denominator being parsley.

1 Make salsa verde.

2 Combine chicken and ⅓ cup of the salsa verde in medium bowl.

3 Cook chicken in heated oiled grill pan until browned both sides and cooked through.

4 Meanwhile, boil, steam or microwave potatoes until tender; drain. Using potato masher, crush potato roughly in large bowl with butter. Cover to keep warm.

5 Serve chicken with potato topped with remaining salsa verde.

SALSA VERDE Combine ingredients in small bowl.

☐ **PER SERVING** 45.3g total fat (14.3g saturated fat); 2897kJ (693 cal); 22.1g carbohydrate; 47.2g protein; 3.5g fibre

Mexican pork cutlets with avocado salsa

PREPARATION TIME 10 MINUTES **COOKING TIME** 10 MINUTES **SERVES** 4

2 tablespoons taco seasoning mix

¼ cup (60ml) olive oil

4 x 235g pork cutlets

3 small tomatoes (270g), seeded, chopped finely

1 small avocado (200g), chopped finely

1 lebanese cucumber (130g), seeded, chopped finely

1 tablespoon lime juice

1 Combine seasoning, 2 tablespoons of the oil and pork in large bowl.

2 Cook pork in heated oiled grill pan until cooked.

3 Meanwhile, combine remaining oil in medium bowl with tomato, avocado, cucumber and juice. Serve pork with salsa.

⬚ **PER SERVING** 42.2g total fat (10.7g saturated fat); 2241kJ (536 cal); 1.2g carbohydrate; 38g protein; 1.2g fibre

Taco seasoning mix is sold in sachets in most supermarkets. If you can't find it, or would prefer to use something else, a mixture of ground cumin, chilli flakes and ground oregano works just as well.

Grilled vegetables with garlic rosemary dressing

PREPARATION TIME 30 MINUTES **COOKING TIME** 30 MINUTES **SERVES** 4

1 medium red capsicum (200g)

1 medium yellow capsicum (200g)

¼ cup (60ml) olive oil

1 clove garlic, crushed

1 teaspoon finely grated lemon rind

2 teaspoons finely chopped fresh rosemary

1 medium red onion (170g), cut into wedges

2 small leeks (400g), trimmed, cut into 2cm pieces

1 medium eggplant (300g), sliced thickly

2 medium zucchini (240g), sliced thickly

4 flat mushrooms (320g), quartered

3 cloves garlic, unpeeled

⅓ cup (100g) mayonnaise

1 tablespoon lemon juice

1 Quarter capsicums, discard seeds and membranes. Roast under grill or in very hot oven, skin-side up, until skin blisters and blackens. Cover capsicum pieces in plastic or paper for 5 minutes; peel away skin, slice thickly.

2 Combine oil, crushed garlic, rind and half the rosemary in small bowl.

3 Brush onion, leek, eggplant, zucchini, mushrooms and unpeeled garlic with oil mixture; cook vegetables, in batches, in heated oiled grill pan until tender.

4 Squeeze cooked garlic into small jug; discard skins. Whisk in remaining rosemary, mayonnaise and juice. Serve vegetables with dressing.

⬚ **PER SERVING** 22.8g total fat (2.9g saturated fat); 1325kJ (317 cal); 16.9g carbohydrate; 7.9g protein; 8.4g fibre

Perfect served just as is, with a few slices of fresh, crusty bread such as sourdough or ciabatta or, for a larger meal, teamed with grilled racks of lamb cutlets. Rosemary marries well with lamb, and best of all, you probably have a whole stack of the herb growing in your garden.

MEXICAN PORK CUTLETS WITH AVOCADO SALSA

Egyptian in origin and delicious in flavour, this nutty mixture forms a perfect crust for meats, as well as being a tasty addition sprinkled into a simple green salad. If you double the dukkah recipe, save the remainder in an airtight container and, next time you have guests around for a drink, simply serve the dukkah in a small bowl, accompanied with fresh bread and good olive oil – it makes the easiest dip in the world.

Dukkah-crusted cutlets with roasted garlic yogurt

PREPARATION TIME 10 MINUTES **COOKING TIME** 20 MINUTES **SERVES** 4

6 cloves garlic, unpeeled

1 teaspoon vegetable oil

1 cup (280g) yogurt

2 tablespoons roasted hazelnuts

2 tablespoons roasted pistachios

2 tablespoons sesame seeds

2 tablespoons ground coriander

1 tablespoon ground cumin

12 french-trimmed lamb cutlets (600g)

1 Preheat oven to 180°C/160°C fan-forced.

2 Place garlic on oven tray; drizzle with oil. Roast 10 minutes. Peel garlic then crush in small bowl with yogurt. Cover; refrigerate.

3 To make dukkah, blend or process nuts until chopped finely. Dry-fry seeds and spices in small frying pan until fragrant; combine with nuts in medium bowl, add lamb, turn to coat in dukkah mixture.

4 Cook lamb, both sides, in heated oiled grill pan until cooked. Serve with garlic yogurt.

　PER SERVING 27.8g total fat (8.7g saturated fat); 1547kJ (370 cal); 5.7g carbohydrate; 22.9g protein; 2.9g fibre

There's a lot to love about lentils: they're high in dietary fibre; nutty and earthy in flavour; low in calories; a good source of vitamin B and protein; and – most of all – simply delicious. We've used brown lentils in this recipe because they hold their shape well when cooked and are easily found in supermarkets.

Beef sausage and lentil salad

PREPARATION TIME 30 MINUTES **COOKING TIME** 40 MINUTES **SERVES** 4

2 cups (400g) brown lentils

2 sprigs fresh thyme

20 baby beetroots (500g), trimmed

8 thick beef sausages (1.2kg)

2 teaspoons olive oil

1 large brown onion (200g), chopped finely

2 teaspoons yellow mustard seeds

2 teaspoons ground cumin

1 teaspoon ground coriander

½ cup (125ml) chicken stock

100g baby spinach leaves

THYME DRESSING

1 teaspoon fresh thyme leaves

1 clove garlic, crushed

½ cup (125ml) red wine vinegar

¼ cup (60ml) olive oil

1 Place ingredients for thyme dressing in screw-top jar; shake well.

2 Cook lentils in large saucepan of boiling water with thyme until lentils are tender; drain, discard thyme. Combine lentils and half the dressing in large bowl.

3 Meanwhile, boil, steam or microwave unpeeled beetroots until tender; drain. When cool enough to handle, peel and halve beetroots.

4 Cook sausages in heated oiled grill pan until cooked. Stand 5 minutes, slice thickly.

5 Heat oil in small saucepan; cook onion, seeds and spices, stirring, until onion softens. Add stock; bring to a boil.

6 Combine onion mixture, spinach, beetroot, sausage and remaining dressing with lentils.

　PER SERVING 94.5g total fat (39.2g saturated fat); 5676kJ (1358 cal); 55.8g carbohydrate; 62.8g protein; 26.4g fibre

Veal cutlets with warm red lentils and cauliflower

PREPARATION TIME 20 MINUTES **COOKING TIME** 30 MINUTES **SERVES** 4

1 cup (200g) red lentils

⅓ cup (80ml) olive oil

1 medium brown onion (150g), chopped finely

1 clove garlic, crushed

2 cups (500ml) chicken stock

150g cherry tomatoes, halved

¼ cup (30g) seeded black olives, chopped coarsely

¼ cup small fresh basil leaves

4 x 200g veal cutlets

1 cup (100g) cauliflower florets

½ cup coarsely chopped fresh flat-leaf parsley

1 Rinse lentils under cold water; drain. Heat 1 tablespoon of the oil in medium frying pan; cook onion and garlic, stirring, until onion softens. Add lentils and stock; bring to a boil. Reduce heat, simmer, uncovered, about 10 minutes or until tender. Add tomatoes, olives and basil.

2 Meanwhile, cook cutlets in heated oiled grill pan until cooked as desired. Transfer to a plate, cover, stand for 5 minutes.

3 Heat remaining oil in medium frying pan; cook cauliflower, stirring, until browned all over and cooked through. Drain on absorbent paper. Sprinkle with parsley.

4 Serve veal cutlets on the lentil mixture with cauliflower.

▭ **PER SERVING** 5.2g total fat (1g saturated fat); 493kJ (118 cal); 5.7g carbohydrate; 11g protein; 2.1g fibre

Pork cutlets with fennel apple relish

PREPARATION TIME 15 MINUTES **COOKING TIME** 20 MINUTES **SERVES** 4

2 tablespoons cider vinegar

¼ cup (60ml) olive oil

1 tablespoon dijon mustard

2 teaspoons caster sugar

4 x 235g pork cutlets

1 large unpeeled green apple (200g), chopped finely

1 small red onion (100g), chopped finely

1 medium fennel (300g), trimmed, chopped finely

1 Whisk vinegar, oil, mustard and sugar in medium bowl.

2 Combine pork and 2 tablespoons of the dressing in large bowl.

3 To make relish, combine apple, onion and fennel in bowl with remaining dressing.

4 Meanwhile, cook drained pork in heated oiled grill pan until cooked as desired, brushing with dressing occasionally. Serve pork with relish.

▭ **PER SERVING** 31.2g total fat (7.9g saturated fat); 1877kJ (449 cal); 9.6g carbohydrate; 32g protein; 2.3g fibre

Fennel can be eaten raw in salads, works well in braises and is a great vegetable to roast or stew; it has a mildly sweet and subtle licorice flavour, which is why it complements the sweet-salty pork and crisp fresh apple in this recipe so well. Fennel belongs to the same plant family as celery and celeriac, which it resembles somewhat in look and texture; it is not related to anise, which it is often mistakenly called because of its taste.

Preparing seafood

The task of tackling the creatures of the sea is as easy as pie if you follow these simple steps.

BUYING FISH
Fresh seafood smells fishy but fresh. Whole fish has clear eyes and is slippery, not slimy. Fillets have a sheen and feel moist, not tacky. Store in refrigerator, covered with foil.

SKINNING FISH FILLETS
Place fillet skin-side down, tail end towards you, dip fingers of one hand in salt and hold tail firmly while you ease a thin filleting knife between flesh and skin, pushing, rather than cutting, the flesh from the skin.

BONING FISH
Cut off head behind gills. Slit belly, remove entrails, then open belly out and "stand" upright. Press along back to loosen backbone, then ease it off the flesh. Cut off at tail.

PREPARING OCTOPUS
Cut off head/body below eyes, slit back of head and pull out entrails. Make a small cut into centre of tentacles, pop out beak. Cut out eyes and discard with beak and entrails. Turn inside out, wash body and tentacles.

BUYING AND PREPARING SASHIMI
Specify sashimi-grade tuna (or kingfish, bream, mackerel or dhufish) when buying. Wrap tightly in plastic wrap and freeze until just firm. Use a heavy, sharp knife to slice fish as thinly as possible immediately on removing from the freezer and unwrapping.

BUTTERFLYING SMALL FISH
Cut off heads, slit entire undersides and discard heads and entrails. Open out, skin upward, and use thumb or rolling pin to press along backbones to make the fish lie flat. Pull out backbones with help of a large, heavy knife slipped underneath.

PIN-BONING
To remove all the tiny, hidden bones from a fillet, run your fingers firmly along it, starting from the tail end, and use tweezers to pull out each bone as you feel it.

FILLETING FISH
For round fish, cut off head, hold tail with salted fingers and, with a thin, filleting knife, cut along backbone from tail end to remove flesh in one piece. For flat fish, first cut down centre then remove fillet on each side.

PREPARING SQUID
Pull head and tentacles from body. Cut off tentacles, press centre and discard beak that pops out, along with head, entrails and quill from inside the body. Pull membrane off body and flaps.

FLAKING SMOKED OR COOKED FISH
Peel off skin, lift flesh from bones and, with your fingers, break flesh into the size of flakes you want, feeling carefully for pin-bones as you go and discarding them.

ROE
Roe consists of eggs collected from female fish. The most famous is sturgeon roe, which is salted to become caviar. Salted salmon eggs make excellent salmon caviar. Imitation caviar is made from lumpfish eggs, dyed black or red.

SCALING FISH
Spread plenty of newspaper and, preferably, work outside as the scales will fly about. Grasp the tail with salted fingers and use a serrated fish-scaler or rigid knife to scrape firmly from tail to head. Repeat on other side.

Chilli coriander lamb with barley salad

PREPARATION TIME 20 MINUTES **COOKING TIME** 30 MINUTES **SERVES** 4

1 tablespoon coriander seeds, crushed lightly

½ teaspoon dried chilli flakes

2 cloves garlic, crushed

4 lamb backstraps (800g)

1 cup (200g) pearl barley

¼ teaspoon ground turmeric

⅓ cup coarsely chopped fresh mint

⅓ cup coarsely chopped fresh coriander

1 small red onion (100g), chopped finely

250g cherry tomatoes, quartered

¼ cup (60ml) lemon juice

2 teaspoons olive oil

1 Combine seeds, chilli, garlic and lamb in medium bowl. Cover; refrigerate until required.
2 Meanwhile, cook barley in large saucepan of boiling water, uncovered, about 20 minutes or until just tender; drain. Rinse under cold water; drain.
3 Cook lamb in heated lightly oiled grill pan until cooked as desired. Cover lamb; stand 5 minutes before slicing thickly.
4 Combine barley in large bowl with turmeric, herbs, onion, tomato, juice and oil; toss gently to combine. Serve salad with lamb.

PER SERVING 10.9g total fat (3.7g saturated fat); 1827kJ (437 cal); 34.2g carbohydrate; 43.4g protein; 7.4g fibre

---

Calamari stuffed with fetta and chilli

PREPARATION TIME 40 MINUTES (PLUS REFRIGERATION TIME) **COOKING TIME** 10 MINUTES **SERVES** 8

8 whole calamari with tentacles (600g)

400g firm fetta cheese

1 teaspoon dried chilli flakes

2 tablespoons olive oil

2 tablespoons coarsely chopped fresh oregano

2 teaspoons finely grated lemon rind

2 tablespoons lemon juice

1 clove garlic, crushed

¼ cup (60ml) olive oil, extra

1 Clean calamari by pulling gently on tentacles to remove. Cut tentacles off below eyes; discard eyes, small black beak in centre of the tentacles and entrails. Remove clear quill from inside body, then remove side flaps and dark membrane. Rinse well; pat dry.
2 Mash cheese, chilli, oil and oregano together in small bowl. Spoon cheese mixture into calamari tubes; secure with toothpicks.
3 Combine calamari and tentacles in large shallow dish with combined rind, juice, garlic and extra oil. Cover; refrigerate 3 hours, turning occasionally.
4 Cook calamari and tentacles in heated oiled grill pan about 3 minutes each side or until browned and filling is heated through.

PER SERVING 23.4g total fat (9.4g saturated fat); 1116kJ (267 cal); 0.3g carbohydrate; 14.3g protein; 0.1g fibre

Char-grilled chilli squid salad

PREPARATION TIME 30 MINUTES (PLUS REFRIGERATION TIME) **COOKING TIME** 5 MINUTES **SERVES** 4

1kg whole baby squid	350g baby egg tomatoes
¼ cup (60ml) olive oil	½ cup firmly packed fresh mint leaves
1 teaspoon sea salt flakes	
2 fresh small red thai chillies, chopped finely	¼ cup firmly packed fresh flat-leaf parsley leaves
2 cloves garlic, chopped finely	100g baby spinach leaves
2 tablespoons fresh oregano leaves, chopped finely	1 tablespoon lemon juice
	1 tablespoon olive oil, extra

Serve this dish as a light meal on a warm summer day: divide crisp butter lettuce or large cos lettuce leaves among serving plates and spoon the squid into the leaves. Accompany with a warmed baguette and a chilled white wine for the perfect patio lunch.

1 Gently separate body and tentacles of squid by pulling on tentacles. Cut head from tentacles just below eyes; discard head. Trim long tentacle from each squid.

2 Remove clear quill from inside body and discard. Peel side flaps from body with salted fingers; peel away dark skin. Wash squid well; pat dry with absorbent paper.

3 Place a palette knife or wooden spatula inside a squid tube (this prevents cutting all the way through). Using a large knife, slice the squid along its length at 1cm intervals, giving a concertina effect. Repeat with remaining squid.

4 Combine squid tubes, tentacles and flaps, oil, salt, chilli, garlic and oregano in medium bowl. Cover; refrigerate for up to 1 hour.

5 Cook squid mixture, in batches, in heated oiled grill pan 5 minutes or until just tender.

6 Serve halved tomatoes, mint, parsley, spinach with squid. Drizzle with combined juice and extra oil.

▭ **PER SERVING** 19.8g total fat (3g saturated fat); 1129kJ (270 cal); 2.4g carbohydrate; 19.0g protein; 2.6g fibre

---

Yakitori

PREPARATION TIME 20 MINUTES (PLUS REFRIGERATION TIME) **COOKING TIME** 10 MINUTES **MAKES** 24

500g chicken breast fillets	1 tablespoon light soy sauce
½ cup (125ml) mirin	1 teaspoon toasted sesame seeds
¼ cup (60ml) kecap manis	1 green onion, sliced thinly

Yakitori, literally "grilled poultry", is a Japanese staple, and you'll find yakitoriya, barbecue stalls or takeaway shops, scattered throughout the streets of every city, where workers gather for a snack after they leave the office.

Soak bamboo skewers in a dish of water at least an hour before using them; this prevents the skewers from scorching.

1 Slice chicken into thin diagonal strips; thread strips loosely onto skewers. Place skewers, in single layer, in large shallow dish.

2 Combine mirin, kecap manis and sauce in small jug. Pour half of the marinade over skewers; reserve remaining marinade. Cover; refrigerate 3 hours or overnight.

3 Simmer reserved marinade in small saucepan over low heat until reduced by half.

4 Meanwhile, cook drained skewers in heated oiled grill pan until chicken is cooked.

5 Serve skewers drizzled with hot marinade; sprinkle with sesame seeds and onion.

▭ **PER SKEWER** 1.2g total fat (0.4g saturated fat); 138kJ (33 cal); 0.2g carbohydrate; 4.7g protein; 0g fibre

Fontina, pancetta and sage chicken

PREPARATION TIME 15 MINUTES **COOKING TIME** 20 MINUTES **SERVES** 4

Fontina is a smooth, firm Italian cow-milk cheese with a creamy, nutty taste and brown or red rind; it's ideal for melting or grilling. If you can't find fontina, havarti cheese or gouda cheese taste just as good.

4 x 200g chicken breast fillets

4 thin slices fontina cheese (100g)

4 slices pancetta (60g)

2 tablespoons coarsely chopped fresh sage

2 tablespoons olive oil

2 cloves garlic, crushed

16 sage leaves

1 Slit a pocket in one side of each fillet but do not cut all the way through. Divide cheese, pancetta and chopped sage among pockets; secure with toothpicks. Brush chicken with combined oil and garlic.

2 Cook chicken in heated oiled grill pan about 20 minutes or until cooked. Remove toothpicks before serving.

3 Cook sage leaves on oiled grill plate until golden brown. Serve chicken topped with sage leaves.

▭ **PER SERVING** 23.3g total fat (8g saturated fat); 1806kJ (432 cal); 0.3g carbohydrate; 55.3g protein; 0.3g fibre

Grilled corn and zucchini salsa

PREPARATION TIME 20 MINUTES **COOKING TIME** 10 MINUTES **MAKES** 7 CUPS

Serve this salsa with grilled chicken, fish or even haloumi, a cheese of Greek Cypriot origin. The salty-sweet taste of haloumi is enhanced when grilled; serve straight from the grill as it becomes tough and rubbery on cooling.

2 corn cobs (800g), trimmed

100g baby zucchini, halved lengthways

2 large avocados (640g), chopped coarsely

200g grape tomatoes, halved

1 medium red onion (170g), sliced thickly

¼ cup coarsely chopped fresh coriander

1 tablespoon sweet chilli sauce

⅓ cup (80ml) lime juice

2 fresh small red thai chillies, sliced thinly

1 Cook corn and zucchini in heated oiled grill pan until tender and browned lightly. Using sharp knife, remove kernels from cobs.

2 Combine corn and zucchini in large bowl with avocado, tomato, onion and coriander. Add remaining ingredients; toss gently to combine.

▭ **PER TABLESPOON** 1.3g total fat (0.3g saturated fat); 84kJ (20 cal); 1.4g carbohydrate; 0.5g protein; 0.5g fibre

1 FONTINA, PANCETTA AND SAGE CHICKEN 2 GRILLED CORN AND ZUCCHINI SALSA
3 CANTONESE BEEF PATTIES WITH GRILLED GAI LAN [P 116]
4 BARRAMUNDI WITH TOMATO, CAPER AND WALNUT DRESSING [P 116]

1

2

3 4

Gai lan, also known as gai larn, chinese broccoli and chinese kale, is a green vegetable that's a favourite for Sunday morning yum cha, steamed and doused with oyster sauce. Here we grill it, releasing its remarkably singular flavour.

Cantonese beef patties with grilled gai lan

PREPARATION TIME 30 MINUTES **COOKING TIME** 15 MINUTES **SERVES** 4

800g beef mince

1 medium brown onion (150g), chopped finely

3 cloves garlic, crushed

2cm piece fresh ginger (10g), grated

1 fresh small red thai chilli, chopped finely

227g can water chestnuts, rinsed, drained, chopped finely

¼ cup finely chopped fresh chives

1 egg

½ cup (35g) fresh breadcrumbs

1 tablespoon hoisin sauce

1 tablespoon water

2 tablespoons oyster sauce

⅓ cup (80ml) hoisin sauce, extra

2 teaspoons sesame oil

1kg gai lan, chopped coarsely

1 Combine beef, onion, two-thirds of the garlic, ginger, chilli, chestnuts, chives, egg, breadcrumbs and hoisin sauce in large bowl; shape mixture into eight patties.

2 Combine the water, oyster sauce, extra hoisin sauce and remaining garlic in small bowl. Reserve ¼ cup (60ml) hoisin mixture.

3 Brush patties with remaining hoisin mixture; cook patties, both sides, in heated oiled grill pan about 10 minutes or until cooked.

4 Heat sesame oil in same grill pan; cook gai lan until wilted. Serve gai lan topped with patties, drizzled with reserved hoisin mixture.

▢ **PER SERVING** 20.2g total fat (6.8g saturated fat); 2077kJ (497 cal); 26.6g carbohydrate; 48g protein; 8.3g fibre

Barramundi, often incorrectly called nile perch, is a firm, white-fleshed fish. Blue-eye, ling or snapper can be used in its place, if you prefer.

Barramundi with tomato, caper and walnut dressing

PREPARATION TIME 15 MINUTES **COOKING TIME** 20 MINUTES **SERVES** 4

250g cherry tomatoes

60g butter

1 tablespoon finely grated lemon rind

2 teaspoons lemon juice

1 teaspoon capers, drained, rinsed, chopped finely

¼ cup (30g) finely chopped walnuts

½ cup coarsely chopped fresh flat-leaf parsley

4 x 185g barramundi fillets

1 Cook tomatoes in heated oiled grill pan until tender.

2 Melt butter in small saucepan, add cooked tomatoes, rind, juice, capers, walnuts and parsley; stir until hot.

3 Cook fish in same heated oiled grill pan.

4 Serve fish topped with tomato, caper and walnut dressing.

▢ **PER SERVING** 19.8g total fat (9.2g saturated fat); 1471kJ (352 cal); 2g carbohydrate; 40.1g protein; 1.9g fibre

Grilled tuna with soba

PREPARATION TIME 15 MINUTES **COOKING TIME** 10 MINUTES **SERVES** 4

Made from a combination of wheat and buckwheat flours, soba can be bought both fresh and dried from Japanese food shops and some supermarkets.

> 4 x 200g tuna steaks
>
> ½ cup (125ml) mirin
>
> 2 teaspoons wasabi paste
>
> ½ cup (125ml) japanese soy sauce
>
> 1 sheet toasted seaweed (yaki-nori)
>
> 300g soba noodles
>
> 6 green onions, sliced thinly
>
> 2 fresh long red chillies, chopped finely

1 Combine tuna with 2 tablespoons of the mirin, half the wasabi and half the soy sauce in large bowl. Cover; refrigerate 10 minutes.

2 Meanwhile, using scissors cut seaweed into four strips; cut each strip crossways into thin pieces.

3 Cook noodles in large saucepan of boiling water, uncovered, until just tender; drain. Rinse under cold water; drain.

4 Meanwhile, cook tuna in heated lightly oiled grill pan until cooked as desired.

5 Combine noodles in medium bowl with onion, chilli and combined remaining mirin, wasabi and soy sauce. Serve noodles with tuna and seaweed.

PER SERVING 12.3g total fat (4.8g saturated fat); 2495kJ (597 cal); 53.6g carbohydrate; 60.8g protein; 3.2g fibre

Salmon with dill and caper dressing

PREPARATION TIME 10 MINUTES **COOKING TIME** 10 MINUTES **SERVES** 4

Instead of serving this as a salad, after grilling the fish, flake it in a bowl with the remaining ingredients and toss it through cooled cooked farfalle or penne for a main-course pasta salad.

> ¼ cup (60g) sour cream
>
> 1 tablespoon capers, drained, rinsed
>
> 2 teaspoons finely chopped fresh dill
>
> 2 teaspoons horseradish cream
>
> 1 teaspoon lime juice
>
> 4 small salmon fillets (600g)

1 Combine sour cream, capers, dill, horseradish and juice in medium bowl.

2 Cook salmon in heated oiled grill pan until cooked as desired.

3 Serve salmon with dill and caper dressing and, if desired, with a mixed green salad, steamed baby potatoes and lime wedges.

PER SERVING 13.9g total fat (4.5g saturated fat); 1045kJ (250 cal); 1.4g carbohydrate; 29.9g protein; 0.1g fibre

Great for the health-conscious as well as the gourmet, rice vermicelli (also known as bee hoon), is so versatile that it is used throughout South-East Asia in an abundance of dishes, presented hot or cold, dry or sauced, wrapped in rice paper or stirred into soups, tossed in a salad or a stir-fry. Made from rice flour, they're a suitable "noodle" for coeliacs; if you can't find vermicelli, you can use thin flat rice noodles instead.

Lemon grass lamb with vietnamese vermicelli salad

PREPARATION TIME 25 MINUTES **COOKING TIME** 20 MINUTES **SERVES** 4

3 lamb backstraps (600g)

10cm stick fresh lemon grass (20g), chopped finely

2 tablespoons light soy sauce

1 tablespoon brown sugar

2 tablespoons vegetable oil

70g rice vermicelli noodles

2 lebanese cucumbers (260g), seeded, sliced thinly

½ small pineapple (450g), chopped coarsely

1 cup (80g) bean sprouts

1 cup loosely packed fresh coriander leaves

1 cup loosely packed fresh mint leaves

1 large carrot (180g), grated coarsely

1 large butter lettuce, trimmed, leaves separated

CHILLI LIME DRESSING

¼ cup (60ml) hot water

2 tablespoons fish sauce

1 tablespoon brown sugar

2 tablespoons lime juice

2 fresh small red thai chillies, chopped finely

1 clove garlic, crushed

1 Combine ingredients for chilli lime dressing in screw-top jar; shake well.

2 Combine lamb, lemon grass, sauce, sugar and oil in medium bowl.

3 Place noodles in medium heatproof bowl; cover with boiling water. Stand until just tender; drain. Rinse under cold water; drain.

4 Place noodles in large bowl with cucumber, pineapple, sprouts, herbs, carrot and 2 tablespoons of the dressing; toss gently to combine.

5 Cook lamb in heated oiled grill pan until cooked as desired. Cover; stand 5 minutes, slice thinly.

6 Top lettuce with salad; serve with lamb, drizzled with remaining dressing.

▭ **PER SERVING** 22.9g total fat (7.2g saturated fat); 1856kJ (444 cal); 20.6g carbohydrate; 35.9g protein; 6g fibre

Beef rissoles with tomato and onion sauce

PREPARATION TIME 20 MINUTES **COOKING TIME** 25 MINUTES **SERVES** 4

1 tablespoon olive oil

1 medium brown onion (150g), sliced thinly

1 clove garlic, sliced thinly

1 tablespoon brown sugar

2 tablespoons malt vinegar

400g can chopped tomatoes

8 beef rissoles (1kg)

1 Heat oil in medium pan; cook onion and garlic, stirring occasionally, about 10 minutes or until soft. Add sugar, vinegar and undrained tomatoes; bring to a boil. Simmer, uncovered, about 10 minutes or until thickened.

2 Meanwhile, cook rissoles in heated oiled grill pan until cooked through.

3 Serve rissoles with tomato and onion sauce and, if desired, steamed green beans and soft polenta.

▭ **PER SERVING** 18.8g total fat (6.3g saturated fat); 1568kJ (375 cal); 8.4g carbohydrate; 42.3g protein; 1.8g fibre

Teriyaki beef

PREPARATION TIME 10 MINUTES **COOKING TIME** 20 MINUTES **SERVES** 4

Make perfect steamed rice to serve with the teriyaki: combine 2 cups white short-grain rice and 4 cups water in a medium heavy-based saucepan; cover tightly, bring to a boil then reduce heat as low as possible. Cook about 15 minutes or until water is absorbed and rice is tender; remove pan from heat. Stand, covered, 10 minutes, then fluff rice with a fork.

½ cup (125ml) mirin

⅓ cup (80ml) light soy sauce

¼ cup (50g) firmly packed brown sugar

1 tablespoon sake

4cm piece fresh ginger (20g), grated

1 clove garlic, crushed

1 teaspoon sesame oil

1 tablespoon sesame seeds

750g beef fillet, sliced thinly

300g fresh baby corn, halved

2 green onions, sliced thinly

1 Combine mirin, sauce, sugar, sake, ginger, garlic, oil and seeds in large bowl. Stir in beef and corn; stand 5 minutes.

2 Drain beef mixture over small saucepan; reserve marinade. Cook beef and corn, in batches, in heated oiled grill pan until cooked as desired.

3 Meanwhile, bring marinade to a boil in pan. Reduce heat, simmer, uncovered, 5 minutes.

4 Serve beef and corn drizzled with hot marinade; sprinkle with onion. Serve with steamed rice, if desired.

▭ **PER SERVING** 12.7g total fat (4.4g saturated fat); 1789kJ (428 cal); 26.8g carbohydrate; 44.4g protein; 3.9g fibre

Beef tortilla stacks

PREPARATION TIME 20 MINUTES **COOKING TIME** 15 MINUTES **SERVES** 4

1/3 cup cooked brown rice

500g beef mince

1/2 small brown onion (40g), chopped finely

1 clove garlic, crushed

1 teaspoon sweet paprika

1 egg

1 tablespoon lemon juice

8 small corn tortillas

200g yogurt

1 lebanese cucumber (130g), chopped finely

100g baby endive, torn

2 medium tomatoes (380g), chopped coarsely

1 Combine rice, beef, onion, garlic, paprika, egg and juice in medium bowl; shape mixture into 20 small, round patties.

2 Heat tortillas in oiled heated grill pan on both sides. Remove from pan; cover to keep warm.

3 Cook patties, in batches, in same oiled heated grill pan until browned both sides and cooked through.

4 Meanwhile, combine yogurt and cucumber in small bowl

5 Divide half the tortillas among serving plates, top with endive, tomato, patties, yogurt sauce and remaining tortillas.

▭ **PER SERVING** 3.1g total fat (3.1g saturated fat); 414kJ (99 cal); 8.9g carbohydrate; 8.1g protein; 1.4g fibre

These beef patties are suitable to freeze, cooked or uncooked. Make double the quantity stated, freeze half, and next time you have a barbecue, all you need to do is thaw the patties then cook them.

Mustard-crumbed beef fillet with rocket salad

PREPARATION TIME 20 MINUTES (PLUS REFRIGERATION TIME) **COOKING TIME** 50 MINUTES **SERVES** 6

1kg piece beef eye fillet

1/4 cup (70g) horseradish

1 tablespoon olive oil

2 tablespoons wholegrain mustard

1 tablespoon coarsely chopped fresh flat-leaf parsley

1/2 cup (35g) fresh breadcrumbs

1 tablespoon butter, melted

ROCKET SALAD

100g baby rocket leaves

1 medium red onion (170g), sliced thinly

8 green onions, sliced thinly

1/4 cup (40g) roasted pine nuts

1/3 cup (80ml) balsamic vinegar

1/3 cup (80ml) olive oil

1 Combine beef, horseradish and oil in large bowl. Cover; refrigerate 3 hours or overnight.

2 Cook beef in heated oiled grill pan, turning, until browned all over. Reduce heat; cook beef, turning occasionally, about 30 minutes or until cooked. Cover; stand 10 minutes.

3 Meanwhile, combine ingredients for rocket salad in large bowl.

4 Preheat grill. Combine mustard, parsley and breadcrumbs in small bowl with half of the butter. Brush beef with remaining butter; press breadcrumb mixture over beef. Place beef under hot grill until crust is browned. Stand 10 minutes; slice thickly. Serve with rocket salad.

▭ **PER SERVING** 34.2g total fat (9.1g saturated fat); 2082kJ (498 cal); 8.7g carbohydrate; 38.4g protein; 1.9g fibre

You can make your own fresh breadcrumbs at home; using slightly stale bread, cut the crusts off, tear into small pieces and place in a food processor. Pulse until you get the size crumb you desire. If your bread isn't stale, it's important to dry it out a little (resting, uncovered, overnight on the kitchen bench or in a slow oven) before processing it or it will just clump. Fresh breadcrumbs can be frozen, in an airtight container or zip lock bag, then thawed before use.

Pork fillet can be used in place of the sausages, if you like. Low in fat and high in taste, the fillet can be cooked in the grill pan, like the sausages; make sure you stand the meat, covered, for at least 5 minutes before cutting it.

Pork sausages with grilled polenta and spicy tomato sauce

PREPARATION TIME 20 MINUTES **COOKING TIME** 15 MINUTES (PLUS REFRIGERATION TIME) **SERVES** 4

1 litre (4 cups) water

1 cup (170g) polenta

1 cup (120g) coarsely grated cheddar cheese

2 teaspoons olive oil

1 medium red onion (170g), sliced thinly

1 clove garlic, crushed

1 fresh small red thai chilli, chopped finely

4 medium tomatoes (600g), chopped coarsely

8 thick pork sausages (960g)

1 Bring the water to a boil in medium saucepan; gradually stir in polenta. Reduce heat, simmer, stirring, until polenta thickens. Stir in cheese. Spread polenta into oiled deep 19cm-square cake pan. Cover; refrigerate about 1 hour or until polenta firms.

2 Meanwhile, heat oil in medium saucepan; cook onion, garlic and chilli, stirring, until onion softens. Add tomato; simmer, covered, until tomato softens.

3 Cut polenta into quarters. Cook polenta and sausages, in batches, in heated oiled grill pan until polenta is browned both sides and sausages are cooked through.

4 Serve sausages on polenta squares, topped with spicy tomato sauce.

▭ **PER SERVING** 65.6g total fat (28.3g saturated fat); 3908kJ (935 cal); 42.2g carbohydrate; 42g protein; 6.8g fibre

Team this speciality with another universal favourite from that nation, Greek salad: combine coarsely chopped tomato, red capsicum and lebanese cucumber, sliced red onion, chunks of greek fetta cheese, a drizzle of olive oil and a sprinkle of fresh oregano (known as rigani in Greece), and serve salad and souvlaki together for a healthy lunch or dinner.

Pork souvlaki

PREPARATION TIME 15 MINUTES (PLUS REFRIGERATION TIME) **COOKING TIME** 25 MINUTES **MAKES** 8

1kg pork fillet, cut into 2cm cubes

⅓ cup (80ml) olive oil

2 tablespoons lemon juice

¼ cup fresh oregano leaves, chopped coarsely

4 cloves garlic, crushed

48 fresh bay leaves

2 lemons, cut into wedges

1 Combine pork, oil, juice, oregano and garlic in large bowl. Cover, refrigerate 3 hours or overnight, stirring occasionally.

2 Thread pork and bay leaves onto eight wooden skewers.

3 Cook souvlaki in heated oiled grill pan until cooked through. Serve with lemon wedges.

▭ **PER SKEWER** 12.1g total fat (2.3g saturated fat); 936kJ (224 cal); 0.7g carbohydrate; 27.7g protein; 0.9g fibre

Prawn and chorizo skewers with bean and tomato salad

PREPARATION TIME 25 MINUTES (PLUS REFRIGERATION TIME) **COOKING TIME** 10 MINUTES **SERVES** 4

24 uncooked medium king prawns (1kg)

4 cloves garlic, crushed

2 tablespoons olive oil

150g green beans, trimmed, halved

3 medium egg tomatoes (225g), quartered

2 tablespoons roasted pine nuts

¼ cup coarsely chopped fresh flat-leaf parsley

8 x 20cm stalks fresh rosemary

2 chorizo sausages (340g), sliced thickly

LIME MUSTARD DRESSING

2 tablespoons olive oil

2 tablespoons lime juice

1 tablespoon wholegrain mustard

2 cloves garlic, crushed

1 Shell and devein prawns, leaving tails intact. Combine prawns in medium bowl with garlic and oil. Cover; refrigerate 3 hours or overnight.

2 Combine ingredients for lime mustard dressing in screw-top jar; shake well.

3 Meanwhile, boil, steam or microwave beans until just tender; drain. Rinse under cold water; drain. Combine beans in medium bowl with tomato, nuts, parsley and dressing.

4 Drain prawns, discard marinade. Remove leaves from bottom two-thirds of each rosemary stalk; thread prawns and chorizo, alternately, onto rosemary skewers. Cook skewers in heated oiled grill pan until prawns are changed in colour and chorizo is browned.

▢ **PER SERVING** 49.9g total fat (12.3g saturated fat); 2730kJ (653 cal); 5.4g carbohydrate; 45g protein; 3.4g fibre

If surf 'n' turf isn't your thing, substitute scallops for the chorizo in this recipe. Scallops and prawns take next to no time to cook, and the skewers can be prepared in advance – pop them in the heated pan just before you're ready to eat.

THE GRILLER

The Griller

Grilled lamb chops used to appear at least once a week on the typical family table. Those chops were not cooked on a char-grill (there was no such thing for home cooks until fairly recently), but under the griller that was, and still is, part of every stove or wall oven.

Changing food habits and the arrival of the char-grill have reduced the role of the overhead griller, but its ability to produce a rich, evenly and deliciously browned surface on everything from chops to the top of a soufflé omelette is still a rewarding part of cooking. Grilling produces much better, though more labour-intensive, toast than you'll get from any automatic toaster, and is still the only way to achieve the homely joy of grilled cheese on toast.

The griller consists of a pierced tray or rack set over a shallow pan to catch the fat and juices that drip from the food as it cooks. Grilling is a healthy cooking method as excess fat ends up in the pan, ready to discard.

USE

Always preheat the griller properly, on high, before you start to cook. The main rule of grilling is that the heat must be fierce when the food goes under it so that it will start to brown immediately. Even if the recipe for a particular food says to grill it at moderate heat, have the griller really hot and turn it down as you start to grill the food.

It is difficult to give times for preheating as grillers differ so much, but try preheating for about 5 minutes for toast and 15 to 20 minutes before grilling any kind of meat. You will soon find out how long your griller needs preheating to produce the results you want.

GRILLING TECHNIQUES

Items to be grilled entirely at high heat must be tender to begin with and fairly small. Brush or spray the food and the tray with melted butter or cooking-oil spray just before starting to cook. The griller must be clean so that old food residue won't make the new food stick. Cleaning the griller also removes old fat which, already broken down by the heat of previous grilling, could smoke or even catch on fire.

GRILLING LARGE ITEMS larger items, such as half a chicken, may still be almost raw inside when they look a perfect golden-brown on the outside. Recipes often give instructions to grill for a certain time at high heat, then reduce the heat and continue cooking until the food is cooked through. To do this, it is better to lower the food from the grill rather than turn the heat down. Remember, you must still keep a close eye on the food and be ready to turn it and, if necessary, protect it with a sheet of foil if it starts to darken.

In some grillers, it is quick and easy to move the pan to a lower position, but if yours is one where repositioning it, especially while hot, is an awkward business, it is better to have an oven tray ready in a moderate oven, and transfer the food to that to finish cooking, turning once, if necessary. It will still look and taste "grilled" rather than "baked", and this can actually make better use of your time, especially if you are cooking for a crowd, rather than leaving it under the griller, as you don't have to watch it so carefully.

GRILLING FISH only thick, skinless fillets or steaks, or small whole fish, are suitable for grilling; thinner pieces are better pan-fried, and large whole fish are better baked.

Fish is so delicate and so easily overcooked that a special approach is called for. Cover the griller pan with a double thickness of foil, with the sides turned up to form a tray; preheat for 10 to 15 minutes. Meanwhile, make tiny slashes round the edge of the fillets to discourage curling; pat the fish dry with paper towels, dust lightly with flour and coat all over in a little melted butter (about 15g per piece of fish) or spray with olive-oil cooking spray.

Brush or spray the preheated foil with butter or oil, place the fish on the foil with a little space between pieces. Grill, basting once or twice with the juices, for about 4 minutes for fillets, or about 7 minutes for thick steaks. Fish is cooked when a toothpick, pushed into the thickest part, runs in easily. Don't turn the pieces – the undersides will cook sufficiently from contact with the hot foil.

Small, whole flat fish, such as sole or flounder, should be prepared and cooked in the same way as fillets. Thicker fish should be prepared in the same way, but slashed two or three times through the thickest part; cook as above, but turn over about halfway through cooking. A small whole fish takes about 8 to 15 minutes to cook, depending on its thickness. Have hot plates ready and serve fish immediately.

GRILLING CHICKEN AND MEAT chicken and meat are grilled directly in the tray of the griller. Brush or spray both food and tray with melted butter or oil just before cooking. Start grilling chicken with the skin-side down and turn halfway through. Check small pieces for doneness by pressing quickly with your fingers or the back of tongs: flesh should feel springy. Check larger pieces by piercing the thickest part with a skewer: juice should run clear with no hint of pink.

Beef is usually cooked rare or medium rare, lamb a little more cooked but still pink, and pork and veal are barely cooked through but still juicy. Check by pressing quickly with your fingers or the back of tongs: rare meat feels soft and spongy, medium-rare feels soft but springy, medium-done feels firm but still springy and well-done feels quite firm.

All meat, including chicken, will be more succulent if it is rested, covered tightly, in a warm place for about 5 minutes before slicing or serving.

CARE

The griller tray can take some effort to clean because the high heat "cooks on" any food residue. Soaking to loosen these bits is better for the tray than scouring or, if you want to avoid the whole question of cleaning, you can cover the entire pan with heavy foil to protect it or use disposable aluminium griller trays, available from supermarkets.

As spatters from grilling food can go far and wide, you should also wipe out the oven or griller compartment after each use.

Za'atar-spiced veal loin chops

PREPARATION TIME 5 MINUTES **COOKING TIME** 20 MINUTES **SERVES** 4

Veal chops are a bigger, meatier cut than is a veal cutlet. While a single chop is sufficient for each diner, it's probably a better call to serve two veal cutlets for a main meal.

1 tablespoon sumac

1 tablespoon toasted sesame seeds

1 teaspoon dried marjoram

2 teaspoons finely chopped fresh thyme

1 tablespoon olive oil

4 x 200g veal loin chops

1 Preheat grill.

2 Combine sumac, sesame seeds, herbs and oil in small bowl.

3 Grill veal until browned both sides and cooked. Sprinkle about 1 tablespoon of the za'atar equally over the veal; reserve remaining za'atar for another use.

4 Serve veal with fattoush (see page 412), if desired.

PER SERVING 9.1g total fat (1.7g saturated fat); 836kJ (200 cal); 0g carbohydrate; 29.4g protein; 0.3g fibre

---

Thai chicken patties with coriander pesto

PREPARATION TIME 15 MINUTES **COOKING TIME** 10 MINUTES **MAKES** 24

Good poultry shops and some supermarkets sell breast and thigh chicken mince and schnitzel. The thigh meat has more flavour than the breast so it's best for a robust spicy dish like this; use breast meat when the recipe contains more subtle, delicate flavours like, for instance, the wontons in a clear Asian vegetable soup.

1 fresh small red thai chilli, chopped finely

7cm piece fresh ginger (35g), grated

1 teaspoon fish sauce

1 teaspoon light soy sauce

2 cloves garlic, crushed

2 teaspoons finely grated lime rind

500g chicken thigh mince

½ small red capsicum (75g), chopped finely

CORIANDER PESTO

¼ cup (35g) roasted unsalted cashews

1 cup loosely packed fresh coriander leaves

1 tablespoon peanut oil

2 teaspoons lemon juice

1 Preheat grill.

2 Combine chilli, ginger, sauces, garlic, rind, chicken and capsicum in medium bowl. Using hands, shape level tablespoons of mixture into patties.

3 Place patties on oiled oven tray; grill about 10 minutes or until cooked through.

4 Meanwhile, make coriander pesto.

5 Serve patties topped with pesto.

CORIANDER PESTO Blend or process ingredients until almost smooth.

PER PATTY 3.2g total fat (0.8g saturated fat); 209kJ (50 cal); 0.7g carbohydrate; 4.4g protein; 0.2g fibre

ZA'ATAR-SPICED VEAL LOIN CHOPS

Grill the fish with its skin on to act as a protective barrier from the initial heat and because it's perfectly delicious when crisped. Grilled crunchy salmon skin has been eaten by the Chinese and Japanese for centuries, and been readily available at sushi restaurants for years. Start grilling, skin-side down, before flipping fillets over. Don't overcook the salmon so that it remains succulent and juicy.

Salmon with macadamia mayonnaise

PREPARATION TIME 10 MINUTES **COOKING TIME** 10 MINUTES **SERVES** 4

2 egg yolks

½ teaspoon coarse cooking salt

½ teaspoon mustard powder

2 tablespoons lemon juice

½ cup (125ml) olive oil

⅓ cup (45g) coarsely chopped roasted macadamias

4 x 200g salmon fillets

1 To make macadamia mayonnaise, combine egg yolks in medium bowl with salt, mustard and half the juice. Gradually add oil in thin, steady stream, whisking constantly until mixture thickens. Whisk in remaining juice and nuts.

2 Meanwhile, preheat grill.

3 Grill salmon, skin-side up, until skin is crisp; turn, grill until cooked as desired. Serve with macadamia mayonnaise.

☐ **PER SERVING** 54.1g total fat (9.2g saturated fat); 2725kJ (652 cal); 0.8g carbohydrate; 41.5g protein; 0.7g fibre

An Italian frittata and Spanish tortilla are essentially the same thing, with perhaps the only difference being that a tortilla is usually thicker and smaller than a frittata. The best known Spanish tortilla is the "tortilla de papas" (with potatoes); it is often served as a tapa in bars before dinner or eaten cold for lunch the next day.

Potato frittata

PREPARATION TIME 5 MINUTES **COOKING TIME** 20 MINUTES **SERVES** 4

600g baby new potatoes

1 tablespoon olive oil

1 medium red capsicum (200g), chopped coarsely

1 small brown onion (80g), chopped coarsely

¼ cup coarsely chopped fresh basil

¼ cup coarsely chopped fresh flat-leaf parsley

10 eggs

½ cup (40g) coarsely grated parmesan cheese

1 Boil, steam or microwave potatoes until just tender; when cool enough to handle, cut potatoes into quarters.

2 Meanwhile, heat oil in large frying pan; cook capsicum and onion, stirring, until softened.

3 Combine potato, herbs and eggs in large bowl. Pour egg mixture into pan; cook, over low heat, about 8 minutes or until edges are set.

4 Meanwhile, preheat grill.

5 Sprinkle top of frittata with cheese. If necessary, cover pan handle with foil then place pan under hot grill until frittata is just set.

☐ **PER SERVING** 22.9g total fat (7.3g saturated fat); 1647kJ (394 cal); 20.1g carbohydrate; 26.8g protein; 3g fibre

Mushroom and fennel gnocchi

PREPARATION TIME 15 MINUTES **COOKING TIME** 15 MINUTES **SERVES** 4

2 tablespoons olive oil

1 clove garlic, crushed

300g baby fennel bulbs, sliced thinly

200g button mushrooms, halved

500g potato gnocchi

½ cup (125ml) vegetable stock

1 teaspoon finely grated lemon rind

¼ cup (60ml) cream

½ cup (60g) seeded black olives

¼ cup finely chopped fresh flat-leaf parsley

1 ½ cups (185g) coarsely grated cheddar cheese

½ cup (40g) coarsely grated parmesan cheese

1 Heat oil in medium flameproof dish; cook garlic, fennel and mushrooms, stirring, until fennel is tender.

2 Cook gnocchi in large saucepan of boiling water, uncovered, until they float to the surface; drain.

3 Preheat grill.

4 Add gnocchi to mushroom mixture with stock, rind, cream, olives and parsley; stir until heated through.

5 Sprinkle combined cheeses over gnocchi mixture; grill until cheese is browned lightly.

☐ **PER SERVING** 43.8g fat (23g saturated fat); 2643kJ (632 cal); 28.8g carbohydrate; 28.8g protein; 5.7g fibre

To make this recipe even more spectacular, prepare your own potato gnocchi (see page 185) instead of buying the ready-made variety. The night before, or the morning of, the day you want to serve this recipe, spread the cooked gnocchi on a lightly oiled tray in a single layer. Cover loosely with plastic wrap and refrigerate until you're ready to stir them into the mushroom and fennel mixture.

Oysters with tomato, bacon and basil

PREPARATION TIME 10 MINUTES **COOKING TIME** 5 MINUTES **MAKES** 12

1 tablespoon olive oil

½ small red onion (50g), chopped finely

1 clove garlic, crushed

2 rindless bacon rashers (130g), chopped finely

2 small tomatoes (150g), seeded, chopped finely

1 tablespoon finely shredded fresh basil

12 oysters on the half shell

2 tablespoons finely grated parmesan cheese

1 Heat oil in small frying pan; cook onion and garlic, stirring, until onion softens. Add bacon; cook, stirring, until browned lightly. Add tomatoes; cook, stirring, until tomato just softens. Stir in basil.

2 Meanwhile, preheat grill.

3 Place oysters on oven tray; divide tomato mixture among oysters, sprinkle with cheese. Grill oysters until cheese melts and is browned lightly.

☐ **PER OYSTER** 4g total fat (1.3g saturated fat); 230kJ (55 cal); 0.4g carbohydrate; 4.4g protein; 0.2g fibre

Buy live oysters and open them yourself to guarantee their freshness and to keep the liquor inside the shell. Scrub them well then place them in the freezer for 15 minutes or so – they will open more easily.

Sprinkling salt or flour thickly on the oven tray creates a bed that will hold the oysters firmly upright when under the grill.

Scallops should smell sweetly briny rather than fishy when fresh. They are extremely perishable so fresh scallops should be used within 1 to 2 days of purchase. When grilling scallops, make sure they and their shells are completely dry because any residual moisture will steam the meat rather than crisp it in its shell. Scallops are ready when the meat is just opaque and easily pulls apart.

Scallops with fennel béchamel

PREPARATION TIME 15 MINUTES **COOKING TIME** 15 MINUTES **SERVES** 4

40g butter
1 baby fennel bulb (130g), trimmed, sliced thinly
2 tablespoons plain flour
1 cup (250ml) milk
24 scallops, roe removed (600g), on the half shell
1 tablespoon finely chopped fresh dill

1 Melt butter in small saucepan; cook fennel, stirring, about 5 minutes or until fennel softens. Add flour; cook, stirring, about 2 minutes or until mixture bubbles and thickens. Gradually stir in milk; cook, stirring, until béchamel boils and thickens.
2 Remove scallops from shells; rinse and dry shells.
3 Preheat grill.
4 Return scallops to shells; grill scallops about 3 minutes or until cooked. Top scallops with béchamel; grill until browned lightly. Sprinkle scallops with dill.

☐ **PER SERVING** 11.8g total fat (7.3g saturated fat); 928kJ (222 cal); 8.6g carbohydrate; 20.4g protein; 0.7g fibre

---

Fish, fresh greens and dairy: this yummy snack is deceptively nutritional – perfect for an after-school or after-sport pick-me-up.

Tuna salad on focaccia

PREPARATION TIME 10 MINUTES **COOKING TIME** 5 MINUTES **SERVES** 4

185g canned tuna in brine, drained
¼ cup (60g) mayonnaise
1 small red onion (100g), chopped finely
¼ cup finely chopped fresh flat-leaf parsley
300g garlic focaccia, cut into quarters
⅓ cup (40g) coarsely grated cheddar cheese

1 Combine tuna, mayonnaise, onion, and parsley in small bowl.
2 Preheat grill.
3 Spread tuna mixture over focaccia pieces; top with cheese. Place on oven tray; grill about 5 minutes or until cheese melts.

☐ **PER SERVING** 11g total fat (3.1g saturated fat); 1388kJ (332 cal); 37.8g carbohydrate; 18.7g protein; 2.6g fibre

1 SCALLOPS WITH FENNEL BECHAMEL **2** TUNA SALAD ON FOCACCIA
3 ANTIPASTO MELT [P 134] **4** WARM POTATO AND KUMARA SALAD [P 134]

Antipasto melt

Tasty and easy for lunch, but even better as a pass-with-drinks before a more formal Italian meal: make sure you cut the pizza base into smaller pieces if serving as finger food.

PREPARATION TIME 5 MINUTES **COOKING TIME** 5 MINUTES **SERVES** 1

1 tablespoon sun-dried tomato pesto

1 small pizza base (112g)

4 drained marinated artichoke quarters (50g)

30g drained bottled char-grilled capsicum

¼ cup (25g) coarsely grated mozzarella cheese

1 Preheat grill.

2 Spread pesto over pizza base; top with artichoke quarters, capsicum, and cheese. Grill about 5 minutes or until cheese melts.

▭ **PER SERVING** 20.8g total fat (6.2g saturated fat); 2199kJ (526 cal); 62.3g carbohydrate; 19.8g protein; 4.6g fibre

---

Warm potato and kumara salad

Grilled kumara cubes can be tossed with a little fresh sage into a plain risotto just before serving, and the grilled kipflers go really well with a small grilled beef steak. And both can be cooked the day before you want to serve this salad and refrigerated overnight as the grilling sufficiently rewarms them.

PREPARATION TIME 20 MINUTES **COOKING TIME** 30 MINUTES **SERVES** 4

750g kipfler potatoes, halved lengthways

500g kumara, chopped coarsely

⅓ cup (80ml) olive oil

1 small red onion (100g), sliced thinly

¼ cup finely chopped fresh dill

¼ cup finely chopped fresh basil

¼ cup (60ml) lemon juice

2 tablespoons capers, rinsed, drained, chopped finely

1 tablespoon wholegrain mustard

1 clove garlic, crushed

1 Boil, steam or microwave potato and kumara, separately, until tender; drain.

2 Preheat grill.

3 Place potato and kumara, in single layer, on oiled oven trays. Brush potato and kumara with a little of the oil; grill, in batches, until browned.

4 Meanwhile, combine remaining oil, onion, dill, basil, juice, capers, mustard and garlic in large bowl. Add potato and kumara; toss gently to combine.

▭ **PER SERVING** 18.7g total fat (2.6g saturated fat); 1605kJ (384 cal); 42.8g carbohydrate; 7.3g protein; 6.5g fibre

Lemon-chilli butterflied chicken

PREPARATION TIME 25 MINUTES **COOKING TIME** 55 MINUTES **SERVES** 4

80g butter, softened

½ teaspoon dried chilli flakes

½ teaspoon cracked black pepper

1 tablespoon finely grated
lemon rind

1 tablespoon finely chopped
fresh rosemary

1.6kg whole chicken

½ cup (35g) stale breadcrumbs

2 teaspoons finely grated
lemon rind, extra

¼ cup (20g) coarsely grated
parmesan cheese

1 Combine butter, chilli, pepper, rind and rosemary in small bowl.

2 Cut along each side of chicken's backbone; discard backbone. Turn chicken skin-side up; press down to flatten. Loosen and lift chicken skin; push butter mixture between skin and flesh.

3 Preheat grill.

4 Place chicken, skin-side down, on oiled wire rack in shallow flameproof baking dish. Grill chicken 40 minutes. Turn chicken; cook about 10 minutes or until chicken is cooked.

5 Meanwhile, combine remaining ingredients in small bowl.

6 Remove chicken from dish; strain juices from dish into small heatproof jug. Return chicken to dish; sprinkle with crumb mixture, drizzle ¼ cup (60ml) of the juices over crumb mixture.

7 Grill chicken about 5 minutes or until topping is browned lightly. Quarter chicken; serve with mixed green salad, if desired.

PER SERVING 50.5g total fat (21.9g saturated fat); 2705kJ (647 cal); 6g carbohydrate; 43.1g protein; 0.5g fibre

This shortcut to a perfect grilled chicken takes very little time but guarantees even cooking through the whole bird. To butterfly means, after you cut out and remove the backbone, you can open the chicken like a book (this shape rather resembles a butterfly) and press it flat. This easy technique will result in a grilled chicken that cooks faster and uniformly.

Chicken with capers, anchovies and rosemary

PREPARATION TIME 15 MINUTES **COOKING TIME** 30 MINUTES **SERVES** 4

¼ cup (50g) drained capers, rinsed, chopped finely

4 cloves garlic, crushed

6 anchovies, chopped finely

2 teaspoons fresh rosemary leaves

8 chicken thigh cutlets (1.6kg)

1 Combine capers, garlic, anchovies and rosemary in small bowl.

2 Cut two deep slashes in each chicken thigh. Place a teaspoon of caper mixture into each of the slashes.

3 Meanwhile, preheat grill.

4 Grill chicken, skin-side down, about 15 minutes; turn chicken, grill a further 15 minutes or until browned and cooked through.

5 Serve with salad leaves and steamed baby potatoes, if desired.

PER SERVING 32.8g total fat (10.8g saturated fat); 1906kJ (456 cal); 1.3g carbohydrate; 39g protein; 0.7g fibre

Thigh cutlets have the bone in but can be sold with their skin on or skinless. While the dish will have less fat content if you use thighs without skin, cooking it under a hot grill crisps the skin, rendering out much of the fat.

Leek frittata with baby spinach salad

PREPARATION TIME 15 MINUTES **COOKING TIME** 25 MINUTES **SERVES** 4

6 eggs

½ cup (125ml) milk

20g butter

1 medium leek (350g), sliced thinly

⅔ cup (80g) frozen peas

2 medium tomatoes (300g), sliced thinly

2 tablespoons finely grated parmesan cheese

80g baby spinach leaves

250g yellow grape tomatoes, halved

½ small red onion (50g), sliced thinly

2 teaspoons olive oil

1 teaspoon red wine vinegar

1 Combine eggs and milk in large jug.

2 Heat butter in medium frying pan; cook leek, stirring, until softened. Add peas, sliced tomato and egg mixture; cook, uncovered, over low heat until frittata is almost set. Remove from heat; sprinkle with cheese.

3 Meanwhile, preheat grill.

4 Grill until frittata sets and top is browned lightly. Stand frittata in pan 5 minutes before cutting into wedges.

5 Meanwhile, place spinach, grape tomatoes and onion in medium bowl with combined oil and vinegar; toss gently to combine. Serve frittata with salad.

☐ **PER SERVING** 16.9g total fat (6.8g saturated fat); 1095kJ (262 cal); 8.9g carbohydrate; 16.2g protein; 5.3g fibre

When you pour the egg mixture into the pan, use a fork to gently move the mixture from side to side as it begins to set, to ensure it cooks evenly. Keep doing this until the egg starts to form a crust around the edge. Give the pan handle a gentle jiggle to make sure the bottom isn't sticking; when the egg mixture just appears set, sprinkle with the cheese and place the pan under a preheated griller. The frittata can be served hot or at room temperature.

Grilled fetta

PREPARATION TIME 5 MINUTES **COOKING TIME** 5 MINUTES **SERVES** 6

300g fetta cheese, halved

2 tablespoons olive oil

1 teaspoon dried chilli flakes

1 teaspoon dried oregano leaves

1 Preheat grill.

2 Place cheese on foil-lined oven tray. Combine oil, chilli and oregano in small bowl; press over cheese.

3 Grill cheese about 5 minutes or until browned lightly. Stand 5 minutes; slice thickly.

☐ **PER SERVING** 17.7g total fat (8.5g saturated fat); 807kJ (193 cal); 0.2g carbohydrate; 8.9g protein; 0g fibre

You can also marinate the fetta (or other cheeses such as haloumi, bocconcini or paneer), cut into chunks, in oil flavoured with lemon myrtle, za'atar, rigani or any dried herb you like, in a glass jar for 3 hours or overnight in the refrigerator before grilling. Great served with grissini or pitta chips and a selection of dips.

LEEK FRITTATA WITH BABY SPINACH SALAD

If you can't find cans of mexibeans, canned refried beans (with and without added green chilli) are available in the Mexican food section of all supermarkets. Finely chop a small fresh red thai chilli and cook it with the garlic and onion to add a bit more heat to your nachos.

Vegie nachos

PREPARATION TIME 15 MINUTES **COOKING TIME** 35 MINUTES **SERVES** 4

1 tablespoon olive oil

1 medium brown onion (150g), chopped finely

1 clove garlic, crushed

400g can chopped tomatoes

420g can mexibeans, rinsed, drained

230g packet corn chips

1 cup (120g) coarsely grated cheddar cheese

½ cup (120g) sour cream

1 tablespoon coarsely chopped fresh coriander

1 Heat oil in medium frying pan; cook onion and garlic, stirring, about 5 minutes or until onion softens. Stir in undrained tomatoes and beans; bring to a boil. Reduce heat, simmer, uncovered, 15 minutes, stirring constantly, until mixture thickens slightly.

2 Preheat grill.

3 Place corn chips onto large ovenproof plate; pour bean mixture over chips, then sprinkle with cheese. Grill nachos until cheese is melted.

4 Serve nachos topped with sour cream and coriander.

PER SERVING 43.4g total fat (21.3g saturated fat); 2867kJ (686 cal); 49.3g carbohydrate; 20.5g protein; 13.3g fibre

---

Everyone's favourite accompaniment to Sunday's baked dinner, "cauliflower cheese" heated under the grill is also a decadent dish to eat on its own with crusty bread and a glass of red. For the perfect rendition, make sure you leave a lot of crunch in the florets: flaccid, soggy cauliflower isn't desirable to anyone.

Cauliflower mornay

PREPARATION TIME 10 MINUTES **COOKING TIME** 20 MINUTES **SERVES** 6

1 small cauliflower (1kg), cut into florets

50g butter

¼ cup (35g) plain flour

2 cups (500ml) milk

¾ cup (90g) coarsely grated cheddar cheese

1 Boil, steam or microwave cauliflower until tender; drain.

2 Melt butter in medium saucepan; cook flour, stirring, until mixture bubbles and thickens. Gradually stir in milk; cook, stirring, until mixture boils and thickens. Stir in half the cheese.

3 Preheat grill.

4 Place cauliflower in shallow 1.5-litre (6-cup) flameproof dish; pour mornay sauce over cauliflower, sprinkle with remaining cheese. Grill about 10 minutes or until browned lightly.

PER SERVING 15.5g total fat (9.9g saturated fat); 970kJ (232 cal); 11.4g carbohydrate; 10.5g protein; 2.9g fibre

Spinach gnocchi

PREPARATION TIME 30 MINUTES **COOKING TIME** 20 MINUTES **SERVES** 4

500g spinach, trimmed

1¼ cups (250g) ricotta cheese

1 cup (80g) finely grated parmesan cheese

1 egg, beaten lightly

¼ teaspoon ground nutmeg

½ cup (70g) plain flour

45g butter, melted

1 Steam or microwave spinach until wilted. Rinse under cold running water; drain well. Squeeze as much liquid as possible from spinach; chop finely.

2 Combine spinach, ricotta, half of the parmesan, egg and nutmeg in medium bowl. Roll level tablespoons of mixture into egg shapes; roll gnocchi lightly in flour.

3 Cook gnocchi, in batches, in large saucepan of boiling water, uncovered, about 3 minutes or until gnocchi float to the surface. Remove from pan with slotted spoon; drain.

4 Preheat grill.

5 Arrange gnocchi in ovenproof dish. Pour butter over gnocchi; sprinkle with remaining parmesan. Grill gnocchi until cheese browns lightly.

☐ **PER SERVING** 24.5g total fat (15.1g saturated fat); 1321kJ (316 cal); 3.7g carbohydrate; 19.2g protein; 3.5g fibre

This dish is also known as naked gnocchi because they are essentially served unsauced. Gnocchi can also be deep-fried, but no matter how you cook them, it's vitally important to squeeze out as much moisture as possible from the spinach to prevent the gnocchi from falling apart when you shape them. You can make the gnocchi to step 3 and refrigerate them overnight.

Bacon and cheese potatoes in jackets

PREPARATION TIME 20 MINUTES **COOKING TIME** 30 MINUTES **SERVES** 6

6 large potatoes (1.8kg)

1 medium brown onion (150g), sliced thinly

3 rindless bacon rashers (195g), chopped coarsely

⅓ cup (80g) sour cream

½ cup (60g) coarsely grated cheddar cheese

2 teaspoons finely chopped fresh chives

1 Boil, steam or microwave potatoes until tender; drain.

2 Cook onion and bacon in heated oiled frying pan until browned lightly.

3 Cut and discard shallow slice from each potato. Scoop two-thirds of potato from each shell; place shells on oven tray. Discard half the potato flesh; combine remainder in bowl with bacon mixture, sour cream and ⅓ cup of the cheese.

4 Preheat grill.

5 Spoon mixture into shells; top with remaining cheese. Grill until cheese browns lightly. Serve sprinkled with chives.

☐ **PER SERVING** 11.2g total fat (6.4g saturated fat); 1275kJ (305 cal); 35g carbohydrate; 12.5g protein; 5.4g fibre

Make grilled potato skins and pass them around at your next party. Scoop the flesh out of baked potatoes, leaving a shell about 5mm thick; refrigerate skins until you are ready to grill them. Brush the inside of each shell with melted butter or olive oil; place, cut-sides down, on oven tray, then brush the outside of the skins. Grill until crisp; turn, sprinkle bacon bits or grated cheese (or both) inside skins' shells and grill until bacon sizzles or cheese melts. Serve with green onion, sour cream or chilli sauce.

Cutting tools

Not just mother's little helpers but something for everyone and every task requiring a little cut and thrust.

PEELER
The swivel-action peeler can be used right- or left-handed. As you draw it towards you, the blade cuts just under the surface to remove the skin of the vegetable or fruit.

ZESTER
The zester has tiny, sharp-edged holes across its end so that, as you press it onto the rind of any citrus fruit and draw it towards you, it cuts fine shreds from the zest without removing any of the bitter white pith beneath.

CANELLE KNIFE
A canelle knife has a V-shaped blade with a sharp indent across its end so that, as you press it on to the skin of citrus fruit and draw it towards you, it cuts matchstick-thick strips (julienne).

EGG SLICER
An egg-slicer works by holding the hard-boiled egg in a shallow, slotted depression while fine wires, which marry with the slots, are pressed down through it. Some egg-slicers have depressions shaped to hold the egg both crosswise and lengthwise.

APPLE-SLICER
An apple-slicer, with sharp blades radiating from a sharp central ring, cores and segments an apple in one operation by being pressed down firmly from above. It works well for medium apples, less so for large or small ones. A good tool to own if symmetry is important, as for a tarte tatin.

CHEESE SLICER [CHEESE PLANE]
The sharpened slit of a cheese slicer, with its edge set at an angle for cutting, will produce even slices from thin to thicker according to how hard it's pressed onto the cheese, which is then served on the slicer's broad blade.

CORER

When the trough-shaped blade of a corer, with its saw-toothed ring at the end, is pushed down through the centre of an apple and twisted, it cuts out a cylinder including the core.

CHERRY STONER

Cherry stoners all work on the principle of holding the cherry in a cup or ring while a plunger stamps out its centre to remove the seed – a more attractive presentation than halving the cherry to stone it.

MELON BALLER

When the sharp-edged metal cup of a melon baller is pressed into the melon flesh and twisted, it cuts out a ball of the flesh. Some ballers have two cups of different sizes, one on each end.

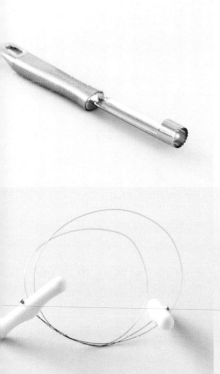

CHEESE WIRE

The oldest way of cutting cheese, and still the best for soft or crumbly varieties, is to draw a wire through it. The one pictured is held by the handgrips in each hand to slide through cheese.

PASTRY WHEEL

A sharp wheel that cuts pastry without pulling or distorting it as a knife may do. Some pastry wheels are fluted to make decorative edges on lattice strips or ravioli, for example. Check that the wheel is set firmly so it won't wobble and create irregular-width strips.

PIZZA CUTTER

Designed like a pastry wheel but larger, a pizza cutter is meant for cutting through melted cheese then cleanly down through the topping and crust of a pizza.

Under your griller, the topping on a crème brûlée transforms itself from a sprinkle of sugar to an ethereally brittle caramelised topping that provides a delicious textural contrast to the creamy custard that lies beneath.

Crème brûlée

PREPARATION TIME 15 MINUTES (PLUS REFRIGERATION TIME) **COOKING TIME** 40 MINUTES **SERVES** 6

1 vanilla bean
3 cups (750ml) thickened cream
6 egg yolks
¼ cup (55g) caster sugar
¼ cup (40g) pure icing sugar

1 Preheat oven to 180°C/160°C fan-forced.

2 Split vanilla bean in half lengthways; scrape seeds into medium heatproof bowl. Place pod in medium saucepan with cream; heat without boiling.

3 Add egg yolks and caster sugar to seeds in bowl; gradually whisk in hot cream mixture. Place bowl over medium saucepan of simmering water; stir over heat about 10 minutes or until custard mixture thickens slightly and coats the back of a spoon. Discard pod.

4 Divide custard among six ½-cup (125ml) ovenproof dishes. Place dishes in large baking dish; pour enough boiling water into baking dish to come halfway up sides of dishes. Bake, uncovered, about 20 minutes or until custards just set. Remove custards from water; cool to room temperature. Cover; refrigerate 3 hours or overnight.

5 Preheat grill.

6 Place custard dishes in shallow flameproof dish filled with ice cubes. Sprinkle custards evenly with sifted icing sugar; using finger, gently smooth sugar over the surface, pressing in gently. Grill until sugar caramelises.

◻ **PER SERVING** 52.1g total fat (32.3g saturated fat); 2358kJ (564 cal); 19.8g carbohydrate; 5.8g protein; 0g fibre

---

Figs have their origins in the long, hot summers of the eastern Mediterranean, and are at their best here from late summer. A magnificent fruit, it can also be grilled sprinkled with combined cinnamon and demerara sugar for dessert. Make sure the figs you use are ready to eat but not overripe or they will lose their shape after being heated under the griller.

Honey grilled figs

PREPARATION TIME 5 MINUTES **COOKING TIME** 5 MINUTES **SERVES** 6

6 large figs (480g)
2 tablespoons caster sugar
¼ cup (90g) honey
1 teaspoon vanilla extract

1 Preheat grill.

2 Cut figs in half lengthways. Place figs on oven tray, cut-side up; sprinkle with sugar.

3 Grill about 5 minutes or until sugar melts and figs are browned lightly.

4 Meanwhile, combine honey and extract in small saucepan; stir over low heat, without boiling, until honey is runny.

5 Serve warm figs drizzled with honey mixture and, if desired, mascarpone cheese.

◻ **PER SERVING** 0.2g total fat (0g saturated fat); 451kJ (108 cal); 24.1g carbohydrate; 1.1g protein; 1.8g fibre

CRÈME BRULEE

A passionfruit is well-named: the fruit's simultaneously sweet and tart taste inspires an almost addictive passion to its seedy, yellow pulp. Its singular flavour marries well with many other creamy desserts such as panna cotta, ice-cream or a bavarois.

Passionfruit and coconut crème brûlée

PREPARATION TIME 15 MINUTES (PLUS REFRIGERATION TIME) **COOKING TIME** 50 MINUTES **SERVES** 4

1 egg
2 egg yolks
2 tablespoons caster sugar
¼ cup (60ml) passionfruit pulp
280ml can coconut cream
½ cup (125ml) cream
1 tablespoon brown sugar

1 Preheat oven to 180°C/160°C fan-forced.

2 Combine egg, egg yolks, caster sugar and passionfruit in medium heatproof bowl.

3 Combine coconut cream and cream in small saucepan; bring to a boil. Gradually whisk hot cream mixture into egg mixture. Place bowl over medium saucepan of simmering water; stir over heat about 10 minutes or until custard thickens slightly.

4 Divide custard among four deep ½-cup (125ml) ovenproof dishes. Place dishes in large baking dish; pour enough boiling water into baking dish to come halfway up sides of dishes. Bake, uncovered, about 30 minutes or until custard is just set. Remove dishes from water; cool. Cover; refrigerate 3 hours or overnight.

5 Preheat grill.

6 Place custard dishes in shallow flameproof dish filled with ice cubes. Sprinkle each custard with 1 teaspoon brown sugar; using finger, gently smooth sugar over the surface. Grill until sugar caramelises.

▭ **PER SERVING** 29.9g total fat (21.3g saturated fat); 1509kJ (361 cal); 16.6g carbohydrate; 5.7g protein; 3.3g fibre

After you've spent hours chopping the ingredients for a Thai dinner, this simple South-East Asian inspired dessert will come as a great relief. You can use palm sugar instead of brown, if you like.

Sweet lime mangoes

PREPARATION TIME 5 MINUTES **COOKING TIME** 8 MINUTES **SERVES** 4

4 small mangoes (1.2kg)
1 tablespoon finely grated lime rind
1 tablespoon lime juice
1 tablespoon brown sugar
½ cup (140g) yogurt

1 Preheat grill.

2 Slice cheeks from mangoes; score each cheek in shallow criss-cross pattern.

3 Place cheeks, cut-side up on oven tray, drizzle with combined rind and juice; sprinkle with brown sugar. Grill until sugar caramelises.

4 Serve mangoes with yogurt.

▭ **PER SERVING** 1.7g total fat (0.7g saturated fat); 798kJ (191 cal); 35.8g carbohydrate; 4.1g protein; 4.1g fibre

Grilled nectarines with passionfruit swirl yogurt

PREPARATION TIME 10 MINUTES **COOKING TIME** 10 MINUTES **SERVES** 4

8 medium nectarines (1.3kg), halved, seeded

2 tablespoons brown sugar

1 tablespoon orange-flavoured liqueur

1 cup (280g) yogurt

2 tablespoons icing sugar

2 tablespoons passionfruit pulp

1 Preheat grill.

2 Place nectarines, cut side up, on oven tray; sprinkle with sugar and liqueur. Grill until browned lightly.

3 Meanwhile, combine yogurt and sifted sugar in serving bowl; swirl with passionfruit pulp.

4 Serve nectarines with passionfruit yogurt.

▭ **PER SERVING** 2.7g total fat (1.5g saturated fat); 1012kJ (242 cal); 40.1g carbohydrate; 6.8g protein; 8.2g fibre

For a really inspired appetiser, wrap pieces of quartered nectarine in thin slices of prosciutto, skewer them and place under a preheated griller, turning occasionally, until the prosciutto is crisp. These are delicious served with a glass of chilled Champagne.

Grilled bananas with vanilla cream

PREPARATION TIME 10 MINUTES **COOKING TIME** 10 MINUTES **SERVES** 4

4 medium bananas (800g), halved lengthways

¼ cup (55g) brown sugar

20g butter

2 tablespoons coconut-flavoured liqueur

1 vanilla bean

⅔ cup (160ml) thickened cream

1 tablespoon icing sugar

1 Preheat grill.

2 Sprinkle bananas with 1 tablespoon of the brown sugar; place on oven tray. Grill bananas until browned lightly.

3 Meanwhile, stir remaining brown sugar, butter and liqueur in small saucepan over low heat until smooth.

4 Split vanilla bean in half lengthways, scrape seeds into small bowl; discard pod. Add cream and icing sugar; beat with electric mixer until soft peaks form.

5 Serve bananas with vanilla cream; drizzle with sauce.

▭ **PER SERVING** 19.1g total fat (12.5g saturated fat); 1659kJ (397 cal); 48g carbohydrate; 3.2g protein; 2.9g fibre

Bananas to be used for grilling should be fairly ripe so that they've produced enough natural sugar to caramelise slightly. They are just as good served with a coconut ice-cream or hazelnut gelato as with this vanilla cream.

Grilled sabayon peaches

PREPARATION TIME 10 MINUTES **COOKING TIME** 15 MINUTES **SERVES** 6

6 medium peaches (900g), sliced thickly

4 egg yolks

2 tablespoons caster sugar

2 tablespoons peach liqueur

2 tablespoons apple juice

1 Arrange peach slices in six shallow 1-cup (125 ml) ovenproof serving dishes.

2 Combine egg yolks, sugar, liqueur and juice in medium bowl. Place bowl over medium saucepan of simmering water, ensuring that water doesn't touch bottom of bowl. Whisk constantly about 8 minutes or until mixture is very thick and creamy.

3 Meanwhile, preheat grill.

4 Spoon warm sabayon evenly over peach slices; grill until sabayon is browned lightly.

PER SERVING 3.9 total fat (1.2 g saturated fat); 562kJ (135 cal) 17.7g carbohydrate; 3.2g protein; 1.8 g fibre

A French variation of the classic Italian zabaglione, a sabayon is a light, frothy custard sauce that is often used as a filling for pies and tarts. It also goes well with poached pears and fresh mango slices.

A flat sabayon is the result of underwhisking: you must whisk vigorously to incorporate as much air as possible

Plums with sour cream

PREPARATION TIME 5 MINUTES **COOKING TIME** 5 MINUTES **SERVES** 4

825g can plums in syrup, drained

½ cup (120g) sour cream

½ cup (140g) honey-flavoured yogurt

⅓ cup (75g) firmly packed brown sugar

1 Preheat grill.

2 Halve plums; discard stones. Divide plums among four shallow 1-cup (250ml) ovenproof serving dishes.

3 Combine sour cream, yogurt and 2 tablespoons of the sugar in small bowl. Spoon sour cream mixture over plums; sprinkle with remaining sugar. Grill plums until browned lightly.

PER SERVING 13.2g total fat (8.6g saturated fat); 1371 kJ (326 cal); 48.4g carbohydrate; 2.9g protein; 1.4g fibre

You can use fresh plums if they are in season; the red-fleshed varieties, like mariposa, lend themselves to being grilled better than the yellow-fleshed variety. Try brushing halved plums with redcurrant jelly then grilling them alongside butterflied pork steaks.

GRILLED SABAYON PEACHES

THE SAUCEPAN

The Saucepan

You need three basic saucepans – small, medium and large – so you can use the right-sized pan for the quantity of food you are cooking. Most cooks have more – the wide, shallow pan that's just right for steamed rice or a pilaf, the extra-big one that can handle spaghetti sauce or soup for a crowd, the handy little one with a pouring lip – plus an extra one or two so you can cook two different things that both need, say, a medium pan, at the same time.

On the other hand, a beginner can survive with just one saucepan for a while. In general, the right buying strategy for saucepans is to invest slowly, as you can afford it, in a few top-quality pans, rather than a crowd of second-rate pans (see Equipment in *The Ideal Kitchen*, pages 11 & 13). You will reach for a saucepan almost every day of your cooking life, so they, of all your kitchen equipment, should be investments in a long and trusty service.

There is, however, an argument for an exception to this rule. A thin, cheap saucepan will do just as good a job as a top-quality one when boiling vegetables and some other foods, or holding a steamer to steam them, since the water or steam will even out any hot spots the cheap pan may develop.

However, the cheap pan won't do anything else well, while the expensive pan will excel at all kinds of cooking, and they'll both take up the same amount of storage space. The cheap pan may also warp and become wobbly on the cooktop and will then have to be replaced, while a quality pan should last a lifetime.

JUDGING QUALITY

Judge a saucepan by its weight and by the material of which it is made. Good saucepans are heavy because they have thick bases to hold the heat and spread it evenly. The saucepan must also respond quickly when the heat is turned up or down, and this depends on whether it is made of material that is a good conductor or a poor one. The different metals, or combinations of metals, of which saucepans are made, have a great effect on how they perform. All these factors are exactly the same by which a frying pan is judged and are explained in detail in *The Frying Pan* (see pages 22 & 23).

The saucepan is, however, designed to hold a much deeper mass of food than a frying pan, and to cook it by surrounding it with even, moist heat. For this reason, the ideal saucepan has fairly thick sides as well as a heavy, thick base. A top-quality saucepan can cook gently and evenly over low heat, without the food scorching or sticking, for a long period.

SHAPES

Tall saucepans conserve moisture, so they are particularly well-suited to long, slow cooking. Wide saucepans, especially those with slightly outward-sloping sides, are easy to see into and their bases are wide enough to brown food properly. Wide saucepans, rather than tall ones, are also better suited for reducing or simmering a sauce, as the larger surface encourages evaporation.

HANDLES

Saucepans are not usually designed to go into the oven, so the handles can be made of plastic, wood or any material that is comfortable to your hand and stays cool when the saucepan is hot.

The handle should be welded on or attached with rivets. A handle attached with screws can work loose and will need frequent retightening. Eventually, the thread of the screw-holes may become too worn to allow proper tightening.

LIDS

Saucepan lids should fit closely but not so tightly that you have to tug to get them off. You will want to check how the food is cooking, so a saucepan with a heatproof glass lid, allowing you to look in without having to lift it, is useful. Any lid should have a knob or handle that can be grasped firmly and stay cool enough to lift it without a pot-holder.

FINISH

Non-stick or not? There are arguments both ways. The answer depends partly on how you treat your cooking equipment. If you (and anyone else who may use the saucepans) are the careful, meticulous type who will always use non-scratching implements and never scrub the pans, then non-stick saucepans may be a good idea. Remember, though, that non-stick linings suffer from high heat, which can be a problem when you brown meat for a braise or curry before adding liquid.

Also, be aware that the quality of non-stick finishes varies greatly. Cheap ones may become degraded and lift off no matter how careful you are. Only tough, high-quality finishes are worth considering; these, not surprisingly, are found in the more expensive, high-quality saucepans on the market. You will probably decide that at least one good non-stick saucepan is worth having for an easy clean-up after scalding milk or making polenta or porridge.

In recent years, some doubts have developed about the safety of non-stick linings once they are damaged (see under Finish in *The Frying Pan*, page 23).

CARE

Before using your saucepans for the first time, be sure to read the manufacturer's instructions on how to care for them. There are often directions for pre-washing new saucepans, as well as cautions about care during cooking and information about how to wash, dry and store them.

Beef massaman curry

PREPARATION TIME 35 MINUTES (PLUS STANDING TIME) **COOKING TIME** 2 HOURS 30 MINUTES
SERVES 4

1kg skirt steak, cut into 3cm pieces

2 cups (500ml) beef stock

5 cardamom pods, bruised

¼ teaspoon ground clove

2 star anise

1 tablespoon grated palm sugar

2 tablespoons fish sauce

2 tablespoons tamarind concentrate

2 x 400ml cans coconut milk

8 baby brown onions (200g), halved

1 medium kumara (400g), chopped coarsely

¼ cup (35g) coarsely chopped roasted unsalted peanuts

2 green onions, sliced thinly

MASSAMAN CURRY PASTE

20 dried long red chillies

1 teaspoon ground coriander

2 teaspoons ground cumin

2 teaspoons ground cinnamon

½ teaspoon ground cardamom

½ teaspoon ground clove

5 cloves garlic, quartered

1 large brown onion (200g), chopped coarsely

2 x 10cm sticks fresh lemon grass (40g), sliced thinly

3 fresh kaffir lime leaves, sliced thinly

4cm piece fresh ginger (20g), chopped coarsely

2 teaspoons shrimp paste

1 tablespoon peanut oil

1 Preheat oven to 180°C/160°C fan-forced; make massaman curry paste.

2 Place beef, 1½ cups of the stock, cardamom, clove, star anise, sugar, sauce, 1 tablespoon of the tamarind and half of the coconut milk in large saucepan; simmer, uncovered, about 1½ hours or until beef is almost tender.

3 Strain beef over large bowl; reserve braising liquid, discard solids. Cover beef to keep warm.

4 Cook 2 tablespoons of the curry paste (reserve remainder for another use) in same pan, stirring, until fragrant. Add remaining coconut milk, tamarind and stock; bring to a boil. Cook, stirring, about 1 minute or until mixture is smooth. Return beef to pan with brown onion, kumara and 1 cup of the reserved braising liquid; simmer, uncovered, about 30 minutes or until beef and vegetables are tender.

5 Stir nuts and green onion into curry off the heat.

MASSAMAN CURRY PASTE Place chillies in small heatproof jug, cover with boiling water; stand 15 minutes, drain. Meanwhile, dry-fry coriander, cumin, cinnamon, cardamom and clove in small frying pan, stirring until fragrant. Place chillies and spices in small shallow baking dish with remaining ingredients. Roast, uncovered, 15 minutes. Blend or process roasted mixture, or crush using mortar and pestle, until smooth.

PER SERVING 52.7g total fat (39.5g saturated fat); 3645kJ (872 cal); 29.2g carbohydrate; 67.4g protein; 7.2g fibre

Duck jungle curry

PREPARATION TIME 40 MINUTES **COOKING TIME** 2 HOURS **SERVES** 4

2kg duck

¼ cup (60ml) peanut oil

1 medium brown onion (150g), chopped coarsely

1 medium carrot (120g), chopped coarsely

2 cloves garlic, halved

4cm piece fresh ginger (20g), sliced thickly

½ teaspoon black peppercorns

2 litres (8 cups) cold water

5 fresh kaffir lime leaves, torn

¼ cup (75g) red curry paste

150g thai eggplants, halved

1 medium carrot (120g), extra, sliced thinly

100g snake beans, cut into 4cm lengths

227g can bamboo shoots, rinsed, drained

2 x 5cm stems (10g) pickled green peppercorns

½ cup firmly packed thai basil leaves

4 fresh small red thai chillies, chopped coarsely

2 tablespoons fish sauce

1 Discard neck then wash duck inside and out; pat dry with absorbent paper. Using sharp knife, separate drumstick and thigh sections from body; separate thighs from drumsticks. Remove and discard wings. Separate breast and backbone; cut breast from bone. You will have six pieces. Cut duck carcass into four pieces; discard any fat from carcass.

2 Heat 1 tablespoon of the oil in large saucepan; cook carcass pieces, stirring occasionally, about 5 minutes or until browned. Add onion, chopped carrot, garlic and ginger; cook, stirring, about 2 minutes or until onion softens. Add black peppercorns, the water and four of the lime leaves; simmer, uncovered, 1 hour 15 minutes, skimming fat from surface of mixture regularly.

3 Strain mixture through muslin-lined sieve into large heatproof jug. Reserve 3 cups of liquid; discard solids and remaining liquid.

4 Preheat oven to 200°C/180°C fan-forced. Heat remaining oil in same cleaned pan; cook thighs, drumsticks and breasts, in batches, until browned. Remove skin from breasts and legs; slice skin thinly. Place sliced duck skin on oven tray; roast, uncovered, about 10 minutes or until crisp.

5 Discard excess oil from pan; reheat pan, cook curry paste, stirring, about 1 minute or until fragrant. Add eggplant, sliced carrot, beans, bamboo shoots, green peppercorns, half of the basil, remaining lime leaf and reserved liquid; simmer, uncovered, 5 minutes. Add duck pieces; simmer, uncovered, about 10 minutes or until vegetables are tender. Stir in chilli and sauce.

6 Place curry in serving bowls; sprinkle with remaining basil and crisped duck skin.

☐ **PER SERVING** 121g total fat (34.4g saturated fat); 5334kJ (1276 cal); 8.1g carbohydrate; 41g protein; 5.4g fibre

Thai red beef curry

PREPARATION TIME 35 MINUTES (PLUS STANDING TIME) **COOKING TIME** 1 HOUR 45 MINUTES **SERVES** 4

1 tablespoon peanut oil

4 x 125g beef scotch fillet steaks

227g can bamboo shoots, drained, rinsed

2 x 400ml cans coconut cream

½ cup (125ml) beef stock

2 tablespoons fish sauce

2 tablespoons lime juice

2 fresh kaffir lime leaves, shredded finely

4 large zucchini (600g), sliced thinly

⅓ cup firmly packed thai basil leaves

RED CURRY PASTE

20 dried long red chillies

1 teaspoon ground coriander

2 teaspoons ground cumin

1 teaspoon hot paprika

2cm piece fresh ginger (10g), chopped finely

3 cloves garlic, quartered

1 medium red onion (170g), chopped coarsely

2 x 10cm sticks fresh lemon grass (40g), sliced thinly

2 tablespoons coarsely chopped fresh coriander root and stem mixture

2 teaspoons shrimp paste

1 tablespoon peanut oil

Kaffir lime leaves are readily available in most greengrocers and many supermarkets; if you can't get fresh, used dried. However, if they are not available at all in your area, at a pinch you can use fresh washed and torn lemon or lime tree leaves.

1 Make red curry paste.

2 Heat oil in large saucepan; cook beef, in batches, until well-browned both sides.

3 Cook ¼ cup of the curry paste (reserve remainder for another use) in same pan, stirring, until fragrant. Return beef to dish with bamboo shoots, coconut cream, stock, sauce, juice and lime leaves; simmer, uncovered, 1 hour 20 minutes. Add zucchini, simmer about 5 minutes or until tender.

4 Serve curry sprinkled with basil.

RED CURRY PASTE Place chillies in small heatproof jug, cover with boiling water; stand 15 minutes, drain. Meanwhile, dry fry ground coriander, cumin and paprika in small frying pan, stirring until fragrant. Blend or process chillies and spices with ginger, garlic, onion, lemon grass, coriander mixture and paste until mixture forms a paste. Add oil to paste; continue to blend until smooth.

PER SERVING 55.5g total fat (40.6g saturated fat); 2897kJ (693 cal); 12.3g carbohydrate; 34.1g protein; 7.2g fibre

Fish yellow curry

PREPARATION TIME 40 MINUTES (PLUS STANDING TIME) **COOKING TIME** 25 MINUTES **SERVES** 4

8 baby new potatoes (320g), halved

400ml can coconut milk

¼ cup (60ml) fish stock

2 tablespoons fish sauce

1 tablespoon lime juice

1 tablespoon grated palm sugar

800g firm white fish fillets, cut into 3cm pieces

3 green onions, sliced thinly

⅓ cup coarsely chopped fresh coriander

1 fresh long red chilli, sliced thinly

1 tablespoon finely chopped fresh coriander

YELLOW CURRY PASTE

2 dried long red chillies

1 teaspoon ground coriander

1 teaspoon ground cumin

½ teaspoon ground cinnamon

2 fresh yellow banana chillies (250g), chopped coarsely

1 teaspoon finely chopped fresh turmeric

2 cloves garlic, quartered

1 small brown onion (80g), chopped finely

10cm stick fresh lemon grass (20g), finely chopped

2 teaspoons finely chopped fresh galangal

1 tablespoon coarsely chopped fresh coriander root and stem mixture

1 teaspoon shrimp paste

1 tablespoon peanut oil

Red, yellow, green and massaman are the most well-known Thai coconut-based curries and are often referred to as "dry" curries. The key ingredients are generally fresh and fragrant: coriander leaves, chillies, lemon grass, garlic, galangal and green onion.

Banana chillies, also known as wax chillies, Hungarian peppers or sweet banana peppers, are almost as mild as capsicum but have a slightly sweet sharpness about their taste. Sold in varying degrees of ripeness, they can be found in pale olive green, yellow and red varieties.

1 Make yellow curry paste.

2 Boil, steam or microwave potatoes until just tender; drain.

3 Meanwhile, place half of the coconut milk in large saucepan; bring to a boil. Boil, stirring, until milk reduces by half and the oil separates from the coconut milk. Add ¼ cup of the curry paste (reserve remainder for another use); cook, stirring, about 1 minute or until fragrant. Add remaining coconut milk, stock, sauce, juice and sugar; cook, stirring, until sugar dissolves.

4 Add fish and potatoes to pan; cook, covered, about 3 minutes or until fish is cooked. Stir in onion and coarsely chopped coriander.

5 Divide curry among serving bowls; sprinkle with chilli and finely chopped coriander.

YELLOW CURRY PASTE Place dried chillies in small heatproof jug, cover with boiling water; stand 15 minutes, drain. Meanwhile, dry-fry ground coriander, cumin and cinnamon in small frying pan, stirring until fragrant. Blend or process spices and chillies with remaining ingredients until mixture is smooth.

▭ **PER SERVING** 23g total fat (18.5g saturated fat); 1960kJ (469 cal); 18.9g carbohydrate; 44.7g protein; 3.9g fibre

Lamb and macadamia curry

PREPARATION TIME 20 MINUTES **COOKING TIME** 2 HOURS **SERVES** 4

Lamb shoulder is a good cut to use for any curry because generally it's a cheaper cut of meat that tenderises beautifully during the long cooking process.

1 cup (140g) roasted unsalted macadamias

2 tablespoons vegetable oil

800g diced lamb shoulder

1 medium brown onion (150g), chopped coarsely

1 clove garlic, crushed

2 fresh small red thai chillies, chopped finely

2cm piece fresh ginger (10g), grated

1 teaspoon ground cumin

1 teaspoon ground turmeric

½ teaspoon ground cinnamon

½ teaspoon ground cardamom

½ teaspoon ground fennel

400g can diced tomatoes

400ml can coconut milk

1 cup (250ml) beef stock

½ cup loosely packed fresh coriander leaves

1 Blend or process half the nuts until finely ground; coarsely chop remaining nuts.

2 Heat half of the oil in large saucepan; cook lamb, in batches, until browned.

3 Heat remaining oil in same pan; cook onion, garlic, chilli and ginger, stirring, until onion softens. Add spices; cook, stirring, until fragrant.

4 Return lamb to pan with ground nuts, undrained tomatoes, coconut milk and stock; bring to a boil. Reduce heat, simmer, covered, about 1¼ hours or until lamb is tender. Uncover; simmer about 15 minutes or until sauce thickens slightly.

5 Serve lamb sprinkled with remaining nuts and coriander.

▭ **PER SERVING** 68.4g total fat (28.4g saturated fat); 3561kJ (852 cal); 11.6g carbohydrate; 47g protein; 5.9g fibre

Lamb meatball korma

PREPARATION TIME 45 MINUTES (PLUS STANDING TIME) **COOKING TIME** 1 HOUR 10 MINUTES **SERVES** 4

A classic Indian curry typical of the affluent Mogul Empire with its rich, luscious content of nuts, cream and cardamom, a korma makes a good "beginner's" curry since it's fairly mild, any hint of spice tempered with the sauce's tomato and coconut content.

½ cup (40g) desiccated coconut

⅓ cup (80ml) hot water

¼ cup (40g) unsalted roasted cashews

500g lamb mince

1 large brown onion (200g), chopped finely

½ cup (35g) stale breadcrumbs

1 egg

2 tablespoons ghee

2 bay leaves

1 cinnamon stick

5 cardamom pods, bruised

5 cloves

1 medium red onion (170g), sliced thinly

2cm piece fresh ginger (10g), grated

2 cloves garlic, crushed

½ teaspoon chilli powder

½ teaspoon ground turmeric

1 teaspoon ground coriander

½ teaspoon ground cumin

2 medium tomatoes (300g), chopped coarsely

1½ cups (375ml) water, extra

¾ cup (180ml) cream

1 Place coconut in small heatproof bowl, cover with the hot water, stand 1 hour; drain. Blend or process coconut and nuts until mixture forms a thick puree.

2 Mix 2 tablespoons of the coconut mixture, lamb, brown onion, breadcrumbs and egg in medium bowl; roll level tablespoons of mixture into balls.

3 Melt half the ghee in large saucepan; cook meatballs, in batches, until just browned. Drain on absorbent paper.

4 Heat remaining ghee in same pan; cook leaves, cinnamon, cardamom and cloves, stirring, until fragrant. Add red onion; cook, stirring, until browned lightly. Add ginger, garlic, chilli, turmeric, coriander and cumin; cook, stirring, 1 minute. Add tomato; cook, stirring, about 5 minutes or until mixture thickens slightly. Add remaining coconut mixture and the extra water; simmer, uncovered, 20 minutes.

5 Return meatballs to pan; simmer, covered, about 20 minutes or until cooked through. Stir in cream; simmer, stirring, until hot.

▭ **PER SERVING** 50.1g total fat (29.5g saturated fat); 2755kJ (659 cal); 17g carbohydrate; 34g protein; 5.5g fibre

Kenyan chicken curry

PREPARATION TIME 30 MINUTES (PLUS REFRIGERATION TIME) **COOKING TIME** 30 MINUTES **SERVES** 6

8cm piece fresh ginger (40g), grated

6 cloves garlic, crushed

2 teaspoons ground turmeric

½ cup (125ml) lemon juice

1 teaspoon ground cumin

3 teaspoons garam masala

1 tablespoon ground coriander

1 teaspoon hot paprika

1 teaspoon chilli flakes

¼ cup (70g) yogurt

1kg chicken thigh fillets, cut into 3cm pieces

⅓ cup (80ml) vegetable oil

3 large brown onions (600g), chopped coarsely

2 teaspoons chilli powder

2 teaspoons ground fenugreek

2 x 400g cans crushed tomatoes

1 stick cinnamon

2 fresh long green chillies, chopped finely

300ml cream

1 tablespoon honey

¼ cup coarsely chopped fresh coriander

This is an authentic Swahili recipe from the kitchens of Lamu, an island off the coast of Kenya whose inhabitants are an amalgam of African and Arab heritage – as is this dish. Use a heavy-based enamelled cast-iron saucepan if you own one.

1 Combine half of the ginger, half of the garlic, half of the turmeric and half of the juice in large bowl with all the cumin, garam masala, ground coriander, paprika, chilli flakes, yogurt and chicken. Cover; refrigerate 30 minutes.

2 Heat half of the oil in large saucepan; cook chicken mixture until browned lightly. Remove from pan.

3 Heat remaining oil in same saucepan; cook onion, chilli powder, fenugreek, remaining ginger, garlic and turmeric, stirring, until onion softens. Add undrained tomatoes, cinnamon, green chilli and remaining juice. Simmer, covered, 10 minutes. Stir in cream and honey; simmer, uncovered, 1 minute. Add chicken mixture; simmer until chicken is cooked through. Remove from heat, stir in fresh coriander.

▭ **PER SERVING** 58.9g total fat (24g saturated fat); 3035kJ (726 cal); 15.6g carbohydrate; 32.5g protein; 4.9g fibre

Chicken green curry

PREPARATION TIME 40 MINUTES **COOKING TIME** 50 MINUTES **SERVES** 4

1 tablespoon peanut oil

3 fresh long green chillies, chopped finely

1 kg chicken thigh fillets, cut into 3cm pieces

2 x 400ml cans coconut milk

2 tablespoons fish sauce

2 tablespoons lime juice

1 tablespoon grated palm sugar

150g pea eggplants

1 large zucchini (150g), sliced thinly

⅓ cup loosely packed thai basil leaves

¼ cup loosely packed fresh coriander leaves

2 green onions, chopped coarsely

GREEN CURRY PASTE

2 teaspoons ground coriander

2 teaspoons ground cumin

10 fresh long green chillies, chopped coarsely

10 fresh small green chillies, chopped coarsely

1 teaspoon shrimp paste

1 clove garlic, quartered

4 green onions, chopped coarsely

10cm stick fresh lemon grass (20g), chopped finely

1cm piece fresh galangal (5g), chopped finely

¼ cup coarsely chopped fresh coriander root and stem mixture

1 tablespoon peanut oil

1 Make green curry paste.

2 Heat oil in large saucepan; cook ⅓ cup of the curry paste (reserve remainder for another use) and about two-thirds of the chilli, stirring, about 2 minutes or until fragrant. Add chicken; cook, stirring, until browned.

3 Add coconut milk, sauce, juice, sugar and eggplants; simmer, uncovered, about 10 minutes or until eggplants are just tender.

4 Add zucchini, basil and coriander; simmer, uncovered, until zucchini is just tender.

5 Serve curry sprinkled with remaining chilli and green onion.

GREEN CURRY PASTE Dry-fry ground coriander and cumin in small frying pan over medium heat, stirring until fragrant. Blend or process spices with chillies, paste, garlic, onion, lemon grass, galangal and coriander mixture until mixture forms a paste. Add oil to paste; continue to blend until smooth.

▭ **PER SERVING** 67.3g total fat (43.2g saturated fat); 3716kJ (889 cal); 17g carbohydrate; 52.9g protein; 6g fibre

Classic pulao

PREPARATION TIME 10 MINUTES (PLUS STANDING TIME) **COOKING TIME** 20 MINUTES **SERVES** 4

1 ⅓ cups (265g) basmati rice, rinsed, drained

2 ½ cups (625ml) chicken stock

pinch saffron threads

50g butter

1 medium brown onion (150g), chopped finely

2 cloves garlic, crushed

1 cinnamon stick

6 cardamom pods

1 bay leaf

⅓ cup (55g) sultanas

½ cup (75g) roasted unsalted cashews

1 Place rice in medium bowl, cover with cold water; stand 20 minutes, drain.

2 Heat stock and saffron in small saucepan.

3 Meanwhile, melt butter in large saucepan; cook onion and garlic, stirring, until onion softens. Stir in cinnamon, cardamom and bay leaf; cook, stirring, 2 minutes.

4 Add rice; cook, stirring, 2 minutes. Add stock mixture and sultanas; simmer, covered, 10 minutes or until rice is tender and liquid is absorbed. Sprinkle with nuts just before serving.

PER SERVING 20.6g total fat (8.8g saturated fat); 2128kJ (509 cal); 68.7g carbohydrate; 10.5g protein; 5g fibre

The world's rice-eating cultures have similar-sounding but differently spelled names for the same basic technique: stirring rice in heated oil, butter or ghee in a saucepan before steaming it in the same pan with water and spices or a seasoned stock. The rice grains in this method remain individual rather than sticky, are light, fluffy and very flavourful. And after the initial combining of ingredients, the rice is never stirred during cooking. Serve this pulao with rogan josh (page 176).

Mexican beans with sausages

PREPARATION TIME 20 MINUTES (PLUS STANDING TIME) **COOKING TIME** 2 HOURS 15 MINUTES **SERVES** 4

1 cup (200g) dried kidney beans

800g beef sausages, chopped coarsely

1 tablespoon olive oil

1 large white onion (200g), chopped coarsely

3 cloves garlic, crushed

1 large red capsicum (350g), chopped coarsely

½ teaspoon ground cumin

2 teaspoons sweet smoked paprika

1 teaspoon dried chilli flakes

2 x 400g cans crushed tomatoes

2 tablespoons coarsely chopped fresh oregano

1 Place beans in medium bowl, cover with cold water; stand overnight, drain. Rinse under cold water, drain. Place beans in medium saucepan of boiling water; return to a boil. Reduce heat, simmer, uncovered, about 30 minutes or until beans are almost tender. Drain.

2 Cook sausages, in batches, in large deep saucepan until browned; drain on absorbent paper.

3 Heat oil in same pan; cook onion, garlic and capsicum, stirring, until onion softens. Add cumin, paprika and chilli; cook, stirring, about 2 minutes or until fragrant. Add beans and undrained tomatoes; bring to a boil. Reduce heat, simmer, covered, about 1 hour or until beans are tender.

4 Return sausages to pan; simmer, covered, about 10 minutes or until sausages are cooked through. Remove from heat; stir in oregano. Serve with tortillas, if desired.

PER SERVING 56.6g total fat (25.2g saturated fat); 3336kJ (798 cal); 28.7g carbohydrate; 36.1g protein; 17.6g fibre

A medium-sized red bean, kidney beans have a slightly floury yet sweet flavour; sold dried or canned. All legumes, from the kidney to the chickpea, contain health-protecting components linked with protection against diseases such as cancer, diabetes and heart disease. They are high in soluble fibre, which acts to lower "bad" cholesterol levels, and, being high in fibre and low in fat, they fill you up without filling you out.

The word dhal is the Hindi generic word for all legumes and pulses. Regarded as meat substitutes, they feature widely in Indian cooking because they are a good source of protein for this largely vegetarian nation.

Omit the coconut cream from the recipe, if you like.

Mixed dhal

PREPARATION TIME 15 MINUTES **COOKING TIME** 1 HOUR 10 MINUTES **SERVES** 4

2 tablespoons ghee

1 medium brown onion (150g), chopped finely

2 cloves garlic, crushed

4cm piece fresh ginger (20g), grated

1 ½ tablespoons black mustard seeds

1 fresh long green chilli, chopped finely

1 tablespoon ground cumin

1 tablespoon ground coriander

2 teaspoons ground turmeric

½ cup (100g) brown lentils

⅓ cup (65g) red lentils

⅓ cup (85g) yellow split peas

⅓ cup (85g) green split peas

400g can crushed tomatoes

2 cups (500ml) vegetable stock

1 ½ cups (375ml) water

140ml can coconut cream

1 Heat ghee in large saucepan; cook onion, garlic and ginger, stirring, until onion softens. Add seeds, chilli and spices; cook, stirring, until fragrant.

2 Add lentils and peas to pan. Stir in undrained tomatoes, stock and the water; simmer, covered, stirring occasionally, about 1 hour or until lentils are tender.

3 Just before serving, add coconut cream; stir over low heat until curry is heated through.

☐ **PER SERVING** 18.4g total fat (12.5g saturated fat); 1898kJ (454 cal); 42.6g carbohydrate; 23.3g protein; 12.7g fibre

Fry the vegetables in peanut or canola oil if you want this to be a totally dairy-free vegetarian dish.

Chickpeas are a major source of protein in cultures which are either predominately vegetarian or where meat is considered a luxury item. Also known as garbanzos, channa or hummus, the canned variety should be well rinsed under cold water to get rid of all the can liquid.

Chickpeas in spicy tomato sauce

PREPARATION TIME 15 MINUTES **COOKING TIME** 45 MINUTES **SERVES** 6

2 tablespoons ghee

2 teaspoons cumin seeds

2 medium brown onions (300g), chopped finely

2 cloves garlic, crushed

4cm piece fresh ginger (20g), grated

1 tablespoon ground coriander

1 teaspoon ground turmeric

1 teaspoon cayenne pepper

2 tablespoons tomato paste

2 x 400g cans diced tomatoes

2 cups (500ml) water

2 x 420g cans chickpeas, rinsed, drained

1 large kumara (500g), cut into 1.5cm pieces

300g spinach, trimmed, chopped coarsely

1 Heat ghee in large saucepan; cook seeds, stirring, until fragrant. Add onion, garlic and ginger; cook, stirring, until onion softens. Add spices; cook, stirring, until fragrant. Add paste; cook, stirring, 2 minutes.

2 Add undrained tomatoes, the water, chickpeas and kumara; simmer, covered, stirring occasionally, about 30 minutes or until kumara is tender and mixture thickens slightly.

3 Just before serving, stir in spinach.

☐ **PER SERVING** 8.1g total fat (4.1g saturated fat); 1037kJ (248 cal); 29.1g carbohydrate; 9.9g protein; 9.4g fibre

Osso buco with semi-dried tomatoes and olives

PREPARATION TIME 30 MINUTES **COOKING TIME** 2 HOURS 45 MINUTES **SERVES** 6

12 pieces veal osso buco (3.6kg)

¼ cup (35g) plain flour

¼ cup (60ml) olive oil

40g butter

1 medium brown onion (150g), chopped coarsely

2 cloves garlic, chopped finely

3 trimmed celery stalks (300g), chopped coarsely

2 large carrots (360g), chopped coarsely

4 medium tomatoes (600g), chopped coarsely

2 tablespoons tomato paste

1 cup (250ml) dry white wine

1 cup (250ml) beef stock

400g can crushed tomatoes

4 sprigs fresh lemon thyme

½ cup (75g) drained semi-dried tomatoes

¼ cup (60ml) lemon juice

1 tablespoon finely grated lemon rind

½ cup (75g) seeded black olives

GREMOLATA

1 tablespoon coarsely grated lemon rind

⅓ cup finely chopped fresh flat-leaf parsley

2 cloves garlic, chopped finely

1 Coat veal in flour; shake off excess. Heat oil in large deep saucepan; cook veal, in batches, until browned all over.

2 Melt butter in same pan; cook onion, garlic, celery and carrot, stirring, until vegetables just soften. Stir in fresh tomato, paste, wine, stock, undrained tomatoes and thyme. Return veal to pan, fitting pieces upright and tightly together in single layer; bring to a boil. Reduce heat, simmer, covered, 1¾ hours. Stir in semi-dried tomatoes; simmer, uncovered, about 30 minutes or until veal is tender.

3 Combine ingredients for gremolata in small bowl.

4 Remove veal from pan; cover to keep warm. Bring sauce to a boil; boil, uncovered, about 10 minutes or until sauce thickens slightly. Stir in juice, rind and olives.

5 Divide veal among serving plates; top with sauce, sprinkle with gremolata. Serve with soft polenta, if desired.

☐ **PER SERVING** 21.4g total fat (6.6g saturated fat); 2855kJ (683 cal); 22.3g carbohydrate; 89g protein; 8.1g fibre

Persian lamb and rhubarb stew

PREPARATION TIME 20 MINUTES **COOKING TIME** 2 HOURS 10 MINUTES **SERVES** 4

40g butter

1kg diced lamb

1 medium brown onion (150g), sliced thinly

¼ teaspoon saffron threads

½ teaspoon ground cinnamon

¼ teaspoon ground turmeric

1 cup (250ml) water

2 cups (500ml) chicken stock

2 tablespoons tomato paste

2¾ cups (300g) coarsely chopped rhubarb

¼ cup finely chopped fresh mint

1 Melt half of the butter in large deep saucepan; cook lamb, in batches, until browned all over.

2 Melt remaining butter in same pan; cook onion, stirring, until soft. Add spices; cook, stirring, until fragrant. Add the water, stock and paste; bring to a boil. Return lamb to pan, reduce heat; simmer, covered, 1 hour 20 minutes, stirring occasionally.

3 Uncover; simmer about 20 minutes or until lamb is tender. Add rhubarb; simmer, uncovered, about 10 minutes or until rhubarb has softened.

4 Stir mint into stew off the heat; serve stew over couscous, if desired.

☐ **PER SERVING** 17.8g total fat (9.7g saturated fat); 1705kJ (408 cal); 5g carbohydrate; 55.2g protein; 3g fibre

---

Braised oxtail in peanut sauce

PREPARATION TIME 30 MINUTES **COOKING TIME** 3 HOURS 20 MINUTES **SERVES** 4

2kg oxtails, cut into 5cm pieces

2 tablespoons plain flour

2 tablespoons vegetable oil

1 large brown onion (200g), chopped coarsely

6 cloves garlic, crushed

1 tablespoon ground coriander

1 tablespoon ground cumin

2 star anise

2 fresh long red chillies, halved lengthways

1 litre (4 cups) beef stock

1 litre (4 cups) water

⅔ cup (200g) red curry paste

⅔ cup (90g) roasted unsalted peanuts, chopped coarsely

300g green beans, trimmed, chopped coarsely

2 green onions, sliced thinly

Here, a traditional Anglo slow-cooked stew gets reinterpreted in the Thai kitchen, proving that once again, East can meet West, especially when it comes to meal-time. Serve the curry with yellow coconut rice (page 176).

1 Coat oxtail in flour; shake off excess. Heat half of the oil in large saucepan; cook oxtail, in batches, until browned.

2 Heat remaining oil in same pan; cook onion and garlic, stirring, until onion softens. Add spices and chilli, cook, stirring, until fragrant. Return oxtail to pan with stock and the water; simmer, covered, 2 hours.

3 Strain beef over large bowl; reserve braising liquid, discard solids. Skim fat from braising liquid.

4 Cook curry paste in same cleaned pan, stirring, until fragrant. Add 4 cups of the reserved braising liquid; bring to a boil. Add oxtail; simmer, uncovered, about 45 minutes or until oxtail is tender.

5 Add nuts and beans; cook, uncovered, about 5 minutes or until beans are tender.

6 Serve curry sprinkled with green onion.

☐ **PER SERVING** 111.7g total fat (36.8g saturated fat); 5626kJ (1346 cal); 15.6g carbohydrate; 70g protein; 6.7g fibre

Baked pumpkin and spinach risotto

PREPARATION TIME 15 MINUTES **COOKING TIME** 40 MINUTES **SERVES** 4

500g butternut pumpkin, chopped coarsely

2 tablespoons olive oil

1½ cups (375ml) chicken stock

1.25 litres (5 cups) water

1 large brown onion (200g), chopped coarsely

2 cloves garlic, crushed

2 cups (400g) arborio rice

½ cup (125ml) dry white wine

500g spinach, trimmed, chopped coarsely

½ cup (80g) pine nuts, toasted

½ cup (40g) coarsely grated parmesan cheese

½ cup (125ml) cream

1 Preheat oven to 220°C/200°C fan-forced.

2 Combine pumpkin with half of the oil in baking dish. Bake, uncovered, 20 minutes or until tender.

3 Meanwhile, combine stock and the water in large saucepan; bring to a boil. Reduce heat; simmer.

4 Heat remaining oil in large saucepan; cook onion and garlic, stirring, until onion is soft. Add rice; stir to coat in mixture. Add wine; stir until almost evaporated.

5 Stir in 1 cup of the hot stock mixture; cook, stirring, over low heat until liquid is absorbed. Continue adding stock mixture, in 1-cup batches, stirring, until liquid is absorbed after each addition. Total cooking time should be about 35 minutes or until rice is just tender.

6 Add spinach, pine nuts, cheese and cream; cook, stirring, until spinach wilts. Gently stir in baked pumpkin.

▭ **PER SERVING** 41.6g total fat (13.8g saturated fat); 3490kJ (835 cal); 91.5g carbohydrate; 19.3g protein; 5.7g fibre

Prawn and asparagus risotto

PREPARATION TIME 25 MINUTES **COOKING TIME** 45 MINUTES **SERVES** 4

500g uncooked medium king prawns

3 cups (750ml) chicken stock

3 cups (750ml) water

10g butter

1 tablespoon olive oil

1 small brown onion (80g), chopped finely

2 cups (400g) arborio rice

½ cup (125ml) dry sherry

10g butter, extra

2 teaspoons olive oil, extra

2 cloves garlic, crushed

500g asparagus, chopped coarsely

⅓ cup (25g) coarsely grated parmesan cheese

⅓ cup coarsely chopped fresh basil

1 Shell and devein prawns; chop prawn meat coarsely.

2 Place stock and the water in large saucepan; bring to a boil. Reduce heat, simmer, covered.

3 Meanwhile, heat butter and oil in large saucepan; cook onion, stirring, until soft. Add rice; stir rice to coat in onion mixture. Add sherry; cook, stirring, until liquid is almost evaporated.

4 Stir in 1 cup simmering stock mixture; cook, stirring, over low heat until liquid is absorbed. Continue adding stock mixture, in 1-cup batches, stirring, until absorbed after each addition. Total cooking time should be about 35 minutes or until rice is tender.

5 Heat extra butter and extra oil in medium frying pan; cook prawn meat and garlic, stirring, until prawn just changes colour.

6 Boil, steam or microwave asparagus until just tender; drain. Add asparagus, prawn mixture and cheese to risotto; cook, stirring, until cheese melts. Stir in basil.

PER SERVING 14.7g total fat (5.5g saturated fat); 2516kJ (602 cal); 82.8g carbohydrate; 26.3g protein; 2.6g fibre

Chicken, pea, sage and prosciutto risotto

PREPARATION TIME 20 MINUTES **COOKING TIME** 45 MINUTES **SERVES** 4

3 cups (750ml) chicken stock

3 cups (750ml) water

10g butter

2 tablespoons olive oil

1 small brown onion (80g), chopped finely

2 cups (400g) arborio rice

½ cup (125ml) dry white wine

350g chicken breast fillets, chopped coarsely

2 cloves garlic, crushed

1½ cups (180g) frozen peas

6 slices prosciutto (90g)

2 tablespoons finely shredded fresh sage

1 Place stock and the water in large saucepan; bring to a boil. Reduce heat, simmer, covered.

2 Heat butter and half of the oil in large saucepan; cook onion, stirring, until soft. Add rice; stir rice to coat in mixture. Add wine; cook, stirring, until liquid is almost evaporated.

3 Stir in 1 cup simmering stock mixture; cook, stirring, over low heat until liquid is absorbed. Continue adding stock mixture, in 1-cup batches, stirring, until absorbed after each addition. Total cooking time should be about 35 minutes or until rice is tender.

4 Meanwhile, heat remaining oil in medium frying pan; cook chicken, stirring, until cooked through. Add garlic; stir until fragrant. Stir chicken mixture and peas into risotto.

5 Cook prosciutto in same frying pan until crisp; drain on absorbent paper then break into coarse pieces. Stir sage and half of the prosciutto into risotto; sprinkle remaining prosciutto over individual risotto servings.

PER SERVING 18.8g total fat (5.1g saturated fat); 2784kJ (666 cal); 84.1g carbohydrate; 24.5g protein; 3.9g fibre

Risottos have become the heroes of many weeknight menus essentially because they can be as versatile as they are simple to prepare. They happily accept leftovers or frozen vegetables as ingredients, and can be chopped and changed to accommodate fussy diners. Pick up a barbecued chicken on your way home and use the coarsely chopped meat here instead of raw chicken breasts.

Turkish pilaf with chicken, onion and almonds

PREPARATION TIME 15 MINUTES **COOKING TIME** 40 MINUTES **SERVES** 4

60g butter

500g chicken strips

1 large brown onion (200g), sliced thinly

4 cloves garlic, crushed

⅓ cup (45g) slivered almonds

1 teaspoon ground allspice

½ teaspoon ground cinnamon

3 drained anchovies, chopped coarsely

2 tablespoons dried currants

1½ cups (300g) basmati rice

2 cups (500ml) chicken stock

1 cup (250ml) water

1 fresh long red chilli, chopped finely

1 Melt a third of the butter in large saucepan; cook chicken, in batches, until just cooked through.

2 Melt remaining butter in same pan; cook onion, garlic and nuts, stirring, until onion softens. Add spices, anchovies and currants; cook, stirring, 2 minutes. Add rice; cook, stirring, 2 minutes. Add stock and the water; bring to a boil. Reduce heat, simmer, covered tightly, 20 minutes or until rice is just tender.

3 Stir chicken into pilaf mixture; cook, covered, until heated through. Serve pilaf sprinkled with chilli, and parsley, if desired.

     PER SERVING 25.1g total fat (10.4g saturated fat); 2696kJ (645 cal); 67g carbohydrate; 36.5g protein; 3.3g fibre

Risotto milanese

PREPARATION TIME 10 MINUTES **COOKING TIME** 40 MINUTES **SERVES** 4

1½ cups (375ml) water

2 cups (500ml) chicken stock

½ cup (125ml) dry white wine

¼ teaspoon saffron threads

20g butter

1 large brown onion (200g), chopped finely

2 cups (400g) arborio rice

¼ cup (20g) finely grated parmesan cheese

1 Place the water, stock, wine and saffron in medium saucepan; bring to a boil. Reduce heat, simmer, covered.

2 Heat butter in large saucepan; cook onion, stirring, until softened. Add rice; stir to coat rice in onion mixture. Stir in ½ cup of the simmering stock mixture; cook, stirring, over low heat, until liquid is absorbed.

3 Continue adding stock mixture, in ½-cup batches, stirring until absorbed after each addition. Total cooking time should be about 35 minutes or until rice is just tender. Gently stir cheese into risotto.

     PER SERVING 6.8g total fat (4.1g saturated fat); 1931kJ (462 cal); 82.7g carbohydrate; 10.7g protein; 1.5g fibre

TURKISH PILAF WITH CHICKEN, ONION AND ALMONDS

Pots & pans

Available in all sorts of shapes, sizes and prices, investing in a good set of pots and pans is a decision you won't regret.

MILK SAUCEPAN WITH LIP
A treasure for comforting and sustaining drinks at any time of day, and just right, too, for making porridge for one. Choose a non-stick finish to make cleaning easy.

DEEP PAN/BASKET FOR FRYING
A metal-mesh frying basket with a long handle, or a perforated metal pan of the same shape, makes deep-frying faster and less messy by letting you add and then remove an entire batch of food at the same time.

PASTA POT WITH STRAINER INSERT
It is like a pot within a pot, with the inner one perforated so that, as you lift it out full of cooked pasta, it drains the water and the pasta is ready to go to the table.

FRYING PAN
A frying pan is wide and shallow for cooking quickly on high heat and allowing food to be tossed and turned easily. It must be heavy and made of material that conducts heat fast and evenly to the entire cooking surface.

GRILL PAN
The grill pan, also called a griddle pan, is ridged to char-grill food, allowing excess fat to run off and giving the surface of the food a stylish black-striped finish. Small, tender cuts of meat, fish steaks, prawns, breads and many fruits and vegetables can be char-grilled.

OMELETTE PAN
An omelette pan is designed specifically to turn out perfect French omelettes, but can also be used for gently frying other things. Ideally, it should be not be washed but cleaned only by wiping out with absorbent paper so that it gradually develops a slick patina.

STOCKPOT

The ideal stockpot is tall and narrow so that the simmering liquid percolates through layers of ingredients to gain the fullest possible flavour. A large, deep saucepan can be used instead.

BOILER

A boiler is large, with two handles for lifting when full. If you want one only for cooking large items in water, a light one will do. If you want it for sauces and preserves too, it should be heavy-based.

WIDE, DEEP PAN

The right pan for frying such items as crumbed fish, chicken or cutlets is wide enough to allow fast evaporation and deep enough to hold the food and its cooking oil without excess spattering.

PAELLA PAN

This a special pan for making the famous Spanish rice dish for which it is named. Very wide and shallow, with flaring sides and two handles, it displays to perfection the decoratively arranged ingredients that are part of the paella tradition.

DOUBLE SAUCEPAN

Consisting of an upper saucepan set over simmering water in a lower one, a double saucepan allows delicate sauces and custards to heat gently so that they will not curdle. An earthenware or glass bowl set over a saucepan can be used instead.

DEEP PAN WITH LID

With the addition of a lid for braises such as lamb shanks, where the food is first browned and then cooked gently under cover. It is also good for steaming rice.

Fettuccine alfredo

PREPARATION TIME 10 MINUTES **COOKING TIME** 10 MINUTES **SERVES** 4

375g fettuccine
80g butter
300ml cream
½ cup (40g) finely grated parmesan cheese

1 Cook pasta in large saucepan of boiling water, uncovered, until just tender.
Drain pasta; return to pan.
2 Meanwhile, melt butter in small saucepan. Add cream; bring to a boil. Reduce heat,
simmer, uncovered, about 5 minutes or until sauce reduces by half.
3 Add cheese; stir over low heat about 2 minutes or until cheese melts.
4 Add sauce to hot pasta; toss gently to combine.

☐ **PER SERVING** 53.1g total fat (34.5g saturated fat); 3382kJ (809 cal); 66.2g carbohydrate; 15.9g protein;
3.1g fibre

Alfredo is named after Roman restaurateur Alfredo di Lelio who is credited with creating this dish in the 1920s. Do not reduce the cream mixture too rapidly or by too much as this sauce can easily turn into a scorched failure. For a lower-fat version, use light cream.

Risoni with spinach and semi-dried tomatoes

PREPARATION TIME 5 MINUTES **COOKING TIME** 25 MINUTES **SERVES** 4

30g butter
2 medium brown onions (300g), chopped finely
3 cloves garlic, crushed
500g risoni pasta
1 litre (4 cups) chicken stock
½ cup (125ml) dry white wine
150g semi-dried tomatoes, halved
100g baby spinach leaves
⅓ cup (25g) finely grated parmesan cheese

1 Melt butter in large saucepan; cook onion and garlic, stirring, until onion softens.
Add risoni; stir to coat in butter mixture.
2 Stir in stock and wine; bring to a boil. Reduce heat, simmer over medium heat, stirring,
until liquid is absorbed and risoni is just tender.
3 Gently stir in tomato, spinach and cheese.

☐ **PER SERVING** 12.4g total fat (6.3g saturated fat); 2830kJ (677 cal); 104.7g carbohydrate; 24.8g protein;
11.2g fibre

Risoni is a very small, rice-shaped pasta similar to orzo that Italian cooks often add to soups, bake in a casserole or, as here, cook similarly to a risotto in stock with a vegetable or two and grated parmesan cheese.

ALFREDO SAUCE (for Fettuccine alfredo)

Baby octopus and eggplant in tomato and caper sauce

PREPARATION TIME 10 MINUTES **COOKING TIME** 25 MINUTES **SERVES** 4

1 tablespoon olive oil

1.2kg whole cleaned
baby octopus

1 clove garlic, sliced thinly

3 shallots (75g), sliced thinly

4 baby eggplants (240g),
sliced thinly

1 medium red capsicum (200g),
sliced thinly

½ cup (125ml) dry red wine

700g bottled tomato
pasta sauce

⅓ cup (80ml) water

¼ cup (50g) baby capers,
rinsed, drained

2 tablespoons coarsely chopped
fresh oregano

1 Heat half of the oil in large saucepan; cook octopus, in batches, until just changed in colour and tender. Cover to keep warm.

2 Heat remaining oil in same pan; cook garlic and shallots, stirring, until shallots soften. Add eggplant and capsicum; cook, stirring, 5 minutes or until vegetables are just tender.

3 Return octopus to pan with wine, sauce and the water; bring to a boil. Reduce heat, simmer, covered, 10 minutes or until sauce thickens slightly. Stir in capers and oregano.

4 If desired, serve topped with extra oregano leaves and steamed rice.

▭ **PER SERVING** 7.2g total fat (0.6g saturated fat); 1586kJ (378 cal); 15.8g carbohydrate; 53.7g protein; 5.8g fibre

Quince and chicken tagine

PREPARATION TIME 25 MINUTES **COOKING TIME** 1 HOUR 50 MINUTES **SERVES** 4

2 medium quinces (700g),
peeled, cored, cut into wedges

40g butter

⅓ cup (115g) honey

3 cups (750ml) water

2 teaspoons orange flower water

2 teaspoons olive oil

4 drumsticks (600g)

4 chicken thigh cutlets (800g),
skin removed

1 large brown onion (200g),
chopped coarsely

3 cloves garlic, crushed

1 teaspoon ground cumin

1 teaspoon ground ginger

pinch saffron threads

2 cups (500ml) chicken stock

2 large zucchini (300g),
chopped coarsely

¼ cup coarsely chopped
fresh coriander

CORIANDER COUSCOUS

1½ cups (300g) couscous

1½ cups (375ml) boiling water

50g baby spinach leaves,
chopped finely

2 tablespoons finely chopped
fresh coriander

2 green onions, sliced thinly

1 Place quince, butter, honey, the water and orange flower water in medium saucepan; bring to a boil. Reduce heat, simmer, covered, 1 hour, stirring occasionally. Uncover, cook, stirring occasionally, about 45 minutes or until quinces are red in colour.

2 Meanwhile, heat oil in large saucepan; cook chicken, in batches, until browned.

3 Cook onion, garlic and spices in same pan, stirring, until onion softens. Add stock and chicken; bring to a boil. Reduce heat, simmer, covered, 20 minutes. Uncover; simmer, about 20 minutes or until chicken is cooked though. Add zucchini; cook, uncovered, about 10 minutes or until zucchini is tender. Stir in quince and ½ cup of the quince syrup.

4 Meanwhile, make coriander couscous.

5 Divide tagine and couscous among serving plates; sprinkle with coriander.

CORIANDER COUSCOUS Combine couscous with the water in large heatproof bowl; cover, stand about 5 minutes or until water is absorbed, fluffing with fork occasionally. Stir in spinach, coriander and onion.

▭ **PER SERVING** 32.6g total fat (12.3g saturated fat); 3913kJ (936 cal); 99g carbohydrate; 56.7g protein; 12.5g fibre

Indian rice pilaf with spiced beef

PREPARATION TIME 10 MINUTES **COOKING TIME** 30 MINUTES **SERVES** 4

2 tablespoons peanut oil

1 small brown onion (80g), sliced thinly

1 clove garlic, crushed

1 teaspoon cumin seeds

1 teaspoon caraway seeds

⅛ teaspoon ground turmeric

1 cup (200g) basmati rice

2 cups (500ml) chicken stock

2 tablespoons dried currants

500g beef mince

2 teaspoons curry powder

⅓ cup (80ml) sweet chilli sauce

¼ cup (60ml) water

4 green onions, sliced thinly

⅔ cup (80g) frozen peas

¼ cup firmly packed fresh coriander leaves

1 Heat half of the oil in large saucepan; cook brown onion, garlic, seeds and turmeric, stirring, until onion softens.

2 Add rice, stir over heat until rice is coated with oil. Stir in stock, bring to a boil. Reduce heat to very low; cook, covered, 12 minutes. Remove from heat; stand, covered, 5 minutes or until rice is tender. Stir in currants.

3 Meanwhile, heat remaining oil in medium saucepan; cook beef, stirring, until browned.

4 Add curry powder; cook until fragrant. Stir in sauce, the water, green onion and peas; cook, stirring, until peas are soft.

5 Serve pilaf topped with spiced mince and coriander.

▭ **PER SERVING** 19.1g total fat (9.8g saturated fat); 2926kJ (700 cal); 93.2g carbohydrate; 35.1g protein; 4.1g fibre

Pulao, pilaf, pilav, pellao all are the same cooked grain (usually rice) dish having different spellings in their respective countries of origin. Most contain spices, some have herbs added, yet others can have meat, vegetables, fruits or nuts and stock tossed into the mix. Their common denominator is that they are all delicious. The secret of a perfect pilaf is to rinse the grain thoroughly to remove excess starch, then to soak it in water or stock briefly. Soaking before cooking softens the grain, giving the cooked pilaf a fluffy and light quality.

Yellow coconut rice

PREPARATION TIME 5 MINUTES (PLUS STANDING TIME) **COOKING TIME** 15 MINUTES **SERVES** 4

In the southern region of Thailand, plentiful coconut milk and fresh turmeric are frequently combined in various dishes. Neither hot like a curry nor wet as a soup, this rich, savoury rice dish makes a good accompaniment to a spicy meal. The flavour of coconut milk is important in this dish, and if you can get fresh turmeric, grate enough to fill a level teaspoon and use it instead of ½ teaspoon of the dried version.

1¾ cups (350g) white long-grain rice

1¼ cups (310ml) water

400ml can coconut cream

½ teaspoon salt

1 teaspoon sugar

½ teaspoon ground turmeric

pinch saffron threads

1 Soak rice in large bowl of cold water for 30 minutes. Pour rice into strainer; rinse under cold water until water runs clear. Drain.

2 Place rice and remaining ingredients in large heavy-based saucepan; cover, bring to a boil, stirring occasionally. Reduce heat, simmer, covered, about 15 minutes or until rice is tender. Remove from heat; stand, covered, 5 minutes.

☐ **PER SERVING** 21.1g total fat (18.2g saturated fat); 2186kJ (523 cal); 73.9g carbohydrate; 7.7g protein; 2.4g fibre

Rogan josh

PREPARATION TIME 25 MINUTES **COOKING TIME** 1 HOUR 50 MINUTES **SERVES** 6

There are many curry pastes available at Asian grocers and supermarkets, some imported from India and others made locally. If you don't want to make your own, this will do the job more than adequately. From Kashmir in India, this medium-hot, deep-red paste is made from fresh chillies or paprika, tomato and aromatic spices.

1 tablespoon vegetable oil

1kg lamb shoulder, diced into 3cm pieces

3 medium brown onions (450g), sliced thinly

4cm piece fresh ginger (20g), grated

2 cloves garlic, crushed

⅔ cup (200g) rogan josh paste

1½ cups (375ml) water

425g can diced tomatoes

1 cinnamon stick

5 cardamom pods, bruised

2 tablespoons coarsely chopped fresh coriander

1 Heat half of the oil in large saucepan; cook lamb, in batches, until browned.

2 Heat remaining oil in same pan; cook onion, stirring, until soft. Add ginger, garlic and paste; cook, stirring, until fragrant.

3 Return lamb to pan; stir to combine with paste mixture. Add the water, undrained tomatoes, cinnamon and cardamom; simmer, covered, about 1½ hours or until lamb is tender. Serve curry sprinkled with coriander.

☐ **PER SERVING** 28.6g total fat (8.3g saturated fat), 1835kJ (439 cal); 7.8g carbohydrate; 35.7g protein; 5.5g fibre

1 YELLOW COCONUT RICE **2** ROGAN JOSH
3 SRI LANKAN FRIED PORK CURRY [P 178] **4** DATE AND TAMARIND CHUTNEY [P 178]

3   4

Sri lankan fried pork curry

PREPARATION TIME 20 MINUTES **COOKING TIME** 1 HOUR 20 MINUTES **SERVES** 4

2 tablespoons vegetable oil

20 fresh curry leaves

½ teaspoon fenugreek seeds

1 large brown onion (200g), chopped finely

4 cloves garlic, crushed

3cm piece fresh ginger (15g), grated

1 tablespoon curry powder

2 teaspoons

1kg pork be

1 tablespo

2 tables conce

1 cir

4 c

1

1 Heat half the oil in large saucepan; cook leaves and s   nd mixture is fragrant. Add onion, garlic and ginger; cook, stirring

2 Add curry powder and cayenne to pan, then pork; sti   Add vinegar, tamarind, cinnamon, cardamom and the water; simmer, cove

3 Heat remaining oil in large frying pan. Transfer pork to pan; co   ring, until pork is browned and crisp.

4 Meanwhile, add coconut milk to curry sauce; simmer, stirring, about 5 minutes or until curry thickens slightly. Return pork to curry; stir to combine.

☐ **PER SERVING** 78.2g total fat (35.7g saturated fat); 3766kJ (901 cal); 8g carbohydrate; 42.1g protein; 3.6g fibre

Date and tamarind chutney

PREPARATION TIME 10 MINUTES **COOKING TIME** 45 MINUTES **MAKES** 2½ CUPS

2 cinnamon sticks

5 cardamom pods, bruised

2 teaspoons cloves

3½ cups (500g) seeded dried dates

1½ cups (375ml) white vinegar

½ cup (110g) firmly packed brown sugar

2 teaspoons coarse cooking salt

¼ cup (60ml) vegetable oil

2 tablespoons tamarind concentrate

2 teaspoons chilli powder

1 Place cinnamon, cardamom and cloves in centre of 20cm muslin square; tie tightly with kitchen string.

2 Place muslin bag in large saucepan with remaining ingredients; bring to a boil, stirring constantly, then reduce heat.

3 Simmer, partially covered, stirring occasionally, about 40 minutes or until dates are soft. Remove and discard spice bag before using.

☐ **PER TABLESPOON** 1.9g total fat (0.2g saturated fat); 343kJ (82 cal); 15g carbohydrate; 0.4g protein; 1.7g fibre

Spiced vegetable biryani

PREPARATION TIME 15 MINUTES **COOKING TIME** 30 MINUTES **SERVES** 4

1 tablespoon vegetable oil

1 clove garlic, crushed

1 medium brown onion (150g), sliced thinly

2 teaspoons garam masala

400g can diced tomatoes

1 medium potato (200g), diced into 1cm pieces

2 medium carrots (240g), chopped coarsely

½ cup (125ml) water

2 medium zucchini (240g), chopped coarsely

1 medium red capsicum (200g), sliced thinly

1 medium brown onion (150g), chopped finely

1½ cups (300g) basmati rice

8 cardamom pods, bruised

½ teaspoon chilli powder

¼ teaspoon ground turmeric

1½ cups (375ml) water, extra

¼ cup (40g) sultanas

1 Heat half of the oil in large saucepan; cook garlic and sliced onion, stirring, until onion softens. Add garam masala; cook, stirring, 1 minute. Stir in undrained tomatoes, potato, carrot and the water; bring to a boil. Reduce heat, simmer, covered, 10 minutes. Add zucchini and capsicum; simmer, covered, about 10 minutes or until vegetables are tender.

2 Meanwhile, heat remaining oil in medium saucepan; cook chopped onion, stirring, until soft. Add rice and spices; cook, stirring, until fragrant. Stir in the extra water and sultanas; bring to a boil. Reduce heat, simmer, covered, about 15 minutes or until rice is just tender and water is absorbed.

3 Place half of the rice mixture in 2 litre (8 cup) serving dish; top with vegetable mixture then remaining rice mixture.

PER SERVING 5.7g total fat (0.7g saturated fat); 1802kJ (431 cal); 84.1g carbohydrate; 10g protein; 7.1g fibre

Cardamom pods act like packaging for the tiny dark-brown seeds inside, keeping them fresh until required. You "bruise" a cardamom pod with the side of a heavy knife, crushing the husk and exposing the seeds. There is no need to separate the seeds and pod before using, nor do you necessarily have to remove the empty pods before serving the biryani.

Rigatoni with zucchini, lemon and mint

PREPARATION TIME 10 MINUTES **COOKING TIME** 10 MINUTES **SERVES** 4

500g rigatoni pasta

¼ cup (60ml) olive oil

2 cloves garlic, crushed

3 medium zucchini (360g), grated coarsely

¾ cup (180g) ricotta cheese

1 cup coarsely chopped fresh mint

½ cup (70g) roasted slivered almonds

2 tablespoons lemon juice

1 Cook pasta in large saucepan of boiling water until just tender; drain.

2 Meanwhile, heat oil in medium saucepan; cook garlic and zucchini, stirring, 2 minutes. Add cheese; cook, stirring, until just heated through.

3 Combine zucchini mixture and pasta in serving bowl with remaining ingredients.

PER SERVING 30.3g total fat (6g saturated fat); 3110kJ (744 cal); 88.9g carbohydrate; 23.9g protein; 8.3g fibre

A large, chunky, tubular pasta with grooves on the exterior, rigatoni works well when tossed with a thick sauce such as this one. You can replace it with tortiglioni or ziti, if you like, but any less substantial pasta will get lost or crushed by the nut and vegetable melange.

Spaghetti napoletana

PREPARATION TIME 15 MINUTES **COOKING TIME** 1 HOUR **SERVES** 4

¼ cup (60ml) olive oil

1 medium brown onion (150g), chopped finely

2 cloves garlic, crushed

¼ cup loosely packed fresh basil leaves

1 teaspoon sea salt

1 tablespoon tomato paste

1kg ripe tomatoes, chopped coarsely

375g spaghetti

1 Heat half of the oil in large saucepan; cook onion, garlic, basil and salt, stirring, until onion softens. Add paste; cook, stirring, 1 minute.

2 Add tomato; bring to a boil. Reduce heat, simmer, uncovered, stirring occasionally, 45 minutes or until sauce thickens. Stir in remaining oil; simmer, uncovered, 5 minutes.

3 Meanwhile, cook pasta in large saucepan of boiling water, uncovered, until just tender; drain and return pasta to pan.

4 Add hot sauce to hot pasta; toss gently to combine.

▭ **PER SERVING** 18.6g total fat (2.6g saturated fat); 903kJ (216 cal); 7.5g carbohydrate; 3.2g protein; 4g fibre

Bolognese sauce

PREPARATION TIME 25 MINUTES **COOKING TIME** 1 HOUR 45 MINUTES **MAKES** 8 CUPS

2 teaspoons olive oil

200g pancetta, chopped finely

1 medium brown onion (150g), chopped finely

1 small carrot (70g), chopped finely

2 trimmed celery stalks (200g), chopped finely

600g beef mince

½ cup (125ml) dry red wine

1 cup (250ml) beef stock

½ cup (140g) tomato paste

2 x 400g cans crushed tomatoes

½ cup coarsely chopped fresh flat-leaf parsley

2 tablespoons coarsely chopped fresh oregano

1 Heat oil in large heavy-based saucepan; cook pancetta, stirring, until crisp. Add onion, carrot and celery; cook, stirring, until vegetables soften. Add beef; cook, stirring occasionally, until beef just changes colour.

2 Add wine; bring to a boil. Reduce heat, simmer 5 minutes. Add stock, paste and undrained tomatoes; bring to a boil. Reduce heat, simmer, covered, 1 hour. Uncover; simmer further 30 minutes or until bolognese thickens. Stir in herbs off the heat.

▭ **PER SERVING (1 CUP)** 10.1g total fat (3.7g saturated fat); 941kJ (225 cal); 7g carbohydrate; 22.3g protein; 3.1g fibre

NAPOLETANA SAUCE (for Spaghetti napoletana)

This is one of the simplest but most delicious of all Italian classic pasta dishes: try it once and you'll be hooked. And best of all, it can be made on a weeknight in less time than it takes your just-opened bottle of red to breathe.

Chilli and garlic spaghettini with breadcrumbs

PREPARATION TIME 10 MINUTES **COOKING TIME** 10 MINUTES **SERVES** 4

375g spaghettini

⅓ cup (80ml) olive oil

50g butter

4 cloves garlic, crushed

4 fresh small red thai chillies, chopped finely

2 cups (140g) stale breadcrumbs

½ cup coarsely chopped fresh flat-leaf parsley

2 teaspoons finely grated lemon rind

1 Cook pasta in large saucepan of boiling water, uncovered, until just tender.

2 Meanwhile, heat half of the oil in large frying pan with butter. After butter melts, add garlic, chilli and breadcrumbs; cook, stirring, until breadcrumbs are browned lightly.

3 Combine drained hot pasta and breadcrumb mixture in large bowl with parsley, rind and remaining oil.

▭ **PER SERVING** 30.9g total fat (9.8g saturated fat); 2959kJ (708 cal); 88.4g carbohydrate; 15.9g protein; 5.6g fibre

Anchovies are one of the most contentious foodstuffs there is: people either love them or hate them, and never the twain shall meet! But there are many popular dishes that wouldn't exist if it were not for these salty, strong-tasting little fish. Think of your classic caesar salad, a pizza with the lot, a bagna cauda – even worcestershire sauce: where would any of these rank without the help of their hit of anchovy?

Penne puttanesca

PREPARATION TIME 10 MINUTES **COOKING TIME** 15 MINUTES **SERVES** 4

500g penne pasta

⅓ cup (80ml) olive oil

3 cloves garlic, crushed

1 teaspoon chilli flakes

5 medium tomatoes (750g), chopped coarsely

200g seeded black olives

8 anchovy fillets, drained, chopped coarsely

⅓ cup (65g) capers, rinsed, drained

⅓ cup coarsely chopped fresh flat-leaf parsley

2 tablespoons finely shredded fresh basil

1 Cook pasta in large saucepan of boiling water, uncovered, until just tender.

2 Meanwhile, heat oil in large frying pan; cook garlic, stirring, until fragrant. Add chilli and tomato; cook, stirring, 5 minutes. Add remaining ingredients; cook, stirring occasionally, about 5 minutes or until sauce thickens slightly.

3 Add drained pasta to sauce; toss gently to combine.

▭ **PER SERVING** 21.1g total fat (3.1g saturated fat); 2884kJ (690 cal); 101.6g carbohydrate; 18.6g protein; 7.9g fibre

Vongole and chorizo linguine

PREPARATION TIME 15 MINUTES (PLUS STANDING TIME) **COOKING TIME** 15 MINUTES **SERVES** 6

750g vongole

375g linguine pasta

1 chorizo sausage (170g), sliced thinly

2 cloves garlic, crushed

2 fresh long red chillies, sliced thinly

250g cherry tomatoes, halved

¾ cup loosely packed small fresh basil leaves

¼ cup (60ml) olive oil

1 Rinse vongole; soak in bowl of cold water 1 hour. Drain.

2 Cook pasta in large saucepan of boiling water, uncovered, until just tender; drain.

3 Cook chorizo in same saucepan until crisp. Remove from pan. Add vongole, garlic, chilli and tomatoes to same heated pan, cook, covered, about 3 minutes or until vongole open.

4 Add chorizo and pasta with basil and oil; toss gently to combine.

☐ **PER SERVING** 21.5g total fat (5g saturated fat); 1868kJ (447 cal); 44.7g carbohydrate; 17.2g protein; 3.1g fibre

Chorizo, a highly seasoned Spanish pork sausage, can be smoked or air-dried, and is as good grilled and eaten on its own as it is used as an ingredient. It is always included in an authentic paella, where it also marries well with clams (another word for vongole).

Pappardelle with chicken and creamy mushroom sauce

PREPARATION TIME 15 MINUTES **COOKING TIME** 12 MINUTES **SERVES** 6

2 tablespoons olive oil

1 clove garlic, crushed

1 small brown onion (80g), chopped finely

250g swiss brown mushrooms, sliced thinly

1 cup (250ml) cream

2 teaspoons finely chopped fresh rosemary

50g butter, chopped

500g pappardelle pasta

1¼ cups (200g) cooked chicken, shredded thinly

½ cup (50g) walnut pieces, roasted

¾ cup (60g) finely grated parmesan cheese

¼ cup chopped fresh flat-leaf parsley

1 Heat oil in medium saucepan; cook garlic and onion, stirring, until onion softens. Add mushrooms; cook, stirring, until tender.

2 Add cream and rosemary to pan; bring to a boil. Reduce heat, simmer, uncovered, about 3 minutes or until sauce thickens. Stir in butter.

3 Meanwhile, cook pasta in large saucepan of boiling water, uncovered, until just tender. Drain pasta; return to pan.

4 Add hot cream sauce to hot pasta with chicken, nuts, half the cheese, and parsley; toss gently to combine. Serve topped with remaining cheese.

☐ **PER SERVING** 43.7g total fat (20.7g saturated fat); 3051kJ (730 cal); 59g carbohydrate; 23.4g protein; 4.7g fibre

Roast the walnuts in an ungreased heavy-based frying pan over medium heat, stirring constantly, until they are golden brown and just fragrant. Remove nuts from the hot pan immediately or they can scorch. You'll find it easier to roast small amounts (say, ½ cup or less) this way rather than in the oven.

Gnocchi with pesto

PREPARATION TIME 30 MINUTES (PLUS REFRIGERATION TIME) **COOKING TIME** 25 MINUTES **SERVES** 8

1kg potatoes, unpeeled

2 eggs, beaten lightly

30g butter, melted

¼ cup (20g) finely grated parmesan cheese

2 cups (300g) plain flour, approximately

PESTO

2 cloves garlic, quartered

¼ cup (40g) toasted pine nuts

¼ cup (20g) finely grated parmesan cheese

1 cup firmly packed fresh basil leaves

⅓ cup (80ml) olive oil

½ cup (125ml) cream

1 Boil or steam whole potatoes until tender; drain. Peel when cool enough to handle. Mash, using ricer, food mill (mouli), or sieve and wooden spoon, into large bowl; stir in eggs, butter, cheese and enough of the flour to make a firm dough.

2 Divide dough into eight equal parts; roll each part on lightly floured surface into 2cm-thick sausage-shape. Cut each sausage-shape into 2cm pieces; roll pieces into balls.

3 Roll each ball along the inside tines of a fork, pressing lightly on top of ball with index finger to form classic gnocchi shape, grooved on one side and dimpled on the other. Place gnocchi, in single layer, on lightly floured tray. Cover; refrigerate 1 hour.

4 Meanwhile, make pesto.

5 Cook gnocchi in large saucepan of boiling water, uncovered, about 3 minutes or until gnocchi float to the surface. Remove from pan with slotted spoon; drain.

6 Return gnocchi to pan with pesto; toss gently to combine.

PESTO Blend or process garlic, pine nuts, cheese and basil until finely chopped. With motor operating, gradually add oil, process until pesto is thick. Just before serving, transfer pesto to small saucepan, add cream; stir over low heat until heated through.

☐ **PER SERVING** 20g total fat (9.5g saturated fat), 1944kJ (465 cal), 44.2g carbohydrate, 11.7g protein, 4.5g fibre

Basil is the traditional herb used in pesto so when in season, make enough of this sauce to see you through winter; it will last for months (without the cream) if you keep it, covered with olive oil in a clean glass jar with a tight-fitting lid, in the refrigerator. Make certain to wipe the inside and lip of the jar with a clean piece of absorbent paper every time you remove any of the pesto. A spoonful stirred into oil and lemon juice makes a marvellous salad dressing.

Chicken and mushroom velouté

PREPARATION TIME 10 MINUTES **COOKING TIME** 15 MINUTES **MAKES** 2½ CUPS

40g butter

2 tablespoons plain flour

2 cups (500ml) hot chicken stock

20g butter, extra

1 small brown onion (80g), chopped finely

150g button mushrooms, sliced thinly

¼ cup (60ml) dry white wine

¼ cup (60ml) cream

1 Melt butter in medium saucepan, add flour; cook, stirring, about 2 minutes or until mixture bubbles and thickens. Stir in hot stock gradually; bring to a boil. Cook, stirring, until velouté boils and thickens. Reduce heat; simmer, uncovered, about 20 minutes or until reduced by half. Strain.

2 Meanwhile, melt extra butter in medium saucepan; cook onion, stirring, until softened. Add mushrooms; cook, stirring, about 5 minutes or until softened.

3 Add wine to pan; cook, stirring, until almost all liquid evaporates. Stir in strained velouté; bring to a boil. Add cream; reduce heat, stir until sauce is heated through.

☐ **PER TABLESPOON** 2.6g total fat (1.7g saturated fat); 130kJ (31 cal); 0.9g carbohydrate; 0.6g protein; 0.2g fibre

Velouté which translates from the French as "texture of velvet", is similar to a béchamel except for the fact that a light stock is added to the roux instead of milk. If you want to serve this sauce with fish, replace the chicken stock with fish, for a vegetarian version, use vegetable stock A velouté is best served as soon as it is made.

If the sauce is lumpy, you may have added the stock too fast or not incorporated it thoroughly between additions. Push the sauce through a fine sieve into medium bowl, discarding any remaining solids.

Sweet chilli dipping sauce

PREPARATION TIME 20 MINUTES (PLUS COOLING TIME) **COOKING TIME** 35 MINUTES **MAKES** 1 CUP

6 fresh long red chillies, chopped finely

1 cup (250ml) white vinegar

1 cup (220g) caster sugar

2 cloves garlic, crushed

1 Place chilli, vinegar and sugar in small saucepan; stir over heat, without boiling, until sugar dissolves. Simmer, uncovered, 15 minutes.

2 Add garlic; simmer, uncovered, about 15 minutes or until mixture reduces by half. Cool.

☐ **PER TABLESPOON** 0.1g total fat (0g saturated fat); 309kJ (74 cal); 18.4g carbohydrate; 0.1g protein; 0.1g fibre

This piquant sauce goes well with spring rolls; salt and pepper squid; grilled chicken tenderloins; thai fish cakes and vietnamese rice paper rolls.

Seafood sauce

PREPARATION TIME 15 MINUTES **COOKING TIME** 30 MINUTES **MAKES** 2 CUPS

1 cup (250ml) dry white wine

30g butter

2 tablespoons plain flour

1 ¼ cups (310ml) hot milk

pinch nutmeg

¾ cup (180ml) cream

250g marinara mix, drained

2 tablespoons finely chopped fresh dill

1 tablespoon lemon juice

1   Bring wine to a boil in medium saucepan. Reduce heat, simmer, uncovered, until reduced by half; transfer to medium heatproof jug.

2   Melt butter in same pan; cook flour, stirring, until mixture bubbles and thickens. Gradually add milk, stirring, until mixture boils and thickens. Stir in nutmeg.

3   Add wine, cream and marinara mix to pan; bring to a boil. Reduce heat, simmer, uncovered, about 5 minutes or until seafood is cooked through. Stir in dill and juice.

▭ **PER TABLESPOON** 5g total fat (3.2g saturated fat); 293kJ (70 cal); 2.1g carbohydrate; 2.7g protein; 0.1g fibre

Instead of using marinara mix, you can use any or a blend of the following seafood: prawns, mussels, calamari and chopped firm white fish fillets. Serve this sauce on fettuccine or other variety of noodle.

A traditional French béchamel is based on a roux, a cooked butter and flour mixture used as a thickening agent for many sauces. Béchamel can be eaten as is, or used as the basis for other sauces.

Tangy barbecue sauce

PREPARATION TIME 5 MINUTES **COOKING TIME** 25 MINUTES **MAKES** 2 CUPS

1 cup (250ml) tomato sauce

½ cup (125ml) cider vinegar

¼ cup (60ml) worcestershire sauce

⅔ cup (150g) firmly packed brown sugar

2 tablespoons american-style mustard

1 fresh small red thai chilli, chopped finely

1 clove garlic, crushed

1 tablespoon lemon juice

1   Combine ingredients in medium saucepan; bring to a boil. Reduce heat, simmer, uncovered, stirring occasionally, 20 minutes.

▭ **PER TABLESPOON** 0.1g total fat (0.0g saturated fat); 163kJ (39 cal); 9.3g carbohydrate; 0.3g protein; 0.3g fibre

Pour this sauce over three or four slabs of American-style pork spareribs in a large shallow dish, cover and marinate the mixture overnight in the refrigerator. Cook the slabs on a heated barbecue plate, brushing them all the while with the barbecue sauce marinade.

THE BOILER

The Boiler

You may or may not need the special utensil called a "boiler". Your largest saucepan or flameproof casserole dish may be able to cope with the jobs a boiler does: cook corned beef, poach a whole chicken or a couple of lobsters, steam or boil a pudding, cook pasta for a crowd, or make as much soup or stock as you want.

However, if you want to get into really large-scale production – any of the above in quantities for a big party, or turning a box of tomatoes into a year's supply of tomato sauce or a surplus of other vegetables into pickles – then you'll need a boiler, characterised by its very large capacity and its two handles, rather than just one handle like a saucepan.

What you need to spend on it depends on what you will use it for. If it's only for foods such as the corned beef, chicken, lobster, pudding or pasta mentioned above, which are cooked in plenty of water, then you will be pleased to hear that this is one piece of kitchen equipment that doesn't need to be expensive. The water will even out any hotspots that a light, cheap boiler may develop, and its lightness will actually be an advantage when it comes to lifting. You can get away with a cheap boiler for making stock or clear soup, too, since the food is surrounded by liquid that is mostly water. It is advisable to check for a base that is a separate plate so that it won't warp readily, but medium-gauge steel or aluminium is adequate – though you should remember that aluminium is not desirable for cooking anything involving tomatoes, fruit, spinach or any of the cabbage family (see Aluminium under Material, *The Frying Pan*, page 22).

If you have ideas of using your boiler for anything that could thicken enough to scorch or stick, such as thickened soups, sauces or pickles etc., then you'll need a utensil of the same quality as a good saucepan (see *The Saucepan*, page 150).

Also, if using a boiler made of thin metal to cook ingredients in water for hours on end, as when making a stock, the ingredients on the bottom of the boiler could eventually become overheated and scorch, so stir gently from time to time and, if you have any doubts, put a heat-spreading mat (see page 40) under the boiler.

HANDLES AND LID

A boiler has two handles for balanced lifting; check that they are riveted or welded on, not screwed on, as screws can work loose, and a wobble when you're carrying a heavy boiler of near-boiling water could be disastrous. Check, too, that the handles will be cool enough to hold when the boiler is hot, and that they are comfortable and shaped to allow a firm grip. If they get too hot, it's better to protect your hands with oven mitts when lifting, rather than with pot-holders, which could slip.

The lid should be well-fitting, but not so tight that it won't allow a little steam to escape, which acts as a safety-valve against pressure build up. The lid handle or knob should either be of a material that will be cool enough to handle when the lid is hot, or shaped to allow you to grip it firmly with a pot-holder.

USE

Although it is called a boiler, more often than not the food should be simmered or poached rather than boiled. It is important to understand these three stages of heating a liquid and be able to recognise them as they give quite different results – for instance, seafood or meat that is boiled when it should be poached will be tough and dry, while pasta needs to be cooked at a brisk boil so the pieces are kept on the move to prevent them sticking together. Check often to see that the liquid is at the right temperature, as shown by the following descriptions:

TO POACH is to cook in a liquid where the surface shivers but no bubbles rise to the top. If the liquid is clear, you can look down and see bubbles on the bottom of the pan, but they don't rise or burst. Fish, chicken and meat should always be poached so that they remain juicy – simmering or boiling makes the tissues contract and squeeze out the juices. If you see little white patches floating in the cooking liquid, turn the heat down: the flecks are protein that has been squeezed out in the juices and "flocculated", cooked into solid form.

TO SIMMER is to cook in a liquid where the surface shudders and bubbles rise one or two at a time. Stock, the flavoursome liquid made by cooking meat, bones and vegetables together in water, is simmered so that the ingredients slowly give up their juices into the water. If you taste the meat remaining after a well-made stock is strained, you will find it almost tasteless: all its flavour is now in the stock.

TO BOIL is to cook in a liquid where bubbles rise quickly and continuously to the surface. It is at a full or "rolling" boil when the surface is rolling or seething with bubbles. This is the right temperature for cooking pasta and most vegetables, especially green ones that need the shortest possible cooking time so they don't lose their colour.

HANDLING

Tipping a heavy boiler to remove the contents can be difficult and even hazardous when it is hot. If possible, lift out the food with a slotted spoon or tongs assisted by a spatula underneath, then ladle out some of the liquid before tipping out the rest. For food in small pieces, such as pasta, ladle out as much liquid as possible into a colander placed in the sink, then tip the remaining contents into the colander. If a poached chicken or corned beef is to be eaten cold, allow it to cool completely in the cooking liquid before removing.

Beef stock

PREPARATION TIME 10 MINUTES (PLUS COOLING AND REFRIGERATION TIME) **COOKING TIME** 5 HOURS
MAKES 3.5 LITRES

Whether you make soup or stock from scratch or not, owning a boiler (stockpot) is a good investment. The better ones are not cheap, and their size can make storage a problem, but their advantages far outweigh these obstacles. Look for a highly polished interior because this makes the pot virtually non-stick as well as resistant to discolouration.

2kg meaty beef bones

2 medium brown onions (300g), chopped coarsely

5.5 litres water (22 cups)

2 trimmed celery stalks (200g), chopped coarsely

2 medium carrots (240g), chopped coarsely

3 bay leaves

2 teaspoons black peppercorns

3 litres water (12 cups), extra

1 Preheat oven to 200°C/180°C fan-forced.

2 Roast bones on an oven tray, uncovered, about 1 hour or until browned.

3 Combine bones and onion with the water, celery, carrot, bay leaves and peppercorns in boiler; bring to a boil. Reduce heat, simmer, uncovered, 3 hours, skimming surface occasionally. Add extra water; simmer, uncovered, 1 hour. Strain stock through muslin-lined sieve or colander into large heatproof bowl; discard solids. Allow stock to cool, cover; refrigerate until cold. Skim and discard surface fat before using.

▭ **PER 1 CUP (250ML)** 2g total fat (0.9g saturated fat); 259kJ (62 cal); 2.3g carbohydrate; 8g protein; 1.1g fibre

---

Chicken stock

PREPARATION TIME 10 MINUTES (PLUS COOLING AND REFRIGERATION TIME) **COOKING TIME** 2 HOURS
MAKES 3.5 LITRES

For a cheat's way to make chicken stock: buy a few barbecued chickens when they're on special, remove and shred the meat then freeze it in one-cup parcels – ready for use at another time, thus saving time and money. Discard the chicken skin but use the bones, along with any carrots, celery or herbs in your vegetable crisper, to make stock and freeze it, too, in 1-cup amounts.

2kg chicken bones

2 medium onions (300g), chopped coarsely

2 trimmed celery stalks (200g), chopped coarsely

2 medium carrots (240g), chopped coarsely

3 bay leaves

2 teaspoons black peppercorns

5 litres (20 cups) water

1 Combine ingredients in boiler; simmer, uncovered, 2 hours, skimming surface occasionally.

2 Strain stock through muslin-lined sieve or colander into large heatproof bowl; discard solids. Allow stock to cool, cover; refrigerate until cold. Skim and discard surface fat before using.

▭ **PER 1 CUP (250ML)** 0.6g total fat (0.2g saturated fat); 105kJ (25 cal); 2.3g carbohydrate; 1.9g protein; 1.1g fibre

Fish stock

PREPARATION TIME 5 MINUTES (PLUS COOLING AND REFRIGERATION TIME) **COOKING TIME** 20 MINUTES
MAKES 2.5 LITRES

> 1.5kg fish bones
>
> 3 litres (12 cups) water
>
> 1 medium onion (150g), chopped coarsely
>
> 2 trimmed celery stalks (200g), chopped coarsely
>
> 2 bay leaves
>
> 1 teaspoon black peppercorns

1 Combine ingredients in boiler; simmer, uncovered, 20 minutes.
2 Strain stock through muslin-lined sieve or colander into large heatproof bowl;
discard solids. Allow stock to cool, cover; refrigerate until cold. Skim and discard
surface fat before using.

◻ **PER 1 CUP (250ML)** 0.2g total fat (0.1g saturated fat); 63kJ (15 cal); 1.1g carbohydrate; 1.9g protein; 0.6g fibre

When stock is cold, after skimming the surface, use a funnel to pour what you're not using at the time into cleaned empty milk cartons and freeze it. Not only does this guarantee thawing only exactly what you need, but you can throw the container away instead of having to wash it! Use 600ml cartons too, as well as litre containers, for those times when you only require a fairly small amount of stock.

Vegetable stock

PREPARATION TIME 10 MINUTES (PLUS COOLING AND REFRIGERATION TIME)
COOKING TIME 1 HOUR 30 MINUTES **MAKES** 3.5 LITRES

> 2 large carrots (360g), chopped coarsely
>
> 2 large parsnips (700g), chopped coarsely
>
> 4 medium onions (600g), chopped coarsely
>
> 10 trimmed celery stalks (1kg), chopped coarsely
>
> 4 bay leaves
>
> 2 teaspoons black peppercorns
>
> 6 litres (24 cups) water

1 Combine ingredients in boiler; simmer, uncovered, 1½ hours.
2 Strain stock through muslin-lined sieve or colander into large heatproof bowl;
discard solids. Allow stock to cool, cover; refrigerate until cold.

◻ **PER 1 CUP (250ML)** 0.2g total fat (0g saturated fat); 151kJ (36 cal); 5.7g carbohydrate; 1.4g protein; 2.9g fibre

Making stock is well worth it, in terms of the quality of the finished dish. For a start, it takes little effort, and it's not rocket science; make it whenever you have some free time and feel like pottering around the kitchen, especially on a cold and dreary weekend when the stock's scent and the warmth pervade the house. Be certain to wash the vegetables well before use but forget about peeling them. While you should bring the stock to a boil initially, slowly simmering it for the duration of cooking time imbues it with the most flavour.

Coconut, chicken and kaffir lime soup

PREPARATION TIME 15 MINUTES **COOKING TIME** 45 MINUTES **SERVES** 4

1 tablespoon peanut oil

600g chicken thigh fillets, cut into 1cm strips

¼ cup (75g) green curry paste

1 litre (4 cups) chicken stock

3¼ cups (800ml) coconut milk

1 long green chilli, chopped finely

8 fresh kaffir lime leaves, shredded finely

125g rice vermicelli noodles

2 tablespoons grated palm sugar

2 tablespoons lime juice

2 tablespoons fish sauce

1 cup (80g) bean sprouts

½ cup loosely packed vietnamese mint leaves

1 long green chilli, sliced thinly

2 limes, cut into thin wedges

1 Heat oil in large frying pan; cook chicken, in batches, until browned lightly.

2 Place paste in boiler; cook, stirring, until fragrant. Add chicken, stock, coconut milk, chopped chilli and lime leaves; bring to a boil. Reduce heat, simmer, uncovered, 30 minutes, skimming fat from surface occasionally. Add vermicelli; cook, uncovered, until vermicelli is just tender. Stir in sugar, juice and sauce.

3 Serve soup sprinkled with sprouts, mint, sliced chilli and lime wedges.

☐ **PER SERVING** 63.9g total fat (41.6g saturated fat); 3478kJ (832 cal); 25g carbohydrate; 38g protein; 6.8g fibre

Green chillies are always fresh chillies, the first stage of ripeness rather than a specific variety. You can keep them frozen for months: buy a large quantity when you find them, wash them thoroughly, allow to air-dry then place, in small amounts, in zip lock plastic bags and freeze until you are ready to use them. Only thaw what you need each time and, for ease, slice or chop them while they're still frozen.

Fish chowder

PREPARATION TIME 15 MINUTES **COOKING TIME** 30 MINUTES **SERVES** 6

60g butter

1 large brown onion (200g), chopped coarsely

2 cloves garlic, crushed

3 rindless bacon rashers (195g), chopped coarsely

¼ cup (35g) plain flour

2 medium potatoes (600g), chopped coarsely

1 litre (4 cups) milk

3 cups (750ml) vegetable stock

600g firm white fish fillets, chopped coarsely

¼ cup finely chopped fresh chives

1 Melt butter in boiler; cook onion, garlic and bacon, stirring, until onion softens.

2 Add flour; cook, stirring, 1 minute. Add potato, milk and stock; bring to a boil. Reduce heat, simmer, covered, about 10 minutes or until potato is just tender.

3 Add fish; simmer, uncovered, about 4 minutes or until fish is cooked through (do not overcook). Serve bowls of soup sprinkled with chives.

☐ **PER SERVING** 30.6g total fat (17.5g saturated fat); 2817kJ (674 cal); 46.2g carbohydrate; 55g protein; 3.7g fibre

A thick and nourishing seafood soup native to the East Coast of the United States, there are basically two kinds of chowder. The one on which our fish version is based, New England chowder, always contains bacon, potatoes and milk or cream thickened with flour, while the second, Manhattan chowder, is thinner and flavoured with tomatoes. Both are always accompanied in the USA by a small hexagonal-shaped saltine biscuit called an "oyster cracker".

1 COCONUT, CHICKEN AND KAFFIR LIME SOUP **2** FISH CHOWDER
3 BEEF AND BARLEY SOUP [P 196] **4** PORK IN ORANGE AND TAMARIND BROTH [P 196]

1

2

3

4

Make the beef and barley base (through to the end of step 2) either the day before or in the morning of the day you want to eat this satisfying soup so that it can chill long enough for the fat to solidify on top; scoop it away before reheating it and adding the vegetables.

Beef and barley soup

PREPARATION TIME 30 MINUTES **COOKING TIME** 1 HOUR 45 MINUTES **SERVES** 6

1 tablespoon olive oil

500g gravy beef, trimmed, diced into 2cm pieces

2 cloves garlic, crushed

2 medium brown onions (300g), chopped finely

¾ cup (150g) pearl barley

3 cups (750ml) beef stock

1.5 litres (6 cups) water

1 bay leaf

1 sprig fresh rosemary

1 sprig fresh thyme

2 medium potatoes (400g), diced into 1cm pieces

2 medium carrots (240g), diced into 1cm pieces

2 medium zucchini (240g), diced into 1cm pieces

2 medium yellow patty-pan squash (60g), diced into 1cm pieces

100g swiss brown mushrooms, chopped coarsely

½ cup finely chopped fresh flat-leaf parsley

1 Heat half of the oil in boiler; cook beef, in batches, until browned.

2 Heat remaining oil in same boiler; cook garlic and onion, stirring, until onion softens. Return beef to pan with barley, stock, the water, bay leaf, rosemary and thyme; bring to a boil. Reduce heat, simmer, covered, about 1 hour or until beef and barley are tender, skimming fat occasionally.

3 Add potato, carrot, zucchini, squash and mushrooms to soup; simmer, covered, about 25 minutes or until vegetables are softened. Remove and discard bay leaf, rosemary and thyme.

4 Serve bowls of soup sprinkled with parsley.

PER SERVING 8.8g total fat (2.6g saturated fat); 1350kJ (323 cal); 30g carbohydrate; 26.9g protein; 7.8g fibre

In a soup like this, one which calls for more water than stock and takes a lot of flavour from its other ingredients (the barbecued pork, tamarind, orange, chilli, etc), you can get away with using commercially made stock. Available both in liquid form in cans, bottles or tetra packs, and as dried cubes or powder, these ready-made stocks can be fairly salty so don't add extra to the broth before tasting it.

Pork in orange and tamarind broth

PREPARATION TIME 15 MINUTES (PLUS STANDING TIME) **COOKING TIME** 30 MINUTES **SERVES** 8

20g dried shiitake mushrooms

2 teaspoons vegetable oil

4 shallots (100g), chopped finely

1 clove garlic, crushed

2 fresh small red thai chillies, chopped finely

2 litres (8 cups) water

1 litre (4 cups) beef stock

2 teaspoons finely grated orange rind

¼ cup (60ml) orange juice

1 tablespoon tamarind concentrate

400g chinese barbecued pork, sliced thinly

100g swiss brown mushrooms, sliced thinly

4 green onions, sliced thinly

1 Place dried mushrooms in small bowl, cover with cold water; stand 1 hour. Drain; remove stems, slice caps thinly.

2 Meanwhile, heat oil in boiler; cook shallot, garlic and chilli, stirring, until shallot softens. Add the water, stock, rind, juice and tamarind; bring to a boil. Add pork, and all the mushrooms; reduce heat, simmer, covered, about 10 minutes or until soup is hot.

3 Serve bowls of soup sprinkled with onion.

▭ **PER SERVING** 9.1g total fat (3.4g saturated fat); 648kJ (155 cal); 4.3g carbohydrate; 13.1g protein; 2.1g fibre

Chicken and risoni soup with herbed meatballs

PREPARATION TIME 30 MINUTES (PLUS REFRIGERATION TIME) **COOKING TIME** 2 HOURS 45 MINUTES
SERVES 4

2.5 litres (10 cups) water

1.6kg whole chicken

1 large tomato (220g), halved

2 trimmed celery stalks (200g), halved

1 medium brown onion (150g), halved

2 fresh flat-leaf parsley stalks

5 black peppercorns

300g chicken mince

1 egg

½ cup (50g) packaged breadcrumbs

2 tablespoons finely chopped fresh flat-leaf parsley

2 tablespoons finely grated parmesan cheese

1 tablespoon olive oil

¾ cup (165g) risoni pasta

2 tablespoons lemon juice

⅓ cup coarsely chopped fresh flat-leaf parsley

1 Place the water in boiler with whole chicken, tomato, celery, onion, parsley stalks and peppercorns; bring to a boil. Reduce heat, simmer, covered, 2 hours.

2 Remove chicken from boiler. Strain broth through muslin-lined sieve or colander into large heatproof bowl; discard solids. Allow broth to cool, cover, refrigerate overnight. When chicken is cool enough to handle, remove and discard skin and bones. Shred meat coarsely; cover, refrigerate overnight.

3 Combine mince, egg, breadcrumbs, finely chopped parsley and cheese in medium bowl; roll rounded teaspoons of mixture into balls. Heat oil in medium saucepan; cook meatballs, in batches, until browned all over.

4 Skim and discard fat from surface of broth. Return broth to boiler; bring to a boil. Reduce heat, simmer, uncovered, 20 minutes. Add meatballs and pasta; simmer, uncovered, about 10 minutes or until meatballs are cooked through and pasta is just tender. Add 2 cups of the reserved shredded chicken (keep remaining chicken for another use), juice and coarsely chopped parsley to boiler; stir soup over medium heat until hot.

▭ **PER SERVING** 45.8g total fat (3.7g saturated fat); 3536kJ (846 cal); 40.4g carbohydrate; 66.3g protein; 4.3g fibre

The obvious uses for a large boiler are, of course, simmering large quantities of stocks and soups, cooking and draining pastas and beans, and cooking various foods that need space for one reason or another: asparagus, artichokes, mussels, dumplings and the like. In addition, their sheer capaciousness renders them capable of poaching a whole chicken, crab or large fish; making gigantic batches of a curry on the weekend to freeze in meal-size portions, and boiling jams, chutneys and the odd Christmas pudding.

Muslin is an inexpensive, finely woven, undyed cotton fabric used in cooking specifically for straining stocks and sauces; coffee filter papers can be used instead. Each piece can be used more than one time if you rinse it well then wash and dry it; new muslin just home from the shop should also be washed and dried before first using it.

Chilli crab laksa

PREPARATION TIME 40 MINUTES (PLUS STANDING TIME) **COOKING TIME** 30 MINUTES **SERVES** 6

3 uncooked mud crabs (2.25kg)

2 tablespoons peanut oil

4 fresh long red chillies, chopped finely

3 cloves garlic, crushed

3cm piece fresh ginger (15g), grated

1 cup (250ml) fish stock

1 cup (270g) laksa paste

3¼ cups (800ml) coconut milk

1.25 litre (5 cups) chicken stock

4 fresh kaffir lime leaves, shredded finely

1 fresh long red chilli, chopped finely, extra

2 tablespoons lime juice

2 tablespoons fish sauce

2 tablespoons grated palm sugar

375g rice stick noodles

4 green onions, sliced thinly

3 cups (240g) bean sprouts

¾ cup loosely packed fresh coriander leaves

Freeze the unused bits of shell and use them at a later date for a fumet (pronounced fuu-may, from the French for aroma), a concentrated seafood stock used to flavour sauces and very nice to have on hand if you want to make a cioppino or a white clam sauce for pasta.

1 Place crabs in large container filled with ice and water; stand 1 hour. Leaving flesh in claws and legs, prepare crab by lifting tail flap and, with a peeling motion, lift off back shell. Remove and discard whitish gills, liver and brain matter; crack claws with back of knife. Rinse crabs well. Using cleaver or heavy knife, chop each body into quarters; crack large claws lightly with back of knife.

2 Heat oil in wok; stir-fry chilli, garlic and ginger until fragrant. Add crab and fish stock, bring to a boil. Reduce heat, simmer, covered, about 20 minutes or until crab is changed in colour. Discard liquid in wok.

3 Meanwhile, cook paste in boiler, stirring, until fragrant. Stir in coconut milk, stock, lime leaves and extra chilli; bring to a boil. Reduce heat, simmer, covered, 20 minutes. Stir in juice, sauce, sugar and crab.

4 Meanwhile, place noodles in large heatproof bowl; cover with boiling water. Stand until tender; drain.

5 Divide noodles and crab among serving bowls; ladle laksa into bowls, top with onion, sprouts and coriander.

PER SERVING 77.5g total fat (40.8g saturated fat); 5856kJ (1401 cal); 84.9g carbohydrate; 84.7g protein; 14.7g fibre

Eating pho is a national institution in Vietnam, and our major cities don't lag behind in the number of restaurants devoted solely to this healthy and flavoursome noodle soup. The noodle used here is the especially popular South-East Asian dried rice noodle which comes in different widths – use thin in soups, wide in stir-fries. All need to be soaked first in hot water until softened.

You really should make your own beef stock (see page 192) for this recipe, and clarify it: even after straining it through muslin, stock can still have some small bits in it. While in most soups, this doesn't matter, the traditional Vietnamese broth used in pho is almost glass-like in its clarity. After the strained stock has cooled completely, whisk a beaten egg into it. Return it to a low simmer and heat it gradually, without stirring; when the stock is hot, the egg will rise to the surface, bringing the solid leftover bits with it. Strain the stock again through muslin and it should be completely clear.

Pho bo

PREPARATION TIME 10 MINUTES **COOKING TIME** 15 MINUTES **SERVES** 4

1 litre (4 cups) water

1 litre (4 cups) beef stock

8cm piece fresh ginger (40g), sliced thinly

1 tablespoon fish sauce

1 tablespoon lime juice

2 cloves garlic, quartered

⅓ cup coarsely chopped fresh coriander root and stem mixture

1 star anise

500g piece beef eye fillet, sliced thinly

375g dried rice stick noodles

8 green onions, sliced thinly

2 cups (160g) bean sprouts

⅓ cup loosely packed vietnamese mint leaves

⅓ cup loosely packed fresh coriander leaves

2 fresh small red thai chillies, chopped finely

2 lemons, cut into wedges

1 Combine the water, stock, ginger, sauce, juice, garlic, coriander mixture and star anise in boiler; bring to a boil. Reduce heat, simmer, uncovered, 10 minutes.

2 Strain broth through muslin-lined sieve into large heatproof bowl; discard solids. Return broth to boiler, add beef; return to a boil. Reduce heat, simmer, uncovered, about 3 minutes or until beef is cooked as desired.

3 Meanwhile, place noodles in large heatproof bowl, cover with boiling water; stand until tender, drain.

4 Divide noodles, onion and sprouts among serving bowls; ladle hot broth into bowls. Serve with herbs, chilli and lemon, so each person can add what they wish.

▭ **PER SERVING** 7.1g total fat (2.9g saturated fat); 1271kJ (304 cal); 24.3g carbohydrate; 33.5g protein; 3g fibre

Corned beef with parsley sauce

PREPARATION TIME 20 MINUTES (PLUS STANDING TIME)
COOKING TIME 2 HOURS 15 MINUTES (PLUS COOLING TIME) **SERVES** 4

1.5kg piece beef corned silverside

2 bay leaves

6 black peppercorns

1 large brown onion (200g), quartered

1 large carrot (180g), chopped coarsely

1 tablespoon malt vinegar

¼ cup (50g) firmly packed brown sugar

PARSLEY SAUCE

30g butter

¼ cup (35g) plain flour

2½ cups (625ml) hot milk

⅓ cup (40g) coarsely grated cheddar cheese

⅓ cup finely chopped fresh flat-leaf parsley

1 tablespoon mild mustard

1 Place beef, bay leaves, peppercorns, onion, carrot, vinegar and half of the sugar in boiler. Add enough water to just cover beef; simmer, covered, about 2 hours or until beef is tender. Cool beef 1 hour in liquid in boiler.

2 Remove beef from boiler; discard liquid. Sprinkle sheet of foil with remaining sugar, wrap beef in foil; stand 20 minutes.

3 Meanwhile, make parsley sauce.

4 Serve beef with sauce and, if desired, steamed potatoes and baby carrots.

PARSLEY SAUCE Melt butter in small saucepan, add flour; cook, stirring, until bubbling. Gradually stir in milk; cook, stirring, until sauce boils and thickens. Remove from heat; stir in cheese, parsley and mustard.

▭ **PER SERVING** 35.8g total fat (193g saturated fat); 3520kJ (842 cal); 31g carbohydrate; 97g protein; 2.5g fibre

Mexican bean and shredded pork soup

PREPARATION TIME 25 MINUTES **COOKING TIME** 2 HOURS 30 MINUTES **SERVES** 6

2 litres (8 cups) water

2 litres (8 cups) chicken stock

1 large carrot (180g), chopped coarsely

1 trimmed celery stalk (100g), chopped coarsely

5 cloves garlic, unpeeled, bruised

6 black peppercorns

3 sprigs fresh oregano

1 bay leaf

1kg piece pork neck

1 tablespoon olive oil

1 large red onion (300g), chopped coarsely

1 medium red capsicum (200g), chopped coarsely

1 medium yellow capsicum (200g), chopped coarsely

2 fresh long red chillies, sliced thinly

2 cloves garlic, crushed

810g can crushed tomatoes

1 teaspoon ground cumin

2 tablespoons coarsely chopped fresh oregano

400g can kidney beans, rinsed, drained

If you can find dried black turtle beans, use them instead of the canned kidney beans called for here. Soak a cup of beans overnight then drain, rinse and add to the boiler with the pork at the start of the recipe. A common ingredient in Caribbean and Mexican soups, salsas and salads, they should not be confused with Chinese black beans, which are fermented soy beans.

1 Place the water and stock in boiler with carrot, celery, bruised garlic, peppercorns, oregano sprigs, bay leaf and pork; bring to a boil. Reduce heat, simmer, covered, 1 hour. Uncover; simmer 1 hour.

2 Transfer pork to medium bowl; using two forks, shred pork coarsely. Strain broth through muslin-lined sieve or colander into large heatproof bowl; discard solids.

3 Heat oil in same cleaned boiler; cook onion, capsicums, chilli and crushed garlic, stirring, until vegetables soften. Return pork and broth to boiler with undrained tomatoes, cumin and chopped oregano; bring to a boil. Reduce heat, simmer, covered, 15 minutes. Add beans; simmer, covered, until soup is hot.

▭ **PER SERVING** 7.4g total fat (1.6g saturated fat); 1490kJ (356 cal); 20.8g carbohydrate; 46.5g protein; 9.1g fibre

Glassware

Most of us have cupboards filled with glasses that we don't know what to do with; it's time to make use of your collection

WHITE WINE
The tall bowl of the glass helps keep the wine cool because the surface area is relatively small. It also holds the delicate aromas for the "nosing" of the wine before drinking.

RED WINE
A red wine glass has a round, wide bowl that gives the wine a chance to breathe, especially if it is swirled around the bowl to enhance the bouquet of a bold red wine.

CHAMPAGNE
The narrow shape shows the bubbles to advantage, and is designed to keep the sparkle in the wine longer because the small surface area limits the rate at which bubbles can escape.

HIGHBALL
A tall, straight glass originally intended for whisky with enough ice and soda or ginger ale to make a long drink; now used for tequila sunrise, Long Island iced tea, gin or vodka and tonic and other long drinks.

MARTINI
A stemmed cocktail glass with a wide, shallow, flared bowl and a base wide enough to balance it. Used for serving martinis, white ladies, sidecars and other short cocktails.

SHOT (JIGGER)
A measure made from stainless steel or glass designed to measure a standard one-drink quantity of spirits, varying from 30ml to 45ml.

WHISKY

Short and wide to hold the usual 30ml to 60ml of whisky and allow the drinker to inhale its aroma. Classic ways to serve are with a little water or soda water, with or without ice, or just neat.

SHERRY

Smaller than a table wine glass because, being more alcoholic, the standard drink is about half the standard amount of table wine. The tall, often tulip-shaped bowl is designed to collect the bouquet for nosing.

BEER

Always tall and may be slightly flared from a small foot, or straight, often with a heavy base to resist being knocked over. Glass or pewter tankards or steins (mugs) are also popular.

TUMBLER

A tall, straight or slightly flared glass for serving water, soft drinks, juices, milk, iced coffee or tea, or long alcoholic drinks.

SAKE

A sake glass is small and curved, with a short foot, and is designed to be cradled in the hand to keep the sake warm. Sake is also served in small, porcelain or lacquer-ware cups without handles.

DESSERT WINE AND LIQUEUR

Dessert wine may be served in a small white wine glass or a classic stemmed tasting glass with a tall, rounded bowl narrowing at the top. Liqueurs are served in miniature stemmed, footed or straight-sided glasses.

White-cut chicken

PREPARATION TIME 20 MINUTES (PLUS STANDING TIME) COOKING TIME 45 MINUTES SERVES 4

It's traditional to serve "white" chicken for Chinese New Year as it symbolises purity and unity for the year ahead. Leaving the bird in the broth ensures that the meat is lusciously tender, juicy and almost lucently white.

Star anise, a dried, star-shaped fruit of a tree native to China, has an astringent aniseed taste and is used to flavour a great many stocks and marinades.

1.6kg whole chicken

2 litres (8 cups) water

¼ cup (60ml) light soy sauce

½ cup (125ml) dark soy sauce

1 cup (250ml) chinese cooking wine

½ cup (135g) coarsely chopped palm sugar

20cm piece fresh ginger (100g), sliced thinly

4 star anise

4 cloves garlic, sliced thinly

1 tablespoon sichuan peppercorns

SOY AND GREEN ONION DRESSING

¼ cup (60ml) dark soy sauce

¼ cup (60ml) rice vinegar

4 green onions, sliced thinly

2 teaspoons peanut oil

½ teaspoon sesame oil

1 Make soy and green onion dressing.

2 Place chicken, breast-side down with remaining ingredients in boiler; bring to a boil. Reduce heat, simmer, uncovered, 25 minutes. Turn chicken breast-side up; simmer, uncovered, 5 minutes. Remove pan from heat; turn chicken breast-side down, stand in poaching liquid 3 hours.

3 Remove chicken from boiler; discard poaching liquid. Using cleaver, cut chicken in half through the centre of the breastplate and along one side of backbone; cut each half into eight pieces. Serve chicken drizzled with dressing.

SOY AND GREEN ONION DRESSING Whisk ingredients in small bowl.

▭ **PER SERVING** 29.1g total fat (8.7g saturated fat); 2608kJ (624 cal); 41g carbohydrate; 46.1g protein; 0.7g fibre

Chicken, chorizo and okra gumbo

PREPARATION TIME 30 MINUTES COOKING TIME 2 HOURS 45 MINUTES SERVES 8

Gumbo is a hearty stew that originated in the US southern state of Louisiana. The one essential to all versions of gumbo is the inclusion of the vegetable, okra – the word gumbo is actually the word for okra in some West African dialects, and the concept of this stew was introduced to the Deep South by African slaves. The okra acts as a thickening agent, as does the roux, and is what makes it a stew rather than a soup.

3 litres (12 cups) water

1.5kg whole chicken

2 medium carrots (240g), chopped coarsely

2 trimmed celery stalks (200g), chopped coarsely

1 medium brown onion (150g), chopped coarsely

12 black peppercorns

1 bay leaf

60g butter

1 small brown onion (80g), chopped finely, extra

2 cloves garlic, crushed

1 medium red capsicum (200g), chopped finely

2 teaspoons dried oregano

1 teaspoon sweet paprika

¼ teaspoon cayenne pepper

¼ teaspoon ground clove

¼ cup (35g) plain flour

¼ cup (70g) tomato paste

400g can crushed tomatoes

100g fresh okra, halved diagonally

1 cup (200g) calrose rice

1 chorizo sausage (170g), sliced thinly

1 Place the water in boiler with chicken, carrot, celery, onion, peppercorns and bay leaf; bring to a boil. Reduce heat, simmer, covered, 1 ½ hours.

2 Remove chicken from pan. Strain broth through muslin-lined sieve or colander into large heatproof bowl; discard solids. When chicken is cool enough to handle, remove and discard skin and bones; shred meat coarsely.

3 Melt butter in same cleaned boiler; cook extra onion and garlic, stirring, until onion softens. Add capsicum, herbs and spices; cook, stirring, until mixture is fragrant. Add flour and paste; cook, stirring, 1 minute. Gradually stir in reserved broth and undrained tomatoes; bring to a boil, stirring. Stir in okra and rice; reduce heat, simmer, uncovered, about 15 minutes, stirring occasionally, or until rice is tender.

4 Meanwhile, heat large oiled frying pan; cook sausage until browned; drain. Add sausage with chicken to gumbo; stir over medium heat until hot.

PER SERVING 26.8g total fat (5.7g saturated fat); 2011kJ (481 cal); 30.5g carbohydrate; 27.8g protein; 3.9g fibre

Pot au feu with stuffed cabbage rolls

PREPARATION TIME 45 MINUTES **COOKING TIME** 1 HOUR 45 MINUTES **SERVES** 6

A classic French pot au feu, which literally translates as "pot on the stove", can be made from a wide variety of different ingredients, the combination varying region to region. All versions, however, usually are made with marrow bones of some kind, and often the marrow itself is served separately, similarly to the way Italians eat osso buco.

2 pieces veal shin (osso buco) (1.5kg)

2 large carrots (360g), chopped coarsely

1 medium leek (350g), chopped coarsely

2 small turnips (300g), chopped coarsely

6 baby brown onions (150g)

1 bay leaf

3 cups (750ml) chicken stock

1 litre (4 cups) water

1 small savoy cabbage (1.2kg)

250g pork mince

250g chicken mince

1 egg

1 small brown onion (80g), chopped finely

½ cup (50g) packaged breadcrumbs

1 Place veal, carrot, leek, turnip, whole onions, bay leaf, stock and the water in boiler; bring to a boil. Reduce heat, simmer, uncovered, about 1 ½ hours or until veal is tender. Remove veal; when cool enough to handle, remove meat from bones and chop it coarsely.

2 Remove 12 large leaves from cabbage; cook, uncovered, in batches, in large saucepan of boiling water 3 minutes. Drain leaves on absorbent paper. Finely chop enough of the remaining cabbage to make ⅓ cup; reserve remaining cabbage for another use.

3 Meanwhile, combine pork, chicken, egg, chopped onion, breadcrumbs and chopped cabbage in large bowl; divide mixture among cabbage leaves. Roll leaves to enclose filling, secure with toothpicks.

4 Return veal meat to vegetable mixture in boiler, add cabbage rolls; bring to a boil. Reduce heat, simmer, uncovered, about 10 minutes or until cabbage rolls are cooked through. Divide cabbage rolls among serving bowls; ladle soup over top.

PER SERVING 9g total fat (2.8g saturated fat); 1634kJ (391 cal); 18.9g carbohydrate; 57.7g protein; 0g fibre

After sundown during Ramadan, many of the Muslims in Morocco and other North African countries break the day's fast by starting their meal with this hearty soup. Recipes vary from family to family but chickpeas and lamb always feature as constant ingredients.

Simmer this dish on the largest burner on your cooktop, on the lowest setting, to distribute the heat over the widest area possible. Keep a watch on the food and don't be afraid to uncover it to give it the occasional stir.

Harira

PREPARATION TIME 25 MINUTES (PLUS STANDING TIME) **COOKING TIME** 2 HOURS 15 MINUTES **SERVES** 8

1 cup (200g) dried chickpeas

20g butter

2 medium brown onions (300g), chopped finely

2 trimmed celery stalks (200g), chopped finely

2 cloves garlic, crushed

4cm piece fresh ginger (20g), grated

1 teaspoon ground cinnamon

½ teaspoon ground black pepper

pinch saffron threads

500g diced lamb

3 large tomatoes (660g), seeded, chopped coarsely

2 litres (8 cups) hot water

½ cup (100g) brown lentils

2 tablespoons plain flour

½ cup (100g) cooked white long-grain rice

½ cup firmly packed fresh coriander leaves

2 tablespoons lemon juice

1 Place chickpeas in medium bowl, cover with water, stand overnight; drain. Rinse under cold water; drain.

2 Melt butter in boiler; cook onion, celery and garlic, stirring, until onion softens. Add ginger, cinnamon, pepper and saffron; cook, stirring, until fragrant. Add lamb; cook, stirring, about 5 minutes or until lamb is browned. Add chickpeas and tomato; cook, stirring, about 5 minutes or until tomato softens.

3 Stir the water into soup mixture; bring to a boil. Reduce heat, simmer, covered, 45 minutes. Add lentils; simmer, covered, 1 hour.

4 Blend flour with ½ cup of slightly cooled broth in a small bowl; return to boiler with rice. Cook, stirring, until soup comes to a boil and thickens slightly. Remove from heat; stir in coriander and juice.

▭ **PER SERVING** 8.6g total fat (4g saturated fat); 1095kJ (262 cal); 23.6g carbohydrate; 20.1g protein; 4.8g fibre

Also called black-eyed peas or cow peas, this small, kidney-shaped, white bean with a single black spot has a fairly thin skin so it cooks somewhat faster than other legumes. The night before, try soaking two or three times the amount of beans called for in our recipe then, freeze what you don't use in 1-cup portions.

Beef, black-eyed bean and spinach soup

PREPARATION TIME 5 MINUTES (PLUS STANDING TIME) **COOKING TIME** 1 HOUR 50 MINUTES **SERVES** 4

1 cup (200g) black-eyed beans

1 tablespoon olive oil

1 medium brown onion (150g), chopped finely

1 clove garlic, crushed

2.5 litres (10 cups) beef stock

¼ cup (60ml) dry red wine

2 tablespoons tomato paste

500g piece beef skirt steak

250g spinach, chopped coarsely

1 Place beans in medium bowl, cover with water, stand overnight, drain. Rinse under cold water; drain.

2 Heat oil in boiler; cook onion and garlic, stirring, until onion softens. Add stock, wine, paste and beef to boiler; bring to a boil. Reduce heat, simmer, covered, 40 minutes. Uncover; simmer 30 minutes.

3 Remove beef from boiler; add beans; bring to a boil. Reduce heat, simmer, uncovered, until beans are tender.

4 Meanwhile, when beef is cool enough to handle, remove and discard fat and sinew. Chop beef coarsely; return to boiler with spinach; simmer, uncovered, until soup is hot.

PER SERVING 13.9g total fat (4.2g saturated fat); 2199kJ (526 cal); 28.3g carbohydrate; 62.6g protein; 12.4g fibre

Pea and ham soup with risoni

PREPARATION TIME 15 MINUTES **COOKING TIME** 1 HOUR 15 MINUTES **SERVES** 6

2 teaspoons olive oil

1 medium brown onion (150g), chopped coarsely

2 teaspoons ground cumin

2.5 litres (10 cups) water

2 trimmed celery stalks (200g), chopped coarsely

2 bay leaves

1.5kg ham bone

1 cup (220g) risoni pasta

2 cups (240g) frozen peas

2 tablespoons finely chopped fresh mint

1 Heat oil in boiler; cook onion, stirring, until softened. Add cumin; cook, stirring, until fragrant. Add the water, celery, bay leaves and bone; bring to a boil. Reduce heat, simmer, covered, 1 hour, skimming occasionally.

2 Remove bone; when cool enough to handle, cut ham from bone, discarding any skin and fat. Shred ham finely.

3 Return soup to a boil; stir in ham, pasta and peas. Cook, uncovered, about 5 minutes or until pasta is tender. Sprinkle bowls of soup with mint.

PER SERVING 3g total fat (0.6g saturated fat); 811kJ (194 cal); 30g carbohydrate; 9g protein; 4.6g fibre

Boiled Christmas pudding

PREPARATION TIME 30 MINUTES (PLUS STANDING TIME) **COOKING TIME** 6 HOURS (PLUS COOLING TIME)
SERVES 12

You need a 60cm square of unbleached calico for the pudding cloth. If calico has not been used before, soak in cold water overnight; next day, boil it for 20 minutes then rinse in cold water.

To store pudding: after removing cloth, allow pudding to come to room temperature then wrap it in plastic wrap and seal tightly in a freezer bag or airtight container. Pudding can be stored in refrigerator up to two months or frozen up to 12 months.

When you're ready to reheat the pudding, thaw frozen pudding three days in refrigerator; remove from refrigerator 12 hours before reheating. Remove plastic wrap; tie dry unfloured cloth around pudding. Boil 2 hours, following instructions in step 5. Hang hot pudding 10 minutes. Remove cloth; stand at least 20 minutes or until skin darkens before serving. To reheat a single serving in microwave oven: cover with plastic wrap, microwave on HIGH for 30 to 60 seconds.

1 ½ cups (250g) raisins
1 ½ cups (240g) sultanas
1 cup (150g) dried currants
¾ cup (120g) mixed peel
1 teaspoon finely grated lemon rind
2 tablespoons lemon juice
2 tablespoons brandy

250g butter, softened
2 cups (440g) firmly packed brown sugar
5 eggs
1 ¼ cups (185g) plain flour
½ teaspoon ground nutmeg
½ teaspoon mixed spice
4 cups (280g) stale breadcrumbs

1 Combine fruit, rind, juice and brandy in large bowl; mix well. Cover tightly with plastic wrap; store in a cool, dark place overnight or up to a week, stirring every day.

2 Beat butter and sugar in large bowl with electric mixer only until combined. Beat in eggs, one at a time, beat only until combined between each addition. Add butter mixture to fruit mixture then sifted dry ingredients and breadcrumbs; mix well.

3 Fill boiler three-quarters full of hot water, cover; bring to a boil. Have ready calico, 2.5m of kitchen string and an extra ½ cup of plain flour. Wearing thick rubber gloves, dip pudding cloth in boiling water; boil 1 minute then remove, carefully squeeze excess water from cloth. Working quickly, spread hot cloth on bench, rub flour into centre of cloth to cover an area about 40cm in diameter, leaving flour a little thicker in centre of cloth where "skin" on the pudding needs to be thickest.

4 Place pudding mixture in centre of cloth. Gather cloth evenly around mixture, avoiding any deep pleats; then pat into round shape. Tie cloth tightly with string as close to mixture as possible. Pull ends of cloth tightly to ensure pudding is as round and firm as possible. Knot two pairs of corners together to make pudding easier to remove.

5 Lower pudding into boiling water; tie free ends of string to handles of boiler to suspend pudding. Cover with tight-fitting lid, boil for 6 hours, replenishing with boiling water as necessary to maintain level.

6 Untie pudding from handles; place wooden spoon through knotted calico loops to lift pudding from water. Do not put pudding on bench; suspend from spoon by placing over rungs of upturned stool or wedging handle in drawer. Pudding must be suspended freely. Twist ends of cloth around string to prevent them from touching pudding. If pudding has been cooked correctly, cloth will dry in patches within a few minutes; hang 10 minutes.

7 Place pudding on board; cut string, carefully peel back cloth. Turn pudding onto a plate then carefully peel cloth away completely. Stand at least 20 minutes or until skin darkens and pudding becomes firm before serving.

PER SERVING 20.6g total fat (12.2g saturated fat); 2788kJ (667 cal); 106.4g carbohydrate; 9.3g protein; 4.4g fibre

THE WOK

The Wok

Firewood has always been scarce in China so fires for cooking could only be small and had to be put to maximum use every moment they were alight. The wok evolved over the centuries as the most efficient design for cooking over flames that provided fierce but perhaps short-lived heat. The technique of stir-frying, the method used most often in wok-cooking, evolved along with the wok itself as the perfect way to cook over very high heat in a very short time.

CHOOSING A WOK

The best woks are to be found in Chinese food stores. Designer woks are usually too heavy and often too shallow. Some have flat bottoms, which do make the wok stand straight on an electric or ceramic burner without support, but this defeats the purpose of the classic design, which is to concentrate intense heat at the centre. Some have non-stick linings, which are not suitable for cooking on high heat. Electric woks don't get hot enough.

Stir-frying works better on gas burners than on electric ones because gas flames surround the wok with the intense heat needed. For cooking on gas, choose a wok made from carbon steel rather than smarter-looking stainless steel or aluminium. You can also use a carbon-steel wok for an electric stove, but most Chinese cooks prefer a cast-iron wok for stir-frying on electric cooktop because it holds the heat better than carbon-steel.

WOK ACCESSORIES

Unless your cooktop has a special wok burner (an especially fierce one shaped to hold the wok), you need a stand to stop the wok from tipping over. For electric or ceramic cooktops, get the kind that is a solid metal ring punched with about six ventilation holes. For a gas cooktop, get one that is a circular wire frame, as the gas flame might not get enough air to function inside the more solid stand.

FOR STIR-FRYING you need a chan (see Asian Utensils page 233). You could make do with an ordinary spatula or large spoon, but a chan is inexpensive and works better because its blade is the right size and its curve fits the curve of the wok.

FOR DEEP-FRYING a wok has the advantage of requiring less oil than an electric or cooktop deep-fryer, but unless you are very confident about handling it safely, you will find an ordinary deep-fryer easier and safer to use. If you do use a wok, be certain that it is quite secure on its stand before adding the oil and please read the Safety and Use sections in

The Deep-fryer on page 57. You will need mesh skimmers and tongs for removing cooked food and any burnt scraps.

FOR STEAMING buy one or more round bamboo steamers with a lid. The 25cm size is the most suitable for home use. Before using a new bamboo steamer, wash it and steam it empty for about 5 minutes. (Also see Using a Wok under Improvising a Steamer in *The Steamer*, on page 241.)

FOR BRAISING you just need a lid.

TECHNIQUES

For all wok-cooking, have the exhaust fan turned on high.

STIR-FRYING

- Have all the required ingredients prepared, measured and immediately at hand. The food should be cut into small, uniform pieces
- Heat the wok until it is very hot before adding the oil, then heat the oil until it just starts to smoke before adding any food. Just before adding the food, use the chan while tilting the wok, to distribute the oil over the side as well as the base.
- Keep the heat high throughout cooking. Cook only small amounts of food at a time, especially when working on an electric burner.
- Keep the food moving constantly so that some of it sears at the bottom of the wok, where the heat is most intense, before being instantly moved around the side of the wok to be replaced by more pieces. One hand should hold the wok while the other holds the chan, and they should work in concert, tilting and moving the wok while tossing and stirring. The entire process should take only minutes.

STEAMING The steamer is placed over about 5cm of boiling water in a wok, the food added and the lid put on. Replenish the water, if necessary, with boiling water.

- Food such as spring rolls can be placed directly on the bamboo base of the steamer, but you may prefer to line the base with baking paper to avoid the possibility of the pieces sticking. Food that releases fat or juice during cooking can be placed on a folded cloth, or a suitable leaf such as lotus or banana, or a heatproof plate, leaving enough space around the sides for the steam to circulate freely.
- Several bamboo steamers can be stacked one above the other so that an entire meal, or enough dim sims for a crowd, can be cooked at the same time.

BRAISING is usually used for tougher cuts of meat and some vegetables. The food is usually browned then simmered, covered, in a stock flavoured with seasonings and spices.

RED-BRAISING is braising in a dark liquid such as soy sauce.

CARE

SEASONING If the wok is covered with heavy machine oil, scrub with a cream cleanser and water, rinse and place over low heat to dry. Add 2 tablespoons of cooking oil and, using a pad of absorbent paper, rub this over the entire inside surface. Heat wok slowly for 10 to 15 minutes and wipe thoroughly with more absorbent paper, which will become black. Repeat several times until the paper wipes clean.

CLEANING Wash with hot water only, removing any stuck-on food with a non-metal brush. Dry with a cloth, then place over low heat to dry thoroughly. With repeated use, the wok gradually acquires a dark, slightly slick surface or patina making it increasingly non-stick.

New iron and steel woks need proper cleaning to remove their protective coating, designed to prevent them rusting in the shop. One way to do this is to fill your wok with hot water and 3 tablespoons of bicarbonate of soda; simmer about 20 minutes to soften the coating then scrub it vigorously to remove the coating.

Sri lankan crab curry

PREPARATION TIME 30 MINUTES **COOKING TIME** 55 MINUTES **SERVES** 4

1 tablespoon peanut oil
2 large brown onions (400g), chopped finely
4 cloves garlic, crushed
3cm piece fresh ginger (15g), grated
1 fresh small red thai chilli, chopped finely
4 dried curry leaves
½ teaspoon fenugreek seeds
1 teaspoon ground cinnamon
1 teaspoon ground turmeric
2 x 400ml cans coconut cream
1 tablespoon fish sauce
2 tablespoons lime juice
2 cooked mud crabs (1.6kg)
½ cup (25g) flaked coconut, toasted

1 Heat oil in wok; stir fry onion, garlic, ginger and chilli until onion softens. Add curry leaves and spices; stir-fry until fragrant. Add coconut cream, sauce and juice; simmer, uncovered, 30 minutes.

2 Meanwhile, prepare crabs. Lift tail flap of each crab then, with a peeling motion, lift off the back of each shell. Remove and discard the gills, liver and brain matter; rinse crabs well. Cut each body in half; separate the claws from bodies. You will have eight pieces.

3 Add half of the crab to wok; simmer, covered, about 10 minutes or until crab is heated through. Transfer crab to large serving bowl; cover to keep warm. Repeat with remaining crab pieces.

4 Spoon curry sauce over crab; sprinkle with coconut.

▭ **PER SERVING**. 52.5g total fat (37.2g saturated fat); 3118kJ (746 calories); 14.4g carbohydrate; 51.9g protein; 6.4g fibre

To segment an orange, first cut off the top and bottom. Stand the orange on a cutting board then, using a short sharp knife, cut off the skin with the inner white pith in long vertical strips. Use the same knife to cut each orange segment at a slight angle between its membrane then lift the segment out carefully. Squeeze out any juice from the remaining orange.

Five-spice and chilli fish with blood orange and broccolini

PREPARATION TIME 20 MINUTES (PLUS REFRIGERATION TIME) **COOKING TIME** 15 MINUTES **SERVES** 4

800g blue-eye fillet, diced into 2cm pieces

¼ cup (60ml) light soy sauce

2 teaspoons five-spice powder

2 cloves garlic, crushed

1 fresh long red chilli, sliced thinly

1 teaspoon finely grated orange rind

5 baby onions (125g), sliced thinly

2 tablespoons peanut oil

350g broccolini, trimmed, chopped coarsely

2 tablespoons water

4 green onions, sliced thickly

4 small blood oranges (720g), segmented

1 Combine fish, 2 tablespoons of the sauce, five-spice, garlic, chilli, rind and baby onion in medium bowl. Cover; refrigerate 1 hour.

2 Heat half of the oil in wok; stir-fry fish mixture, in batches, until fish is cooked.

3 Heat remaining oil in wok; stir-fry broccolini with the water and remaining sauce until just tender. Return fish mixture to wok; add green onion and orange, stir-fry until just hot.

☐ **PER SERVING** 11g total fat (1.9g saturated fat); 1400kJ (335 cal); 13.4g carbohydrate; 41.9g protein; 7.1g fibre

Use a wok lid for steaming or braising as in this recipe. It should fit inside the rim of the wok and be domed to allow for the steaming of whole chickens or ducks.

Mussels with kaffir lime and thai basil

PREPARATION TIME 30 MINUTES **COOKING TIME** 10 MINUTES **SERVES** 4

1.5kg small black mussels

1 tablespoon peanut oil

3cm piece fresh ginger (15g), sliced thinly

1 clove garlic, sliced thinly

2 shallots (50g), sliced thinly

2 fresh long red chillies, sliced thinly

½ teaspoon ground turmeric

¼ cup (60ml) kecap manis

¼ cup (60ml) fish stock

¼ cup (60ml) water

2 tablespoons lime juice

2 fresh kaffir lime leaves, shredded finely

½ cup firmly packed fresh coriander leaves

½ cup firmly packed thai basil leaves

1 Scrub mussels under cold water; remove beards.

2 Heat oil in wok; stir-fry ginger, garlic, shallot, chilli and turmeric until mixture is fragrant. Add kecap manis, stock and the water; bring to a boil. Add mussels; reduce heat, simmer, covered, about 5 minutes or until mussels open (discard any that do not).

3 Remove from heat, add remaining ingredients; toss gently to combine.

☐ **PER SERVING** 5.6g total fat (1.1g saturated fat); 405kJ (97 cal); 3.9g carbohydrate; 7.5g protein; 0.7g fibre

Garlic and chilli seafood stir-fry

PREPARATION TIME 25 MINUTES **COOKING TIME** 20 MINUTES **SERVES** 4

720g uncooked medium
king prawns

2 cleaned squid hoods (300g)

6 cleaned baby octopus (540g)

¼ cup (60ml) peanut oil

6 cloves garlic, sliced thinly

2cm piece fresh ginger (10g),
sliced thinly

2 fresh long red chillies,
sliced thinly

2 tablespoons chinese
cooking wine

1 teaspoon caster sugar

4 green onions, cut in 4cm pieces

CHILLI FRIED SHALLOTS

1 tablespoon fried shallots

1 teaspoon sea salt flakes

½ teaspoon dried chilli flakes

1 Shell and devein prawns, leaving tails intact. Cut squid down centre to open out; score inside in diagonal pattern then cut into thick strips. Quarter octopus lengthways.

2 Combine ingredients for chilli fried shallots in small bowl.

3 Heat 1 tablespoon of the oil in wok; stir-fry prawns until changed in colour, remove from wok. Heat another tablespoon of the oil in wok; stir fry squid until cooked through, remove from wok. Heat remaining oil in wok; stir-fry octopus until tender, remove from wok.

4 Stir-fry garlic, ginger and chilli until fragrant. Return seafood to wok with remaining ingredients; stir-fry until hot. Serve stir-fry sprinkled with chilli fried shallots.

◻ **PER SERVING** 16.3g total fat (2.9g saturated fat); 1593kJ (381 cal); 2.7g carbohydrate; 53.7g protein; 1.1g fibre

---

Sang choy bow

PREPARATION TIME 15 MINUTES **COOKING TIME** 15 MINUTES **SERVES** 4

2 teaspoons sesame oil

1 small brown onion (80g),
chopped finely

2 cloves garlic, crushed

2cm piece fresh ginger (10g),
grated

500g pork mince

2 tablespoons water

100g shiitake mushrooms,
chopped finely

2 tablespoons light soy sauce

2 tablespoons oyster sauce

1 tablespoon lime juice

2 cups (160g) bean sprouts

4 green onions, sliced thinly

¼ cup coarsely chopped
fresh coriander

12 large butter lettuce leaves

Spoon the filling on smaller leaves such as witlof, betel or radicchio and serve on platters as finger food with cocktails. Accompany them with other trays containing gow gee, mini-spring rolls and dim sum to give the evening a Chinese restaurant theme.

1 Heat oil in wok; cook brown onion, garlic and ginger until onion just softens. Add pork; stir-fry until pork is just changed in colour.

2 Add the water, mushrooms, sauces and juice; stir-fry until mushrooms are just tender. Remove from heat. Add sprouts, green onion and coriander; toss gently to combine.

3 Divide lettuce leaves among serving plates; spoon sang choy bow into leaves.

◻ **PER SERVING** 11.5g total fat (3.6g saturated fat); 1066kJ (255 cal); 6.5g carbohydrate; 29.3g protein; 4.1g fibre

Sweet basil chicken and snake bean stir-fry

PREPARATION TIME 20 MINUTES (PLUS REFRIGERATION TIME) **COOKING TIME** 20 MINUTES **SERVES** 4

There are more than two dozen different varieties of basil, and the one used here is Thai basil, also known as horapa, which has very small leaves and purplish stems. It has a slight licorice or aniseed taste, and is one of the basic flavours that typify Thai cuisine.

800g chicken thigh fillets, sliced thinly

¼ cup (60ml) fish sauce

1 tablespoon grated palm sugar

¼ teaspoon ground white pepper

1 tablespoon peanut oil

3 cloves garlic, sliced thinly

2cm piece fresh ginger (10g), sliced thinly

½ teaspoon dried chilli flakes

250g snake beans, cut into 5cm lengths

2 medium yellow capsicums (400g), sliced thinly

⅓ cup (80ml) chinese cooking wine

⅓ cup (80ml) lemon juice

1 tablespoon dark soy sauce

½ cup loosely packed thai basil leaves, torn

1 Combine chicken, fish sauce, sugar and pepper in large bowl. Cover; refrigerate 1 hour.

2 Heat oil in wok; stir-fry chicken mixture about 10 minutes. Add garlic, ginger, chilli, beans and capsicum; stir-fry until beans are tender.

3 Add wine, juice and soy sauce; bring to a boil. Simmer, uncovered, 2 minutes. Remove from heat; stir in basil.

PER SERVING 19.4g total fat (5.2g saturated fat); 1693kJ (405 cal); 8.8g carbohydrate; 42.4g protein; 3.3g fibre

---

Chow mein

PREPARATION TIME 30 MINUTES **COOKING TIME** 25 MINUTES **SERVES** 4

Chow mein literally translates as "fried noodles", and there are many variations of this Chinese dish. If you can't find fresh thin egg noodles, use a dried wheat variety, cooked according to the packet instructions.

We used button mushrooms here but you can use whichever variety you prefer so long as they are sliced thinly.

1 tablespoon vegetable oil

500g beef mince

1 medium brown onion (150g) chopped finely

2 cloves garlic, crushed

1 tablespoon curry powder

1 large carrot (180g), chopped finely

2 trimmed celery stalks (200g), sliced thinly

150g mushrooms, sliced thinly

1 cup (250ml) chicken stock

⅓ cup (80ml) oyster sauce

2 tablespoons light soy sauce

450g fresh thin egg noodles

½ cup (60g) frozen peas

½ cup (55g) frozen sliced green beans

½ small wombok (400g) shredded coarsely

1 Heat oil in wok; stir-fry mince, onion and garlic until mince is browned. Add curry powder; stir-fry about 1 minute or until fragrant. Add carrot, celery and mushrooms; stir-fry until vegetables soften.

2 Add stock, sauces and noodles, stir-fry gently until combined; bring to a boil. Add peas, beans and wombok; reduce heat, simmer, uncovered, tossing occasionally about 5 minutes or until vegetables are just soft.

PER SERVING 14.1g total fat (4.1g saturated fat); 2537kJ (607 cal); 71.3g carbohydrate; 43.8g protein; 8.2g fibre

Chicken larb with thai pickle

PREPARATION TIME 15 MINUTES **COOKING TIME** 15 MINUTES (PLUS STANDING TIME) **SERVES** 4

¼ cup (60ml) chicken stock

2 tablespoons lime juice

1 tablespoon fish sauce

1 tablespoon grated palm sugar

500g chicken mince

1 clove garlic, crushed

2 shallots (50g), sliced thinly

2 tablespoons finely chopped fresh coriander

1 tablespoon finely chopped fresh mint

1 fresh long red chilli, sliced thinly

1 medium iceberg lettuce, shredded coarsely

THAI PICKLE

½ cup (110g) white sugar

½ cup (125ml) white vinegar

1 tablespoon coarse cooking salt

½ cup (125ml) water

1 small red capsicum (150g), sliced thinly

½ cup (40g) bean sprouts

1 lebanese cucumber (130g), seeded, sliced thinly

1 Make thai pickle.

2 Meanwhile, place stock, juice, sauce and sugar in large saucepan; bring to a boil. Add chicken and garlic, reduce heat; simmer, stirring, about 5 minutes or until chicken is cooked through. Cool 10 minutes. Stir in shallot, herbs and chilli.

3 Serve larb with drained thai pickle on lettuce, with steamed jasmine rice, if desired.

THAI PICKLE Place sugar, vinegar, salt and the water in small saucepan; bring to a boil. Cool 5 minutes. Place capsicum, sprouts and cucumber in medium bowl; pour vinegar mixture over capsicum mixture. Cover; stand 30 minutes.

PER SERVING 10.5g total fat (3.1g saturated fat); 1438kJ (344 cal); 34.1g carbohydrate; 26.7g protein; 2.9g fibre

Palm sugar, also called jaggery, jawa or gula melaka, is made from the sap of the sugar palm tree. It is creamy to dark brown in colour and usually sold in rock-hard cakes; substitute brown sugar if it is unavailable.

Mixed mushrooms and chicken with crispy noodles

PREPARATION TIME 15 MINUTES **COOKING TIME** 20 MINUTES **SERVES** 4

1 tablespoon peanut oil

1kg chicken thigh fillets, sliced thinly

2 cloves garlic, crushed

8 green onions, chopped coarsely

200g shiitake mushrooms, chopped coarsely

100g oyster mushrooms, chopped coarsely

200g gai lan, chopped coarsely

⅓ cup (80ml) vegetarian mushroom oyster sauce

100g enoki mushrooms

50g fried noodles

1 Heat oil in wok; stir-fry chicken, in batches, until browned and cooked through.

2 Return chicken to wok with garlic and onion; stir-fry until onion just softens. Add shiitake mushrooms; stir-fry until just tender. Add oyster mushrooms, gai lan and sauce; stir-fry until vegetables are just tender.

3 Remove from heat; toss enoki mushrooms and noodles into stir-fry.

PER SERVING 24.3g total fat (6.9g saturated fat); 1977kJ (473 cal); 10.7g carbohydrate; 51.1g protein; 4.5g fibre

Chilli jam beef

PREPARATION TIME 10 MINUTES **COOKING TIME** 10 MINUTES **SERVES** 4

2 tablespoons vegetable oil

800g beef strips

1 medium brown onion (150g), chopped coarsely

2 cloves garlic, crushed

115g baby corn, halved lengthways

150g snow peas, halved crossways

½ cup (160g) chilli jam

2 teaspoons finely grated lime rind

2 tablespoons lime juice

1 Heat half of the oil in wok; cook beef, in batches, until browned.

2 Heat remaining oil in wok; cook onion and garlic, stirring, until onion softens. Add corn; cook, stirring, until corn is just tender.

3 Return beef to wok with peas, jam, rind and juice; stir-fry until sauce thickens slightly.

PER SERVING 24.7g total fat (7g saturated fat); 2057kJ (492 cal); 19.6g carbohydrate; 46.4g protein; 3g fibre

1 MIXED MUSHROOMS AND CHICKEN WITH CRISPY NOODLES **2** CHILLI JAM BEEF
3 STIR-FRIED ASIAN GREENS IN BLACK BEAN SAUCE [P 222] **4** HOKKIEN MEE [P 222]

Stir-fried asian greens in black bean sauce

PREPARATION TIME 10 MINUTES **COOKING TIME** 15 MINUTES **SERVES** 4

2 cups (400g) jasmine rice

1 tablespoon peanut oil

150g sugar snap peas, trimmed

400g gai lan, chopped coarsely

200g snake beans, trimmed, cut into 5cm lengths

2 cloves garlic, sliced thinly

1 fresh small red thai chilli, chopped finely

2 medium zucchini (240g), sliced thickly

2 tablespoons black bean sauce

1 tablespoon kecap manis

1 teaspoon sesame oil

⅓ cup (50g) roasted unsalted cashews, chopped coarsely

1 Cook rice in large saucepan of boiling water, uncovered, until just tender; drain.

2 Meanwhile, heat peanut oil in wok; stir-fry peas, gai lan stems, beans, garlic, chilli and zucchini until stems are just tender.

3 Add sauces, sesame oil, gai lan leaves and nuts; stir fry until leaves are just wilted.

4 Serve stir-fry with rice.

☐ **PER SERVING** 13.3g total fat (2.6 saturated fat); 2274kJ (544 cal); 89.5 carbohydrate; 15.4g protein; 8.8g fibre

Hokkien mee

PREPARATION TIME 15 MINUTES **COOKING TIME** 15 MINUTES **SERVES** 4

450g hokkien noodles

1 tablespoon peanut oil

600g piece beef eye fillet, sliced thinly

1 medium brown onion (150g), sliced thinly

2 cloves garlic, crushed

1 medium red capsicum (200g), sliced thinly

115g baby corn, halved lengthways

150g snow peas, trimmed, halved diagonally

2 baby buk choy (300g), chopped coarsely

¼ cup (60ml) char siu sauce

1 tablespoon dark soy sauce

¼ cup (60ml) chicken stock

1 Place noodles in medium heatproof bowl, cover with boiling water; separate with fork, drain.

2 Heat half of the oil in wok; stir-fry beef, in batches, until browned.

3 Heat remaining oil in wok; stir-fry onion, garlic and capsicum until tender.

4 Return beef to wok with noodles, corn, snow peas, buk choy, sauces and stock, stir-fry until vegetables are just tender and beef is cooked as desired.

☐ **PER SERVING** 32.3g total fat (13.8g saturated fat); 3382kJ (809 cal); 75.5g carbohydrate; 47.1g protein; 13.3g fibre

Nasi goreng

PREPARATION TIME 25 MINUTES **COOKING TIME** 15 MINUTES **SERVES** 4

16 cooked medium king prawns (720g)

1 tablespoon peanut oil

175g dried chinese sausages, sliced thickly

1 medium brown onion (150g), sliced thinly

1 medium red capsicum (200g), sliced thinly

2 fresh long red chillies, sliced thinly

2 cloves garlic, crushed

2cm piece fresh ginger (10g), grated

1 teaspoon shrimp paste

4 cups (600g) cold cooked white long-grain rice

2 tablespoons kecap manis

1 tablespoon light soy sauce

4 green onions, sliced thinly

1 tablespoon peanut oil, extra

4 eggs

1 Shell and devein prawns.

2 Heat half the oil in wok; stir-fry sausage, in batches, until browned.

3 Heat remaining oil in wok; stir-fry brown onion, capsicum, chilli, garlic, ginger and paste, until vegetables just soften. Add prawns and rice; stir-fry 2 minutes. Return sausage to wok with sauces and half of the green onion; stir-fry until combined.

4 Heat extra oil in large frying pan; fry eggs, one side only, until just set. Divide nasi goreng among serving plates, top each with an egg; sprinkle with remaining green onion.

▭ **PER SERVING** 25.7g total fat (7.4g saturated fat); 2730kJ (653 cal); 48.5g carbohydrate; 54.7g protein; 3.3g fibre

A typical Malaysian and Indonesian dish, where it makes use of the night before's leftover rice by being eaten at breakfast with a fried egg on top. Nasi goreng simply translates as "fried rice".

Chicken and thai basil fried rice

PREPARATION TIME 15 MINUTES **COOKING TIME** 10 MINUTES **SERVES** 4

¼ cup (60ml) peanut oil

1 medium brown onion (150g), chopped finely

3 cloves garlic, crushed

2 fresh long green chillies, chopped finely

1 tablespoon brown sugar

500g chicken breast fillets, chopped coarsely

2 medium red capsicums (400g), sliced thinly

200g green beans, chopped coarsely

4 cups (600g) cooked jasmine rice

2 tablespoons fish sauce

2 tablespoons light soy sauce

½ cup loosely packed thai basil leaves

1 Heat oil in wok; stir-fry onion, garlic and chilli until onion softens. Add sugar; stir-fry until dissolved. Add chicken; stir-fry until lightly browned. Add capsicum and beans; stir-fry until vegetables are just tender and chicken is cooked through.

2 Add rice and sauces; stir-fry, tossing gently to combine. Remove from heat; stir in basil.

▭ **PER SERVING** 19.7g total fat (4g saturated fat); 2445kJ (585 cal); 64g carbohydrate; 34.8g protein; 5g fibre

Always cool cooked rice as quickly as possible, as cooling it slowly at room temperature creates an ideal environment for bacteria to multiply. It will cool more quickly if removed from its hot container and spread on a tray, or rinsed in a colander under cold water.

Pad thai

PREPARATION TIME 25 MINUTES **COOKING TIME** 10 MINUTES **SERVES** 4

500g uncooked medium king prawns

¼ cup (85g) tamarind concentrate

⅓ cup (80ml) sweet chilli sauce

2 tablespoons fish sauce

⅓ cup firmly packed fresh coriander leaves

¼ cup (35g) roasted unsalted peanuts

¼ cup (20g) fried shallots

2 cups (160g) bean sprouts

4 green onions, sliced thinly

375g dried rice stick noodles

1 tablespoon peanut oil

2 cloves garlic, crushed

4cm piece fresh ginger (20g), grated

3 fresh small red thai chillies, chopped finely

250g pork mince

2 eggs, beaten lightly

1 lime, quartered

1 Shell and devein prawns, leaving tails intact.

2 Combine tamarind and sauces in small jug.

3 Combine coriander, nuts, shallots, half the sprouts and half the onion in medium bowl.

4 Place noodles in large heatproof bowl, cover with boiling water, stand until tender; drain.

5 Meanwhile, heat oil in wok; stir-fry garlic, ginger and chilli until fragrant. Add pork; stir-fry until cooked. Add prawns; stir-fry 1 minute. Add egg; stir-fry until set. Add tamarind mixture, remaining sprouts, remaining onion and noodles; stir-fry until combined.

6 Divide mixture among serving bowls; sprinkle with coriander mixture, serve with lime.

▭ **PER SERVING** 17.5g total fat (3.9g saturated fat); 1827kJ (437 cal); 30.3g carbohydrate; 36.8g protein; 4.9g fibre

Mongolian garlic lamb

PREPARATION TIME 10 MINUTES **COOKING TIME** 10 MINUTES **SERVES** 4

800g lamb backstraps, sliced thinly

3 cloves garlic, crushed

1 tablespoon cornflour

¼ cup (60ml) dark soy sauce

⅓ cup (80ml) sweet sherry

2 tablespoons peanut oil

1 tablespoon brown sugar

1 teaspoon sesame oil

8 green onions, sliced thinly

1 Combine lamb, garlic, cornflour, half of the sauce and half of the sherry in large bowl.

2 Heat peanut oil in wok; stir-fry lamb mixture, in batches, until lamb is browned.

3 Return lamb to wok with sugar, sesame oil, remaining sauce and remaining sherry; stir-fry until sauce thickens slightly. Remove from heat; serve stir-fry sprinkled with onion.

▭ **PER SERVING** 28g total fat (9.8g saturated fat); 2057kJ (492 cal); 12.4g carbohydrate; 43.1g protein; 0.8g fibre

Honey and five-spice lamb with buk choy

PREPARATION TIME 15 MINUTES **COOKING TIME** 10 MINUTES **SERVES** 4

¼ teaspoon five-spice powder

¼ cup (60ml) oyster sauce

2 tablespoons honey

2 tablespoons rice vinegar

2 cloves garlic, crushed

600g lamb fillets, sliced thinly

400g fresh thin rice noodles

1 tablespoon sesame oil

2 fresh long red chillies,
sliced thinly

2cm piece fresh ginger (10g),
cut into matchsticks

1 medium red onion (150g),
sliced thickly

500g baby buk choy,
chopped coarsely

¼ cup firmly packed fresh
coriander leaves

1 tablespoon crushed peanuts

1 Combine five-spice, sauce, honey, vinegar and garlic in small bowl.

2 Combine lamb with 1 tablespoon of the five-spice mixture in medium bowl.

3 Place noodles in large heatproof bowl; cover with boiling water. Separate noodles
with fork; drain.

4 Heat oil in wok; stir-fry lamb, in batches, until browned. Return lamb to wok, add
remaining five-spice mixture, chilli, ginger and onion; stir-fry until onion softens. Add
noodles and buk choy; stir-fry until hot.

5 Serve stir-fry sprinkled with coriander and nuts.

PER SERVING 12.2g total fat (3.3g saturated fat); 1781kJ (426 cal) 40.7g carbohydrate; 36.1g protein; 5.3g fibre

Chilli rice noodles with lamb

PREPARATION TIME 20 MINUTES **COOKING TIME** 15 MINUTES **SERVES** 4

400g fresh thin rice noodles

1 tablespoon peanut oil

500g lamb mince

3 cloves garlic, crushed

2 fresh small red thai chillies,
chopped finely

400g buk choy, sliced thinly

2 tablespoons tamari

1 tablespoon fish sauce

2 tablespoons kecap manis

4 green onions, sliced thinly

1 cup firmly packed
thai basil leaves

3 cups (240g) bean sprouts

1 Place noodles in medium heatproof bowl; cover with boiling water, separate with
fork, drain.

2 Heat oil in wok; stir-fry lamb until browned. Add garlic and chilli; stir-fry until fragrant.
Add noodles, buk choy, tamari, sauce and kecap manis; stir-fry until buk choy just wilts

3 Remove from heat; stir in onion, basil and sprouts.

PER SERVING 14.4g total fat (4.7 saturated fat); 1877kJ (449 cal); 44.5 carbohydrate; 34.3g protein; 5.3g fibre.

Although traditional soy sauce is made with nearly equal amounts of soy beans and wheat, tamari is normally made with soy beans and such a small amount of wheat that it is considered free from wheat gluten and thus suitable for coeliacs. Thick and a deep rich brown in colour, tamari possesses a unique flavour; it is actually the predecessor of shoyu (soy sauce).

Mee krob

PREPARATION TIME 35 MINUTES **COOKING TIME** 20 MINUTES **SERVES** 4

A much loved Thai dish, the name literally means "crispy noodles". It is made with rice vermicelli noodles and a sauce that is predominantly sweet but balanced with acid, usually vinegar or lime juice.

150g fresh silken firm tofu

vegetable oil, for deep-frying

125g rice vermicelli noodles

2 tablespoons peanut oil

2 eggs

1 tablespoon water

2 cloves garlic, crushed

2 fresh small red thai chillies, chopped finely

1 small green thai chilli, chopped finely

2 tablespoons grated palm sugar

2 tablespoons fish sauce

2 tablespoons tomato sauce

1 tablespoon rice wine vinegar

200g pork mince

200g cooked shelled small prawns, chopped coarsely

6 green onions, sliced thinly

¼ cup firmly packed fresh coriander leaves

1 Pat tofu all over with absorbent paper; cut into slices, then cut each slice into 1cm-wide matchsticks. Spread tofu on absorbent-paper-lined tray; cover tofu with more absorbent paper, stand at least 10 minutes.

2 Meanwhile, heat vegetable oil in wok; deep-fry vermicelli quickly, in batches, until puffed. Drain on absorbent paper.

3 Using same heated oil, deep-fry drained tofu, in batches, until lightly browned. Drain on absorbent paper

4 Heat 2 teaspoons of the peanut oil in cleaned wok; add half of the combined eggs and water, swirl wok to make thin omelette. Cook, uncovered, until egg is just set. Remove from wok; roll omelette, cut into thin strips. Heat 2 more teaspoons of the peanut oil in wok; repeat process with remaining egg mixture.

5 Combine garlic, chillies, sugar, sauces and vinegar in small bowl; pour half of the chilli mixture into small jug, reserve.

6 Combine pork in bowl with remaining half of the chilli mixture. Heat remaining peanut oil in same wok; stir-fry pork mixture about 5 minutes or until pork is cooked through. Add prawns; stir-fry 1 minute. Add tofu; stir-fry, tossing gently to combine.

7 Remove wok from heat; stir in the reserved chilli mixture and half of the onion. Add vermicelli; toss gently to combine.

8 Serve mee krob sprinkled with remaining onion, omelette strips and coriander.

▭ **PER SERVING** 20.7g total fat (4.5g saturated fat); 1509kJ (361 cal); 17.6g carbohydrate; 25.6g protein; 1.9g fibre

Beef kway teow

PREPARATION TIME 10 MINUTES **COOKING TIME** 10 MINUTES **SERVES** 4

¼ cup (60ml) oyster sauce

2 tablespoons kecap manis

2 tablespoons chinese cooking wine

1 teaspoon sambal oelek

3 cloves garlic, crushed

2cm piece fresh ginger (10g), grated

2 tablespoons peanut oil

500g beef strips

450g fresh wide rice noodles

6 green onions, cut into 2cm lengths

1 small red capsicum (150g), sliced thinly

1 small green capsicum (150g), sliced thinly

¼ cup coarsely chopped garlic chives

2 cups (160g) bean sprouts

1 Combine sauces, wine, sambal, garlic and ginger in small jug.

2 Heat half of the oil in wok; stir-fry beef, in batches, until browned lightly.

3 Place noodles in large heatproof bowl, cover with boiling water; separate with fork, drain.

4 Heat remaining oil in wok; stir-fry onion and capsicums until tender.

5 Return beef to wok with sauce mixture, noodles, chives and sprouts; stir-fry until hot.

PER SERVING 17.7g total fat (4.8g saturated fat); 2195kJ (525 cal); 53g carbohydrate; 34.4g protein; 3.8g fibre

Beef in satay sauce

PREPARATION TIME 10 MINUTES **COOKING TIME** 20 MINUTES **SERVES** 4

1 tablespoon peanut oil

750g beef strips

1 fresh long red chilli, sliced thinly

1 medium brown onion (150g), sliced thinly

1 medium red capsicum (200g), sliced thinly

½ cup (140g) peanut butter

½ cup (125ml) coconut cream

¼ cup (60ml) sweet chilli sauce

1 tablespoon light soy sauce

1 Heat half of the oil in wok; stir-fry beef, in batches, until browned and cooked through.

2 Heat remaining oil in wok; stir-fry chilli, onion and capsicum until soft; remove from wok.

3 Combine peanut butter, coconut cream and sauces in wok; bring to a boil. Return beef and onion mixture to wok; stir-fry until hot.

PER SERVING 42.2g total fat (15g saturated fat); 2629kJ (629 cal); 10.6g carbohydrate; 49.8g protein; 6.1g fibre

Ginger beef stir-fry

PREPARATION TIME 20 MINUTES **COOKING TIME** 10 MINUTES **SERVES** 4

2 tablespoons peanut oil

600g beef rump steak, sliced thinly

6cm piece fresh ginger (30g), cut into matchsticks

2 cloves garlic, crushed

120g snake beans, cut into 5cm lengths

8 green onions, sliced thinly

2 teaspoons grated palm sugar

2 teaspoons oyster sauce

1 tablespoon fish sauce

1 tablespoon dark soy sauce

½ cup loosely packed thai basil leaves

1 Heat half of the oil in wok; stir-fry beef, in batches, until browned all over.
2 Heat remaining oil in wok; stir-fry ginger and garlic until fragrant. Add beans, stir-fry until just tender.
3 Return beef to wok with onion, sugar and sauces; stir-fry until sugar dissolves and beef is cooked as desired. Remove from heat; stir in basil.

PER SERVING 19.4g total fat (6.2g saturated fat); 1421kJ (340 cal); 4.6g carbohydrate; 55.9g protein; 1.9g fibre

Always ensure the wok is hot before adding the oil and the oil is hot before adding the raw ingredients. This will ensure the food does not stick to the wok. Don't add too many ingredients at a time or else the heat level will be lowered and the food will stew instead of fast-fry.

Singapore noodles

PREPARATION TIME 30 MINUTES **COOKING TIME** 15 MINUTES **SERVES** 4

250g dried thin egg noodles

2 tablespoons peanut oil

4 eggs, beaten lightly

3 cloves garlic, crushed

3cm piece fresh ginger (15g), grated

1 medium white onion (150g), sliced thinly

2 tablespoons mild curry paste

227g can water chestnuts, drained, chopped coarsely

3 green onions, chopped diagonally

200g chinese barbecued pork, sliced

500g uncooked medium prawns, shelled, deveined

2 tablespoons light soy sauce

2 tablespoons oyster sauce

1 Cook noodles in large saucepan of boiling water, uncovered, until just tender; drain.
2 Meanwhile, heat half of the oil in wok; add half of the egg, swirl wok to make thin omelette. Cook, uncovered, until egg is just set. Remove from wok; roll omelette, cut into thin strips. Repeat with remaining egg.
3 Heat remaining oil in wok; stir-fry garlic and ginger 1 minute. Add white onion and paste; stir-fry until fragrant.
4 Add water chestnuts, green onion, pork and prawns; stir-fry until prawns are just changed in colour. Add noodles, sauces and omelette; stir-fry until sauce thickens and noodles are heated through.

PER SERVING 27.4g total fat (7.1g saturated fat); 2679kJ (641 cal); 54.6g carbohydrate; 40.7g protein; 6.2g fibre

A recipe rather than the name of a particular noodle, this stir-fry is usually made with rice vermicelli noodles and is probably no more authentically Singaporean than fortune cookies. Its origins are a bit of a mystery, but it is thought that it evolved in the Chinese restaurants of London and some of the Chinatowns in California and New York in the middle of the last century. It always contains curry powder, or paste, which gives it its identifying colour and flavour.

To stabilise the round-bottomed wok on a gas stove, use a wok ring. They come in different sizes and depths to fit a variety of burners and are sold in all Asian grocery or utensil shops.

Spiced coconut prawn stir-fry

PREPARATION TIME 10 MINUTES **COOKING TIME** 10 MINUTES **SERVES** 4

1.25kg uncooked medium king prawns

1 medium brown onion (150g), sliced thinly

2 cloves garlic, sliced thinly

2 fresh long red chillies, sliced thinly

1 teaspoon ground turmeric

2 teaspoons yellow mustard seeds

1/4 teaspoon cardamom seeds

1/2 teaspoon ground cumin

500g cauliflower, cut into florets

200g broccoli, cut into florets

140ml can coconut milk

2 tablespoons mango chutney

1 Shell and devein prawns, leaving tails intact. Combine prawns and remaining ingredients in large bowl.

2 Stir-fry ingredients in heated oiled wok until vegetables are just tender.

☐ **PER SERVING** 8.7g total fat (6.5g saturated fat); 1225kJ (293 cal); 11.9g carbohydrate; 38.5g protein; 6g fibre

Pomegranate molasses is thicker, browner and more concentrated in flavour than grenadine, the sweet, red pomegranate syrup used in cocktails. It possesses tart and fruity qualities similar to balsamic vinegar and is available at Middle Eastern food stores, specialty food shops and some delicatessens.

Sweet and sour duck with broccolini

PREPARATION TIME 25 MINUTES **COOKING TIME** 10 MINUTES **SERVES** 4

1kg chinese barbecued duck

2 small red onions (200g), cut into thin wedges

1 fresh small red thai chilli, chopped finely

250g broccolini, chopped into 3cm pieces

1/4 cup (60ml) chicken stock

1/4 cup (90g) honey

1/4 cup (60ml) rice vinegar

1 tablespoon dark soy sauce

2 teaspoons pomegranate molasses

4 green onions, cut into 3cm lengths

1 tablespoon sesame seeds, toasted

1 Quarter duck; discard bones. Slice duck meat thickly, keeping skin intact. Stir-fry duck in heated oiled wok, in batches, until skin is crisped.

2 Heat oiled wok; stir-fry red onion and chilli until onion softens slightly. Add broccolini, stock, honey, vinegar, sauce and molasses; stir-fry, until sauce thickens slightly.

3 Remove from heat; stir in duck and green onion, sprinkle with seeds.

☐ **PER SERVING** 38.9g total fat (11.3g saturated fat); 2437kJ (583 cal); 24.7g carbohydrate; 33g protein; 3.7g fibre

SPICED COCONUT PRAWN STIR-FRY

Asian utensils

If you're seriously into cooking Asian food, take a tip from the experts and tool up on their traditional equipment.

WOK

The wok's curved shape evolved over many years as the most efficient for cooking for a short time over fierce heat. It can be used for stir-frying, deep-frying, steaming or braising.

WOK DRAINING RACK

The draining rack is attached to the side of the wok, above the cooking area, for draining just-cooked food and keeping it warm while the cook finishes other components of the meal, such as rice or noodles.

WOK RING

A wok ring holds the wok steady. For electric cooktops, buy a solid-metal design with ventilation holes. For gas, buy a wire-frame design to ensure the flame gets enough air.

DEEP-FRYING BASKET

To add and remove large amounts of food when deep-frying, use a long-handled wire-mesh basket. It can also be used when stir-frying or boiling.

WOK LADLE

Used by Asian chefs to take up and add stock and other ingredients to the wok as needed. Experienced chefs can measure by eye how much they need, but home cooks should re-measure their ingredients.

WIRE MESH SKIMMER

The long-handled skimmer is used for removing cooked food from boiling water or deep-frying fat in a wok. It is also useful for skimming off burnt scraps that may float to the surface during deep-frying.

WOK LID/COVER

Flat or domed wok lids are available. The most useful shape is one with sufficient doming to accommodate a whole chicken. The lid should fit snugly just inside the rim of the wok.

COOKING CHOPSTICKS

Extra-long wooden or bamboo chopsticks are used by both Chinese and Japanese cooks for stirring noodles and turning foods in hot oil and removing them when cooked. Some are joined with string at one end.

WOK CHAN

The angle and curved edge of a chan's wide, shovel-like blade are designed to fit the curve of a wok. It is used to keep food moving and turning constantly.

DUMPLING PRESS

A dumpling press shapes a filled Chinese dumpling neatly and trims and presses the edges together all in one operation as its hinged halves are closed together.

STEAMING BASKETS

Bamboo steaming baskets, unlike metal steamers, allow the steam to dissipate so that it doesn't condense and drip. They can be stacked to cook different foods at the same time.

CLEAVER

Cleavers are, for Asian cooks, what knives are for Western ones – basic tools for all kinds of cutting, from chopping through bones to fine shredding. Like knives, they come in various blade weights and thicknesses.

Cauliflower, paneer and pea balti stir-fry

PREPARATION TIME 20 MINUTE **COOKING TIME** 25 MINUTES **SERVES** 4

1 tablespoon sesame seeds

2 tablespoons vegetable oil

6 dried curry leaves

¼ teaspoon black mustard seeds

1 teaspoon ground coriander

1 teaspoon hot chilli powder

1 teaspoon ground cumin

2 cloves garlic, crushed

400g can diced tomatoes

1kg cauliflower, cut into florets

½ cup (125ml) water

1 cup (120g) frozen peas, thawed

400g paneer cheese, cut into 2cm cubes

¼ cup coarsely chopped fresh coriander

1 Heat wok; toast sesame seeds just until fragrant. Remove from wok; reserve seeds.

2 Heat oil in wok; stir-fry leaves and mustard seeds until seeds pop.

3 Add ground coriander, chilli, cumin and garlic to wok; stir-fry until fragrant. Add undrained tomatoes; bring to a boil. Reduce heat, simmer, stirring, about 5 minutes or until mixture thickens slightly.

4 Add cauliflower and the water; stir-fry until cauliflower is almost tender. Add peas, cheese and chopped coriander; stir-fry until hot. Remove from heat; sprinkle with reserved seeds.

PER SERVING 34.9g total fat (16.7g saturated fat); 2002kJ (479 cal); 11.4g carbohydrate; 26.6g protein; 8.1g fibre

Curry leaves are commonly used as seasoning in Indian and Sri Lankan cooking, much as we use bay leaves. When fresh, they have a short shelf life and can be stored in the refrigerator for up to a week. Dried, they keep indefinitely in an airtight container. The fresher they are, the better the flavour.

Cheese is not generally produced and eaten in India with paneer the notable exception. It is available cryovac-packed in some supermarkets or loose, in brine, in Indian food shops. In a stir-fry you can substitute haloumi if paneer is not available.

Pumpkin, basil and chilli stir-fry

PREPARATION TIME 10 MINUTES **COOKING TIME** 15 MINUTES **SERVES** 4

⅓ cup (80ml) peanut oil

1 large brown onion (200g), sliced thinly

2 cloves garlic, sliced thinly

4 fresh small red thai chillies, sliced thinly

1kg pumpkin, chopped coarsely

250g sugar snap peas

1 teaspoon grated palm sugar

¼ cup (60ml) vegetable stock

2 tablespoons light soy sauce

¾ cup loosely packed opal basil leaves

4 green onions, sliced thinly

½ cup (75g) roasted unsalted peanuts

1 Heat oil in wok; cook brown onion, in batches, until browned and crisp. Drain on absorbent paper.

2 Stir-fry garlic and chilli in wok until fragrant. Add pumpkin; stir-fry until browned all over and just tender. Add peas, sugar, stock and sauce; stir-fry until sauce thickens slightly.

3 Remove from heat; stir in basil, green onion and nuts until well combined. Serve topped with fried onion.

PER SERVING 18.5g total fat (3.5g saturated fat); 1321kJ (316 cal); 22.2g carbohydrate; 12.3g protein; 6.7g fibre

Opal basil has large, purple leaves and a sweet, almost gingery flavour. Thai basil, which has an aniseed flavour, can be substituted but don't use holy basil which has an almost hot, spicy flavour similar to clove which would dramatically alter the flavour of this dish.

CAULIFLOWER, PANEER AND PEA BALTI STIR-FRY

If you do not have a blender or processor, use a mortar and pestle to make the garlic paste. The theory when using a mortar and pestle is that, by adding and processing the ingredients one at a time, each builds on the next to form a well-integrated mixture. The grinding motion releases the essential oils and flavour of each of the ingredients.

Chiang mai pork and eggplant

PREPARATION TIME 20 MINUTES **COOKING TIME** 25 MINUTES **SERVES** 4

3 fresh small red thai chillies, halved

6 cloves garlic, quartered

1 medium brown onion (150g), chopped coarsely

500g baby eggplants

¼ cup (60ml) peanut oil

700g pork leg steaks, sliced thinly

1 tablespoon fish sauce

1 tablespoon light soy sauce

1 tablespoon grated palm sugar

4 purple shallots (100g), sliced thinly

150g snake beans, cut into 5cm lengths

1 cup loosely packed thai basil leaves

1 Blend or process chilli, garlic and onion until mixture forms a paste.

2 Quarter eggplants lengthways; slice each piece into 5cm lengths. Cook eggplant in large saucepan of boiling water until just tender; drain. Pat dry with absorbent paper.

3 Heat 2 tablespoons of the oil in wok; stir-fry eggplant, in batches, until browned lightly. Drain on absorbent paper.

4 Heat remaining oil in wok; stir-fry pork, in batches, until browned and cooked as desired.

5 Stir-fry garlic paste in wok about 3 minutes or until fragrant and browned lightly. Add sauces and sugar; stir-fry until sugar dissolves.

6 Add shallot and beans; stir-fry until beans are just tender. Return eggplant and pork to wok; stir-fry, tossing gently, until hot. Remove from heat; toss basil into stir-fry.

▭ **PER SERVING** 19.3g total fat (4.1g saturated fat); 1676kJ (401 cal); 10.7g carbohydrate; 43.5g protein; 5.7g fibre

A new, well cleaned wok needs "seasoning" before use to prepare the metal to accept food without making it stick. Heat the wok until very hot then carefully wipe the entire inner surface with a soft cloth or bamboo brush drenched in peanut oil. Tilt the wok from side to side to ensure the entire surface is in contact with heat so that oil is burned into it. Allow the wok to cool completely then rinse it in warm water and repeat the heating and oiling process. This process will turn the wok's surface from silver to shiny black.

Sweet and sour pork

PREPARATION TIME 10 MINUTES (PLUS REFRIGERATION TIME) **COOKING TIME** 15 MINUTES **SERVES** 4

500g pork fillet, sliced thinly

½ teaspoon five-spice powder

2 teaspoons chinese cooking wine

1 tablespoon light soy sauce

1 tablespoon sesame oil

1 large red capsicum (350g), chopped coarsely

1 medium green capsicum (200g), chopped coarsely

1 medium red onion (170g), sliced thinly

1 small pineapple (900g), chopped coarsely

SWEET AND SOUR SAUCE

¼ cup (60ml) water

2 tablespoons caster sugar

2 tablespoons white wine vinegar

2 tablespoons light soy sauce

2 tablespoons tomato sauce

1 Combine pork, five-spice, wine and sauce in medium bowl; refrigerate 15 minutes.

2 Heat half of the oil in wok; stir-fry capsicums and onion until onion softens. Remove from wok.

3 Heat remaining oil in wok; stir-fry pork, in batches, until browned and just cooked through.

4 Meanwhile, combine ingredients for sweet and sour sauce in small jug.

5 Add sweet and sour sauce to wok; bring to a boil. Return capsicum mixture and pork to wok; stir-fry until hot.

6 Top stir-fry with pineapple and, if desired, serve with steamed rice and chinese broccoli.

☐ **PER SERVING** 15g total fat (4g saturated fat); 1580kJ (378 cal); 26.9g carbohydrate; 31g protein; 4.4g fibre

Stir-fried pork, buk choy and water chestnuts

PREPARATION TIME 15 MINUTES (PLUS REFRIGERATION TIME) **COOKING TIME** 15 MINUTES **SERVES** 4

¼ cup (60ml) light soy sauce

2 tablespoons oyster sauce

1 tablespoon honey

1 tablespoon chinese cooking wine

1 teaspoon five-spice powder

½ teaspoon sesame oil

1 clove garlic, crushed

600g pork fillets, sliced thinly

2 tablespoons peanut oil

600g baby buk choy, chopped coarsely

227g can water chestnuts, rinsed, drained, sliced thickly

½ cup (75g) roasted unsalted cashews

2 fresh long green chillies, sliced thinly

1 tablespoon water

If you don't have a bottle of chinese cooking wine in your pantry, you can use a tablespoon of sake (japanese rice wine), mirin or even dry sherry in this recipe.

Marinating overnight ensures that the marinade flavours fully penetrate the ingredients of the dish.

1 Combine 2 tablespoons of the soy sauce, 1 tablespoon of the oyster sauce, honey, wine, five-spice, sesame oil, garlic and pork in large bowl. Cover; refrigerate 3 hours or overnight.

2 Stir-fry pork in oiled wok, in batches, until browned.

3 Heat peanut oil in wok; stir-fry buk choy, water chestnuts, nuts and chilli until tender.

4 Return pork to wok with the water and remaining soy and oyster sauces; stir-fry until hot.

☐ **PER SERVING** 23g total fat (4.5g saturated fat); 1827kJ (437 cal); 15.8g carbohydrate; 39.1g protein; 4.1g fibre

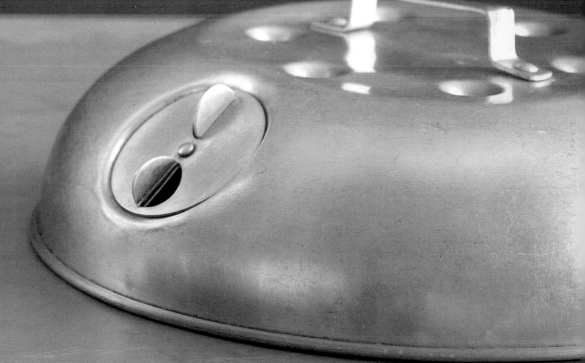

THE STEAMER

The Steamer

You may be attracted to the idea of steaming because it is healthy, because it makes for a simple clean-up, or because it's quicker and easier to serve the vegetables and other foods since you don't have to drain them. All these points are true, but the main reason to cook with steam is for the pure flavours and wonderful textures that will reward you; from fresh-tasting carrots and pearly new potatoes to fragrant fish and chicken cooked to juicy perfection – not to mention the host of Asian snacks to be found in Chinese and South-East Asian food stores or the frozen-food cabinet of your supermarket, needing only steaming to become great party food.

TYPES OF STEAMER

The principle of steaming is that the food sits in a perforated container above boiling water (or other liquid) and cooks in the steam, which is forced to circulate under pressure because it is prevented from escaping by a well-fitting lid.

COLLAPSIBLE METAL STEAMERS consist of perforated, overlapping stainless-steel petals, arranged in a circle, that unfold and expand to fit your pot. They are attached to a perforated base with short legs to hold the food above the boiling water, and there is a central post with a handle for lifting out the whole apparatus when the food is cooked. The only point you need to watch is that the food doesn't fall off as you lift it out as the petals open wide until they are almost flat.

PIERCED METAL STEAMERS look like thin saucepans with holes in the bottom. They have recessed bases to fit into the top of a saucepan of a matching size. The saucepan lid becomes the lid of the steamer. Some of these steamers have saucepan-style handles, some don't and have to be lifted out using potholders. They can be stacked so that different dishes can be cooked together.

BAMBOO STEAMERS are made primarily to use with a wok, but their recessed bases will fit into the top of any saucepan of a matching size. They come in sizes from tiny to giant and have matching lids, which are sold separately. Some cooks think that food from bamboo steamers tastes better than food from metal steamers. Bamboo steamers can be stacked so that different dishes can be cooked together. They are attractive and can be taken straight to the table for serving. If you plan to do this, line the base with vine or other leaves for an appealing presentation.

IMPROVISING A STEAMER

Even in the absence of any of the above equipment, you can improvise as follows:

USING A WOK Place food on baking paper or a heatproof plate on a wire rack set over a little boiling water in a wok. The sloping sides of the wok will hold the rack above the water. Cover with the wok's own or another well-fitting lid, or improvise with a double layer of foil, greased underneath and tucked closely round the sides of the wok.

USING A FRYING PAN OR SAUCEPAN Place food on baking paper or a heatproof plate on a wire rack set over a little boiling water in a deep frying pan, wide saucepan, flameproof casserole or baking dish. If the rack is not high enough to clear the water, set it on upturned ramekins or cups. Cover with the vessel's own lid or another well-fitting lid, or you can improvise with foil as described above under Using a Wok.

USING A CASSEROLE DISH OR BOILER Place food in a metal colander, which has a base, standing in a little boiling water in a larger flameproof casserole dish or boiler. The bottom of the rounded colander must be clear of the water. Cover with the vessel's own lid, or you can improvise with foil as described above under Using a Wok.

STEAMING IN THE OVEN Wrap food in foil lined with wet baking paper, or in wet leaves (vine, banana or cabbage); place on a rack set on an oven tray in a preheated moderate oven.

STEAMING TECHNIQUES

While you can place food directly on the base of the steamer, placing it on baking paper will prevent it from sticking, and make it easy to lift out fragile food, such as fish, without breaking it. Food that releases fat or juice during cooking can be placed on a folded cloth, or a sturdy leaf such as banana, or a heatproof plate, leaving enough space around the sides for the steam to circulate freely.

Always have the water boiling and plenty of steam flowing before adding the food. Make sure the lid is not too tight-fitting and will allow a little steam to escape, or the pressure could build up dangerously. Take care when opening any steamer as steam can inflict severe burns. Open at a safe distance from your face, and protect your hands and arms.

VEGETABLES Steamed vegetables retain more of their vitamin content than boiled vegetables because their water-soluble vitamins are not released into the cooking water. Similarly, steaming retains flavour components that would be lost in the cooking water with boiled vegetables. There is, however, an important exception to steam's excellent performance with vegetables: it turns green vegetables a dull olive colour. To minimise this colour change, steam green vegetables only very briefly.

SEAFOOD Slash whole fish two or three times in the thickest part on each side before cooking to allow the steam to penetrate. Flavourings such as ginger, lemon, herbs or onion can be placed in the cavity of a whole fish or sprinkled over other seafood before steaming.

CHICKEN Whole chicken or chicken pieces may be steamed with added flavourings, as described above for seafood.

GRAIN Couscous, the fine semolina staple of North African cooking, is steamed over the pot of meat and vegetables for the meal. Cooked rice and other grains may be reheated by steaming.

These are just as good served at room temperature as they are served hot, and they make perfect finger-food for a cocktail party or for inclusion on a large selection of mezze dishes.

Stuffed vine leaves with yogurt dip

PREPARATION TIME 25 MINUTES (PLUS STANDING TIME) **COOKING TIME** 15 MINUTES **SERVES** 6

1 cup (160g) burghul

1 cup (250ml) boiling water

1 tablespoon olive oil

1 green onion, chopped finely

¼ cup (35g) toasted slivered almonds

2 tablespoons finely chopped raisins

2 tablespoons finely chopped fresh mint

1 tablespoon finely chopped fresh coriander

1 tablespoon finely chopped fresh flat-leaf parsley

2 teaspoons ground cinnamon

2 teaspoons finely grated lemon rind

1 tablespoon lemon juice

40 grapevine leaves in brine (200g), rinsed, drained

YOGURT DIP

¾ cup (200g) yogurt

1 tablespoon finely chopped fresh mint

1 tablespoon finely chopped fresh coriander

1 teaspoon lemon juice

5cm piece fresh ginger (25g), grated

1 Combine burghul and the boiling water in medium heatproof bowl. Cover; stand 5 minutes. Stir in oil, onion, nuts, raisins, herbs, cinnamon, rind and juice.

2 Line base of large bamboo steamer with about 10 vine leaves.

3 Place one of the remaining leaves, vein-side up, on board; place 1 tablespoon of the burghul mixture in centre of leaf. Fold in two opposing sides; roll to enclose filling. Repeat with remaining leaves and burghul mixture.

4 Place rolls, in single layer, on leaves in steamer over wok of boiling water; steam, covered, about 15 minutes or until rolls are heated through.

5 Meanwhile, combine ingredients for yogurt dip in small bowl.

6 Serve rolls with yogurt dip.

☐ **PER SERVING** 8g total fat (1.5g saturated fat); 836kJ (200 cal); 21.3g carbohydrate; 7g protein; 7g fibre

Don't crowd the gow gees in your steamer. Cook them in separate batches, or, if necessary, simultaneously in two different steamers.

Steam gow gees within an hour of making them; if the pastry becomes wet from the filling, it becomes gooey and unpalatable. They can be frozen, uncooked, in single layers in freezer wrap, for up to 3 months. Do not defrost them before steaming, but allow about 2 minutes extra for each batch.

Chicken gow gees

PREPARATION TIME 30 MINUTES (PLUS REFRIGERATION TIME) **COOKING TIME** 10 MINUTES **SERVES** 4

400g lean chicken mince

2 green onions, chopped finely

2 cloves garlic, crushed

2cm piece fresh ginger (10g), grated

¼ teaspoon five-spice powder

½ cup (50g) packaged breadcrumbs

1 tablespoon hoisin sauce

2 tablespoons coarsely chopped fresh coriander

1 tablespoon coarsely chopped thai basil

1 egg

24 gow gee wrappers

SWEET CHILLI DIPPING SAUCE

⅓ cup (80ml) sweet chilli sauce

¼ cup (60ml) red wine vinegar

¼ cup coarsely chopped fresh coriander

1 Combine chicken, onion, garlic, ginger, five-spice, breadcrumbs, sauce, herbs and egg in large bowl. Roll level tablespoons of the mixture into balls; place balls on tray. Cover; refrigerate 30 minutes.

2 Meanwhile, make sweet chilli dipping sauce.

3 Brush one wrapper with water; place one chicken ball in centre of wrapper. Fold wrapper over to completely enclose chicken ball. Pleat edge of wrapper along join; repeat process with remaining wrappers and chicken balls.

4 Place gow gees, in single layer, about 1cm apart in baking-paper-lined steamer set over wok of boiling water; steam, covered, about 8 minutes or until gow gees are cooked through.

SWEET CHILLI DIPPING SAUCE Place ingredients in screw-top jar; shake well.

▭ **PER SERVING** 11.2g total fat (3.2g saturated); 1547kJ (370 cal); 42.2g carbohydrate; 23.2g protein; 2.6g fibre

If you are steaming several layers of food, place the one having the longest cooking time on the bottom layer.

Hot and sour fish in banana leaves

PREPARATION TIME 25 MINUTES (PLUS REFRIGERATION TIME) **COOKING TIME** 20 MINUTES **SERVES** 4

4 medium whole bream (1.8kg)

1 large banana leaf

4 fresh small red thai chillies, sliced thinly

2 fresh kaffir lime leaves, shredded finely

2 green onions, sliced thinly

¼ cup loosely packed fresh coriander leaves

¼ cup loosely packed thai basil leaves

2 x 10cm sticks fresh lemon grass (40g)

LIME AND SWEET CHILLI DRESSING

¼ cup (60ml) sweet chilli sauce

2 tablespoons fish sauce

2 tablespoons lime juice

2 tablespoons peanut oil

1 clove garlic, crushed

1 teaspoon grated fresh ginger

1 Make lime and sweet chilli dressing.

2 Score fish both sides through thickest part of flesh; place on large tray, drizzle with half of the lime and sweet chilli dressing. Cover; refrigerate 1 hour.

3 Meanwhile, trim banana leaf into four 30cm squares. Using tongs, dip one square at a time into wok of boiling water; remove immediately. Rinse under cold water; pat dry with absorbent paper.

4 Place leaves on work surface. Combine chilli, lime leaves, onion, coriander and basil in small bowl. Halve lemon grass sticks lengthways, then halve crossways; you will have eight pieces.

5 Place two pieces cut lemon grass on each leaf; place one fish on each. Top fish with equal amounts of the herb mixture then fold opposite corners of the leaf to enclose centre part of fish; secure each parcel with cotton string.

6 Place parcels, in single layer, in large bamboo steamer set over wok of boiling water; steam, covered, in two batches, about 15 minutes or until fish is cooked through.

7 Serve fish still in parcel, sprinkled with remaining dressing.

LIME AND SWEET CHILLI DRESSING Place ingredients in screw-top jar; shake well.

☐ **PER SERVING** 16.4g total fat (4.1g saturated); 1150kJ (275 cal); 4.1g carbohydrate; 27.3g protein; 1.3g fibre

Garlic and lemon thyme chicken

PREPARATION TIME 10 MINUTES **COOKING TIME** 12 MINUTES **SERVES** 4

8 outside cos lettuce leaves

4 small single skinless chicken breast fillets (720g), trimmed

2 cloves garlic, crushed

3 teaspoons chopped fresh lemon thyme

20 baby carrots, trimmed

1 bunch asparagus, trimmed, halved

150g sugar snap peas, trimmed

1 Remove thick centre rib from the lettuce leaves. Overlap two lettuce leaves, place one piece of chicken on leaves. Repeat with remaining lettuce and chicken. Sprinkle chicken with garlic and thyme. Roll up chicken in lettuce.

2 Place chicken and carrots in baking-paper-lined bamboo steamer set over wok of boiling water; steam, covered, 10 minutes. Add asparagus and peas; cover, steam for further 3 minutes or until chicken is cooked through and vegetables are just tender.

3 Serve chicken and vegetables with lemon wedges, if desired.

☐ **PER SERVING** 10.2g total fat (3.1g saturated); 1221kJ (292 cal); 8.3g carbohydrate; 41.5g protein; 5.4g fibre

Bamboo steamers are inexpensive so buy two or more to have on hand for vegetable, pastry and meat dishes: different foods' flavours will permeate the wood and affect the taste of the next lot of food you cook in the steamer.

As a rule, when steaming, the water should never touch the food. However, some vegetables, such as asparagus, have a tough or stringy base or shoot that needs to be submerged.

While a tight-fitting lid will keep most of the water in the pan or wok, if you're steaming for long periods of time, it's not a bad idea to check occasionally, that the water has not totally evaporated.

Salmon with burnt orange sauce

PREPARATION TIME 10 MINUTES   **COOKING TIME** 25 MINUTES   **SERVES** 4

½ cup (110g) caster sugar

⅓ cup (80ml) water

1 teaspoon finely grated orange rind

¼ cup (60ml) orange juice

1 tablespoon olive oil

1 tablespoon rice wine vinegar

4 x 200g salmon fillets

350g watercress, trimmed

1   Combine sugar and the water in small saucepan; stir, without boiling, until sugar dissolves, bring to a boil. Reduce heat, simmer, uncovered, without stirring, until mixture is a light caramel colour.

2   Remove pan from heat; allow bubbles to subside. Carefully stir in rind and juice; return pan to low heat. Stir until any pieces of caramel melt. Remove pan from heat; stir in oil and vinegar.

3   Meanwhile, place fish in large bamboo steamer set over wok of boiling water; steam, covered, 15 minutes. Serve fish with watercress, drizzled with sauce.

◻ **PER SERVING** 19.1g total fat (3.8g saturated fat); 1940kJ (464 cal); 29.4g carbohydrate; 41.6g protein; 3.4g fibre

Almost every vegetable can be steamed, and this is an excellent way to cook them because they retain their shape, flavour, colour and goodness. Trim and prepare the vegetables as you would normally then layer them evenly in the steamer basket. Food can still be overcooked in a steamer though, especially green vegetables, which will lose their bright colour and look dull and dry, so keep an eye on them.

Asian greens with char siu sauce

PREPARATION TIME 5 MINUTES   **COOKING TIME** 10 MINUTES   **SERVES** 4

1 fresh long red chilli, sliced thinly

350g broccolini, trimmed

150g snow peas, trimmed

2 baby buk choy (300g), halved

2 tablespoons char siu sauce

2 teaspoons sesame oil

1 tablespoon peanut oil

1 tablespoon toasted sesame seeds

1   Layer chilli, broccolini, snow peas and buk choy in baking-paper-lined bamboo steamer over wok of boiling water; steam, covered, 5 minutes or until vegetables are just tender.

2   Place vegetables, sauce and sesame oil in large bowl.

3   Heat peanut oil in small saucepan until hot; pour over vegetable mixture then toss to combine. Serve sprinkled with seeds.

◻ **PER SERVING** 9.5g total fat (1.4g saturated); 635kJ (152 cal); 7g carbohydrate; 6.6g protein; 5.6g fibre

1 SALMON WITH BURNT ORANGE SAUCE **2** ASIAN GREENS WITH CHAR SIU SAUCE
3 VINE-LEAF-WRAPPED SWORDFISH WITH TOMATO-OLIVE SALSA [P 248] **4** COCONUT FISH [P 248]

1
2
3   4

If you are unable to find fresh grapevine leaves, buy those that come cryovac-packed in brine; they can be found in most Greek or Middle-Eastern food stores. Be sure to rinse them in cold water and dry with absorbent paper before using.

Vine-leaf-wrapped swordfish with tomato-olive salsa

PREPARATION TIME 20 MINUTES **COOKING TIME** 20 MINUTES **SERVES** 4

16 large fresh grapevine leaves

4 x 200g swordfish steaks

TOMATO-OLIVE SALSA

3 cloves garlic, crushed

1 cup loosely packed fresh flat-leaf parsley leaves

¼ cup coarsely chopped fresh chives

3 small tomatoes (270g), chopped coarsely

½ cup (75g) seeded black olives, quartered lengthways

2 tablespoons capers, drained, rinsed

2 tablespoons lemon juice

2 teaspoons olive oil

1 Trim vine leaves; using metal tongs, dip, one at a time, in medium saucepan of boiling salted water. Rinse immediately under cold water; drain on absorbent paper.

2 Overlap four vine leaves slightly to form a rectangle large enough to wrap each piece of fish; fold leaves around fish to enclose completely. Place fish parcels in large steamer fitted over wok of boiling water; steam, covered, about 15 minutes or until cooked as desired.

3 Meanwhile, make tomato-olive salsa.

4 Place fish parcels in serving bowls; pull back vine leaves to uncover fish, top with salsa.

TOMATO-OLIVE SALSA Combine ingredients in medium bowl.

☐ **PER SERVING** 7.1g total fat (1.8g saturated); 1124kJ (269 cal); 6.8g carbohydrate; 42.6g protein; 2.9g fibre

---

Using fresh coconut for dishes like this will enhance the flavour immeasurably, and you'll find that many greengrocers and supermarkets now sell plastic bags of shredded or grated fresh coconut in their Asian ingredient section. Another option is to buy a halved coconut at the greengrocer or Asian food store, remove and shred the flesh then freeze what you don't use here in the compartments of an ice-cube tray. After they're frozen, save them in an air-tight plastic bag in your freezer for future use.

Coconut fish

PREPARATION TIME 10 MINUTES **COOKING TIME** 25 MINUTES **SERVES** 4

2 cups coarsely chopped fresh coriander

2 fresh small red thai chillies, chopped coarsely

2 cloves garlic, quartered

4 cm piece fresh ginger (20g), peeled, chopped coarsely

1 tablespoon cumin seeds

⅔ cup (50g) shredded coconut

1 tablespoon peanut oil

4 medium whole snapper (1.8kg)

1 Blend or process coriander, chilli, garlic, ginger and seeds until chopped finely.

2 Combine coriander mixture with coconut and oil in small bowl; mix well.

3 Score each fish three times both sides; place fish on large sheet of foil. Press coconut mixture onto fish; fold foil over to enclose fish.

4 Place fish in large bamboo steamer; steam fish, covered, over wok of boiling water about 25 minutes or until cooked through. Serve with lemon wedges, steamed long-grain white rice and stir-fried buk choy, if desired.

☐ **PER SERVING** 15.5g total fat (9.6g saturated); 1241kJ (297 cal); 1.9g carbohydrate; 36.3g protein; 2.9g fibre

Fish with chilli and ginger

PREPARATION TIME 10 MINUTES **COOKING TIME** 10 MINUTES **SERVES** 4

10cm piece fresh ginger (50g), cut into 4cm strips

2 green onions, cut into 4cm strips

2 baby buk choy (300g), quartered

4 x 200g snapper cutlets

¼ cup (60ml) light soy sauce

1 teaspoon sesame oil

1 long fresh red chilli, sliced

1 cup loosely packed fresh coriander leaves

1 Cut ginger and onions into long thin strips.

2 Place buk choy on large heatproof plate inside large bamboo steamer; top with fish. Sprinkle ginger and onion over fish, then spoon over sauce and oil. Place steamer over wok of boiling water; steam fish, covered, about 5 minutes or until just cooked through.

3 Serve fish topped with chilli and coriander.

▭ **PER SERVING** 4.9g total fat (1.3g saturated); 823kJ (187 cal); 2.3g carbohydrate; 34.8g protein; 1.8g fibre

If your steamer isn't large enough in circumference to accommodate a dinner plate, sit your biggest colander over a deep stockpot or pasta boiler. Just make certain that all the holes of the colander fall below the lip of the pan or too much steam will escape.

Bream with black bean and chilli sauce

PREPARATION TIME 5 MINUTES **COOKING TIME** 8 MINUTES **SERVES** 4

500g gai lan, cut into 8cm lengths

4 x 200g bream fillets

1 tablespoon black bean garlic sauce

1 tablespoon water

5cm piece fresh ginger (25g), sliced thinly

1 tablespoon peanut oil

2 fresh small red thai chillies, sliced thinly

1 Place gai lan stems in single layer on large heatproof plate inside large bamboo steamer; top with fish. Place steamer over wok of boiling water; steam, covered, 5 minutes.

2 Add gai lan leaves, pour over combined sauce and the water; sprinkle with ginger. Steam, covered, 3 minutes or until fish is cooked through and vegetables are tender.

3 Meanwhile, heat oil and chilli in small saucepan.

4 Serve fish on gai lan; drizzle with hot oil mixture just before serving with steamed rice or noodles, if desired.

▭ **PER SERVING** 8.1g total fat (2.1g saturated); 1133kJ (271 cal); 3g carbohydrate; 43.9g protein; 5g fibre

Choy sum or buk choy can be used instead of the gai lan in this recipe.

Steaming methods

Easy and healthy, steaming is an age-old technique allowing foods' inherent quality to shine, pure and simple.

COLLAPSIBLE METAL STEAMER
Perforated, overlapping stainless steel petals expand to fit the pot. Make sure the water does not touch the base, and the food doesn't drop as the petals flatten when lifted out.

BAMBOO STEAMER
Made to sit over boiling water in a wok, but also easily fitted into the top of a saucepan. Bamboo steamers can be stacked – put longest cooking foods in the bottom one, and quicker-cooking foods near the top.

DIY
For a do-it-yourself steamer (see also page 241), place food on a plate sitting on an upturned ramekin in a deep pan. The vessel's own lid becomes the lid of the steamer.

CLAY POT
Clay-pot cooking is an ancient method of steaming/baking food in an unglazed clay pot that has been soaked in water so it steams as it heats. Food cooked in a clay pot is deliciously concentrated in flavour.

PUDDING STEAMER
A steamed pudding cooks in a covered steamer or basin standing in boiling water in a closed saucepan. The pudding cooks in the steam from its own moisture content, the water providing steady, moderate, non-drying heat.

ELECTRIC RICE COOKER
Most Asian cooks, and many Western ones, swear by the automatic rice cooker. Some cooks find its results a little clumpy (the way Asians like rice for easy eating with chopsticks) and prefer the classic cooktop method.

EN PAPILLOTE

Food enclosed in an *en papillote* (paper) case (see page 548) placed on a plate in a steamer or microwave oven, or on a tray in the oven will steam or bake. Diners open their own packages.

STEAMING IN A WRAPPER

Wrap food in damp banana, cabbage, vine or other leaves to cook in a steamer, microwave oven, closed barbecue or lidded oven dish. The leaves make an attractive presentation and add their own subtle flavour.

PRESSURE COOKER

A pressure cooker steams under high pressure, cooking food in about a third of the normal time. You can use it for meats, grains, pulses (dried beans and peas) and many other foods.

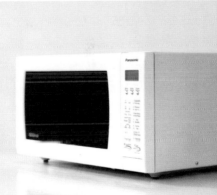

ASIAN STEAMBOAT

A steamboat, also called a Mongolian hot pot and not strictly speaking a method of cooking by steaming, is a chimneyed firepot with a moat of simmering stock into which diners dip finely sliced food to cook.

SAUCEPAN STEAMER INSERT

A steamer insert for a pan or pot comes as a set, complete with lid. The base of the insert is peppered with small holes so the simmering water beneath steams the food in the insert.

MICROWAVE OVEN

Microwave cooking, in which electromagnetic waves penetrate food, cause its moisture content to heat rapidly, steaming it from the inside. Enclosed foods in a microwave oven generate outer steam as well, cooking like conventionally steamed food.

Scallops take very little time to cook. They are very delicate, and their flavour and texture will suffer if overcooked – they become chewy if cooked too long. When the flesh is opaque and the centre still slightly translucent, the scallops are ready to eat.

Wash and keep the scallop shells from this recipe so that you can use them in the future for a range of fish dishes.

Scallops with sugar snap pea salad

PREPARATION TIME 20 MINUTES **COOKING TIME** 5 MINUTES **SERVES** 4

250g sugar snap peas, trimmed

20 scallops on the half shell (800g), roe removed

100g cherry tomatoes, halved

1 medium lebanese cucumber (130g), seeded, sliced thinly

½ cup loosely packed fresh mint leaves

BALSAMIC DRESSING

1 teaspoon finely grated lemon rind

2 tablespoons lemon juice

1 clove garlic, crushed

1 tablespoon olive oil

2 teaspoons balsamic vinegar

LEMON DRESSING

1 tablespoon finely grated lemon rind

¼ cup (60ml) lemon juice

1 clove garlic, crushed

1 tablespoon olive oil

1 Make balsamic dressing. Make lemon dressing.

2 Boil, steam or microwave peas until just tender; drain.

3 Remove scallops from shell; reserve shells. Place scallops, in single layer, in large steamer fitted over large saucepan of boiling water; steam scallops, covered, 2 minutes or until cooked as desired.

4 Meanwhile, rinse and dry scallop shells.

5 Place peas in medium bowl with tomato, cucumber, mint and balsamic dressing; toss gently to combine.

6 Return scallops to shells; drizzle with lemon dressing. Serve scallops with salad.

BALSAMIC DRESSING Place ingredients in screw-top jar; shake well.
LEMON DRESSING Place ingredients in screw-top jar; shake well.

PER SERVING 9.9g total fat (1.4g saturated); 652kJ (156 cal); 5.5g carbohydrate; 10g protein; 2.9g fibre

Try lining the bamboo steamer with fresh pandanus leaves instead of oiling it. Pandanus, also called screwpine, is available fresh and frozen from Asian grocers, and adds a sensational aromatic flavour to many of our favourite South-East Asian foods. Discard the leaves once the purses are ready to eat.

Pork and prawn chinese purses

PREPARATION TIME 30 MINUTES **COOKING TIME** 10 MINUTES **MAKES** 24

200g uncooked medium king prawns

400g pork mince

1 teaspoon sichuan peppercorns, toasted, crushed

1 egg white

1 teaspoon sesame oil

1 clove garlic, crushed

2cm piece fresh ginger (10g), grated

3 green onions, chopped finely

24 gow gee wrappers

DIPPING SAUCE

¼ cup (60ml) light soy sauce

1 tablespoon water

1 tablespoon lime juice

1 fresh small red thai chilli, sliced thinly

1 Shell and devein prawns; chop prawn meat coarsely.

2 Combine prawn in medium bowl with pork, pepper, egg white, oil, garlic, ginger and onion.

3 Place one wrapper on your hand; place 1 level tablespoon of the pork mixture into centre of wrapper. Gently cup your hand and gather sides of wrapper to form pleats, leaving top open. Repeat with remaining wrappers and pork mixture.

4 Place purses, without touching, in oiled bamboo steamer. Steam, covered, in batches, over wok of boiling water about 10 minutes or until cooked through.

5 Meanwhile, combine ingredients for dipping sauce in small bowl.

6 Serve purses with dipping sauce.

▭ **PER PURSE** 1.5g total fat (0.5g saturated fat); 226kJ (54 cal); 4.7g carbohydrate; 4.5g protein; 0.1g fibre

Tea-smoked salmon with broccolini and jasmine rice

PREPARATION TIME 15 MINUTES (PLUS REFRIGERATION TIME) **COOKING TIME** 20 MINUTES **SERVES** 4

½ cup (125ml) water

½ cup (125ml) mirin

1 tablespoon brown sugar

1 tablespoon sea salt

4 x 200g salmon fillets, with skin

½ cup (110g) caster sugar

1 cup (65g) green tea leaves

2½ cups (500g) jasmine rice

350g broccolini, trimmed, halved

1 lemon, cut into 8 wedges

Chinese kitchens have tea-smoked food in woks for centuries. The tea and sugar combine to add both flavour and sweetness to the fish while the rice helps disperse the heat evenly. When the wok is covered, the contents will start to smoke dynamically. The fish is cooked when the flesh is firm to the touch but not dried out; the skin may be too pungent with smoked-tea residue so you might prefer to discard it.

1 Combine the water, mirin, brown sugar and salt in medium bowl; stir to dissolve sugar. Add fish; stir to coat in mirin mixture. Cover; refrigerate 1 hour.

2 Meanwhile, line large wok with three layers of foil. Place caster sugar, tea and 1 cup of the jasmine rice on foil in wok; stir gently to combine.

3 Cook remaining rice in large saucepan of boiling water, uncovered, until just tender; drain. Cover to keep warm.

4 Meanwhile, discard marinade; place fish in large bamboo steamer. Turn heat to high under wok; when tea mixture starts to smoke, sit steamer over tea mixture. Cover steamer tightly; wind two dampened tea towels in gap between steamer and wok to contain smoke. Cook fish 10 minutes.

5 Boil, steam or microwave broccolini until just tender; drain.

6 Serve fish with rice, broccolini and lemon wedges.

▭ **PER SERVING** 15.1g total fat (3.3g saturated); 3733kJ (893 cal); 131g carbohydrate; 50.2g protein; 3.9g fibre

Spinach-wrapped chicken with anchovy and tomato

PREPARATION TIME 15 MINUTES **COOKING TIME** 20 MINUTES **SERVES** 4

24 large trimmed spinach leaves (150g)

4 anchovy fillets, drained, chopped finely

2 tablespoons baby capers, drained, rinsed

1 tablespoon olive oil

¼ cup (35g) drained semi-dried tomatoes, chopped coarsely

½ teaspoon cracked black pepper

2 cloves garlic, crushed

4 x 200g chicken breast fillets

LEMON DRESSING

2 tablespoons olive oil

1 teaspoon finely grated lemon rind

2 tablespoons lemon juice

1 clove garlic, crushed

1 Bring large saucepan of water to a boil; add spinach, one leaf at a time, drain immediately. Place in large bowl of iced water, stand 3 minutes. Drain spinach thoroughly on absorbent paper.

2 Combine anchovy, capers, oil, tomato, pepper and garlic in small bowl.

3 Divide spinach into four portions; spread leaves flat on board, slightly overlapping and large enough to enclose chicken. Place one chicken fillet on each spinach portion. Top chicken with anchovy mixture. Wrap spinach around chicken to completely enclose.

4 Place chicken parcels in baking-paper-lined bamboo steamer set over wok of boiling water; steam, covered, about 20 minutes or until chicken is cooked through.

5 Meanwhile, whisk ingredients for lemon dressing in small bowl. Serve chicken with dressing.

PER SERVING 26.1g total fat (5.6g saturated fat); 1894kJ (453 cal); 4.4g carbohydrate; 49.2g protein; 2.5g fibre

Wrap the chicken in large parboiled cabbage, silver beet, lettuce or fresh grapevine leaves, if you prefer any of them over spinach. This dish incorporates mostly Mediterranean flavours so use a wrapper that follows the theme. Corn husks, banana and lotus leaves also make good wrappers but keep them for Hispanic or Asian dishes.

Spinach dumplings with fresh tomato and herb sauce

PREPARATION TIME 30 MINUTES (PLUS STANDING TIME) **COOKING TIME** 20 MINUTES **SERVES** 4

Almost like quenelle or gnocchi made with spinach, these dumplings can also be served, without the tomato sauce, drizzled with a burnt sage butter as the perfect accompaniment for veal scaloppine.

2 x 250g packets frozen spinach, thawed

200g ricotta cheese

1 clove garlic, crushed

1 egg white

1 tablespoon plain flour

¼ cup (20g) finely grated parmesan cheese

1½ cups (105g) stale breadcrumbs

¼ teaspoon ground nutmeg

1 tablespoon finely chopped fresh chives

2 tablespoons finely grated parmesan cheese, extra

FRESH TOMATO AND HERB SAUCE

½ cup (125ml) dry white wine

4 medium tomatoes (600g), chopped finely

2 tablespoons finely chopped fresh flat-leaf parsley

1 teaspoon white sugar

1 Squeeze excess liquid from spinach. Combine spinach in large bowl with ricotta, garlic, egg white, flour, parmesan, breadcrumbs, nutmeg and chives; roll level tablespoons of the mixture into balls. Place balls, in single layer, about 2cm apart in baking-paper-lined bamboo steamer fitted over wok of boiling water. Steam, covered, about 10 minutes or until dumplings are hot.

2 Meanwhile, make fresh tomato and herb sauce.

3 Serve dumplings with sauce and extra parmesan.

FRESH TOMATO AND HERB SAUCE Bring wine to a boil in medium saucepan. Reduce heat, simmer, uncovered, until reduced by half. Add tomato; return to a boil. Boil, uncovered, about 10 minutes or until thickened slightly. Stir in parsley and sugar.

☐ **PER SERVING** 10.2g total fat (5.5g saturated fat); 1233kJ (295 cal); 25.7g carbohydrate; 19.4g protein; 9.3g fibre

---

Ocean trout in baby buk choy parcels

PREPARATION TIME 20 MINUTES (PLUS STANDING TIME) **COOKING TIME** 15 MINUTES **SERVES** 4

Wombok leaves can be substituted for the buk choy if you prefer. They may have to be submerged in boiling water for an instant to make them supple enough to wrap around the fish without tearing or breaking. Tie the parcels with cotton kitchen string to ensure the filling stays completely enclosed within the leaves while the parcels are steaming.

4 dried shiitake mushrooms

2 green onions, chopped finely

3cm piece fresh ginger (15g), grated

5cm stick fresh lemon grass (10g), chopped finely

2 cloves garlic, crushed

1 teaspoon sambal oelek

2 tablespoons light soy sauce

4 ocean trout fillets (600g)

4 large baby buk choy (600g)

1½ cups (300g) jasmine rice

GINGER DRESSING

2cm piece fresh ginger (10g), grated

2 tablespoons rice wine vinegar

1 tablespoon vegetable oil

1 teaspoon sesame oil

2 tablespoons mirin

1 tablespoon light soy sauce

1 Place mushrooms in small heatproof bowl, cover with boiling water, stand 20 minutes; drain. Discard stems; chop caps finely.

2 Meanwhile, place ingredients for ginger dressing in screw-top jar; shake well.

3 Combine mushroom, onion, ginger, lemon grass, garlic, sambal and sauce in small bowl; divide mushroom mixture over flesh side of fish fillets. Carefully insert fillets, mushroom-side up, inside leaves of each bok choy; wrap leaves around fillets then tie parcels with kitchen string.

4 Place parcels in large steamer fitted over wok of boiling water; steam, covered, about 10 minutes or until fish is cooked as desired.

5 Meanwhile, cook rice in large saucepan of boiling water, uncovered, until rice is just tender; drain. Divide rice among plates; top with parcels, drizzle with dressing.

▭ **PER SERVING** 12.3g total fat (2.2g saturated fat); 2195kJ (525 cal); 64.6g carbohydrate; 37.1g protein; 3.6g fibre

Veal and tomato dolmades

PREPARATION TIME 40 MINUTES (PLUS COOLING TIME) **COOKING TIME** 35 MINUTES **MAKES** 36

200g packet grapevine leaves in brine

1 tablespoon olive oil

1 large red onion (300g), chopped finely

4 cloves garlic, crushed

500g veal mince

400g can crushed tomatoes

¼ cup (30g) seeded green olives, chopped finely

¼ cup (35g) drained sun-dried tomatoes, chopped finely

1 tablespoon tomato paste

1 Place leaves in large heatproof bowl, cover with boiling water; stand 10 minutes, drain. Rinse under cold water; drain. Pat 36 similar-size, well-shaped leaves dry with absorbent paper; reserve remaining leaves for another use.

2 Heat oil in large frying pan; cook onion and garlic, stirring, until onion softens. Add mince; cook, stirring, until just changed in colour.

3 Add remaining ingredients; bring to a boil. Reduce heat, simmer, uncovered, 5 minutes or until liquid is almost evaporated; cool 15 minutes.

4 Place leaves, vein-side up, on board. Spoon 1 tablespoon of the filling near stem in centre of 1 leaf; roll once toward tip of leaf to cover filling then fold in two sides. Continue rolling toward tip of leaf; place, seam-side down, in baking-paper-lined steamer. Repeat with remaining leaves and filling mixture, placing rolls about 1cm apart in steamer.

5 Place steamer over wok of boiling water. Steam, covered, about 15 minutes or until dolmades are heated through.

6 Serve dolmades hot or cold, drizzled with lemon juice, if desired.

▭ **PER DOLMADE** 1.6g total fat (0.5g saturated); 146kJ (35 cal); 1.4g carbohydrate; 3.6g protein; 0.7g fibre

Stuffed grapevine leaves – called dolmades or dolmas – are delicious staples found in every Middle Eastern cuisine but we've created a rather Italian variation on the classic with absolutely no lessening of the delectability of the dish. Leaves preserved in brine are available in Greek and Lebanese grocery stores so keep a package in a cool, dark place in your kitchen and you'll always have them on hand. These leaves still need to be covered with hot water or they will be too salty and strong-flavoured. Line the steamer with any leftover vine leaves instead of baking paper if you have enough to cover the base completely.

Don't sit the steamer over the pan until the water is at a rolling boil. This helps minimise cooking time, thereby maximising the retention of nutrients and flavour. Make certain the pan or wok, steamer and lid are totally secure-fitting to prevent the steam escaping, which can slow cooking time and cause uneven cooking.

Citrus-ginger bream

PREPARATION TIME 20 MINUTES **COOKING TIME** 15 MINUTES **SERVES** 4

1 medium lemon (140g)

2 medium oranges (480g)

2 cloves garlic, crushed

2cm piece fresh ginger (10g), grated

4 x 250g whole bream

2 cups (400g) jasmine rice

⅓ cup loosely packed fresh basil leaves, torn

1 Using vegetable peeler, peel rind carefully from lemon and one orange; cut rind into thin strips. Squeeze juice of both oranges and lemon into large bowl. Stir in rind, garlic and ginger. Score fish both sides; add to bowl, coat in marinade.

2 Fold 80cm-long piece of foil in half crossways; place one fish on foil, spoon a quarter of the marinade onto fish. Fold foil over fish to tightly enclose. Repeat process with remaining fish and marinade.

3 Place fish parcels in large steamer fitted over wok of boiling water; steam, covered, about 15 minutes or until cooked as desired.

4 Meanwhile, cook rice in large saucepan of boiling water, uncovered, until tender; drain. Divide rice among serving plates; top with fish, drizzle with cooking juices, sprinkle with basil.

☐ **PER SERVING** 7.4g total fat (2.5g saturated); 2341kJ (560 cal); 86.4g carbohydrate; 33.7g protein; 3.4g fibre

The perfect end to a Thai meal, these custards can be served with thinly sliced mango cheeks instead of the papaya mixture if you prefer.

Coconut custards with papaya

PREPARATION TIME 15 MINUTES **COOKING TIME** 15 MINUTES **SERVES** 4

½ cup (135g) grated palm sugar

⅓ cup (80ml) water

3 eggs

⅔ cup (160ml) coconut cream

2 tablespoons milk

1 teaspoon vanilla extract

1 large red papaya (580g)

2 teaspoons grated lime rind

1 tablespoon lime juice

1 tablespoon grated palm sugar, extra

1 Stir sugar and the water in small saucepan over low heat until sugar is dissolved.

2 Whisk eggs, coconut cream and milk until combined. Gradually whisk hot sugar syrup into egg mixture, then stir in extract. Strain custard into heatproof jug.

3 Pour custard into four ⅔-cup (160ml) heatproof dishes. Place dishes in bamboo steamer over wok of boiling water, cover dishes with a sheet of baking paper. Steam, covered, about 15 minutes or until just set.

4 Meanwhile, peel and seed papaya; cut into quarters. Combine papaya in medium bowl with rind, juice and extra sugar.

5 Cool custards 5 minutes; serve with papaya mixture.

☐ **PER SERVING** 13.5g total fat (9.1g saturated fat); 1492kJ (357 cal); 54.4g carbohydrate; 7.3g protein; 3g fibre

CITRUS-GINGER BREAM

THE BARBECUE

The Barbecue

Barbecuing often means entertaining – a pleasantly informal and relaxed way of entertaining – although it does call for some forethought to ensure the cook doesn't get so frazzled that it stops being fun. The clue to enjoying your role as a barbecue cook, whether for family or friends, is to limit the amount of food you barbecue to just as much as you can handle comfortably, and have the rest of the meal ready to appear from the kitchen.

TYPES OF BARBECUE

OPEN FIRE The most basic form of barbecue is simply an open fire with a grill or metal plate, supported on bricks, over it. It is perfect for the beach or the bush (always checking, of course, whether you're allowed to light fires there).

TROLLEY A barbecue fitted with wheels. Most modern trolley barbecues are fitted with hoods so they can be used open or closed. When closed, they can be used for roasting large items; the hood is usually fitted with an external temperature gauge.

KETTLE BARBECUES are meant to be used in the closed position for all cooking, and usually have temperature gauges. Both the kettle barbecue and any trolley barbecue that can be used closed cook food by two different methods: direct, where the food sits on a grill or grill plate situated directly over the heat source; or indirect, where the heat source is shoved to the outside edges of the barbecue and the grill is situated over the area free of heat. Indirect cooking is best for roasting large pieces of meat, such as a leg of lamb or pork.

HIBACHI AND OTHER PORTABLE BARBECUES Hibachi are open, portable, cast-iron barbecues in an ancient Japanese design, just large enough to take food for two or three people. They use solid fuel, such as charcoal or heat beads. Modern portable barbecues come in many models powered by solid fuel, gas or electricity. Most have hoods and many are sold as indoor/outdoor barbecues.

ELECTRIC BARBECUES come in portable models, as described above, and also in full-size models, although these tend to be at the smaller end of the scale. Most have a hood.

FUELS

GAS Liquid petroleum gas (LPG) is clean and efficient. It is available at service stations or large hardware stores, and there are also home-delivery services. It is good policy to keep a spare bottle in case the gas runs out while you're still cooking. Safety is an important issue when using a gas bottle. Never try to repair or alter any part of the bottle.

BRIQUETTES AND HEAT BEADS are made from compressed charcoal and other materials that may include sawdust or makeweights, such as clay. These products vary considerably in quality: look on the bag, where the list of ingredients should include about 70 per cent carbon and no more than about 5 per cent un-named "other ingredients". Follow directions on the bag for use.

CHARCOAL Most serious cooks prefer real charcoal, which is made from hardwood, for the flavour it gives the food. It is about 90 per cent carbon and usually makes a hotter fire than briquettes. It is not as widely available as briquettes, but can be bought from selected service stations and large hardware stores. Charcoal can throw sparks, so don't wear floaty or highly-flammable clothing.

WOOD is a wonderful fuel, especially for its smell, but you must use the right kind. Don't burn stained or treated wood, such as old fencing or decking, any wood that has been treated for termites, or painted wood, all of which can give off unpleasant or hazardous fumes. In particular, don't burn any of the numerous poisonous woods whose fumes can make you sick or even kill you; the best known of these are oleander and poinsettia, but there are many others. If in doubt, buy your wood from a supplier of firewood for heating. Allow time for it to burn down to grey and red embers before starting to cook. Wood also can throw sparks, so don't wear floaty or highly-flammable clothing.

A NOTE ON FIRE-STARTERS Commercial fire-starters work efficiently but smell awful, and it is hard to prevent the lingering smell from tainting the food.

BARBECUING TECHNIQUES

Brush or spray food with oil or melted butter just before cooking. Also oil the grill, unless the manufacturer's instructions direct otherwise. Baste food frequently with more butter or oil (or with a marinade or sauce according to the recipe) while it is cooking.

STEAKS, CHOPS AND CHICKEN PIECES Cook the first side (skin-side down for chicken pieces) until browned to your liking, then turn only once and cook until done as you want it (see Grilling Techniques in *The Grill Pan*, page 101). Don't worry if the second side isn't as brown as the first – serve it best side up. Rest meat and chicken in the warmth next to the barbecue for 5 minutes before serving.

SAUSAGES Cook at a moderate heat, moving to side of grill or plate if over-browning before they are cooked through. An easier way is to poach the sausages ahead of time, then brown them quickly on the barbecue. Use a hinged wire grill for a lot of sausages so you can turn or move them all at once.

ROASTS Follow the manufacturer's directions for roasting on your barbecue.

FISH Give fish your undivided attention while it is cooking and remove as soon as flesh turns white (or pink for salmon or trout). Whole fish is cooked when a skewer will slide easily into the thickest part. For whole fish, slash sides two or three times before cooking and use a greased fish-shaped hinged wire grill, if possible, to help turn it without breaking. Otherwise, lift carefully with two spatulas, one at each end.

CARE

Clean barbecue according to manufacturer's directions, or clean while hot – but turned off – with hot water and a wire brush; dry with a cloth and leave for an hour or two in the open air to dry thoroughly. Spray metal parts with oil and wipe off surplus before covering.

Pork neck with five-spice star-anise glaze

PREPARATION TIME 15 MINUTES **COOKING TIME** 1 HOUR 20 MINUTES (PLUS STANDING TIME) **SERVES** 6

1kg piece pork neck
1 clove garlic, sliced thinly
4cm piece fresh ginger (20g), sliced thinly
2 x 100g packets baby asian greens

FIVE-SPICE STAR-ANISE GLAZE
1¼ cups (310ml) water
1 cup (220g) firmly packed brown sugar
3 fresh long red chillies, chopped finely
1 star anise
1 teaspoon five-spice powder
⅓ cup (80ml) light soy sauce
¼ cup (60ml) rice vinegar

1 Make five-spice star-anise glaze. Reserve 1 cup (250ml) of glaze.
2 Make several shallow cuts in pork. Press garlic and ginger into cuts; brush ¼ cup (60ml) of the remaining glaze over pork.
3 Cook pork on heated oiled barbecue grill plate, covered, over low heat, 30 minutes. Turn pork; cook, covered, 30 minutes. Increase heat to high; cook, uncovered, 5 minutes, turning and brushing with remaining glaze constantly. Remove pork from heat. Cover; stand 15 minutes, slice thickly.
4 Meanwhile, place reserved glaze in small saucepan; simmer about 5 minutes or until thickened slightly. Cool.
5 Combine greens with reserved glaze in medium bowl; serve with pork.

FIVE-SPICE STAR-ANISE GLAZE Combine the water and sugar in medium saucepan; simmer about 10 minutes or until glaze thickens slightly. Remove from heat; stir in remaining ingredients.

▭ **PER SERVING** 13.4g total fat (4.5g saturated fat); 1714kJ (410 cal); 36.4g carbohydrate; 36.5g protein; 0.6g fibre

Naan, one of a variety of ready-to-eat Indian breads, simply requires a brief warming in your microwave oven or on top of a heated barbecue grill; it is readily available in supermarkets, delicatessens and specialty food shops. Distinctive because it is both leavened and baked at high heat in an oven (traditionally, against the inside wall of a heated tandoor, an Indian clay-brick oven), naan is thick and doughy, and usually served with other tandoor-cooked foods like chicken or fish.

Chicken tikka with herbed yogurt

PREPARATION TIME 20 MINUTES (PLUS REFRIGERATION TIME) **COOKING TIME** 20 MINUTES **SERVES** 4

800g chicken thigh fillets, cut into strips

4cm piece fresh ginger (20g), grated

3 cloves garlic, crushed

2 tablespoons lemon juice

3 teaspoons ground cumin

2 teaspoons ground coriander

½ teaspoon garam masala

½ teaspoon chilli powder

½ teaspoon salt

2 tablespoons tomato paste

1 ½ cups (420g) yogurt

⅓ cup coarsely chopped fresh coriander

⅓ cup coarsely chopped fresh mint

8 fresh long red chillies

1 Combine chicken, ginger, garlic, juice, 2 teaspoons of the cumin, coriander, garam masala, chilli powder, salt, paste and ⅓ cup of the yogurt in large bowl. Cover; refrigerate overnight. Thread the chicken onto skewers.

2 Cook remaining cumin in small heated frying pan until fragrant. Combine cumin in small bowl with remaining yogurt and herbs.

3 Cook fresh chillies on heated oiled barbecue grill plate until browned and just tender. Cook chicken on same grill plate until browned and cooked through.

4 Serve chicken, chillies and herbed yogurt with warmed naan bread and lemon wedges, if desired.

☐ **PER SERVING** 16.4g total fat (5.6g saturated fat); 1522kJ (364 cal); 10.3g carbohydrate; 43.3g protein; 1.5g fibre

Sear the steaks over high heat and turn them only once, just as if you were pan-frying, to avoid toughening the meat. Resting the steaks, covered, allows the juices to settle before cutting into the meat.

Char-grilled T-bones with potato pancakes

PREPARATION TIME 20 MINUTES **COOKING TIME** 30 MINUTES **SERVES** 4

3 fresh long red chillies, chopped finely

2cm piece fresh ginger (10g), grated

2 cloves garlic, crushed

2 tablespoons olive oil

4 x 300g beef T-bone steaks

4 trimmed corn cobs (1kg)

4 medium potatoes (800g), grated coarsely

50g butter

1 Combine chilli, ginger, garlic and oil in large bowl; add steaks, turn to coat in mixture. Cook steaks on heated oiled barbecue grill plate. Cover; stand 5 minutes.

2 Meanwhile, cook corn, turning occasionally, on same grill plate until tender.

3 To make potato pancakes, squeeze excess moisture from potato; divide into four portions. Heat half of the butter on heated oiled barbecue flat plate; cook potato portions, flattening with spatula, until browned both sides.

4 Spread corn with remaining butter; serve with steaks and potato pancakes.

☐ **PER SERVING** 33.1g total fat (13g saturated fat); 3118kJ (746 cal); 53.4g carbohydrate; 52.8g protein; 11.4g fibre

Harissa spatchcock with rocket and cucumber salad

PREPARATION TIME 25 MINUTES **COOKING TIME** 20 MINUTES **SERVES** 4

4 x 500g spatchcocks

1 tablespoon harissa paste

1 teaspoon finely grated
lemon rind

¼ cup (60ml) olive oil

2 teaspoons cumin seeds

1 teaspoon ground coriander

¾ cup (200g) yogurt

1 clove garlic, crushed

2 lebanese cucumbers (260g)

150g baby rocket leaves

2 tablespoons lemon juice

1 Rinse spatchcocks under cold water; pat dry inside and out with absorbent paper.
Using kitchen scissors, cut along each side of each spatchcock's backbone; discard
backbones. Place spatchcocks, skin-side up, on board; using heel of hand, press down
on breastbones to flatten spatchcock.

2 Combine paste, rind and 1 tablespoon of the oil in large bowl, add spatchcock; rub
mixture all over spatchcocks.

3 Cook spatchcocks on heated oiled barbecue grill plate, uncovered, 10 minutes. Cook,
covered, over low heat, about 10 minutes or until spatchcocks are cooked through.

4 Meanwhile, dry-fry cumin and coriander in small frying pan, stirring, until fragrant.
Cool 10 minutes. Combine spices with yogurt and garlic in small bowl.

5 Using vegetable peeler, slice cucumber lengthways into ribbons. Combine cucumber
in large bowl with rocket, juice and remaining oil.

6 Serve spatchcocks with yogurt and salad.

☐ **PER SERVING** 55.2g total fat (15.4g saturated fat); 3043kJ (728 cal); 4.9g carbohydrate; 52.8g protein; 1.5g fibre

The word spatchcock is used both to describe a small chicken (poussin), no more than 6 weeks old and weighing a maximum 500g, and a cooking technique, where a small chicken is split open, then flattened and barbecued or grilled.

Kipflers with aïoli

PREPARATION TIME 20 MINUTES **COOKING TIME** 20 MINUTES **SERVES** 4

1kg kipfler potatoes

AIOLI

2 egg yolks

2 tablespoons lemon juice

2 cloves garlic, crushed

¾ cup (180ml) olive oil

1 tablespoon hot water

1 Cut potatoes in half lengthways. Cook on heated oiled barbecue grill plate until tender.

2 Meanwhile, make aïoli.

3 Serve potatoes with aïoli.

AIOLI Blend or process egg yolks, juice and garlic until combined. With motor operating,
gradually add oil; process until thick. Stir in the water.

☐ **PER SERVING** 44.1g total fat (6.6g saturated fat); 2366kJ (566 cal); 33.2g carbohydrate; 7.7g protein; 5.3g fibre

We cut these potatoes in half before cooking them on the barbecue but you can wrap them well them in foil, whole, and cook them either on the barbecue grill or inside the barbecue, alongside the outer edge of the heat.

A commercial blend of black, white, green and pink peppercorns, coriander seeds and allspice, called pepper medley, is sold in grinders in all supermarkets. You can use it for this recipe if you prefer.

Roasted peppered pork

PREPARATION TIME 10 MINUTES **COOKING TIME** 1 HOUR 30 MINUTES (PLUS STANDING TIME) **SERVES** 6

1 tablespoon coarse cooking salt

1 tablespoon green peppercorns, crushed

1 tablespoon pink peppercorns, crushed

1 tablespoon white peppercorns, crushed

1 tablespoon black peppercorns, crushed

1kg piece pork shoulder

cooking-oil spray

1 Combine salt and peppercorns in small bowl.

2 Score rind of pork, coat pork with oil-spray. Rub pepper mixture over pork.

3 Place pork in disposable aluminium baking dish; cook in barbecue, covered, using indirect heat, about 1 ½ hours or until cooked.

4 Cover pork; stand 10 minutes, slice thickly.

☐ **PER SERVING** 19.2g total fat (7.3g saturated fat); 1371kJ (328 cal); 0g carbohydrate; 39g protein; 0g fibre

---

Never chop mint too long before you want to use it because it tends to blacken quickly. Mint and fresh pineapple blended together with fresh ice makes a perfect summer drink when sipped out on the patio with lunch made on the barbecue.

Lobster tails with lime butter and pineapple mint salsa

PREPARATION TIME 20 MINUTES **COOKING TIME** 10 MINUTES **SERVES** 4

100g butter

1 teaspoon finely grated lime rind

1 fresh small red thai chilli, chopped finely

2cm piece fresh ginger (10g), grated

4 uncooked small lobster tails in shells (660g)

PINEAPPLE MINT SALSA

1 small pineapple (900g), chopped coarsely

2 tablespoons lime juice

½ cup finely chopped fresh mint

1 fresh long red chilli, chopped finely

1 Combine ingredients for pineapple mint salsa in medium bowl.

2 Melt butter in small saucepan; cook rind, chilli and ginger, stirring, 2 minutes.

3 Using scissors, cut soft shell from underneath lobster tails to expose meat; cut lobster tails in half lengthways. Brush with butter mixture; cook, in batches, on heated oiled barbecue grill plate until cooked through.

4 Serve lobster tails with salsa.

☐ **PER SERVING** 21.9g total fat (13.8g saturated fat); 1538kJ (368 cal); 10.1g carbohydrate; 31.1g protein; 3.1g fibre

---

1 ROASTED PEPPERED PORK **2** LOBSTER TAILS WITH LIME BUTTER AND PINEAPPLE MINT SALSA
3 ITALIAN-STYLE CHICKEN BURGERS [P 270] **4** PIRI PIRI CHICKEN THIGH FILLETS [P 270]

1

2

3

4

Preheat the grill plate of your barbecue for at least 10 minutes before cooking, and oil it lightly before heating. Never spray oil on an already hot barbecue.

A grill plate is a wonderful tool: here, it's used to cook the burgers, toast the bread and crisp the focaccia, making cleaning-up practically a thing of the past.

Italian-style chicken burgers

PREPARATION TIME 20 MINUTES **COOKING TIME** 30 MINUTES **SERVES** 4

500g chicken mince

¼ cup (35g) sun-dried tomatoes, drained, chopped finely

1 tablespoon finely chopped fresh basil

1 egg

1 cup (70g) stale breadcrumbs

3 cloves garlic, crushed

4 slices pancetta (60g)

1 square loaf focaccia (440g)

½ cup (150g) mayonnaise

40g baby rocket leaves

120g bocconcini cheese, sliced thickly

1 Combine chicken, tomato, basil, egg, breadcrumbs and about a third of the garlic in large bowl; shape mixture into four patties.

2 Cook patties on heated oiled barbecue grill plate about 30 minutes or until cooked.

3 Cook pancetta on same grill plate until crisp. Drain.

4 Quarter focaccia; slice each square in half horizontally. Toast cut sides on same grill plate.

5 Combine mayonnaise with remaining garlic, spread on focaccia bases; sandwich rocket, patties, pancetta and cheese between focaccia quarters.

▭ **PER SERVING** 34.9g total fat (9.3g saturated fat); 3357kJ (803 cal); 71.5g carbohydrate; 47.6g protein; 5.6g fibre

This world-famous barbecue sauce is thought to have originated when Portuguese traders took the seeds of the small hot piri-piri ("pepper-pepper" in Swahili) chilli from their African colonies of Angola and Mozambique back to Europe.

If you can get them, buy dried pequin chillies for piri-piri sauce and grind them without removing the seeds. The pequin, thai and birds-eye chilli are very similar in appearance and in heat quotient (HOT!). A great way to enliven barbecued chicken, this sauce hits the mark with plenty of heat and flavour.

Piri piri chicken thigh fillets

PREPARATION TIME 10 MINUTES **COOKING TIME** 15 MINUTES **SERVES** 4

4 fresh long red chillies, chopped coarsely

1 teaspoon dried chilli flakes

2 cloves garlic, quartered

1 teaspoon sea salt

2 tablespoons olive oil

1 tablespoon cider vinegar

2 teaspoons brown sugar

8 x 125g chicken thigh fillets

1 Using mortar and pestle, grind fresh chilli, chilli flakes, garlic and salt to make piri piri paste.

2 Combine paste with oil, vinegar, sugar and chicken in medium bowl. Cook chicken mixture on heated oiled barbecue grill plate until cooked through.

3 Serve chicken with lime wedges, if desired.

▭ **PER SERVING** 27.2g total fat (6.8g saturated fat); 1822kJ (436 cal); 1.8g carbohydrate; 46.6g protein; 0.3g fibre

Grilled beef and vegetable burgers

PREPARATION TIME 15 MINUTES **COOKING TIME** 10 MINUTES **SERVES** 4

600g beef mince

2 teaspoons ground cumin

2 cloves garlic, crushed

¼ cup finely chopped
fresh coriander

4 baby eggplants (240g),
sliced thickly

3 medium egg tomatoes (225g),
sliced thickly

1 medium brown onion (150g),
sliced thinly

8 large slices sourdough bread

½ cup (130g) hummus

2 teaspoons lemon juice

1 teaspoon olive oil

100g rocket, trimmed

1 Combine mince, cumin, garlic and coriander in medium bowl. Using your hands, shape mixture into four patties to fit the size of the bread slices.

2 Cook patties, eggplant, tomatoes and onion on heated oiled barbecue grill plate until patties and vegetables are browned and cooked through.

3 Meanwhile, cook bread on heated oiled barbecue flat plate until browned on both sides. Transfer to a plate.

4 Combine hummus, juice and oil in small bowl.

5 Layer four toasted bread slices with rocket, eggplant, patties, tomatoes, hummus and onion. Top with remaining bread slices before serving.

PER SERVING 21.2g total fat (6.2g saturated fat); 2913kJ (697 cal); 71.6g carbohydrate; 48.1g protein; 12.6g fibre

You can make kofta out of the mince mixture by kneading it extremely well with slightly wet hands then moulding it like a thick cigar around fairly long, sturdy skewers [wooden butchers skewers or long metal ones are better than bamboo]. Grill directly on an oiled barbecue, turning to brown all over; wrap a piece of Lebanese bread around the cooked kofta, using it like an oven mitt to pull the meat off the skewer.

Chilli-rubbed hickory-smoked steaks

PREPARATION TIME 10 MINUTES (PLUS REFRIGERATION AND STANDING TIME)
COOKING TIME 10 MINUTES **SERVES** 4

1 tablespoon finely grated
lemon rind

2 teaspoons chilli powder

2 teaspoons dried thyme

1 teaspoon sweet smoked paprika

2 tablespoons olive oil

2 cloves garlic, crushed

4 x 200g beef rib-eye steaks

100g hickory smoking chips

2 cups (500ml) water

1 Combine rind, chilli powder, thyme, paprika, oil and garlic in large bowl with steaks. Cover; refrigerate 3 hours or overnight.

2 Soak chips in the water in medium bowl; stand 3 hours or overnight.

3 Place drained chips in smoke box alongside steaks on barbecue. Cook steaks, covered, using indirect heat, about 10 minutes or until cooked.

PER SERVING 27.3g total fat (8.9g saturated fat); 1726kJ (413 cal); 0.4g carbohydrate; 41.1g protein; 0.7g fibre

Wood chips add a fabulous dimension to barbecued food. Hickory is one of the most intensely flavoured and sweet woods to use; also available are mesquite (delicately spicy) and cherry (provides an acidic fruit nuance). These woods are available packed in bags of either chips or chunks.

Chilli prawns with mango salad

PREPARATION TIME 25 MINUTES **COOKING TIME** 10 MINUTES **SERVES** 4

1kg uncooked large king prawns

½ teaspoon ground turmeric

1 teaspoon chilli powder

2 teaspoons sweet paprika

2 cloves garlic, crushed

MANGO SALAD

2 large mangoes (1.2kg), chopped coarsely

1 small red onion (100g), sliced thinly

1 fresh long red chilli, sliced thinly

1½ cups (120g) bean sprouts

½ cup coarsely chopped fresh coriander

2 teaspoons fish sauce

2 teaspoons grated palm sugar

2 tablespoons lime juice

1 tablespoon peanut oil

1 Place ingredients for mango salad in medium bowl; toss gently to combine.

2 Shell and devein prawns, leaving tails intact. Combine prawns in large bowl with turmeric, chilli, paprika and garlic.

3 Cook prawn mixture, in batches, on heated oiled barbecue grill plate until browned lightly. Serve immediately with salad.

☐ **PER SERVING** 5.9g total fat (1g saturated fat); 1229kJ (294 cal); 30.3g carbohydrate; 29.5g protein; 5.1g fibre

Spanish-style seafood

PREPARATION TIME 20 MINUTES **COOKING TIME** 15 MINUTES **SERVES** 4

500g uncooked medium prawns

650g whiting fillets

½ cup (125ml) olive oil

2 cloves garlic, crushed

1 teaspoon sweet paprika

2 teaspoons finely grated lemon rind

2 large zucchini (300g), sliced lengthways

1 large red capsicum (350g), quartered

GARLICKY MAYONAISE

½ cup (150g) mayonnaise

1 clove garlic, crushed

1 tablespoon lemon juice

This is a perfect example of how an entire meal can be cooked on the barbecue. And to add even more zing to the mayonnaise, roast a few unpeeled garlic cloves, wrapped in oiled foil, on the barbecue until softened. Cool slightly then squeeze the roasted flesh straight into the mayonnaise.

1 Peel and devein prawns, leaving tails intact. Combine prawns, fish, ⅓ cup (80ml) of the oil, half of the garlic, paprika and rind in medium bowl.

2 Combine ingredients for garlicky mayonnaise in small bowl.

3 Heat remaining oil on barbecue grill plate; cook zucchini and capsicum until browned and tender. Cook prawns and whiting on grill plate until browned both sides and just cooked.

4 Serve seafood with vegetables, mayonnaise and, if desired, lemon wedges.

☐ **PER SERVING** 42.5g total fat (5.8g saturated fat); 2604kJ (623 cal); 12g carbohydrate; 46.7g protein; 2.7g fibre

CHILLI PRAWNS WITH MANGO SALAD

Mexican char-grilled scallops with corn salsa

PREPARATION TIME 25 MINUTES (PLUS REFRIGERATION TIME) **COOKING TIME** 20 MINUTES **SERVES** 4

Corn, eaten in your hands straight from the cob, cooked on the barbecue is just the best. Remove the silk and leave the husks, twist-tied to hold them closed, then submerge the cobs under cold water for an hour or even overnight. This prevents the husks burning when you grill the cobs, on a grill plate or in a kettle barbecue around the inside edge, away from the coals, for between 15 and 30 minutes, until the kernels are tender and slightly browned.

36 scallops (900g), roe removed

2 cloves garlic, crushed

2 tablespoons lime juice

1 tablespoon olive oil

2 corn cobs (800g), trimmed

200g grape tomatoes, halved

1 large avocado (320g), chopped coarsely

1 medium red onion (170g), chopped finely

1 medium green capsicum (200g), chopped finely

2 fresh small red thai chillies, chopped finely

¼ cup coarsely chopped fresh coriander

8 corn tortillas

2 limes, cut into wedges

LIME DRESSING

¼ cup (60ml) lime juice

½ teaspoon ground cumin

2 teaspoons olive oil

1 Combine scallops, garlic, juice and oil in large bowl. Cover; refrigerate 3 hours or overnight.

2 Place ingredients for lime dressing in screw-top jar; shake well.

3 Cook corn on heated oiled barbecue grill plate until browned lightly and just tender. Using sharp knife, cut corn kernels from cobs. Place kernels in large bowl with tomato, avocado, onion, capsicum, chilli, coriander and dressing; toss gently to combine.

4 Cook drained scallops, in batches, on same grill plate until browned lightly and cooked as desired. Cover to keep warm.

5 Using tongs, place tortillas, one at a time, briefly, on grill plate to lightly brown both sides (work quickly as tortillas toughen if overcooked). Wrap tortillas in tea towel to keep warm.

6 Serve scallops with salsa, tortillas and lime wedges.

PER SERVING 24.1g total fat (4.4g saturated fat); 2416kJ (578 cal); 50.6g carbohydrate; 37.8g protein; 12.2g fibre

Whole snapper wrapped in banana leaf

PREPARATION TIME 45 MINUTES **COOKING TIME** 45 MINUTES **SERVES** 6

In Indonesia, particularly on Java, food is often wrapped in banana leaves before steaming or grilling, a process called "pepesan", which gives a special flavour to the food. The leaves are either par-boiled or made pliable over high heat before use. Fresh banana leaves are available in greengrocers and some large supermarkets.

3 large banana leaves

⅓ cup (110g) thai chilli jam

2 tablespoons light soy sauce

1 tablespoon chinese rice wine

1 whole snapper (2kg)

6cm piece fresh ginger (30g), cut into matchsticks

1 small carrot (70g), cut into matchsticks

2 cloves garlic, crushed

227g can drained, rinsed bamboo shoots, cut into matchsticks

2 green onions, chopped coarsely

½ cup firmly packed fresh coriander leaves

2 limes, cut into wedges

1 Trim two banana leaves to make one 30cm x 50cm rectangle and two 15cm x 30cm rectangles. Using metal tongs, dip one piece at a time into large saucepan of boiling water; remove immediately. Rinse under cold water; pat dry. Trim remaining banana leaf to fit barbecue grill plate.

2 Combine jam, sauce and wine in small bowl.

3 Score fish both sides through thickest part of flesh; place on large tray, brush both sides with jam mixture.

4 Combine ginger, carrot, garlic, bamboo and onion in medium bowl.

5 Place 30cm x 50cm leaf on work surface. Place one 15cm x 30cm leaf in centre of larger leaf; top with fish. Pour over any remaining jam mixture. Top fish with ginger mixture and remaining 15cm x 30cm leaf. Fold corners of banana leaf into centre to enclose fish; tie parcel at 10cm intervals with kitchen string to secure.

6 Place remaining trimmed leaf onto heated barbecue grill plate; place fish parcel on leaf. Cook, over medium heat, about 40 minutes or until fish is cooked, turning halfway through cooking time.

7 Serve fish sprinkled with coriander leaves and lime wedges.

PER SERVING 3.6g total fat (1.1g saturated fat); 719kJ (172 cal); 6.2g carbohydrate; 27g protein; 1.2g fibre

Char-grilled bream and vegetables with chilli basil butter sauce

PREPARATION TIME 20 MINUTES **COOKING TIME** 30 MINUTES **SERVES** 4

4 baby cauliflowers (500g), halved

2 trimmed corn cobs (500g), cut into 2cm rounds

400g baby carrots, trimmed

2 tablespoons olive oil

4 x 240g whole bream

CHILLI BASIL BUTTER SAUCE

80g butter

2 fresh small red thai chillies, chopped finely

⅓ cup firmly packed fresh basil leaves, shredded finely

1 tablespoon lemon juice

Try softening the butter to room temperature in a small bowl then mix in the chilli, basil and juice. Place the mixture on a piece of plastic wrap, shape into a rectangular block; wrap tightly, place in freezer until just firm. Serve each fish topped with a slice of the chilled butter.

1 Combine vegetables with half of the oil in large bowl. Cook vegetables on heated oiled barbecue grill plate about 20 minutes or until browned all over and cooked through.

2 Meanwhile, make chilli basil butter sauce.

3 Score each fish three times both sides; brush all over with remaining oil. Cook fish on same grill plate about 5 minutes each side or until cooked as desired.

4 Serve fish and vegetables drizzled with sauce.

CHILLI BASIL BUTTER SAUCE Melt butter in small saucepan; add chilli, basil and juice, stir until combined.

PER SERVING 32.2g total fat (13.9g saturated fat); 2608kJ (624 cal); 22.7g carbohydrate; 56.4g protein; 9.3g fibre

Nam jim is a generic term for a thai dipping sauce; most versions include fish sauce and chillies, but the remaining ingredients are up to the cook's discretion.

Salmon with nam jim and herb salad

PREPARATION TIME 30 MINUTES **COOKING TIME** 10 MINUTES **SERVES** 4

4 x 220g salmon fillets, skin-on

NAM JIM

3 fresh long green chillies, chopped coarsely

2 fresh small red thai chillies, chopped coarsely

2 cloves garlic, quartered

1 shallot (25g), quartered

2cm piece fresh ginger (10g), quartered

⅓ cup (80ml) lime juice

2 tablespoons fish sauce

1 tablespoon grated palm sugar

1 tablespoon peanut oil

¼ cup (35g) finely chopped roasted unsalted cashews

HERB SALAD

1½ cups loosely packed fresh mint leaves

1 cup loosely packed fresh coriander leaves

1 cup loosely packed fresh basil leaves, torn

1 medium red onion (170g), sliced thinly

2 lebanese cucumbers (260g), seeded, sliced thinly

1 Make nam jim.

2 Cook salmon, both sides, on heated oiled barbecue grill plate until cooked as desired.

3 Meanwhile, combine ingredients for herb salad in medium bowl.

4 Serve salmon and herb salad topped with nam jim.

NAM JIM Blend or process chillies, garlic, shallot, ginger, juice, sauce, sugar and oil until smooth; stir in nuts.

PER SERVING 25g total fat (5.1g saturated fat); 1952kJ (467 cal); 10.9g carbohydrate; 46.6g protein; 4.4g fibre

Barbecue tips

Imparting a delicious flavour on foods, barbecuing is a great way to cook meats, seafood and vegies, just to name a few

MARINADE
Marinating food before cooking, adds flavour and/or tenderises food. Marinades usually contain oil and an acid ingredient such as wine or lemon juice.

DRY RUBS
A blend of crushed dried herbs and/or spices, rubbed lightly onto meats about 20 minutes before barbecuing, adds flavour. Prevent spices from burning by brushing lemon juice over meat during cooking.

FLAT PLATE AND GRILL BARS
Eggs, fish, soft foods, such as tomatoes, and easily burnt foods, such as breads, are best cooked on the solid steel plate of the barbecue. Meats are mostly cooked on the bars.

BUTTERFLIED CHICKEN
One of the best things about barbecuing a butterflied chicken or turkey is that it reduces the cooking time by about half. For something special, rub under the skin with combined butter, garlic and herbs before cooking – this will result in a crisp-skinned, beautifully moist barbecued bird.

FISH
Fish is inclined to stick to grill bars so cook it on the solid steel plate, first oiling both fish and plate. Alternatively, cook whole fish in a special hinged fish grill, oiling fish and grill before placing over heat.

LONG TONGS
Special, long barbecue tongs with flat metal blades and wooden or heat-resistant plastic handles are an essential tool for a barbecue cook, making it easy to turn and move food as required.

COOKING STEAK ON BARBECUE

Slash through fat to prevent from curling; oil meat and grill. Cook, without turning, until well browned. Turn only once, cooking other side just until done as you like (see page 263).

COVERING FOOD ON AN OPEN BARBECUE

If your barbecue doesn't have a hood and food requires covering to protect it from drying out, move it to the side of the barbecue if necessary, make a tent of foil, or use a domed lid, and place over food.

SKEWERS

Metal skewers come in round and flat shapes, the latter being better to stop food from slipping round as it is turned. Bamboo skewers must be soaked in water before using, to prevent burning.

LONG BASTING BRUSH

Basting (brushing) the food, as it cooks, with oil or a marinade or sauce as the recipe directs, is an essential part of successful barbecuing. Use a special long-handled barbecue basting brush with heatproof bristles and a heat-resistant handle.

SCRAPER

When cooking is finished, use a metal scraper (such as a paint scraper) to loosen food residues from the bars and plate of the barbecue, picking them up or mopping them off with absorbent paper or disposable cloths as you go.

WIRE BRUSH FOR CLEANING

Wire brushes are available wherever barbecue accessories are sold (as well as hardware stores). As soon as possible after barbecuing, with heat turned off, and while the barbecue is still hot, clean all cooking surfaces with a wire brush dipped in water. Cool barbecue, spray with oil, wipe off surplus before covering.

Garlic and rosemary smoked lamb

PREPARATION TIME 10 MINUTES (PLUS REFRIGERATION AND SOAKING TIMES)
COOKING TIME 50 MINUTES **SERVES** 6

1kg boned, rolled lamb loin

4 cloves garlic, halved

8 fresh rosemary sprigs

1 teaspoon dried chilli flakes

1 tablespoon olive oil

250g smoking chips

1 Pierce lamb in eight places with sharp knife; push garlic and rosemary into cuts. Rub lamb with oil; sprinkle with chilli. Cover; refrigerate 3 hours or overnight.

2 Soak smoking chips in large bowl of water 2 hours.

3 Cook lamb, uncovered, on heated oiled barbecue grill plate until browned all over. Place drained smoking chips in smoke box on barbecue next to lamb. Cook lamb, covered, using indirect heat, about 40 minutes or until cooked as desired.

PER SERVING 17.8g total fat (7.1g saturated fat); 1250kJ (299 cal); 0.2g carbohydrate; 35g protein; 0.3g fibre

Barbecue smoking does not preserve meat (it's not like smoking bacon) but does help tenderise it and enhance its flavour. The wood chips are soaked in cold water so that they will smoulder rather than burn. Flavour can be added to the chips by adding various dried herbs, spices or even a little whisky to the soaking water.

Butterflied lamb with fresh mint sauce

PREPARATION TIME 15 MINUTES (PLUS REFRIGERATION TIME) **COOKING TIME** 50 MINUTES **SERVES** 10

½ cup (125ml) water

½ cup (110g) firmly packed brown sugar

1½ cups (375ml) cider vinegar

½ cup finely chopped fresh mint

1 teaspoon salt

¼ teaspoon coarsely ground black pepper

¼ cup (90g) honey

1 tablespoon wholegrain mustard

2kg butterflied leg of lamb

¼ cup loosely packed fresh rosemary leaves

1 To make mint sauce, stir the water and sugar in small saucepan over heat, without boiling, until sugar dissolves. Simmer, uncovered, without stirring, about 5 minutes or until syrup thickens slightly. Combine syrup with vinegar, mint, salt and pepper in medium jug.

2 Place a quarter of the mint sauce in large shallow dish with honey and mustard, add lamb; coat well in mint sauce mixture. Cover; refrigerate 2 hours or overnight, turning occasionally.

3 Cook drained lamb, covered, fat-side down, on heated oiled barbecue grill plate about 10 minutes or until browned. Turn lamb, sprinkle with rosemary; cook, covered, further 35 minutes or until lamb is cooked as desired. Cover; stand lamb 10 minutes.

4 Serve sliced lamb with remaining mint sauce.

PER SERVING 8.1g total fat (3.6g saturated fat); 1170kJ (280 cal); 18.3g carbohydrate; 33g protein; 0.3g fibre

A disposable aluminium baking dish provides a handy container in which to rest the cooked meat and transport it from barbecue to carving board. Large ones, available at supermarkets and barbecue supply stores, are indispensable (as well as disposable!) when roasting a turkey or baking a ham on the barbecue.

The mint sauce can be made several days ahead; keep refrigerated.

GARLIC AND ROSEMARY SMOKED LAMB

Marinating the ribs is optional, but it does tenderise the meat and helps it to remain moist during cooking.

Texan-style spareribs

PREPARATION TIME 20 MINUTES (PLUS REFRIGERATION TIME) **COOKING TIME** 1 HOUR 20 MINUTES
SERVES 8

3kg american-style pork spareribs

2 tablespoons sweet paprika

1 tablespoon ground cumin

1 teaspoon cayenne pepper

2 x 800ml bottles beer

1 cup (250ml) barbecue sauce

¼ cup (60ml) water

¼ cup (60ml) maple syrup

¼ cup (60ml) cider vinegar

1 Place ribs on large tray. Combine spices in small bowl, rub spice mixture all over ribs. Cover; refrigerate 3 hours or overnight.

2 Bring beer to a boil in medium saucepan. Reduce heat, simmer, uncovered, 15 minutes. Divide beer and ribs between two disposable aluminium baking dishes; cook on heated barbecue, covered, using indirect heat, 45 minutes. Remove ribs from baking dishes; discard beer.

3 Meanwhile, combine sauce, the water, syrup and vinegar in small saucepan; bring to a boil. Reduce heat, simmer, uncovered, 5 minutes.

4 Cook ribs, uncovered, on heated oiled barbecue grill plate, turning and brushing with sauce occasionally, about 15 minutes or until browned all over.

☐ **PER SERVING** 17.5g total fat (6.1g saturated fat); 2123kJ (508 cal); 25.4g carbohydrate; 49.8g protein; 0.4g fibre

Portobello is another name for mature swiss brown mushrooms. Large, dark brown mushrooms with full-bodied flavour, these are ideal for barbecuing, and can be stuffed and grilled for a starter or light lunch.

Barbecued vegetables and haloumi with lemon basil dressing

PREPARATION TIME 10 MINUTES **COOKING TIME** 10 MINUTES **SERVES** 4

150g baby spinach leaves

200g char-grilled red capsicum, sliced thickly

250g grilled artichokes, halved

½ cup (80g) seeded green olives

8 portobello mushrooms (400g)

400g haloumi cheese, sliced thickly

LEMON BASIL DRESSING

2 tablespoons lemon juice

⅓ cup (80ml) olive oil

1 clove garlic, crushed

2 tablespoons finely shredded fresh basil

1 Combine spinach, capsicum, artichokes and olives in large bowl.

2 Cook mushrooms on heated oiled barbecue grill plate, loosely covered with foil, about 5 minutes or until browned and tender. Cover to keep warm.

3 Cook cheese on grill plate, in batches, over high heat until browned lightly on both sides.

4 Meanwhile, make lemon basil dressing.

5 Divide spinach salad among serving dishes, top with mushrooms, cheese and dressing.

LEMON BASIL DRESSING Combine ingredients in screw-top jar; shake well.

☐ **PER SERVING** 40.8g total fat (14.2g saturated fat); 2169kJ (519 cal); 9.3g carbohydrate; 27.8g protein; 3.9g fibre

Lemon and garlic lamb kebabs with greek salad

PREPARATION TIME 25 MINUTES **COOKING TIME** 5 MINUTES **SERVES** 4

8 x 15cm stalks fresh rosemary

800g lamb fillets, diced into 3cm pieces

3 cloves garlic, crushed

2 tablespoons olive oil

2 teaspoons finely grated lemon rind

1 tablespoon lemon juice

GREEK SALAD

5 medium egg tomatoes (375g), cut into wedges

2 lebanese cucumbers (260g), halved lengthways, sliced thinly

1 medium red capsicum (200g), diced into 2cm pieces

1 medium green capsicum (200g), diced into 2cm pieces

1 medium red onion (170g), sliced thinly

¼ cup (40g) seeded black olives

200g fetta cheese, diced into 2cm pieces

2 teaspoons fresh oregano leaves

¼ cup (60ml) olive oil

2 tablespoons cider vinegar

Lamb and rosemary have long been regarded as possessing a special affinity, and the idea in using the stalks as skewers is to infuse the meat with the herb's flavour.

1 Remove leaves from bottom two-thirds of each rosemary stalk; sharpen trimmed ends to a point.

2 Thread lamb onto rosemary skewers. Brush kebabs with combined garlic, oil, rind and juice. Cover; refrigerate until required.

3 Place ingredients for greek salad in large bowl; toss gently to combine.

4 Cook kebabs on heated oiled barbecue grill plate, brushing frequently with remaining garlic mixture, until cooked. Serve kebabs with greek salad.

PER SERVING 52.5g total fat (18.9g saturated fat); 3085kJ (738 cal); 11.2g carbohydrate; 54.1g protein; 4.1g fibre

Pumpkin with walnut dressing

PREPARATION TIME 15 MINUTES **COOKING TIME** 15 MINUTES **SERVES** 4

800g pumpkin, sliced thickly

WALNUT DRESSING

½ cup (55g) toasted chopped walnuts

¼ cup (60ml) lemon juice

½ cup (125ml) olive oil

1 tablespoon dijon mustard

2 tablespoons finely chopped fresh chives

Kumara can be substituted for the pumpkin or, even better, use a mixture of both. Try sprinkling the pumpkin with a mixture of crushed pistachios and brown sugar while it is on the barbecue.

1 Cook pumpkin on heated oiled barbecue flat plate until browned all over and tender.

2 Meanwhile, make walnut dressing.

3 Serve pumpkin drizzled with dressing.

WALNUT DRESSING Place ingredients in screw-top jar; shake well.

PER SERVING 38g total fat (5.2g saturated fat); 1772kJ (429 cal); 13.8g carbohydrate; 6.3g protein; 3.8g fibre

Throw a few tarragon stalks and leftover leaves onto the coals if you're using heat beads.

Steak sandwich with tarragon and tomato salsa

PREPARATION TIME 15 MINUTES **COOKING TIME** 15 MINUTES **SERVES** 4

4 x 125g beef scotch fillet steaks

2 cloves garlic, crushed

1 tablespoon dijon mustard

1 tablespoon olive oil

8 thick slices bread (360g)

⅓ cup (100g) mayonnaise

40g trimmed watercress

TARRAGON AND TOMATO SALSA

2 cloves garlic, crushed

3 large egg tomatoes (270g), quartered, sliced thinly

½ small red onion (50g), sliced thinly

1 tablespoon finely chopped fresh tarragon

1 Combine beef, garlic, mustard and half of the oil in medium bowl.

2 Make tarragon and tomato salsa.

3 Cook beef on heated oiled barbecue grill plate until cooked as desired. Remove from heat, cover; stand 5 minutes.

4 Meanwhile, brush both sides of bread with remaining oil; cook on barbecue. Spread one side of each slice with mayonnaise; sandwich watercress, beef and salsa between slices.

TARRAGON AND TOMATO SALSA Combine ingredients in medium bowl.

▭ **PER SERVING** 21.6g total fat (4.6g saturated fat); 2161kJ (517 cal); 43.3g carbohydrate; 35g protein; 4.2g fibre

Indirect cooking is barbecuing that approximates an oven, when lower temperatures and longer cooking times are required. The food sits over the unheated centre of the barbecue so the interior heat circulates around the food, cooking it through without burning it. Flare-ups are not an issue with indirect heat as any dripping fat doesn't fall onto the heat source.

Barbecued scotch fillet

PREPARATION TIME 10 MINUTES (PLUS REFRIGERATION TIME)

COOKING TIME 1 HOUR 30 MINUTES (PLUS STANDING TIME) **SERVES** 6

¼ cup (60ml) barbecue sauce

2 tablespoons american mustard

4 cloves garlic, crushed

½ cup (125ml) beer

1.4kg piece beef scotch fillet

1 Combine sauce, mustard, garlic and beer in large bowl; add beef, turn to coat in mixture. Cover; refrigerate 3 hours or overnight.

2 Place beef and marinade in lightly oiled disposable aluminium baking dish. Cook in barbecue, covered, using indirect heat, about 1½ hours or until cooked as desired. Cover; stand 15 minutes, slice thinly.

▭ **PER SERVING** 14.2g total fat (5.9g saturated fat); 1488kJ (356 cal); 5.9g carbohydrate; 49.7g protein; 0.6g fibre

STEAK SANDWICH WITH TARRAGON AND TOMATO SALSA

Sweet chilli barbecued corn with herb and lime butter

PREPARATION TIME 20 MINUTES (PLUS REFRIGERATION TIME) **COOKING TIME** 20 MINUTES **SERVES** 8

8 corn cobs in husks (3.2kg)

2 cups (500ml) milk

²⁄₃ cup (160ml) sweet chilli sauce

HERB AND LIME BUTTER

125g butter, softened

2 teaspoons finely grated lime rind

2 teaspoons lime juice

1 tablespoon coarsely chopped fresh coriander

1 Gently peel husks down each corn cob, keeping husks attached at the base. Remove as much silk as possible then bring husks back over corn cobs to enclose completely.

2 Place corn cobs in large bowl; add milk and enough cold water to completely submerge corn. Cover; refrigerate 3 hours or overnight.

3 Meanwhile, make herb and lime butter.

4 Drain corn, peel back husks; spread equal amounts of chilli sauce over each cob then bring husks back over cobs to enclose completely. Do not allow husks to dry out; cook as soon as possible after draining.

5 Cook corn on heated oiled barbecue grill plate about 25 minutes or until tender, turning occasionally. Serve with herb and lime butter.

HERB AND LIME BUTTER Combine ingredients in small bowl. Spoon butter mixture onto piece of plastic wrap; enclose in plastic wrap. Shape into log; refrigerate until firm.

▭ **PER SERVING** 18.6g total fat (10.4g saturated fat); 1647kJ (394 cal); 44.7g carbohydrate; 12g protein; 11.3g fibre

---

Barbecued ham

PREPARATION TIME 15 MINUTES **COOKING TIME** 1 HOUR 45 MINUTES (PLUS STANDING TIME) **SERVES** 10

7kg cooked leg of ham

2 tablespoons dijon mustard

²⁄₃ cup (150g) firmly packed brown sugar

½ cup (125ml) pineapple juice

½ cup (125ml) sweet sherry

¼ cup (55g) firmly packed brown sugar, extra

2 cloves garlic, halved lengthways

¼ teaspoon ground clove

1 medium pineapple (1.25kg), halved, sliced thickly

1 Cut through rind about 10cm from shank end of leg in decorative pattern; run thumb around edge of rind just under skin to remove rind. Start pulling rind from shank end to widest edge of ham; discard rind.

2 Using sharp knife, make shallow cuts in one direction diagonally across fat at 3cm intervals, then shallow-cut in opposite direction, forming diamonds. Do not cut through top fat or fat will spread apart during cooking.

3 Place ham in disposable aluminium baking dish; rub with combined mustard and sugar. Cook ham on heated barbecue, covered, using indirect heat, 1 hour.

4 Meanwhile, stir juice, sherry, extra sugar, garlic and clove in small saucepan over heat until sugar dissolves. Reduce heat, simmer, uncovered, about 10 minutes or until glaze reduces by half. Brush ham with glaze; cook, covered, using indirect heat, a further 45 minutes, brushing several times with glaze during cooking. Cover ham with foil; stand 15 minutes before slicing.

5 Meanwhile, cook pineapple on heated oiled barbecue flat plate, brushing with remaining glaze during cooking.

6 Serve ham with pineapple.

▭ **PER SERVING (2 SLICES)** 5.9g total fat (0g saturated fat), 920kJ (220 cal); 9.3g carbohydrate; 30.8g protein; 0.5g fibre

Veal cutlets with green olive salsa

PREPARATION TIME 20 MINUTES **COOKING TIME** 15 MINUTES **SERVES** 4

2 tablespoons olive oil

2 cloves garlic, crushed

1 tablespoon finely chopped fresh oregano

2 teaspoons finely grated lemon rind

1 tablespoon lemon juice

4 x 125g veal cutlets

GREEN OLIVE SALSA

1 tablespoon lemon juice

¼ cup coarsely chopped fresh flat-leaf parsley

½ cup (80g) seeded, finely chopped large green olives

1 small green capsicum (150g), chopped finely

1 tablespoon olive oil

1 clove garlic, crushed

1 tablespoon finely chopped fresh oregano

Kipflers, being small, are quick and easy to cook in a barbecue. Prick the scrubbed potatoes, rub with butter or olive oil then double-wrap individually in foil (with a sprig of herb or an unpeeled clove of garlic, if you wish) and place directly on the coals. After about 30 minutes, stick a bamboo skewer through the foil into a potato to see if it's cooked through.

1 Make green olive salsa.

2 Combine oil, garlic, oregano, rind and juice in small bowl; brush mixture over veal. Cook veal on heated oiled barbecue grill plate until browned both sides and cooked as desired.

3 Serve veal with salsa and barbecued kipfler potatoes, if desired.

GREEN OLIVE SALSA Combine ingredients in small bowl.

▭ **PER SERVING** 16.3g total fat (2.7g saturated fat); 1112kJ (266 cal); 5.8g carbohydrate; 23.4g protein; 1.2g fibre

THE CASSEROLE DISH

The Casserole Dish

Many of the world's most famous and beloved dishes are casseroles: beef bourguignon, cassoulet, osso buco, chile con carne, Hungarian goulash, steak and kidney, any number of curries, even proper baked beans, which are a far cry from the canned kind. A luscious casserole, especially one of the comforting old favourites, such as oxtail or lamb shanks, always gets a big welcome from dinner-party guests and, of course, families love casseroles, too.

A casserole is the busy cook's friend because, once in the oven, it looks after itself while you get on with other things, and most casseroles can be made up to a day ahead and are all the better for reheating.

TYPES OF CASSEROLE DISHES

The basic principle of casseroling is that ingredients are cooked slowly with liquid in a covered vessel in the oven, so they become tender and their flavours blend. Time and the gentle heat of the oven, surrounding the casserole dish on all sides, are vital factors in the process.

The familiar chicken or beef casserole, with the meat brown but moist and served in its thickened gravy, is an example of a particular type of casserole called a braise: this is where the meat is browned on the cooktop before adding the liquid and cooking it in the oven. Another kind of braise is the pot roast, where the meat is in one large piece, such as a whole chicken or a joint of beef, lamb or pork. Braising can be carried out entirely on the cooktop, but most cooks find they get a better result, with no danger of scorching, by using the oven.

Sturdy vegetables, such as carrots, turnips or potatoes, can be browned then casseroled with a little water or stock, in the same way as meat. More delicate vegetables, such as celery, leeks or witlof, are braised by turning in melted butter on the cooktop, sometimes with added flavourings, such as garlic or herbs, then casseroling in the butter and a little stock.

CHOOSING A CASSEROLE DISH

The most important thing to keep in mind when you're shopping for a casserole dish is whether you want a flameproof one. This means a dish that is not only ovenproof but can go directly onto a cooktop burner in the same way as a saucepan or frying pan. As mentioned previously, many casserole recipes call for browning ingredients on the cooktop before adding liquid and completing the cooking in the oven. With a flameproof casserole dish, you can do all this in the one utensil. Check that it has a thick, cast base, like a good frying pan, so that it will brown evenly. A flameproof casserole dish is very versatile, able to operate as an extra saucepan or boiler when the occasion demands. With an ovenproof, but not flameproof, casserole dish, you must do the browning in a frying pan and then transfer the food to the dish before continuing with the recipe.

Also consider the size of the dish. It should be in keeping with the volume of food you will be cooking. Too small and the food cannot be properly bathed by the moisture (both liquid and steam), that tenderises it; too large and the moisture will be too diffuse to blend the flavours.

If you have only one casserole dish, make it a flameproof one that will take a whole chicken or duck comfortably; if that is sometimes too large for your recipe, make more and freeze the extra – one of the best things about casseroles is that they freeze beautifully (except for potato, which goes mushy, so leave it out for freezing; add fresh pieces and simmer an extra 10 minutes or so when reheating).

MATERIALS

FLAMEPROOF Most flameproof casserole dishes are made from metal such as stainless steel, plain or enamelled cast-iron, titanium or plain or hard-anodised aluminium. For descriptions of how these materials perform and how to care for them, read the Material and Care sections on pages 22 & 23 in *The Frying Pan*.

There are also flameproof casserole dishes made from "pyroceram", a space-age transparent ceramic material that can withstand extreme temperature changes without breaking. It is, however, a poor conductor, developing hot spots when used over direct heat.

OVENPROOF but not flameproof casserole dishes are made from many materials from fine porcelain and glass to rugged earthenware and stoneware. They are usually attractive enough to go straight from oven to table, and also can be used as serving dishes for other types of food, such as vegetables or soup.

BRAISING TECHNIQUES

MEAT AND CHICKEN When browning pieces of meat, including chicken, in a flameproof casserole dish (as in the first step of braising), heat half the butter or oil to start with; brown the meat in small batches and leave plenty of room between the pieces. Add the rest of the butter as needed. Steam will not escape as readily as it would from a frying pan because the casserole dish is deeper, so keep the heat high and allow more space for the steam to be driven off or the meat will stew instead of brown. If the butter used to brown the meat has become very dark, pour it off and use a fresh lot for the vegetables if the recipe also calls for them to be fried.

If you dust the meat with flour before browning, the flour will thicken the juices slightly to make a gravy that clings instead of running off. Another method is to thicken the liquid slightly with *beurre manié* (a kneaded butter and flour mixture), made by mixing softened butter with flour in equal proportions – that is, 60g butter to 3 tablespoons plain flour. Place a small piece on the end of a whisk and beat it into the simmering liquid, which will thicken almost immediately; repeat until it is as thickened as you want it.

REDUCED-FAT BRAISING If you feel your braises are too fatty, don't reduce the butter or oil in the recipe as this helps produce flavour; instead, make the casserole at least a few hours ahead. When cooked, pour off the liquid into a bowl; refrigerate the liquid until the fat solidifies on the surface. Remove the fat, return the juices to the casserole then reheat.

Pork, chicken and black-eyed bean cassoulet

PREPARATION TIME 20 MINUTES (PLUS STANDING TIME) **COOKING TIME** 2 HOURS 45 MINUTES **SERVES** 4

1 cup (200g) black-eyed beans

1 tablespoon olive oil

500g boned pork belly, rind removed, sliced thinly

8 chicken drumettes (640g)

4 thin pork sausages (320g)

1 trimmed celery stalk (100g), sliced thinly

1 medium brown onion (150g), chopped coarsely

1 small leek (200g), sliced thinly

1 teaspoon fresh thyme leaves

½ cup (125ml) dry white wine

400g can diced tomatoes

2 cups (500ml) chicken stock

3 cups (210g) stale breadcrumbs

½ cup finely chopped fresh flat-leaf parsley

50g butter, melted

1 Place beans in medium bowl, cover with cold water; stand 3 hours or overnight, drain. Rinse under cold water; drain.

2 Preheat oven to 180°C/160°C fan-forced.

3 Heat oil in large flameproof casserole dish; cook pork, chicken and sausages, in batches, until browned all over.

4 Cook celery, onion, leek and thyme in same dish, stirring, until onion softens. Add wine; cook, stirring, 5 minutes. Return pork, chicken and sausages to dish with undrained tomatoes, stock and beans; cook, covered in oven 40 minutes.

5 Uncover; sprinkle with combined breadcrumbs, parsley and butter. Cook, uncovered, in oven about 40 minutes or until meat is tender and top is lightly browned. Serve with a curly endive salad dressed with white wine vinaigrette, if desired.

PER SERVING 65.2g total fat (25.3g saturated fat); 4314kJ (1032 cal); 51.3g carbohydrate; 57g protein; 9.9g fibre

Ragoût, a word derived from the French ragoûter, means "to stimulate the appetite"; it is traditionally a slowly cooked meat and vegetable stew, often rabbit and other game. Here, however, we make it with vegetables alone, with no lessening of flavour.

Veal shin on mushroom ragoût

PREPARATION TIME 15 MINUTES **COOKING TIME** 2 HOURS 15 MINUTES **SERVES** 4

40g butter

4 pieces veal shin (osso buco) (1kg)

2 cloves garlic, crushed

1 tablespoon fresh rosemary leaves

½ cup (125ml) port

1 cup (250ml) beef stock

MUSHROOM RAGOUT

40g butter

2 cloves garlic, crushed

1 large flat mushroom (100g), sliced thickly

200g swiss brown mushrooms, trimmed

200g shiitake mushrooms, sliced thickly

1 medium red capsicum (200g), sliced thickly

1 medium green capsicum (200g), sliced thickly

½ cup (125ml) beef stock

2 tablespoons port

1 Preheat oven to 160°C/140°C fan-forced.

2 Melt butter in medium flameproof casserole dish; cook veal, uncovered, until browned both sides. Add garlic, rosemary, port and stock; cook, covered, in oven 2¼ hours.

3 Meanwhile, make mushroom ragoût.

4 Divide veal and ragoût among serving dishes; serve with soft polenta, if desired.

MUSHROOM RAGOUT Heat butter in large frying pan; cook garlic, mushrooms and capsicums, stirring, until vegetables are browned lightly and tender. Stir in stock and port; cook, covered, 30 minutes.

▭ **PER SERVING** 17.8g total fat (11.1g saturated fat); 1743kJ (417 cal); 11g carbohydrate; 41.1g protein; 4.3g fibre

Many fresh leafy herbs turn black if cut or shredded and left exposed to air so it's best to leave this process until just before the mint is needed. Be sure to use a very sharp knife, too, or the mint can blacken through bruising.

Veal with eggplant, olives and capers

PREPARATION TIME 20 MINUTES **COOKING TIME** 2 HOURS 30 MINUTES **SERVES** 6

1.5kg diced veal

⅓ cup (50g) plain flour

2 tablespoons olive oil

10 spring onions, trimmed, halved

4 cloves garlic, crushed

1 tablespoon capers, drained, rinsed, chopped finely

1 large eggplant (500g), chopped coarsely

10 medium tomatoes (1.3kg) chopped coarsely

¼ cup (70g) tomato paste

1 cup (250ml) dry white wine

2 teaspoons finely chopped fresh thyme

2 bay leaves

¼ cup (40g) seeded black olives

2 tablespoons pine nuts, roasted

2 tablespoons finely chopped fresh mint

1 Preheat oven to 180°C/160°C fan-forced.

2 Toss veal in flour; shake away excess flour. Heat oil in large flameproof casserole dish; cook veal, in batches, until browned.

3 Cook onion, garlic, capers and eggplant in same dish, stirring 5 minutes. Add veal; stir in tomato, tomato paste, wine, thyme and bay leaves. Cook, covered, in oven about 2 hours or until veal is tender. Discard bay leaves.

4 Serve topped with olives, nuts and mint.

PER SERVING 16.5g total fat (2.8g saturated fat); 2416kJ (578 cal); 22.7g carbohydrate; 66.6g protein; 22.2g fibre

Chile con carne with corn dumplings

PREPARATION TIME 25 MINUTES **COOKING TIME** 2 HOURS 45 MINUTES **SERVES** 6

2 tablespoons olive oil

1.5kg chuck steak, cut into 4cm cubes

2 medium brown onions (300g), chopped coarsely

2 cloves garlic, crushed

1 large green capsicum (350g), chopped coarsely

2 teaspoons sweet paprika

2 teaspoons ground cumin

2 teaspoons chilli powder

2 x 400g cans chopped tomatoes

2 tablespoons tomato paste

1 cup (250ml) beef stock

400g can red kidney beans, rinsed, drained

CORN DUMPLINGS

½ cup (75g) self-raising flour

½ cup (85g) polenta

50g butter, chopped

1 egg, beaten lightly

¼ cup (30g) coarsely grated cheddar cheese

¼ cup coarsely chopped fresh coriander

130g can corn kernels, drained

1 tablespoon milk, approximately

Use leftover chile con carne (the Mexican term for our everyday chilli with meat) as a topping for nachos, a filling for tacos or even served solo on a piece of toasted Turkish bread topped with coleslaw for an easy dinner.

1 Heat half of the oil in large flameproof casserole dish; cook steak, in batches, until browned all over.

2 Heat remaining oil in same dish; cook onion, garlic and capsicum, stirring until vegetables soften. Add spices; cook, stirring until fragrant. Return steak to dish with undrained tomatoes, paste and stock; bring to a boil. Reduce heat, simmer, covered, 2½ hours or until tender.

3 Shred a quarter of the steak coarsely with two forks; return to dish with kidney beans. Simmer, uncovered, until thickened slightly.

4 Meanwhile, make corn dumplings; drop level tablespoons of dumpling mixture, about 2cm apart, on top of steak mixture. Simmer, covered, about 20 minutes or until dumplings are cooked through.

CORN DUMPLINGS Place flour and polenta in medium bowl; rub in butter. Stir in egg, cheese, coriander, corn and enough milk to make a soft, sticky dough.

PER SERVING 28.2g total fat (11.7g saturated fat); 2784kJ (666 cal); 37g carbohydrate; 62.1g protein; 7.4g fibre

Molluscs & crustaceans

Serving guests beautiful seafood is a cinch when you know how to do it like the pros.

PREPARING CRAB (1)
Twist off legs and claws, lift tail flap and then, with a peeling motion, lift off back shell. Discard whitish gills, liver and brain matter, reserving some of the "mustard" for sauces.

PREPARING CRAB (2)
Rinse crab, crack body shell and pick out meat, breaking shell as needed. Crack claws with nutcrackers, break legs in half and extract meat from these, using a skewer to help.

PREPARING LOBSTER (1)
Turn lobster upside down and, with a heavy knife, cut tail and chest in half; turn lobster around and cut head in half. Pull halves apart, use a spoon to remove liver and brain matter.

BUYING PRAWNS
Buy uncooked (green) or raw prawns for Asian dishes, barbecuing, garlic prawns, etc. They should have a pleasant sea smell. Cooked prawns, for salads, sandwiches or a feast with lemon wedges and brown bread, should smell prawny but sweet.

PREPARING PRAWNS (1)
Hold head with one hand and body with the other, and twist to detach head. Peel away shell, with legs, from the body, leaving the tail intact, if you wish, for a decorative effect. Discard head and shell.

PREPARING PRAWNS (2)
Make a shallow slit along back to expose the black vein (gut). Slip the tip of a small, pointed knife under vein and gently lift it out. If it breaks, be sure to remove all the pieces. Discard vein.

PREPARING LOBSTER (2)

Remove meat from tail with your fingers. For whole tail meat for medallions, twist tail off; cut away soft under-shell and remove meat in one piece.

PREPARING OYSTERS (1)

Protecting your non-opening hand with either a tea-towel wrapped around oyster or a tough glove, lever an oyster knife or other short, pointed, rigid-bladed knife between shells at hinge, and twist to pop shells apart.

PREPARING OYSTERS (2)

Cut through muscle joining oyster to shell, discard top shell; try to save oyster liquor for added natural flavour. Place on a plate or tray with a bed of rock salt to hold the oysters upright.

PREPARING MUSSELS

Scrub shells with a stiff brush and cleanse by soaking several hours in water with a handful of oatmeal or cornmeal added. Pull hairy "beard" sharply down and away from the hinge, and discard.

PREPARING PIPIS, CLAMS AND COCKLES

Wash in several changes of water, scrub shells with a stiff brush and cleanse by soaking in salted water (100g sea salt per 4 litres) for several hours.

PREPARING SCALLOPS

Scallops bought on or off the shell are usually prepared already – simply remove any small brown parts that are left. If recipe specifies white meat only, gently detach the orange roe with fingers and, if you wish, keep it for another dish.

This recipe can be made, up to step 4, in a slow cooker or a pressure cooker if you have one; make sure you follow the instructions stated in your cookers' manual.

Beef stew with parsley dumplings

PREPARATION TIME 20 MINUTES **COOKING TIME** 2 HOURS 30 MINUTES **SERVES** 4

1kg beef chuck steak, diced into 5cm pieces

2 tablespoons plain flour

2 tablespoons olive oil

20g butter

2 medium brown onions (300g), chopped coarsely

2 cloves garlic, crushed

2 medium carrots (240g), chopped coarsely

1 cup (250ml) dry red wine

2 tablespoons tomato paste

2 cups (500ml) beef stock

4 sprigs fresh thyme

PARSLEY DUMPLINGS

1 cup (150g) self-raising flour

50g butter

1 egg, beaten lightly

¼ cup (20g) coarsely grated parmesan cheese

¼ cup finely chopped fresh flat-leaf parsley

⅓ cup (50g) drained sun-dried tomatoes, chopped finely

¼ cup (60ml) milk

1 Preheat oven to 180°C/160°C fan-forced.

2 Coat beef in flour; shake off excess. Heat oil in large flameproof casserole dish; cook beef, in batches, until browned all over.

3 Melt butter in same dish; cook onion, garlic and carrot, stirring, until vegetables soften. Add wine; cook, stirring, until liquid reduces to ¼ cup. Return beef to dish with paste, stock and thyme; bring to a boil. Cover; cook in oven 1¾ hours.

4 Meanwhile, make parsley dumplings.

5 Remove dish from oven; drop level tablespoons of the dumpling mixture, about 2cm apart, onto top of stew. Cook, uncovered, in oven about 20 minutes or until dumplings are browned lightly and cooked through. Serve with a mixed green salad dressed with vinaigrette, if desired.

PARSLEY DUMPLINGS Place flour in medium bowl; rub in butter. Stir in egg, cheese, parsley, tomato and enough milk to make a soft, sticky dough.

☐ **PER SERVING** 39.8g total fat (17.6g saturated fat); 3541kJ (847 cal); 44.7g carbohydrate; 64g protein; 6.9g fibre

You can use dijon or, if you can find it, green peppercorn dijon, instead of wholegrain mustard in this recipe.

Chicken pot roast with mustard cream sauce

PREPARATION TIME 25 MINUTES **COOKING TIME** 1 HOUR 50 MINUTES **SERVES** 4

1.6kg chicken

1 tablespoon olive oil

12 shallots (300g), halved

20 baby carrots (400g), trimmed

3 small parsnips (360g), chopped coarsely

1 cup (250ml) dry white wine

2 cups (500ml) chicken stock

2 bay leaves

200g swiss brown mushrooms

2 tablespoons cream

2 tablespoons wholegrain mustard

1 Preheat oven to 200°C/180°C fan-forced.

2 Wash chicken under cold water; pat dry inside and out with absorbent paper.

3 Heat oil in large flameproof casserole dish; cook chicken until browned all over. Remove chicken. Cook shallots, carrots and parsnip in same dish, stirring, about 5 minutes or until vegetables are browned lightly.

4 Return chicken to dish with wine, stock and bay leaves; bring to a boil. Cook, covered, in oven 30 minutes. Uncover; cook about 30 minutes or until chicken is cooked through. Add mushrooms; cook, uncovered, about 10 minutes or until mushrooms are tender.

5 Remove chicken and vegetables from dish; cover to keep warm. Add cream and mustard to dish; bring to a boil. Boil, uncovered, about 5 minutes or until sauce thickens slightly.

6 Serve chicken with vegetables and mustard cream sauce.

▭ **PER SERVING** 42.2g total fat (13.8g saturated fat); 2859kJ (684 cal); 16.9g carbohydrate; 46.7g protein; 6.6g fibre

Chicken and merguez cassoulet

PREPARATION TIME 25 MINUTES (PLUS STANDING TIME) **COOKING TIME** 2 HOURS 45 MINUTES **SERVES** 4

1½ cups (290g) lima beans

1 tablespoon vegetable oil

8 chicken thigh cutlets (1.3kg), halved

6 merguez sausages (480g)

1 large brown onion (200g), chopped coarsely

2 medium carrots (240g), diced into 1cm pieces

2 cloves garlic, chopped finely

4 sprigs fresh thyme

2 tablespoons tomato paste

1 teaspoon finely grated lemon rind

425g can diced tomatoes

1 cup (250ml) chicken stock

1 cup (250ml) water

2 cups (140g) fresh breadcrumbs

1 Place beans in medium bowl, cover with cold water; stand overnight, drain. Rinse under cold water; drain. Cook beans in large saucepan of boiling water, uncovered, 10 minutes; drain.

2 Heat oil in large flameproof casserole dish; cook chicken, in batches, until browned all over. Cook sausages, in batches, in same dish until browned all over. Drain on absorbent paper; halve sausages. Reserve 1 tablespoon of oil from dish; discard remainder.

3 Preheat oven to 160°C/140°C fan-forced.

4 Heat reserved oil in same dish; cook onion, carrot, garlic and thyme, stirring, until onion softens. Add paste; cook, stirring, 2 minutes. Return chicken to dish with drained beans, rind, undrained tomatoes, stock and the water; bring to a boil. Cover; cook in oven 40 minutes. Uncover; cook in oven further 1¼ hours or until liquid is almost absorbed and beans are tender.

5 Preheat grill.

6 Sprinkle cassoulet with breadcrumbs; place under hot grill until breadcrumbs are browned lightly. Serve with a green onion couscous, if desired.

▭ **PER SERVING** 60.2g total fat (19.2g saturated fat); 4974kJ (1190 cal); 64.5g carbohydrate; 89.2g protein; 19.2g fibre

If your grill is too small to brown the top of the cassoulet, place it, uncovered, in a moderately hot oven, about 10 minutes or until the breadcrumb crust browns lightly

To make the green onion couscous, place 2 cups chicken stock in medium saucepan; bring to a boil. Remove from heat, stir in 2 cups couscous and 30g butter, cover; stand 5 minutes or until stock is absorbed, fluffing with fork occasionally. Add 2 thinly sliced green onions; toss gently to combine.

Maple syrup-glazed lamb shanks

PREPARATION TIME 10 MINUTES **COOKING TIME** 2 HOURS **SERVES** 4

⅓ cup (80ml) pure maple syrup

1 cup (250ml) chicken stock

1 tablespoon dijon mustard

1 ½ cups (375ml) orange juice

8 french-trimmed lamb shanks (2kg)

1 Combine syrup, stock, mustard and juice in large deep flameproof casserole dish, add lamb; turn lamb to coat in syrup mixture. Bring to a boil then cover tightly. Reduce heat, cook lamb, turning every 20 minutes, about 2 hours or until lamb is tender.

2 Serve lamb with roast potatoes and just-wilted baby spinach leaves, if desired.

▭ **PER SERVING** 25g total fat (11.4g saturated fat); 2332kJ (558 cal); 25.7g carbohydrate; 57.1g protein; 0.3g fibre

To make perfect roast potatoes to accompany the shanks, boil, steam or microwave 6 halved medium potatoes for 5 minutes then drain. Pat dry with absorbent paper; cool 10 minutes. Gently rake rounded sides of potatoes with fork; place potato in single layer, cut-side down, on lightly oiled oven tray. Brush potatoes with 2 tablespoons olive oil; roast, uncovered, in a hot oven, 50 minutes or until browned lightly and crisp.

Sour pork curry

PREPARATION TIME 30 MINUTES **COOKING TIME** 2 HOURS 15 MINUTES (PLUS STANDING TIME) **SERVES** 4

1 tablespoon vegetable oil

1kg pork neck

1 teaspoon shrimp paste

2cm piece fresh galangal (10g), chopped finely

5 dried long red chillies, chopped finely

3 fresh long red chillies, chopped finely

¼ cup coarsely chopped coriander root and stem mixture

2 tablespoons fish sauce

¾ cup (235g) tamarind concentrate

2 tablespoons caster sugar

2 cups (500ml) chicken stock

1 litre (4 cups) water

½ cup fresh thai basil leaves, chopped coarsely

1 Heat oil in large flameproof casserole dish; cook pork, uncovered, until browned all over. Remove from dish.

2 Preheat oven to 160°C/140°C fan-forced.

3 Add shrimp paste, galangal, dried and fresh chillies and coriander mixture to same dish; cook, stirring, until fragrant. Add sauce, tamarind, sugar, stock and the water; bring to a boil. Return pork to dish, cover; cook in oven 1 hour. Uncover; cook 1 hour.

4 Remove pork from dish, cover; stand 10 minutes before slicing thickly. Stir basil into curry sauce off the heat.

▭ **PER SERVING** 9.3g total fat (2.1g saturated fat); 1680kJ (402 cal); 18.3g carbohydrate; 59.7g protein; 1.5g fibre

Galangal is a rhizome with a hot ginger-citrusy flavour; used similarly to ginger and garlic, as a seasoning and as an ingredient. Sometimes known as thai or siamese ginger, it also comes in a dried powdered form called laos. Fresh ginger can be substituted but the flavour of the dish will not be the same.

1 MAPLE SYRUP-GLAZED LAMB SHANKS **2** SOUR PORK CURRY
3 BEEF, BARLEY AND MUSHROOM STEW [P 302] **4** LAMB CHOP AND LENTIL STEW [P 302]

1 2

3 4

A nutritious grain used in soups and stews, high fibre pearl barley has had the husk discarded and been hulled and polished so just the "pearl" of the original grain remains, much the same as white rice.

Use either of the two kinds of mushrooms for this recipe if you don't want to use two different varieties.

Beef, barley and mushroom stew

PREPARATION TIME 35 MINUTES **COOKING TIME** 2 HOURS 20 MINUTES **SERVES** 4

1kg beef chuck steak, diced into 3cm pieces

¼ cup (35g) plain flour

2 tablespoons olive oil

20g butter

2 medium brown onions (300g), chopped finely

3 cloves garlic, crushed

1 medium carrot (120g), chopped finely

1 trimmed celery stalk (100g), chopped finely

4 sprigs fresh thyme

1 sprig fresh rosemary

1 bay leaf

½ cup (100g) pearl barley

2 cups (500ml) beef stock

½ cup (125ml) dry white wine

2 cups (500ml) water

200g swiss brown mushrooms, quartered

200g button mushrooms, quartered

1 Preheat oven to 160°C/140°C fan-forced.

2 Coat beef in flour; shake off excess. Heat oil in large flameproof casserole dish; cook beef, in batches, until browned all over.

3 Melt butter in same dish; cook onion, garlic, carrot, celery and herbs, stirring, until vegetables soften. Add barley, stock, wine and the water; bring to a boil. Return beef to dish, cover; cook in oven 1½ hours.

4 Stir in mushrooms; cook, uncovered, in oven about 30 minutes or until beef and mushrooms are tender. Serve with parsnip mash sprinkled with fresh thyme, if desired.

PER SERVING 25.9g total fat (9g saturated fat); 2621 kJ (627 cal); 28.7g carbohydrate; 60.4g protein; 8.2g fibre

Lamb chop and lentil stew

PREPARATION TIME 20 MINUTES **COOKING TIME** 1 HOUR 45 MINUTES **SERVES** 4

1 cup (200g) brown lentils

1 tablespoon vegetable oil

1.5kg lamb neck chops

2 medium brown onions (300g), chopped coarsely

2 cloves garlic, crushed

4 rindless bacon rashers (260g), chopped coarsely

1 teaspoon caraway seeds

2 teaspoons ground cumin

½ cup (125ml) dry red wine

⅓ cup (90g) tomato paste

2 cups (500ml) beef stock

425g can diced tomatoes

½ cup coarsely chopped fresh coriander

1 Cook lentils in large saucepan of boiling water, uncovered, about 15 minutes or until tender; drain.

2 Preheat oven to 180°C/160°C fan-forced.

3 Meanwhile, heat oil in large flameproof casserole dish; cook chops, in batches, until browned. Cook onion, garlic and bacon in same heated dish, stirring, until onion is just browned and bacon is crisp. Add spices; cook, stirring, until fragrant. Add wine, paste, stock and undrained tomatoes; bring to a boil.

4 Return chops to dish; stir in lentils, Cook, covered, in oven 1 hour 10 minutes.

5 Stir coriander into stew just before serving, if desired, with kumara mash.

PER SERVING 47.2g total fat (19.3g saturated fat); 3357kJ (803 cal); 15.9g carbohydrate; 71.6g protein; 5.1g fibre

---

Braised oxtail with orange gremolata

PREPARATION TIME 20 MINUTES **COOKING TIME** 3 HOURS 15 MINUTES **SERVES** 4

1.5kg oxtails, cut into 5cm pieces

2 tablespoons plain flour

2 tablespoons olive oil

1 medium brown onion (150g), chopped coarsely

2 cloves garlic, crushed

½ cup (125ml) sweet sherry

400g can crushed tomatoes

1 cup (250ml) beef stock

1 cup (250ml) water

4 sprigs fresh thyme

2 bay leaves

10cm strip orange rind

4 medium tomatoes (600g), chopped coarsely

ORANGE GREMOLATA

¼ cup finely chopped fresh flat-leaf parsley

1 tablespoon finely grated orange rind

1 clove garlic, crushed

Traditionally made from finely chopped parsley, grated lemon rind and crushed garlic, gremolata is an aromatic accompaniment to the Italian dish osso buco. Here, we've used orange rind for something different; you could use lemon rind, or even a combination of the two, if you prefer.

1 Preheat oven to 160°C/140°C fan-forced.

2 Coat oxtail in flour; shake off excess. Heat half of the oil in large flameproof casserole dish; cook oxtail pieces, in batches, until browned all over.

3 Heat remaining oil in same dish; cook onion and garlic, stirring, until onion softens. Return oxtails to dish with sherry, undrained tomatoes, stock, the water, herbs and rind, cover; cook in oven about 3 hours or until oxtail is tender. Stir in chopped tomato.

4 Meanwhile, combine ingredients for orange gremolata in small bowl.

5 Serve oxtail sprinkled with gremolata on mashed potato, if desired.

PER SERVING 75.1g total fat (26.5g saturated fat); 4004kJ (958 cal); 16.1g carbohydrate; 46.9g protein; 4.4g fibre

Lamb shanks massaman

PREPARATION TIME 30 MINUTES **COOKING TIME** 2 HOURS 30 MINUTES **SERVES** 4

1 tablespoon vegetable oil

8 french trimmed lamb shanks (2kg)

2 large brown onions (400g), chopped coarsely

400ml can coconut milk

2 tablespoons tamarind concentrate

2 cups (500ml) beef stock

700g piece pumpkin, trimmed, cut into 2cm cubes

¼ cup (35g) roasted unsalted peanuts, chopped coarsely

2 green onions, sliced thinly

MASSAMAN CURRY PASTE

20 dried red chillies

1 teaspoon ground coriander

2 teaspoons ground cumin

2 teaspoons ground cinnamon

½ teaspoon ground cardamom

½ teaspoon ground clove

5 cloves garlic, quartered

1 large brown onion (200g), chopped coarsely

2 x 10cm sticks fresh lemon grass (40g), sliced thinly

3 fresh kaffir lime leaves, sliced thinly

4cm piece fresh ginger (20g), chopped coarsely

2 teaspoons shrimp paste

1 tablespoon peanut oil

Having a spicy flavour reminiscent of many Indian or Pakistani dishes, massaman curries evolved from foods originally introduced to Thailand by Muslim traders from India and Pakistan. Massaman paste remains a favourite of Muslim communities in southern Thailand for use in hot and sour curries and sauces.

1 Preheat oven to 180°C/160°C fan-forced.

2 Make massaman curry paste.

3 Heat half of the oil in large flameproof casserole dish; cook lamb, in batches, until browned all over.

4 Heat remaining oil in same dish; cook onion and ½ cup of the curry paste (freeze remaining paste for another use), stirring, 2 minutes. Add coconut milk, tamarind and stock; bring to a boil. Remove from heat, add lamb; cook in oven, covered, 2 hours. Remove lamb from dish; cover to keep warm.

5 Add pumpkin to dish; bring to a boil. Reduce heat; simmer, uncovered, about 10 minutes or until pumpkin is tender.

6 Divide lamb, pumpkin and sauce among serving plates, sprinkle with nuts and onion.

MASSAMAN CURRY PASTE Place chillies in small heatproof jug, cover with boiling water, stand 15 minutes; drain, reserve chillies. Meanwhile, dry fry coriander, cumin, cinnamon, cardamom and clove in small frying pan, stirring, until fragrant. Place chillies and roasted spices in small shallow baking dish with remaining ingredients. Roast in oven, uncovered, 15 minutes. Blend or process roasted mixture until smooth.

PER SERVING 57.2g total fat (31.4g saturated fat); 3628kJ (868 cal); 20.7g carbohydrate; 65.7g protein; 6g fibre

Family beef casserole

PREPARATION TIME 15 MINUTES **COOKING TIME** 2 HOURS 15 MINUTES **SERVES** 6

2 tablespoons vegetable oil

2kg beef chuck steak, chopped coarsely

2 medium brown onions (300g), sliced thinly

2 medium carrots (240g), sliced thickly

3 cloves garlic, crushed

¼ cup finely chopped fresh parsley

¼ cup (70g) tomato paste

2 teaspoons french mustard

1 cup (250ml) dry red wine

½ cup (125ml) beef stock

1 Preheat oven to 160°C/140°C fan-forced.

2 Heat oil in large flameproof casserole dish; cook beef, in batches, until browned.

3 Cook onion, carrot and garlic in same dish, stirring, until onion is soft.

4 Return beef to dish; stir in parsley, paste, mustard, wine and stock. Cook, covered, in oven about 1¾ hours or until beef is tender.

☐ **PER SERVING** 21.4g total fat (7.1g saturated fat); 2203kJ (527 cal); 6.1g carbohydrate; 69.2g protein; 2.6g fibre

---

Serve the casserole with creamy polenta on the side. A flour-like cereal made from corn, polenta is a versatile ingredient to store in your pantry. It tastes great when cooked as follows – bring 2 cups milk and 2 cups water to a boil in large saucepan. Gradually add 1 cup polenta, stirring constantly. Reduce heat; simmer, stirring, about 5 minutes or until polenta thickens. Stir in ½ cup finely grated parmesan cheese and ½ cup cream.

Braised pork with pears and cider

PREPARATION TIME 10 MINUTES **COOKING TIME** 2 HOURS 15 MINUTES **SERVES** 4

2 tablespoons olive oil

1kg piece pork neck

3cm piece fresh ginger (15g), sliced thinly

2 cloves garlic, sliced thinly

½ teaspoon ground fennel

3 cups (750ml) sweet cider

2 cups (500ml) chicken stock

2 large pears (660g), peeled, cut into thick wedges

½ cup coarsely chopped fresh flat-leaf parsley

1 Preheat oven to 160°C/140°C fan-forced.

2 Heat oil in large flameproof casserole dish; cook pork until browned all over. Remove from dish.

3 Cook ginger and garlic in same dish, stirring, until fragrant. Add fennel; cook, stirring, 1 minute. Add cider and stock; bring to a boil. Return pork to dish, cover; cook in oven 1 hour. Uncover; cook in oven 30 minutes. Add pear; cook, uncovered, about 30 minutes or until pear is tender. Remove pork, cover, stand 5 minutes before slicing thickly.

4 Serve pork with braising liquid, sprinkled with parsley.

☐ **PER SERVING** 29.8g total fat (8.3g saturated fat); 2805kJ (671 cal); 34.7g carbohydrate; 55.1g protein; 3.5g fibre

Non-alcoholic cider can be substituted for the sweet cider in this recipe. Although apple juice and cider are both made from apples, their differences not only lie in the flavour, but also the process by which the liquid is obtained. Cider is produced from whole washed, mashed and pressed apples, while apple juice is made from crushed apple flesh only.

Spanish chicken casserole

PREPARATION TIME 10 MINUTES **COOKING TIME** 1 HOUR 25 MINUTES **SERVES** 4

1 tablespoon olive oil

4 chicken drumsticks (600g)

4 chicken thigh cutlets (800g)

1 large brown onion (200g), chopped finely

4 medium potatoes (800g), quartered

½ cup (80g) roasted pine nuts

½ cup (80g) roasted almonds

3 cups (750ml) chicken stock

1 cup (250ml) dry white wine

⅓ cup (80ml) lemon juice

4 cloves garlic, crushed

2 tablespoons fresh thyme leaves

½ cup coarsely chopped fresh flat-leaf parsley

500g baby green beans, trimmed

1 Preheat oven to 180°C/160°C fan-forced.

2 Heat oil in large flameproof casserole dish; cook chicken, in batches, until browned.

3 Cook onion in same dish, stirring, until soft. Return chicken to dish with potato, nuts, stock, wine, juice, garlic, thyme and half of the parsley; bring to a boil. Cover; cook in oven about 1 hour or until chicken is cooked through.

4 Meanwhile, boil, steam or microwave beans until tender; drain.

5 Serve chicken with beans; sprinkle with remaining parsley.

▭ **PER SERVING** 61.4g total fat (12.4g saturated fat); 4050kJ (969 cal); 35g carbohydrate; 57g protein; 10.4g fibre

If you wouldn't drink it, don't cook with it: that's the general rule of thumb for choosing wine for cooking. Cheap, inferior quality wines will impart a less pleasant flavour than a great drinking wine. However, if you wish to forego the wine in this recipe, replace it with water, white grape juice or even ginger ale.

Apples, pork and prunes

PREPARATION TIME 25 MINUTES **COOKING TIME** 1 HOUR 30 MINUTES **SERVES** 4

2 tablespoons vegetable oil

2 small leeks (400g), sliced thinly

4 forequarter pork chops (1.75kg)

¼ cup (35g) plain flour

1 litre (4 cups) chicken stock

½ cup (100g) white long-grain rice

4 medium apples (600g), sliced thickly

1 cup (170g) seeded prunes

2 tablespoons coarsely chopped fresh sage

1 Preheat oven to 180°C/160°C fan-forced.

2 Heat one-third of the oil in large flameproof casserole dish; cook leek, stirring, until soft. Remove from dish.

3 Trim fat and bone from chops; cut pork into 5cm pieces. Toss pork in flour; shake away excess flour. Heat remaining oil in dish; cook pork, stirring, until browned. Return leek to dish with stock; cook, covered, in oven 45 minutes.

4 Remove dish from oven; skim off any fat. Stir in rice, apple, prunes and half of the sage; cook, covered, 20 minutes or until pork is tender. Serve sprinkled with remaining sage.

▭ **PER SERVING** 41.5g total fat (12.2g saturated fat); 3599kJ (861 cal); 58.2g carbohydrate; 59.5g protein; 8.8g fibre

The classic Alsatian combination of apple, pork and prune is used here to highlight the best produce of this French region. The prunes become soft and gelatinous during cooking while the apple imparts a subtly sweet flavour: both fruits complement pork perfectly. Serve in true Alsatian style with a glass of just-chilled riesling.

Ask your butcher to roll and tie the pork shoulder for you. Serve the pork with a big loaf of thick, crusty Italian bread to mop up all the wonderful sauce on your plate.

Italian braised pork

PREPARATION TIME 25 MINUTES **COOKING TIME** 2 HOURS 50 MINUTES **SERVES** 6

2 tablespoons olive oil

1.5kg pork shoulder, rolled and tied

2 cloves garlic, crushed

1 medium brown onion (150g), chopped coarsely

½ small fennel bulb (100g), chopped coarsely

8 slices hot pancetta (120g), chopped coarsely

1 tablespoon tomato paste

½ cup (125ml) dry white wine

400g can chopped tomatoes

1 cup (250ml) chicken stock

1 cup (250ml) water

2 sprigs fresh rosemary

2 large fennel bulbs (1kg), halved, sliced thickly

SPICE RUB

1 teaspoon fennel seeds

2 teaspoons dried oregano

½ teaspoon cayenne pepper

1 tablespoon cracked black pepper

1 tablespoon sea salt

2 teaspoons olive oil

1 Preheat oven to 180°C/160°C fan-forced.

2 Heat oil in large flameproof casserole dish; cook pork, uncovered, until browned.

3 Meanwhile, combine ingredients for spice rub in small bowl.

4 Remove pork from dish; discard all but 1 tablespoon of the oil in dish. Cook garlic, onion, chopped fennel and pancetta in same dish, stirring, until onion softens. Add paste; cook, stirring, 2 minutes.

5 Meanwhile, rub pork with spice rub.

6 Return pork to dish with wine, undrained tomatoes, stock, the water and rosemary; bring to a boil. Cover; cook in oven 1 hour.

7 Add sliced fennel; cook, covered, in oven 1 hour. Remove pork from dish; discard rind. Cover to keep warm.

8 Cook braising liquid in dish over medium heat, uncovered, until thickened slightly. Return sliced pork to dish; serve pork and sauce with warm italian bread, if desired.

PER SERVING 32.8g total fat (10.7g saturated fat); 2525kJ (604 cal); 7.5g carbohydrate; 66.5g protein; 4.6g fibre

Eggplant, tomato and chickpea casserole

PREPARATION TIME 20 MINUTES **COOKING TIME** 1 HOUR **SERVES** 4

Serve this casserole accompanied with a warmed loaf of ciabatta and thick plain yogurt to which you have added a spoonful of finely chopped rinsed and drained preserved lemon rind – it adds just the right note!

2 medium eggplants (600g), sliced thickly

2 tablespoons olive oil

10 spring onions (250g), trimmed

150g green beans, trimmed, halved

2 cloves garlic, crushed

3 trimmed celery stalks (300g), sliced thinly

2 x 310g cans chickpeas, rinsed, drained

4 large tomatoes (1kg), peeled, chopped finely

¼ cup finely chopped fresh flat-leaf parsley

¼ cup finely chopped fresh oregano

1 tablespoon tomato paste

1 Preheat oven to 180°C/160°C fan-forced. Preheat grill.

2 Place eggplant slices on greased oven tray; brush lightly with about half of the oil. Place under hot grill until browned both sides.

3 Heat remaining oil in large flameproof casserole dish; cook onion, stirring, until onion is browned lightly. Boil, steam or microwave beans until tender; drain.

4 Stir in eggplant, garlic, celery, chickpeas, tomato and herbs. Cook, covered, in oven 45 minutes or until vegetables are tender. Remove from oven; stir in paste and beans.

☐ **PER SERVING** 12.2g total fat (1.6g saturated fat); 1262kJ (302 cal); 28.1g carbohydrate; 12.9g protein; 14.7g fibre

---

Vegetable cassoulet

PREPARATION TIME 20 MINUTES (PLUS STANDING TIME) **COOKING TIME** 1 HOUR 25 MINUTES **SERVES** 4

This is a vegetarian version of a traditional cassoulet from Languedoc in France, which is made with various cuts of meat, like pork sausages, pork belly, duck and mutton.

½ cup (100g) dried borlotti beans

½ cup (100g) dried great northern beans

2 teaspoons olive oil

4 shallots (100g), halved

3 cloves garlic, sliced thinly

2 medium carrots (240g), chopped coarsely

200g mushrooms, halved

1 cup (250ml) dry white wine

2 medium zucchini (240g), chopped coarsely

1½ cups (375ml) vegetable stock

700g bottled tomato pasta sauce

1 teaspoon finely chopped fresh thyme

BREAD TOPPING

1 tablespoon olive oil

1 small brown onion (80g), chopped finely

2 teaspoons finely grated lemon rind

1 clove garlic, crushed

2 teaspoons finely chopped fresh thyme

½ ciabatta (220g), diced into 2cm pieces

2 tablespoons coarsely chopped fresh flat-leaf parsley

1 Place beans in medium bowl, cover with water; stand overnight, drain. Rinse under cold water; drain. Place beans in medium saucepan of boiling water; return to a boil. Reduce heat, simmer, uncovered, about 15 minutes or until beans are just tender.

2 Preheat oven to 180°C/160°C fan-forced.

3 Heat oil in large flameproof casserole dish; cook shallot, garlic, carrot and mushrooms, stirring, until vegetables are just tender. Add wine; bring to a boil. Boil, uncovered, until liquid is reduced by half. Add zucchini, stock, sauce, thyme and drained beans; return to a boil. Remove from heat; transfer to oven. Cook, covered, 50 minutes.

4 Meanwhile, make bread topping.

5 Sprinkle cassoulet with bread topping; cook, uncovered, in oven about 10 minutes or until bread topping is browned.

BREAD TOPPING Heat oil in large frying pan; cook onion, stirring, until soft. Add rind, garlic, thyme and bread; cook, stirring, about 10 minutes or until bread browns lightly. Stir in parsley.

☐ **PER SERVING** 11.4g total fat (1.8g saturated fat); 2128kJ (509 cal); 68.3g carbohydrate; 22.7g protein; 19.6g fibre

Ratatouille

PREPARATION TIME 15 MINUTES **COOKING TIME** 40 MINUTES **SERVES** 12

2 medium green zucchini (240g)
2 medium yellow zucchini (240g)
1 large eggplant (500g)
1 medium red capsicum (200g)
1 medium green capsicum (200g)
1 cup (250ml) olive oil
2 medium red onions (340g), chopped coarsely

4 cloves garlic, chopped finely
2 x 400g cans chopped tomatoes
1 fresh long red chilli
1 strip orange rind
½ teaspoon coriander seeds
2 bay leaves
1 sprig fresh basil
1 tablespoon red wine vinegar

1 Chop zucchini, eggplant and capsicums into 2cm cubes. Heat 2 tablespoons of the oil in large flameproof casserole dish over high heat; cook green zucchini, stirring, until browned. Remove from pan. Repeat using another 2 tablespoons oil with each vegetable.

2 Heat remaining 2 tablespoons of oil in same dish; cook onion and garlic, stirring, until onion is soft. Add undrained tomatoes; bring to a boil. Simmer, uncovered, until thickened to a sauce consistency.

3 Add vegetables, chilli, rind, seeds, bay leaves and basil to dish; simmer, covered, over low heat about 40 minutes or until vegetables are soft and mixture is thickened. Add vinegar; remove chilli, rind and bay leaves.

4 Serve ratatouille either hot, cold or at room temperature as a side dish or as a starter with bread.

☐ **PER SERVING** 19.4g total fat (2.7g saturated fat); 895kJ (214 cal); 6.3g carbohydrate; 2.6g protein; 3.3g fibre

Provençale in origin, variations of this famous French vegetable dish also feature in the cuisines of many other European countries: the Spanish have pisto, the Maltese eat kapunata and the Italians serve caponata. Regardless of where it comes from or what it's called, Mediterranean garden vegetables are the key ingredient and can be served as a meal with lentils or rice, for example, or as a side dish with crusty bread.

THE BAKING DISH

The Baking Dish

Ask a dozen people what their favourite dish is, and it's good odds that at least half of them will name a roast. Many of us have got out of the habit of making what our mothers called a "baked dinner" because we think it takes too long (yes, it does take time, but not much of *your* time – you can read the paper while it's in the oven) or that our household is too small to make a roast worthwhile. The answer to that is to buy one of the "mini" roasts now available or, better still, buy a traditional-size roast and enjoy both the baked dinner and the lovely follow-up dishes you can make with the leftovers. Some of these have become beloved classics in their own right, for example, shepherd's pie using leftover lamb, or a chicken and mushroom pie or club sandwich using leftover chicken.

The clue to success with dishes such as the pies is to make enough extra-flavoursome gravy with the roast to have plenty left over. Rev up the gravy flavour by roasting quartered onions in the baking dish with the meat, and using these (chopped) and a good-quality liquid stock (available in tetra packs at the supermarket) rather than water; a dash of red or white wine doesn't hurt either.

The only good thing about not having roasts as much as we used to, is that, when they do appear, they are such a treat – try doing a plain roast chicken or leg of lamb the next time you have friends to dinner and wait for their exclamations of delight.

The words "roast" and "bake" have come to be interchangeable when we are talking about meat, chicken or fish, and the utensil we are calling a baking dish here can also be called a roasting pan. Until recent years, we would say "bake" when we were talking about vegetables, but nowadays we often say "roast" for them, too. In practice, there is no problem – it's always clear what is meant.

CHOOSING A BAKING DISH

You can roast successfully in any old warped, thin baking dish, but when it comes to making the gravy, the pan will not only wobble on the cooktop, but will scorch if you don't stir it madly. Having a good, heavy baking dish is not as vital as having a top-notch saucepan, but once you have quality saucepans, a quality baking dish is a further worthwhile investment.

You can also roast in dishes that are not made primarily for that purpose, such as shallow pottery, glass or china ovenproof dishes. Purpose-made baking dishes are virtually always metal.

A good baking dish should feel heavy for its size because it is made from metal thick enough to resist warping and hot spots. It should have a plain flat bottom, not a raised pattern: these are meant to let the juices run away into the corners, but they are a nuisance when deglazing or making gravy.

Plain aluminium or, even better, because it is stronger, an aluminium alloy, are the choices of many chefs. These pans are heavy enough, but not too heavy, and perform better on top of the stove than stainless-steel pans, which look smarter but can't match aluminium's superb conductivity. The major disadvantage of aluminium – its way of reacting with acid foods to produce off flavours (see Aluminium under Material in *The Frying Pan*, page 22) – doesn't come into most roasting, and should you want to roast tomatoes, for instance, you could always do them in a ceramic ovenproof dish.

The best aluminium and stainless-steel baking dishes have handles to make lifting easier when they have a heavy roast on board. The Rolls-Royce of aluminium baking dishes is one in the wonder metal, hard-anodised aluminium, which has all the virtues of plain aluminium without the disadvantages, and is stick-resistant, too. This is a fairly new material on the domestic market, but the professionals have been using them for years.

Baking dishes are also available in enamelled cast-iron, which has the advantage over the other materials mentioned of being approved for washing in the dishwasher. These dishes are also suitable for serving, and can double as an oven dish for lasagne or moussaka.

For information on the performance of all these materials and the way to care for them, read the sections on Material and Care in *The Frying Pan,* pages 22 & 23.

ROASTING TECHNIQUES

TURNING THE PAN Many ovens are hotter towards the back than at the front. Check once or twice during cooking time and turn the pan around, if necessary, to even out cooking.

BULB BASTER This looks like a huge eye-dropper with a metal stem and a rubber bulb. It makes it easy to suck up pan juices and distribute them over the food as it cooks.

RACK Some cooks like to place the roast on a rack, some don't. Some baking dishes come with flat racks, but these don't leave room for the vegetables to go on the bottom of the dish where they brown best. Separate V-shaped racks with adjustable sides are also available.

JUDGING DONENESS A meat thermometer will tell you a roast's internal temperature, but use the manufacturers' markings for "rare", "medium-rare" or "well-done" as a guide only – your idea of medium rare may be different from theirs.

Other ways of checking doneness:

- For poultry, insert a fine skewer into the thickest part of the poultry and check the colour of the juices that run out: pink means underdone, clear means cooked through. For whole birds, run the skewer between the thigh and the body.

- For meat, insert a skewer as described above to check the juices: red for rare, pink for medium-rare, and clear for well-done. You can also check by pressing quickly with a finger – raw meat feels mushy and it becomes progressively springier, then firm, as it changes from rare to medium-rare to well-done – but this technique takes experience; you will probably need to practise it on steaks and work up to roasts.

- Seafood is cooked when it changes from translucent to opaque, or from grey to white or, for salmon and trout, from reddish to pink. A whole fish is cooked when a toothpick is inserted without resistance into the thickest part of the fish. Always remove fish from the oven before it's fully cooked, as it will finish cooking in its own heat by the time it's served.

RESTING Stand all smaller pieces of meat and poultry in a warm place for 5 minutes, or 15 minutes for joints of meat or whole birds, before serving or carving. This makes the meat more succulent by allowing the juices to settle into the tissues.

Slow-roasted leg of lamb with artichokes and lemon

PREPARATION TIME 30 MINUTES **COOKING TIME** 4 HOURS **SERVES** 4

½ cup coarsely chopped fresh flat-leaf parsley

½ cup (75g) seeded black olives, quartered

4 drained anchovy fillets

4 cloves garlic, quartered

2 teaspoons finely grated lemon rind

2 tablespoons lemon juice

2 tablespoons capers, rinsed, drained

2 tablespoons olive oil

2kg leg of lamb

800g jerusalem artichokes (800g), halved lengthways

2 small red onions (200g), cut into wedges

2 medium lemons (280g), cut into wedges

12 cloves garlic, unpeeled

1 Preheat oven to 140°C/120°C fan-forced.

2 Blend or process parsley, olives, anchovies, quartered garlic, rind, juice, capers and 1 tablespoon of the oil until mixture is chopped coarsely.

3 Using sharp knife, pierce lamb down to the bone at 3cm intervals along the length of the leg. Spread olive mixture all over lamb, pressing into cuts.

4 Combine artichokes in large shallow baking dish with onion, lemon, unpeeled garlic and remaining oil.

5 Place lamb on artichoke mixture; cover tightly with foil. Roast in oven 4 hours. Serve lamb with vegetable mixture.

PER SERVING 30.4g total fat (10.4g saturated fat); 2888kJ (691 cal); 4.6g carbohydrate; 87.8g protein; 8.7g fibre

Looking like a knobbly parsnip, the Jerusalem artichoke is a crisp tuber with the texture of a fresh water chestnut and its own unique earthy taste. It's a great winter vegetable, suiting casseroles, roasts and savoury pies, plus it makes a wonderful cream soup. After they're peeled, keep submerged in acidulated water to stop them from discolouring. If they are not available, you can simply cook peeled chats (baby potatoes) with the lamb, adding them to the baking dish midway through roasting time.

Lamb rendang

PREPARATION TIME 30 MINUTES **COOKING TIME** 3 HOURS 15 MINUTES (PLUS STANDING TIME) **SERVES** 4

2 teaspoons coriander seeds

¼ teaspoon ground turmeric

2 large brown onions (400g), chopped coarsely

4 cloves garlic, quartered

2 x 10cm sticks fresh lemon grass (40g), chopped coarsely

2cm piece fresh galangal (10g), sliced thinly

4 fresh small red thai chillies, chopped coarsely

2 fresh long red chillies, chopped coarsely

2 tablespoons coarsely chopped coriander root and stem mixture

2 tablespoons peanut oil

1.5kg butterflied leg of lamb

400ml can coconut milk

1 Dry-fry spices in small frying pan, stirring, about 1 minute or until fragrant. Blend or process spices with onion, garlic, lemon grass, galangal, chillies and coriander mixture until mixture forms a paste.

2 Preheat oven to 150°C/130°C fan-forced.

3 Heat half of the oil in large flameproof baking dish; cook lamb, turning occasionally, until browned all over. Remove from dish.

4 Heat remaining oil in same dish; cook onion paste, stirring, until fragrant. Add coconut milk; bring to a boil.

5 Return lamb to dish; cook in oven, uncovered, turning occasionally, about 3 hours or until liquid has evaporated. Cover lamb; stand 10 minutes before serving.

PER SERVING 50.2g total fat (28.8g saturated fat); 3490kJ (835 cal); 8.1g carbohydrate; 86.5g protein; 3.7g fibre

Lamb shanks with risoni and tomato

PREPARATION 15 MINUTES **COOKING** 2 HOURS 50 MINUTES **SERVES** 4

8 french-trimmed lamb shanks (2kg)

½ cup (75g) plain flour

2 tablespoons olive oil

4 cloves garlic, crushed

½ cup (125ml) dry white wine

400g can chopped tomatoes

2 tablespoons tomato paste

1 litre (4 cups) chicken stock

1 cup (220g) risoni pasta

3 small zucchini (270g), chopped coarsely

½ cup coarsely chopped fresh flat-leaf parsley

1 teaspoon finely grated lemon rind

1 Preheat oven to 160°C/140°C fan-forced.

2 Toss lamb in flour, shake away excess flour. Heat oil in large, flameproof baking dish; cook lamb until well browned.

3 Add garlic to dish, cook until fragrant, but not coloured. Add wine; boil until almost evaporated. Stir in tomatoes, paste and stock; bring to a boil. Cover dish tightly with foil; cook in oven 2 hours.

4 Add risoni and zucchini to dish; cook, covered, further 40 minutes or until lamb is tender. Stir in parsley and rind.

▭ **PER SERVING** 36g total fat (13.2g saturated fat); 3628kJ (868 cal); 58.6g carbohydrate; 69g protein; 6.2g fibre

Tamarind-glazed lamb rack with tat soi and orange salad

PREPARATION TIME 10 MINUTES **COOKING TIME** 25 MINUTES **SERVES** 4

¼ cup (60ml) tamarind concentrate

¼ cup (60ml) orange juice

2 teaspoons sesame oil

1 tablespoon brown sugar

4 x 4 french-trimmed lamb cutlet racks (600g)

2 large oranges (600g)

100g tat soi leaves

100g shiitake mushrooms, sliced thickly

1 Preheat oven to 200°C/180°C fan-forced.

2 Combine tamarind, juice, oil and sugar in small saucepan; reserve 2 tablespoons of the mixture in large bowl. Bring remaining mixture in pan to a boil. Reduce heat, simmer, uncovered, about 2 minutes or until mixture thickens slightly.

3 Place lamb on wire rack inside large shallow baking dish; brush hot tamarind glaze over lamb. Cook, uncovered, in oven about 20 minutes or until lamb is cooked as desired. Cover lamb; stand 10 minutes.

4 Meanwhile, segment oranges over reserved tamarind mixture in bowl. Add tat soi and mushrooms; toss gently to combine.

5 Cut each lamb rack in half; place two halves on each serving plate, serve with salad.

▭ **PER SERVING** 15.4g total fat (6.2g saturated fat); 1132kJ (271 cal); 15.7g carbohydrate; 17.7g protein; 3.4g fibre

Tat soi's dark-green, spoon-shaped leaves are usually eaten raw in salads, but can also be combined with other Asian greens in soups, curries and stir-fries. Also known as rosette, pak choy and flat cabbage, it is a member of the same family as buk choy, and has the same mild flavour.

Beef cut from the shoulder, bolar blade and oyster blade, lends itself to long, slow cooking as does, generally, any meat coming from a moving, muscular part of the animal. The fat and gelatinous content of these cuts renders down after a long cooking into meat that is rich, tender and almost viscous. The beauty here, of course, is that these cuts are the least expensive and the long cooking brings out unbelievable flavour. Trim the piece of beef well of fat but leave some of the gristle, because this adds both flavour and a syrupy consistency to the pan juices; browning the meat well will add depth of colour.

Slow-roasted beef and garlic with mustard cream

PREPARATION TIME 15 MINUTES **COOKING TIME** 4 HOURS 35 MINUTES **SERVES** 6

18 baby onions (720g)

2.5kg piece beef bolar blade or chuck

2 tablespoons olive oil

½ cup (125ml) dry red wine

salt

2 sprigs fresh thyme

2 bulbs garlic, tops removed

1 cup (250ml) beef stock

MUSTARD CREAM

½ cup (120g) sour cream

2 tablespoons wholegrain mustard

1 Preheat oven to 120°C/100°C fan-forced.

2 Place onions in heatproof bowl; cover with boiling water and stand 5 minutes. Drain, peel away skins.

3 Heat a large flameproof baking dish. Rub beef all over with oil. Cook beef in dish until browned all over. Add wine; simmer, uncovered, until reduced by half. Remove dish from heat; sprinkle beef with salt and thyme leaves.

4 Add garlic, peeled onions and stock to dish. Cover tightly with lid or foil; roast in oven 2½ hours. Remove foil; baste meat with pan juices. Roast, uncovered, a further 2 hours. Stand, covered, about 30 minutes before slicing.

5 Make mustard cream.

6 Serve beef with onions, garlic, strained pan juices, mustard cream and steamed green beans, if desired.

MUSTARD CREAM Combine the sour cream and mustard in a bowl.

☐ **PER SERVING** 35.8g total fat (17g saturated fat); 3122kJ (747 cal); 9.1g carbohydrate; 91.4g protein; 9.2g fibre

The cuisines of Beijing and Shantung, probably the best known cooking styles of Northeastern China, are light and elegant, respected for their artful use of seasonings rather than for their richness. Using flavourings like garlic, ginger, soy sauce and vinegar in marinades, rather than part of what is to be consumed, help identify their subtle technique.

Shantung chicken

PREPARATION TIME 10 MINUTES (PLUS REFRIGERATION TIME) **COOKING TIME** 1 HOUR 20 MINUTES **SERVES** 4

1 clove garlic, crushed

2cm piece fresh ginger (10g), grated

1 tablespoon dark soy sauce

1 tablespoon dry sherry

2 teaspoons sichuan peppercorns, crushed

2 teaspoons peanut oil

1.6kg whole chicken

SHANTUNG SAUCE

⅓ cup (75g) caster sugar

½ cup (125ml) water

2 tablespoons white wine vinegar

1 fresh small red thai chilli, chopped finely

1   Combine garlic, ginger, soy sauce, sherry, pepper and oil in large bowl with chicken. Cover; refrigerate overnight.

2   Preheat oven to 220°C/200°C fan-forced.

3   Half-fill a large baking dish with water; place chicken on oiled wire rack set over dish. Roast, uncovered, about 1 hour 20 minutes or until cooked through.

4   Meanwhile, make shantung sauce.

5   Remove chicken from oven; when cool enough to handle, remove and discard skin and bones. Chop meat coarsely; serve drizzled with sauce.

SHANTUNG SAUCE Stir sugar and the water in small saucepan over low heat until sugar dissolves. Bring to a boil; boil, uncovered, without stirring, about 5 minutes or until sauce thickens slightly. Remove from heat; stir in vinegar and chilli.

☐ **PER SERVING** 28.3g total fat (8.6g saturated fat); 2107kJ (504 cal); 19.2g carbohydrate; 42.1g protein; 0.2g fibre

Roast chicken with herb stuffing

PREPARATION TIME 30 MINUTES **COOKING TIME** 1 HOUR 45 MINUTES (PLUS STANDING TIME) **SERVES** 4

1.5kg chicken

15g butter, melted

HERB STUFFING

1½ cups (105g) stale breadcrumbs

1 trimmed celery stalk (100g), chopped finely

1 small white onion (80g), chopped finely

1 teaspoon finely chopped fresh rosemary

1 teaspoon finely chopped fresh thyme

¼ cup coarsely chopped fresh flat-leaf parsley

1 egg

1   Preheat oven to 200°C/180°C fan-forced.

2   Make seasoning.

3   Remove and discard any fat from cavity of chicken. Fill cavity with seasoning; do not pack in tightly as bread expands during cooking and seasoning will become a solid mass.

4   Place chicken on board, breast-side up. Secure chicken with string by looping string around tail end, bring string around ends of drumsticks. Following the creases between drumsticks and body, take string towards wing end of chicken.

5   Turn chicken breast-side down and secure string around wings.

6   Place chicken on rack over baking dish. Half-fill baking dish with water; it should not touch the chicken. Using small pastry brush, brush chicken with butter; roast 15 minutes. Reduce oven temperature to 180°C/160°C fan-forced; roast further 1½ hours. Pierce skin and flesh of chicken in thickest part of drumstick; juices will be clear if chicken is cooked. Or, wriggle leg of chicken and it will feel quite loose at the joint; this indicates chicken is cooked. Stand chicken, covered, 10 minutes before breaking or cutting into serving-sized pieces. Serve with roasted vegetables, if desired.

HERB STUFFING Using hand or wooden spoon, combine ingredients in medium bowl.

☐ **PER SERVING** 29.7g total fat (10.3g saturated fat); 2190kJ (524 cal); 18.7g carbohydrate; 44.8g protein; 1.8g fibre

This recipe offers you a good opportunity to use a V-shaped roasting rack set into a large shallow baking dish. Place the chicken in it, breast-side down, and after oven has been turned to moderate for about an hour, wearing oven gloves and using a piece of foil, carefully turn the bird over for the last 30 minutes of cooking time. The poultry juices from the back will flow into the breast, making it moist, tender and golden brown.

When the chicken is cooked, allow it to stand in the rack, covered, for 5 minutes then pour any juices from the inside of the chicken into the baking dish. Tilt juices into one corner of the dish; skim away as much fat as possible. Place dish over a medium heat and make chicken gravy right in the baking dish to serve with the carved chicken.

Slow-roasted turkey with zucchini, lemon and wild rice seasoning

PREPARATION TIME 40 MINUTES **COOKING TIME** 4 HOURS 45 MINUTES **SERVES** 10

4kg turkey

50cm square muslin

100g butter, melted

1 litre (4 cups) water

40g butter, extra

¼ cup (35g) plain flour

⅓ cup (80ml) port

2 cups (500ml) chicken stock

ZUCCHINI, LEMON AND WILD RICE SEASONING

50g butter

1 large brown onion (200g), chopped coarsely

2 cloves garlic, crushed

⅓ cup (60g) wild rice

½ cup (125ml) dry white wine

1 cup (250ml) water

⅔ cup (130g) basmati rice

2 cups (500ml) chicken stock

2 medium zucchini (240g), grated coarsely

2 teaspoons finely grated lemon rind

2 teaspoons lemon thyme leaves

1 cup (70g) stale breadcrumbs

If you can find the commercial blend of white long-grain and dark brown wild rice, use a cup of it in the seasoning, preparing it according to package directions. Wild rice is not, in fact, a true rice at all. It is the seed of a flowering aquatic grass native to the cold climates of North America. It has a distinctively nutty flavour and a crunchy, resilient texture.

1 Make zucchini, lemon and wild rice seasoning.

2 Preheat oven to 150°C/130°C fan-forced.

3 Discard neck from turkey. Rinse turkey under cold water, pat dry inside and out. Fill neck cavity loosely with seasoning; secure skin over opening with toothpicks or poultry pins. Fill large cavity loosely with seasoning; tie legs together with string, tuck wing tips under turkey.

4 Place turkey on oiled wire rack in flameproof baking dish. Dip muslin in melted butter and place over turkey. Add the water to baking dish, cover dish with foil. Roast 4 hours.

5 Remove foil and muslin from turkey, brush with pan juices. Increase oven temperature to 200°C/180°C fan-forced; roast further 30 minutes or until turkey is cooked. Remove turkey from oven; cover, stand 20 minutes.

6 Drain pan juices into large jug; skim fat from top of juices, discard. You will need about 2 cups of juice.

7 Place same baking dish over medium heat, melt extra butter, add flour; cook, stirring, until well browned. Gradually stir in port, reserved juices and stock; cook, stirring, until mixture boils and thickens. Strain into large jug.

8 Serve turkey with gravy.

ZUCCHINI, LEMON AND WILD RICE SEASONING Heat butter in large frying pan; cook onion and garlic, stirring, until onion is soft. Add wild rice; cook, stirring, 1 minute. Add wine; simmer, covered, about 10 minutes or until almost all the liquid is absorbed. Add the water; simmer, covered, about 10 minutes, until liquid is absorbed. Add basmati rice; cook, stirring, 1 minute. Add stock; simmer, covered, 10 minutes or until all liquid is absorbed and rice is tender. Stir in zucchini, rind and thyme; cool. Stir in breadcrumbs.

    PER SERVING 41.8g total fat (18.1g saturated fat); 2788kJ (667 cal); 22g carbohydrate; 46.7g protein; 1.4g fibre

The word spatchcock can be used to both describe a small chicken (poussin), no more than 6 weeks old, weighing approximately 500g, and the cooking technique where it is split open, then flattened and roasted, baked or grilled. The flavours here are somewhat Indian in nature, and the spatchcock would go nicely with the classic pulao on page 161.

Spicy roast spatchcocks

PREPARATION TIME 15 MINUTES (PLUS REFRIGERATION TIME) **COOKING TIME** 30 MINUTES **SERVES** 4

4 x 500g spatchcocks

2 teaspoons sweet paprika

2 cloves garlic, crushed

1 teaspoon cumin seeds

2 teaspoons yellow mustard seeds

2 tablespoons finely chopped fresh coriander

2 green onions, chopped finely

⅓ cup (110g) mango chutney

2 tablespoons olive oil

VINAIGRETTE

⅓ cup (80ml) olive oil

2 tablespoons lemon juice

½ teaspoon sugar

1 Using kitchen scissors, cut along each side of each spatchcock's backbone; discard backbones. Cut spatchcocks in half along breastbones.

2 Combine spatchcocks in large bowl with paprika, garlic, seeds, coriander, onion, chutney and oil. Cover; refrigerate 3 hours or overnight.

3 Preheat oven to 220°C/200°C. Drain spatchcocks; reserve marinade.

4 Place spatchcocks, skin-side up, on rack in baking dish. Bake, uncovered, 30 minutes or until cooked through, brushing with marinade several times during cooking.

5 Place ingredients for vinaigrette in screw-top jar; shake well.

6 Serve spatchcocks drizzled with vinaigrette.

▭ **PER SERVING** 18.9g total fat (4.6g saturated fat); 999kJ (239 cal); 3.7g carbohydrate; 14g protein; 0.3g fibre

Arrange peeled batons or wedges of potatoes (sebago or pontiac are good) in the bottom of the baking dish for about the last 40 minutes of chicken cooking time, turning them and brushing them with juices accumulating in the bottom of the dish. They will crisp and taste of the chorizo and lemon – just delicious.

Chorizo-stuffed roast chicken

PREPARATION TIME 25 MINUTES (PLUS COOLING TIME) **COOKING TIME** 1 HOUR 35 MINUTES **SERVES** 4

20g butter

1 medium brown onion (150g), chopped finely

1 chorizo sausage (170g), diced into 1cm pieces

1½ cups (110g) stale breadcrumbs

½ cup (100g) ricotta cheese

1 egg

¼ cup finely chopped fresh flat-leaf parsley

¼ cup (35g) roasted slivered almonds

1.6kg chicken

2 medium lemons (280g), cut into wedges

SPINACH AND RED ONION SALAD

150g baby spinach leaves

1 small red onion (100g), sliced thinly

1 tablespoon red wine vinegar

2 tablespoons olive oil

1 Melt half of the butter in medium frying pan; cook onion and chorizo, stirring, until onion softens. Cool 10 minutes. Combine chorizo mixture in medium bowl with breadcrumbs, cheese, egg, parsley and nuts.

2 Preheat oven to 200°C/180°C fan-forced.

3 Wash chicken under cold water; pat dry inside and out with absorbent paper. Tuck wing tips under chicken. Trim skin around neck; secure neck flap to underside of chicken with skewers.

4 Fill cavity with chorizo mixture, fold over skin to enclose stuffing; secure with skewers. Tie legs together with string. Place chicken and lemon in baking dish. Rub chicken all over with remaining butter; roast, uncovered, about 1½ hours or until chicken is cooked through, basting occasionally with juices.

5 Meanwhile, place ingredients for spinach and red onion salad in large bowl; toss gently to combine.

6 Serve chicken with stuffing, lemon and salad.

☐ **PER SERVING** 68.4g total fat (21.4g saturated fat); 4042kJ (967 cal); 24.4g carbohydrate, 60.3g protein, 5.8g fibre

Spiced chicken with roasted eggplant

PREPARATION TIME 25 MINUTES **COOKING TIME** 1 HOUR 20 MINUTES **SERVES** 6

1½ teaspoons coriander seeds

¾ teaspoon cumin seeds

1 teaspoon black peppercorns

1½ teaspoons sea salt flakes

½ teaspoon ground cinnamon

¾ teaspoon chilli powder

1 tablespoon plain flour

1 tablespoon olive oil

2kg whole chicken

1 lemon, halved

1 cup (250ml) chicken stock

2 large eggplants (1kg), halved, scored deeply

⅓ cup coarsely chopped fresh flat-leaf parsley

Eggplant prepared this way is sometimes called "eggplant caviar" on menus and in cookbooks, because its taste is similarly deep and rich, and its seeds somewhat resemble caviar. Slow-roasting eggplant gives it a distinctively smoky flavour, and the lemon juice keeps the flesh from darkening.

1 Preheat the oven to 180°C/160°C fan-forced.

2 Using a mortar and pestle or small spice mill, crush coriander, cumin, peppercorns and salt until finely ground. Transfer to a small bowl, add cinnamon, chilli powder, flour and oil. Rub spice mixture evenly all over chicken.

3 Squeeze lemon, reserve 1 tablespoon of the juice. Stuff lemon halves into cavity of the chicken. Tie legs of chicken together; tuck wings under body. Place chicken on wire rack in a baking dish. Add stock; cover tightly with foil. Bake 20 minutes.

4 Add eggplants, cut-side down, to same dish; bake, uncovered, further 1 hour.

5 Transfer chicken to serving dish; cover to keep warm. Carefully scoop eggplant flesh into medium bowl, add reserved juice and parsley; stir to combine.

6 Serve chicken with warm eggplant mixture and lemon wedges, if desired.

☐ **PER SERVING** 25.8g total fat (7.5g saturated fat); 1735kJ (415 cal); 6.3g carbohydrate; 38g protein; 4.1g fibre

Preparing poultry

You needn't pay a butcher to do your chicken chores – with our tips, you'll find it just as easy to do at home.

CLEANING

Remove any feathers or quills and loose fat. Press the two oil glands near base of tail to empty them. Wash bird in cold water and dry inside and out with absorbent paper.

JOINTING (1)

Using poultry shears or strong scissors, cut off legs and thighs together, then cut them apart. Cut off wings. Cut backbone section from chicken. The back can be served with another portion such as a wing.

JOINTING (2)

Trim breast section and cut down centre into halves. You can vary these instructions by cutting off a top corner of the breast with each wing, to give more equal portions.

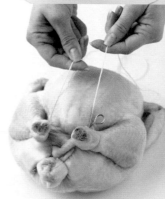

STUFFING

To stuff cavity, spoon in enough stuffing to fill loosely, allowing room for swelling while cooking. To stuff under skin, use fingers to loosen skin from neck end and push stuffing in to cover breast.

TRUSSING (1)

If cavity is gaping, push poultry pins (small, fine skewers) across cavity through skin and lace up with string in a zigzag pattern, pulling firmly and tying to bring sides together. Lay bird on its back, tail towards you, wingtips tucked under body.

TRUSSING (2)

Place centre of string under tail and cross ends around tail (also known as "parson's nose"), then take around legs and tie legs and tail together. Bring string up between legs and body, wrap round wings, turn bird over and tie firmly between wings.

BONING (1)

Cut off wingtips and cut through skin along centre back. Using a small pointed knife pressed against bone, work blade between flesh and bone on each side, cutting through wing and thigh joints.

BONING (2)

Hold up leg and thigh with one hand, cut around top of thighbone and scrape off flesh; repeat with leg. Cut and scrape flesh from wings in the same way. Small birds, such as quail, may have wings and legs left intact.

SPATCHCOCKING (BUTTERFLYING)

Cut along each side of backbone with poultry shears; remove backbone. Pull bird open, turn over, press breastbone to break it. Skewer through breast, wings, thighs and legs to keep flat.

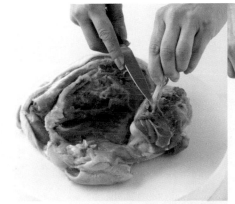

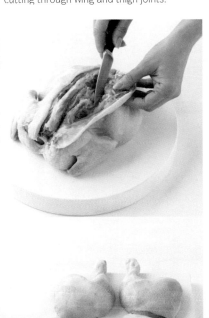

CHINESE CHOPPING (1)

Use a cleaver and/or poultry shears or strong scissors. Cut through alongside breastbone and right through backbone, then cut both pieces in half.

CHINESE CHOPPING (2)

Cut off wings, legs and thighs and chop each into three pieces. Cut breast, on the bone, from each half-chicken and cut each breast into three pieces. You should now have 24 pieces.

SKINNING CHICKEN PIECES

For skinless chicken pieces, freeze until just firm, not hard, then grasp skin with a clean cloth, such as a disposable cloth or a paper towel. Pull skin away from the meat and cut off if necessary.

Roast beef fillet with herb and walnut topping

PREPARATION TIME 20 MINUTES **COOKING TIME** 35 MINUTES (PLUS STANDING TIME) **SERVES** 6

This is perfect special-occasion or dinner-party fare: a prized cut of beef spectacularly presented that is neither difficult nor time-consuming to prepare. Serve it with the fennel and potato gratin on page 352 and a lightly chilled sparkling merlot, and you'll have a meal ready for royalty (or even your mother-in-law).

750g piece beef fillet

1 tablespoon olive oil

½ cup coarsely chopped fresh flat-leaf parsley

¼ cup coarsely chopped fresh dill

1 clove garlic, crushed

2 teaspoons finely grated lemon rind

2 teaspoons lemon juice

¼ cup (30g) coarsely chopped roasted walnuts

1 tablespoon olive oil, extra

1 Preheat oven to 200°C/180°C fan-forced. Rub beef with oil.

2 Combine remaining ingredients in small bowl.

3 Cook beef, in flameproof baking dish, over high heat until browned all over.

4 Roast beef, uncovered, in oven, 15 minutes. Remove beef, sprinkle with three-quarters of the herb and walnut mixture. Cover, return to oven; roast further 10 minutes or until cooked. Remove from oven, stand, covered, 10 minutes.

5 Serve beef, sliced, sprinkled with remaining herb and walnut mixture.

PER SERVING 17.1g total fat (4.2g saturated fat); 1104kJ (264 cal); 0.3g carbohydrate; 27.2g protein; 0.7g fibre

Crisp-skinned thai chilli snapper

PREPARATION TIME 15 MINUTES (PLUS REFRIGERATION TIME) **COOKING TIME** 45 MINUTES **SERVES** 4

If snapper is unavailable, use any of your favourite whole firm-fleshed fish for this recipe. Cooking times will change slightly for each different kind and thickness of fish you select.

1 whole snapper (1.2 kg)

4 cloves garlic, crushed

¼ cup finely chopped fresh lemon grass

¼ cup finely chopped fresh coriander

2 fresh small red thai chillies, chopped finely

4cm piece fresh ginger (20g), grated

1 tablespoon thai red curry paste

2 tablespoons lime juice

⅓ cup (80ml) sweet chilli sauce

½ cup firmly packed fresh coriander leaves, extra

1 Make four deep slits diagonally across both sides of fish; place in baking dish.

2 Combine garlic, lemon grass, chopped coriander, chilli, ginger, paste, juice and half the sauce in medium bowl; pour over fish.

3 Preheat oven to 180°C/160°C fan-forced.

4 Bake fish, covered with foil, about 35 minutes or until fish is almost tender.

5 Brush fish with remaining sauce; place under preheated grill until skin is browned and crisp. Serve sprinkled with extra coriander leaves.

PER SERVING 4.3g total fat (1g saturated fat); 677kJ (162 cal); 5.3g carbohydrate; 24.2g protein; 2.4g fibre

---

1 ROAST BEEF FILLET WITH HERB AND WALNUT TOPPING **2** CRISP-SKINNED THAI CHILLI SNAPPER
3 WHOLE FISH IN A SALT CRUST WITH GREMOLATA [P 330]
4 ROAST PORK FILLET WITH PEAR AND APRICOT RELISH [P 330]

1

2

3 4

Cooking food in a salt crust
isn't a recent innovation –
the Chinese were cooking
chicken in a salt crust more
than 1000 years ago,
having discovered that it
helped retain the juices and
enhanced the flavour.

It's important to press the
dampened salt firmly all
over the fish so that none of
it is exposed directly to the
heat of the oven. If the fish
is too long for your baking
dish, trim its tail. After
cooking, the crust should
be very hard and browned.

Whole fish in a salt crust with gremolata

PREPARATION TIME 10 MINUTES **COOKING TIME** 35 MINUTES **SERVES** 4

1kg whole snapper, cleaned, scales left on

1.5kg coarse cooking salt, approximately

GREMOLATA

¼ cup finely chopped fresh flat-leaf parsley

1 clove garlic, crushed

2 teaspoons finely grated lemon rind

1 tablespoon olive oil

1 Preheat oven to 240°C/220°C fan-forced.

2 Combine gremolata ingredients in small bowl.

3 Wash fish, pat dry inside and out with absorbent paper. Fill cavity of fish with half the gremolata.

4 Place half the salt in baking dish large enough to hold fish; place fish on salt.

5 Place remaining salt in large sieve or colander and run quickly under cold water until salt is damp. Press salt firmly over fish to completely cover fish.

6 Bake 35 minutes. Remove fish from oven; stand 5 minutes.

7 Using a hammer or meat mallet and old knife, break open the crust then lift away with the scales and skin. Serve fish with remaining gremolata.

PER SERVING 3.1g total fat (0.6g saturated fat); 280kJ (67 cal); 0.1g carbohydrate; 9.7g protein; 0.2g fibre

Another, rather Indian, way
to cook pork fillets is by
rubbing them all over with
a paste made from peanut
oil and crushed garam
masala (a blend of spices
that includes cloves,
cardamom, cinnamon,
cumin, coriander and
fennel) before placing the
baking dish in the oven.
Serve the pork with
steamed basmati rice and
the date and tamarind
chutney on page 178.

Roast pork fillet with pear and apricot relish

PREPARATION TIME 10 MINUTES **COOKING TIME** 20 MINUTES **SERVES** 4

410g can sliced pears in natural juice

410g can apricot halves in natural juice

600g pork fillets

1 tablespoon olive oil

½ cup (125ml) water

2 tablespoons white wine vinegar

1 fresh long red chilli, chopped finely

¼ cup (40g) sultanas

2 tablespoons white sugar

1 Preheat oven to 240°C/220°C fan-forced.

2 Drain pears over small bowl. Reserve juice; chop pears coarsely. Drain apricots, discarding juice. Chop apricots coarsely.

3 Place pork in oiled baking dish; drizzle with oil. Roast, uncovered, about 20 minutes or until cooked as desired. Cover; stand 5 minutes then slice thickly.

4 Meanwhile, bring pear, apricot, reserved juice and remaining ingredients to a boil in medium saucepan. Reduce heat, simmer, uncovered, about 20 minutes or until relish thickens slightly. Serve pork with relish and steamed snow peas, if desired.

PER SERVING 8g total fat (1.8g saturated fat); 1400kJ (335 cal); 29.2g carbohydrate; 34.2g protein; 3.3g fibre

Apple-stuffed pork loin with braised red cabbage

PREPARATION TIME 1 HOUR **COOKING TIME** 2 HOURS 15 MINUTES **SERVES** 8

2.5kg boneless pork loin
with 20cm flap

2 tablespoons coarse cooking salt

3 cups (750ml) sparkling cider

½ cup (125ml) chicken stock

3 teaspoons white sugar

APPLE STUFFING

30g butter

3 large green apples (600g),
peeled, cored, cut into thin wedges

1 medium leek (350g),
sliced thinly

1 medium brown onion (150g),
sliced thinly

½ teaspoon ground cinnamon

2 tablespoons white sugar

1 cup (70g) stale breadcrumbs

1 tablespoon finely grated
lemon rind

1 cup coarsely chopped fresh
flat-leaf parsley

BRAISED CABBAGE

40g butter

¼ teaspoon caraway seeds

4 sprigs thyme

1 bay leaf

1 medium brown onion (150g),
chopped finely

1 medium green apple (150g),
peeled, grated coarsely

1 medium red cabbage (1.5kg),
sliced thinly

½ cup (125ml) red wine vinegar

1¼ cups (310ml) water

When you order the pork loin, ask your butcher to leave a flap measuring about 20cm in length to make it possible to roll the loin. And, since his knives are probably sharper than yours, why not see if he will remove the rind for the crackling.

1   Preheat oven to 240°C/220°C fan-forced.

2   Place pork on board, rind-side up. Run sharp knife about 5mm under rind, gradually lifting rind away from pork. Place rind in large shallow baking dish. Using sharp knife, make shallow cuts in one direction diagonally across fat at 3cm intervals, then shallow-cut in opposite direction, forming diamonds; rub with salt. Roast, uncovered, in oven about 30 minutes or until crackling is browned and crisp. Chop crackling into serving pieces; reserve. Reduce oven temperature to 180°C/160°C fan-forced.

3   Meanwhile, make apple stuffing.

4   Slice through the thickest part of pork horizontally, without cutting all the way through. Open pork out to form one large piece; press stuffing against the loin along length of pork. Roll pork to enclose stuffing; secure with kitchen string at 2cm intervals.

5   Place pork on rack in large shallow flameproof baking dish; pour 2½ cups of the cider into dish. Roast, uncovered, in oven about 1½ hours or until cooked through.

6   Meanwhile, make braised cabbage.

7   Remove pork from baking dish; cover to keep warm. Place baking dish over heat, add stock, sugar and remaining cider; cook, stirring, until sauce thickens slightly.

8   Serve pork, braised cabbage and crackling drizzled with sauce.

APPLE STUFFING Heat butter in large frying pan; cook apple, leek, onion, cinnamon and sugar, stirring, until leek and onion soften. Remove from heat, stir in breadcrumbs, rind and parsley.

BRAISED CABBAGE Cook butter, caraway seeds, thyme and bay leaf in large heavy-based saucepan, stirring, until fragrant. Add onion and apple; cook, stirring, until onion softens. Add cabbage, vinegar and the water; cook, covered, over low heat, stirring occasionally, 1 hour. Discard thyme and bay leaf.

▭ **PER SERVING** 28.6g total fat (11.9g saturated fat); 2834kJ (678 cal); 35.6g carbohydrate; 64.1g protein; 10.7g fibre

The olives must be seeded before being added to this recipe. An olive pipper is a great kitchen tool; it can pop the seeds out of cherries as well as olives. Plus it can be used to perform the reverse task, re-stuffing seeded olives with bits of anchovy, fetta or sun-dried tomato.

Snapper with roasted tomatoes, capsicums and olives

PREPARATION TIME 15 MINUTES **COOKING TIME** 40 MINUTES **SERVES** 4

2 tablespoons olive oil

1 medium red onion (170g), cut into thick wedges

2 medium red capsicums (400g), sliced thickly

250g cherry tomatoes

4 cloves garlic, unpeeled, bruised

1kg whole snapper

1 cup (120g) seeded green olives

¼ cup coarsely chopped fresh flat-leaf parsley

1 Preheat oven to 220°C/200°C fan-forced.

2 Combine half of the oil, the onion, capsicum, tomatoes and garlic in large baking dish; roast, uncovered, 20 minutes.

3 Rinse snapper in cold water; pat dry with absorbent paper. Score snapper diagonally on both sides; place in same dish on top of vegetables, drizzle with remaining oil. Roast, uncovered, for 20 minutes or until snapper is just cooked through.

4 Transfer snapper to platter, cover. Add olives to vegetables in dish; toss to combine. Serve snapper with roasted vegetables, parsley and, if desired, lemon wedges.

☐ **PER SERVING** 11.3g total fat (1.9g saturated fat); 1045kJ (250 cal); 13.1g carbohydrate; 22.1g protein; 4g fibre

Easy, quick and foolproof, this mussel dish makes a great appetiser to a Thai main course such as the crisp-skinned chilli snapper on page 328.

Bean sprouts, also known as bean shoots, are the tender new growths of assorted beans and seeds germinated for consumption as sprouts. The most readily available are mung bean, soy bean, alfalfa and snow pea sprouts. In Thailand, the tiny root hanging off the end of every sprout is picked off but we consider this job unnecessary.

Baked mussels infused with asian-flavours

PREPARATION TIME 20 MINUTES **COOKING TIME** 20 MINUTES **SERVES** 4

1.5kg large black mussels

8cm piece fresh ginger (40g), cut into matchsticks

1 clove garlic, sliced thinly

2 fresh kaffir lime leaves, shredded finely

2 fresh long red chillies, sliced thinly

1 medium carrot (120g), cut into matchsticks

1 medium red capsicum (200g), cut into matchsticks

⅓ cup (80ml) water

¼ cup (60ml) kecap manis

¼ cup (60ml) lime juice

½ cup (40g) bean sprouts

⅔ cup loosely packed fresh coriander leaves

1 Preheat oven to 220°C/200°C fan-forced.

2 Scrub mussels; remove beards. Combine mussels in large baking dish with ginger, garlic, lime leaves, chilli, carrot, capsicum, the water, kecap manis and juice.

3 Cook, covered, in oven about 20 minutes or until mussels open (discard any that do not). Remove from oven; stir in sprouts and coriander.

☐ **PER SERVING** 1.6g total fat (0.4g saturated fat); 414kJ (99 cal); 8.2g carbohydrate; 11.2g protein; 2.1g fibre

SNAPPER WITH ROASTED TOMATOES, CAPSICUMS AND OLIVES

Roast veal rack with herb stuffing

PREPARATION TIME 20 MINUTES **COOKING TIME** 35 MINUTES **SERVES** 4

1 small brown onion (80g), chopped finely

1 clove garlic, crushed

½ trimmed celery stalk (50g), chopped finely

¾ cup (45g) stale breadcrumbs

1 tablespoon dijon mustard

1 teaspoon finely chopped fresh thyme

1 tablespoon finely chopped fresh flat-leaf parsley

1 teaspoon finely grated lemon rind

2 teaspoons sea salt

2 teaspoons cracked black pepper

800g veal rack (4 cutlets), trimmed

1 medium brown onion (150g), chopped coarsely

1½ cups (375ml) beef stock

2 teaspoons olive oil

2 teaspoons balsamic vinegar

½ cup (125ml) beef stock, extra

1 Preheat oven to 220°C/200°C fan-forced.

2 Cook finely chopped onion, garlic and celery in heated lightly oiled small frying pan, stirring, until vegetables soften. Add breadcrumbs; cook until breadcrumbs brown lightly. Remove from heat; stir in mustard, herbs, rind, half of the salt and half of the pepper. Cool 10 minutes.

3 Using sharp knife, make a tunnel through veal rack, close to bone; fill with herb mixture.

4 Place coarsely chopped onion and stock in large flameproof baking dish; add veal, drizzle with oil, sprinkle with remaining salt and pepper. Roast, uncovered, in oven about 30 minutes or until cooked as desired. Remove veal from dish, cover; stand 10 minutes.

5 Stir vinegar and extra stock into veal juices in dish; bring to a boil. Strain into medium jug; serve with veal and steamed green beans, if desired.

▭ **PER SERVING** 6.8g total fat (1.7g saturated fat); 1145kJ (274 cal); 11.7g carbohydrate; 40.2g protein; 1.8g fibre

Slow-roasted duck with sour cherry, apple and walnut salad

PREPARATION TIME 40 MINUTES **COOKING TIME** 2 HOURS **SERVES** 4

680g jar morello cherries

½ cup (125ml) chicken stock

½ cup (125ml) port

1 cinnamon stick

3 cloves

1 clove garlic, crushed

4 duck marylands (1.2kg), excess fat removed

2 small green apples (260g)

1 cup (100g) roasted walnuts, chopped coarsely

3 green onions, sliced thinly

1 cup firmly packed fresh flat-leaf parsley leaves

2 tablespoons olive oil

1 tablespoon lemon juice

1 Preheat oven to 160°C/140°C fan-forced.

2 Strain cherries over small bowl. Combine cherry juice with stock, port, cinnamon, cloves and garlic in large baking dish. Place duck on wire rack over baking dish; cover tightly with oiled foil. Roast, covered, in oven about 2 hours or until duck meat is tender. Strain pan liquid into large jug; skim away fat (this is the cherry sauce).

3 Cut apples into thin slices; cut slices into matchstick-sized pieces. Place apple and seeded cherries in large bowl with nuts, onion, parsley, oil and juice; toss gently to combine. Serve duck with salad and reheated cherry sauce.

☐ **PER SERVING** 30.5g total fat (3.6g saturated fat); 1990kJ (476 cal); 25.9g carbohydrate; 15g protein; 5g fibre

Braised sweet ginger duck

PREPARATION TIME 20 MINUTES **COOKING TIME** 1 HOUR 50 MINUTES **SERVES** 4

2kg duck

3 cups (750ml) water

½ cup (125ml) chinese cooking wine

⅓ cup (80ml) light soy sauce

¼ cup (55g) firmly packed brown sugar

1 star anise

3 green onions, halved

3 cloves garlic, quartered

10cm piece fresh ginger (50g), unpeeled, chopped coarsely

2 teaspoons sea salt

1 teaspoon five-spice powder

800g baby buk choy, halved

1 Preheat oven to 180°C/160°C fan-forced.

2 Discard neck from duck, wash duck; pat dry with absorbent paper. Score duck in thickest parts of skin; cut duck in half through breastbone and along both sides of backbone, discard backbone. Tuck wings under duck.

3 Place duck, skin-side down, in baking dish. Combine the water, wine, sauce, sugar, star anise, onion, garlic and ginger; add to dish. Cook, covered, about 1 hour.

4 Increase oven temperature to 220°C/200°C fan-forced. Remove duck from braising liquid; strain liquid through muslin-lined sieve into large saucepan. Place duck, skin-side up, on wire rack in same dish. Rub combined salt and five-spice all over duck; roast duck, uncovered, in oven about 30 minutes or until skin is crisp.

5 Skim fat from surface of braising liquid; bring to a boil. Reduce heat, simmer, uncovered, 10 minutes. Add buk choy; simmer, covered, about 3 minutes or until buk choy is just tender.

6 Cut duck halves into two pieces; divide buk choy, braising liquid and duck among serving plates. Serve with steamed jasmine rice, if desired.

☐ **PER SERVING** 105.7g total fat (31.7g saturated fat); 4974kJ (1190 cal); 17.9g carbohydrate; 40.8g protein; 3.5g fibre

Choose a fresh duck having a wide, plump breast and taut rather than loose-looking skin. Scoring and salting help dry the duck, as the fat just under the skin drains away while it's cooking. Placing the duck skin-side-up on a rack and increasing the oven temperature during the last half hour of cooking guarantees a crisp skin.

Roast beef with Yorkshire puddings and red wine gravy

PREPARATION TIME 25 MINUTES **COOKING TIME** 1 HOUR 15 MINUTES **SERVES** 6

1 tablespoon port

2 tablespoons wholegrain mustard

1½ tablespoons worcestershire sauce

2kg piece boneless beef sirloin

1 cup (250ml) dry red wine

1½ cups (375ml) water

40g butter

2 tablespoons plain flour

1½ cups (375ml) beef stock

YORKSHIRE PUDDINGS

1 cup (150g) plain flour

1 teaspoon salt

1 cup (250ml) milk

2 eggs

1 Preheat oven to 220°C/200°C fan-forced.

2 Combine port, mustard and 1 tablespoon of the sauce in small bowl; rub all over beef. Place beef on wire rack in medium, flameproof baking dish. Combine ½ cup (125ml) of the wine and the water; pour into dish. Roast, uncovered, 10 minutes.

3 Reduce oven temperature to 180°C/160°C fan-forced; roast a further 45 minutes for medium or until cooked as desired. Add extra water if pan juices evaporate.

4 Meanwhile, make batter for Yorkshire puddings.

5 Transfer beef to plate, cover to keep warm. Increase oven temperature to 240°C/220°C fan forced. Drain all pan juices into small heatproof bowl; freeze 10 minutes. Scrape solidified fat from top of pan juices. Divide 2 tablespoons of the fat (if necessary, use olive oil) among two 12-hole mini muffin pans; place in oven about 3 minutes to heat pans. Remove muffin pans from oven; immediately divide pudding batter among hot pans.

6 Return muffin pans to oven; bake 15 minutes or until well browned and risen.

7 Melt butter in same flameproof baking dish, add flour; cook, stirring, over heat until mixture is well browned. Gradually stir in remaining wine, then stock, remaining sauce and reserved pan juices; cook, stirring, until gravy boils and thickens slightly. Strain into jug.

8 Serve beef with Yorkshire puddings, red wine gravy and fresh peas, if desired.

YORKSHIRE PUDDINGS Sift flour and salt into medium bowl. Whisk in combined milk and eggs until batter is smooth. Cover; stand 30 minutes.

PER SERVING 23.5g total fat (11.3g saturated fat); 2784kJ (666 cal); 24.8g carbohydrate; 79.7g protein; 1.4g fibre

Folklore has it that, at meal-time in the poorer rural families of pre-industrial England, Yorkshire pudding was served first, on its own with gravy, to fill the children and leave the more expensive meat for the adults. How tastes have changed! Today, most of us head straight for the comfort-food qualities of these stick-to-the-ribs, hot, moist, popover-like puddings made from the drippings of rare roast beef.

If you want to make this recipe but don't want to feed 10 people, there are 101 delicious ideas for using up leftover pork. One that everyone knows, of course, is to use it in fried rice; one perhaps not so familiar but quite remarkable is to shred the meat and make burritos. Heat the shredded pork with sliced roasted green chillies (fresh, not bottled, jalapeños are good, as is the long green thai variety) and homemade tomato, onion and coriander salsa then wrap spoonfuls of it up in warmed flour tortillas. Serve with a drizzle of lime juice, some shredded lettuce and a dollop of sour cream – very moreish.

Leg of pork with apple and onion compote

PREPARATION TIME 30 MINUTES **COOKING TIME** 3 HOURS **SERVES** 10

4kg leg of pork

2 tablespoons fresh sage leaves

2 cloves garlic, sliced thinly

1 tablespoon olive oil

2 tablespoons salt

1 teaspoon fennel seeds

APPLE AND ONION COMPOTE

40g butter

3 large brown onions (600g), sliced thinly

2 tablespoons white sugar

¼ cup (60ml) cider vinegar

¾ cup (180ml) water

4 large apples (800g), peeled, sliced

1 Preheat oven to 240°C/220°C fan-forced.

2 Using the point of a sharp knife, pierce pork about 12 times all over (including underside), gently twisting to make a small hole. Press sage and garlic evenly into holes.

3 Rub pork rind with oil then salt, rub underside of pork with seeds. Place pork on wire rack in baking dish. Roast 30 minutes or until rind blisters.

4 Reduce oven temperature to 180°C/160°C fan-forced; roast pork a further 2½ hours or until cooked as desired.

5 Meanwhile, make apple and onion compote.

6 Serve pork with compote and steamed green beans, if desired.

APPLE AND ONION COMPOTE Heat butter in large frying pan; cook onion, stirring occasionally, about 10 minutes. Add sugar; cook, stirring occasionally, about 10 minutes or until onion caramelises. Stir in vinegar, the water and apples; bring to a boil. Reduce heat, simmer, covered, about 15 minutes or until apples are soft.

▭ **PER SERVING** 28.6g total fat (10.4g saturated fat); 2433kJ (582 cal); 14.6g carbohydrate; 65.6g protein; 2.1g fibre

Asian-style braised pork neck

PREPARATION TIME 10 MINUTES **COOKING TIME** 2 HOURS 30 MINUTES **SERVES** 4

1 tablespoon peanut oil

1kg piece pork neck

2 cinnamon sticks

2 star anise

½ cup (125ml) light soy sauce

½ cup (125ml) chinese rice wine

¼ cup (55g) firmly packed brown sugar

5cm piece fresh ginger (25g), sliced thinly

4 cloves garlic, quartered

1 medium brown onion (150g), chopped coarsely

1 cup (250ml) water

1 Preheat oven to 160°C/140°C fan-forced.

2 Heat oil in medium deep flameproof baking dish; cook pork, uncovered, until browned all over. Remove from heat.

3 Add combined spices, sauce, wine, sugar, ginger, garlic, onion and the water to pork; turn pork to coat in mixture. Cook, uncovered, in oven about 2 hours or until pork is tender, turning every 20 minutes.

4 Remove pork from dish; cover to keep warm. Strain braising liquid through muslin-lined strainer over medium saucepan; bring to a boil. Reduce heat, simmer, uncovered, about 5 minutes or until sauce thickens slighly. Serve pork drizzled with sauce.

▭ **PER SERVING** 18.7g total fat (5.6g saturated fat); 2040kJ (488 cal); 18.1g carbohydrate; 54.9g protein; 1.2g fibre

Duxelles-filled leg of lamb with roasted vegetables

PREPARATION TIME 30 MINUTES **COOKING TIME** 1 HOUR 45 MINUTES **SERVES** 4

40g butter

150g swiss brown mushrooms, chopped finely

1 clove garlic, crushed

3 shallots (75g), chopped finely

½ cup (125ml) balsamic vinegar

1.2kg easy carve lamb leg

1 teaspoon sea salt

2 large parsnips (700g)

2 large carrots (360g)

1 large kumara (500g)

2 large potatoes (600g)

2 tablespoons olive oil

½ cup (125ml) beef stock

1 Melt butter in large frying pan; cook mushrooms, garlic and shallot, stirring, until shallot softens. Add half of the vinegar; bring to a boil. Reduce heat, simmer duxelles, uncovered, about 5 minutes or until liquid has evaporated.

2 Fill lamb cavity with duxelles; rub lamb all over with salt.

3 Preheat oven to 180°C/160°C fan-forced.

4 Halve parsnips, carrots and kumara first crossways, then lengthways; cut pieces into thick slices. Cut potatoes into wedges. Place vegetables, in single layer, in large shallow flameproof baking dish; drizzle with oil. Place lamb on wire rack over vegetables, roast, uncovered, about 1 hour 30 minutes or until lamb is cooked as desired and vegetables are tender. Remove lamb and vegetables from dish, cover lamb; stand 10 minutes.

5 Meanwhile, place dish containing juices over heat; stir in stock and remaining vinegar, bring to a boil. Strain sauce into small jug.

6 Serve vegetables with sliced lamb, drizzled with sauce.

▭ **PER SERVING** 34.3g total fat (13.9g saturated fat); 3432kJ (821 cal); 50.5g carbohydrate; 76.5g protein; 11g fibre

Duxelles (pronounced deu-zehl) is the term for a classic French preparation believed to have been first devised in the 17th Century by La Varenne, one of the first cookbook authors, who created this mixture while chef for the Marquis d'Uxelles. Finely chopped shallots and mushrooms are sautéed in butter until the moisture evaporates and the result is a soft, almost essence-like, paste. A duxelles is used to flavour stuffings, sauces and soups, but we probably know it best as a fundamental part of a pâté or beef wellington.

Roast pork belly with plum sauce

PREPARATION TIME 20 MINUTES **COOKING TIME** 1 HOUR 55 MINUTES **SERVES** 4

800g boned pork belly, rind-on

1 teaspoon olive oil

2 teaspoons salt

1 cup (250ml) water

1 ½ cups (375ml) chicken stock

2 tablespoons light soy sauce

¼ cup (60ml) chinese cooking wine

¼ cup (55g) firmly packed brown sugar

2 cloves garlic, sliced thinly

3cm piece fresh ginger (15g), sliced thinly

1 cinnamon stick, crushed

1 teaspoon dried chilli flakes

⅓ cup (80ml) orange juice

6 cloves

1 teaspoon fennel seeds

4 plums (450g), halved

CUCUMBER SALAD

1 lebanese cucumber (130g)

1 fresh long green chilli, sliced thinly

⅔ cup coarsely chopped fresh mint

1 tablespoon olive oil

1 tablespoon lemon juice

1 teaspoon caster sugar

1 Preheat oven to 180°C/160°C fan-forced.

2 Place pork on board, rind-side up. Using sharp knife, score rind by making shallow cuts diagonally in both directions at 3cm intervals; rub oil, then salt into cuts.

3 Combine the water, stock, sauce, wine, sugar, garlic, ginger, cinnamon, chilli, juice, cloves and seeds in large shallow baking dish. Place pork in dish, rind-side up; roast, uncovered, 1 hour 20 minutes. Increase oven temperature to 240°C/220°C fan-forced; roast pork, uncovered, a further 15 minutes or until crackling is crisp.

4 Remove pork from dish; cover to keep warm. Strain liquid in baking dish into medium saucepan, skim away surface fat; bring to a boil. Add plums; reduce heat, simmer, uncovered, about 15 minutes or until plum sauce thickens.

5 Meanwhile, make cucumber salad.

6 Serve thickly sliced pork with plum sauce and salad.

CUCUMBER SALAD Using vegetable peeler, cut cucumber lengthways into ribbons. Place cucumber in large bowl with remaining ingredients; toss gently to combine.

⬜ **PER SERVING** 51g total fat (16.2g saturated fat); 3010kJ (720 cal); 25.6g carbohydrate; 39.1g protein; 3.4g fibre

A traditionally popular cut of pork in both Chinese and Korean cooking, belly is usually marinated and cooked as a whole slab, similar to the way we treat spareribs. Here, the meat is imbued with Asian flavours as it roasts over the scented broth.

Ginger and garlic used in a marinade or spiced broth that is to be discarded don't have to be peeled nor should either be so finely chopped that bits can find their way through the sieve when the liquid is strained.

THE GRATIN DISH

The Gratin Dish

The word "gratin" comes from a French word for "scrape", referring to the action of grating cheese, or bread for breadcrumbs – the usual ingredients for the golden-brown topping that characterises food cooked *au gratin*. *Le gratin* is also French slang for the "top people" in society – the equivalent of our term "the upper crust". One of the most rewarding things about a gratin dish is that it gives food instant class: in the same way that putting a frame around a picture suddenly brings it to life, food presented in a gratin dish always seems special.

CHOOSING A GRATIN DISH

A gratin dish is a shallow ovenproof dish with flaring sides so that it is considerably wider at the top than at the base, ensuring plenty of the delicious browned top to go with the food underneath. Gratin dishes are usually made using ceramic-type materials, most commonly porcelain, but sometimes other kinds of pottery. As they are designed to go to the table, they are often beautifully decorated. Even plain ones are elegant: the classic shape is round or oval with shell-like "ears" for handles. Less commonly, you may find metal gratin dishes in handsome finishes like copper, mirror-finished stainless steel or enamelled cast-iron.

Because of their shallowness and flaring shape, you need a gratin dish larger than you might expect to serve several people. Depending on appetites and what else is being served, you might need an oval dish with a top 23cm long to serve two or three people as a main course or a solo lunch dish, an oval dish 29cm long to serve four, or an oval dish 32cm long to serve six (the measurements are for the dish only, not counting "ears" or other handles). It is easier, for many occasions, to use individual gratin dishes, which save you the trouble of serving and are invariably greeted with the same sort of delight as when people get their very own soufflés or omelettes. Individual dishes come in various sizes; one attractive option for a small entrée-sized dish is to buy the natural scallop shells that are available in some kitchen shops.

USE

The longer you have gratin dishes, the more uses you find for them. Their primary purpose is to hold food topped with a layer that will brown in the heat of the oven or the griller, but they are also useful for frittatas and the baked-egg dishes the French call *en cocotte* and Americans call "shirred". They also make elegant serving dishes. A small oval gratin dish is the perfect serving dish for a filled avocado half, while larger ovals look beautiful with fish fillets or slender vegetables such as asparagus, baby leeks, green beans and baby carrots.

TOPPINGS Some foods don't need a separate topping because they will themselves brown when baked or grilled – scalloped potatoes or food in a rich custard such as those used for quiche fillings, for example. The traditional added toppings are cheese and breadcrumbs, but you can make a gratin using any food that will brown. The classics that head the list are:

- Grated or shaved cheddar, parmesan or any hard or semi-hard cheese
- Dried or fresh breadcrumbs dotted with butter or tossed in melted butter
- A mixture of the above two items
- Mashed potato, plain or mixed with another mashed vegetable such as pumpkin, sweet potato, parsnip or celeriac, preferably mashed with no milk, only butter and/or cream so that it will brown better; or, to reduce the fat content by about a third, mashed with equal quantities of butter and instant full-cream milk powder
- Small bread cubes tossed in melted butter or oil
- Sliced and buttered brioche, croissant, fruit bread or any other sweet bread, or plain bread, arranged in an overlapping pattern to cover the top completely. Be sure to butter right to the edges; cut large slices into quarters. For desserts, bread may be sprinkled with sugar after assembly.

FOODS TO COOK AU GRATIN The food that goes under the topping is usually cooked separately as the shallowness of a gratin dish lends itself only to brief cooking times. The job of the gratin dish is only to heat the food and brown the topping. The main exceptions are foods such as scallops, which call for such brief cooking that the short heating and browning time will cook them to perfection. Any food in a sauce or gravy, or foods that provide their own moisture such as tomato mixtures or sliced fruits, also can be used.

LEFTOVERS The thing you may enjoy most about your gratin dish is the way you can use it to make fabulous leftovers, in fact, you may join the many cooks who deliberately cook "too much" the first time to ensure they will have enough leftovers for the recipes they want. The most famous example is shepherd's pie, which not only uses the last of a lamb roast, but has become a beloved classic in its own right.

Cooked vegetables that would be boring if simply reheated are a new treat if you add a little fried onion or mushroom and heat them in a cheese sauce with a crunchy topping; cooked seafood is exquisite when baked in an egg custard like those used for quiche fillings.

TECHNIQUES

Whether cooking in a preheated oven or under the grill, place the gratin dish or dishes on an oven tray, in order to catch any spills. In the oven, check it a couple of times during cooking and be ready to move it to a hotter part of the oven if it is not browning, if it is browning too quickly, move it to a cooler part and, if necessary, lay a piece of baking paper over the top to protect it from the heat. If you are browning the top under the grill, check constantly and be ready to remove it the moment it is delicately golden brown.

CARE

A gratin dish can be washed by hand or go into the dishwasher. If it has baked-on brown bits that are resistant to brushing with an ordinary washing-up brush, soak in hot water with a few drops of detergent, overnight if necessary, rather than attacking it with scouring products or pads that may damage the glaze.

In the English-speaking world, the hard, slightly yellow root vegetable that slightly resembles a large dried turnip is called a swede in England and Australia, a neep in Scotland and rutabaga in the United States. Because this vegetable thrives in the cold, it has always been popular in Scandinavia, especially in Sweden, hence the name. Still under-appreciated here, the swede is deserving of more attention; it's a great tasting vegetable with a delicate sweetness and flavour that hints of the freshness of cabbage and turnip.

Winter vegetable gratin

PREPARATION TIME 25 MINUTES   **COOKING TIME** 1 HOUR 50 MINUTES   **SERVES** 4

40g butter
¼ cup (35g) plain flour
2 cups (500ml) milk
pinch ground nutmeg
3 medium potatoes (600g)
2 medium carrots (240g)
1 large swede (450g)
1 large kumara (500g)
½ cup (35g) stale breadcrumbs
¾ cup (60g) finely grated parmesan cheese

1   Preheat oven to 200°C/180°C fan-forced. Oil 1.5-litre (6-cup) gratin dish.

2   Melt butter in medium saucepan, add flour; cook, stirring, 1 minute. Remove from heat, gradually stir in milk; cook, stirring, until mixture boils and thickens. Stir in nutmeg.

3   Using sharp knife, mandoline or V-slicer, slice potatoes, carrots, swede and kumara thinly; pat dry with absorbent paper.

4   Layer potato slices in dish; pour a third of the white sauce over potato slices. Layer with carrot, another third of the white sauce, then swede, remaining white sauce and finally kumara.

5   Cover dish; cook about 1½ hours or until vegetables are tender. Uncover; top with combined breadcrumbs and cheese; cook, uncovered, about 20 minutes or until top is browned lightly. Stand 10 minutes before serving.

▭ **PER SERVING** 18.7g total fat (11.8g saturated fat); 2044kJ (489 cal); 57g carbohydrate; 18.7g protein; 8.8g fibre

Kitchen extras

Help is at hand with tools designed to facilitate a specific purpose. If you're serious about cooking, you'll love these aids.

MEAT MALLET

Usually double-sided with a plain and a waffle face. The waffle points can tear food if used with too much force. The plain side is especially good for pounding schnitzel.

FOOD MILL

A hand-operated "food mill" uses a rotating curved blade to push food through a perforated disc into the container beneath. Interchangeable fine, medium and coarse discs govern the texture of the puree.

RICER

Used to make the super-smooth potato called Paris mash. The potato goes into the container and, as the flat side is pressed down, it falls through the perforated base in fine, soft flakes.

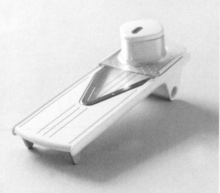  

V-SLICER

Cheaper and simpler to use than the Italian mandoline (but just as dangerously sharp), the V-slicer combines German efficiency and performance with its razor-sharp, flexible thin blades that slice, dice, shred and julienne.

MORTAR AND PESTLE

For grinding spices, chillies and other aromatics and making curry pastes. An electric spice/coffee grinder or a food processor will do it faster, but many good cooks swear by the superior flavour and texture of ingredients ground this slower, time-honoured way.

HAND GRATERS

Razor-sharp blades grate food cleanly and fast without "chewing" it or clogging. Comes in varying degrees of fineness/coarseness, length and width. Expensive compared to other graters, but worth it.

MULTI-PURPOSE SKEWERS

Wooden butcher skewers are used to secure rolled meats and the like; they are also used in cake decorating. Trussing skewers are great for testing cakes and trussing poultry.

SALAD SPINNER

Quickly dries washed salad leaves, herbs and shredded cabbage, whirling them so fast in a slotted container that centrifugal force makes the water fly off through the slots into an outer container and is discarded.

MANDOLINE

Slices vegetables and firm fruits, cheese or meats, such as salami and prosciutto, into paper-thin or thick slices. It also waffle-cuts, juliennes and cuts chips.

SQUARE GRATER

The best of the traditional graters is a sturdy, square one that is comfortable to grasp and presents a generous surface to each pass of the food. Different faces grate fine or coarse and shreds or slices.

GARLIC PRESS

The traditional garlic press does a good, quick job of crushing peeled cloves efficiently although is fiddly to clean. Pressing rather than mincing liberates more of the garlic's flavouring.

MEZZALUNA

The mezzaluna or "half-moon" is the classic Italian chopping instrument used by holding the two handles and rocking the sharp blade rapidly through the food. Can be used on a board or in a bowl shaped to match its curve. Chops parsley very finely without bruising it.

Smashed roast potato and thyme gratin

PREPARATION TIME 15 MINUTES **COOKING TIME** 30 MINUTES **SERVES** 4

50g butter

1 medium brown onion (150g), sliced thinly

600g roast potatoes, halved

2 tablespoons plain flour

1 cup (250ml) milk

2 teaspoons finely chopped fresh thyme

1 cup (120g) coarsely grated cheddar cheese

1 Preheat oven to 220°C/200°C fan-forced. Oil four 1-cup (250ml) gratin dishes.

2 Melt 10g of the butter in medium saucepan; cook onion, stirring, until softened.

3 Meanwhile, use potato masher to gently crush potato in large bowl; stir in onion mixture.

4 Melt remaining butter in same pan, add flour; cook, stirring, until mixture thickens and bubbles. Gradually stir in milk; cook, stirring, until mixture boils and thickens. Remove from heat; stir in thyme and half of the cheese.

5 Stir cheese sauce into potato mixture. Spoon gratin mixture into dishes; sprinkle each with remaining cheese. Bake about 20 minutes or until browned lightly.

☐ **PER SERVING** 29.1g total fat (16.5g saturated fat); 2128kJ (509 cal); 42.8g carbohydrate; 17.1g protein; 4.8g fibre

Macaroni cheese

PREPARATION TIME 10 MINUTES **COOKING TIME** 50 MINUTES **SERVES** 4

300g macaroni

4 rindless bacon rashers (260g), chopped coarsely

50g butter

⅓ cup (50g) plain flour

1 litre (4 cups) hot milk

1 cup (125g) coarsely grated cheddar cheese

½ cup (40g) coarsely grated pecorino cheese

2 tablespoons wholegrain mustard

½ cup (35g) stale breadcrumbs

20g butter, chopped, extra

1 Cook pasta in large saucepan of boiling water, uncovered, until just tender; drain.

2 Preheat oven to 200°C/180°C fan-forced. Oil 2-litre (8-cup) gratin dish.

3 Cook bacon in medium frying pan, stirring, until crisp; drain.

4 Melt butter in same pan, add flour; cook, stirring, 1 minute. Gradually add milk; cook, stirring, until mixture boils and thickens. Cool 2 minutes; stir in cheeses and mustard.

5 Combine pasta, cheese sauce and bacon in large bowl; transfer mixture to dish. Top with breadcrumbs; dot with extra butter.

6 Bake about 30 minutes or until top is browned lightly.

☐ **PER SERVING** 43.9g fat (26.4g saturated fat); 3616kJ (865 cal); 78.7g carbohydrate; 37.8g protein; 3.5g fibre

Fish mornay pies

PREPARATION TIME 25 MINUTES **COOKING TIME** 35 MINUTES **SERVES** 4

2½ cups (625ml) milk

½ small brown onion (40g)

1 bay leaf

6 black peppercorns

4 x 170g fish fillets, skinned

3 large potatoes (900g), chopped coarsely

600g celeriac, chopped coarsely

1 egg yolk

½ cup (40g) finely grated parmesan cheese

¾ cup (180ml) cream

60g butter

¼ cup (35g) plain flour

2 tablespoons coarsely chopped fresh flat-leaf parsley

1 Place milk, onion, bay leaf and peppercorns in large frying pan; bring to a boil. Add fish, reduce heat; simmer, covered, about 5 minutes or until cooked through. Remove fish from pan; divide fish among four 1½-cup (375ml) gratin dishes. Strain milk through sieve into medium jug. Discard solids; reserve milk.

2 Boil, steam or microwave potato and celeriac, separately, until tender; drain. Push potato and celeriac through sieve into large bowl; stir in yolk, cheese, ¼ cup of the cream and half of the butter until smooth. Cover to keep warm.

3 Meanwhile, melt remaining butter in medium saucepan, add flour; cook, stirring, about 3 minutes or until mixture bubbles and thickens slightly. Gradually stir in reserved milk and remaining cream; cook, stirring, until mixture boils and thickens. Stir in parsley.

4 Preheat grill.

5 Divide mornay mixture among dishes; cover each with potato mixture. Place dishes on oven tray; grill until browned lightly.

▭ **PER SERVING** 47.8g total fat (28.9g saturated fat); 3520kJ (842 cal); 43.4g carbohydrate; 53.9g protein; 8.7g fibre

A mornay is basically a béchamel sauce with a little cream, an egg yolk and some grated cheese stirred into the mix. The word has also come to mean the name of a dish which makes use of a mornay in its composition.

Celeriac, like fennel, lends itself tastefully to a creamy, cheesy mix. A member of the celery family, celeriac is a tuberous brown-skinned root having a coarse, off-white flesh that tastes like an earthy, more pungent celery. Sometimes called knob celery, it is widely eaten throughout Northern Europe, raw in salads, mashed like potato or fried into chips.

Pumpkin gratin

PREPARATION TIME 10 MINUTES **COOKING TIME** 50 MINUTES **SERVES** 4

750g butternut pumpkin

2 cloves garlic, halved

¼ cup (60ml) cream

⅓ cup (25g) coarsely grated parmesan cheese

1 Preheat oven to 200°C/180°C fan-forced. Oil 1-litre (4-cup) gratin dish.

2 Peel pumpkin, remove seeds; chop into even pieces. Place pumpkin pieces in dish with garlic; roast about 25 minutes or until pumpkin is almost cooked through.

3 Pour cream over pumpkin; sprinkle with cheese. Cook another 25 minutes or until pumpkin is tender.

▭ **PER SERVING** 9.5g total fat (6.1g saturated fat); 660kJ (158 cal); 11.2g carbohydrate; 6g protein; 2.3g fibre

A special, "dressed-up" way to serve this common household veg all too often hidden away in a mash, soup or scone: here it's eaten standing proud as golden-brown chunks enhanced with garlic and cream. The same treatment can be given to other humble vegetables – turnips, parsnips or kumara all take on a life of their own in a gratin.

Scalloped potatoes

PREPARATION TIME 20 MINUTES   **COOKING TIME** 1 HOUR 10 MINUTES (PLUS STANDING TIME)   **SERVES** 6

1.2kg potatoes, peeled
150g leg ham, chopped finely
300ml cream
¾ cup (180ml) milk
¾ cup (90g) coarsely grated cheddar cheese

1   Preheat oven to 180°C/160°C fan-forced. Oil 1.5-litre (6-cup) gratin dish.
2   Using sharp knife, mandoline or V-slicer, cut potatoes into very thin slices; pat dry with absorbent paper. Layer a quarter of the potato in dish; top with a third of the ham. Continue layering remaining potato and ham, finishing with potato.
3   Heat cream and milk in small saucepan until almost boiling; pour over potato mixture.
4   Cover dish with foil; bake 30 minutes. Remove foil; bake a further 20 minutes. Top with cheese; bake, uncovered, about 20 minutes or until potato is tender. Stand 10 minutes before serving.

☐ **PER SERVING** 28.9g total fat (18.6g saturated fat); 1764kJ (422 cal); 25.2g carbohydrate; 14.6g protein; 2.7g fibre

Fennel and potato gratin

PREPARATION TIME 20 MINUTES   **COOKING TIME** 1 HOUR 15 MINUTES   **SERVES** 8

800g potatoes, peeled
2 small fennel bulbs (400g), sliced thinly
1 tablespoon plain flour
1¾ cups (430ml) cream
¼ cup (60ml) milk
20g butter
¾ cup (90g) coarsely grated cheddar cheese
¾ cup (50g) stale breadcrumbs

1   Preheat oven to 180°C/160°C fan-forced. Oil 2-litre (8-cup) gratin dish.
2   Using sharp knife, mandoline or V-slicer, cut potatoes into very thin slices; pat dry with absorbent paper. Layer a quarter of the potato slices into dish; top with a third of the fennel. Continue layering remaining potato and fennel, finishing with potato.
3   Blend flour with a little of the cream in medium jug to form a smooth paste; stir in remaining cream and milk. Pour cream mixture over potato; dot with butter.
4   Cover dish with foil; bake about 1 hour or until vegetables are just tender. Remove foil, top with combined cheese and breadcrumbs; bake about 15 minutes or until top is browned lightly.

☐ **PER SERVING** 15.2g total fat (9.9g saturated fat); 803kJ (192 cal); 9.8g carbohydrate; 3.8g protein; 1.3g fibre

1 SCALLOPED POTATOES **2** FENNEL AND POTATO GRATIN
3 CREAMED POTATOES WITH ROSEMARY AND CHEESE [P 354] **4** POTATOES BYRON [P 354]

1

2

3 4

Creamed potatoes with rosemary and cheese

PREPARATION TIME 15 MINUTES **COOKING TIME** 1 HOUR 20 MINUTES (PLUS STANDING TIME) **SERVES** 6

This warm and homely dish takes no time at all to get into the oven, and once there, it will fill the kitchen with the pine-tree-and-lemon aroma of rosemary – a perfect gratin to serve with lamb kebabs, marinated in olive oil, lemon juice and garlic then skewered on whittled lengths of trimmed rosemary stems.

1kg potatoes, peeled

300ml cream

2 cloves garlic, crushed

2 chicken stock cubes, crumbled

½ teaspoon cracked black pepper

1 tablespoon finely chopped fresh rosemary

½ cup (40g) finely grated parmesan cheese

1 Preheat oven to 180°C/160°C fan-forced. Oil 2.5-litre (10-cup) gratin dish.

2 Using sharp knife, mandoline or V-slicer, cut potatoes into thin slices; pat dry with absorbent paper.

3 Combine cream, garlic, stock cubes, pepper and rosemary in small bowl.

4 Layer a quarter of the potato slices, slightly overlapping, in dish; top with a quarter of the cream mixture. Continue layering with remaining potato and cream mixture.

5 Press potato firmly with spatula to completely submerge in cream, cover dish with foil; bake 1 hour. Remove foil; sprinkle with cheese. Bake a further 20 minutes or until potato is tender and cheese browns lightly. Stand 10 minutes before serving.

PER SERVING 15.7g total fat (1375g saturated fat); 329kJ (20.4 cal); 20.4g carbohydrate; 7.1g protein; 2.4g fibre

Potatoes byron

PREPARATION TIME 10 MINUTES (PLUS COOLING TIME) **COOKING TIME** 1 HOUR 10 MINUTES **SERVES** 4

Supposedly named for the poet Lord Byron who declined all other food at a dinner party except this dish. When prepared by the French or in restaurant kitchens, this dish is artfully arranged in a very shallow gratin dish and heated under a salamander, a piece of equipment resembling a griller which can be either wall-mounted or hand-held, depending on whether a professional or domestic tool is used. It heats from the top so is quite hot, making it perfect for rapid browning of a gratin.

1kg potatoes, unpeeled

60g butter, chopped

½ cup (125ml) cream

¼ cup (20g) finely grated parmesan cheese

¼ cup (30g) finely grated gruyère cheese

1 Preheat oven to 180°C/160°C fan-forced. Oil four 1-cup (250ml) gratin dishes.

2 Pierce skin of each potato with fork; place on oven tray. Bake about 1 hour or until tender. Cover; cool 10 minutes. Increase oven temperature to 220°C/200°C fan-forced.

3 Split potatoes in half lengthways; scoop flesh into medium bowl, discard potato skins. Mash potato with butter.

4 Place 7.5cm cutter in centre of one dish; pack mashed potato into cutter. Carefully remove cutter; repeat, packing remaining potato into cutter in each dish. Pour cream evenly over dishes; sprinkle with combined cheeses.

5 Bake, uncovered, about 10 minutes or until heated through and browned lightly.

PER SERVING 30.2g total fat (19.7g saturated fat); 1910kJ (457 cal); 33.8g carbohydrate; 10.8g protein; 5g fibre

Baked tortellini and vegetables

PREPARATION TIME 15 MINUTES **COOKING TIME** 35 MINUTES **SERVES** 4

500g cheese and spinach tortellini

1 tablespoon olive oil

200g button mushrooms, sliced thinly

2 medium zucchini (240g), chopped coarsely

1 medium red capsicum (200g), chopped coarsely

700g bottled tomato pasta sauce

4 green onions, sliced thinly

¼ cup coarsely chopped fresh flat-leaf parsley

2 cups (250g) coarsely grated cheddar cheese

1 Preheat oven to 200°C/180°C fan-forced. Oil 3-litre (12-cup) gratin dish.

2 Cook pasta in large saucepan of boiling water, uncovered, until just tender; drain, reserve ½ cup of the cooking liquid.

3 Meanwhile, heat oil in large frying pan; cook mushrooms, zucchini and capsicum, stirring, until vegetables are just tender. Stir in sauce and reserved cooking liquid, then pasta, onion and parsley. Spoon mixture into dish; sprinkle with cheese.

4 Bake about 20 minutes or until browned lightly.

▭ **PER SERVING** 36.1g total fat (19.6g saturated fat); 2592kJ (620 cal); 38.5g carbohydrate; 31.6g protein; 8.3g fibre

Refrigerated or frozen ring-shaped tortellini, available in supermarkets and delicatessens, are machine-made or handmade small filled pasta cases made from durum wheat semolina and fresh eggs, then stuffed with combinations of various meats, cheeses and/or vegetables. These are cooked in large pots of boiling water and served with various sauces and cheese, just like dried unfilled pasta.

Zucchini gratin

PREPARATION TIME 15 MINUTES **COOKING TIME** 40 MINUTES **SERVES** 6

7 medium zucchini (840g)

60g butter

2 medium brown onions (300g), chopped finely

¼ cup finely shredded fresh basil

3 eggs

¾ cup (180g) crème fraîche or sour cream

¾ cup (90g) coarsely grated gruyère cheese

1 Peel five of the zucchini, then coarsely grate all zucchini. Melt half of the butter in large frying pan; cook zucchini, stirring, over medium heat, about 10 minutes or until softened and excess liquid is evaporated.

2 Meanwhile, melt remaining butter in medium frying pan; cook onion, over medium heat, stirring, about 5 minutes or until very soft. Add onion and basil to zucchini; mix well.

3 Preheat oven to 200°C/180°C fan-forced. Oil shallow 2-litre (8-cup) gratin dish.

4 Whisk eggs, crème fraîche and half of the cheese in medium bowl.

5 Spread zucchini mixture into dish, top with egg mixture; swirl with knife to mix lightly. Sprinkle with remaining cheese.

6 Bake about 25 minutes or until browned lightly and just set.

▭ **PER SERVING** 28.1g total fat (17g saturated fat); 1329kJ (318 cal); 6g carbohydrate; 11.2g protein; 3g fibre

One of the many beauties of making a gratin topping is that ingredients can be chopped and changed at will. You're only restricted by what's in the fridge or pantry – and by what your cooking knowledge tells you will or will not work. Here, you can combine the final half of the cheese with a quarter cup of coarsely ground yellow polenta for a nice hint of corn and a tad more crunch. Serve the gratin with char-grilled red capsicum pieces and meaty young veal chops.

Za'atar is a blend of roasted dried spices, usually including sesame seeds, wild marjoram, thyme and sumac. It's available from Middle-Eastern food shops, delicatessens and most supermarkets. Make your own by combining 1 tablespoon sumac, 1 tablespoon roasted sesame seeds, 1 teaspoon dried marjoram, 2 teaspoons dried thyme. Try it sprinkled on your morning toast that's been spread with softened fetta or ricotta cheese. Keep what you don't use stored, in a glass jar with a tight-fitting lid, in the fridge.

Potato, spinach and za'atar frittatas

PREPARATION TIME 20 MINUTES **COOKING TIME** 40 MINUTES **SERVES** 4

4 medium potatoes (800g), sliced thinly
1 tablespoon za'atar
2 cloves garlic, crushed
6 eggs
½ cup (125ml) cream
40g baby spinach leaves
1 tablespoon roasted sesame seeds

1 Preheat oven to 180°C/160°C fan-forced. Oil four 1½-cup (375ml) gratin dishes.
2 Boil, steam or microwave potatoes until tender; drain. Combine potato with za'atar in medium bowl.
3 Whisk garlic, eggs and cream in small jug. Divide half the potato mixture among dishes; top with half the egg mixture, then spinach. Top with remaining potato mixture and remaining egg mixture.
4 Bake frittatas about 30 minutes or until almost firm. Stand 10 minutes to allow to firm. Serve frittatas sprinkled with sesame seeds.

☐ **PER SERVING** 32.3g total fat (12.8g saturated fat); 1906kJ (456 cal); 24.3g carbohydrate; 15.7g protein; 3.6g fibre

You can buy cannelloni, large tubular pasta, instead of shells if you like, and stuff them with the filling. Another alternative that will save you time is to roll the filling in sheets of fresh lasagne, which needs no parboiling before being baked. Try stirring ½ teaspoon ground cinnamon into the spinach and cheese mixture.

Ricotta and spinach stuffed pasta shells

PREPARATION TIME 20 MINUTES **COOKING TIME** 1 HOUR 5 MINUTES **SERVES** 4

32 large pasta shells (280g)
500g spinach
250g ricotta cheese
500g cottage cheese

600ml bottled tomato pasta sauce
1 cup (250ml) vegetable stock
1 tablespoon finely grated parmesan cheese

1 Cook pasta in large saucepan of boiling water, uncovered, 3 minutes; drain. Cool slightly.
2 Preheat oven to 180°C/160°C fan-forced. Oil 2-litre (8-cup) gratin dish.
3 Boil, steam or microwave spinach until just wilted; drain. Chop spinach finely; squeeze out excess liquid.
4 Combine spinach in large bowl with ricotta and cottage cheese; spoon spinach mixture into pasta shells.
5 Combine sauce and stock in dish. Place pasta shells in dish; sprinkle with parmesan. Bake, covered, about 1 hour or until pasta is tender.

☐ **PER SERVING** 17.3g total fat (9.8g saturated fat); 2596kJ (621 cal); 69.3g carbohydrate; 41.6g protein; 9.1g fibre

POTATO, SPINACH AND ZA'ATAR FRITTATAS

THE
OVENPROOF
DISH

The Ovenproof Dish

There are, of course, ovenproof dishes in many shapes from soufflé dishes and pie dishes to casseroles and gratin dishes; all those are discussed in other chapters. Here, we are talking about the shallow, straight-sided oven dish you reach for when you want to make lasagne, moussaka and bread and butter pudding, or to bake stuffed apples, tomatoes or capsicums.

And, of course, there are also individual ovenproof dishes, usually a little deeper in proportion to their width than the larger ones, which are useful for pastitso (a Greek version of lasagne) or pot pies, and for serving french onion soup with its topping of bread covered in melted cheese.

These dishes are deep enough to accommodate the layers of the lasagne or moussaka, or to hold the apples or vegetables upright while they cook, while their large surface areas encourage evaporation, so the finished dish will be moist but not wet, and delicately golden on top.

CHOOSING AN OVENPROOF DISH

MATERIAL

This kind of dish is designed for gentle cooking, so it is usually made from earthenware or stoneware, which takes up heat slowly and holds it steadily. There are also enamelled cast-iron ovenproof dishes (which may be sold as baking dishes and double for both roles), and ovenproof glass dishes. All work well, although glass can cause the food to scorch more readily than the other materials. Some authorities recommend reducing the temperature by at least 10°C below that given in the recipe if you are using glass.

SHAPE AND SIZE

These dishes are usually oval or rectangular. Ovals are better for dishes that you spoon out to serve, such as a pudding; rectangular dishes are better for recipes that you cut into squares to serve, such as lasagne.

Consider the quantities you will be cooking when choosing an ovenproof dish. The food should fill it about three-quarters full before baking – much less and it will "hide" in the dish instead of looking generous, much more and it may overflow as it expands with cooking. Baked apples and other whole fruits and vegetables call for a dish into which they just fit comfortably so they stand upright and make a pleasing repeated pattern, like well-drilled soldiers, when carried to the table.

USE

PASTA AND OTHER SUBSTANTIAL DISHES You will often find rectangular oven dishes marked "lasagne dish", but they are perfect for any baked pasta – cannelloni, pastitso, rigatoni or other shapes in a rich sauce.

They are also the right dishes for such national specialities as Greek moussaka and Lebanese baked kibbeh, or for picnic pies such as egg and bacon or a double-crust meat pie with a firm filling.

FISH An oval ovenproof dish is just the right shape for poaching fish fillets or small whole fish. Make a *court bouillon* (seasoned stock) by combining 1 cup water, ½ cup dry white wine or ¼ cup verjuice or 1 tablespoon white wine vinegar, a few slices of onion, some flat-leaf parsley stalks and a bay leaf in a small saucepan, simmer for 5 minutes then strain. Put the fish into the greased dish, pour hot *court bouillon* over, lay a piece of baking paper loosely over the top and poach in a preheated 180°C/160°C fan-forced oven until the fillets turn white (or a lighter pink, for salmon or trout), or when a toothpick easily pierces the thickest part of a whole fish. This may take only 5 minutes, so it's important to observe the golden rule of fish cookery: don't leave the stove. Check frequently and, when the fish is cooked, remove immediately from the oven and lift out of the cooking liquid using two long metal spatulas (egg slides or fish slice), one at each end, to prevent it breaking.

FRUIT Poach sliced, halved or whole fruit in a sugar syrup of 1 cup water to ¼ to ½ cup sugar (depending on the sweetness of the fruit) with a vanilla bean, a strip of lemon rind or any other flavourings you wish. Arrange fruit in the dish, pour hot syrup over, lay a piece of buttered greaseproof paper loosely over and poach in a preheated 180°C/160°C fan-forced oven until tender.

VEGETABLES Baking vegetables with herbs, garlic, lemon or other delicious flavours turns them into the stars of a vegetarian table, or brilliant accompaniments to plain grilled, roasted or cold meats. Vegetables such as leeks, witlof, radicchio, eggplant , celeriac or carrots are excellent cooked this way. The usual method is to blanch them (or briefly fry eggplant), then bake them until tender in a foil covered ovenproof dish with your choice of flavouring ingredients, and a little cream or stock drizzled over. When cooked, remove the foil, sprinkle with breadcrumbs, grated cheese or a mixture of these, and bake a little longer until golden.

Vegetables that brown by themselves, such as potato, parsnip, carrot, pumpkin and sweet potato, can be coated in oil with the flavouring ingredients, drizzled with a little water or stock, covered with foil and baked until almost tender, then finished by baking, uncovered, until they are golden. Eggplant Parmigiana, is another vegetable classic from the ovenproof dish. Fried eggplant slices are topped with gently fried onion slices, tomato slices and cheese, and then baked.

FRENCH ONION SOUP If the ovenproof dishes in which the soup will be served are flameproof, you can put them on an oven tray, float the toasted bread on top, cover with grated cheese and place under the griller until the cheese is bubbling. If dishes are not flameproof, put dishes on an oven tray in the hottest part of a hot oven until the cheese bubbles. Place the dishes on larger, unheated plates for serving, to reduce the risk of burns.

CARE

An ovenproof dish is cared for in the same way as a gratin dish, see page 345.

Chicken and leek lasagne

PREPARATION TIME 25 MINUTES   **COOKING TIME** 1 HOUR 10 MINUTES   **SERVES** 4

60g butter

1 large leek (500g), sliced thinly

¼ cup (35g) plain flour

2 teaspoons dijon mustard

2 cups (500ml) chicken stock, warmed

3 cups (480g) shredded barbecued chicken

4 fresh lasagne sheets (200g), trimmed to fit ovenproof dish

⅔ cup (80g) coarsely grated cheddar cheese

1 Preheat oven to 180°C/160°C fan-forced. Oil shallow 2-litre (8-cup) ovenproof dish.

2 Melt butter in medium saucepan; cook leek, stirring, until soft. Add flour; cook, stirring, until mixture bubbles and thickens. Gradually stir in mustard and stock; stir over medium heat until mixture boils and thickens. Reserve ⅔ cup of the white sauce; stir chicken into remaining sauce.

3 Cover base of dish with lasagne sheet; top with about a quarter of the warm chicken mixture. Repeat layering with remaining lasagne sheets and chicken mixture, finishing with chicken mixture; top with reserved white sauce and cheese.

4 Bake lasagne, covered, 30 minutes; uncover, bake a further 20 minutes or until browned lightly. Stand 5 minutes before serving.

▭ **PER SERVING** 24.8g total fat (8.5g saturated fat); 1685kJ (403 cal); 15.5g carbohydrate; 28.8g protein; 2.4g fibre

Beef lasagne with four cheeses

PREPARATION TIME 25 MINUTES   **COOKING TIME** 55 MINUTES   **SERVES** 6

2 teaspoons olive oil

1 medium brown onion (150g), chopped finely

2 cloves garlic, crushed

500g lean beef mince

2 x 425g cans crushed tomatoes

½ cup (140g) tomato paste

½ teaspoon sugar

½ cup finely chopped fresh basil

¼ cup finely chopped fresh oregano

500g ricotta cheese

1 cup (80g) finely grated parmesan cheese

1 cup (100g) coarsely grated mozzarella cheese

¼ teaspoon ground nutmeg

4 eggs

200g large curly instant lasagne sheets

1 cup (100g) pizza cheese

1 Heat oil in large saucepan; cook onion and garlic, stirring, until onion softens. Add mince; cook, stirring, until mince changes colour. Add undrained tomatoes, tomato paste and sugar; cook, stirring, until sauce thickens. Remove from heat; stir in basil and oregano.

2 Preheat oven to 180°C/160°C fan-forced.

3 Beat ricotta, parmesan, mozzarella and nutmeg in medium bowl with electric mixer until well combined. Add eggs, one at a time, beating until just combined between additions.

4 Place a third of the lasagne sheets in shallow 2.5-litre (10-cup) ovenproof dish; top with half of the meat sauce and half of the cheese mixture. Top with another third of the lasagne sheets, remaining meat sauce, remaining lasagne sheets then remaining cheese mixture. Top with pizza cheese.

5 Bake lasagne, uncovered, about 45 minutes or until top browns lightly. Stand 5 minutes before serving.

PER SERVING 32.7g total fat (17.2g saturated fat); 2671kJ (639 cal); 33.2g carbohydrate; 50.9g protein; 4.1g fibre

Chicken, mushroom and asparagus creamy pasta bake

PREPARATION TIME 20 MINUTES **COOKING TIME** 30 MINUTES **SERVES** 4

375g rigatoni

60g butter

600g chicken breast fillets, diced into 1cm pieces

100g button mushrooms, sliced thinly

2 tablespoons plain flour

2 cups (500ml) milk

½ cup (40g) coarsely grated romano cheese

1¼ cups (150g) coarsely grated cheddar cheese

170g asparagus, trimmed, chopped coarsely

¼ cup coarsely chopped fresh flat-leaf parsley

1 Preheat oven to 200°C/180°C fan-forced.

2 Cook pasta in large saucepan of boiling water, uncovered, until just tender; drain.

3 Meanwhile, heat 20g of the butter in large frying pan; cook chicken, in batches, until browned and cooked through.

4 Heat remaining butter in same pan; cook mushrooms, stirring, until tender. Add flour; cook, stirring, 1 minute. Gradually stir in milk; stir over medium heat until mixture boils and thickens. Stir in chicken, ¼ cup of the romano, ¾ cup of the cheddar and asparagus.

5 Combine chicken mixture and pasta in 2.5-litre (10-cup) ovenproof dish; sprinkle with remaining cheeses. Bake, uncovered, about 15 minutes or until top browns lightly.

6 Serve pasta bake sprinkled with parsley, and a mixed green salad, if desired.

PER SERVING 37.3g total fat (22.3g saturated fat); 3775kJ (903 cal); 75.2g carbohydrate; 64g protein; 4.8g fibre

Romano is a variety of pecorino, an Italian generic sheep-milk cheese, named specifically after the area in which it is made, Rome. A hard cheese, straw-coloured and grainy in texture, it's mainly used for grating. A spicy variation of romano is pepato, where whole black peppercorns are added to the cheese as it's made, before ageing; using pepato in this pasta bake adds a complementary note of piquancy.

Baked risotto with spicy sausage and cherry tomatoes

PREPARATION TIME 15 MINUTES **COOKING TIME** 1 HOUR **SERVES** 4

5 thin spicy Italian-style sausages (400g)

3½ cups (875ml) chicken stock

2 teaspoons olive oil

1 large brown onion (200g), chopped finely

1 clove garlic, crushed

1½ cups (300g) arborio rice

250g cherry tomatoes

2 tablespoons fresh marjoram leaves

1 Preheat oven to 180°C/160°C fan-forced.

2 Cook sausages, uncovered, in heated large frying pan until browned all over and cooked through. Drain on absorbent paper; slice thickly.

3 Meanwhile, bring stock to a boil in medium saucepan. Reduce heat, simmer, covered.

4 Heat oil in same frying pan; cook onion and garlic, stirring, until onion softens. Add rice; stir to coat in onion mixture. Stir in stock and sausages.

5 Place risotto mixture in large shallow ovenproof dish. Cover dish with foil; bake 15 minutes, stirring halfway during cooking time. Uncover; bake another 15 minutes. Add tomatoes; bake about 15 minutes or until tomatoes soften and rice is tender.

6 Serve risotto sprinkled with marjoram.

☐ **PER SERVING** 29.1g total fat (13g saturated fat); 2587kJ (619 cal); 67.1g carbohydrate; 20.1g protein; 5g fibre

Vegetarian lasagne

PREPARATION TIME 40 MINUTES **COOKING TIME** 1 HOUR 30 MINUTES **SERVES** 4

3 medium red capsicums (600g)

1 medium eggplant (300g), sliced thinly

1 tablespoon coarse cooking salt

3 medium zucchini (360g), sliced thinly

1 medium kumara (400g), sliced thinly

cooking-oil spray

2 cups (500g) bottled tomato pasta sauce

250g instant lasagne sheets

2½ cups (250g) coarsely grated mozzarella cheese

⅓ cup (25g) coarsely grated parmesan cheese

WHITE SAUCE

40g butter

2 tablespoons plain flour

1¼ cups (310ml) milk

¼ cup (20g) coarsely grated parmesan cheese

1 Quarter capsicums; discard seeds and membranes. Roast under grill or in very hot oven, skin-side up, until skin blisters and blackens. Cover capsicum pieces in plastic or paper for 5 minutes; peel away skin.

2 Preheat oven to 200°C/180°C fan-forced. Place eggplant in colander, sprinkle all over with salt; stand 20 minutes. Rinse eggplant under cold water; drain on absorbent paper.

3 Meanwhile, make white sauce.

4 Place eggplant, zucchini and kumara, in single layer, on oven trays; coat with oil spray. Roast, uncovered, about 20 minutes or until browned and tender.

5 Oil deep rectangular 2-litre (8-cup) ovenproof dish. Spread ⅔ cup of the pasta sauce into dish; top with a quarter of the lasagne sheets, ⅓ cup of the pasta sauce, eggplant and a third of the mozzarella. Layer cheese with another quarter of the lasagne sheets, ⅓ cup of the pasta sauce, capsicum, and another third of the mozzarella. Layer mozzarella with another quarter of the lasagne sheets, ⅓ cup of the pasta sauce, zucchini, kumara, remaining mozzarella, remaining lasagne sheets and remaining pasta sauce. Top with white sauce, sprinkle with parmesan.

6 Bake lasagne, uncovered, about 30 minutes or until browned lightly. Stand 10 minutes before serving.

WHITE SAUCE Heat butter in small saucepan, add flour; cook stirring, until mixture thickens and bubbles. Gradually stir in milk; stir until mixture boils and thickens. Remove from heat; stir in cheese.

◻ **PER SERVING** 32.5g total fat (19g saturated fat); 3189kJ (763 cal); 82g carbohydrate; 37.5g protein; 9.9g fibre

Moussaka

PREPARATION TIME 40 MINUTES (PLUS STANDING TIME)
COOKING TIME 1 HOUR 30 MINUTES (PLUS STANDING TIME) **SERVES** 6

2 large eggplants (1kg), sliced thinly

1 tablespoon coarse cooking salt

¼ cup (60ml) olive oil

1 large brown onion (200g), chopped finely

2 cloves garlic, crushed

1kg lamb mince

425g can crushed tomatoes

½ cup (125ml) dry white wine

1 teaspoon ground cinnamon

¼ cup (20g) finely grated parmesan cheese

WHITE SAUCE
80g butter

⅓ cup (50g) plain flour

2 cups (500ml) milk

1 Place eggplant in colander, sprinkle all over with salt; stand 30 minutes. Rinse under cold water; drain. Pat dry with absorbent paper.

2 Heat oil in large frying pan; cook eggplant, in batches, until browned both sides. Drain on absorbent paper.

3 Cook onion and garlic in same pan, stirring, until onion softens. Add mince; cook, stirring, until mince changes colour. Stir in undrained tomatoes, wine and cinnamon; bring to a boil. Reduce heat, simmer, uncovered, about 30 minutes or until liquid has evaporated.

4 Meanwhile, preheat oven to 180°C/160°C fan-forced. Oil shallow 2-litre (8-cup) rectangular ovenproof dish.

5 Make white sauce.

6 Place a third of the eggplant, overlapping slices slightly, in dish; spread half of the meat sauce over eggplant. Repeat layering with another third of the eggplant, remaining meat sauce and remaining eggplant. Spread white sauce over top layer of eggplant, sprinkle with cheese.

7 Bake moussaka, uncovered, about 40 minutes or until top browns lightly. Cover; stand 10 minutes before serving.

WHITE SAUCE Melt butter in medium saucepan, add flour; cook, stirring, until mixture thickens and bubbles. Gradually stir in milk; stir until mixture boils and thickens.

◻ **PER SERVING** 36.6g total fat (16.5g saturated fat); 2420kJ (579 cal); 18g carbohydrate; 41.8g protein; 5.3g fibre

Oven-baked casseroles are common in Greek cooking, and moussaka is often considered the country's national dish. Some versions call for artichokes, potatoes and zucchini, or a combination but this one with eggplant is the classic known around the globe.

Ovenproof & baking dishes

Big and small, deep and shallow, these dishes all play an important role on the culinary stage.

DUTCH OVEN

A large casserole, wider than it is deep, usually made from stainless steel, enamelled or plain cast iron, or anodised aluminium. Great for pot-roasting and braising.

TIMBALE

A tall mould that gives its name to the dishes made in it, such as layered rice-and-vegetable mixtures. Today, timbale usually means an individual serving, but there is also a tradition of festive large moulds called timbales.

DARIOLE

A small, straight-sided mould for individual servings of savoury or sweet dishes such as mousses, rice mixtures, jellies and custards; used for classic British castle puddings.

FLAMEPROOF DISH

A flameproof oven dish is more useful than one that is only ovenproof, as it can also go on top of the stove to brown food before it is finished in the oven. Available in various metals and ceramics.

OVENPROOF DISH

A multi-purpose dish which comes in a variety of shapes, sizes and depths, usually made from earthenware, glass or enamelled cast iron, for food that is to be cooked in the oven.

BAKING DISHES

Also called roasting pans, baking dishes are intended mainly for cooking large joints of meat (see page 314), but are also useful for party-sized lasagne and the like. They come in various sizes and metals.

RAMEKIN

Small ceramic dishes in many sizes and shapes, in which foods of many kinds, from soups to desserts, are cooked or heated and served. Small ones are also useful servers for nibbles.

SOUFFLE DISH

Soufflé dishes come in individual or large sizes and are designed specifically for cooking and serving soufflés (see page 542), but can also be used for other cooking or serving duties.

PIZZA STONE

A flat pizza stone goes into the oven to be heated before the pizza is placed onto it for baking. The hot stone gives a crisp crust. To use, follow the manufacturer's instructions.

GRATIN DISH

A gratin dish is shallow and flared so that there will be plenty of the delicious browned topping to go with the food underneath. It is designed to cook the food and also to go to the table as an attractive serving piece.

SCALLOP SHELL

The scallop shell is one of nature's most beautiful designs and is the perfect shape for an individual entrée cooked au gratin (with a browned topping). Both natural ones and porcelain dishes made to resemble them are available.

CASSEROLE DISH

A casserole dish or two of the right size for your household, plus a big one for entertaining, are good investments. There are hundreds of shapes, sizes, colours and patterns to choose from.

Black bean, corn and chipotle stew

PREPARATION TIME 15 MINUTES (PLUS STANDING TIME) **COOKING TIME** 1 HOUR **SERVES** 4

1 ½ cups (300g) dried black beans

2 chipotle chillies

½ cup (125ml) boiling water

1 tablespoon cumin seeds

2 trimmed corn cobs (500g)

2 teaspoons olive oil

1 large brown onion (200g), chopped finely

810g can crushed tomatoes

8 small white corn tortillas

SALSA

1 small red onion (100g), chopped coarsely

1 small tomato (90g), chopped coarsely

½ cup coarsely chopped fresh coriander

1 lebanese cucumber (130g), chopped coarsely

1 tablespoon olive oil

2 tablespoons lemon juice

1 Place beans in medium bowl, cover with water; stand overnight, drain. Rinse under cold water; drain. Place beans in medium saucepan of boiling water; return to a boil. Reduce heat, simmer, uncovered, about 15 minutes or until beans are just tender.

2 Preheat oven to 200°C/180°C fan-forced.

3 Place chillies and the boiling water in small bowl; stand 15 minutes. Discard stalks; blend or process chilli and its soaking liquid until smooth.

4 Meanwhile, dry-fry cumin in large frying pan, stirring, until fragrant; remove from pan.

5 Cook corn on heated oiled grill plate (or grill or barbecue) until browned lightly and just tender. When cool enough to handle, cut kernels from cobs with sharp knife.

6 Heat oil in same large pan; cook onion, stirring, until soft. Add drained beans, chilli mixture, cumin, undrained tomatoes and half of the corn; bring to a boil. Transfer to large ovenproof dish; cook, uncovered, in oven about 20 minutes or until sauce thickens.

7 Meanwhile, heat tortillas according to manufacturer's instructions.

8 Combine remaining corn with salsa ingredients in medium bowl.

9 Serve stew with tortillas and salsa.

☐ **PER SERVING** 10.4g total fat (1.3g saturated fat); 1839kJ (440 cal); 61.3g carbohydrate; 26.2g protein; 19.5g fibre

In Mexican (and all Latin- and South-American) cooking, each variety of chilli has two names, distinguishing the fresh from the dried since the flavours are immensely different. Chipotle (pronounced chee-poat-lay) is the name given to a jalapeño (pronounced hah-lah-pain-yo) chilli once it's been dried and smoked. Having a deep, intensely smoky flavour, rather than a searing heat, chipotles are so dark brown they're almost black in colour and wrinkled in appearance. They are available from specialty spice stores and gourmet delicatessens.

Full of protein and fibre, cholesterol-free and low in fat, black beans (also known as turtle beans) make a tasty and healthy addition to stews, soups, salsas and salads, and go well with corn and chillies – the three are staples of the Mexican kitchen. Used in many of our favourite recipes, black beans can be soaked overnight in quantity, parboiled then frozen in user-friendly amounts, ready-to-go when a menu dictates.

No matter how you intend to cook it, raw mince requires careful handling and storage. It should be purchased as near to possible as when you intend to use it and kept, re-packaged from the shop, in the coldest part of your refrigerator. A non-plastic storage container (one having a perforated insert to keep the meat above its draining juices) is recommended for storage. The longest you should refrigerate minced meat is two days: always remember that the more cutting or preparation given meat, the briefer the allowable uncooked keeping time.

Italian cottage pie

PREPARATION TIME 25 MINUTES **COOKING TIME** 1 HOUR **SERVES** 6

1 tablespoon olive oil

1 medium brown onion (150g), chopped finely

2 cloves garlic, crushed

200g mushrooms, sliced thinly

1 large carrot (180g), cut into 1cm cubes

1 medium eggplant (300g), cut into 1cm cubes

750g lamb mince

1 tablespoon plain flour

½ cup (125ml) dry red wine

425g can crushed tomatoes

2 tablespoons tomato paste

1 tablespoon worcestershire sauce

2 tablespoons finely chopped fresh oregano

800g potatoes, chopped coarsely

20g butter

⅓ cup (80ml) milk

¼ cup (20g) finely grated parmesan cheese

SOFT POLENTA

1¼ cups (310ml) chicken stock

¾ cup (180ml) milk

½ cup (85g) polenta

¼ cup (20g) finely grated parmesan cheese

1 Preheat oven to 200°C/180°C fan-forced. Oil deep 2.5-litre (10-cup) ovenproof dish.

2 Heat oil in large frying pan; cook onion, garlic, mushrooms, carrot and eggplant, stirring, until onion softens. Add lamb; cook, stirring, until browned. Add flour; cook, stirring, 1 minute. Add wine; bring to a boil, stirring. Stir in undrained tomatoes, tomato paste, sauce and oregano. Reduce heat, simmer, uncovered, about 10 minutes or until mixture thickens slightly.

3 Meanwhile, make soft polenta.

4 Boil, steam or microwave potato until tender; drain. Mash potatoes with butter and milk in large bowl until smooth. Using wooden spoon, gently swirl hot polenta mixture into potato mixture.

5 Spoon mince mixture into dish; top with potato polenta mixture, sprinkle with cheese. Bake, uncovered, in oven about 25 minutes or until cheese browns lightly.

6 Serve with baby rocket leaves in balsamic vinaigrette, if desired.

SOFT POLENTA Bring stock and milk to a boil in large saucepan. Gradually add polenta to stock mixture, stirring constantly. Reduce heat, cook, stirring, about 10 minutes or until polenta thickens. Stir in cheese.

PER SERVING 19.4g total fat (8.8g saturated fat); 2040kJ (488 cal); 37.1g carbohydrate; 37.5g protein; 6.7g fibre

Lamb biryani

PREPARATION TIME 35 MINUTES (PLUS REFRIGERATION TIME) **COOKING TIME** 2 HOURS 30 MINUTES
SERVES 8

1.5kg boneless lamb shoulder, cut into 2cm cubes

5cm piece fresh ginger (25g), grated

3 cloves garlic, crushed

2 fresh small red thai chillies, chopped finely

2 tablespoons finely chopped fresh coriander

3 teaspoons garam masala

large pinch ground tumeric

½ teaspoon ground chilli powder

1 teaspoon salt

1 cup (280g) thick yogurt

80g ghee or butter

1 cup (140g) flaked almonds

⅓ cup (55g) sultanas

3 large brown onions (600g), sliced thickly

1 cup (250ml) water

500g basmati rice, washed, drained

large pinch saffron threads

2 tablespoons hot milk

fresh coriander leaves, extra

1 Combine lamb, ginger, garlic, chilli, coriander, garam masala, tumeric, chilli powder, salt and yogurt in medium bowl. Cover; refrigerate overnight.

2 Heat half of the ghee in large, heavy-based saucepan; cook almonds and sultanas until browned lightly. Remove from pan with a slotted spoon.

3 Heat remaining ghee in same pan; cook onion, covered, over medium heat 5 minutes or until onion is soft. Uncover; cook a further 5 minutes or until onions are lightly browned. Remove half of the onion mixture from pan; reserve.

4 Add lamb mixture to onion in pan, cook, stirring, until lamb is browned lightly. Add water; bring to a boil. Simmer, covered, over low heat, stirring occasionally, 1 hour. Uncover; simmer a further 30 minutes or until lamb is tender.

5 Meanwhile, cook rice in large saucepan of boiling about 5 minutes or until half-cooked; drain.

6 Combine saffron and milk in small bowl; stand 15 minutes.

7 Preheat oven to 180°C/160°C fan-forced. Oil 3.5-litre (14-cup) ovenproof dish.

8 Spread half of the lamb mixture into dish, top with half the rice. Layer with remaining lamb, then remaining rice. Drizzle saffron and milk mixture over rice. Cover dish tightly with greased foil and lid; bake about 40 minutes or until rice is tender.

9 Serve biryani topped with reheated reserved onions, almond mixture and extra coriander leaves.

▭ **PER SERVING** 38.2g total fat (15.9g saturated fat); 3281kJ (785 cal); 61.5g carbohydrate; 47g protein; 3.6g fibre

An elaborate layered dish inspired by moghul royalty, the regal biryani is still a spectacular Indian curry fit for a king. Perfect for entertaining, our version takes time but is worth every bit of effort.

Masala simply means blended flavours, so it can be whole spices, a paste or a powder, and can include herbs as well as spices and other seasonings. Traditional dishes are usually based on and named after particular masalas. Garam masala, used here, is a North Indian blend of spices based on varying proportions of cinnamon, cardamom, cloves, coriander, fennel and cumin, roasted and ground together. Black pepper and chilli can be added for a hotter version.

Pastitso

PREPARATION TIME 30 MINUTES **COOKING TIME** 1 HOUR 45 MINUTES **SERVES** 6

250g macaroni

2 eggs, beaten lightly

¾ cup (60g) coarsely grated parmesan cheese

2 tablespoons stale breadcrumbs

MEAT SAUCE

1 tablespoon olive oil

2 medium brown onions (300g), chopped finely

750g beef mince

400g can chopped tomatoes

⅓ cup (95g) tomato paste

½ cup (125ml) beef stock

¼ cup (60ml) dry white wine

½ teaspoon ground cinnamon

1 egg, beaten lightly

TOPPING

90g butter

½ cup (75g) plain flour

3½ cups (875ml) milk

1 cup (80g) coarsely grated parmesan cheese

2 egg yolks

1 Preheat oven to 180°C/160°C fan-forced. Oil shallow 2.5-litre (10-cup) ovenproof dish.

2 Cook pasta in large saucepan of boiling water, uncovered, until just tender; drain.

3 Combine warm pasta, egg and cheese in large bowl. Press pasta mixture over base of dish.

4 Make meat sauce.

5 Make topping.

6 Top pasta evenly with meat sauce, pour over topping; smooth surface then sprinkle with breadcrumbs. Bake, uncovered, about 1 hour or until browned lightly. Stand 10 minutes before serving.

MEAT SAUCE Heat oil in large saucepan; cook onion, stirring, until onion is soft. Add beef; cook, stirring, until beef is well browned. Stir in undrained tomatoes, tomato paste, stock, wine and cinnamon; simmer, uncovered, until thick. Cool 10 minutes; stir in egg.

TOPPING Melt butter in medium saucepan, add flour; stir over heat until bubbling. Remove from heat, gradually stir in milk. Stir over heat until sauce boils and thickens; stir in cheese. Cool 5 minutes; stir in egg yolks.

PER SERVING 41.7g total fat (21.8g saturated fat); 3398kJ (813 cal); 54.4g carbohydrate; 54g protein; 3.8g fibre

The tortilla (pronounced tor-tee-yah) is a pliable, thin unleavened bread that originated in Mexico and is still the bread product eaten daily by Hispanics everywhere. Tortillas are made either of wheat flour or ground corn meal, and can be purchased fresh, frozen or packaged from supermarkets. While enchiladas are traditionally made in Mexican kitchens with corn tortillas, the flour variety is perfectly acceptable and generally easier to obtain.

Enchilada (pronounced enn-chee-lah-dah) simply means "in chilli" and in Mexico is usually just street food, a corn tortilla eaten dipped in chilli sauce.

Chicken enchiladas

PREPARATION TIME 50 MINUTES   **COOKING TIME** 35 MINUTES   **SERVES** 10

3 chipotle chillies

1 cup (250ml) boiling water

500g chicken breast fillets

1 tablespoon vegetable oil

1 large red onion (300g), chopped finely

2 cloves garlic, crushed

1 teaspoon ground cumin

1 tablespoon tomato paste

2 x 425g cans crushed tomatoes

1 tablespoon finely chopped fresh oregano

²⁄₃ cup (160g) sour cream

1½ cups (240g) coarsely grated cheddar cheese

10 small flour tortillas

1   Cover chillies with the water in small heatproof bowl; stand 20 minutes. Remove stems from chillies; discard stems. Blend or process chillies with soaking liquid until smooth.

2   Meanwhile, place chicken in medium saucepan of boiling water; return to a boil. Reduce heat, simmer, covered, about 10 minutes or until chicken is cooked through. Remove chicken from poaching liquid; cool 10 minutes. Discard poaching liquid (or keep for another use); shred chicken finely.

3   Preheat oven to 180°C/160°C fan-forced. Oil shallow rectangular 3-litre (12-cup) ovenproof dish.

4   Heat oil in large frying pan; cook onion, stirring, until soft. Reserve half of the onion in small bowl.

5   Add garlic and cumin to remaining onion in pan; cook, stirring, until fragrant. Add chilli mixture, tomato paste, undrained tomatoes and oregano; bring to a boil. Reduce heat, simmer, uncovered, 1 minute. Remove sauce from heat.

6   Meanwhile, combine shredded chicken, reserved onion, half of the sour cream and a third of the cheese in medium bowl.

7   Warm tortillas according to manufacturer's instructions. Dip tortillas, one at a time, in tomato sauce in pan; place on board. Place ¼ cup of the chicken mixture along edge of each tortilla; roll enchiladas to enclose filling.

8   Spread ½ cup tomato sauce into dish. Place enchiladas, seam-side down, in dish (they should fit snugly, without overcrowding). Pour remaining tomato sauce over enchiladas; sprinkle with remaining cheese. Cook, uncovered, in oven about 15 minutes or until cheese melts and enchiladas are heated through. Sprinkle with coriander leaves, if desired. Serve with remaining sour cream.

☐ **PER SERVING** 9.4g total fat (9.4g saturated fat); 1593kJ (381 cal); 29.4g carbohydrate; 22g protein; 3.1g fibre

Beef and eggplant bake with polenta crust

PREPARATION TIME 20 MINUTES (PLUS STANDING TIME)

COOKING TIME 1 HOUR 20 MINUTES (PLUS STANDING TIME) **SERVES** 6

2 medium eggplants (600g), sliced thickly

2 tablespoons coarse cooking salt

1 tablespoon olive oil

1 medium brown onion (150g), chopped coarsely

1 medium red capsicum (200g), chopped coarsely

1 clove garlic, crushed

500g beef mince

2 tablespoons tomato paste

½ cup (125ml) dry red wine

400g can whole tomatoes

1 cup firmly packed fresh basil leaves

1 tablespoon fresh oregano leaves

2 cups (500ml) chicken stock

2 cups (500ml) milk

1 cup (170g) polenta

1½ cups (150g) coarsely grated mozzarella cheese

Also known as cornmeal, polenta is a flour-like cereal made from either white or yellow dried corn (maize) available ground both fine and coarse and in varying degrees in between; it is also the word for the name of the dish made with it. It's a staple in northern Italy where it is eaten either soft and creamy like a potato mash or fried into crisp pieces. Many cultures use it in sweet dishes: North Americans eat it for breakfast doused in maple syrup; Mexicans use it as the basis for the sweet tamales; and the Italians also use it in biscuits and cakes.

1 Place eggplant in colander, sprinkle all over with salt; stand 30 minutes. Rinse eggplant; drain on absorbent paper.

2 Meanwhile, heat oil in medium frying pan; cook onion, capsicum and garlic, stirring, until onion softens. Add beef; cook, stirring, until beef changes colour. Add tomato paste; cook, stirring, 2 minutes. Add wine; cook, stirring, 5 minutes. Add undrained tomatoes; bring to a boil. Reduce heat, simmer, uncovered, stirring occasionally, about 15 minutes or until liquid is almost evaporated. Chop about a quarter of the basil leaves coarsely; stir into sauce with oregano.

3 Preheat oven to 220°C/200°C fan-forced.

4 Cook eggplant on heated oiled grill plate (or grill or barbecue) until just browned.

5 Meanwhile, combine stock and milk in medium saucepan; bring to a boil. Gradually add polenta, stirring constantly. Reduce heat, simmer, stirring, about 10 minutes or until polenta thickens.

6 Arrange half of the eggplant in shallow 3-litre (12-cup) ovenproof dish; top with half of the beef mixture. Top with remaining eggplant then remaining beef mixture and remaining basil. Spread polenta over basil; sprinkle with cheese.

7 Bake, uncovered, about 20 minutes or until top is browned lightly. Stand 10 minutes before serving with a mixed green salad, if desired.

⬛ **PER SERVING** 19.9g total fat (8.7g saturated fat); 1877kJ (449 cal); 32g carbohydrate; 32.3g protein; 4.7g fibre

Baked custard

PREPARATION TIME 5 MINUTES **COOKING TIME** 45 MINUTES **SERVES** 6

Custard is usually baked in a water bath (bain-marie) in the oven mainly to prevent a crust from forming on the top before the interior is cooked. Only a fine line separates cooking custard until it just thickens to a soft set before it congeals to a curdle, and a water bath also slows heat transfer, helping cook the custard in the oven without it curdling.

6 eggs

1 teaspoon vanilla extract

⅓ cup (75g) caster sugar

1 litre (4 cups) hot milk

¼ teaspoon ground nutmeg

1 Preheat oven to 160°C/140°C fan-forced. Grease shallow 1.5-litre (6-cup) ovenproof dish.

2 Whisk eggs, extract and sugar in large bowl; gradually whisk in hot milk. Pour custard mixture into dish; sprinkle with nutmeg.

3 Place ovenproof dish in larger baking dish; add enough boiling water to come halfway up sides of ovenproof dish. Bake, uncovered, about 45 minutes. Remove custard from baking dish; stand 5 minutes before serving.

▭ **PER SERVING** 11.8g total fat (5.9g saturated fat); 995kJ (238 cal); 20.7g carbohydrate; 12.3g protein; 0g fibre

---

Chocolate bread and butter pudding

PREPARATION TIME 20 MINUTES **COOKING TIME** 50 MINUTES **SERVES** 6

Some of the world's great recipes are based on using yesterday's stale bread rather than wasting it: just think about panzanella, fattoush, French toast and half a dozen wintry Italian soups. Bread and butter pudding is another classic example. And we're not just talking plain white bread alone here: brioche, panettone, challah and croissant all make a mean bread and butter pudding.

1½ cups (375ml) milk

2 cups (500ml) cream

⅓ cup (75g) caster sugar

1 vanilla bean

4 eggs

2 small brioche (200g), sliced thickly

100g dark eating chocolate, chopped coarsely

⅓ cup (40g) coarsely chopped roasted pecans

1 Preheat oven to 180°C/160°C fan-forced. Grease shallow 2-litre (8-cup) ovenproof dish.

2 Combine milk, cream and sugar in small saucepan. Split vanilla bean in half lengthways; scrape seeds into pan then place pod in pan. Stir over heat until hot; strain into large heatproof jug, discard pod.

3 Whisk eggs in large bowl; whisking constantly, pour hot milk mixture into eggs.

4 Layer brioche, chocolate and nuts, overlapping brioche slightly, in dish. Pour hot milk mixture over brioche.

5 Place ovenproof dish in larger baking dish; add enough boiling water to come halfway up sides of ovenproof dish. Bake, uncovered, about 45 minutes or until pudding sets. Remove pudding from baking dish; stand 5 minutes before serving.

▭ **PER SERVING** 50.1g total fat (27.8g saturated fat); 2796kJ (669 cal); 45g carbohydrate; 12.6g protein; 1.4g fibre

1 BAKED CUSTARD **2** CHOCOLATE BREAD AND BUTTER PUDDING
3 LEMON DELICIOUS PUDDING [P 380] **4** QUEEN OF PUDDINGS [P 380]

Lemon delicious pudding

PREPARATION TIME 20 MINUTES **COOKING TIME** 45 MINUTES **SERVES** 6

125g butter, melted

2 teaspoons finely grated lemon rind

1 ½ cups (330g) caster sugar

3 eggs, separated

½ cup (75g) self-raising flour

⅓ cup (80ml) lemon juice

1 ⅓ cups (330ml) milk

1 Preheat oven to 180°C/160°C fan-forced. Grease six 1-cup (250ml) ovenproof dishes.

2 Combine butter, rind, sugar and yolks in large bowl. Stir in sifted flour then juice. Gradually stir in milk; mixture should be smooth and runny.

3 Beat egg whites in small bowl with electric mixer until soft peaks form; fold into lemon mixture, in two batches.

4 Place ovenproof dishes in large baking dish; divide lemon mixture among dishes. Add enough boiling water to baking dish to come halfway up sides of ovenproof dishes. Bake, uncovered, about 45 minutes.

▭ **PER SERVING** 22g total fat (13.5g saturated fat); 2069kJ (495 cal); 67.1g carbohydrate; 6.7g protein; 0.5g fibre

Queen of puddings

PREPARATION TIME 20 MINUTES **COOKING TIME** 40 MINUTES **SERVES** 6

2 cups (140g) stale breadcrumbs

1 tablespoon caster sugar

1 teaspoon vanilla extract

1 teaspoon finely grated lemon rind

2½ cups (625ml) milk

60g butter

4 eggs, separated

¼ cup (80g) raspberry jam, warmed

¾ cup (165g) caster sugar, extra

1 Preheat oven to 180°C/160°C fan-forced. Grease six ¾-cup (180ml) ovenproof dishes; place on oven tray.

2 Combine breadcrumbs, sugar, extract and rind in large bowl. Heat milk and butter in medium saucepan until almost boiling, pour over breadcrumb mixture; stand 10 minutes. Stir in egg yolks.

3 Divide mixture among dishes. Bake about 30 minutes. Carefully spread top of hot puddings with jam.

4 Beat egg whites in small bowl with electric mixer until soft peaks form; gradually add extra sugar, beating until sugar dissolves. Spoon meringue over puddings; bake, uncovered, about 10 minutes.

▭ **PER SERVING** 16.6g total fat (9.3g saturated fat); 1843kJ (441 cal); 60.5g carbohydrate; 11.4g protein; 1.2g fibre

Fruit mince and brioche pudding

PREPARATION TIME 20 MINUTES **COOKING TIME** 50 MINUTES **SERVES** 6

475g jar fruit mince

2 tablespoons brandy

300g brioche, sliced thickly

1 tablespoon demerara sugar

CUSTARD

1 ½ cups (375ml) milk

2 cups (500ml) cream

⅓ cup (75g) caster sugar

½ teaspoon vanilla extract

4 eggs

1 Preheat oven to 160°C/140°C fan-forced. Grease shallow 2-litre (8-cup) ovenproof dish.

2 Make custard.

3 Combine fruit mince and brandy in small bowl.

4 Spread brioche slices with half of the fruit mixture, overlap brioche slightly, in dish. Pour custard over brioche; sprinkle with sugar.

5 Place ovenproof dish in larger baking dish; add enough boiling water to come halfway up sides of ovenproof dish. Bake about 45 minutes or until pudding sets. Remove pudding from baking dish; stand 5 minutes before serving.

CUSTARD Combine milk, cream, sugar and extract in medium saucepan; bring to a boil. Whisk eggs in large bowl; whisking constantly, gradually pour hot milk mixture into eggs.

☐ **PER SERVING** 50.5g total fat (29.9g saturated fat); 3632kJ (869 cal); 85.6g carbohydrate; 13.4g protein; 3.5g fibre

One of the most popular of French breads, brioche can be found in the shape of a loaf or roll. The most recognisable shape, however, is the delightful "brioche à tête" or brioche with a head, formed by placing a small ball of dough on top of a larger one. Use whatever shape is most readily available in this recipe; since it's sliced, it makes no difference to the look of the pudding.

Blackberry clafoutis

PREPARATION TIME 10 MINUTES **COOKING TIME** 25 MINUTES **SERVES** 4

2 teaspoons caster sugar

1 cup (150g) frozen blackberries

⅓ cup (80ml) milk

⅔ cup (160ml) cream

1 teaspoon vanilla extract

4 eggs

½ cup (110g) caster sugar, extra

1 tablespoon plain flour

1 tablespoon icing sugar

1 Preheat oven to 180°C/160°C fan forced. Grease four shallow ¾-cup (180ml) ovenproof dishes; sprinkle inside of dishes with caster sugar. Divide blackberries evenly among dishes; place dishes on oven tray.

2 Bring milk, cream and extract to a boil in small saucepan. Remove from heat.

3 Whisk eggs and extra caster sugar in small bowl until creamy; whisk in flour and strained milk mixture. Pour mixture over blackberries.

4 Bake, uncovered, about 20 minutes or until browned and set.

5 Dust clafoutis with sifted icing sugar and serve warm.

☐ **PER SERVING** 23.5g total fat (13.6g saturated fat); 1664kJ (398 cal); 36.8g carbohydrate; 8.9g protein; 2.4g fibre

Clafoutis is originally from the Limousin region of central France where, in the local dialect, the word means "brimming over". It is one of the world's easiest desserts to make: a sweet batter is poured into an ovenproof dish (or, in this recipe, dishes) "brimming" with fruit which is then baked. How easy – and delicious – is that? Traditionally, cherries native to the region were used, but our version uses frozen blackberries – available year round.

Chocolate self-saucing pudding

PREPARATION TIME 20 MINUTES **COOKING TIME** 45 MINUTES **SERVES** 6

60g butter

½ cup (125ml) milk

½ teaspoon vanilla extract

¾ cup (165g) caster sugar

1 cup (150g) self-raising flour

1 tablespoon cocoa powder

¾ cup (165g) firmly packed brown sugar

1 tablespoon cocoa powder, extra

2 cups (500ml) boiling water

1 Preheat oven to 180°C/160°C fan-forced. Grease 1.5-litre (6-cup) ovenproof dish.

2 Melt butter with milk in medium saucepan. Remove from heat; stir in extract and caster sugar then sifted flour and cocoa. Spread mixture into dish.

3 Sift brown sugar and extra cocoa over mixture; gently pour boiling water over mixture.

4 Bake pudding, uncovered, about 40 minutes or until centre is firm. Stand 5 minutes before serving.

PER SERVING 9.7g total fat (6.2g saturated fat); 1676kJ (401 cal); 73.4g carbohydrate; 3.8g protein; 1.1g fibre

As the word means, an extract is made by actually extracting the flavour from a food product. In the case of vanilla, pods are soaked, usually in alcohol but sometimes in water, to capture the authentic flavour. Essences are either a distilled concentration of a food or an artificial creation of it. Both extracts and essences keep indefinitely if stored in a cool dark place.

Sour cherry baked custards

PREPARATION TIME 15 MINUTES **COOKING TIME** 25 MINUTES **SERVES** 4

1 cup (200g) drained morello cherries

3 eggs

1 teaspoon vanilla extract

½ cup (110g) caster sugar

2 cups (500ml) hot milk

2 teaspoons custard powder

1 tablespoon cold milk

½ teaspoon ground cinnamon

1 Preheat oven to 160°C/140°C fan-forced.

2 Pat cherries dry with absorbent paper; divide among four shallow ¾-cup (180ml) ovenproof dishes.

3 Whisk eggs, extract and sugar in large jug. Gradually whisk hot milk into egg mixture.

4 Blend custard powder with cold milk in small bowl until smooth; whisk into egg mixture. Pour mixture over cherries.

5 Bake custards, uncovered, about 25 minutes or until just set. Serve warm or cooled sprinkled with cinnamon.

PER SERVING 9.6g total fat (4.7g saturated fat); 1233kJ (295 cal); 43.6g carbohydrate; 10.5g protein; 0.9g fibre

When a recipe calls for sour cherries, reach for the morellos. They are available at supermarkets in large glass jars so it's a great idea to keep one in your pantry. Somewhat bitter and tangy, the morello variety is used in jams, preserves, pies and savoury dishes, particularly as an accompaniment to game birds and meats.

CHOCOLATE SELF-SAUCING PUDDING

Do you know the difference between butterscotch and caramel? Butterscotch is a blend of butter and brown sugar (thinned with another sweetener and/or water to became saucy), whereas caramel is the result of cooking caster or white sugar until it liquefies ("caramelises") into a thick, viscous liquid ranging in colour from golden to deep brown. Caramel sauce is made with this caramelised sugar, plus butter and milk.

Butterscotch ginger dumplings

PREPARATION TIME 15 MINUTES **COOKING TIME** 35 MINUTES **SERVES** 4

1 cup (150g) self-raising flour

2 tablespoons caster sugar

60g butter, chopped

⅓ cup (80ml) water

2 tablespoons finely chopped glacé ginger

¼ cup (20g) flaked almonds

BUTTERSCOTCH SAUCE

30g butter

½ cup (110g) firmly packed brown sugar

2 tablespoons golden syrup

1½ cups (375ml) water

1 Preheat oven to 180°C/160°C fan-forced.

2 Sift flour into large bowl, add sugar; rub in butter. Add the water and ginger; mix to a soft dough. Divide dough into eight equal portions; shape into oval dumplings. Place in shallow 1.5-litre (6-cup) ovenproof dish.

3 Make butterscotch sauce; pour sauce over dumplings.

4 Bake dumplings, uncovered, 20 minutes. Remove from oven, spoon sauce over dumplings; sprinkle with almonds. Bake, uncovered, further 10 minutes or until dumplings are browned. Serve warm with cream or ice-cream, if desired.

BUTTERSCOTCH SAUCE Stir ingredients in small saucepan over low heat until sugar dissolves. Bring to a boil; remove from heat.

▭ **PER SERVING** 21.1g total fat (12.1g saturated fat); 2211kJ (529 cal); 78.3g carbohydrate; 4.9g protein; 1.9g fibre

We used golden delicious apples, a crisp, almost citrus-coloured apple with excellent flavour and good keeping properties, in this sponge. It's probably the best cooking apple around, but you can substitute it with green- skinned granny smiths if you prefer. If you prepare the apples for any length of time before finishing the recipe, after they've been peeled and sliced, cover them with acidulated water (cold water into which white vinegar or lemon juice or pulp has been added) to prevent discolouring.

Apple sponge

PREPARATION TIME 15 MINUTES **COOKING TIME** 35 MINUTES **SERVES** 4

4 large apples (800g)

¼ cup (55g) caster sugar

¼ cup (60ml) water

SPONGE TOPPING

2 eggs

⅓ cup (65g) caster sugar

1 tablespoon cornflour

2 tablespoons plain flour

2 tablespoons self-raising flour

1 Preheat oven to 180°C/160°C fan-forced.

2 Peel, core, quarter and slice apples; place in medium saucepan with sugar and water. Cook, covered, about 10 minutes or until apples are tender.

3 Meanwhile, make sponge topping.

4 Spoon hot apple mixture into deep round 1.5-litre (6-cup) ovenproof dish; spread with topping. Bake, uncovered, about 25 minutes.

SPONGE TOPPING Beat eggs in small bowl with electric mixer 7 minutes or until thick and creamy. Gradually add sugar, beating until dissolved between additions. Fold in sifted flours.

▭ **PER SERVING** 2.9g total fat (0.8g saturated fat); 1275kJ (305 cal); 62.1g carbohydrate; 5g protein; 3.4g fibre

Ginger crème caramels

PREPARATION TIME 25 MINUTES **COOKING TIME** 40 MINUTES (PLUS REFRIGERATION TIME) **SERVES** 6

¾ cup (165g) caster sugar

¾ cup (180ml) water

2 tablespoons finely chopped glacé ginger

4 eggs

1 teaspoon vanilla essence

¼ cup caster sugar, extra

1¼ cups (310ml) milk

¾ cup (180ml) cream

1 Preheat oven to 180°C/160°C fan-forced.

2 Stir sugar, water and ginger in medium saucepan over heat, without boiling, until sugar is dissolved. Bring to a boil; boil, uncovered, without stirring, 2 minutes. Strain sugar syrup; return to same pan. Return to a boil; boil, uncovered, without stirring, about 3 minutes or until golden brown.

3 Pour caramel mixture into six ¾-cup (180ml) ovenproof dishes; place ovenproof dishes into baking dish.

4 Whisk eggs, essence and extra sugar in medium bowl.

5 Combine milk and cream in medium saucepan, bring to a boil. Remove from heat, allow bubbles to subside; gradually whisk into egg mixture. Strain custard mixture into medium jug; pour custard over caramel in dishes. Pour enough boiling water into baking dish to come half-way up sides of ovenproof dishes.

6 Bake, uncovered, about 25 minutes or until custard is just set. Remove dishes from water, cool to room temperature; refrigerate overnight.

7 To serve, turn custards onto serving plates, with extra glacé ginger and fresh strawberries, if desired.

PER SERVING 16.7g total fat (9.7g saturated fat); 1509kJ (361 cal); 45.7g carbohydrate; 6.9g protein; 0g fibre

Glacé ginger is fresh ginger root preserved in a sugar syrup; it has a smooth, rich flavour with an added hint of subtle heat. It can be eaten as a snack as well as (by far its most common use) used to add a flavourful burst of ginger when baking. Crystallised ginger can be substituted if rinsed with warm water and dried before using.

THE SALAD BOWL

The Salad Bowl

You don't need to buy a special salad bowl, just look in your cupboards. Pasta bowls, ramekins or small gratin dishes will hold individual or two-person salads; a soufflé dish, an attractive casserole or oven dish, the cut-glass bowl that was a wedding present, a good-looking mixing bowl or any other capacious bowl will hold big salads; a shallow ovenproof dish or a deep serving or fruit platter is perfect for decoratively arranged or "composed" Middle Eastern, Thai or French salads.

The traditional wooden bowl is nice to have, too, but its role as the one correct salad bowl dates back to the days when it was the fashion to rub the bowl with garlic and wash it as little as possible, in the belief that lingering aromas from past salads were desirable. Ideas change, and now we rinse it with warm water to remove used oil, dry it and rub in a little fresh oil to keep the wood in good condition.

When you think salad, you may be thinking of anything from a refreshing side dish to a chic entrée, from a meal in a bowl to a substantial party dish, or something with a bit of flair to have before or after an evening out. It can be cold or warm, casual or elegant, vegetarian or not, health-conscious or recklessly rich. You can go for a salad with its origins in Asian, French, Middle Eastern, Greek, American, Italian or other cuisines. The following list indicates only some of the possibilities, to help you decide.

GREEN Some people say a green salad should consist of green leaves only, others allow fresh herbs, sprouts or shoots, or other green vegetables such as celery or green onion.

SINGLE-VEGETABLE Just about any vegetable, cooked or raw, can star in its own salad. Tomato, cucumber, asparagus, beetroot, green bean and zucchini are popular.

MIXED VEGETABLE Use just a few vegetables that are complementary to one another, such as tomato, capsicum and onion, or shaved fennel and peas, or warm char-grilled capsicum, zucchini, onion and eggplant, rather than a jumble – though there are exceptions, such as Italian caponata, which combines cooked eggplant, capsicum, celery, onion and tomato, plus garlic, olives, pine nuts and sultanas to glorious effect.

POTATO A potato salad may be dressed with vinaigrette only, or be creamy with sour cream or mayonnaise. The best creamy potato salads are first dressed with vinaigrette while still warm. Hot or German potato salad is made by combining warm potatoes and crisp bacon, and dressing with a warm sweet-sour dressing made with bacon dripping.

CHICKPEA, BEAN OR LENTIL These are substantial and savoury. The other ingredients should include flavours strong enough to balance, but not overwhelm, the main one – onion, garlic, lemon, olives, tahini, strong-flavoured vegetables, herbs and spices.

RICE Salads made from rice can be dull, but also can be very good if they include plenty of other textures such as ham, seafood, diced vegetables (green or red onion, celery, peas, capsicum, seeded tomato, radish or young raw zucchini), herbs (flat-leaf parsley, basil, mint or dill) and just enough dressing to moisten.

OTHER GRAINS AND BREAD The most famous grain salad is tabbouleh, the refreshing Middle Eastern salad of burghul with lots of parsley, in a lemony dressing. Salads using bread include Middle Eastern fattoush, with crisped pieces of pitta combined with tomato, capsicum, cucumber, radish and green onion in a lemon/garlic dressing, and Italian panzanella, with pieces of stale ciabatta crust mixed with tomato, celery, cucumber and onion in a garlic, red wine vinegar and basil dressing. Chunks of sourdough bread, either straight from the loaf or brushed with oil and oven-toasted, can be substituted for the ciabatta.

CHICKEN A universal favourite, an excellent choice for a family party when you want to please all ages. It can be classic – sliced, with lemon mayonnaise, lettuce or watercress and such vegetables as asparagus, peas, new potatoes, celery, green onions, mushrooms, tomato, cucumber or capsicum; homely – bite-size chunks of chicken folded through a rice salad; or stylish – sliced and served on a bed of snow peas, sugar peas, snow pea sprouts and baby leaves, with a lemon mustard vinaigrette.

EGG OR CHEESE Eggs, plain or stuffed, go with mayonnaise, curry sauces, watercress or lettuce, ham, smoked fish and caviar. Cheddars go well with apples, celery and crisp baby leaves; parmesan is good with sliced pear; blue cheese is sublime with figs and walnuts; fried or grilled haloumi is lovely with tomato and mint or lemon thyme, or a green salad.

FRUIT Some fruits lend themselves to savoury salads, such as the classic Waldorf salad of apple, celery and walnuts, or a gingered melon salad to go with ham or pork, but most fruit salads are desserts. The best use only a few fruits, or even just one, rather than a jumble of many, and have bite-size pieces rather than a small dice.

SEAFOOD Goes well with citrus and other sharp flavours such as green mango. Asian-style salads often combine just-grilled seafood with a bed of raw vegetables with chilli and herbs such as mint and coriander, and a sour/sweet/salty dressing, which includes fish sauce, lime juice and a little sugar. Cold seafood, especially salmon, goes beautifully with cucumber salad. Smoked trout and salmon go with lettuce, eggs and creamy potato salad.

MEAT Range from cold, rare roast beef with new potatoes and salad vegetables to Asian-style salads such as cold roast pork with green mango and bean sprouts, or the brilliant Thai salad of warm char-grilled beef with cooling herbs and vegetables that offset a chilli blast.

DRESSINGS

VINAIGRETTE To make a classic vinaigrette, mix together a good wine vinegar or fresh lemon juice, a good olive or nut oil (or a mixture of these), a dollop of french mustard and a pinch of salt and pepper.

MAYONNAISE Homemade mayonnaise is still the ideal, but many of the expensive ones sold under chefs' names are also good. The better commercial ones are fine for salads with plenty of flavour of their own. For lighter-flavoured salads, commercial mayonnaise whisked together with your own vinaigrette makes a nice creamy dressing.

Potato salad

PREPARATION TIME 20 MINUTES (PLUS REFRIGERATION TIME) **COOKING TIME** 20 MINUTES **SERVES** 8

2kg potatoes, peeled

2 tablespoons cider vinegar

8 green onions, sliced thinly

¼ cup finely chopped fresh flat-leaf parsley

MAYONNAISE

2 egg yolks

1 teaspoon dijon mustard

2 teaspoons lemon juice

1 cup (250ml) vegetable oil

2 tablespoons hot water, approximately

Make sure the parsley is perfectly dry before chopping it; squeeze it in a double thickness of absorbent paper after you rinse it well. You don't have to be fanatical about plucking the leaves off the stems. Just cut off the stems as close to the leaves as possible and start to chop from that cut end, practically "shaving" the leaves with a really sharp knife.

1 Cut potatoes into 1.5cm pieces. Place potato in large saucepan, barely cover with cold water; cover, bring to a boil. Reduce heat, simmer, uncovered, stirring occasionally, until just tender; drain. Spread potato on a tray; sprinkle with vinegar. Cool 10 minutes. Cover; refrigerate until cold.

2 Meanwhile, make mayonnaise.

3 Place potato in large bowl with mayonnaise, onion and parsley; toss gently to combine.

MAYONNAISE Blend or process egg yolks, mustard and juice until smooth. With motor operating, gradually add oil in a thin, steady stream; process until mixture thickens. Add as much of the hot water as required to thin mayonnaise.

◻ **PER SERVING** 30.4g total fat (4.1g saturated fat); 1739kJ (416 cal); 28.4g carbohydrate; 6.1g protein; 3.7g fibre

Ruby red grapefruit, smoked salmon and mizuna salad

PREPARATION TIME 15 MINUTES **SERVES** 4

This salad is almost too pretty to eat with its contrasting pinks of the salmon and grapefruit peering through the pale green curls of the mizuna. Serve this as a light lunch in summer, accompanied with chilled pink Champagne and be prepared to impress your guests.

300g sliced smoked salmon

2 ruby red grapefruits (700g)

2 tablespoons olive oil

1 teaspoon dijon mustard

150g mizuna

⅓ cup (50g) roasted unsalted cashews, chopped coarsely

½ small red onion (50g), sliced thinly

1 Reserve four slices of salmon; cut remaining slices into thick pieces.

2 Segment grapefruits over large bowl. Add oil, mustard, mizuna, nuts, onion and salmon pieces; toss gently to combine.

3 Divide salad among serving plates; top with reserved salmon slices.

◻ **PER SERVING** 19.1g total fat (3g saturated fat); 1229kJ (294 cal); 8.6g carbohydrate; 21.1g protein; 2.4g fibre

POTATO SALAD

Adding about 125g softened rice vermicelli to this salad will bulk it up enough to make a sufficient main-course salad for four. At a pinch, use the shredded meat of a takeaway barbecued chicken instead of cooking the raw poultry called for in the recipe.

Vietnamese chicken salad

PREPARATION TIME 20 MINUTES **COOKING TIME** 15 MINUTES **SERVES** 4

500g chicken breast fillets

1 large carrot (180g)

½ cup (125ml) rice wine vinegar

2 teaspoons salt

2 tablespoons caster sugar

1 medium white onion (150g), sliced thinly

1½ cups (120g) bean sprouts

2 cups (160g) finely shredded savoy cabbage

¼ cup firmly packed vietnamese mint leaves

½ cup firmly packed fresh coriander leaves

1 tablespoon crushed roasted peanuts

2 tablespoons fried shallots

VIETNAMESE DRESSING

2 tablespoons fish sauce

¼ cup (60ml) water

2 tablespoons caster sugar

2 tablespoons lime juice

1 clove garlic, crushed

1 Place chicken in medium saucepan of boiling water; return to a boil. Reduce heat, simmer, uncovered, about 10 minutes or until cooked through. Cool chicken in poaching liquid 10 minutes; discard liquid (or reserve for another use). Shred chicken coarsely.

2 Meanwhile, cut carrot into matchstick-sized pieces. Combine carrot in large bowl with vinegar, salt and sugar, cover; stand 5 minutes. Add onion, cover; stand 5 minutes. Add sprouts, cover; stand 3 minutes. Drain pickled vegetables; discard liquid.

3 Place pickled vegetables in large bowl with chicken, cabbage, mint and coriander.

4 Place ingredients for vietnamese dressing in screw-top jar; shake well. Pour dressing over salad in bowl; toss gently to combine. Sprinkle with nuts and shallots.

☐ **PER SERVING** 8.9g total fat (2.3g saturated fat); 1271kJ (304 cal); 24.3g carbohydrate; 31g protein; 5.1g fibre

Tamarind is one of the ingredients used in the chicken's sauce to add to the balance of flavours that immediately identify it as Thai: sour, hot, sweet and salty.

Tamarind concentrate is the distillation of tamarind pulp into a condensed paste that's ready to use, with no soaking or straining required, adding zing to marinades, dipping sauces and dressings.

Tamarind, lime and honey chicken salad

PREPARATION TIME 35 MINUTES (PLUS REFRIGERATION TIME) **COOKING TIME** 20 MINUTES **SERVES** 4

¼ cup (60ml) peanut oil

¼ cup (60ml) tamarind concentrate

1 tablespoon honey

2 teaspoons dark soy sauce

½ teaspoon finely grated lime rind

1 tablespoon lime juice

1 clove garlic, crushed

800g chicken breast fillets

½ small wombok (350g), trimmed, shredded finely

4 green onions, sliced thinly

2 lebanese cucumbers (260g), halved widthways, seeded, cut into matchsticks

500g red radishes, trimmed, sliced thinly, cut into matchsticks

½ cup loosely packed fresh mint leaves

½ cup loosely packed fresh coriander leaves

⅔ cup (50g) fried shallots

HONEY LIME DRESSING

1 tablespoon honey

2 tablespoons lime juice

1 teaspoon sesame oil

1 tablespoon dark soy sauce

1 fresh long red chilli, chopped finely

1 Combine 1 tablespoon of the oil, tamarind, honey, sauce, rind, juice, garlic and chicken in large bowl. Cover; refrigerate 3 hours or overnight.

2 Place ingredients for honey lime dressing in screw-top jar; shake well.

3 Heat remaining oil in large frying pan; cook chicken mixture, in batches, until cooked through. Stand 5 minutes; slice thickly. Cover to keep warm.

4 Meanwhile, place dressing in large bowl with remaining ingredients; toss gently to combine. Divide salad among serving plates; top with chicken.

▢ **PER SERVING** 27.2g total fat (6.1g saturated fat); 2161kJ (517 cal); 19.5g carbohydrate; 46.5g protein; 4.5g fibre

Beetroot, pumpkin and spinach salad with fetta polenta

PREPARATION TIME 20 MINUTES (PLUS REFRIGRATION TIME) **COOKING TIME** 1 HOUR 15 MINUTES **SERVES** 4

2 cups (500ml) water

2 cups (500ml) vegetable stock

1 cup (170g) polenta

200g fetta cheese, crumbled

10 small beetroots (600g)

2 tablespoons olive oil

700g peeled pumpkin, cut into 4cm pieces

150g baby spinach leaves

¾ cup (75g) toasted walnuts, chopped coarsely

WALNUT VINAIGRETTE

2 tablespoons walnut oil

¼ cup (60ml) olive oil

¼ cup (60ml) lemon juice

1 Preheat oven to 200°C/180°C fan-forced. Grease 20cm x 30cm lamington pan; line with baking paper.

2 Combine the water and stock in large saucepan; bring to a boil. Gradually add polenta, stirring constantly. Reduce heat; cook, stirring, about 10 minutes or until polenta thickens. Stir in cheese. Spread polenta into pan; cool 10 minutes. Cover; refrigerate about 1 hour or until polenta is firm.

3 Meanwhile, discard beetroot stems and leaves; quarter unpeeled beetroots. Place in large shallow baking dish, drizzle with half of the oil, roast, uncovered, 15 minutes. Add pumpkin, drizzle with remaining oil; roast, uncovered, about 30 minutes or until vegetables are tender.

4 Place ingredients for walnut vinaigrette in screw-top jar; shake well.

5 When cool enough to handle, peel beetroot. Place in large bowl with dressing; toss gently to combine.

6 Turn polenta onto board; trim edges. Cut polenta into 12 pieces; cook, in batches, on heated oiled grill plate (or grill or barbecue) until browned both sides and heated through.

7 Add pumpkin, spinach and nuts to beetroot mixture; toss gently to combine. Divide polenta pieces among serving plates; top with salad.

▢ **PER SERVING** 58.8g total fat (13.3g saturated fat); 3403kJ (814 cal); 51.8g carbohydrate; 23g protein; 9.3g fibre

Here's a handy tip to ensure your walnuts roast evenly: place ¾ cup unroasted nuts in a small microwave-safe bowl; microwave on HIGH about 2 minutes, pausing and stirring every 30 seconds, until the nuts are fragrant and slightly browner in colour. Spread the walnuts on absorbent paper until cool. This technique works well for almonds, pine nuts, hazelnuts and cashews too.

The skins from roasted walnuts can impart a bitter taste so, before chopping them, removes nut skins by rubbing the still-slightly-warm roasted nuts together inside a clean tea towel.

Goat cheese, fig and prosciutto salad

PREPARATION TIME 10 MINUTES **COOKING TIME** 5 MINUTES **SERVES** 4

6 slices prosciutto (90g)

120g baby rocket leaves, trimmed

4 large fresh figs (320g), quartered

150g soft goat cheese, crumbled

HONEY CIDER DRESSING

¼ cup (60ml) cider vinegar

2 tablespoons olive oil

1 tablespoon wholegrain mustard

1 tablespoon honey

1 Preheat grill.

2 Place ingredients for honey cider dressing in screw-top jar; shake well.

3 Crisp prosciutto under grill; drain, chop coarsely.

4 Serve rocket topped with fig, cheese and prosciutto; drizzle with dressing.

PER SERVING 16.9g total fat (5.7g saturated fat); 1062kJ (254 cal); 13.7g carbohydrate; 11.1g protein; 2.6g fibre

---

Duck salad with mandarin and pomegranate

PREPARATION TIME 25 MINUTES **COOKING TIME** 5 MINUTES **SERVES** 4

150g sugar snap peas, trimmed

1kg chinese barbecued duck

2 small mandarins (200g), segmented

1 red mignonette lettuce (280g)

⅓ cup (60g) pomegranate pulp

¾ cup (120g) roasted slivered almonds

LEMON DIJON DRESSING

1 clove garlic, crushed

1 teaspoon dijon mustard

2 tablespoons lemon juice

2 tablespoons olive oil

1 Boil, steam or microwave peas until just tender; drain. Rinse under cold water; drain.

2 Remove meat, leaving skin on, from duck; discard bones. Chop meat coarsely; place in large bowl with peas, mandarin, lettuce, pomegranate and nuts.

3 Place ingredients for lemon dijon dressing in screw-top jar; shake well. Pour dressing over salad; toss gently to combine.

PER SERVING 58.3g total fat (12.7g saturated fat); 2876kJ (688 cal); 8.9g carbohydrate; 33.3g protein; 6.5g fibre

---

1 GOAT CHEESE, FIG AND PROSCIUTTO SALAD **2** DUCK SALAD WITH MANDARIN AND POMEGRANATE
3 SALADE NICOISE [P 398] **4** LAMB AND FETTA SALAD WITH WARM WALNUT DRESSING [P 398]

1   2

3   4

Salade niçoise

PREPARATION TIME 15 MINUTES **COOKING TIME** 5 MINUTES **SERVES** 4

200g baby green beans, trimmed

2 tablespoons olive oil

1 tablespoon lemon juice

2 tablespoons white wine vinegar

4 medium tomatoes (600g), cut into wedges

4 hard-boiled eggs, quartered

425g can tuna in springwater, drained, flaked

½ cup (80g) drained caperberries, rinsed

½ cup (60g) seeded small black olives

¼ cup firmly packed fresh flat-leaf parsley leaves

440g can drained whole baby new potatoes, rinsed, halved

1 Boil, steam or microwave beans until tender; drain. Rinse under cold water; drain.

2 Whisk oil, juice and vinegar in large bowl, add beans and remaining ingredients; toss gently to combine.

PER SERVING 16.9g total fat (3.7g saturated fat); 1522kJ (364 cal); 19.5g carbohydrate; 30.9g protein; 5.2g fibre

Lamb and fetta salad with warm walnut dressing

PREPARATION TIME 15 MINUTES **COOKING TIME** 10 MINUTES **SERVES** 4

1 tablespoon vegetable oil

600g lamb fillets

200g fetta cheese, crumbled

250g witlof, trimmed, leaves separated

150g baby spinach leaves, trimmed

WARM WALNUT DRESSING

2 cloves garlic, crushed

1 teaspoon finely grated lemon rind

¼ cup (60ml) olive oil

2 tablespoons cider vinegar

½ cup (55g) coarsely chopped roasted walnuts

1 Heat oil in large frying pan; cook lamb, uncovered, about 10 minutes. Cover; stand 5 minutes then slice thickly.

2 Make warm walnut dressing.

3 Combine lamb in medium bowl with cheese, witlof and spinach.

4 Serve salad drizzled with dressing.

WARM WALNUT DRESSING Cook garlic, rind, oil and vinegar in small saucepan, stirring, until hot. Remove from heat; stir in nuts.

PER SERVING 52.8g total fat (16.8g saturated fat); 2742kJ (656 cal); 1.2g carbohydrate; 43.8g protein; 3.2g fibre

Pork and lychee salad

PREPARATION TIME 20 MINUTES (PLUS STANDING TIME) **COOKING TIME** 10 MINUTES **SERVES** 4

1 tablespoon peanut oil

300g pork fillet

565g can lychees, rinsed, drained, halved

1 medium red capsicum (200g), sliced thinly

10cm stick fresh lemon grass (20g), sliced thinly

2 fresh kaffir lime leaves, shredded finely

100g watercress, trimmed

2 tablespoons coarsely chopped vietnamese mint

2 tablespoons drained thinly sliced pickled ginger

2 tablespoons fried shallot

PICKLED GARLIC DRESSING

1 tablespoon drained finely chopped pickled garlic

2 fresh small red thai chillies, seeded, sliced thinly

1 tablespoon rice vinegar

1 tablespoon lime juice

1 tablespoon fish sauce

1 tablespoon grated palm sugar

1 Place ingredients for pickled garlic dressing in screw-top jar; shake well.

2 Heat oil in wok; cook pork, turning, until browned all over and cooked as desired. Cover, stand 10 minutes; slice thinly. Place pork in medium bowl with dressing; toss to coat pork all over. Stand 10 minutes.

3 Meanwhile, combine lychees, capsicum, lemon grass, lime leaves, watercress and mint in large bowl.

4 Add pork to lychee mixture; toss gently to combine. Serve sprinkled with pickled ginger and fried shallot.

☐ **PER SERVING** 6.9g total fat (1.5g saturated fat); 911kJ (218 cal); 18.1g carbohydrate; 19.1g protein; 3.3g fibre

We rinsed and drained a whole 565g can of lychees for this recipe but if fresh lychees are available, substitute 300g of these, peeled and halved. You can also try using rambutan or longan in this salad if you like.

Sweet and subtle pickled garlic, or kratiem dong, is the whole young green bulb, pickled unpeeled in vinegar brine. Eaten as a snack by the Thais, it can be served as a condiment to be sprinkled over salads or noodle dishes, or used in a dressing, as here.

Tabbouleh

PREPARATION TIME 30 MINUTES (PLUS REFRIGERATION TIME) **SERVES** 4

¼ cup (40g) burghul

3 medium tomatoes (450g)

3 cups coarsely chopped fresh flat-leaf parsley

3 green onions, chopped finely

¼ cup coarsely chopped fresh mint

¼ cup (60ml) lemon juice

¼ cup (60ml) olive oil

1 Place burghul in medium shallow bowl. Halve tomatoes, scoop pulp from tomato over burghul. Chop tomato flesh finely; spread over burghul. Cover; refrigerate 1 hour.

2 Combine burghul mixture in large bowl with remaining ingredients.

☐ **PER SERVING** 14.1g total fat (2g saturated fat); 790kJ (189 cal); 9.2g carbohydrate; 3.4g protein; 5.6g fibre

Tabbouleh is traditionally made with a far greater amount of chopped fresh parsley than burghul: some non-Lebanese cooks use too much burghul which absorbs the lemon juice and tomato liquid, and results in an overly dry, heavy salad. This recipe softens the burghul with the juice from the tomatoes instead of water, which contributes to a stronger, fresher tasting salad.

Croutons provide a crunchy addition to most salads. Make a large amount at once and keep what you don't use on the day in an airtight container for up to a week.

The eggs in our caesar have been "coddled", cooked so gently that they remain soft and runny enough to coat the salad's leaves. Traditionally, raw egg was used to dress a caesar but in recent times health concerns have led cooks towards cooking them slightly to kill off any harmful bacteria.

Classic caesar salad

PREPARATION TIME 30 MINUTES **COOKING TIME** 15 MINUTES **SERVES** 4

½ loaf ciabatta (220g)
1 clove garlic, crushed
⅓ cup (80ml) olive oil
2 eggs
3 baby cos lettuces, trimmed, leaves separated
1 cup (80g) flaked parmesan cheese

CAESAR DRESSING
1 clove garlic, crushed
1 tablespoon dijon mustard
2 tablespoons lemon juice
2 teaspoons worcestershire sauce
2 tablespoons olive oil

1 Preheat oven to 180°C/160°C fan-forced.

2 Cut bread into 2cm cubes; combine garlic and oil in large bowl with bread. Toast bread on oven tray until croutons are browned.

3 Place ingredients for caesar dressing in screw-top jar; shake well.

4 Bring water to a boil in small saucepan, add eggs; cover pan tightly, remove from heat. Remove eggs from water after 2 minutes. When cool enough to handle, break eggs into large bowl; add lettuce, mixing gently so egg coats leaves.

5 Add cheese, croutons and dressing to bowl; toss gently to combine.

▭ **PER SERVING** 39.1g total fat (9.1g saturated fat); 2366kJ (566 cal); 33.1g carbohydrate; 18.4g protein; 5.6g fibre

---

A traditional wooden salad bowl should be capacious so that the ingredients can be tossed heartily enough to combine them and the dressing. When cleaning it, wipe your bowl out with a warm damp cloth then allow it to air-dry, in the sun if possible. Season a wooden bowl before using it for the first time (then after every second or third use) by rubbing it with a piece of absorbent paper or soft cloth wet with olive oil; the oil helps prevent water and dressings from permeating the bowl's interior.

Oakleaf and mixed herb salad with dijon vinaigrette

PREPARATION TIME 10 MINUTES **SERVES** 6

1 green oakleaf lettuce, leaves separated
¼ cup coarsely chopped fresh chives
½ cup firmly packed fresh flat-leaf parsley leaves
½ cup firmly packed fresh chervil leaves

DIJON VINAIGRETTE
2 tablespoons olive oil
2 tablespoons white wine vinegar
1 tablespoon dijon mustard
2 teaspoons white sugar

1 Place ingredients for dijon vinaigrette in screw-top jar; shake well.

2 Place salad ingredients in medium bowl with dressing; toss gently to combine.

▭ **PER SERVING** 6.2g total fat (0.9g saturated fat); 288kJ (69 cal); 2g carbohydrate; 0.7g protein; 1.1g fibre

Warm lentil and chorizo salad

PREPARATION TIME 15 MINUTES **COOKING TIME** 25 MINUTES **SERVES** 6

1 ¼ cups (250g) french green lentils

1 small brown onion (80g), quartered

1 bay leaf

2 chorizo sausages (340g), sliced thinly

3 shallots (75g), sliced thinly

2 trimmed celery stalks (200g), sliced diagonally

1 cup coarsely chopped fresh flat-leaf parsley

MACADAMIA DRESSING

½ cup (125ml) red wine vinegar

⅓ cup (80ml) macadamia oil

1 Cook lentils, onion and bay leaf in large saucepan of boiling water, uncovered, about 15 minutes or until lentils are tender; drain. Discard onion and bay leaf.

2 Cook chorizo in large frying pan, stirring occasionally, until browned. Drain; cool 10 minutes.

3 Combine ingredients for macadamia dressing in screw-top jar; shake well.

4 Combine lentils and chorizo in large bowl with shallot, celery, parsley and dressing.

☐ **PER SERVING** 30.2g total fat (8.1g saturated fat); 1860kJ (445 cal); 19.1g carbohydrate; 21.8g protein; 7.3g fibre

French green lentils (also called Bondi or Matilda lentils), grown in this country, are a local cousin to the expensive import, lentils du puy. They have a sensational nutty, earthy flavour and hold up well when being boiled without disintegrating or becoming muddy.

Leek and smoked chicken salad with orange mustard dressing

PREPARATION TIME 35 MINUTES **SERVES** 4

1 small leek (200g)

1 large carrot (180g)

1 medium red capsicum (200g), sliced thinly

1 medium yellow capsicum (200g), sliced thinly

500g smoked chicken breast, sliced thinly

200g snow peas, trimmed, sliced thinly

1 green mignonette lettuce, trimmed, torn

ORANGE MUSTARD DRESSING

2 tablespoons orange juice

2 tablespoons apple cider vinegar

2 teaspoons finely grated orange rind

1 tablespoon wholegrain mustard

1 tablespoon sour cream

¼ cup (60ml) olive oil

1 Place ingredients for orange mustard dressing in screw-top jar; shake well.

2 Cut leek into 8cm lengths. Cut each in half lengthways; slice into matchstick-sized pieces. Cut carrot into 8cm pieces. Cut each lengthways into thin slices; cut slices into matchstick-sized pieces.

3 Place leek and carrot in large bowl with dressing and remaining ingredients; toss gently to combine.

☐ **PER SERVING** 25.1g total fat (5.7g saturated fat); 1756kJ (420 cal); 10.6g carbohydrate; 35.6g protein; 5.5g fibre

Citrus rind is loaded with aromatic oil that adds great flavour to a salad dressing. Zesting citrus is generally better than chopping the rind with a knife: it's difficult to avoid taking some of the bitter white pith along with the rind when paring the citrus, and a zester helps release the rind's oil. Zest citrus onto a saucer or piece of baking paper to make it easy to transfer as much of it as possible into the bowl or pan.

Chickpea and kumara salad

PREPARATION TIME 20 MINUTES (PLUS STANDING TIME) **COOKING TIME** 30 MINUTES **SERVES** 4

1 cup (200g) dried chickpeas

1 medium red onion (170g), chopped coarsely

1 medium red capsicum (200g), sliced thickly

1 medium kumara (400g), cut into 1cm pieces

2 cloves garlic, unpeeled

⅓ cup (80ml) olive oil

¼ cup (60ml) lemon juice

1 teaspoon english mustard

150g baby spinach leaves

1 Place chickpeas in medium bowl, cover with cold water; stand overnight, drain. Rinse under cold water; drain.

2 Preheat oven to 220°C/200°C fan-forced.

3 Place chickpeas in medium saucepan of boiling water; return to a boil. Reduce heat, simmer, uncovered, about 1 hour or until chickpeas are tender. Drain.

4 Meanwhile, toss onion, capsicum, kumara, garlic and 1 tablespoon of the oil in shallow baking dish. Roast, uncovered, in oven about 30 minutes or until kumara is tender. Cool 10 minutes; remove garlic from dish.

5 Using back of fork, crush peeled garlic in large bowl; whisk in remaining oil, juice and mustard. Add chickpeas, roasted vegetables and spinach; toss gently to combine.

▭ **PER SERVING** 21.5g total fat (3g saturated fat); 1685kJ (403 cal); 34.9g carbohydrate; 12.7g protein; 10.3g fibre

Chickpeas are a major source of protein in cultures either predominantly vegetarian or where meat is considered a luxury item. Used in so many of our favourite foods (think hummus and salsa), chickpeas can be soaked, parboiled then frozen in user-friendly amounts, ready to go when your menu dictates. One cup of dried chickpeas will double in quantity after soaking.

Smoked trout, peach and watercress salad with lemon buttermilk dressing

PREPARATION TIME 10 MINUTES **SERVES** 4

600g piece hot-smoked ocean trout

200g watercress, trimmed

2 medium peaches (460g), cut into thin wedges

LEMON BUTTERMILK DRESSING

¼ cup (60ml) buttermilk

1 tablespoon lemon juice

1 teaspoon finely grated lemon rind

1 teaspoon white sugar

1 Place ingredients for lemon buttermilk dressing in screw-top jar; shake well.

2 Discard skin and bones from fish; break fish into large pieces in medium bowl. Add watercress and peach; toss gently to combine.

3 Serve salad drizzled with dressing.

▭ **PER SERVING** 8.1g total fat (2g saturated fat); 1170kJ (280 cal); 8.7g carbohydrate; 40.7g protein; 3.3g fibre

Buttermilk was originally the liquid left after churning butter but today it is a commercially made product which, in spite of the name's implications, is low in fat but still an excellent source of protein. Use leftover buttermilk when making scones, pancakes, waffles or panna cotta.

Techniques with eggs & vegetables

Careful food preparation leads to a beautiful end result – it's a lot easier than you imagine.

SEPARATING EGGS
Carefully crack the egg into a cup. Tip egg onto your hand held over a bowl, let the white run through your fingers, then drop the yolk into another bowl.

PREPARING FRESH ASPARAGUS
Hold middle and bottom of each stem and bend it until it snaps; set lower stems aside for soup. You can also peel asparagus with a swivel-bladed peeler, and, if necessary, trim off any remaining woody parts with a knife.

PEELING TOMATOES
Remove the cores from tomatoes and drop, one at a time, into boiling water for 10 seconds. Remove from pan, run under cold water and, starting from the core end, pull off the skin.

BEETROOT MATCHSTICKS
Remove skin and halve vertically. Lay each half on its flat side and cut lengthways into thin slices. Stack slices two or three at a time and cut lengthways again into narrow strips.

CUTTING CARROT INTO JULIENNE
Trim off ends and peel. Cut into 5cm to 6cm lengths; lay each on its side and cut in half lengthwise. Lay each piece on its flat side and cut lengthwise into thin slices, then stack slices two or three at a time and cut lengthwise again into narrow strips.

DICING POTATO
Peel potatoes and halve lengthways. Lay each half on its flat side and cut lengthways into slices the width of required dice. Stack three or four slices at a time; cut lengthways to same width, then across into dice.

PEELING GARLIC

Place clove on its side and whack it with the flat blade of a heavy knife to split the skin. Peel with fingers, trim the root end, cut in half lengthways, lift out and discard greenish shoot.

ROASTING AND PEELING CAPSICUM

Hold capsicum on a carving fork over gas flame, or place under very hot griller, turning until blistered and blackened all over. Seal in a paper or plastic bag for 10 minutes, or place under a bowl to steam, then peel away skin.

CHOPPING AN ONION FINELY

Remove skin, halve onion vertically. Place flat-side down and make four horizontal cuts, going to root but not through it. Cut lengthways into narrow slices, then across into a tiny dice.

CUTTING CUCUMBER RIBBONS

Wash cucumber, trim off ends and, if very long, cut into shorter lengths. Hold cucumber and draw a swivel-bladed peeler down the side, towards you, to cut into fine ribbons.

BRUISING CARDAMOM

Place whole cardamom pods on a board and hammer gently with a meat mallet or hit gently with the flat blade of a heavy knife to split skin, but not shatter apart.

SEPARATING LETTUCE LEAVES

Using a pointed knife, cut out the core in a cone shape or, bash lettuce, core-side down, on bench to release the core. Hold lettuce upside-down under running water and bounce up and down to loosen the leaves, then gently pull them apart.

Thai beef salad

PREPARATION TIME 25 MINUTES (PLUS REFRIGERATION TIME) **COOKING TIME** 10 MINUTES **SERVES** 4

¼ cup (60ml) fish sauce

¼ cup (60ml) lime juice

500g beef rump steak

3 lebanese cucumbers (390g), seeded, sliced thinly

4 fresh small red thai chillies, sliced thinly

4 green onions, sliced thinly

250g cherry tomatoes, halved

¼ cup firmly packed vietnamese mint leaves

½ cup firmly packed fresh coriander leaves

½ cup firmly packed fresh thai basil leaves

1 tablespoon grated palm sugar

2 teaspoons dark soy sauce

1 clove garlic, crushed

1 Combine 2 tablespoons of the fish sauce and 1 tablespoon of the juice in medium bowl, add beef; toss beef to coat in marinade. Cover; refrigerate 3 hours or overnight.

2 Drain beef; discard marinade. Cook beef on heated oiled grill plate (or grill or barbecue) until cooked as desired. Cover beef, stand 5 minutes; slice beef thinly.

3 Meanwhile, combine cucumber, chilli, onion, tomato and herbs in large bowl.

4 Place sugar, soy sauce, garlic, remaining fish sauce and remaining juice in screw-top jar; shake well. Add beef and dressing to salad; toss gently to combine.

▭ **PER SERVING** 8.7g total fat (3.8g saturated fat); 986kJ (236 cal); 8.2g carbohydrate; 30.6g protein; 3.4g fibre

Everyone's favourite, our version of yum nuah is one you'll find so simple and so yummy that you'll make your own from now on. It's best if you assemble the salad just before serving as the beef should still be slightly warm and the vegetables and herbs crisp.

The hallmark of an authentic Thai salad is the appearance of stacks of fresh vietnamese mint leaves, coriander leaves and thai basil leaves. Tossed into or strewn over a salad, this trio of leaves combines to create the signature flavour of Thai food.

Cajun-spiced beef and garlicky bean salad

PREPARATION TIME 15 MINUTES **COOKING TIME** 10 MINUTES **SERVES** 4

750g piece beef fillet

1 tablespoon cajun spice mix

420g can mixed beans, rinsed, drained

2 lebanese cucumbers (260g), halved lengthways, sliced thinly

4 small tomatoes (360g), cut into wedges

1 medium red onion (170g), sliced thinly

1 medium avocado (250g), sliced thickly

½ cup finely chopped fresh coriander

GARLIC VINAIGRETTE

¼ cup (60ml) lemon juice

¼ cup (60ml) olive oil

2 cloves garlic, crushed

1 Combine ingredients for garlic vinaigrette in small bowl.

2 Sprinkle beef with spice mix; cook on heated oiled grill plate (or grill or barbecue). Cover; stand 5 minutes then slice thinly.

3 Place remaining ingredients in large bowl with dressing; toss gently to combine.

4 Serve salad topped with beef.

▭ **PER SERVING** 35.3g total fat (8.8g saturated fat); 2445kJ (585 cal); 16.3g carbohydrate; 47.5g protein; 7.5 g fibre

A blend of herbs and spices usually consisting of basil, paprika, onion, fennel, thyme, cinnamon and cayenne, cajun spice mix is available from most supermarkets and specialty food stores. It's used in the spicy rub for traditional "blackened" Cajun meat or fish dishes, both for colour and for flavour.

THAI BEEF SALAD

Nut oils (hazelnut, walnut and macadamia) deserve to find their way into more salad dressings. While they can be relatively expensive and possess a short shelf life, they add flavour and interest to a salad, and are an appealing alternative to olive oil. Bear in mind that these oils are quite potent so don't use them with a heavy hand. Since they can turn rancid quickly, buy in small bottles and keep tightly sealed in the fridge. Refrigerated nut oils coagulate so bring to room temperature before using.

Green bean and tomato salad with mustard hazelnut dressing

PREPARATION TIME 10 MINUTES **COOKING TIME** 10 MINUTES **SERVES** 4

200g green beans, trimmed

250g cherry tomatoes, halved

MUSTARD HAZELNUT DRESSING

½ cup (70g) roasted hazelnuts, skinned, chopped coarsely

2 tablespoons hazelnut oil

2 tablespoons cider vinegar

1 teaspoon wholegrain mustard

1 Combine ingredients for mustard hazelnut dressing in screw-top jar; shake well.

2 Boil, steam or microwave beans until tender; drain. Rinse under cold water; drain.

3 Combine beans, tomato and dressing in medium bowl; toss gently.

▭ **PER SERVING** 20.2g total fat (1.8g saturated fat); 920kJ (220 cal); 3.6g carbohydrate; 4.2g protein; 4.3g fibre

Prawn, snowpea and wild rice salad

PREPARATION TIME 20 MINUTES **COOKING TIME** 20 MINUTES **SERVES** 4

24 uncooked medium king prawns (1kg)

1½ cups (300g) white and wild rice blend

150g snow peas, trimmed, halved lengthways

1 small red onion (100g), sliced thinly

½ cup coarsely chopped fresh flat-leaf parsley

150g snow pea tendrils

RASPBERRY VINEGAR DRESSING

⅓ cup (80ml) raspberry vinegar

2 tablespoons olive oil

1 tablespoons dijon mustard

2 cloves garlic, crushed

1 tablespoons lemon juice

2 teaspoons white sugar

1 Shell and devein prawns, leaving tails intact.

2 Place ingredients for raspberry vinegar dressing in screw-top jar; shake well.

3 Cook rice in large saucepan of boiling water, uncovered, until tender; drain.

4 Meanwhile, boil, steam or microwave peas until just tender.

5 Cook prawns on heated lightly oiled grill plate (or grill or barbeque) until changed in colour.

6 Place rice, peas and prawns in large bowl with onion, parsley, tendrils and dressing; toss gently to combine.

▭ **PER SERVING** 10.7g total fat (1.5g saturated fat); 1902kJ (455 cal); 51.6g carbohydrate; 34.9g protein; 4.6g fibre

Spinach salad with mushrooms, poached egg and anchovy dressing

PREPARATION TIME 20 MINUTES **COOKING TIME** 10 MINUTES **SERVES** 4

40g butter

2 flat mushrooms (160g), sliced thickly

100g swiss brown mushrooms, sliced thickly

100g shiitake mushrooms, sliced thickly

4 eggs

270g char-grilled capsicum in oil, drained, sliced thinly

300g baby spinach leaves

ANCHOVY DRESSING

2 tablespoons coarsely chopped fresh sage

1 tablespoon capers, rinsed, drained

6 anchovy fillets, drained

2 tablespoons balsamic vinegar

¼ cup (60ml) olive oil

2 tablespoons water

This fresh take on a classic spinach salad makes a main course for lunch. Accompany it with crisp cheese toasts made by toasting one side of sliced oil-brushed french bread under a preheated grill then turning and sprinkling the other side with coarsely grated parmesan cheese. When the cheese starts to bubble, take it out from under the grill and allow to cool before serving.

1 Blend or process ingredients for anchovy dressing until combined.

2 Melt butter in large frying pan; cook mushrooms, stirring, until tender. Cover to keep warm.

3 Half-fill a large shallow frying pan with water; bring to a boil. Break eggs into cup, one at a time, then slide into pan. When all eggs are in pan, allow water to return to a boil. Cover pan, turn off heat; stand about 4 minutes. Remove eggs, one at a time, using slotted spoon, and place on absorbent-paper-lined saucer to blot up poaching liquid.

4 Place mushrooms in large bowl with capsicum and half of the dressing; toss to combine.

5 Serve spinach topped with mushroom mixture, egg and remaining dressing.

PER SERVING 32.6g total fat (9.4g saturated fat); 1559kJ (373 cal); 4.6g carbohydrate; 14.2g protein; 4.6g fibre

---

Bean and coriander salad

PREPARATION TIME 10 MINUTES **COOKING TIME** 5 MINUTES **SERVES** 4

400g green beans, halved crossways

1 cup loosely packed fresh coriander leaves

4 small tomatoes (120g), quartered

1 medium red onion (150g), sliced thinly

DRESSING

1 teaspoon coarsely grated lime rind

2 tablespoons lime juice

1 clove garlic, crushed

1 teaspoon white sugar

1 Boil, steam or microwave beans until just tender; drain. Rinse under cold water; drain.

2 Combine ingredients for dressing in small jug.

3 Place beans in medium bowl with remaining ingredients and dressing; toss gently to combine.

PER SERVING 0.3g fat (0g saturated fat); 213kJ (51 cal); 6.6g carbohydrate; 3.5g protein; 4g fibre

The classic main-course
"salade composé" found in
most French bistros makes
a particularly good evening
meal in summer since the
ingredients need very little,
if any, cooking. Translated,
it means simply a composed,
or arranged salad, rather
than a tossed one, and can
contain meat or seafood,
or neither, and a variety of
vegetables and condiments
typically drizzled with a
traditional vinaigrette.

Mesclun is a classic baby
leaf salad mix (derived from
the Provençal patois, mescla,
which means "to mix"); it
traditionally consists of
coral lettuce, rocket, cos,
red oakleaf, curly endive
and a few nasturtium petals.

Salade composé

PREPARATION TIME 15 MINUTES **COOKING TIME** 20 MINUTES **SERVES** 4

1 small french bread stick

2 cloves garlic, crushed

¼ cup (60ml) olive oil

6 rindless bacon rashers (390g),
sliced thickly

150g mesclun

6 medium egg tomatoes (450g),
sliced thinly

4 hard-boiled eggs,
halved lengthways

RED WINE VINAIGRETTE

¼ cup (60ml) red wine vinegar

3 teaspoons dijon mustard

⅓ cup (80ml) olive oil

1 Preheat grill.

2 Cut bread into 1cm slices. Brush both sides of bread with combined garlic and oil;
toast under grill.

3 Cook bacon in large frying pan until crisp; drain on absorbent paper.

4 Meanwhile, place ingredients for red wine vinaigrette in screw-top jar; shake well.

5 Layer bread and bacon in large bowl with mesclun and tomato, top with egg; drizzle
with vinaigrette.

PER SERVING 48.3g total fat (9.9g saturated fat); 2575kJ (616 cal); 19.7g carbohydrate; 25.2g protein;
3.5g fibre

A thick paste that combines
a variety of the best
produce of the south of
France, tapenade is
traditionally made from
black olives, olive oil,
capers, anchovies and
Mediterranean herbs.
While it is frequently
used as an ingredient in
dressings and sauces, it is
most usually eaten on its
own as a spread or dip.

Warm pasta provençale salad

PREPARATION TIME 15 MINUTES **COOKING TIME** 15 MINUTES **SERVES** 6

375g rigatoni

600g lamb fillets

¾ cup (115g) seeded black olives,
chopped coarsely

1 cup (150g) drained semi-dried
tomatoes in oil, chopped coarsely

400g can artichoke hearts,
drained, quartered

1 small red onion (100g),
sliced thinly

60g baby rocket leaves

½ cup (120g) olive tapenade

2 tablespoons olive oil

2 tablespoons lemon juice

1 Cook pasta in large saucepan of boiling water until just tender; drain.

2 Meanwhile, cook lamb, uncovered, in heated oiled large frying pan until cooked as
desired. Cover; stand 5 minutes then slice thickly.

3 Place drained pasta and lamb in large bowl with remaining ingredients; toss gently to
combine. Serve warm.

PER SERVING 16.9g total fat (3.4g saturated fat); 2203kJ (527 cal); 57.4g carbohydrate; 32g protein;
7.5g fibre

SALADE COMPOSE

Green (unripe) papayas are readily available in various sizes at many Asian shops and growers' markets. Select one that is very hard and slightly shiny, which indicates that it is freshly picked. It's imperative that it be totally unripe – the flesh so light green it is almost white. A firm papaya will soften rapidly if you don't use it within one or two days. Green papaya has very little taste, but acts as a sponge to absorb the combined thai flavours (hot, sour, sweet and salty) of the other ingredients. Assemble this salad just before serving.

Green papaya salad

PREPARATION TIME 20 MINUTES (PLUS STANDING TIME) **SERVES** 4

10cm stick fresh lemon grass (20g)

1 small green papaya (650g)

2 cups (160g) bean sprouts

1 cup (100g) coarsely grated fresh coconut

¾ cup loosely packed fresh coriander leaves

¾ cup loosely packed fresh mint leaves

2 purple shallots (50g), sliced thinly

½ cup (70g) roasted unsalted peanuts, chopped coarsely

CHILLI CITRUS DRESSING

¼ cup (60ml) lime juice

¼ cup (60ml) lemon juice

1 tablespoon grated palm sugar

2 teaspoons fish sauce

1 fresh small red thai chilli, chopped finely

1 Soak lemon grass in medium bowl of boiling water, uncovered, about 4 minutes or until tender. Drain; slice lemon grass thinly.

2 Meanwhile, place ingredients for chilli citrus dressing in screw-top jar; shake well.

3 Peel papaya, quarter lengthways, discard seeds; grate papaya coarsely.

4 Place lemon grass and papaya in large bowl with sprouts, coconut, coriander, mint, shallot and dressing; toss gently to combine.

5 Divide salad among serving bowls then sprinkle with nuts.

PER SERVING 15.5g total fat (7.3g saturated fat); 1049kJ (251 cal); 16.3g carbohydrate; 7.9g protein; 8.4g fibre

Fattoush

PREPARATION TIME 15 MINUTES **COOKING TIME** 5 MINUTES **SERVES** 4

2 large pitta breads (160g)

4 medium tomatoes (600g), cut into wedges

2 lebanese cucumbers (260g), seeded, sliced thinly

1 medium green capsicum (200g), cut into 2cm pieces

3 green onions, sliced thinly

1 cup coarsely chopped fresh flat-leaf parsley

½ cup coarsely chopped fresh mint

½ cup (125ml) olive oil

¼ cup (60ml) lemon juice

2 cloves garlic, crushed

1 Preheat grill.

2 Toast bread under grill until crisp; break into small pieces.

3 Combine tomato, cucumber, capsicum, onion and herbs in large bowl.

4 Just before serving, add bread to salad with combined oil, juice and garlic; toss gently to combine.

PER SERVING 29.8g total fat (4.2g saturated fat); 1726kJ (413 cal); 27.1g carbohydrate; 7g protein; 5.7g fibre

Moroccan couscous salad with preserved lemon dressing

PREPARATION TIME 20 MINUTES **SERVES** 4

1 ½ cups (300g) couscous

1 ½ cups (375ml) boiling water

20g butter

400g can chickpeas, rinsed, drained

⅓ cup (55g) sultanas

⅓ cup (50g) roasted pine nuts

100g baby rocket leaves, chopped coarsely

¾ cup finely chopped fresh flat-leaf parsley

1 cup (120g) seeded green olives

PRESERVED LEMON DRESSING

1 tablespoon finely grated lemon rind

¼ cup (60ml) lemon juice

¼ cup (60ml) olive oil

2 tablespoons drained, rinsed, finely chopped preserved lemon

1 Combine couscous and the water in large heatproof bowl. Cover; stand 5 minutes or until water is absorbed, fluffing with fork occasionally. Stir in butter. Stand 10 minutes.

2 Place ingredients for preserved lemon dressing in screw-top jar; shake well.

3 Combine couscous in large bowl with remaining ingredients and dressing.

▭ **PER SERVING** 29g total fat (5.5g saturated fat); 268kJ (686 cal); 85.6g carbohydrate; 17.2g protein; 6.5g fibre

An indispensable ingredient in Moroccan cooking and used as a flavouring by many modern chefs, the preserved lemon's silken texture and distinctive taste is a result of the citrus fruit being preserved for at least a month in a mixture of salt and oil or lemon juice. Rinsed well, it can be chopped and stirred into yogurt or a salad dressing without being cooked, or added to a simmering tagine or casserole, adding piquancy to a finished dish.

Stuffed zucchini flowers and radicchio salad

PREPARATION TIME 20 MINUTES **COOKING TIME** 10 MINUTES **SERVES** 4

2 tablespoons finely chopped fresh sage

2 teaspoons finely grated lemon rind

1 small red onion (100g), chopped finely

100g firm goat cheese, grated coarsely

100g ricotta cheese

24 baby zucchini with flowers attached

250g yellow teardrop tomatoes

1 tablespoon olive oil

1 teaspoon balsamic vinegar

100g radicchio leaves, torn

1 Preheat oven to 240°C/220°C fan-forced. Oil oven tray.

2 Beat sage, rind, onion, goat cheese and ricotta in small bowl with wooden spoon until combined.

3 Remove and discard stamens from centre of zucchini flowers; fill flowers with cheese mixture, twist petal tops to enclose filling. Place filled flowers on oven tray. Place tomatoes, in single layer, in small shallow baking dish; drizzle with combined oil and vinegar. Roast flowers and tomatoes about 10 minutes or until flowers are browned lightly and tomatoes are softened.

4 Place tomatoes and pan juices in medium bowl with radicchio; toss gently to combine. Serve salad with zucchini flowers.

▭ **PER SERVING** 11.8g total fat (5g saturated fat); 694kJ (166 cal); 5.3g carbohydrate; 8.2g protein; 3.6g fibre

Life may be too short to stuff cherry tomatoes but there's definitely time for stuffing zucchini flowers – the Italians have been doing it for centuries. Indeed, this recipe makes use of many of the best-loved of the Italian flavours we're acquainted with: olive oil, balsamic vinegar, ricotta and radicchio, in addition to the tiny baby zucchini with their attached flowers. Delicious.

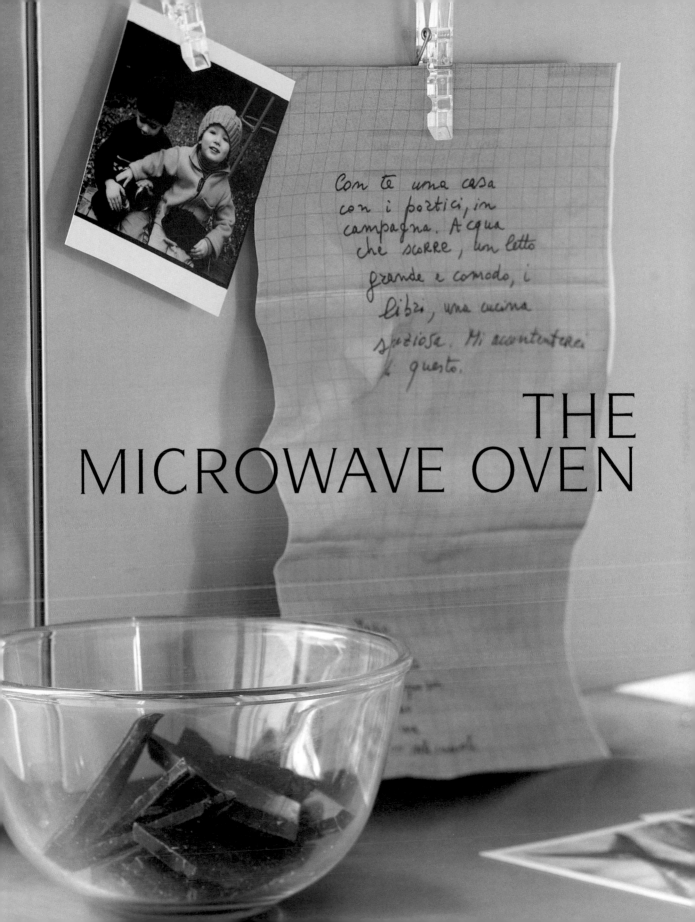

THE
MICROWAVE OVEN

The Microwave Oven

The key to loving your microwave oven is to use it for what it does well and not to ask it to do things it cannot. It is an auxiliary item, albeit an invaluable one, to your cooktop and oven, not a substitute for either. Microwave cooking is, simply stated, akin to steaming. What's happening when you use your oven is that the microwaves penetrate the food, rapidly heating the inherent moisture (water, fat, sugar, etc) which causes the food to cook in a very short time through the internal conduction of heat.

MICROWAVE TRIUMPHS

REHEATING anything: from the cup of tea or coffee you've let stand too long to a filled plate for a latecomer's dinner. Leftovers such as soup and rice; cheese, white and pasta sauces; stews, casseroles or any sauced meat or poultry dishes. Previously cooked fruit or vegetables also reheat well in a microwave oven, as do commercial frozen dinners, vegetables and other foods; packaged flatbreads like tortillas, pitta and chapati become supple and warmed through in seconds.

MELTING AND SOFTENING chocolate and butter, honey that's been refrigerated, dried pulses and beans.

COOKING vegetables without loss of crunch, colour or vitamins, and perfectly moist fish and chicken fillet meat, as well as, if not better than, by any other means. A piece or two of bacon "fries" on absorbent paper in a microwave oven with no frying pan to wash-up; stocks, stews and ragoûts can be made in half the time or less; classic savoury sauces and concentrated meat glazes you rarely take the time to make are no trouble at all. Plain rice steams flawlessly in a microwave oven (and in less time than in a purpose-built rice cooker), and making risotto and polenta in a microwave oven is just a piece of cake.

DIVIDENDS TO THE COOK include cutting back on washing-up time (you'll dirty fewer dishes and bowls and never have to scrub burnt food from the ones you use); maintaining a cool kitchen in the heat of summer, eliminating spatter and unpleasant smells; taking for granted how quick and simple microwave cooking is, and how perfect the results.

MICROWAVE LIMITATIONS

SPONTANEOUS COOKS may feel constrained by having to follow recipes to the letter when cooking in the microwave oven, but this is advisable until you get to know your microwave.

Some foods cook unevenly. This can be a benefit (see Placement of Food, below), but it can also be a problem. The revolving turntable in your microwave oven is designed to even out the cooking by moving the food constantly, but this works only up to a point.

BROWNING FOOD is an impossibility since, in microwave cooking, the food's surface gets no warmer than its interior. You cannot make a roast or a soufflé in it. Some manufacturers have tried to overcome this by supplying browning dishes that, unlike most utensils recommended for the microwave (see Utensils for Microwaving, below) will get hot enough to brown the food due to their metallised cooking surfaces or metallised patterns underneath.

Because microwaving creates steam, that is, pressure, foods that are self-enclosed like eggs, potatoes and sausages can burst like overfilled balloons inside the oven. Some parts of some foods have a tendency to dry out as they become overcooked, while others become soggy.

Unlike conventional cooking, microwave cooking calls for increased cooking times as the quantity of food increases. Cooking times also change according to the power level (wattage) used. For these reasons, it is important to stick to the recipe exactly – you can't simply double or halve it, or cook it at a different wattage, and expect it to work.

UTENSILS FOR MICROWAVING

Dishes, cups and plates made of glass, china, earthenware, plastic and paper are fine to use for microwave cooking, so long as they don't have metallic decorations, such as gold rims on cups. Remember that, depending on their composition, some such utensils remain cool while others heat up, so don't risk it by using a delicate porcelain cup or thin glass bowl. Most ordinary plastic bowls and measuring jugs stand up to microwave heating without distorting, though it would not be wise to attempt longer cooking in them. Paper towels are useful for heating small items, such as a bread roll.

Because microwaves cannot penetrate metal, most metal containers are not suitable for use in the microwave oven. Small pieces of foil can be used to shield part of the food, for instance, the thin end of a fish fillet, to stop it overcooking. Usually the foil is removed at a given time to allow the shielded part to catch up.

COVERING FOOD Cover food to be microwaved with plastic wrap, a plastic bag or absorbent paper to prevent spattering. If covering the dish tightly with plastic wrap, which speeds up heating and conserves moisture, make a doubled pleat in its top, leave a corner lifted or stab the cover a couple of times with a fork to prevent an excessive build-up of steam. When removing plastic wrap, do so with caution to avoid being burned by a burst of steam

PLACEMENT OF FOOD

In general, food near the walls of the microwave oven cooks faster than food at the centre. Arrange foods accordingly, either in rings with the thickest or longest-cooking items on the outside and the quickest-cooking ones toward the centre, or arrange like the spokes of a wheel with the tougher or thicker parts to the outside and the more tender or thinner parts in the centre (it won't matter if they overlap as the microwaves will penetrate them).

This is a great advantage in cooking, for example, asparagus or fish fillets, since the asparagus tips or thin tail ends of the fish won't overcook in the time it takes for the outer parts to be cooked sufficiently.

Combination short soup

PREPARATION TIME 55 MINUTES **COOKING TIME** 20 MINUTES **SERVES** 6

Stock can be made in the microwave oven quickly and with great success. Buy a kilo of chicken bones – a carcass or two, wing tips or necks, breast bones – and place in 2.5 litre microwave-safe dish with 1 litre water, and a quartered white onion, carrot and celery stalk. Cover tightly in microwave-safe plastic wrap and cook on HIGH (100%) for 30 minutes. You'll have to double this method for the amount required here but during the time it takes to make the stock you can get the rest of the soup components ready.

1 medium carrot (120g)

2 litres (8 cups) chicken stock

250g spinach, shredded

200g chinese barbecued pork, sliced

230g can sliced bamboo shoots, rinsed, drained

½ cup (40g) bean sprouts

4 green onions, chopped

1 tablespoon light soy sauce

PORK AND VEAL POUCHES

150g minced pork and veal

1 green onion, chopped

1 clove garlic, crushed

1 tablespoon oyster sauce

16 gow gee wrappers

1 egg white, beaten lightly

1 Cut carrot into 4cm-long thin strips. Make pork and veal pouches.

2 Bring stock to a boil in large microwave-safe bowl, covered, on HIGH (100%) about 10 minutes. Add pouches; cook, uncovered, on MEDIUM-HIGH (70%) about 4 minutes or until cooked through.

3 Add carrot and remaining ingredients to soup; cook, uncovered, on MEDIUM-HIGH (70%) 2 minutes.

PORK AND VEAL POUCHES Combine mince, onion, garlic and sauce in small bowl. Brush each wrapper with egg white, place rounded teaspoons of mince mixture in centre of each wrapper; pinch edge together to enclose filling.

▭ **PER SERVING** 8.6g total fat (3.5g saturated fat); 986kJ (236 cal); 18.7g carbohydrate; 19.1g protein; 3.6g fibre

Fish with ginger and kaffir lime

PREPARATION TIME 5 MINUTES **COOKING TIME** 6 MINUTES **SERVES** 4

The microwave oven takes a star turn when it comes to cooking fish. Fish fillets will always remain moist and cook through evenly in a microwave oven. When in doubt, slightly undercook the fish.

4 x 180g white fish fillets

3 green onions, sliced thinly

5cm piece fresh ginger (25g), sliced thinly

4 fresh kaffir lime leaves, shredded finely

2 teaspoons sesame oil

1 Place fillets on large microwave-safe plate; top each with onion, ginger and lime leaves, drizzle with oil. Cover with plastic wrap; cook on HIGH (100%) about 6 minutes or until fish is just cooked through.

2 Serve with wedges of lime and steamed jasmine rice, if desired.

▭ **PER SERVING** 3.4g total fat (0.5g saturated fat); 648kJ (155 cal); 6.3g carbohydrate; 30.4g protein; 0.2g fibre

Mexican chilli beef

PREPARATION TIME 10 MINUTES **COOKING TIME** 40 MINUTES **SERVES** 4

1 tablespoon olive oil

1 medium onion (150g), chopped

2 cloves garlic, crushed

1kg minced beef

1 long red chilli, chopped finely

400g can crushed tomatoes

1 cup (250ml) beef stock

¾ cup (190g) tomato paste

425g can mexebeans

2 tablespoons coarsely chopped fresh flat-leaf parsley

1 Cook oil, onion and garlic in large microwave-safe bowl, uncovered, on HIGH (100%) 4 minutes, stirring once during cooking.

2 Stir in beef; cook, uncovered, on HIGH (100%) 10 minutes, stirring twice.

3 Add chilli, undrained tomatoes, stock and paste; cook, uncovered, on HIGH (100%) about 25 minutes or until thick, stirring twice.

4 Stir in beans; cook, uncovered, on HIGH (100%) 2 minutes. Stir in parsley.

☐ **PER SERVING** 22.9g total fat (8.1g saturated fat); 2337kJ (559 cal); 23.8g carbohydrate; 59.8g protein; 9.4g fibre

By cooking the chilli beef down until it thickens, you'll have a tasty filling for enchiladas or burritos, or a topping for nachos. Tortillas reheat beautifully in a microwave oven, but because they soften rather than crisp, warming them this way is only suitable when you want to fill and roll them. To make nachos, toast the corn chips briefly under a preheated grill.

Chinese-style pork spareribs

PREPARATION TIME 15 MINUTES (PLUS REFRIGERATION TIME) **COOKING TIME** 20 MINUTES **SERVES** 4

1kg pork spareribs

¼ cup (60ml) dry sherry

2 tablespoons light soy sauce

2 tablespoons tomato sauce

2 tablespoons honey

2 tablespoons lemon juice

2 teaspoons grated fresh ginger

2 cloves garlic, crushed

2 teaspoons cornflour

1 tablespoon water

1 Remove rind and excess fat from ribs; cut ribs into 3cm lengths.

2 Combine sherry, sauces, honey, juice, ginger and garlic in large bowl with pork. Cover, refrigerate 3 hours or overnight.

3 Drain pork, reserve marinade in small microwave-safe bowl. Place pork on rack in single layer over shallow microwave-safe dish; cook, covered, on HIGH (100%) about 15 minutes or until pork is tender, turning occasionally during cooking.

4 Add blended cornflour and the water to reserved marinade; cook on HIGH (100%) about 5 minutes or until mixture boils and thickens, stirring occasionally. Serve over ribs.

☐ **PER SERVING** 9.1g total fat (3g saturated fat); 1087kJ (260 cal); 15.5g carbohydrate; 24.7g protein; 0.4g fibre

Spicy marinated spareribs on the table in 20 minutes? Thanks to cooking in a microwave oven, it's a definite after-work meal possibility. Pause cooking every 5 minutes, turn and brush the ribs with the marinade then, if you like, finish them off with a final brushing under a preheated grill for a crisp, blackened look.

Chicken minestrone

PREPARATION TIME 25 MINUTES **COOKING TIME** 25 MINUTES **SERVES** 4

500g chicken thigh fillets, chopped

1 medium brown onion (150g), sliced thinly

1 clove garlic, crushed

2 rindless bacon rashers (130g), chopped coarsely

1 trimmed celery stalk (100g), sliced thickly

1 medium carrot (120g), chopped coarsely

400g can crushed tomatoes

300g can kidney beans, rinsed, drained

3 cups (750ml) chicken stock

40g macaroni

2 tablespoons chopped fresh oregano

1 tablespoon finely chopped fresh flat-leaf parsley

1 Cook chicken, onion, garlic, bacon, celery and carrot in large microwave-safe bowl, covered, on MEDIUM-HIGH (70%) 15 minutes, stirring once during cooking.

2 Add undrained tomatoes, beans, stock and pasta; cook, uncovered, on MEDIUM-HIGH (70%) about 10 minutes or until pasta is just tender. Stir in herbs.

⬜ **PER SERVING** 15.1g total fat (4.9g saturated fat); 1634kJ (391 cal); 22.4g carbohydrate; 38.3g protein; 6.6g fibre

There are as many versions of minestrone as there are regions in Italy, but this version simplifies the process with no loss of goodness or flavour. There's no greasy frying pan to wash up after the bacon and vegies are softened, and the cooking time is practically halved from the usual cooktop method.

Creamy broccoli and bacon pasta

PREPARATION TIME 20 MINUTES **COOKING TIME** 15 MINUTES **SERVES** 4

500g fresh fettuccine

1.5 litres (6 cups) boiling water

30g butter

1 small brown onion (80g), chopped finely

2 rindless bacon rashers (130g), chopped coarsely

1 clove garlic, crushed

250g broccoli, chopped finely

2 teaspoons cornflour

1 tablespoon water, extra

1 chicken stock cube

300ml cream

2 tablespoons finely grated parmesan cheese

1 Place pasta with the boiling water in large microwave-safe bowl; cook, uncovered, on HIGH (100%) about 5 minutes or until pasta is tender, stirring once during cooking. Drain pasta; cover to keep warm.

2 Cook butter, onion, bacon and garlic in large microwave-safe bowl, uncovered, on HIGH (100%) 4 minutes, stirring once during cooking. Add broccoli; cook, covered, on HIGH (100%) 2 minutes.

3 Stir in blended cornflour and the extra water, crumbled stock cube, cream and cheese; cook, uncovered, on HIGH (100%) about 3 minutes or until sauce boils and thickens slightly, stirring once during cooking. Toss pasta through hot sauce.

⬜ **PER SERVING** 46g total fat (28.2g saturated fat); 3749kJ (897 cal); 90.3g carbohydrate; 26.9g protein; 7.1g fibre

This dish can be made with any long flat pasta – fettuccine, pappardelle, tagliatelle or linguine are all good. Broccolini, peas, button mushrooms and baby spinach leaves can be substituted for the broccoli but the microwave cooking times will have to be adjusted.

1 CHICKEN MINESTRONE **2** CREAMY BROCCOLI AND BACON PASTA
3 PORK WITH CARAMELISED APPLES [P 422] **4** SPICED APRICOT AND CHICKEN TAGINE [P 422]

1

2

3

4

Pork with caramelised apples

PREPARATION TIME 20 MINUTES **COOKING TIME** 30 MINUTES **SERVES** 6

Admittedly the microwave oven isn't crash-hot for browning meat but, here, cooking the pork in a frying pan or under a grill is a waste of effort: it's a white meat to begin with, plus the colour of the combined port and jam in the sauce obscures the look of the meat. And, as is the case with most microwave-oven recipes, a bonus is the time-saving factor; while the pork is cooking, you can be preparing the remaining called-for ingredients.

800g pork fillets
2 teaspoons cornflour
1 tablespoon water
⅓ cup (80ml) orange juice
¼ cup (60ml) chicken stock
2 tablespoons port

2 tablespoons blackberry jam
20g butter
2 medium red apples (300g), sliced thickly
2 tablespoons brown sugar

1 Cook pork in large shallow microwave-safe dish, uncovered, on MEDIUM (55%) 5 minutes; drain. Turn pork; cook, uncovered, on MEDIUM (55%) 5 minutes. Repeat once more or until pork is almost tender; cover, stand 5 minutes.

2 Blend cornflour with the water in medium microwave-safe jug, stir in juice, stock, port and jam; cook, uncovered, on HIGH (100%) about 2 minutes or until sauce boils and thickens, whisking once during cooking.

3 Melt butter in large shallow microwave-safe dish, uncovered, on HIGH (100%) 30 seconds. Stir in apple and sugar; cook, uncovered, on HIGH (100%) about 5 minutes or until apples are soft, stirring once during cooking. Serve pork with apples and sauce.

PER SERVING 5.9g total fat (2.9g saturated fat); 1058kJ (253 cal); 17.8g carbohydrate; 29.6g protein; 1g fibre

Spiced apricot and chicken tagine

PREPARATION TIME 25 MINUTES **COOKING TIME** 30 MINUTES **SERVES** 4

Interestingly enough, a tagine actually cooks by steaming, just like your microwave oven. With its circular, shallow base and tall coned lid, a tagine is the unglazed clay container used to make the traditional Moroccan stew of the same name. When the steam rises to the top of the conical lid, it condenses and drips or slides back down into the food in a continuous cycle. So a classic chicken tagine is a natural for microwave cooking. Serve the tagine with steamed couscous with plumped raisins and finely chopped fresh coriander tossed into it.

1kg chicken thigh fillets, chopped
1 tablespoon olive oil
2 cloves garlic, crushed
1 large brown onion (200g), chopped finely
¼ teaspoon ground cinnamon
½ teaspoon ground cumin
½ teaspoon ground ginger
½ teaspoon ground turmeric

1 cup (250ml) hot chicken stock
1 tablespoon honey
1 cup (150g) dried apricots
1 tablespoon cornflour
1 tablespoon water
½ cup (80g) blanched almonds
2 tablespoons coarsely chopped fresh coriander

1 Combine chicken, oil, garlic, onion and spices in large microwave-safe bowl; cook, covered, on MEDIUM-HIGH (70%) 15 minutes, stirring once during cooking.

2 Add stock, honey and apricots; cook, uncovered, on MEDIUM-HIGH (70%) about 5 minutes or until apricots are tender. Stir in blended cornflour and the water; cook, uncovered, on MEDIUM-HIGH (70%) about 3 minutes or until mixture boils and thickens slightly, stirring once during cooking.

3 Cook nuts on microwave-safe plate, uncovered, on HIGH (100%) about 3 minutes or until browned lightly, stirring twice during cooking. Stir nuts and coriander into tagine.

PER SERVING 34.1g total fat (7g saturated fat); 2688kJ (643 cal); 27.8g carbohydrate; 53.8g protein; 6.2g fibre

Quick lamb curry with mango relish

PREPARATION TIME 25 MINUTES **COOKING TIME** 15 MINUTES **SERVES** 4

¼ cup (65g) madras curry paste

1 medium brown onion (150g), sliced thinly

1 tablespoon grated fresh ginger

2 cloves garlic, crushed

480g lamb fillets, sliced thinly

⅓ cup (95g) yogurt

2 teaspoons cornflour

½ cup (125ml) beef stock

1 tablespoon coarsely chopped fresh coriander

MANGO RELISH

1 medium mango (430g), chopped coarsely

1 tablespoon finely chopped fresh coriander leaves

2 teaspoons white wine vinegar

½ teaspoon sweet chilli sauce

1 Make mango relish.

2 Cook paste, onion, ginger and garlic in large microwave-safe bowl, covered, on HIGH (100%) 4 minutes, stirring once during cooking.

3 Add lamb; cook, covered, on MEDIUM-HIGH (70%) about 5 minutes or until lamb is just cooked, stirring once during cooking.

4 Stir in yogurt and blended cornflour and stock; cook, uncovered, on MEDIUM-HIGH (70%) about 5 minutes or until mixture boils and thickens slightly, stirring twice during cooking. Stir in coriander. Serve with mango relish.

MANGO RELISH Combine ingredients in medium bowl. Cover; refrigerate until required.

▭ **PER SERVING** 10.3g total fat (2.9g saturated fat); 966kJ (231 cal); 5.9g carbohydrate; 27g protein; 2.5g fibre

The steam generated by microwave cooking helps keep robust dishes such as curries, tagines, stews and ragoûts moist, concentrates their flavours, and cooks them evenly and quickly. A curry like this can be made the night before, or even the morning of, the day you want to serve it. Refrigeration for several hours brings out the flavours and melds them to a delicious whole; all that you have to do is reheat it on 50% for just about as long as it takes you to steam some basmati rice on top of the stove.

Satay chicken tenderloins

PREPARATION TIME 10 MINUTES **COOKING TIME** 15 MINUTES **SERVES** 4

750g chicken tenderloins

2 large browns onions (400g), cut into wedges

2 cups (500ml) bottled satay sauce

250g cherry tomatoes, halved

⅓ cup finely shredded fresh basil

¾ cup (200g) yogurt

2 tablespoons sweet chilli sauce

1 Combine chicken, onion and half of the satay sauce in large microwave-safe bowl; cook, uncovered, on HIGH (100%) 10 minutes, stirring twice during cooking.

2 Add remaining satay sauce; cook, covered, on HIGH (100%) about 2 minutes or until chicken is cooked through.

3 Add tomatoes and basil; cook, uncovered, on HIGH (100%) 2 minutes.

4 Serve chicken drizzled with combined yogurt and chilli sauce.

▭ **PER SERVING** 42.3g total fat (13.5g saturated fat); 3219kJ (770 cal); 43.5g carbohydrate; 51.4g protein; 6.1g fibre

This surprisingly disparate combination of ingredients combines to make a zesty and savoury meal: a culinary confirmation that the whole can be greater than the sum of its parts! Double the yogurt and chilli sauce mixture, drizzling half over the chicken and serving the other half as a dip for our potato wedges on page 560.

Teas

Delicious hot or cold, a cup of tea is the perfect hug in a mug; test-drive the new and wonderful flavours out there.

ICED TEA
Made with teabags or, better, with loose tea leaves (use a hinged infuser for one cup). Hot tea is poured over ice cubes, with a spoon in the glass to prevent it cracking.

SUN TEA
Made by mixing tea leaves and cold water in a screw-top jar and leaving in the sun for several hours. Resulting tea is "cleaner" tasting than ordinary tea, and makes crystal-clear iced tea.

CHAI
Chai means tea in Hindi, Chinese and several other languages. In India, tea may be plain or spiced (*masala chai*). The favourite Indian way to make tea is to boil leaves with milk and sugar.

WHITE TEA
White tea is made by plucking buds of the tea bush while they are still covered with fine white hair. Many health benefits are claimed for it. Once reserved for Chinese emperors, it is now available in larger supermarkets.

YERBA MATE
The traditional "tea" of South America, is made with a species of holly native to several countries there. It tastes strongly herbal and grassy, and is becoming popular worldwide as an alternative to coffee as it is gentler on the stomach.

FRUIT TEA
Similar in nature to a herbal tea, fruit teas are also a tisane, and are made from dried fruits, often with the addition of spices. Flavours such as raspberry, blackcurrant and strawberry are common, and their delicious sweet-nature makes them a perfect afternoon pick-me-up.

HERBAL TEA

Made from dried herbs such as peppermint. Herbal infusions fall under the banner of *tisanes*, which differs from a regular tea because they generally contain no leaves of the tea bush.

GREEN TEA

Green tea is dried, unfermented leaves of the tea bush, camellia sinensis. Jasmine, a blend of jasmine blossom and tea, is the most popular. Matcha is a powdered Japanese blend, good for making green tea ice-cream.

BLACK TEA

Produced by fermenting the leaves of the tea bush, which turns them black and changes the flavour. This makes the tea stronger and more astringent than green tea.

BUBBLE TEA

A fashionable drink, especially among the young, being a mixture of tea and pearl tapioca, which forms bubbles when shaken. It is drunk cold. Also called black pearl tea or boba tea, it comes in many flavour and colour variations.

ROOIBOS TEA

A popular "tea" of southern Africa, made from the leaves of the rooibos or honey bush. It contains no oxalic acid or caffeine, and is widely believed to be good for problems associated with allergies and the nervous system.

PU-ERH TEA

A post-fermented tea, meaning that it is usually aged for years after harvesting and fermenting – hence its other name of vintage tea. Available loose or in cakes, it is often claimed to aid weight loss.

If you ever needed convincing about cooking (as opposed to reheating) in a microwave oven, making a risotto will convert you: it does so effortlessly, fairly quickly and seamlessly. Microwave cooking tends to make starchy foods absorb too much liquid too slowly – exactly the brief required of a perfect risotto.

Asparagus and chicken risotto

PREPARATION TIME 10 MINUTES **COOKING TIME** 15 MINUTES **SERVES** 4

300g asparagus, chopped

2 tablespoons olive oil

1½ cups (300g) arborio rice

1 clove garlic, crushed

1 litre (4 cups) boiling
chicken stock

2 cups (340g) coarsely chopped
cooked chicken

¼ cup (20g) coarsely grated
parmesan cheese

¼ cup (60ml) cream

1 Cook asparagus in large microwave-safe bowl, covered, on HIGH (100%) 1 minute. Rinse under cold water; drain.

2 Combine oil, rice and garlic in large microwave-safe bowl; cook, covered, on HIGH (100%) 1 minute. Add 2 cups (500ml) of the boiling stock; cook, covered, on HIGH (100%) 5 minutes. Add remaining boiling stock; cook, covered, on HIGH (100%) 5 minutes, stirring twice during cooking.

3 Gently stir asparagus and remaining ingredients into risotto; cook, covered, on HIGH (100%) 2 minutes. Stand, covered, 5 minutes.

▭ **PER SERVING** 24.6g total fat (8.9g saturated fat); 2521kJ (6.3 cal); 62.3g carbohydrate; 32.2g protein; 1.5g fibre

---

Hard vegetables like pumpkin, kumara, kohlrabi and potatoes cook quickly, do not absorb too much additional moisture, and retain their shape and colour well when cooked in a microwave oven.

Ghee, Indian clarified butter, is a fat that can be heated to a high temperature without burning since all the milk solids have been removed.

Spinach and pumpkin curry

PREPARATION TIME 15 MINUTES **COOKING TIME** 30 MINUTES **SERVES** 4

1 tablespoon flaked almonds

1kg butternut pumpkin

2 tablespoons ghee

2 medium onions (300g), sliced

2 cloves garlic, crushed

1 teaspoon grated fresh ginger

2 small green chillies, sliced thinly

1 teaspoon ground coriander

1 teaspoon ground cumin

300ml cream

250g spinach, chopped coarsely

2 tablespoons coarsely chopped
fresh coriander

1 Cook nuts in small shallow microwave-safe dish, uncovered, on HIGH (100%) 4 minutes or until nuts are browned lightly, stirring twice during cooking.

2 Peel pumpkin, cut into 3cm pieces.

3 Combine ghee and onion in large microwave-safe bowl; cook, uncovered, on HIGH (100%) about 10 minutes or until browned lightly, stirring three times during cooking.

4 Add garlic, ginger, chilli and spices; cook, uncovered, on HIGH (100%) 30 seconds. Add pumpkin and cream; cook, covered, on HIGH (100%) about 12 minutes or until pumpkin is just tender, stirring gently twice during cooking. Add spinach and coriander; cook, uncovered, on HIGH (100%) 1 minute. Just before serving, sprinkle with nuts.

▭ **PER SERVING** 45.4g total fat (27.9g saturated fat); 2249kJ (538 cal); 21.1g carbohydrate; 9.5g protein; 6.1g fibre

Mushroom risotto

PREPARATION TIME 10 MINUTES **COOKING TIME** 30 MINUTES **SERVES** 4

40g butter

1 medium brown onion (150g), chopped finely

2 cloves garlic, crushed

2 cups (400g) arborio rice

500g mixed mushrooms, quartered

2½ cups (625ml) chicken stock

1¾ cups (430ml) boiling water

2 green onions, sliced thinly

¼ cup (20g) finely grated parmesan cheese

1 Place butter, brown onion and garlic in large microwave-safe bowl; cook on HIGH (100%) 2 minutes or until onion softens. Add rice and mushrooms, stirring well; cook, covered, on HIGH (100%) 3 minutes.

2 Stir in stock and the water; cook, covered, on HIGH (100%) about 20 minutes, stirring every 5 minutes, or until rice is just tender. Stir in green onions and cheese.

▭ **PER SERVING** 11.4g total fat (6.9g saturated fat); 2128kJ (509 cal); 83g carbohydrate; 15.5g protein; 4.8g fibre

Instead of mixed mushrooms, try a mix of finely sliced swiss browns and frozen peas. Cook these together first with half of the butter then remove them from the microwave oven and follow the directions as in step 1. Stir the mushroom and pea mixture in along with the green onions and cheese (and a tablespoon of cream if you're feeling decadent: it adds gloss and a softness to the risotto) just before serving.

Sticky toffee pudding

PREPARATION TIME 25 MINUTES **COOKING TIME** 25 MINUTES **SERVES** 8

1 cup (170g) seeded dried dates, chopped coarsely

1¼ cups (310ml) hot water

1 teaspoon bicarbonate of soda

80g butter, chopped

¾ cup (165g) raw sugar

2 eggs

1¼cups (185g) self-raising flour

CARAMEL SAUCE

¾ cup (150g) firmly packed brown sugar

⅔ cup (160ml) cream

30g butter

1 Grease 21cm microwave-safe ring pan, line base with baking paper.

2 Combine dates and the water in medium microwave-safe bowl; cook, uncovered on HIGH (100%) 4 minutes, stirring once during cooking. Stir in soda (mixture will foam); cool 5 minutes.

3 Blend or process date mixture with remaining ingredients until combined; spread into pan. Cook, uncovered, on MEDIUM-HIGH (70%) 8 minutes. Stand 5 minutes before turning onto wire rack to cool.

4 Make caramel sauce.

5 Serve warm pudding with hot sauce.

CARAMEL SAUCE Combine ingredients in medium microwave-safe bowl; cook, uncovered, on HIGH (100%) about 7 minutes or until caramel has thickened, whisking after each minute.

▭ **PER SERVING** 21.6g total fat (13.6g saturated fat); 2090kJ (500 cal); 70g carbohydrate; 7.9g protein; 2.9g fibre

Making one of the all-time great sweets has just become a whole lot easier – putting a hot dessert back on the menu without stress and easing up on the washing-up too.

There are purpose-built microwave egg poachers and muffin pans on the market; if you own one or the other, make individual puddings in it, working out the correct cooking time.

Cherry-choc self-saucing pudding

PREPARATION TIME 10 MINUTES **COOKING TIME** 15 MINUTES **SERVES** 8

60g butter, chopped

1 ½ cups (225g) self-raising flour

1 cup (220g) caster sugar

⅓ cup (35g) cocoa powder

1 ¼ cups (310ml) milk

1 teaspoon vanilla extract

2 x 55g Cherry Ripe bars, chopped coarsely

½ cup (110g) firmly packed brown sugar

1 tablespoon cocoa powder, extra

2 cups (500ml) boiling water

50g butter, chopped, extra

1 Melt butter in deep 3-litre (12-cup) microwave-safe dish, uncovered, on HIGH (100%) about 1 minute or until melted. Add sifted flour, caster sugar and cocoa with milk and extract; whisk until smooth. Stir in Cherry Ripe.

2 Combine brown sugar and sifted extra cocoa in medium jug; gradually stir in the boiling water. Add extra butter; stir until butter melts. Carefully pour syrup mixture evenly over pudding mixture.

3 Cook pudding, uncovered, on HIGH (100%) about 15 minutes or until just cooked in centre. Stand 5 minutes before serving. Serve with cream, if desired.

☐ **PER SERVING** 16.9g total fat (11.3g saturated fat); 1948kJ (466 cal); 71.1g carbohydrate; 5.8g protein; 2g fibre

---

Orange and raspberry self-saucing pudding

PREPARATION TIME 5 MINUTES **COOKING TIME** 15 MINUTES **SERVES** 4

¼ cup (20g) flaked almonds

30g butter

¾ cup (110g) self-raising flour

⅓ cup (80ml) milk

⅔ cup (150g) firmly packed brown sugar

2 teaspoons finely grated orange rind

¾ cup (110g) frozen raspberries

¼ cup (60ml) orange juice

¾ cup (180ml) boiling water

The same thing that prevents "baking" a cake in a microwave oven is exactly what makes it so good for making a self-saucing pudding. The steaming action of the microwaves guarantees success, and in about a third of the cooking time required by a conventional oven.

1 Grease shallow 1.5-litre (6-cup) microwave-safe dish.

2 Cook nuts in small microwave-safe bowl, uncovered, in microwave oven on HIGH (100%) about 2 minutes or until browned lightly.

3 Place butter in medium microwave-safe bowl; cook, uncovered, in microwave oven on HIGH (100%) 30 seconds. Add flour, milk and half of the sugar; whisk until smooth. Stir in rind and raspberries; spread into dish. Sprinkle remaining sugar over pudding mixture; carefully pour over combined juice and boiling water. Place pudding on microwave-safe rack; cook, uncovered, on MEDIUM-HIGH (70%) about 12 minutes. Stand 5 minutes.

4 Sprinkle nuts over pudding; serve with cream or ice-cream, if desired.

☐ **PER SERVING** 5.4g total fat (2.6g saturated fat); 803kJ (192 cal); 32g carbohydrate; 2.6g protein; 1.6g fibre

CHERRY-CHOC SELF-SAUCING PUDDING

Apple and pear crumble

PREPARATION TIME 25 MINUTES **COOKING TIME** 12 MINUTES **SERVES** 4

3 large apples (600g), peeled, cored, sliced

3 small pears (540g), peeled, cored, sliced

1 tablespoon caster sugar

1 tablespoon honey

CRUMBLE TOPPING

½ cup (75g) self-raising flour

1 teaspoon ground cinnamon

¾ cup (65g) rolled oats

⅓ cup (30g) desiccated coconut

75g cold butter

⅓ cup (75g) firmly packed brown sugar

1 Place apple, pear, sugar and honey in shallow 2-litre (8-cup) microwave-safe dish; cook, covered, on HIGH (100%) 5 minutes or until fruit is just tender, stirring once during cooking.
2 Meanwhile, make crumble topping; sprinkle over apple and pear mixture. Cook, uncovered, on HIGH (100%) about 6 minutes or until topping is firm.

CRUMBLE TOPPING Combine flour, cinnamon, oats and coconut in bowl. Rub in butter using fingertips; stir in sugar.

☐ **PER SERVING** 22.1g total fat (14.7g saturated fat); 2232kJ (534 cal); 55.1g carbohydrate; 4.9g protein; 7.1g fibre

This is an easy and yummy dessert to make at any time of year but especially on a cold winter night. Brown coconut (and nuts) in the microwave oven; arrange in a single layer on a shallow microwave-safe tray or on a double thickness of baking paper and cook, uncovered, on HIGH (100%) until just lightly browned. The length of time will depend on what you're toasting and how much there is; remember to remove the food when just lightly browned as it continues to colour for a few minutes out of the oven.

Poached peaches with custard

PREPARATION TIME 20 MINUTES (PLUS REFRIGERATION) **COOKING TIME** 20 MINUTES **SERVES** 4

3 cups (750ml) water

1 cup (250ml) orange juice

1½ cups (330g) caster sugar

4 medium firm peaches (800g)

1 teaspoon cornflour

2 teaspoons water, extra

CUSTARD

1 cup (250ml) milk

3 egg yolks

⅓ cup (75g) caster sugar

1 Combine the water, juice and sugar in large microwave-safe bowl; cook, uncovered, on HIGH (100%) 3 minutes or until sugar dissolves, stirring twice during cooking. Add peaches; cook, covered, on HIGH (100%) 6 minutes or until tender. Cover; refrigerate 3 hours.
2 Meanwhile, make custard.
3 Remove peaches from syrup; peel peaches. Reserve syrup.
4 Strain 1 cup (250ml) of the reserved syrup into microwave-safe jug; stir in blended cornflour and the extra water. Cook, uncovered, on HIGH (100%) 3 minutes or until it boils and thickens slightly, whisking twice during cooking; cool. Serve peaches with syrup and custard.

CUSTARD Heat milk in microwave-safe jug on MEDIUM-HIGH (70%) 1 minute. Whisk in combined yolks and sugar; cook, uncovered, on MEDIUM (55%) 5 minutes or until thickened slightly, whisking twice during cooking. Cover surface with plastic wrap; refrigerate until required.

☐ **PER SERVING** 6.9g total fat (2.9g saturated fat); 2424kJ (580 cal); 120g carbohydrate; 6.3g protein; 2.5g fibre

One of the many fruits that poach perfectly in the microwave oven, these peaches come to the table with their own custard. To add a hint of spice, a cinnamon stick can be cooked along with the water, juice and sugar; discard it when adding the peaches.

Apricot citrus marmalade

PREPARATION TIME 25 MINUTES (PLUS STANDING TIME) **COOKING TIME** 30 MINUTES

MAKES ABOUT 3½ CUPS (1.125KG)

1 medium orange (180g)

1 large lemon (180g)

1 tablespoon water

¾ cup (110g) dried apricots

2 cups (500ml) water, extra

2½ cups (550g) caster sugar, approximately

1 Remove and reserve seeds from unpeeled quartered orange and lemon. Place seeds and the water in small bowl; cover, stand overnight.

2 Roughly chop orange, lemon and apricots; blend or process until finely chopped. Combine fruit with the extra water in large glass microwave-safe bowl; cook, covered, on HIGH (100%) about 20 minutes or until rind is soft, stirring once during cooking. Do not uncover; stand fruit mixture overnight.

3 Drain seeds over fruit mixture; discard seeds.

4 Measure fruit mixture; allow 1 cup (220g) sugar for every 1 cup fruit mixture. Return fruit mixture and sugar to same bowl; cook, uncovered, on HIGH (100%) 5 minutes, stirring twice during cooking.

5 Cook, uncovered, without stirring, on HIGH (100%) further 5 minutes or until marmalade jells when tested. Skim surface, pour into hot sterilised jars; seal while hot.

▭ **PER TABLESPOON** 0g total fat (0g saturated fat); 138kJ (33 cal); 8g carbohydrate; 0.1g protein; 0.2g fibre

The microwave oven does a good job of drying citrus rind, a nice ingredient to have on hand for baking or adding to stir-fries. Peel wide strips of rind from oranges, lemons, limes, mandarins and the like, avoiding the pith. For one orange or two lemons, spread the strips in a single layer on a double thickness of absorbent paper and cover with a single piece; microwave, on HIGH (100%) 2 minutes. Pause to check if they are dried sufficiently; if not, microwave 30 to 60 seconds. Once cooled, keep tightly sealed in a glass jar. Store refrigerated for 2 months.

Rhubarb berry jam

PREPARATION TIME 20 MINUTES **COOKING TIME** 30 MINUTES **MAKES** ABOUT 3 CUPS (960G)

4 cups (440g) chopped rhubarb

500g fresh or frozen blackberries

1 teaspoon finely grated orange rind

1 tablespoon orange juice

1 tablespoon lemon juice

1¾ cups (385g) caster sugar

1 Cook rhubarb, berries, rind and juices in large glass microwave-safe bowl, uncovered, on HIGH (100%) 10 minutes, stirring once during cooking.

2 Add sugar, stir until it dissolves; cook, uncovered, on HIGH (100%) about 20 minutes or until jam jells when tested, stirring 3 times during cooking.

3 Pour jam into hot sterilised jars; seal while hot.

▭ **PER TABLESPOON** 0g total fat (0g saturated fat); 117kJ (28 cal); 6.3g carbohydrate; 0.2g protein; 0.7g fibre

Making jam when fruits are in season is an undertaking we all contemplate but seldom follow through on because it's just not worth the work if you're not making large quantities. With a microwave oven, you can size-down in quantity and still get a perfect set to your jam.

Store refrigerated for 2 months.

THE PIE DISH

The Pie Dish

A pie brings a smile to everyone's face. Even the look of the classic pie dish, with its wide rim to support a generous crust, has a motherly air that says comfort. You can, however, make a pie in just about any dish that can go into the oven. The usual definition of a pie, as opposed to a tart, is that a pie has a top crust, although there are exceptions. It may have a bottom crust as well.

CHOOSING A PIE DISH

You may choose not to buy a special pie dish or dishes, but to use ramekins, an ovenproof dish, a pudding basin, a soufflé dish, a cake pan or even a baking dish for your pies. The purpose of the wide rim on a classic pie dish is to hold an extended double crust, fluted or decoratively marked in some way to make the pie look handsome and impressive.

MATERIALS

Traditional pie dishes are available in the thin, enamelled metalware as well as in earthenware. Other pie dishes and plates are made in various metals including aluminium, stainless steel and black-finished steel, and in ovenproof glass and ceramics such as earthenware, china and porcelain. Because metal conducts heat much more rapidly than ceramic materials, metal is generally considered better for browning bottom crusts on pies. Ceramic performs well for one-crust pies because it takes up heat slowly, which heats the filling gently and evenly. Ceramic dishes also work well for two-crust pies with a long cooking period.

PIE FILLINGS

A pie is a wonderful way to use leftovers. Leftover meat needs flavoursome gravy (see *The Baking Dish*, page 314). Seafood, vegetables, eggs or ham need a sauce and a flavour boost from a freshly cooked addition such as onion, garlic, mushrooms or herbs.

PIE CRUSTS

A bottom crust may be shortcrust, puff, or even fillo pastry for a pie that does not have a top crust, but is called a pie anyway because it is too deep to be described as a tart.

The top crust may be shortcrust or puff pastry, or mashed potato, scone dough, dumpling or a crumble topping. Non-pastry toppings are placed over the cooked filling. Pastry crusts, both top and bottom, call for a little more work. The following instructions are for pastry crusts – see Handling Pastry on pages 440 & 441 for illustrated steps (also read the section on Making a Pastry Shell in *The Flan Tin & The Quiche Tin*, page 456).

ONE-CRUST PIE TOP If the filling is not firm enough to mound in the centre to support the top crust, place a greased pie funnel or upturned egg cup in the centre of the dish, then fill the dish with the cold filling. If the filling will mound, a funnel will not be needed.

Roll out pastry as the recipe directs. If using a traditional pie dish, roll out a shape, about 3cm larger all round, than the top of the dish. Cut a pastry strip from around the edge of the rolled-out pastry as wide as the rim to make a collar. Moisten the rim of the dish with water and press collar on to it, slightly overlapping the ends. If you break the collar or it seems a bit thin, patch it with small scraps of pastry. Although pastry will stretch, be gentle; over-stretching will cause the pastry to shrink during baking. Moisten collar with a little water. Then use your floured hands or a floured rolling pin with pastry rolled round loosely, to place lid loosely on the pie. Press edges firmly onto the collar, hold up the dish on one hand (as if you were holding a tray of drinks) and, with the other hand, trim off pastry overhang with a sharp knife slanted slightly under the rim. If using a pie funnel, cut a hole to uncover the opening. If not using a funnel, cut a few slits in the crust to allow the steam to escape.

If using a dish without a rim cut the pastry a little larger than the top, dampen edges of the dish and pastry then position the pastry. Press pastry onto the dish then trim.

FLUTING EDGES If using puff pastry, use your knuckle to press the pastry all round, just inside the edge, to push it a little beyond the edge of the dish to allow for shrinkage during baking and at the same time tapping the cut edge with a knife blade held horizontally, to "knock up" the pastry and give a flaky finish. Next, draw the back of a knife vertically across the edge at 2cm to 3cm intervals all round, pulling the pastry in slightly to notch it, while with your other thumb you press the pastry down just inside the edge.

If using shortcrust pastry, press edge of the pastry out slightly beyond the edge of the dish as described above, then flute by pressing just inside the edge with a thumb and pinching pastry with the other thumb and forefinger, or notch with the back of a knife, or simply mark all round with a fork or tip of a spoon.

If you wish, decorate the pie with shapes, cut from pastry trimmings, moisten them underneath and secure them in place. Traditionally, sweet pies were only decorated in the centre, presumably to make them easy to identify when a home had a larder full of pies.

TWO-CRUST PIE Reserve about a third of the pastry (or amount directed by recipe) for top crust. Roll out remaining pastry to a shape that will line the dish with about a 2cm overhang. Using a floured rolling pin, lift and transfer pastry to dish; ease pastry in loosely without stretching it. Use your fingertips to eliminate air pockets.

If filling is very liquid, it could make the pastry soggy, to help avoid this, brush bottom and sides of crust with beaten egg or egg white (or for a sweet pie, warmed sieved jam) and allow to dry for a few minutes. Place funnel (if using) and filling in dish; dampen the edges of bottom crust. Roll out top crust and place over filling. Press both crusts together, trim off overhang, flute or mark sides and decorate, if desired, as described above.

RESTING All pastry tends to shrink when it is cooked because the gluten content of the flour, which becomes elastic when it is moistened and handled, shrinks back when heated. To minimise this, always rest pastry for 30 minutes in the refrigerator after rolling out, then rest assembled pie again before baking. This allows the gluten to relax.

Curried chicken pies

PREPARATION TIME 50 MINUTES **COOKING TIME** 1 HOUR 45 MINUTES (PLUS STANDING TIME) **SERVES** 6

1.6kg chicken

90g butter

1 small leek (200g), chopped finely

1 medium white onion (150g), chopped finely

1 medium red capsicum (200g), chopped finely

2 trimmed celery stalks (200g), chopped finely

3 teaspoons curry powder

¼ teaspoon chilli powder

¼ cup (35g) plain flour

⅓ cup (80g) sour cream

½ cup finely chopped fresh flat-leaf parsley

2 sheets ready-rolled puff pastry

1 egg, beaten lightly

1 Place chicken in large saucepan, add enough water to just cover chicken; bring to a boil. Reduce heat, simmer, uncovered, 1 hour. Remove pan from heat; when cool enough to handle, remove chicken from stock. Reserve 1¾ cups (430ml) of the stock for this recipe.

2 Preheat oven to 200°C/180°C fan-forced.

3 Remove skin and bones from chicken; chop chicken flesh roughly.

4 Heat butter in large frying pan; cook leek, onion, capsicum and celery, stirring, until vegetables are soft. Add curry powder and chilli powder; cook, stirring, until fragrant.

5 Stir in flour. Add reserved stock, stirring over heat until mixture boils and thickens; reduce heat, simmer 1 minute, remove from heat.

6 Add sour cream, chicken and parsley to vegetable mixture. Spoon mixture into six 1¼-cup (310ml) pie dishes.

7 Cut pastry into six rounds large enough to cover top of each dish. Lightly brush pastry with egg. Place pies on oven tray.

8 Bake pies 10 minutes; reduce oven temperature to 180°C/160°C fan-forced. Bake further 15 minutes or until pastry is golden brown.

▭ **PER SERVING** 52.8g total fat (25.4g saturated fat); 3001 kJ (718 cal); 28.5g carbohydrate; 33.3g protein; 3g fibre

Meat pies

PREPARATION TIME 35 MINUTES (PLUS REFRIGERATION TIME) **COOKING TIME** 1 ¼ HOURS **SERVES** 8

2 cups (300g) plain flour

125g cold butter, chopped

2 eggs, beaten lightly

2 tablespoons iced water, approximately

2 sheets ready-rolled puff pastry

1 egg yolk

FILLING

30g butter

2 medium brown onions (300g), chopped coarsely

900g beef mince

¼ cup (60ml) worcestershire sauce

¼ cup (60ml) dark soy sauce

2 cups (500ml) beef stock

½ teaspoon ground allspice

2 tablespoons cornflour

2 tablespoons water, extra

1 Sift flour into bowl; rub in butter. Add eggs and enough water to make ingredients come together. Knead dough on floured surface until smooth. Cover; refrigerate 30 minutes.

2 Meanwhile, make filling. Preheat oven to 200°C/180°C fan-forced.

3 Divide dough into eight portions; roll each portion on floured surface large enough to line eight 11cm pie dishes. Trim away excess pastry. Place dishes on oven tray. Cover pastry with baking paper, fill with dried beans or rice. Bake about 8 minutes, remove paper and beans; bake further 8 minutes or until pastry is browned lightly. Cool.

4 Spoon cold filling into pastry cases. Cut eight 12cm rounds from puff pastry, brush edges of pastry with a little egg yolk, gently press puff pastry tops onto pies; trim edges. Brush tops with a little more egg yolk. Make two small slits in centre of pies, return to trays; bake about 15 minutes or until browned lightly. Serve hot with tomato sauce.

FILLING Heat butter in frying pan; cook onion, stirring, until soft. Add mince; stir over heat until browned. Stir in sauces, stock and allspice; bring to a boil. Simmer, covered, 20 minutes. Stir in blended cornflour and the extra water until it boils and thickens.

▭ **PER SERVING** 35.7g total fat (15.1g saturated fat); 2713kJ (649 cal); 48.3g carbohydrate; 32.6g protein; 2.5g fibre

Beef carbonade pies

PREPARATION TIME 25 MINUTES **COOKING TIME** 3 HOURS 20 MINUTES **SERVES** 8

2kg beef round steak, cut into 3cm pieces

½ cup (75g) plain flour

40g butter

¼ cup (60ml) vegetable oil

4 medium brown onions (600g), sliced thickly

2 large carrots (360g), chopped coarsely

2 cloves garlic, crushed

2¾ cups (680ml) stout

2 tablespoons brown sugar

¼ cup (60ml) cider vinegar

3 sprigs fresh thyme

1 bay leaf

2 sheets ready-rolled puff pastry

1 tablespoon milk

1 egg

1 Coat beef in flour; shake off excess. Heat butter and 2 tablespoons of the oil in large deep saucepan; cook beef, in batches, until browned all over.

2 Heat remaining oil in same pan; cook onion, carrot and garlic, stirring, until onion softens. Return beef to pan with stout, sugar, vinegar, thyme and bay leaf; bring to a boil. Reduce heat, simmer, covered, 1½ hours.

3 Uncover; simmer, stirring occasionally, about 1 hour or until beef is tender and sauce thickens. Discard herbs.

4 Meanwhile, preheat oven to 220°C/200°C fan-forced.

5 Divide beef mixture among eight 1¼-cup (310ml) pie dishes. Cut each pastry sheet into four squares; top each dish with one pastry square. Brush pastry squares with combined milk and egg; place dishes on oven tray. Bake, uncovered, about 15 minutes or until pastry is puffed and browned lightly.

☐ **PER SERVING** 55.9g total fat (14.4g saturated fat); 2930kJ (701 cal); 32.4g carbohydrate, 58.2g protein; 3.1g fibre

---

Shepherd's pie

PREPARATION TIME 20 MINUTES **COOKING TIME** 45 MINUTES **SERVES** 4

30g butter

1 medium brown onion (150g), chopped finely

1 medium carrot (120g), chopped finely

½ teaspoon dried mixed herbs

4 cups (750g) chopped cooked lamb

¼ cup (70g) tomato paste

¼ cup (60ml) tomato sauce

2 tablespoons worcestershire sauce

2 cups (500ml) beef stock

2 tablespoons plain flour

⅓ cup (80ml) water

POTATO TOPPING

5 medium potatoes (1kg), chopped coarsely

60g butter, chopped

¼ cup (60ml) milk

Shepherd's pie is traditionally made from cooked lamb (and any of the vegies, too, leftover with the Sunday roast). A similar potato-topped pie but usually made with minced beef is called cottage pie.

1 Preheat oven to 200°C/180°C fan-forced. Oil shallow 2.5-litre (10-cup) pie dish.

2 Make potato topping.

3 Meanwhile, heat butter in large saucepan, cook onion and carrot, stirring, until tender. Add mixed herbs and lamb; cook, stirring, 2 minutes. Stir in tomato paste, sauces and stock, then blended flour and water; stir over heat until mixture boils and thickens. Spoon mixture into dish.

4 Place heaped tablespoons of potato topping on lamb mixture. Bake, uncovered, about 20 minutes or until browned lightly and heated through.

POTATO TOPPING Boil, steam or microwave potatoes until tender; drain. Mash with butter and milk until smooth.

☐ **PER SERVING** 36.2g total fat (20.2g saturated fat); 2976kJ (712 cal); 44.7g carbohydrate; 48.8g protein; 6g fibre

Handling pastry

Many believe the secret to good pastry-making rests with the cook having cold hands and a warm heart.

KNEADING

Not really an appropriate word for pastry, as kneading dough should be done quickly and lightly, until the ingredients come together in a smooth ball.

STORING AND FREEZING

Pastry can be stored, tightly wrapped in plastic wrap and enclosed in a plastic bag, in the refrigerator for up to a week, or frozen for up to a month. Allow to return to room temperature before rolling or shaping.

DUSTING

Dusting the work surface lightly but evenly with flour, or sometimes sugar for sweet dough, prevents pastry from sticking. Keep some flour in a dredger (mug with pierced lid) for this purpose.

BLIND BAKING

A pastry case can be baked blind (empty) to ensure crispness. Line with baking paper and weigh down with raw rice or dried beans, then bake as directed. Rice and beans can be reused for blind baking but not eating.

FLUTING

To flute the edge of a tart shell or pie crust, press from just inside the edge with a thumb pinched between the other thumb and finger. For a sunburst effect, press edge flat and cut 1cm slits around crust at 2cm intervals.

LATTICING

For a latticed top crust, cut pastry into narrow strips and lay a row of strips parallel across the top. Trim to fit; press ends onto dampened pastry around the rim. Repeat with strips laid across the first ones.

ROLLING

Dust rolling pin with flour, or roll dough between sheets of greaseproof or baking paper. Roll from centre out, lifting and turning dough a quarter-turn. Never turn dough over.

LINING A PAN WITH PASTRY

Dust pastry lightly with flour, roll loosely around lightly floured rolling pin and unroll over pan. Ease in gently, taking care not to stretch it; press to fit. Trim edges and rest pastry in the refrigerator before baking.

DOCKING OR PRICKING PASTRY

A docker has a spiked roller to prick holes in uncooked dough so that it will not puff up when baked. Alternatively, you can use a fork to prick the pastry all over.

WORKING WITH FILLO PASTRY

Work with one sheet of fillo at a time, keeping the rest covered with baking paper, then a damp tea-towel. Brush with oil or melted butter, stack another piece on top and repeat. Don't freeze fillo as the layers will stick together.

WORKING WITH READY-MADE PUFF PASTRY

If not making your own puff pastry, try to buy commercial pastry made with butter. Use it chilled, and always cut edges with a sharp knife and without dragging pastry so it will rise evenly in delicate layers.

WORKING WITH CHOUX PASTRY

Use choux pastry as soon as it is made, while still warm. Pipe small, high mounds or finger lengths, or drop heaped teaspoons, well separated, onto baking-paper-lined oven trays; bake as directed.

A regular-size store-bought barbecued chicken will give you enough meat for this quick and easy recipe. Discard the skin and bones before coarsely chopping the flesh.

Chicken, leek and mushroom pies

PREPARATION TIME 15 MINUTES **COOKING TIME** 45 MINUTES **SERVES** 4

1 tablespoon vegetable oil

1 medium leek (350g), sliced thinly

2 rindless bacon rashers (130g), sliced thinly

200g mushrooms, halved

1 tablespoon plain flour

1 cup (250ml) chicken stock

⅓ cup (80ml) cream

1 tablespoon dijon mustard

3 cups (480g) coarsely chopped barbecued chicken

1 sheet ready-rolled puff pastry, quartered

1 Preheat oven to 200°C/180°C fan-forced.

2 Heat oil in medium saucepan; cook leek, bacon and mushrooms, stirring, until leek softens. Stir in flour; cook, stirring, until mixture thickens and bubbles. Gradually add stock; cook, stirring, until mixture boils and thickens. Stir in cream, mustard and chicken.

3 Divide mixture among four 1-cup (250ml) pie dishes; top each with a pastry quarter. Bake, uncovered, about 20 minutes or until browned.

☐ **PER SERVING** 44.7g total fat (13.1g saturated fat); 2780kJ (665 cal); 20.4g carbohydrate; 44.5g protein; 3.7g fibre

---

Russet burbank potatoes will give you the best results for the rösti topping. If you can't get them, buy a dry white (not waxy) type of potato.

Fish pie with caper rösti topping

PREPARATION TIME 10 MINUTES **COOKING TIME** 25 MINUTES **SERVES** 4

600g white fish fillets, chopped coarsely

100g uncooked small prawns, shelled, deveined

¼ cup (35g) plain flour

25g butter

½ cup (120g) sour cream

½ cup (60g) frozen peas

¼ cup coarsely chopped fresh dill

CAPER ROSTI TOPPING

500g russet burbank potatoes, peeled, grated coarsely

2 tablespoons rinsed baby capers, drained

25g butter, melted

1 Make caper rösti topping.

2 Coat seafood in flour; shake off excess. Heat butter in large frying pan; cook seafood, in batches, 3 minutes. Return seafood to pan with sour cream, peas and dill; cook, stirring occasionally, about 5 minutes or until seafood is cooked through.

3 Preheat grill. Spread seafood into shallow 2.5-litre (10-cup) square pie dish; top with caper rösti topping. Grill about 10 minutes or until topping is tender and golden brown.

CAPER ROSTI TOPPING Squeeze excess moisture from potato; combine with capers and butter in medium bowl.

☐ **PER SERVING** 23.4g total fat (14.8g saturated fat); 1910kJ (457 cal); 23g carbohydrate; 37.3g protein; 3g fibre

---

1 CHICKEN, LEEK AND MUSHROOM PIES **2** FISH PIE WITH CAPER ROSTI TOPPING
3 LAMB AND ROSEMARY PIES [P 444] **4** BEEF BOURGUIGNON PIES [P 444]

1 2

3 4

Diced lamb can be bought from supermarkets and butchers. If you prefer to dice the lamb yourself, shoulder meat is very good. Ask the butcher to bone the shoulder for you, and discard as much fat as possible.

Lamb and rosemary pies

PREPARATION TIME 20 MINUTES **COOKING TIME** 25 MINUTES **SERVES** 4

2 tablespoons olive oil

400g diced lamb

4 baby onions (100g), quartered

1 tablespoon plain flour

¼ cup (60ml) dry red wine

¾ cup (180ml) beef stock

1 tablespoon tomato paste

1 tablespoon fresh rosemary leaves

2 sheets ready-rolled puff pastry

1 egg

4 fresh rosemary sprigs

20g butter

1 Heat half of the oil in large saucepan; cook lamb, in batches, uncovered, until browned all over. Heat remaining oil in same pan; cook onion, stirring, until soft. Add flour; cook, stirring, until mixture bubbles and thickens. Gradually add wine, stock, paste and rosemary leaves; stir until mixture boils and thickens. Stir in lamb; cool 10 minutes.

2 Preheat oven to 200°C/180°C fan-forced. Oil four holes of 6-hole (¾-cup/180ml) texas muffin pan.

3 Cut two 13cm rounds from opposite corners of each pastry sheet; cut two 9cm rounds from remaining corners of each sheet. Place larger rounds in pan holes to cover bases and sides; trim any excess pastry, prick bases with fork.

4 Spoon lamb mixture into pastry cases; brush around edges with a little egg. Top pies with smaller rounds; gently press around edges to seal. Brush pies with remaining egg; press one rosemary sprig into top of each pie.

5 Bake pies, uncovered, about 15 minutes or until browned lightly. Stand 5 minutes in pan before serving. Serve with peas, if desired.

▭ **PER SERVING** 42.4g total fat (18.6g saturated fat); 2687kJ (643 cal); 34.2g carbohydrate; 28.7g protein; 1.8g fibre

---

This is the perfect recipe for freezing ahead, for pies that you want to serve at a later date – they'll keep up to 3 months. Cook the filling as instructed until the meat is tender, without adding the mushrooms, then cool the filling before freezing it. Simply stir in the mushrooms after you thaw the filling mixture and finish the recipe from there.

Beef bourguignon pies

PREPARATION TIME 30 MINUTES **COOKING TIME** 2 HOURS **SERVES** 6

12 pickling onions (480g)

6 rindless bacon rashers (390g), sliced thinly

2 tablespoons olive oil

400g mushrooms

1kg gravy beef, trimmed, cut into 2cm pieces

¼ cup (35g) plain flour

1 tablespoon tomato paste

2 teaspoons fresh thyme leaves

1 cup (250ml) dry red wine

2 cups (500ml) beef stock

2 sheets ready-rolled butter puff pastry

cooking-oil spray

½ cup finely chopped fresh flat-leaf parsley

1 Peel onions, leaving roots intact; halve lengthways.

2 Cook bacon in heated large heavy-based saucepan, stirring, until crisp; drain on absorbent paper. Reheat same pan; cook onion, stirring, until browned all over, remove from pan. Heat 2 teaspoons of the oil in same pan; cook mushrooms, stirring, until just browned, remove from pan.

3 Coat beef in flour; shake off excess. Heat remaining oil in same pan; cook beef, in batches, until browned all over. Add bacon and onion with tomato paste and thyme; cook, stirring, 2 minutes. Add wine and stock; bring to a boil. Reduce heat, simmer, covered, 1 hour. Add mushrooms; simmer, uncovered, about 40 minutes or until beef is tender, stirring occasionally.

4 Meanwhile, preheat oven to 220°C/200°C fan-forced.

5 Place pastry sheets on board; using 1¼-cup (310ml) pie dish, cut lid for one pie by tracing around upper-rim of dish with tip of sharp knife. Repeat process until you have six lids. Place lids on oiled oven tray, spray with cooking-oil spray; bake, uncovered, about 5 minutes or until browned lightly.

6 Meanwhile, stir parsley into beef bourguignon then divide among six 1¼-cup (310ml) pie dishes; top each with pastry lid. Serve pies with hot chips, if desired.

PER SERVING 34.2g total fat (13.4g saturated fat); 2796kJ (669 cal); 29.8g carbohydrate; 51.7g protein; 4g fibre

Tomato tarte tatin

PREPARATION TIME 20 MINUTES **COOKING TIME** 1 HOUR (PLUS STANDING TIME) **SERVES** 8

2 large red onions (400g), sliced thinly

½ cup (125ml) balsamic vinegar

2 cups (440g) raw sugar

12 medium egg tomatoes (900g), halved

1 tablespoon water

2 sheets ready-rolled puff pastry with canola oil

Don't try to dissolve the raw sugar; just move the pan around over the heat so that the melting of the sugar is even. Stir the sugar gently and only a few times during the crystallising process.

1 Preheat oven to 200°C/180°C fan-forced.

2 Heat large oiled frying pan; cook onion, stirring, until onion softens. Add vinegar and 1 tablespoon of the sugar to pan; cook, stirring, until onion caramelises.

3 Place tomatoes, cut side up, in single layer on oven tray; bake, uncovered, 20 minutes or until softened and browned lightly.

4 Meanwhile, oil eight 10cm pie dishes. Combine remaining sugar with the water in large heavy-based saucepan; stir over low heat to combine. Cook, shaking pan constantly and stirring occasionally, until mixture crystallises. Continue cooking, stirring occasionally until mixture turns to a thick, dark syrup. Divide sugar mixture among pie dishes. Arrange three tomato halves, cut-side down, in each dish; top with onion mixture.

5 Cut four 10cm-rounds from each pastry sheet; top each dish with pastry round. Bake, uncovered, about 15 minutes or until pastry is browned lightly. Stand 2 minutes before turning onto serving plates.

PER SERVING 9.6g total fat (0.7g saturated fat); 1726kJ (413 cal); 75.1g carbohydrate; 4.2g protein; 2.8g fibre

Leeks can take a surprisingly long time to soften. Younger, smaller leeks will take less time to cook than the larger ones. It's important to clean a leek well before using it: discard the tough green leaves and base of the root end then slice the white part of the leek in half lengthways. Clasping it together with one hand, hold one half of the leek under cold running water and fan the layers apart with the other hand, washing out any grit hidden among the leaves.

Farmhouse chicken pie

PREPARATION TIME 30 MINUTES **COOKING TIME** 45 MINUTES **SERVES** 6

60g butter

1 medium leek (350g), sliced thickly

⅓ cup (50g) plain flour

¾ cup (180ml) milk

1 cup (250ml) chicken stock

3 cups (480g) coarsely chopped cooked chicken

1 cup (85g) chopped broccoli

1 small red capsicum (150g), chopped finely

310g can corn kernels, drained

¼ cup coarsely chopped fresh flat-leaf parsley

2 sheets ready-rolled puff pastry

1 egg

1 Melt butter in medium saucepan; cook leek, stirring, about 1 minute or until leek is soft. Add flour; cook, stirring, until mixture bubbles. Remove from heat, gradually stir in milk and stock; cook, stirring, over heat until mixture boils and thickens. Remove from heat; stir in chicken, broccoli, capsicum, corn and parsley.

2 Preheat oven to 200°C/180°C fan-forced.

3 Spoon filling into 23cm pie dish. Cut 3cm wide strips from one sheet of pastry and place them around the lip of dish. Brush strips lightly with egg. Place second sheet of pastry over filling and lip to cover dish. Trim edge, scallop edge firmly to seal, decorate with pastry scraps, if desired. Brush top of pastry with egg.

4 Bake pie, uncovered, about 10 minutes; reduce oven temperature to 180°C/160°C fan-forced, bake further 20 minutes or until pastry is brown.

▭ **PER SERVING** 29.4g total fat (9.1g saturated fat); 2291kJ (548 cal); 37.3g carbohydrate; 29.3g protein; 4.2g fibre

This is a cheat's tarte tatin, but it works like a charm in about quarter of the time.

French apple tart

PREPARATION TIME 10 MINUTES **COOKING TIME** 30 MINUTES **SERVES** 6

50g butter

⅓ cup (75g) firmly packed brown sugar

¼ cup (60ml) cream

¼ teaspoon ground cinnamon

3 medium apples (450g), peeled, cored, sliced thickly

1 sheet ready-rolled puff pastry

1 Preheat oven to 240°C/220°C fan-forced.

2 Stir butter, sugar, cream and cinnamon in medium saucepan over low heat until sugar dissolves; bring to a boil. Add apple; reduce heat, simmer, uncovered, without stirring, about 5 minutes or until apple is tender.

3 Spread apple mixture into 23cm pie dish. Cut 24cm round from pastry sheet; place round on top of apple mixture. Bake, uncovered, about 20 minutes or until pastry is browned lightly. Stand 5 minutes; turn tart, apple-side up, onto serving plate.

▭ **PER SERVING** 16.9g total fat (10.3g saturated fat); 1175kJ (281 cal); 29.7g carbohydrate; 2g protein; 1.5g fibre

Blackberry and apple pie

PREPARATION TIME 50 MINUTES (PLUS REFRIGERATION TIME)

COOKING TIME 1 HOUR 5 MINUTES (PLUS STANDING TIME) **SERVES** 8

9 medium apples (1.4kg)

2 tablespoons caster sugar

1 tablespoon cornflour

1 tablespoon water

300g frozen blackberries

1 tablespoon cornflour, extra

1 tablespoon demerara sugar

PASTRY

2 cups (300g) plain flour

⅔ cup (110g) icing sugar

185g cold butter, chopped

2 egg yolks

1 tablespoon iced water, approximately

Tossing the blackberries in cornflour will prevent them colouring the apple mixture too much, and will also help hold and contain the natural juice of the berries.

1 Make pastry; cover, refrigerate 30 minutes. Roll two-thirds of the dough between sheets of baking paper until large enough to line greased 23cm pie dish. Ease dough into dish; trim edge. Cover; refrigerate 30 minutes. Roll remaining pastry between sheets of baking paper until large enough to cover pie.

2 Meanwhile, peel and core apples; slice thinly. Place in large saucepan with caster sugar, cook, covered, over low heat, about 10 minutes or until apples are just tender. Strain over small saucepan; reserve cooking liquid. Blend cornflour with the water, stir into reserved cooking liquid; stir over heat until mixture boils and thickens. Place apples in large bowl, gently stir in cornflour mixture.

3 Toss blackberries in extra cornflour, stir gently into apple mixture.

4 Preheat oven to 220°C/200°C fan-forced.

5 Spoon fruit mixture into pastry case; top with remaining rolled out pastry. Press edges together, trim with knife; decorate edge. Brush pastry with a little water; sprinkle with demerara sugar. Using knife, make three cuts in top of pastry to allow steam to escape. Place pie on oven tray; bake, uncovered, 20 minutes. Reduce oven temperature to 200°C/180°C fan-forced, bake, uncovered, a further 30 minutes or until pastry is browned lightly. Stand 10 minutes before serving.

PASTRY Process flour, icing sugar and butter until crumbly. Add egg yolks and enough of the water to make ingredients just come together. Knead dough on floured surface until smooth.

PER SERVING 21.1g total fat (13g saturated fat); 2107kJ (504 cal); 69.4g carbohydrate; 5.9g protein; 6.3g fibre

Apple pie

PREPARATION TIME 45 MINUTES (PLUS REFRIGERATION TIME) **COOKING TIME** 1 HOUR 10 MINUTES
SERVES 8

10 medium granny smith apples (1.5kg), peeled, cored, sliced thickly

½ cup (125ml) water

¼ cup (55g) caster sugar

1 teaspoon finely grated lemon rind

¼ teaspoon ground cinnamon

1 tablespoon caster sugar, extra

PASTRY

1 cup (150g) plain flour

½ cup (75g) self-raising flour

¼ cup (35g) cornflour

¼ cup (30g) custard powder

1 tablespoon caster sugar

100g cold butter, chopped

1 egg, separated

¼ cup (60ml) iced water, approximately

1 Make pastry; cover, refrigerate 30 minutes.

2 Place apple and the water in large saucepan; bring to a boil. Reduce heat, simmer, covered, 10 minutes or until apples soften. Drain; stir in sugar, rind and cinnamon. Cool.

3 Preheat oven to 220°C/200°C fan-forced. Grease deep 25cm pie dish.

4 Divide pastry in half. Roll one half between sheets of baking paper until large enough to line dish. Spoon apple mixture into dish; brush pastry edge with egg white.

5 Roll remaining pastry large enough to cover filling. Press edges together. Brush pastry with egg white; sprinkle with extra sugar.

6 Bake pie, uncovered, 20 minutes. Reduce oven temperature to 180°C/160°C fan-forced; bake, uncovered, a further 25 minutes.

PASTRY Process dry ingredients and butter until crumbly. Add egg yolk and enough of the water to process until combined. Knead on floured surface until smooth.

PER SERVING 11.4g total fat (7g saturated fat); 1438kJ (344 cal); 53.9g carbohydrate; 4.3g protein; 3.7g fibre

Old-fashioned cherry pie

PREPARATION TIME 30 MINUTES (PLUS REFRIGERATION AND COOLING TIME)
COOKING TIME 1 HOUR 15 MINUTES **SERVES** 8

2¼ cups (335g) plain flour

⅔ cup (110g) icing sugar

185g cold butter, chopped

1 egg

2 teaspoons iced water, approximately

600g frozen pitted cherries

2 tablespoons cornflour

1 tablespoon lemon juice

⅓ cup (75g) white sugar

½ teaspoon ground cinnamon

20g butter, extra, cut into 1cm cubes

1 egg, beaten lightly, extra

1 Process flour, icing sugar and butter until crumbly. Add egg and enough of the water to process until the ingredients just come together. Knead on a lightly floured surface until smooth. Cover; refrigerate 30 minutes.

2 Stand thawed cherries in a colander over a bowl 30 minutes to drain well.

3 Grease a 23cm pie dish. Roll two-thirds of the pastry between sheets of baking paper until large enough to line pie dish. Lift pastry into dish, smooth over base and side. Trim edge; cover, freeze 10 minutes.

4 Preheat oven to 180°C/160°C fan-forced. Place pie dish on oven tray. Cover pastry with baking paper, fill with dried beans or rice. Bake about 15 minutes, remove paper and beans. Wrap foil around pastry edges of pie dish to prevent over-browning; bake further 20 minutes or until base is browned and cooked through. Cool.

5 Combine drained cherries, cornflour, juice, ¼ cup of the white sugar and cinnamon in a medium bowl. Spoon filling into pastry case. Dot with extra butter. Roll out remaining pastry until large enough to cover pie. Brush edges with a little extra egg, place pastry over filling. Press edges together, trim with a knife; crimp edge gently if desired. Brush pastry lightly with a little more of the egg. Sprinkle with remaining white sugar. Bake about 40 minutes or until browned.

☐ **PER SERVING** 23g total fat (14.3g saturated fat); 2073kJ (496 cal); 63.6g carbohydrate; 7.1g protein; 2.9g fibre

Custard tart

PREPARATION TIME 30 MINUTES (PLUS REFRIGERATION TIME) **COOKING TIME** 55 MINUTES **SERVES** 8

1¼ cups (185g) plain flour

¼ cup (35g) self-raising flour

¼ cup (55g) caster sugar

90g cold butter, chopped

1 egg, beaten lightly

2 teaspoons water, approximately

ground nutmeg

CUSTARD

3 eggs, beaten lightly

1 teaspoon vanilla essence

2 tablespoons caster sugar

2 cups (500ml) milk

1 Sift flours and sugar into bowl; rub in butter. Add egg and enough water to make ingredients cling together. Press dough into a ball; knead on floured surface until smooth. Cover; refrigerate 30 minutes.

2 Preheat oven to 220°C/200°C fan-forced. Grease deep 23cm pie dish.

3 Roll dough on floured surface until large enough to line dish. Lift pastry into pie dish, gently ease into side of dish; trim edge. Use scraps of pastry to make a double layer of pastry around edge of dish, joining pastry strips with a little water. Trim edge, pinch a frill around edge of pastry.

4 Place pie dish on oven tray. Cover pastry with baking paper, fill with dried beans or rice. Bake 10 minutes. Remove paper and beans; bake further 10 minutes or until pastry is browned lightly. Cool.

5 Reduce oven temperature to 180°C/160°C fan-forced. Make custard.

6 Pour custard into pastry case; bake 15 minutes. Sprinkle custard evenly with nutmeg; bake further 15 minutes or until custard is just set, cool. Refrigerate until cold.

CUSTARD Whisk eggs, essence and sugar in bowl until combined. Heat milk until hot; quickly whisk into egg mixture.

PER SERVING 14.6g total fat (8.5g saturated fat); 1258kJ (301 cal); 33.4g carbohydrate; 8.1g protein; 1g fibre

---

Tarte tatin

PREPARATION TIME 40 MINUTES (PLUS REFRIGERATION TIME) **COOKING TIME** 1 HOUR 45 MINUTES **SERVES** 8

6 large apples (1.2kg)

100g unsalted butter, chopped

1 cup (220g) firmly packed brown sugar

2 tablespoons lemon juice

PASTRY

1 cup (150g) plain flour

2 tablespoons caster sugar

80g cold unsalted butter, chopped

2 tablespoons sour cream

1 Peel, core and quarter apples. Melt butter in large heavy-based frying pan, add apple, sprinkle evenly with sugar and juice. Cook, uncovered, over low heat, for about 1 hour, turning apple as it caramelises.

2 Place apple, rounded-sides down, in 23cm pie dish; drizzle with 1 tablespoon of the caramel in pan. Reserve remaining caramel. Pack apple tightly to avoid any gaps, cover; refrigerate while preparing pastry.

3 Make pastry; cover, refrigerate 30 minutes.

4 Preheat oven to 200°C/180°C fan-forced.

5 Roll dough between sheets of baking paper until large enough to cover apple. Peel away one sheet of paper; invert pastry over apple. Remove remaining paper; tuck pastry around apple. Bake, uncovered, 30 minutes or until browned. Carefully turn onto serving plate.

6 Reheat reserved caramel over low heat; drizzle over apple.

PASTRY Process flour, sugar, butter and sour cream until ingredients just come together. Knead dough on floured surface until smooth.

PER SERVING 21.1g total fat (13.7g saturated fat); 1860kJ (445 cal); 59.5g carbohydrate; 2.7g protein; 2.9g fibre

The best apples to use are golden delicious as they soak up the caramel but retain their shape; granny smith would be our second choice.

The original was a caramelised apple dessert tart named after the "demoiselles Tatin", two French sisters who created it in the late 1800s. Traditionally made in a heavy cast-iron frying pan with an ovenproof handle, the pan is covered with pastry once the apples have caramelised then transferred directly to the oven for baking. We have adapted the recipe to allow it to be cooked without such a pan. Pears or quinces can be used instead of apples, if desired.

Quince and rhubarb pie

PREPARATION TIME 30 MINUTES (PLUS REFRIGERATION TIME) **COOKING** 2 HOURS 30 MINUTES **SERVES** 8

2 cups (440g) caster sugar

2 cups (500ml) water

4 medium quinces (1.2kg), peeled, quartered

2 strips lemon rind

500g rhubarb, chopped coarsely

¼ cup (60ml) lemon juice, approximately

1 cup (150g) plain flour

⅓ cup (55g) icing sugar

100g cold butter, chopped

1 egg, separated

1 tablespoon iced water, approximately

1 tablespoon raw sugar

1 Stir caster sugar and the water in medium saucepan over low heat until sugar has dissolved. Add quince and rind; bring to a boil. Simmer, covered, about 2 hours, or until quince is tender and rosy in colour. Add rhubarb; cook 5 minutes, or until rhubarb softens. Add juice to taste, to reduce sweetness. Cool quince and rhubarb in syrup.

2 Meanwhile, process flour, icing sugar and butter until crumbly. Add egg yolk and enough of the iced water to process until ingredients just come together. Knead gently on floured surface until smooth. Cover; refrigerate 30 minutes.

3 Preheat oven to 180°C/160°C fan-forced. Grease 23cm pie dish.

4 Drain fruit mixture; reserve ⅓ cup (80ml) of the syrup. Spoon fruit mixture and reserved syrup into pie dish.

5 Roll out pastry until large enough to cover fruit mixture. Using a 1cm cutter, randomly cut out rounds from pastry; reserve rounds. Place pastry with holes over fruit mixture, trim edge with a knife. Place reserved rounds on pastry in between holes; brush a little of the lightly beaten egg white over pastry; sprinkle with raw sugar.

6 Place pie dish on oven tray; bake, uncovered, about 30 minutes or until well browned (cover edge of pastry with foil after 20 minutes to prevent over-browning). Stand 10 minutes. Serve with double cream, if desired.

PER SERVING 11.6g total fat (7g saturated fat); 2119kJ (507 cal); 90.3g carbohydrate; 4.4g protein; 10.6g fibre

Strawberry rhubarb pie

PREPARATION TIME 45 MINUTES (PLUS REFRIGERATION TIME) **COOKING TIME** 1 HOUR **SERVES** 8

1½ cups (225g) self-raising flour

½ cup (75g) plain flour

125g cold butter, chopped

1 egg, separated

¼ cup (60ml) water, approximately

1 tablespoon caster sugar

FILLING

4 large trimmed rhubarb stalks (500g), chopped coarsely

250g punnet strawberries

¼ cup (55g) caster sugar

¼ cup (35g) cornflour

⅓ cup (80ml) water

1 Make filling

2 Sift flours into large bowl, rub in butter. Make well in centre, stir in egg yolk and enough water to make ingredients cling together. Knead gently on lightly floured surface until smooth. Cover; refrigerate 30 minutes.

3 Preheat oven to 200°C/180°C fan-forced. Grease deep 23cm pie dish.

4 Roll out two-thirds of the pastry large enough to line dish. Lift pastry into dish; trim edge. Spoon filling into pastry case; brush edge of pastry with egg white. Roll out remaining pastry large enough to cover filling, press edges together gently. Pinch a frill around edge.

5 Bake, uncovered, 20 minutes. Reduce oven temperature to 180°C/160°C fan-forced; bake further 30 minutes or until pastry is golden brown. Brush hot pastry with egg white, sprinkle with sugar.

FILLING Place rhubarb and strawberries in large saucepan; bring to a boil. Reduce heat, simmer, covered, about 10 minutes or until rhubarb is soft. Stir in sugar. Add blended cornflour and the water, stirring, over high heat until mixture boils and thickens. Remove from heat; cool to room temperature.

☐ **PER SERVING** 14.1g total fat (8.7g saturated fat); 1208kJ (289 cal); 32.6g carbohydrate; 5.9g protein; 4g fibre

Lime chiffon pie

PREPARATION TIME 20 MINUTES (PLUS REFRIGERATION TIME) **COOKING TIME** 15 MINUTES **SERVES** 6

After the custard is made, cover the surface of hot mixture with a piece of plastic wrap to seal the air out and stop a skin forming on the custard.

250g plain sweet biscuits
125g butter, melted
4 eggs, separated
⅓ cup (75g) caster sugar
3 teaspoons gelatine
2 teaspoons finely grated lime rind
⅓ cup (80ml) lime juice
⅓ cup (80ml) water
⅓ cup (75g) caster sugar, extra

1 Grease deep 23cm pie dish.

2 Process biscuits until fine; add butter, process until combined. Press mixture firmly over base and side of dish. Refrigerate 30 minutes.

3 Combine egg yolks, sugar, gelatine, rind, juice and the water in medium heatproof bowl. Whisk over medium saucepan of simmering water until mixture thickens slightly. Remove from heat; pour into large bowl. Cover; cool.

4 Beat egg whites in small bowl with electric mixer until soft peaks form; gradually add extra sugar, beating until sugar dissolves. Fold meringue into filling mixture, in two batches.

5 Spread filling into crumb crust; refrigerate 3 hours.

☐ **PER SERVING** 27.3g total fat (15.6g saturated fat); 2094kJ (501 cal); 54.9g carbohydrate; 8.7g protein; 0.9g fibre

THE FLAN TIN & THE QUICHE TIN

The Flan Tin & The Quiche Tin

Flan, quiche, tart? They all mean a delicious combination of luscious filling and crisp pastry crust baked in a shallow tin, dish or ring. The British tend to call it a flan, the French call it a tarte except when they call it a quiche, which is a tarte with a savoury custard filling, thought to have originated in the province of Lorraine. We usually say quiche for the savoury-custard kind and tart for all others, savoury or sweet. And occasionally, none of these rules apply and we say pecan pie or lemon meringue pie because in America, where they originated, those were their names.

CHOOSING A TIN

A loose-based, round or rectangular metal flan tin with plain or fluted sides, or a metal ring (always called a flan ring), will give you a flan that stands by itself. Alternatively, you can choose an attractive ceramic dish in which to bake the flan and serve it; the best of these are left unglazed underneath for better heat conduction so the crust browns nicely.

MAKING A PASTRY SHELL

The thing that sets a first-class flan or quiche apart is a crisp and tender crust. Shortcrust pastry is the traditional choice.

SHORTCRUST PASTRY Your aim when making shortcrust pastry is to rub together flour and small pieces of butter (or other fat, as the recipe directs) so that they coat each other evenly but the butter remains firm. The mixture is moistened with water and mixed together to form a dough. It is important to do this with minimum handling so the gluten in the flour won't develop and form tiny elastic strands making the pastry tough.

Shortcrust pastry may be plain, using only water, or may be enriched by using a mixture of water and egg yolk. For sweet pastry, sugar is added.

The pastry should be kept cool at every stage so the butter remains firm; it will melt during baking and leave minute pockets throughout the pastry, making it tender when cooked. Have the butter diced and well chilled, the water or water/egg-yolk mixture ice cold and, if possible, make the pastry when the kitchen is cool. If you are interrupted, put the bowl in the fridge until you can continue.

Rub in the butter by picking up some flour and butter between thumbs and fingertips (keeping it well away from your warm palms), rubbing together briefly and dropping it, repeating this until the mixture resembles coarse breadcrumbs. Pour all but a little of the liquid around the bowl onto the flour/butter mix, then use a round-tipped table knife to "cut" the liquid through the dry mixture until it just starts to cling together. Gather up the dough with your fingers and, if any dry mixture is left in the bowl, sprinkle with just enough of the reserved liquid to moisten it and use the ball of dough to pick it up.

Place the dough on a sheet of plastic wrap and shape it into a thick round or rectangle, depending on the shape of your tin; wrap in plastic wrap and rest it in the refrigerator for 30 minutes or more.

MAKING PASTRY IN A FOOD PROCESSOR Many chefs consider the food processor makes better shortcrust pastry than handmade, but you must be quick with the pulse button to prevent it from overmixing. Place flour and diced butter in the bowl, then combine, using the metal blade, with short bursts of power. Add all the liquid at once and mix with just a few brief bursts, stopping immediately the mixture starts to come together. Rest in the refrigerator for at least 30 minutes before rolling out. If the kitchen is hot or, you have hot fingertips, the processor is a good option. The tricky bit is when you come to adding the liquid. Most pastry recipes will specify an amount of liquid, followed by "approximately". This is because every batch of pastry you make will need a slightly different amount of liquid, due to factors such as the temperature of the room and the ingredients, the absorbency of the flour, and the accuracy of your measuring. So, if you're making the pastry by hand, you can "feel" how much liquid the pastry needs; this is not possible when using the processor where there is a tendancy to add too much.

ROLLING OUT If possible, roll the pastry on a cool surface, either directly on a lightly floured surface with a lightly floured rolling pin, or between two sheets of baking paper, greaseproof paper or plastic wrap. Start each stroke from the centre and turn pastry as you go, so that you are always rolling directly away from yourself, not at an angle. Roll up to but not over the edge of the pastry, until you have a sheet roughly the shape of your tin or dish and 4cm to 5cm larger, depending on the depth of the tin.

LINING Lift pastry loosely over the rolling pin and unroll pastry over the tin, dish, or ring placed on a flat oven tray. Gently ease the pastry in, taking care not to stretch it; press gently against the base and sides to eliminate air pockets. If using a dish, hold it on the flat of one hand and use a small, sharp knife, held at a slight outward angle, to trim away surplus pastry. If using a tin or ring, run the rolling pin over the top to cut off the surplus. Place your two thumbs a little below the inside edge, and press the pastry gently upward to push it just a shade above the edge. Rest the pastry again in the refrigerator for at least 30 minutes, covering it lightly with plastic wrap to stop it drying out.

BAKING The pastry case may now be filled and baked as directed, or partly baked "blind" (empty) to ensure crispness before the filling is added, or completely blind-baked to hold a pre-cooked filling. As a precaution against a soggy pastry (due to a liquid filling), an unbaked or blind-baked case may be brushed with beaten egg or egg white or, for a sweet tart, with warmed sieved jam; allow the pastry case to dry before the filling is added.

BAKING BLIND Line the pastry in the tin or dish with a crumpled piece of baking paper cut a little larger than the tin or dish. Fill paper with dried beans or uncooked rice (or ceramic baking beads or pie weights) to prevent the pastry from puffing up; bake as directed.

Instead of being lined and weighted, pastry cases, especially small ones, are often pricked all over with a fork, or a special tool called a docker (see Handling Pastry, page 441) to discourage rising. If you do this, check once or twice during baking, and be ready to push down with your fingers or a spoon any parts that are puffing up.

A firm, pale yellow, cow-milk cheese from the Fribourg canton in Switzerland, gruyère is also produced in many regions of France. It has a sweet, nutty taste and is delicious eaten as is or used in cooking – try making macaroni cheese with gruyère for a flavour sensation.

Asparagus and gruyère tart

PREPARATION TIME 25 MINUTES (PLUS REFRIGERATION AND FREEZING TIME)
COOKING TIME 55 MINUTES (PLUS COOLING TIME) **SERVES** 4

25g butter

1 small white onion (80g), sliced thinly

12 asparagus spears, halved crossways

2 eggs

1 teaspoon plain flour

¾ cup (180ml) cream

50g gruyère cheese, grated coarsely

PASTRY

¾ cup (110g) plain flour

75g cold butter, chopped

1 tablespoon finely grated parmesan cheese

pinch sweet paprika

1 egg yolk

1 teaspoon iced water, approximately

1 Make pastry; cover, refrigerate 30 minutes. Roll pastry until large enough to line 10cm x 34cm rectangular loose-based flan tin. Lift pastry into tin, ease into sides, trim edges. Freeze 30 minutes.

2 Preheat oven to 180°C/160°C fan-forced.

3 Cover pastry with baking paper, fill with dried beans or rice, place on oven tray; bake 15 minutes. Remove paper and beans; bake further 10 minutes. Cool.

4 Increase oven temperature to 200°C/180°C fan-forced.

5 Meanwhile, heat butter in large frying pan; cook onion over low heat without browning, about 10 minutes or until very soft.

6 Cook asparagus in small saucepan of boiling water 1 minute; drain. Place into bowl of iced water; drain.

7 Whisk eggs, flour and cream in medium jug.

8 Place onion on pastry base, top with asparagus and gruyère. Place tart on oven tray, gently pour egg mixture over asparagus. Bake about 20 minutes or until browned lightly and set.

PASTRY Process flour, butter, parmesan and paprika until crumbly. Add egg yolk and enough iced water to process until mixture just comes together. Knead pastry on lightly floured surface until smooth.

PER SERVING 48.9g total fat (30.5g saturated fat); 2445kJ (585 cal); 23.6g carbohydrate; 14.2g protein; 2.3g fibre

...sted vegetable tart

...ATION TIME 2 HOURS (PLUS REFRIGERATION TIME) **COOKING TIME** 1 HOUR 5 MINUTES **SERVES** 6

90g cold butter, chopped

1¼ cups (185g) plain flour

½ cup (40g) coarsely grated parmesan cheese

1 egg yolk

1 tablespoon chopped fresh chives

3 teaspoons iced water, approximately

½ large butternut pumpkin (600g), chopped coarsely

10 baby beetroot (250g), trimmed

10 shallots (250g), peeled

8 cloves garlic

2 tablespoons olive oil

ROAST GARLIC CREAM

1 tablespoon finely chopped fresh dill

¾ cup (180g) sour cream

2 tablespoons milk

Garlic is easy to roast and has a more mellow taste than it does raw or fried. Make it and freeze it by the tablespoon wrapped tightly in plastic wrap. Roasted garlic can be whisked with lemon juice and olive oil into a mayonnaise-like emulsion and spread on toast for a sandwich, dolloped onto chunks of grilled chicken or lamb, or added to salad dressings and dips. Roasted garlic beaten with softened butter adds a whole new dimension of flavour to mashed potato or steamed corn cobs.

1 Process butter, flour and cheese until crumbly. Add egg yolk, chives and enough water to process until mixture just clings together. Cover; refrigerate 30 minutes.

2 Preheat oven to 200°C/180°C fan-forced.

3 Meanwhile, combine pumpkin, beetroot, shallots and garlic with oil in large baking dish. Bake, uncovered, about 45 minutes or until tender.

4 Roll dough between two sheets of baking paper until large enough to line base and sides of 10cm x 34cm rectangular, loose-based flan tin. Carefully lift pastry into tin, ease into sides, trim edges. Place flan tin on oven tray; refrigerate 30 minutes.

5 Peel skin from beetroot, wearing disposable gloves. Squeeze flesh from garlic skins; reserve garlic for roast garlic cream. Cover vegetables to keep warm.

6 Reduce oven temperature to 180°C/160°C fan-forced. Cover pastry with baking paper, fill with dried beans or rice; bake 15 minutes. Remove paper and beans; bake further 10 minutes or until browned.

7 Make roast garlic cream.

8 Fill tart with vegetables; serve warm with roast garlic cream.

ROAST GARLIC CREAM Combine reserved garlic in small bowl with remaining ingredients.

☐ **PER SERVING** 34.5g total fat (19g saturated fat); 1998kJ (478 cal); 31.3g carbohydrate; 9.9g protein; 3.3g fibre

Flan, tart & pie dishes

Armed with insider information on dishes, and a little of your own creativity, watch your pie and tart repertoire grow.

SPRINGFORM TIN
A tin with a removable side, used for rich cakes and moulded desserts. The side is held together with a clip which, when undone, allows it to expand and be lifted off.

FLUTED SHALLOW TIN
This tin is used for quiches and other shallow tarts. It has a removable base which fits inside so that, when the tart is cooked, the tin can be placed on a jar or another raised support and the side will fall away.

INDIVIDUAL FLUTED TINS
Come in all-in-one or with separate removable bases. If not non-stick, grease extra thoroughly, getting into all the crevices, to facilitate removal of the cooked tart.

TARTLET PANS
These small, round-bottomed pans in a frame make pastry shells to be filled with lemon curd, fruit, etc. Non-stick are best, but for pastry containing sugar the pans should also be greased.

PLAIN RINGS
Metal rings, designed to stand on an oven tray, come in many sizes. For tarts, quiches and flans, they are lined with pastry; they can also be used to shape pavlovas and moulded desserts, and small ones can hold eggs for cooking.

INDIVIDUAL FLUTED CERAMIC DISHES
Tarts are made in these dishes in the usual way – lining with pastry and adding filling either before or after baking – but the tart is served in its dish rather than being turned out.

CERAMIC AND GLASS PIE/TART PLATES

The best ceramic tart plates are unglazed underneath for better conduction of heat so that the crust will brown. However, glass is a better heat conductor than ceramic.

INDIVIDUAL METAL PIE TINS

These are the tins for the classic meat pie and other small, covered pies that are shallow enough to be manageable for eating with the hands. Grease well to ensure easy removal from tin.

CERAMIC AND GLASS DEEP PIE DISHES

These are used for deep sweet or savoury pies that may have a top crust only or both a top and base crust. In both cases, it is best to serve the pie from the dish to avoid any unecessary mess.

DEEP INDIVIDUAL PIE DISHES

These ceramic pie dishes are designed to go to the table, so they are suitable for pies that cannot be turned out, such as those with only a top crust or a topping, such as mashed potato. .

FLUTED DEEP TIN

In either individual or large sizes, this tin is for deep tarts with fillings such as vegetables in a sauce or egg and bacon. The crust must be sturdy. Side is removable, as for a shallow tin.

RECTANGULAR FLUTED TIN

This is a variation on the classic round tin. The rectangular shape not only looks stylish, but is also better for serving small portions (for example, to go with drinks) as it can be cut into neat squares or bars. Side is removable, as for deep and shallow tins.

Quiche lorraine

PREPARATION TIME 30 MINUTES (PLUS REFRIGERATION AND STANDING TIME)

COOKING TIME 1 HOUR (PLUS COOLING TIME) **SERVES** 6

Named after the region straddling the French-German border, the classic quiche lorraine is thought to be the original quiche. The pastry used for the first quiches is thought to have been a bread dough, which morphed over the centuries to the crisp shortcrust identified with the open tart today. With its creamy custardy filling and buttery shell, it's still practically everyone's favourite.

1¾ cups (260g) plain flour

150g cold butter, chopped

1 egg yolk

2 teaspoons lemon juice

⅓ cup (80ml) iced water, approximately

1 medium brown onion (150g), chopped finely

3 rindless bacon rashers (195g), chopped coarsely

3 eggs

300ml cream

½ cup (125ml) milk

¾ cup (90g) coarsely grated cheddar cheese

1 Sift flour into bowl; rub in butter. Add egg yolk, juice and enough water to make ingredients cling together. Knead gently on lightly floured surface until smooth. Cover; refrigerate 30 minutes.

2 Preheat oven to 220°C/200°C fan-forced.

3 Roll dough between two sheets of baking paper until large enough to line deep 23cm loose-based flan tin. Lift pastry into tin, press into base and side; trim edge.

4 Cover pastry with baking paper, fill with dried beans or rice; bake 10 minutes. Remove paper and beans; bake further 10 minutes or until golden brown. Cool to room temperature.

5 Reduce oven temperature to 180°C/160°C fan-forced.

6 Cook onion and bacon in oiled small frying pan until onion is soft; drain away excess fat, cool. Spread into pastry case.

7 Whisk eggs in medium bowl. Add cream, milk and cheese; whisk until just combined. Pour into pastry case. Bake, uncovered, about 35 minutes or until filling is set and brown. Stand 5 minutes before removing from tin.

PER SERVING 56.4g total fat (34.3g saturated fat); 3056kJ (731 cal); 35.4g carbohydrate; 20.8g protein; 2g fibre

Sun-dried tomato and zucchini quiche

PREPARATION TIME 30 MINUTES (PLUS REFRIGERATION TIME) **COOKING TIME** 1 HOUR **SERVES** 6

Baking pastry before adding the filling is called "blind-baking", used when a filling is very wet or doesn't need baking. The pastry is eased into the tin, lined with baking paper and weighed down with dried beans, uncooked rice or "baking beans" (also called pie weights) to keep it from puffing up or blistering. The beans and rice are no longer suitable to eat but, once cool, can be stored in an airtight jar for next time.

½ cup (100g) cottage cheese

100g butter, softened

1⅓ cups (200g) plain flour

1 tablespoon olive oil

1 medium brown onion (150g), sliced thinly

¼ cup (35g) drained, finely chopped sun-dried tomatoes

⅓ cup (70g) drained sun-dried zucchini

¼ cup finely shredded fresh basil

¾ cup (90g) coarsely grated gruyère cheese

¼ cup (20g) finely grated parmesan cheese

3 eggs

¾ cup (180ml) cream

¼ cup (30g) coarsely grated cheddar cheese

1 Combine cottage cheese and butter in large bowl; stir in flour. Press dough into a ball; knead gently on floured surface until smooth. Cover; refrigerate 30 minutes.

2 Preheat oven to 220°C/200°C fan-forced.

3 Roll dough on floured surface until large enough to line 24cm-round flan tin. Lift pastry into tin, press into base and side; trim edge. Place tin on oven tray.

4 Cover pastry with baking paper, fill with dried beans or rice; bake 10 minutes. Remove paper and beans; bake further 10 minutes or until browned.

5 Heat oil in medium saucepan; cook onion until soft. Drain on absorbent paper.

6 Reduce oven temperature to 180°C/160°C fan-forced.

7 Spread onion, tomato, zucchini, basil, gruyère and parmesan into pastry case. Top with combined eggs and cream; sprinkle with cheddar cheese.

8 Bake about 35 minutes or until set.

☐ **PER SERVING** 44g total fat (25.9g saturated fat); 2483kJ (594 cal); 29.1g carbohydrate; 20.2g protein; 2.7g fibre

---

Caramelised onion and goat cheese tartlets

PREPARATION TIME 25 MINUTES (PLUS REFRIGERATION TIME) **COOKING TIME** 45 MINUTES **SERVES** 4

1 cup (150g) plain flour

80g cold butter, chopped

1 egg yolk

2 tablespoons iced water, approximately

100g soft goat cheese

2 tablespoons coarsely chopped fresh chives

CARAMELISED ONION

2 tablespoons olive oil

4 large brown onions (800g), sliced thinly

⅓ cup (80ml) port

2 tablespoons red wine vinegar

2 tablespoons brown sugar

Caramelising breaks down an onion's natural sugar, resulting in a concentration of flavour that gives its sweet taste. The onion mass significantly reduces during the caramelisation process so even though you begin with a frying pan filled with raw onion, it will cook down substantially. A general rule is to use one onion per diner when caramelising.

1 Process flour and butter until mixture is crumbly. Add egg yolk and enough of the water to process until ingredients just come together. Cover; refrigerate 30 minutes.

2 Meanwhile, make caramelised onion.

3 Preheat oven to 200°C/180°C fan-forced. Grease four 10.5cm loose-based flan tins.

4 Divide dough into four portions. Roll one portion of dough between sheets of baking paper until large enough to line tin. Lift pastry into tin, press into base and side, trim edge; prick base all over with fork. Repeat with remaining pastry.

5 Place tins on oven tray; cover pastry with baking paper, fill with dried beans or rice. Bake, uncovered, 10 minutes. Remove paper and beans; bake about 5 minutes.

6 Divide onion mixture and cheese among tartlets. Bake, uncovered, about 5 minutes or until heated through. Sprinkle tartlets with chives.

CARAMELISED ONION Heat oil in large frying pan; cook onion, stirring, until soft. Add port, vinegar and sugar; cook, stirring occasionally, about 25 minutes or until onion caramelises.

☐ **PER SERVING** 31.5g total fat (15.2g saturated fat); 2165kJ (518 cal); 43.6g carbohydrate; 11g protein; 4g fibre

Easy ham and zucchini quiche

PREPARATION TIME 15 MINUTES **COOKING TIME** 45 MINUTES **SERVES** 4

⅓ cup (50g) plain flour

1 ½ cups (375ml) milk

3 eggs

3 slices ham (60g), chopped coarsely

3 green onions, chopped finely

1 cup (125g) coarsely grated cheddar cheese

1 medium zucchini (120g), grated coarsely

2 tablespoons finely chopped fresh flat-leaf parsley

1 Preheat oven to 160°C/140°C fan-forced. Oil 20cm round quiche dish.

2 Whisk flour and milk in medium bowl until smooth; whisk in eggs. Stir in remaining ingredients; pour mixture into dish.

3 Bake, uncovered, about 45 minutes or until filling is set.

4 Sprinkle with extra chopped parsley and serve with salad and bread, if desired.

☐ **PER SERVING** 19g total fat (10.6g saturated fat); 1313kJ (314 cal); 14.5g carbohydrate; 20.8g protein; 1.2g fibre

Always use full-cream rather than light or skim milk for a quiche or savoury pie filling. Try substituting chopped speck for the ham and use a nutty, good-melting swiss cheese like raclette or appenzeller instead of cheddar to make this easy-peasy pie really something special.

Smoked salmon pie

PREPARATION TIME 10 MINUTES **COOKING TIME** 35 MINUTES **SERVES** 6

1kg potatoes, peeled, chopped coarsely

40g butter, softened

¼ cup (60g) sour cream

200g smoked salmon, chopped coarsely

2 eggs, separated

2 green onions, chopped finely

1 Preheat oven to 200°C/180°C fan-forced.

2 Boil, steam or microwave potato until tender; drain. Mash potato in large bowl with butter and sour cream. Stir in salmon, one of the egg yolks, egg whites and onion.

3 Spoon mixture into deep 22cm-round loose-based flan tin; smooth top with spatula, brush with remaining egg yolk. Bake, uncovered, about 25 minutes or until pie is heated through and browned lightly.

☐ **PER SERVING** 12.9g total fat (7g saturated fat); 1049kJ (251 cal); 19.1g carbohydrate; 13.6g protein; 2.3g fibre

Replace the smoked salmon with smoked ocean trout to inject a different edge to this all-in-one main course. Look for pre-packed hot-smoked ocean trout, sold vacuum-packed in the refrigerated section of some supermarkets or in large fish shops.

1 EASY HAM AND ZUCCHINI QUICHE **2** SMOKED SALMON PIE
3 ALMOND PEAR FLAN [P 466] **4** PECAN PIE [P 466]

1

2

3

4

Almond pear flan

PREPARATION TIME 30 MINUTES (PLUS REFRIGERATION TIME) **COOKING TIME** 45 MINUTES **SERVES** 10

1 ¼ cups (185g) plain flour

90g cold butter, softened

¼ cup (55g) caster sugar

2 egg yolks

3 firm ripe medium pears (690g), peeled, cored, quartered

2 tablespoons apricot jam, warmed, strained

ALMOND FILLING

125g butter

⅓ cup (75g) caster sugar

2 eggs

1 cup (120g) almond meal

1 tablespoon plain flour

1 Process flour, butter, sugar and egg yolks until just combined. Knead on floured surface until smooth. Cover; refrigerate 30 minutes.

2 Meanwhile, make almond filling.

3 Preheat oven to 180°C/160°C fan-forced. Grease 23cm-round loose-based flan tin.

4 Roll dough between sheets of baking paper. Lift pastry into tin, press into base and side; trim edge. Spread filling into pastry case; arrange pears over filling.

5 Bake, uncovered, about 45 minutes. Brush flan with jam.

ALMOND FILLING Beat butter and sugar in small bowl with electric mixer until just combined. Add eggs, one at a time; fold in meal and flour.

PER SERVING 26.7g total fat (12.7g saturated fat); 1785kJ (427 cal); 38.8g carbohydrate; 6.8g protein; 2.9g fibre

Pecan pie

PREPARATION TIME 25 MINUTES (PLUS REFRIGERATION TIME) **COOKING TIME** 1 HOUR **SERVES** 10

1 cup (120g) pecans, chopped coarsely

2 tablespoons cornflour

1 cup (220g) firmly packed brown sugar

60g butter, melted

2 tablespoons cream

1 teaspoon vanilla extract

3 eggs

⅓ cup (40g) pecans, extra

2 tablespoons apricot jam, warmed, strained

PASTRY

1 ¼ cups (185g) plain flour

⅓ cup (55g) icing sugar

125g cold butter, chopped

1 egg yolk

1 teaspoon iced water

1 Make pastry; cover, refrigerate 30 minutes.

2 Grease 24cm-round loose-based flan tin. Roll dough between sheets of baking paper until large enough to line tin. Lift pastry into tin, press into base and side; trim edge. Cover; refrigerate 30 minutes. Preheat oven to 180°C/160°C fan-forced.

3 Place tin on oven tray. Cover pastry with baking paper, fill with dried beans or rice; bake 10 minutes. Remove paper and beans; bake further 5 minutes. Cool.

4 Reduce oven temperature to 160°C/140°C fan-forced.

5 Combine chopped nuts and cornflour in medium bowl. Add sugar, butter, cream, extract and eggs; stir until combined. Pour mixture into shell, sprinkle with extra nuts.

6 Bake, uncovered, about 45 minutes. Cool; brush pie with jam.

PASTRY Process flour, icing sugar and butter until crumbly. Add egg yolk and enough of the water to process until ingredients just come together. Knead dough on floured surface until smooth.

⬚ **PER SERVING** 30.8g total fat (12.5g saturated fat); 2048kJ (490 cal); 46.5g carbohydrate; 6.1g protein; 2.1g fibre

Brushing it with warmed sieved apricot jam gives a lovely glaze and sheen to the finished pie. Serve pecan pie with a delish maple-flavoured ice cream, prepared the night before: stir 2 tablespoons of maple syrup and ½ teaspoon ground cinnamon into 1 litre slightly softened good-quality French vanilla ice-cream. Freeze overnight.

Sour cherry custard tart

PREPARATION TIME 40 MINUTES (PLUS REFRIGERATION TIME)
COOKING TIME 30 MINUTES (PLUS COOLING TIME) **SERVES** 4

300ml thickened cream

1 vanilla bean, split lengthways, seeds scraped

½ cup (110g) caster sugar

3 eggs, beaten lightly

1 cup (200g) drained sour cherries

PASTRY

1 cup (150g) plain flour

⅓ cup (55g) icing sugar

100g cold butter, chopped

1 egg yolk

2 teaspoons iced water, approximately

1 Make pastry; cover, refrigerate 30 minutes.

2 Grease 24cm-round loose-based flan tin. Roll dough between sheets of baking paper until large enough to line tin. Lift pastry into tin, press into base and side; trim edge. Refrigerate 20 minutes.

3 Preheat oven to 200°C/180°C fan-forced.

4 Cover pastry with baking paper, fill with dried beans or rice; bake 15 minutes. Reduce oven temperature to 160°C/140°C fan-forced. Remove paper and beans; bake, uncovered, further 10 minutes or until browned, cover edges with foil if overbrowning. Cool.

5 Meanwhile, heat cream, vanilla bean and seeds, and caster sugar in medium saucepan, stirring, until sugar dissolves. Remove from heat. Cool slightly. Stir in eggs; strain into jug.

6 Place cherries in pastry case; gently pour custard over cherries.

7 Bake, uncovered, about 30 minutes or until custard is just set. Cool.

PASTRY Process flour, icing sugar and butter until just combined. Add egg yolk and enough of the water to process until mixture just comes together. Knead dough lightly until smooth.

⬚ **PER SERVING** 54.2g total fat (33.5g saturated fat); 3566kJ (853 cal); 78.8g carbohydrate; 12g protein; 2.3g fibre

This custard is what the French call a crème anglaise (english cream). There are two types of custard: one cooked and baked in a water bath in the oven (think crème brûlée) and the other (as here) cooked on top of the stove which results in a rich, smooth-textured, pourable custard. Traditionally a vanilla bean is added to the mixture but flavoured extracts can be used, as can citrus zests, spirits or liqueurs, or even melted chocolate.

Lemon tart

PREPARATION TIME 30 MINUTES (PLUS REFRIGERATION TIME)
COOKING TIME 55 MINUTES (PLUS REFRIGERATION TIME) **SERVES** 8

1 ¼ cups (185g) plain flour
⅓ cup (55g) icing sugar
¼ cup (30g) almond meal
125g cold butter, chopped
1 egg yolk

LEMON FILLING
1 tablespoon finely grated lemon rind
½ cup (125ml) lemon juice
5 eggs
¾ cup (165g) caster sugar
1 cup (250ml) thickened cream

1 Process flour, icing sugar, almond meal and butter until crumbly. Add egg yolk, process until ingredients just come together. Knead dough on floured surface until smooth. Cover; refrigerate 30 minutes.
2 Grease 24cm-round loose-based flan tin. Roll pastry between sheets of baking paper until large enough to line tin. Lift pastry into tin, press into base and side; trim edge. Cover; refrigerate 30 minutes.
3 Preheat oven to 200°C/180°C fan-forced.
4 Place flan tin on oven tray. Cover pastry case with baking paper, fill with dried beans or rice; bake, uncovered, 15 minutes. Remove paper and beans; bake further 10 minutes.
5 Meanwhile, whisk ingredients for lemon filling in medium bowl; stand 5 minutes.
6 Reduce oven temperature to 180°C/160°C fan-forced.
7 Strain filling into pastry case; bake about 30 minutes or until filling has set slightly, cool.
8 Refrigerate tart until cold. Serve dusted with sifted icing sugar, if desired.

▭ **PER SERVING** 30.7g total fat (17.4g saturated fat); 2040kJ (488 cal); 45.9g carbohydrate; 8.6g protein; 1.3g fibre

Pecan ganache tart

PREPARATION TIME 35 MINUTES (PLUS REFRIGERATION TIME)
COOKING TIME 20 MINUTES (PLUS REFRIGERATION TIME) **SERVES** 10

½ cup (60g) pecans
1 ½ cups (225g) plain flour
90g cold butter, chopped
1 egg
1 tablespoon iced water, approximately

GANACHE FILLING
300ml carton thickened cream
300g dark eating chocolate, melted
2 tablespoons Kahlua
1 cup (120g) pecans, chopped roughly

CREAMY TOPPING
¼ cup (40g) icing sugar
300ml thickened cream
2 teaspoons gelatine
2 tablespoons water
1 tablespoon Kahlua

1 Blend or process nuts until finely chopped (do not over-process). Sift flour into medium bowl; rub in butter, stir in nuts. Add egg and enough of the water until ingredients come together. Knead dough on floured surface until smooth. Cover; refrigerate 30 minutes.

2 Preheat oven to 200°C/180°C fan-forced.

3 Roll dough large enough to line 23cm flan tin. Lift pastry into tin, ease into base and side; trim edge. Place tin on oven tray. Cover pastry with baking paper, fill with dried beans or rice; bake 10 minutes. Remove paper and beans; bake further 10 minutes or until browned lightly. Cool to room temperature.

4 Meanwhile, combine ingredients for ganache filling in medium bowl.

5 Spread filling into pastry case; refrigerate about 2 hours or until filling starts to set.

6 Make creamy topping; pour over filling. Refrigerate tart several hours or until set. Decorate with whipped cream and extra pecans, if desired.

CREAMY TOPPING Sift icing sugar into medium bowl, stir in cream. Sprinkle gelatine over the water in small bowl, stand bowl in small saucepan of simmering water; stir until gelatine dissolves. Cool. Stir gelatine mixture into cream mixture, stir in liqueur.

▭ **PER SERVING** 53.2g total fat (26.3g saturated fat); 2859kJ (684 cal); 41.5g carbohydrate; 8.3g protein; 2.7g fibre

Rich chocolate tart

PREPARATION TIME 25 MINUTES (PLUS REFRIGERATION TIME) **COOKING TIME** 55 MINUTES **SERVES** 10

4 egg yolks

2 eggs

¼ cup (55g) caster sugar

⅓ cup (80ml) thickened cream

300g dark eating chocolate, melted

1 teaspoon vanilla extract

PASTRY

1¼ cups (185g) plain flour

¼ cup (25g) cocoa powder

⅓ cup (55g) icing sugar

150g cold butter, chopped

2 egg yolks

1 teaspoon iced water, approximately

1 Make pastry; cover, refrigerate 30 minutes. Grease 24cm-round loose-based flan tin.

2 Roll dough between sheets of baking paper until large enough to line base and side of tin. Lift pastry into tin, press into base and side; trim edge. Cover; refrigerate 30 minutes.

3 Preheat oven to 180°C/160°C fan-forced. Place tin on oven tray. Cover pastry case with baking paper, fill with dried beans or rice; bake 15 minutes. Remove paper and beans; bake, uncovered, further 10 minutes or until browned lightly. Cool.

4 Reduce oven temperature to 160°C/140°C fan-forced.

5 Beat egg yolks, eggs and caster sugar in small bowl with electric mixer until thick and creamy. Fold in cream, chocolate and extract. Pour chocolate mixture into pastry case.

6 Bake, uncovered, about 30 minutes or until filling is set. Cool 10 minutes.

PASTRY Process flour, sifted cocoa, sugar and butter until crumbly. Add egg yolks and enough of the water to process until ingredients just come together. Knead dough on floured surface until smooth.

▭ **PER SERVING** 28.8g total fat (16.8g saturated fat); 1952kJ (467 cal); 44.1g carbohydrate; 7.5g protein; 1.2g fibre

Serve with fresh raspberries and double cream for a taste of the sublime.

Cocoa powder is made when chocolate liquor is pressed to remove most of the cocoa butter. The remaining solids are processed to make a fine, unsweetened powder, which tastes bitter and imparts a deep chocolate flavour to baked items such as brownies, biscuits, pie and tart fillings and cakes. Used alone in cakes, cocoa powder gives full flavour and dark colour, but it can also be used in recipes with other chocolate (unsweetened or dark) to produce a result with a more intense flavour.

Lemon meringue pie

PREPARATION TIME 30 MINUTES (PLUS REFRIGERATION TIME) **COOKING TIME** 35 MINUTES **SERVES** 10

½ cup (75g) cornflour

1 cup (220g) caster sugar

½ cup (125ml) lemon juice

1¼ cups (310ml) water

2 teaspoons finely grated lemon rind

60g unsalted butter, chopped

3 eggs, separated

½ cup (110g) caster sugar, extra

PASTRY

1½ cups (225g) plain flour

1 tablespoon icing sugar

140g cold butter, chopped

1 egg yolk

2 tablespoons iced water, approximately

1 Make pastry; cover, refrigerate 30 minutes.

2 Grease 24cm-round loose-based fluted flan tin. Roll dough between sheets of baking paper until large enough to line tin. Lift pastry into tin, press into base and side; trim edge. Cover; refrigerate 30 minutes.

3 Preheat oven to 220°C/200°C fan-forced.

4 Place tin on oven tray. Cover pastry case with baking paper; fill with dried beans or rice; bake 15 minutes. Remove paper and beans; bake, uncovered, further 10 minutes. Cool. Turn oven off.

5 Meanwhile, combine cornflour and sugar in medium saucepan; gradually stir in juice and the water until smooth. Cook, stirring, over high heat, until mixture boils and thickens. Reduce heat, simmer, stirring, 1 minute. Remove from heat; stir in rind, butter and egg yolks. Cool 10 minutes.

6 Spread filling into pastry case. Cover; refrigerate 2 hours.

7 Preheat oven to 220°C/200°C fan-forced.

8 Beat egg whites in small bowl with electric mixer until soft peaks form; gradually add extra sugar, beating until sugar dissolves.

9 Roughen surface of filling with fork before spreading with meringue mixture. Bake about 2 minutes or until browned lightly.

PASTRY Process flour, icing sugar and butter until crumbly. Add egg yolk and enough of the water to process until ingredients come together. Knead dough on floured surface until smooth.

PER SERVING 18.9g total fat (11.6g saturated fat); 1772kJ (424 cal); 57.7g carbohydrate; 5g protein; 0.9g fibre

Prune and custard tart

PREPARATION TIME 20 MINUTES (PLUS REFRIGERATION TIME)
COOKING TIME 35 MINUTES (PLUS COOLING AND STANDING TIME) **SERVES** 8

1 ½ cups (250g) seeded prunes
2 tablespoons brandy
300ml cream
3 eggs
⅔ cup (150g) caster sugar
1 teaspoon vanilla extract

PASTRY

1 ¼ cups (185g) plain flour
⅓ cup (55g) icing sugar
¼ cup (30g) almond meal
125g cold butter, chopped
1 egg yolk
1 tablespoon iced water, approximately

When adding the hot cream to the egg mixture, place the bowl on a damp tea towel to keep it stable while you whisk. Spoon in the hot cream slowly: the eggs need time to cope with the heat and could curdle if hit with too much cream too quickly. You can use fresh dates instead of prunes for this tart if you prefer.

1 Make pastry; cover, refrigerate 30 minutes.

2 Grease 26cm-round loose-based flan tin. Roll pastry between sheets of baking paper until large enough to line tin. Lift pastry into tin; press into side and base. Trim edge; prick base all over with fork. Cover; refrigerate 20 minutes.

3 Preheat oven to 200°C/180°C fan-forced.

4 Place tin on oven tray. Cover pastry with baking paper, fill with dried beans or rice; bake 10 minutes. Remove paper and beans; bake further 5 minutes or until browned.

5 Reduce oven temperature to 150°C/130°C fan-forced.

6 Blend or process prunes and brandy until mixture forms a paste; spread into pastry case.

7 Bring cream to a boil in small saucepan; remove from heat. Whisk eggs, sugar and extract in small bowl until combined; gradually add cream, whisking continuously until combined. Pour into pastry case; bake, uncovered, about 20 minutes or until custard just sets. Stand 10 minutes. Serve tart warm or cold dusted with icing sugar, if desired.

PASTRY Process flour, sugar, meal and butter until crumbly. Add egg yolk and enough of the water to process until ingredients just come together.

▭ **PER SERVING** 34g total fat (20g saturated fat); 2353kJ (563 cal); 52.9g carbohydrate; 7.5g protein; 3.6g fibre

Bakewell tart

PREPARATION TIME 30 MINUTES (PLUS REFRIGERATION TIME) **COOKING TIME** 25 MINUTES **SERVES** 8

100g butter
2 tablespoons caster sugar
1 egg yolk
1 cup (150g) plain flour
½ cup (60g) almond meal
1 ½ tablespoons raspberry jam
2 tablespoons apricot jam

FILLING

125g butter
½ cup (110g) caster sugar
2 eggs
¾ cup (90g) almond meal
2 tablespoons rice flour
½ teaspoon grated lemon rind

LEMON ICING

⅓ cup (55g) icing sugar
2 teaspoons lemon juice

A short pastry topped with jam, almond meal, egg and lemon rind, English folklore has the bakewell tart originating in the Derbyshire town of the same name, the result of a culinary mistake by a cook in the local hostelry during the mid-1800s.

1 Beat butter, sugar and egg yolk in small bowl with electric mixer until combined. Stir in sifted flour and almond meal, in two batches. Knead dough on floured surface until smooth. Cover; refrigerate 30 minutes.

2 Roll dough between sheets of baking paper until large enough to line 24cm flan tin. Lift pastry into tin, ease into base and side; trim edge.

3 Preheat oven to 200°C/180°C fan-forced.

4 Make filling.

5 Spread base of pastry with raspberry jam; spread filling over jam.

6 Place tin on oven tray; bake, uncovered, 25 minutes or until browned lightly.

7 Heat apricot jam in small saucepan; strain. Brush top of hot tart with hot jam; cool.

8 Meanwhile, make lemon icing; pipe or drizzle over tart.

FILLING Beat butter and sugar in small bowl with electric mixer until mixture is light and fluffy; beat in eggs one at a time. Stir in almond meal, rice flour and rind.

LEMON ICING Sift icing sugar into small bowl; stir in juice until smooth.

▭ **PER SERVING** 34.7g total fat (16.5g saturated fat); 2249kJ (538 cal); 48g carbohydrate; 7.8g protein; 2.4g fibre

---

Banoffee pie

PREPARATION TIME 45 MINUTES (PLUS REFRIGERATION TIME) **COOKING TIME** 35 MINUTES **SERVES** 8

395g can sweetened condensed milk

75g butter, chopped

½ cup (110g) firmly packed brown sugar

2 tablespoons golden syrup

2 large bananas (460g), sliced thinly

300ml thickened cream, whipped

PASTRY

1 ½ cups (225g) plain flour

1 tablespoon icing sugar

140g cold butter, chopped

1 egg yolk

2 tablespoons iced water, approximately

1 Make pastry; cover, refrigerate 30 minutes.

2 Grease 24cm-round loose-based fluted flan tin. Roll dough between sheets of baking paper until large enough to line tin. Lift dough into tin; press into base and side. Trim edge; prick base all over with fork. Cover; refrigerate 30 minutes.

3 Preheat oven to 200°C/180°C fan-forced.

4 Place tin on oven tray. Cover dough with baking paper, fill with dried beans or rice; bake 10 minutes. Remove paper and beans; bake further 10 minutes. Cool.

5 Meanwhile, cook condensed milk, butter, sugar and syrup in medium saucepan over medium heat, stirring, about 10 minutes or until mixture is caramel-coloured. Stand 5 minutes; pour into pastry case. Cool.

6 Arrange banana slices over caramel; top with whipped cream.

PASTRY Process flour, sugar and butter until crumbly. Add egg yolk and enough of the water to process until ingredients come together. Knead dough on floured surface until smooth.

▭ **PER SERVING** 41.6g total fat (27g saturated fat); 3005kJ (719 cal); 76.3g carbohydrate; 9.2g protein; 1.9g fibre

It is believed that this dessert, originally called banoffi pie (the sound of this made-up word coming from a mix of banana and toffee), was developed by an East Sussex restaurateur in 1971. A pie crust with a rich caramel base, banana centre and top of whipped cream, it is still as popular today as it was more than 30 years ago. It's best to use a flan tin with a removable base, but if you don't have one, use a similar size springform pan.

THE TERRINE DISH
& THE BREAD TIN

The Terrine Dish & The Bread Tin

A terrine is a combination of meats, seafood and/or vegetables, with other ingredients to flavour and bind the mixture, cooked in a deep mould and served cold. Terrines have been made for centuries as a way to transform ingredients, whether humble or luxurious, into something new, and often beautiful, as the various components can be arranged in layers to reveal patterns when the terrine is sliced.

On the other hand, terrines can be homely. Familiar, old-fashioned brawn and other British-style potted meats, with shredded or diced meat set in its own spiced, jellied stock, are relations of classic terrines. We are used to seeing them in humble basins but, chilled in a traditional terrine dish and cut into slices, they could stand beside more elaborate creations. The rustic French dish, rillettes, consisting of shredded pork, rabbit or duck set in its own spiced fat, or English potted shrimps set in the spiced butter in which they were cooked, are other family concoctions usually seen in simple dishes but lacking only a handsome terrine dish to go up in the world.

Terrine dishes can also be used for cooking mixtures that are entirely puréed, usually known as pâtés or parfaits; some of these are served by slicing, some are meant to be taken from the dish with a serving knife or spatula in chunks or dollops.

Any terrine or pâté can be presented in a pastry crust: the dish is lined with pastry, the mixture arranged in it and a pastry lid fitted in place, in the same way as when making a pie (see *The Pie Dish*, pages 434 & 435). After cooking, melted jellied stock is poured in through a hole in the crust to fill the gap left due to the filling shrinking during cooking, then the whole creation – now a pâté en croûte – is chilled. Layered fruit or ice-cream desserts are chilled or frozen in a terrine mould and served in slices.

CHOOSING A TERRINE DISH

Traditional terrine dishes are usually lidded; if not, they must be covered with foil during cooking. They come in various types of ceramic – ovenproof earthenware, china or porcelain – and in enamelled cast-iron. These are good looking and often highly decorative because they are intended to go to the table. The classic shapes are rectangular – the best for terrines to be precisely sliced to show their decorative layering – or round or oval, better for mixtures to be cut into more rustic slices or taken in portions with a knife.

Small rectangular metal moulds, about 4.5cm x 8cm (base measurements) x 3cm deep, are available in framed sets like patty pans. A terrine of the light jellied type, set in these, would make charming individual servings, while richer pâté or rillettes would serve two. The same moulds can be used for miniature fruit or chocolate cakes to give as Christmas presents, or for miniature loaves of bread or individual meat loaves.

There are also metal terrine moulds with drop sides so the terrine or pâté can be easily removed and served on a plate, or sliced into individual servings. This is the most convenient type for a pâté en croûte or an ice-cream terrine.

Alternatively, you may choose a metal or ovenproof glass mould in a loaf shape, more prosaically known as a bread tin or glass loaf pan. These are perfect for turning out a terrine for serving, and will also serve you for baking a meatloaf or baking breads.

ACCOMPANIMENTS

Simple accompaniments are best for terrines and pâtés: unbuttered hot toast, Melba toast or sliced baguette or sourdough, with cornichons (baby pickled cucumbers) for meat terrines. Brawn and similar potted meats are traditionally served with hot mustard and vinegar and, if used as a summer lunch dish, with salads.

THE BREAD TIN

If you're serious about bread-making, buy two good quality, standard loaf-sized heavy bread tins. They'll last you a lifetime and the resulting crusty bread will make you glad you bought them. Any good cookware shop will sell them. Breadmaking is easier than cake- and pastry-making because you don't have to be careful not to over-handle the dough – indeed, you need to thump and push it around (knead it) to develop its gluten content so it will form the countless little elastic strands that make it strong and elastic. Even small children can give a hand with the kneading, which they enjoy.

KNEADING You can knead with a bread hook attachment in an electric mixer, or by hand. The way to knead is to turn the dough out on to a floured work surface, fold it towards you then push it firmly away with the heel of your hand, turn it a little and repeat. Frequently pick up the dough and slap it down hard on the work surface. Continue until the dough is smooth and elastic enough for a dent made with a fingertip to spring back (but be aware that some sweet, butter-rich doughs will always be to too soft for this test; simply knead them as the recipe directs and don't worry).

RISING Bread dough needs to be strong to swell without breaking as the fermentation process caused by the yeast produces gas, dispersed in thousands of tiny pockets throughout the loaf, to give the bread its lightness and good chewy texture. This happens slowly and the yeast needs warmth to do its work, so the next step after kneading is to put the dough into a greased bowl, cover with greased plastic wrap and then a damp cloth, and leave in a warm place for an hour or so, or as recipe directs, until it is rather more than doubled in volume and, if you make a dent with a fingertip, it does not puff back up, showing that the gluten has reached the limit of its elasticity.

KNOCKING DOWN The next step is to punch the dough down so as to divide the gas pockets even further, to even out the warmth and moisture, which build up in the centre of the dough during fermentation, and to return the dough to a state where it can be shaped. Rising and knocking down are sometimes done twice.

PROVING AND BAKING The bread is placed in the greased tin and left for one last short rise, called "proving". It then goes into the hot oven where the "oven spring" takes place during the first 15 minutes of baking: that is, the heat makes the gas in the air pockets expand rapidly to inflate the dough to its final shape before the crust sets. Bread is cooked when it sounds hollow if you knock the underside with your knuckles. Cool, right-side up, on a wire rack.

Potato terrine

PREPARATION TIME 1 HOUR **COOKING TIME** 2 HOURS 15 MINUTES (PLUS STANDING TIME) **SERVES** 8

There are now silicone loaf tins on the market, and their high sides and good heat transmission help guarantee even cooking, foolproof release and easy clean-up.

All you need for a brunch or lunch for friends is to accompany this terrine with a salad of mixed baby leaves tossed with cherry tomatoes, kalamata olives and roasted baby beetroots.

2 large potatoes (600g)
1 medium red capsicum (200g)
1 large eggplant (500g)
cooking-oil spray
1 large leek (500g)
⅓ cup (80ml) olive oil
3 cloves garlic, crushed
2 tablespoons finely chopped fresh thyme

1 teaspoon ground black pepper
10 slices prosciutto (150g)
250g mozzarella cheese, sliced
1 cup loosely packed fresh basil leaves

SAFFRON VINAIGRETTE
⅓ cup (80ml) olive oil
2 tablespoons lemon juice
pinch saffron threads

1 Preheat oven to 180°C/160°C fan-forced. Oil 1.5-litre (6-cup) ovenproof terrine dish.

2 Cut potatoes into 2mm slices. Cook potato in large saucepan of boiling water about 4 minutes or until potatoes are just beginning to soften; drain.

3 Quarter capsicum, remove seeds and membranes. Roast under preheated grill, skin-side up, until skin blisters and blackens. Cover capsicum pieces in plastic or paper 5 minutes; peel away skin.

4 Cut eggplant lengthways into 5mm slices; coat slices, both sides, with oil-spray. Cook eggplant, in large frying pan, until browned both sides; drain on absorbent paper.

5 Cut white part of leek into 7cm lengths; cut lengths in half. Boil, steam or microwave leek until tender. Drain, rinse under cold water; drain.

6 Combine oil, garlic, thyme and pepper in small bowl.

7 Cover base and long sides of dish with prosciutto, allowing prosciutto to overhang edges. Place half of the potato, overlapping, over base, brush with herb oil mixture; top with half of the cheese, brush with herb oil mixture. Layer capsicum, eggplant, basil and leek, brushing each layer with herb oil mixture. Top leek layer with remaining cheese then remaining potato, brushing with herb oil mixture between layers; press down firmly. Cover terrine with prosciutto slices.

8 Cover terrine with foil, place on oven tray; cook in oven 1 hour. Uncover, cook further 40 minutes. Remove from oven, pour off any liquid. Cool 5 minutes; cover top of terrine with plastic wrap, weight with two large heavy cans for 1 hour.

9 Combine ingredients for saffron vinaigrette in jar; shake well. Serve with sliced terrine.

PER SERVING 27.1g total fat (7.4g saturated fat); 1476kJ (353 cal); 12.8g carbohydrate; 15.1g protein; 4.3g fibre

Glazed meatloaf with salami

PREPARATION TIME 15 MINUTES **COOKING TIME** 45 MINUTES **SERVES** 8

1kg beef mince

1 medium brown onion (150g), chopped finely

1 clove garlic, crushed

1 medium carrot (120g), coarsely grated

100g sliced salami, chopped coarsely

1 egg, beaten lightly

1 cup (70g) stale breadcrumbs

½ cup finely chopped fresh flat-leaf parsley

GLAZE

½ cup (125ml) tomato sauce

¼ cup (60ml) worcestershire sauce

2 tablespoons malt vinegar

2 tablespoons brown sugar

1 Preheat oven to 200°C/180°C fan-forced. Oil 1.5-litre (6-cup) ovenproof terrine dish.

2 Make glaze.

3 Combine all ingredients in large bowl with ⅓ cup (80ml) of the glaze. Press meatloaf mixture into dish.

4 Bake, uncovered, 25 minutes; turn out onto baking-paper-lined oven tray. Brush meatloaf with remaining glaze; bake further 20 minutes or until browned lightly and cooked through.

GLAZE Stir ingredients in small jug until sugar has dissolved.

☐ **PER SERVING** 14.4g total fat (5.4g saturated fat); 1333kJ (319 cal); 15.5g carbohydrate; 30.9g protein; 1.5g fibre

---

White bread

PREPARATION TIME 20 MINUTES (PLUS STANDING TIME) **COOKING TIME** 45 MINUTES **MAKES** 18 SLICES

3 teaspoons (10g) dry yeast

½ cup (125ml) warm water

2 teaspoons sugar

2½ cups (375g) plain flour

1 teaspoon salt

30g butter, melted

½ cup (125ml) warm milk

1 Combine yeast, the water and sugar in small bowl, whisk until yeast dissolves. Cover; stand in warm place about 10 minutes or until mixture is frothy.

2 Sift flour and salt into large bowl, stir in butter, milk and yeast mixture. Knead dough on floured surface 10 minutes or until smooth and elastic; place in oiled bowl. Cover; stand in warm place about 1 hour or until mixture has doubled in size.

3 Preheat oven to 220°C/200°C fan-forced. Oil 14cm x 21cm loaf pan.

4 Turn dough onto floured surface; knead until smooth. Roll dough to 18cm x 35cm rectangle, roll up from short side like a swiss roll. Place in pan; cut four diagonal slashes across top. Cover; stand in warm place about 20 minutes or until risen.

5 Bake about 45 minutes; turn bread onto wire rack to cool.

☐ **PER SLICE** 1.9g total fat (1.1g saturated fat); 393kJ (94 cal); 15.9g carbohydrate; 2.7g protein; 0.9g fibre

Duck liver parfait with red onion jam

PREPARATION TIME 25 MINUTES **COOKING TIME** 40 MINUTES (PLUS REFRIGERATION TIME) **SERVES** 8

30g butter

6 shallots (150g), chopped finely

2 cloves garlic, crushed

½ teaspoon ground allspice

1 tablespoon finely chopped
fresh thyme

1 teaspoon cracked black pepper

⅔ cup (160ml) brandy

400g duck livers, trimmed

¾ cup (180ml) cream

4 eggs

150g butter, melted, cooled

2 bay leaves, halved

2 sprigs thyme, halved

100g butter, extra

RED ONION JAM

50g butter

4 medium red onions (680g),
sliced thinly

¼ cup (55g) sugar

¾ cup (180ml) dry red wine

¼ cup (60ml) port

¼ cup (60ml) red wine vinegar

You can use chicken livers in this recipe if duck liver is not readily available. Clean them by discarding their membranes and separating the livers' lobes.

Double the red onion jam recipe and keep the extra quantity, covered and refrigerated, for up to two weeks. It is fabulous spread on ciabatta topped with cold roast beef or thick slabs of a mature cheddar cheese, if desired, instead of toasted brioche.

Remove tiny portions of the parfait from the terrine using a small ice-cream scoop and serve them on individual pieces of sourdough bread.

1 Preheat oven to 150°C/130°C fan-forced.

2 Melt butter in small frying pan; cook shallot and garlic, stirring, until shallot softens. Add allspice, thyme, pepper and brandy; bring to a boil. Reduce heat, simmer, uncovered, about 2 minutes or until liquid is reduced to about 1 tablespoon.

3 Blend or process shallot mixture with livers, cream, eggs and melted butter until mixture is smooth. Push parfait mixture through fine sieve into medium bowl; repeat process through same cleaned sieve.

4 Pour parfait mixture into greased 1.5-litre (6-cup) ovenproof terrine dish; place terrine in baking dish. Pour enough boiling water into baking dish to come halfway up sides of terrine; cover terrine with foil. Cook, covered, in oven, about 40 minutes or until parfait is just set. Remove terrine from baking dish; cool parfait 10 minutes.

5 Meanwhile, make red onion jam.

6 Decorate parfait with bay leaves and thyme. Melt extra butter in small saucepan; cool 2 minutes, then carefully pour butter fat over parfait, leaving milk solids in pan. Cover parfait in terrine; refrigerate 3 hours or overnight.

7 Turn parfait onto board. Using hot, wet knife, cut parfait into eight slices; serve with red onion jam and, if desired, toasted brioche.

RED ONION JAM Melt butter in large frying pan; cook onion and sugar, stirring occasionally, over medium heat, about 20 minutes or until onion starts to caramelise. Add wine, port and vinegar; bring to a boil. Reduce heat, simmer, uncovered, about 30 minutes or until jam thickens.

PER SERVING 48.3g total fat (30.2g saturated fat); 2558kJ (612 cal); 14.8g carbohydrate; 14.6g protein; 1.5g fibre

Liver and asparagus terrine

PREPARATION TIME 40 MINUTES **COOKING TIME** 1 HOUR 30 MINUTES (PLUS COOLING TIME) **SERVES** 4

12 slices prosciutto (180g)

¼ cup (60ml) olive oil

1 large brown onion (200g), chopped finely

4 cloves garlic, crushed

¼ cup (60ml) cream

250g mushrooms, sliced thinly

⅓ cup (25g) coarsely grated parmesan cheese

400g chicken livers, halved, trimmed

700g chicken mince

250g asparagus, trimmed

4 large potatoes (1.2 kg), chopped coarsely

CELERIAC COLESLAW

½ cup (150g) whole-egg mayonnaise

200g celeriac, grated coarsely

2 tablespoons dijon mustard

2 tablespoons lemon juice

Wrapping the uncooked terrine mixture completely in prosciutto ensures that the loaf remains moist and flavoursome.

For an interesting presentation of this whole-meal dish, cut the potato into baton shapes before roasting them. Arrange the batons on serving plates log-cabin style and "roof" each cabin with a terrine slice. Surround the log cabin with coleslaw.

1 Preheat oven to 180°C/160°C fan-forced. Oil 1.5-litre (6-cup) ovenproof terrine dish.

2 Line base and sides of dish with prosciutto slices, allowing 7cm overhang on long sides of dish.

3 Heat 1 tablespoon of the oil in large frying pan; cook onion and garlic, stirring, until onion softens. Stir in cream; transfer to medium bowl.

4 Heat 1 tablespoon of the remaining oil in same pan; cook mushrooms, stirring, until browned. Stir in cheese; transfer to another medium bowl.

5 Heat remaining oil in same pan; cook liver, stirring, over high heat, about 2 minutes or until browned, but not cooked through. Drain on absorbent paper.

6 Combine liver and mince with onion mixture in medium bowl. Spread one third of the mince mixture into dish, top with asparagus. Cover with another third of the mince mixture; top with mushroom mixture, then top with remaining mince mixture. Fold prosciutto slices over to cover mince mixture.

7 Bake, uncovered, in oven about 1 hour or until mixture is cooked through. Remove terrine from oven; drain juices from dish. Cool 20 minutes in dish before slicing.

8 Meanwhile, place potato on oiled oven tray. Roast, uncovered, alongside terrine, about 1 hour or until potato is tender and browned lightly.

9 Combine ingredients for celeriac coleslaw in medium bowl. Serve terrine with potato and coleslaw.

▭ **PER SERVING** 55.8g total fat (15.4g saturated fat); 4285kJ (1025 cal); 50.4g carbohydrate; 74.9g protein; 10.5g fibre

Breads

This is just a small sample of the breads of the world available to us now.

SOURDOUGH
Sourdough does not use commercial yeast, but instead a piece of dough from the last batch, to start fermentation. Sourdough is delicious with unsalted butter.

PUMPERNICKEL
A dark, dense sourdough of German origin, made with a high proportion of rye flour and meal to wheat flour, frequently with added molasses for colour and flavour. Good with smoked salmon or German sausage.

RYE
Rye bread uses both rye and wheat flours, the latter contributing gluten for good texture, since rye has only a little. It comes in various degrees of heaviness, darkness and sweetness.

ROTI
A wheaten Indian flatbread, shaped by rotating the dough on a round iron plate called a tawa and pushing it down to move air bubbles to where they are wanted. Chapatis and phulkas are close relations.

BAGUETTE
The very long, very narrow loaf that is everyone's idea of typical French bread. Wonderfully light and crisp-crusted, its perfection is brief as it stales very quickly. Baguette slices make good bases for party savouries, or toasted, as croûtons.

FOCACCIA
A thick, leavened Italian flatbread, often baked with a savoury topping and cut into squares for serving warm as a snack, or split after baking and cooling and filled with meats and vegetables to eat as a sandwich.

CIABATTA

The word means "slipper" in Italian, referring to the long, narrow shape of this white, crisp-crusted, often rather holey sourdough loaf. A classic accompaniment to antipasto.

TURKISH BREAD

Also known as pide, Turkish bread is a long, flattish, round-ended loaf with a chewy texture. Widely served in the form of thick toast as part of café breakfasts, and good for mopping up sauce or gravy.

NAAN

An irregular shaped, leavened Indian flatbread baked on the inner wall of a tandoor (clay oven with a live fire), good naan is blistered and light. Excellent with curries.

CHALLAH

Also called barches or khalleh, this rich, sweet, braided Jewish bread is, traditionally eaten on Shabbat (the Sabbath) and holidays except Passover, when leavened bread is forbidden. It is quite similar to the French brioche.

BAGEL

A small, ring-shaped bread roll that is boiled before it is baked, giving it a dense, chewy texture. Bagels are a traditional Jewish breakfast treat, often split and spread with cream cheese or sour cream, topped with smoked salmon.

LAVASH

A thin, soft Armenian flatbread. Lavash is traditionally baked on the inside wall of a clay oven with a live fire. Similar to tortillas, it is supple when fresh but becomes stale and brittle rapidly.

Make individual terrines by dividing the cold risotto and remaining ingredients into six portions and arranging them in the same order, in small individual plastic-lined loaf pans, that we give for the terrine dish. Cover each with plastic wrap and weight with small unopened cans of food; refrigerate 3 hours or overnight then turn the tiny loaves out onto a crisp red radicchio leaf and serve with grissini.

Risotto terrine

PREPARATION TIME 20 MINUTES

COOKING TIME 45 MINUTES (PLUS COOLING, REFRIGERATION AND STANDING TIME) **SERVES** 6

1 medium green capsicum (200g)	1 clove garlic, crushed
1 medium red capsicum (200g)	1½ cups (300g) arborio rice
8 medium egg tomatoes (600g), halved	½ cup (125ml) dry white wine
3½ cups (875ml) vegetable stock	20g butter
1 tablespoon olive oil	½ cup (40g) coarsely grated parmesan cheese
1 medium brown onion (150g), chopped finely	50g baby spinach leaves

1 Preheat oven to 180°C/160°C fan-forced.

2 Quarter capsicums; discard seeds and membranes. Place tomato and capsicum on oven tray; roast, uncovered, skin-side up, about 40 minutes or until tomato and capsicum soften. Cover capsicum pieces with plastic or paper 5 minutes; peel away skin.

3 Meanwhile, place stock in medium saucepan; bring to a boil. Reduce heat, simmer, covered.

4 Heat oil in large saucepan; cook onion and garlic, stirring, until onion softens. Add rice; stir to coat rice in onion mixture. Stir in wine; cook, stirring, until wine is absorbed. Add ½ cup of the simmering stock; cook, stirring, over low heat, until stock is absorbed. Continue adding stock, in ½-cup batches, stirring, until stock is absorbed after each addition. Total cooking time should be about 35 minutes or until rice is tender. Stir in butter and cheese. Cool to room temperature.

5 Line 1.5-litre (6-cup) terrine dish with plastic wrap. Layer half of the tomato, cut-side down, then half of the spinach, half of the risotto, all of the capsicum, remaining tomato, remaining spinach and remaining risotto. Cover terrine; weight with another dish filled with heavy cans. Refrigerate 3 hours or overnight. Serve terrine at room temperature.

PER SERVING 9g total fat (4g saturated fat); 1371kJ (328 cal); 46.1g carbohydrate; 10.1g protein; 3.1g fibre

Purchase the flours, grains and seeds called for here by weight from a health-food store that sells them in bulk, if you can. Unless you intend to make this bread on a regular basis, buying 500g packages of each could be a waste. If you do have to buy large amounts, keep what you don't use in a tightly sealed glass jar, under refrigeration if you have the space.

Mixed grain loaf

PREPARATION TIME 20 MINUTES (PLUS STANDING TIME) **COOKING TIME** 45 MINUTES **MAKES** 18 SLICES

¼ cup (50g) cracked buckwheat	1 teaspoon salt
½ cup (80g) burghul	1 tablespoon linseeds
¼ cup (50g) kibbled rye	2 teaspoons olive oil
3 teaspoons (10g) dry yeast	1 egg yolk
1 teaspoon sugar	1 teaspoon milk, extra
¾ cup (180ml) warm milk	2 teaspoons sesame seeds
¼ cup (60ml) warm water	2 teaspoons cracked buckwheat, extra
2¼ cups (335g) white plain flour	
½ cup (80g) wholemeal plain flour	

1 Place buckwheat, burghul and kibbled rye in small heatproof bowl, cover with boiling water. Cover; stand 30 minutes. Rinse well, drain well.

2 Combine yeast, sugar, milk and the water in small bowl, whisk until yeast dissolves. Cover; stand in warm place about 10 minutes or until mixture is frothy.

3 Sift flours and salt into large bowl, add grain mixture and linseeds. Stir in oil and yeast mixture; mix to a soft dough. Knead dough on floured surface about 10 minutes or until dough is smooth and elastic. Place dough in large oiled bowl; cover, stand in warm place about 1 hour or until dough has doubled in size.

4 Preheat oven to 220°C/200°C fan-forced. Oil 14cm x 21cm loaf pan.

5 Turn dough onto floured surface, knead until smooth. Divide dough into three pieces. Shape each piece into a 30cm sausage. Plait sausages together, place into pan. Cover; stand in warm place about 30 minutes or until risen.

6 Brush dough with combined egg yolk and extra milk, sprinkle evenly with combined sesame seeds and extra buckwheat. Bake about 45 minutes; turn onto wire rack to cool.

PER SLICE 2g total fat (0.5g saturated fat); 568kJ (136 cal); 23.4g carbohydrate, 4.5g protein; 2.5g fibre

---

Cinnamon spiral loaf

PREPARATION TIME 20 MINUTES (PLUS STANDING TIME) **COOKING TIME** 35 MINUTES **MAKES** 18 SLICES

2 teaspoons (7g) dry yeast

¼ teaspoon sugar

½ cup (125ml) warm water

3 cups (450g) plain flour

1 teaspoon salt

⅔ cup (160ml) warm milk

40g butter, melted

2 teaspoons butter, melted, extra

⅓ cup (80g) chocolate hazelnut spread

2 teaspoons sugar, extra

1 teaspoon ground cinnamon

If you don't have chocolate hazelnut spread such as Nutella on hand, substitute it with dark brown sugar: combine the cinnamon with ⅓ cup firmly packed dark brown sugar and sprinkle it evenly over the melted butter you've spread on the dough in step 4.

1 Combine yeast, sugar and the water in small bowl, whisk until yeast has dissolved. Cover; stand in warm place about 10 minutes or until mixture is frothy.

2 Sift flour and salt into large bowl. Stir in milk, butter and yeast mixture, mix to a soft dough. Knead dough on floured surface about 5 minutes or until smooth and elastic. Place dough in oiled bowl; cover; stand in warm place about 1 hour or until dough has almost doubled in size.

3 Preheat oven to 220°C/200°C fan-forced. Oil 14cm x 21cm loaf pan.

4 Turn dough onto floured surface, knead until smooth. Shape dough into 20cm x 26cm rectangle. Brush with extra butter, spread evenly with chocolate hazelnut spread, leaving a 1cm border; sprinkle with combined extra sugar and cinnamon. Roll up from short side, like a swiss roll. Place into pan, cover with plastic wrap, stand in warm place 40 minutes or until dough has doubled in size. Remove plastic.

5 Bake 10 minutes. Reduce oven temperature to 180°C/160°C fan-forced. Bake further 25 minutes; turn onto wire rack to cool.

PER SLICE 4.3g total fat (2.2g saturated fat); 589kJ (141 cal); 21.5g carbohydrate; 3.4g protein; 1.1g fibre

Potato, olive and sun-dried tomato bread

PREPARATION TIME 15 MINUTES **COOKING TIME** 1 HOUR **SERVES** 8

This substantial loaf coupled with a pot of homemade pureed soup (think tomato, broccoli or pumpkin) makes the perfect meal for a cold winter's night. Use leftover mashed potatoes if you have them, or cook and mash the potato in the morning so that you can get the bread in the oven within a few minutes of getting home from work.

1 large potato (200g), peeled, chopped coarsely

30g butter

2 cups (300g) self-raising flour

1 cup (250ml) milk

½ cup (60g) thickly sliced green olives

½ cup (75g) drained sun-dried tomatoes, sliced thickly

1 cup (100g) coarsely grated mozzarella cheese

1 Preheat oven to 220°C/200°C fan-forced. Oil 14cm x 21cm loaf pan; line base with baking paper.

2 Boil, steam or microwave potato until tender; drain. Mash potato in large bowl with butter until smooth.

3 Add flour, milk, olives, tomato and cheese to potato mixture; mix to combine. Spoon into pan; bake about 50 minutes. Turn bread onto wire rack to cool.

PER SERVING 8g total fat (4.7g saturated fat); 1116kJ (267 cal); 36.8g carbohydrate; 9.9g protein; 3.4g fibre

Terrine de campagne

PREPARATION TIME 20 MINUTES **COOKING TIME** 2 HOURS (PLUS REFRIGERATION TIME) **SERVES** 6

This classic French "country-style" pâté takes its name from the loaf-shaped mould in which it is prepared. Like the words casserole and tagine, terrine can mean both the vessel and the food that is cooked in it. As a general rule, the difference in a pâté and a terrine is mainly textural, with the former being smooth and spreadable while a terrine is usually chunky, rustic and sliced with a knife.

350g chicken thigh fillets, chopped coarsely

400g boned pork belly, rind removed, chopped coarsely

300g piece calves liver, trimmed, chopped coarsely

3 rindless bacon rashers (195g), chopped coarsely

3 cloves garlic, crushed

2 teaspoons finely chopped fresh thyme

10 juniper berries, crushed

2 tablespoons port

¼ cup (60ml) dry white wine

1 egg

¼ cup (35g) toasted, shelled pistachios

1 Preheat oven to 150°C/130°C fan-forced. Oil 1.5-litre (6-cup) ovenproof terrine dish.

2 Mince or process meats, separately, until coarsely minced; combine in large bowl with remaining ingredients.

3 Press meat mixture into dish; cover with foil. Place terrine dish in baking dish; pour enough boiling water into baking dish to come halfway up side of terrine dish. Cook in oven 1 hour. Uncover; cook further 1 hour or until cooked through.

4 Remove terrine dish from baking dish; cover terrine with baking paper. Weight with another dish filled with heavy cans; cool 10 minutes then refrigerate overnight.

5 Turn terrine onto serving plate; serve sliced terrine, at room temperature, with french bread and cornichons, if desired.

PER SERVING 30.1g total fat (9.6g saturated fat); 2019kJ (483 cal); 3.6g carbohydrate; 46.2g protein; 0.8g fibre

1 POTATO, OLIVE AND SUN-DRIED TOMATO BREAD **2** TERRINE DE CAMPAGNE
3 CHICKEN, BASIL AND SUN-DRIED TOMATO TERRINE [P 492] **4** CHOCOLATE BANANA BREAD [P 492]

1

2

3

4

Chicken, basil and sun-dried tomato terrine

PREPARATION TIME 20 MINUTES **COOKING TIME** 1 HOUR (PLUS COOLING AND REFRIGERATION TIME)
SERVES 8

This terrine is perfect picnic fare: make it the day before; refrigerate it overnight; transport it, still covered, in the terrine, wrapped well in several sections of old newspaper to ensure it stays cold and protected. Make sure you also take a loaf or two of the best and freshest bread you can find.

Place the boiling water in the baking dish in the oven just as you are starting to cook the terrine so you don't have to carry the entire water bath across your kitchen.

600g chicken breast fillets, chopped coarsely

350g chicken thigh fillets, chopped coarsely

300g chicken mince

½ cup (80g) roasted pine nuts

½ cup coarsely chopped fresh basil

½ cup (75g) drained semi-dried tomatoes, chopped coarsely

¼ cup (60ml) cream

CAPSICUM SALSA

1 cup (200g) drained char-grilled capsicum, chopped finely

¼ teaspoon cayenne pepper

1 Preheat oven to 180°C/160°C fan-forced. Oil 1.5-litre (6-cup) terrine dish; line base and two long sides with baking paper, extending paper 3cm above sides.

2 Combine ingredients in large bowl; press mixture into dish, fold sides of baking paper over chicken mixture, cover with foil.

3 Place terrine in baking dish; pour enough boiling water into baking dish to come halfway up side of terrine. Bake about 1 hour or until chicken is cooked. Cool to room temperature; drain away excess liquid. Cover; refrigerate 3 hours or overnight.

4 Combine ingredients for capsicum salsa in small bowl.

5 Serve sliced terrine with salsa.

PER SERVING 20.4g total fat (5.1g saturated fat); 1451 kJ (347 cal); 5.1g carbohydrate; 35.1g protein; 2g fibre

Chocolate banana bread

PREPARATION TIME 15 MINUTES **COOKING TIME** 1 HOUR **SERVES** 12

You need approximately 2 large overripe bananas (460g) for this recipe. Pecans are a great substitute for walnuts, if you prefer their flavour.

If you wish, soften the butter then fold the chopped nuts into it; roll the butter mixture in a piece of plastic wrap into a short, fat log and refrigerate it until it firms. Cut rounds of chilled butter to melt onto the hot bread slices.

1 cup mashed banana

¾ cup (165g) caster sugar

2 eggs, beaten lightly

¼ cup (60ml) olive oil

¼ cup (60ml) milk

⅔ cup (100g) self-raising flour

⅔ cup (100g) wholemeal self-raising flour

¾ cup (90g) coarsely chopped roasted walnuts

¼ cup (45g) finely chopped dark eating chocolate

WHIPPED NUT BUTTER

100g butter

¼ cup (30g) finely chopped toasted walnuts

1　Preheat oven to 180°C/160°C fan-forced. Grease 14cm x 21cm loaf pan; line base and long sides with baking paper.

2　Combine banana and sugar in large bowl; stir in eggs, oil and milk. Add remaining ingredients; stir until combined.

3　Spread mixture into pan; bake about 1 hour. Stand bread in pan 5 minutes; turn onto wire rack to cool.

4　Make whipped nut butter. Serve bread warm with whipped nut butter.

WHIPPED NUT BUTTER　Beat butter in small bowl with electric mixer until light and fluffy; stir in nuts.

▭ **PER SERVING** 20.7g total fat (6.7g saturated fat); 1409kJ (337 cal); 31.7g carbohydrate; 5.1g protein; 2.4g fibre

Fruit and nut loaf

PREPARATION TIME 25 MINUTES (PLUS STANDING TIME)　**COOKING TIME** 45 MINUTES　**MAKES** 18 SLICES

2 teaspoons (7g) dry yeast

¼ cup (55g) caster sugar

2 tablespoons warm water

⅔ cup (160ml) warm milk

1 cup (150g) plain flour

1 egg, beaten lightly

2 teaspoons flenly grated orange rind

2 cups (300g) plain flour, extra

1 teaspoon salt

½ teaspoon ground cinnamon

100g butter, softened

¼ cup (40g) sultanas

¼ cup (40g) raisins

¼ cup (55g) dried currants

¼ cup (30g) chopped walnuts, roasted

1 egg yolk

1 tablespoon caster sugar, extra

½ teaspoon ground cinnamon, extra

1　Combine yeast, 2 teaspoons of the sugar and the water in large bowl, whisk until yeast has dissolved. Whisk in milk and sifted flour. Cover; stand in warm place about 30 minutes or until mixture is frothy.

2　Stir in egg and rind, then sifted extra flour, salt, cinnamon and remaining sugar. Stir in butter, fruit and nuts. Knead dough on floured surface until smooth. Place dough into greased bowl; cover, stand in warm place about 1½ hours or until dough has doubled in size.

3　Preheat oven to 220°C/200°C fan-forced. Oil 14cm x 21cm loaf pan, line base with baking paper.

4　Turn dough onto floured surface, knead until smooth, place into pan. Cover loosely with greased plastic wrap, stand in warm place about 30 minutes or until risen slightly. Remove plastic wrap.

5　Brush dough with egg yolk, sprinkle with combined extra sugar and extra cinnamon; bake 10 minutes. Reduce oven temperature to 180°C/160°C fan-forced; bake further 35 minutes. Turn onto wire rack to cool.

▭ **PER SLICE** 7g total fat (3.5g saturated fat); 803kJ (192 cal); 27.2g carbohydrate; 4.1g protein; 1.5g fibre

This bread is just as good a few days after you bake it (if there's any left!): toast thick slices under a hot grill and serve it buttered for breakfast or spread with cream cheese for an after-school snack.

Use the best quality loaf pan you have when baking any bread. Steel pans conduct heat superbly so the bread emerges from the oven baked evenly with a crisp crust and tender centre. Never wash good metal pans in the dishwasher but do so by hand and dry them completely.

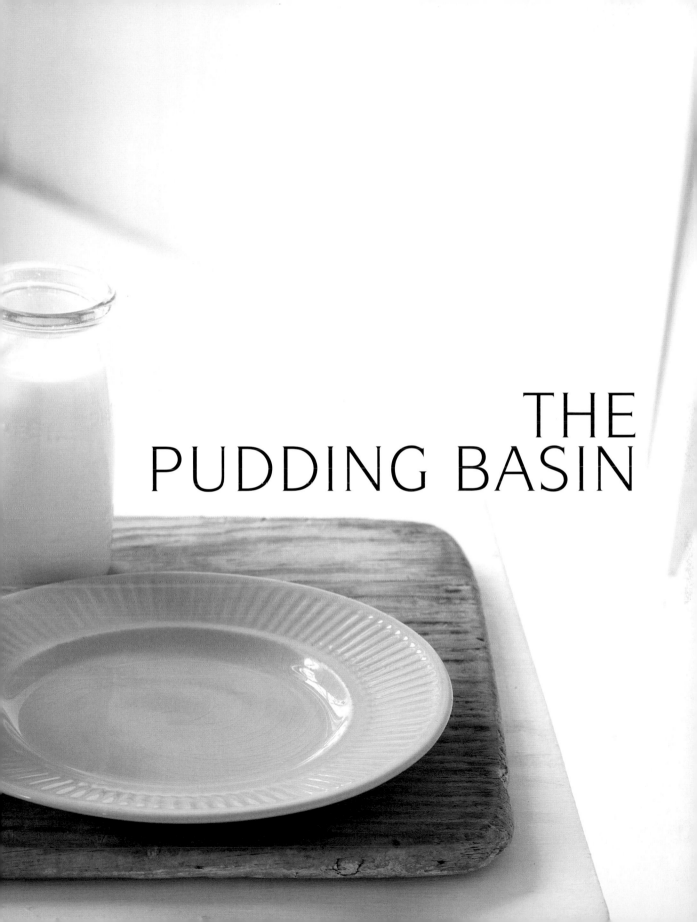

THE
PUDDING BASIN

The Pudding Basin

A traditional pudding basin is one with a deep, indented outside rim so the pudding cover can be tied in place underneath. It is still the one to use for a steamed pudding, and is also the one generally preferred for uncooked puddings, such as summer puddings or frozen Christmas puddings, simply because we seem to like that time-honoured shape for anything called a pudding.

When not on pudding duty, this classic basin performs as a useful member of the great bowl family, which serves us for mixing, moulding, heating, chilling, certain kinds of cooking, serving, storing and a hundred other jobs. Most cooks accumulate quite a few bowls; beginners can start with just three inexpensive mixing bowls – small, medium and large – and go from there.

BASINS

You could make a pudding in any heatproof bowl, but the traditional earthenware one with the rim is the easiest for securing the cover, which stops the condensed steam inside the lid falling onto the pudding and wetting it (alternatively, you can buy a metal pudding steamer with a clip-on lid). As you are cooking in water, which will keep everything at an even temperature, slow-conducting earthenware and fast-conducting metal perform equally well, provided that you protect the bottom of the basin from overheating by raising it from the base of the boiler.

STEAMED PUDDING To cook a steamed pudding, put an upturned plate or saucer into a boiler or saucepan large enough to hold the pudding basin and leave a little space around and above it; add the water to a depth that comes halfway up the pudding basin when you put it in, and put the lid on. To make a pudding cover, cut a sheet of baking paper or greased greaseproof paper or aluminium foil in a circle about 5cm larger than the top of the basin; make a 3cm-wide pleat across the middle of the paper/foil.

Make the pudding mixture and put it in the greased basin. Turn heat on high under prepared boiler. Grease the prepared pudding cover and secure it over the basin by tying it under the rim with kitchen string; if you wish, take the string across the top a couple of times, bringing it under the length used for tying the cover on, to make a handle for lifting out the pudding. (Alternatively, you can use the untraditional, but quite efficient, method of securing the cover with a large rubber band slipped down over the rim, and using rubber-gloved hands to lift the pudding out.)

If you have a basin with a clip-on lid, simply grease, put in the pudding mixture and cover it loosely with a round of baking paper or greased greaseproof paper cut to fit, then put on the greased lid and close with clips.

Lower pudding basin onto the plate or saucer, then put the lid on the boiler; adjust the heat to keep the water at a steady boil and steam for the time directed in the recipe, checking from time to time and adding more boiling water as needed to maintain the same level. After taking the pudding basin out, leave it for a minute or two to allow pudding to shrink a little from the sides, then run a thin knife, such as a palette knife, around side (see *The Cake Pan*, page 513) and turn out onto a warm serving plate.

Rich puddings such as Christmas pudding can be made ahead and reheated by steaming exactly the same way as the first time.

BOWLS

MIXING You can buy mixing bowls in earthenware and other ceramics, glass, various metals and various types of plastic. All have their virtues. Earthenware and heatproof glass bowls are probably the most useful all-rounders. Unlike plastic, they can stand heat and can be cleaned to be absolutely grease-free (vital for whisking egg whites). Unlike metal, they don't make a terrible noise when you use metal tools in them. On the other hand, plastic is unbreakable and lighter, and a metal bowl is unbreakable and better when you want to warm or chill the contents of the bowl quickly. Our advice is to start with earthenware or glass, then add bowls in other materials as you discover a use for them.

Whatever else you have, it is a good idea to have one earthenware bowl that will sit snugly into one of your saucepans so you can make a double boiler (where the saucepan is filled with 5cm of simmering water and the bowl sits on the top of the pan without touching with water). Many experienced cooks prefer this arrangement to metal or glass double boilers for making such delicate sauces as hollandaise and béarnaise, because earthenware takes up the heat slowly and gently, protecting the sauce from overheating.

Classic pudding basins make good bowls for beating cream and creamy mixtures because their shape, fairly deep in proportion to their width, keeps most of the particles that fly off the beaters inside the bowl, not on the counter or your clothes. On the other hand, make sure you have a good size, wide-open bowl that you can get your hands into to gather shortcrust pastry gently together. When you have a serious amount of mixing to do, stand the bowl on a damp cloth to hold it steady.

UTILITY These are the bowls you reach for to mix the filling for Chinese dumplings, hold a chopped onion until it's time to add it to the pan, soak saffron in before it goes into a pilaf, or the egg yolks and whites as you separate them, or any other everyday job. A few light, inexpensive stainless-steel bowls are a good buy for these tasks.

COPPER These are horrendously expensive and you can live without them, but if you become a meringue or soufflé enthusiast, a pure copper bowl that will whisk egg whites to new heights, while making them stronger and more elastic, will give you joy and confidence. It is the copper itself, reacting with the egg whites, that makes this happen. Clean the inside with vinegar and salt just before each use, and use a metal balloon whisk or hand-held electric beaters (purists will be horrified, but they are much quicker and work perfectly so long as you keep turning the bowl). Use brass and copper cleaner to keep the outside glowing, and hang it up where you can enjoy its beauty.

Summer pudding

PREPARATION TIME 30 MINUTES (PLUS REFRIGERATION TIME) **COOKING TIME** 25 MINUTES **SERVES** 6

3 eggs

½ cup (110g) caster sugar

1 tablespoon cornflour

¾ cup (110g) self-raising flour

1 teaspoon butter

¼ cup (60ml) boiling water

⅓ cup (75g) caster sugar, extra

½ cup (125ml) water

2 cups (300g) frozen blackberries

3⅓ cups (500g) frozen mixed berries

¼ cup (80g) blackberry jam

1 Preheat oven to 180°C/160°C fan-forced. Grease 25cm x 30cm swiss roll pan; line base with baking paper, extending paper 5cm over long sides.

2 Beat eggs in small bowl with electric mixer until thick and creamy. Gradually add sugar, beating until sugar dissolves; transfer mixture to large bowl.

3 Fold triple-sifted flours into egg mixture. Pour combined butter and boiling water down side of bowl; fold into egg mixture. Spread mixture into pan; bake 15 minutes. Cool in pan.

4 Meanwhile, combine extra sugar and the water in medium saucepan; bring to a boil. Stir in berries; return to a boil. Reduce heat; simmer, uncovered, until berries soften. Strain over medium bowl; reserve syrup and berries separately.

5 Turn cake onto board. Line 1.25-litre (5-cup) pudding basin with plastic wrap, extending wrap 10cm over side of basin. Cut circle slightly smaller than top edge of basin from cake using tip of sharp knife; cut second circle exact size of base of basin from cake. Cut remaining cake into 10cm long strips.

6 Place small cake circle in base of basin and use cake strips to line side of basin. Pour ⅔ cup of the reserved syrup into small jug; reserve. Fill basin with berries; cover with remaining syrup, top with large cake circle. Cover pudding with overhanging plastic wrap, weight pudding with saucer; refrigerate 3 hours or overnight.

7 Stir jam and two tablespoons of the reserved syrup in small saucepan until heated through. Turn pudding onto serving plate; brush with remaining reserved syrup then jam mixture. Serve with whipped cream, if desired.

▭ **PER SERVING** 3.7g total fat (1.3g saturated fat); 1338kJ (320 cal); 60.6g carbohydrate; 7.3g protein; 5.8g fibre

Chocolate chip pudding

PREPARATION TIME 25 MINUTES **COOKING TIME** 2 HOURS **SERVES** 8

125g butter, chopped

2 teaspoons finely grated
orange rind

1 cup (220g) caster sugar

4 eggs

½ cup (60g) almond meal

½ cup (125ml) orange juice

½ cup (50g) stale cake crumbs

1 cup (150g) self-raising flour

1 cup (150g) plain flour

⅔ cup (130g) Choc Bits

CHOCOLATE SAUCE

½ cup (125ml) thickened cream

100g dark eating chocolate,
chopped

1 Grease 1.5-litre (6 cup) pudding basin.

2 Beat butter, rind and sugar in small bowl with electric mixer until light and fluffy. Beat
in eggs, one at a time, beating well between additions. Mixture will curdle at this stage but
will reconstitute later. Transfer mixture to large bowl. Stir in almonds, juice, crumbs and
sifted flours, in two batches; stir in Choc Bits.

3 Pour mixture into basin, cover with greased round of baking paper, then foil; secure
with string or lid. Place basin in large saucepan with enough boiling water to come halfway
up side of basin; boil, covered, about 2 hours or until firm. Replenish water when necessary.

4 Make chocolate sauce; serve with pudding.

CHOCOLATE SAUCE Stir ingredients in small saucepan, over heat, without boiling, until
mixture is smooth and heated through.

> **PER SERVING** 33.8g total fat (18.2g saturated fat); 2700kJ (646 cal); 73.8g carbohydrate; 10.6g protein; 2.4g fibre

Ginger pudding

PREPARATION TIME 25 MINUTES **COOKING TIME** 2 HOURS **SERVES** 6

185g butter, chopped

½ cup (110g) firmly packed
brown sugar

½ cup (175g) golden syrup

¼ cup (90g) honey

¼ cup (60ml) water

2 eggs, beaten lightly

1½ cups (225g) plain flour

1½ cups (225g) self-raising flour

1½ tablespoons ground ginger

1 teaspoon bicarbonate of soda

2 tablespoons finely chopped
glacé ginger

1 Grease 1.5-litre (6-cup) pudding basin; line base with baking paper.

2 Stir butter, sugar, golden syrup, honey and the water in medium saucepan, over heat,
until butter is melted; bring to a boil. Remove from heat; cool to room temperature.

3 Stir eggs into butter mixture, then sifted dry ingredients and ginger; mix well. Spoon into
basin, cover with greased foil, secure with string or lid. Place basin in boiler with enough
boiling water to come halfway up side of basin; boil, covered, about 2 hours or until firm.

> **PER SERVING** 27.2g total fat (16.9g saturated fat); 2926kJ (700 cal); 102g carbohydrate; 9.8g protein; 2.7g fibre

Steamed Christmas pudding

PREPARATION TIME 1 HOUR **COOKING TIME** 6 TO 7 HOURS **SERVES** 12

4 cups (750g) mixed dried fruit

½ cup (125ml) dark rum

250g butter, softened

2½ cups (500g) firmly packed dark brown sugar

1 tablespoon parisian essence

4 eggs

1 cup (150g) plain flour

1 teaspoon mixed spice

4 cups (280g) stale breadcrumbs

1 large apple (200g), grated coarsely

1 Combine fruit and rum in large bowl. Cover; stand overnight or up to a week.

2 Grease 2-litre (8-cup) pudding basin. Line base with baking paper.

3 Beat butter, sugar and essence in small bowl with electric mixer until just combined. Beat in eggs, one at a time, beating until combined between additions. Add butter mixture to fruit mixture, then stir in sifted flour and spice, then breadcrumbs and apple; mix well.

4 Spoon pudding mixture into basin. Cover with pleated baking paper and foil; secure with string and then lid.

5 Place basin in boiler with enough boiling water to come halfway up side of basin; boil, covered, 6 to 7 hours or until firm. Replenish water when necessary. Stand pudding 15 minutes before turning onto a plate. serve wedges with custard, cream or ice-cream, if desired.

PER SERVING 20.4g total fat (12.2g saturated fat); 2867kJ (686 cal); 108.3g carbohydrate; 8.4g protein; 5.3g fibre

Around Christmas time you should be able to find dark brown, and sometimes black, sugar – both of these are good for puddings. You can use parisian essence to darken the mixture, but we prefer to use the darker sugar.

This pudding can be made up to three months ahead and kept refrigerated, or up to one year ahead and frozen.

REHEATING PUDDINGS Steam (in the pudding basin) for 2 hours, following the cooking instructions at left.

TO MICROWAVE To reheat a whole, large pudding, cover with microwave-safe plastic wrap, microwave on MEDIUM (50%) for about 15 minutes. To reheat a single serve, cover with microwave-safe plastic wrap and microwave on HIGH (100%) for 30 to 60 seconds.

College pudding

*Use any flavoured jam
you like; marmalade is
really good too, as is
golden syrup.*

*Make sure you always use
cotton kitchen string, not
synthetic, in cooking. The
synthetic variety witll melt,
stretch or break when
exposed to heat.*

PREPARATION TIME 15 MINUTES **COOKING TIME** 25 MINUTES **SERVES** 4

⅓ cup (110g) raspberry jam

1 egg

½ cup (110g) caster sugar

1 cup (150g) self-raising flour

½ cup (125ml) milk

25g butter, melted

1 tablespoon boiling water

1 teaspoon vanilla extract

1 Grease four 1-cup (250ml) metal moulds; divide jam among moulds.

2 Beat egg and sugar in small bowl with electric mixer until thick and creamy. Fold in sifted flour and milk, in two batches. Fold in combined butter, the water and extract.

3 Spoon pudding mixture onto jam. Cover each mould with pleated baking paper and foil; secure with kitchen string.

4 Place puddings in large saucepan with enough boiling water to come halfway up sides of moulds. Cover pan with tight-fitting lid; boil 25 minutes. Replenish water when necessary. Stand puddings 5 minutes before turning onto plates. Serve with cream, if desired.

PER SERVING 8.1g total fat (4.7g saturated fat); 1676kJ (401 cal); 73.7g carbohydrate; 6.5g protein; 1.8g fibre

White chocolate frozen Christmas pudding

*Decorate pudding with
fresh or frozen (thawed)
cherries and dust with
icing sugar just before
serving, if desired.*

*This recipe can be made
1 week ahead. Add
chocolate coating up to
3 hours before serving.*

PREPARATION TIME 25 MINUTES (PLUS STANDING AND FREEZING TIMES) **SERVES** 12

½ cup (75g) craisins

½ cup (115g) finely chopped glacé pineapple

¼ cup (60ml) brandy

2 litres vanilla ice-cream, softened

2 cups (280g) vienna almonds, chopped coarsely

360g white eating chocolate, melted

1 Line 17.5cm 1.75-litre (7-cup) pudding basin with plastic wrap, extending plastic 5cm over edge of basin.

2 Combine fruit and brandy in large bowl; stand 30 minutes.

3 Stir ice-cream and nuts into fruit mixture until combined. Pack ice-cream mixture into basin. Cover with foil; freeze overnight.

4 Turn pudding onto tray; remove plastic wrap, return pudding to freezer.

5 Cut a piece of paper into 35cm circle to use as a guide. Cover paper with a large sheet of plastic wrap. Spread chocolate into the circle over plastic wrap. Quickly drape plastic, chocolate-side down, over pudding. Smooth pudding with hands before gently peeling away plastic wrap. Trim base; centre pudding on serving plate.

PER SERVING 28.4g total fat (13.3g saturated fat); 2174kJ (520 cal); 54.1g carbohydrate; 8.6g protein; 1.8g fibre

1 COLLEGE PUDDING **2** WHITE CHOCOLATE FROZEN CHRISTMAS PUDDING **3** GOLDEN SYRUP STEAMED PUDDING [P 504] **4** QUINCE AND SPICE STEAMED PUDDING WITH ORANGE SYRUP [P 504]

1

2

3

4

Golden syrup steamed pudding

PREPARATION TIME 15 MINUTES **COOKING TIME** 1 HOUR **SERVES** 6

60g butter

¼ cup (90g) golden syrup

½ teaspoon bicarbonate of soda

1 cup (150g) self-raising flour

2 teaspoons ground ginger

½ cup (125ml) milk

1 egg

SYRUP

⅓ cup (115g) golden syrup

2 tablespoons water

30g butter

1 Grease 1.25-litre (5-cup) pudding basin.

2 Stir butter and syrup in small saucepan over low heat until smooth. Remove from heat, stir in soda; transfer mixture to medium bowl. Stir in sifted dry ingredients, then combined milk and egg, in two batches. Spread mixture into basin. Cover with pleated baking paper and foil; secure with lid.

3 Place basin in large saucepan with enough boiling water to come halfway up side of basin; boil, covered, about 1 hour. Replenish water when necessary. Stand pudding for 5 minutes before turning onto plate.

4 Meanwhile, make syrup. Serve pudding with syrup and, if desired, cream.

SYRUP Stir ingredients in small saucepan over heat until smooth; bring to a boil. Reduce heat; simmer, uncovered, 2 minutes.

☐ **PER SERVING** 14.3g total fat (9g saturated fat); 1367kJ (327 cal); 44.5g carbohydrate; 4.5g protein; 1g fibre

Quince and spice steamed pudding with orange syrup

PREPARATION TIME 25 MINUTES **COOKING TIME** 2 HOURS **SERVES** 8

800g quinces

½ cup (125ml) water

1 tablespoon brown sugar

2 teaspoons finely grated orange rind

100g butter

½ cup (110g) firmly packed brown sugar, extra

2 eggs

1½ cups (225g) self-raising flour

½ teaspoon bicarbonate of soda

2 teaspoons ground ginger

1 teaspoon mixed spice

½ cup (125ml) milk

ORANGE SYRUP

1 medium orange (240g)

1 cup (220g) caster sugar

1½ cups (375ml) water

6 cardamom pods, bruised

1 cinnamon stick

2 star anise

1 Grease 1.5-litre (6-cup) pudding basin.

2 Peel quinces; cut into quarters, core, then chop fruit coarsely. Place quince in large saucepan with the water, sugar and rind; cook, covered, over low heat, stirring occasionally, about 30 minutes or until quince softens. Cool to room temperature.

3 Beat butter and extra sugar in small bowl with electric mixer until light and fluffy. Beat in eggs, one at a time, beating until combined between additions. Stir in sifted flour, soda, ginger and spice until smooth; stir in milk and cooled quince mixture. Spread mixture into basin. Cover with pleated baking paper and foil; secure with lid.

4 Place basin in large saucepan with enough boiling water to come halfway up side of basin; cover pan with tight-fitting lid. Boil 1 ½ hours; replenish water as necessary. Stand pudding 5 minutes before turning onto plate.

5 Meanwhile, make orange syrup.

6 Pour half of the syrup over hot pudding. Serve pudding with remaining syrup and, if desired, whipped cream.

ORANGE SYRUP Using knife, cut rind from orange; cut rind into thin strips. Squeeze juice from orange (you need ⅓ cup). Stir rind and juice in small saucepan with remaining ingredients over heat, without boiling, until sugar dissolves. Reduce heat, simmer, uncovered, without stirring, about 10 minutes or until syrup thickens slightly. Discard spices.

▭ **PER SERVING** 12.7g total fat (7.6g saturated fat); 1848kJ (442 cal); 72.4g carbohydrate; 5.6g protein; 6.7g fibre

Spicy fig and ginger pudding

PREPARATION TIME 25 MINUTES **COOKING TIME** 1 HOUR 40 MINUTES **SERVES** 8

¾ cup (135g) finely chopped dried figs

¼ cup (55g) finely chopped glacé ginger

60g butter

½ cup (110g) firmly packed brown sugar

¼ cup (60ml) water

1 ⅓ cups (200g) plain flour

1 teaspoon ground ginger

1 teaspoon mixed spice

¾ cup (180ml) milk

1 tablespoon malt vinegar

1 teaspoon bicarbonate of soda

Pudding basins can be placed on an old, unloved saucer during the steaming process. This simply lifts the pudding from the bottom of the pan in case the pan boils dry.

1 Grease 1.5-litre (6-cup) pudding basin.

2 Stir figs, ginger, butter, sugar and water in medium saucepan over heat until butter is melted. Cool to room temperature.

3 Sift flour and spices into large bowl, make well in centre. Bring milk to a boil in small saucepan, remove from heat, quickly stir in vinegar and sifted soda. Stir hot milk mixture and fig mixture into flour.

4 Pour mixture into basin, cover with greased round of paper, then foil, secure with string or lid. Place basin in large saucepan with enough boiling water to come halfway up side of basin; boil, covered, about 1 ½ hours or until firm.

5 Turn pudding onto serving plate, serve hot with whipped cream, if desired.

▭ **PER SERVING** 7.5g total fat (4.7g saturated fat); 1137kJ (272 cal); 44.7g carbohydrate; 4.1g protein; 3.7g fibre

Sugars & syrups

White sugar no longer reigns supreme in the sugar world – it's time to acquaint yourself with the sweet newcomers.

PALM SUGAR/JAGGERY
Made by boiling down the sap of various types of palm tree to concentrate it into a thick syrup, which sets as it dries. The blocks are then chipped or grated for use.

DEMERARA
A large-crystal, light brown sugar named after the Demerara district in Guyana. Used for sprinkling on cereal and desserts, and is great for sweetening coffee as it dissolves slowly, and has a slight caramel flavour.

RAW
Granulated sugar that has not been through the final refining that makes white sugar. It is golden with larger crystals than white sugar, and has a richer flavour with a hint of caramel.

CASTER
White sugar that has been ground a little finer. Mainly used in baking, as its smaller crystals dissolve more readily during mixing pastry, meringue, sponges, biscuits and butter cakes.

CUBES
Small-grained crystallised sugar pressed into blocks, dried and cut into little cubes. Used as a table sugar, in champagne cocktails and for rubbing over oranges or lemons to soak up flavoursome oils from the skin.

MUSCOVADO
A fine-grained, moist sugar that comes in two types, light and dark. Light muscovado has a light toffee flavour, and is good for sticky toffee sauce and caramel ice-cream. Dark muscovado is used in sweet and spicy sauces.

ICING

Two types are available: pure icing sugar and icing sugar mixture, the latter having some cornflour added to prevent lumping. Pure icing sugar is mostly used in cake decorating.

BROWN

Comes in light or dark types, both soft and moist. Brown sugar, without further description, means light brown, which has a light caramel flavour. Dark brown has a stronger caramel/fudge flavour.

WHITE

Sugar, without further description, means granulated white sugar, the everyday kind used for sweetening tea, sprinkling on cornflakes and in many kinds of cooking.

CORN SYRUP

A sweet syrup made by heating cornstarch with water under pressure. It comes in light and dark types and is used in baking, and confectionery. It is sometimes mixed with other sugars such as honey.

GLUCOSE SYRUP

Also known as liquid glucose, is a form of sugar that is chemically different from ordinary sugar and will not crystallise, making it useful for preventing crystallisation in confectionery cooking.

MAPLE SYRUP

The boiled down sap of the rock or sugar maple and the black maple, both of which are native to north-eastern America. Used on the table for pancakes and in cooking. There are many imitations so check that it is labelled "pure maple syrup".

Bombe refers to the shape of this famous dessert. They're easy, quick (if you ignore the freezing time), taste divine and look spectacular. Change the ice-cream flavour, fruit and liqueur to combinations you like and that meld well with one another.

Mango bombe alaska

PREPARATION TIME 20 MINUTES (PLUS FREEZING TIME) **COOKING TIME** 5 MINUTES **SERVES** 6

2 litres mango ice-cream, softened

¼ cup (60ml) orange juice

2 tablespoons orange-flavoured liqueur

16cm-round unfilled packaged sponge cake

1 large mango (600g), sliced thinly

4 egg whites

1 cup (220g) caster sugar

1 Line 15cm 1.375-litre (5½-cup) pudding basin with plastic wrap, extending plastic 5cm over edge of basin.

2 Pack ice-cream into basin, cover with foil; freeze about 2 hours or until firm.

3 Preheat oven to 240°C/220°C fan-forced.

4 Combine juice and liqueur in small jug. Trim top of cake to flatten; split cake in half horizontally through centre. Place bottom layer of cake on oven tray; brush with half of the juice mixture. Top with mango, then with remaining cake half; brush with remaining juice mixture.

5 Invert ice-cream from basin onto cake; working quickly, trim cake to exact size of ice-cream. Return to freezer.

6 Beat egg whites in small bowl with electric mixer until soft peaks form; gradually add sugar, beating until sugar dissolves between additions.

7 Remove bombe from freezer; spread meringue over to enclose bombe completely. Bake, uncovered, about 3 minutes or until browned lightly. Lift onto serving plate; serve immediately.

▭ **PER SERVING** 22.8g total fat (13.9g saturated fat); 3173kJ (759 cal); 117.5g carbohydrate; 14g protein; 1.8g fibre

Tangelos are a citrus fruit that's a cross between a mandarin and grapefruit. They not only taste good but have a wonderful colour.

Buttermilk despite its rich-sounding name is low in fat. In this recipe, it adds to the flavour and texture of the pudding and, combined with the soda, also serves as a raising agent.

Tangelo syrup pudding

PREPARATION TIME 25 MINUTES **COOKING TIME** 1 HOUR 40 MINUTES **SERVES** 8

2 large tangelos (420g)

125g butter

½ cup (110g) caster sugar

2 eggs

1 cup (150g) wholemeal self-raising flour

½ cup (75g) white self-raising flour

½ teaspoon bicarbonate of soda

¼ cup (60ml) buttermilk

SYRUP

½ cup (110g) caster sugar

60g butter

1 Grease 1.75-litre (7-cup) pudding basin; line base with baking paper.

2 Squeeze juice from tangelos, reserve juice for syrup; you will need ⅔ cup juice. Blend or process remaining skin and pulp until smooth.

3 Beat butter and sugar in small bowl with electric mixer until light and fluffy. Beat in eggs, one at a time, beating until combined between additions. Stir in sifted dry ingredients and buttermilk, in two batches. Stir in pureed tangelo pulp. Pour mixture into basin, cover with greased round of paper, then foil; secure with string or cover with lid.

4 Place basin in large saucepan with enough boiling water to come halfway up side of basin; boil, covered, 1½ hours.

5 Make syrup.

6 Stand wire rack over shallow tray, turn pudding onto rack, pour hot syrup over pudding. Serve pudding with any remaining syrup and, if desired, cream.

SYRUP Stir sugar, reserved juice and butter in small saucepan over heat, without boiling, until sugar is dissolved; bring to a boil. Reduce heat, simmer, uncovered, without stirring, 3 minutes.

☐ **PER SERVING** 20.9g total fat (13.1g saturated fat); 1622kJ (388 cal), 43.7g carbohydrate; 4.8g protein; 3.1g fibre

---

Date pudding

PREPARATION TIME 25 MINUTES **COOKING TIME** 2 HOURS 40 MINUTES **SERVES** 10

3 cups (420g) coarsely chopped dried dates

90g butter

¾ cup (165g) firmly packed brown sugar

¾ cup (180ml) water

1 tablespoon malt vinegar

2 eggs

1 tablespoon brandy

2 cups (300g) plain flour

½ cup (75g) self-raising flour

1 teaspoon bicarbonate of soda

1 teaspoon ground cinnamon

1 teaspoon mixed spice

½ cup (125ml) milk

1 Grease 2-litre (8-cup) pudding basin.

2 Stir dates, butter, sugar and the water in medium saucepan, over heat, without boiling, until butter is melted and sugar dissolved; bring to a boil. Reduce heat, simmer, uncovered, 5 minutes. Stir in vinegar; cool to room temperature.

3 Stir eggs and brandy into date mixture, then stir in sifted dry ingredients and milk in two batches. Spoon mixture into basin, cover with greased foil, secure with string or lid.

4 Place basin in large saucepan with enough boiling water to come halfway up side of basin; boil, covered, about 2½ hours. Replenish water when necessary.

5 Serve pudding warm with custard or cream.

☐ **PER SERVING** 9.4g total fat (5.6g saturated fat); 1634kJ (391 cal); 65.8g carbohydrate; 6.4g protein; 5.4g fibre

Maintaining the correct level of boiling water in the boiler or large saucepan is the most important part of this cooking method. The best way to make sure the water doesn't boil dry is to check it every 20 to 30 minutes; you can also put a couple of marbles in the water the jiggling sound of the marbles will keep you on the alert. The trouble is is that you can get used to this sound after a while – so keep checking, and keep a kettle of water "on the boil".

THE CAKE PAN

The Cake Pan

There is a special kind of satisfaction in turning out a good cake, and it's one that anyone can enjoy since cake-making is more a matter of care and attention than any special skill.

You do need the right pan – the size and shape directed in the recipe – because a different pan could need a different oven temperature or baking time. Check on this well ahead of when you plan to start. Check on other things as well: even if you've made the recipe before, it's all too easy to get ready to make a cake and then think, "Oh, I'd forgotten I'm nearly out of caster sugar". Give yourself time to take cold things like butter and eggs out of the fridge early so they will be at room temperature, if that's what the recipe calls for. If you're liable to interruptions while you're cooking, try to make cakes when things are relatively quiet; you may want to shift some of the preparation, such as preparing the pan and measuring ingredients, to an earlier quiet time. Then, when the time comes, you can give your full attention to the mixing and baking.

CHOOSING CAKE PANS

There are a multitude of different cake pans, but some are called for constantly and those are the ones to start with.

A basic collection would be:
- Deep 20cm- and 22cm-diameter round cake pan
- Deep 19cm- and 23cm-square cake pan
- 20cm x 30cm lamington pan
- 14cm x 21cm loaf pan

And you may want to add:
- 20cm ring pan
- 25cm x 30cm swiss roll pan
- 19cm x 29cm slice pan
- 23cm round springform pan
- two 8cm x 26cm bar pans

And on into the glorious world of baba pans, heart-shaped pans, nut-roll tins, recessed pans, kugelhopf pans and more.

MATERIALS

Plain uncoated aluminium cake pans do an excellent job. Pans with a non-stick coating perform well unless the coating gets scratched or starts to wear off (read more about non-stick coatings in the Finish section of *The Frying Pan*, page 23). Steel does not conduct heat as evenly as aluminium; if using steel pans, or non-stick or anodised aluminium pans, bake at 10°C below the temperature given in the recipe.

There is also a new kind of aluminium on the market, called hard-anodised aluminium, which is already available in cake pans for the restaurant trade. It is very expensive but is harder than stainless steel, so it won't get the dings that ordinary aluminium is liable to. It has a superbly smooth, impervious finish and releases food well.

Another new material is silicone, which does not brown as well as metal but is wonderfully non-stick and flexible, so you can twist it to "pop" cakes out. Depending on its shape, silicone baking ware, once filled, may need to be supported on an oven tray.

BAKING TECHNIQUES

PREPARING CAKE PANS For information and pictures showing various ways to prepare cake pans for different kinds of cakes, see Preparing Cake Pans on pages 572 & 573.

STEPS IN BAKING Cake mixtures should be baked as soon as they are ready, as standing around in the kitchen could prematurely activate the raising agent. Have the oven shelf in the right place so that the top of the baked cake is in the centre of the oven, and set the temperature as the recipe directs before starting to mix.

When the recipe tells you to fold in the flour, sift it over the mixture through a sieve, then use the edge of a large metal spoon to cut down repeatedly through the mixture, lifting up some from the bottom each time and dropping it back onto the surface, and turning the bowl a little each time. If the recipe says to add flour and liquid alternately, do this in two or three batches, starting and ending with flour.

Open the oven door a little, about halfway through baking time, to check the cake is cooking evenly. Many ovens have hot spots, so you may need to turn the cake at this point. If so, open and close the door gently and as quickly as possible. Check again about three-quarters of the way through baking time and, if cake is browning too much, lightly top with foil, shiny-side up, to protect it from the heat.

TURNING OUT OF THE PAN Unless otherwise instructed, allow the cake to cool in the pan for up to 10 minutes or until it shrinks a little away from the sides. If the cake doesn't shrink from the pan, run a thin, flexible blade between the cake and the side(s) of the pan. Place a wire rack over the pan, hold the rack and pan together with both oven-mitted hands, turn over and rap on the work surface, then gently lift the pan straight up and off the cake. Immediately put another rack on the bottom of the cake, and turn cake top-side up so the wire pattern will not mark the cake top. To avoid marking a very delicate cake, cover the first rack with a sheet of baking paper.

STORING CAKE IN FREEZER Most un-iced, unfilled cakes will freeze beautifully and, if you slice them first, you will be able to take out just as many slices as you need. Cover and leave them at room temperature to thaw, which takes only 10 to 15 minutes.

The best way to freeze sliced cake is to arrange the slices in a single layer, not touching, on an oven tray lined with plastic wrap; cover them with another sheet of plastic and put the tray in the freezer until they are frozen. They can then go into a freezer bag.

Lime and poppy seed syrup cake

PREPARATION TIME 20 MINUTES **COOKING TIME** 1 HOUR **SERVES** 33

¼ cup (40g) poppy seeds

½ cup (125ml) milk

250g butter, softened

1 tablespoon finely grated lime rind

1¼ cups (275g) caster sugar

4 eggs

2¼ cups (335g) self-raising flour

¾ cup (110g) plain flour

1 cup (240g) sour cream

LIME SYRUP

½ cup (125ml) lime juice

1 cup (250ml) water

1 cup (220g) caster sugar

1 Preheat oven to 180°C/160°C fan-forced. Grease base and sides of deep 23cm-square cake pan. Combine poppy seeds and milk in small jug; soak 10 minutes.

2 Beat butter, rind and sugar in small bowl with electric mixer until light and fluffy. Add eggs, one at a time, beating until combined between additions; transfer mixture to large bowl. Stir in sifted flours, cream and poppy seed mixture, in two batches.

3 Spread mixture into pan; bake about 1 hour.

4 Meanwhile, stir ingredients for lime syrup in small saucepan over heat, without boiling, until sugar dissolves. Simmer, uncovered, without stirring, 5 minutes.

5 Stand cake 5 minutes, turn onto wire rack over tray. Pour hot lime syrup over hot cake.

PER SERVING 10.6g total fat (6.4g saturated fat); 869kJ (208 cal); 21.1g carbohydrate; 2.8g protein; 0.8g fibre

Chocolate fudge brownies

PREPARATION TIME 20 MINUTES (PLUS COOLING TIME) **COOKING TIME** 1 HOUR 5 MINUTES **MAKES** 16

150g butter, chopped

300g dark eating chocolate, chopped coarsely

1½ cups (330g) firmly packed brown sugar

3 eggs

1 teaspoon vanilla extract

¾ cup (110g) plain flour

¾ cup (140g) dark Choc Bits

½ cup (120g) sour cream

¾ cup (110g) roasted macadamias, chopped coarsely

1 Preheat oven to 180°C/160°C fan-forced. Grease 19cm x 29cm rectangular slice pan; line base with baking paper, extending paper 5cm over sides.

2 Stir butter and chocolate in medium saucepan over low heat until smooth. Cool 10 minutes.

3 Stir in sugar, eggs and extract then sifted flour, Choc Bits, sour cream and nuts. Spread mixture into pan; bake 40 minutes. Cover pan with foil; bake 20 minutes. Cool in pan.

PER BROWNIE 24.8g total fat (12.7g saturated fat); 1722kJ (412 cal); 42.8g carbohydrate; 4.2g protein; 1g fibre

Dark chocolate mud cake

PREPARATION TIME 20 MINUTES (PLUS COOLING TIME) **COOKING TIME** 2 HOURS 40 MINUTES **SERVES** 16

This chocolate mud cake is one of our most requested recipes of all time. It's easy to make and mix, slow to bake, keeps well and is delicious to eat. If you don't like coffee flavour, leave out the instant coffee, change the liqueur, or even substitute the liqueur with milk.

675g dark eating chocolate, chopped coarsely

400g unsalted butter, chopped

1½ tablespoons instant coffee granules

1¼ cups (310ml) water

1¼ cups (275g) firmly packed brown sugar

1¾ cups (260g) plain flour

½ cup (75g) self-raising flour

4 eggs

⅓ cup (80ml) coffee-flavoured liqueur

DARK CHOCOLATE GANACHE

½ cup (125ml) cream

400g dark eating chocolate, chopped coarsely

1 Preheat oven to 160°C/140°C fan-forced. Grease deep 19cm-square cake pan; line with baking paper.

2 Stir chocolate, butter, coffee, the water and sugar in large saucepan over low heat until smooth. Cool 15 minutes.

3 Whisk in sifted flours, eggs and liqueur. Pour mixture into pan; bake about 2½ hours. Cool cake in pan.

4 Meanwhile, make dark chocolate ganache.

5 Turn cake, top-side up, onto plate; spread with ganache.

DARK CHOCOLATE GANACHE Bring cream to a boil in small saucepan; remove from heat, add chocolate, stir until smooth. Refrigerate, stirring occasionally, about 30 minutes or until spreadable.

☐ **PER SERVING** 45.7g total fat (28.3g saturated fat); 3135kJ (750 cal); 75.3g carbohydrate; 7.8g protein; 1.7g fibre

Chocolate peppermint cake

PREPARATION TIME 20 MINUTES (PLUS REFRIGERATION TIME) **COOKING TIME** 1 HOUR **SERVES** 14

Chocolate ganache can be used before or after it sets. Here, it's used as a glaze so should be as pourable as unwhipped cream and as cool as possible. If it's too warm, it will melt the peppermint cream.

125g unsalted butter, chopped

2 teaspoons instant coffee granules

¾ cup (180ml) water

100g dark eating chocolate, chopped coarsely

1 cup (220g) caster sugar

1 egg

¾ cup (110g) self-raising flour

½ cup (75g) plain flour

2 tablespoons cocoa powder

PEPPERMINT CREAM

125g unsalted butter, softened

3 cups (480g) icing sugar

2 tablespoons milk

½ teaspoon peppermint essence

green food colouring

CHOCOLATE GANACHE

300g dark eating chocolate, chopped coarsely

1 cup (250ml) cream

1 Preheat oven to 150°C/130°C fan-forced. Grease two 8cm x 26cm bar cake pans; line bases and sides with baking paper.

2 Stir butter, coffee, the water, chocolate and sugar in medium saucepan over low heat until smooth. Transfer mixture to medium bowl. Whisk in egg with sifted flours and cocoa. Pour mixture equally between pans; bake about 45 minutes. Stand cakes 5 minutes; turn, top-side up, onto wire rack to cool.

3 Meanwhile, make peppermint cream.

4 Using serrated knife, split cooled cakes in half. Place bottom layers on wire rack over tray. Spread each with about a quarter of the peppermint cream; top with cake tops. Place remaining peppermint cream in piping bag fitted with 2cm fluted tube. Pipe remaining cream along centre of each cake top; refrigerate 1 hour.

5 Meanwhile, make chocolate ganache. Using metal spatula and working quickly, pour ganache over cakes, smoothing sides. Stand at room temperature until ganache sets.

PEPPERMINT CREAM Beat butter in small bowl with electric mixer until as pale as possible. Gradually beat in sifted icing sugar, milk and essence. Tint pale green.

CHOCOLATE GANACHE Stir chocolate and cream in small saucepan over low heat until smooth.

⬜ **PER SERVING** 17.7g total fat (11.3g saturated fat); 1797kJ (430 cal); 64.3g carbohydrate; 2.7g protein; 0.7g fibre

Boiled raisin chocolate cake

PREPARATION TIME 20 MINUTES **COOKING TIME** 1 HOUR 20 MINUTES (PLUS COOLING AND STANDING TIME)
SERVES 12

2 cups (300g) raisins
2 cups (500ml) water
1 teaspoon bicarbonate of soda
⅓ cup (35g) cocoa powder
2 teaspoons ground cinnamon
½ teaspoon ground clove
1 teaspoon vanilla extract
250g butter, softened

1½ cups (330g) caster sugar
4 eggs
1½ cups (225g) plain flour
1 cup (150g) self-raising flour

CHOCOLATE GLAZE
200g dark eating chocolate, chopped coarsely
100g butter, chopped

Originally a trademark for a particular deep-sided fluted tube pan, a bundt pan today is just a generic name for that style of cake pan. When making a cake in a bundt pan, it's extremely important that all the creases of the flutes are well greased before pouring in the cake mixture.

1 Preheat oven to 180°C/160°C fan-forced. Grease 24cm bundt pan well.

2 Combine raisins and the water in medium saucepan; bring to a boil. Reduce heat, simmer, uncovered, 10 minutes. Remove from heat; stir in sifted soda and cocoa, then spices and extract. Cool to room temperature.

3 Beat butter and sugar in medium bowl with electric mixer until light and fluffy. Add eggs, one at a time, beating until just combined between additions; stir in sifted flours and raisin mixture, in two batches.

4 Spread mixture into pan; bake about 1 hour 10 minutes. Stand cake 5 minutes; turn onto wire rack to cool.

5 Stir ingredients for chocolate glaze in medium heatproof bowl over medium saucepan of simmering water until smooth. Pour over cake; stand 30 minutes before serving.

⬜ **PER SERVING** 31.4g total fat (19.5g saturated fat); 2658kJ (636 cal); 79.2g carbohydrate; 7.6g protein; 2.7g fibre

Tiramisu roulade

PREPARATION TIME 35 MINUTES **COOKING TIME** 20 MINUTES (PLUS REFRIGERATION TIME) **SERVES** 8

The combination of coffee, cream, mascarpone and sponge is irresistible to almost everyone. This dessert is at its best when made ahead and refrigerated several hours before serving.

2 tablespoons coffee-flavoured liqueur

¼ cup (60ml) water

2 tablespoons caster sugar

1 tablespoon instant coffee granules

1 tablespoon boiling water

3 eggs

½ cup (110g) caster sugar, extra

½ cup (75g) plain flour

2 tablespoons flaked almonds

COFFEE LIQUEUR CREAM

1 cup (250g) mascarpone cheese

½ cup (125ml) thickened cream

2 tablespoons coffee-flavoured liqueur

1 Preheat oven to 220°C/200°C fan-forced. Grease 25cm x 30cm swiss roll pan; line base and two long sides with baking paper, extending paper 5cm over long sides.

2 Combine liqueur with the water and sugar in small saucepan; bring to a boil. Reduce heat, simmer, uncovered, without stirring, about 5 minutes or until syrup thickens slightly. Remove from heat, stir in half of the coffee; reserve syrup.

3 Dissolve remaining coffee in the boiling water.

4 Beat eggs and extra sugar in small bowl with electric mixer about 5 minutes or until sugar is dissolved and mixture is thick; transfer to large bowl, fold in dissolved coffee.

5 Meanwhile, sift flour twice onto paper. Sift flour over egg mixture then fold gently into mixture. Spread sponge mixture into pan; sprinkle with almonds. Bake about 15 minutes.

6 Meanwhile, place a piece of baking paper cut the same size as swiss roll pan on bench; sprinkle evenly with about 2 teaspoons of caster sugar. Turn sponge onto sugared paper; peel away lining paper. Use serrated knife to cut crisp edges from all sides of sponge. Roll sponge from long side, using paper as a guide; cool.

7 Meanwhile, beat ingredients for coffee liqueur cream in small bowl with electric mixer until firm peaks form. Unroll sponge, brush with reserved syrup. Spread cream over sponge then re-roll sponge. Cover roulade with plastic wrap; refrigerate 30 minutes before serving.

PER SERVING 26g total fat (15.1g saturated fat); 1668kJ (399 cal); 31g carbohydrate; 6.6g protein; 1.1g fibre

Sticky (or toffee) date pudding became popular here in the 1980s, and has now become a family stand-by. This is a smart twist on an old favourite.

Upside-down toffee date and banana cake

PREPARATION TIME 20 MINUTES **COOKING TIME** 1 HOUR 10 MINUTES **SERVES** 8

1½ cups (330g) caster sugar

1½ cups (375ml) water

3 star anise

2 medium bananas (400g), sliced thinly

1 cup (140g) seeded dried dates

¾ cup (180ml) water, extra

½ cup (125ml) dark rum

1 teaspoon bicarbonate of soda

60g butter, chopped

½ cup (110g) firmly packed brown sugar

2 eggs

2 teaspoons mixed spice

1 cup (150g) self-raising flour

½ cup mashed banana

300ml thickened cream

1 Preheat oven to 180°C/160°C fan-forced. Grease deep 22cm-round cake pan; line with baking paper.

2 Stir caster sugar, the water and star anise in medium saucepan over low heat, without boiling, until sugar dissolves; bring to a boil. Boil syrup, uncovered, without stirring, about 5 minutes or until thickened slightly. Strain ½ cup of the syrup into small heatproof jug; reserve to flavour cream. Discard star-anise.

3 To make toffee, continue boiling remaining syrup, uncovered, without stirring, about 10 minutes or until toffee is golden brown. Pour hot toffee into cake pan; top with sliced banana.

4 Combine dates, the extra water and rum in small saucepan; bring to a boil then remove from heat. Stir in soda; stand 5 minutes. Process date mixture with butter and brown sugar until almost smooth. Add eggs, spice and flour; process until just combined. Stir in mashed banana.

5 Pour mixture into pan; bake about 40 minutes. Turn cake, still in pan, onto serving plate; stand 2 minutes. Remove pan then baking paper.

6 Beat cream in small bowl with electric mixer until firm peaks form. Stir in reserved syrup. Serve cake with cream.

PER SERVING 21.7g total fat (13.7g saturated fat); 2595kJ (916 cal); 90.4g carbohydrate; 5.5g protein; 3.5g fibre

You'll need about four passionfruits for this recipe. If you don't like the look or the crunch of the seeds, then push the pulp through a sieve, using only the juice. If you do this, you'll probably need about six passionfruits.

Passionfruit buttermilk cake

PREPARATION TIME 20 MINUTES **COOKING TIME** 45 MINUTES (PLUS COOLING TIME) **SERVES** 8

250g butter, softened

1 cup (220g) caster sugar

3 eggs, separated

2 cups (300g) self-raising flour

¾ cup (180ml) buttermilk

¼ cup (60ml) passionfruit pulp

PASSIONFRUIT ICING

1½ cups (240g) icing sugar

¼ cup (60ml) passionfruit pulp, approximately

1 Preheat oven to 180°C/160°C fan-forced. Grease and flour 24cm bundt tin; tap out excess flour.

2 Beat butter and sugar in small bowl with electric mixer until light and fluffy. Add egg yolks, beating until just combined. Transfer mixture to large bowl; stir in sifted flour and buttermilk, in two batches, then passionfruit.

3 Beat egg whites in small bowl with electric mixer until soft peaks form. Fold into cake mixture in two batches. Spread mixture into tin.

4 Bake about 40 minutes. Stand cake in pan 5 minutes; turn onto wire rack to cool.

5 Make passionfruit icing; drizzle over cake.

PASSIONFRUIT ICING Sift icing sugar into heatproof bowl; stir in enough passionfruit pulp to make a firm paste. Stand bowl over small saucepan of simmering water, stir until icing is a pouring consistency.

☐ **PER SERVING** 28.6g total fat (17.9g saturated fat); 2679kJ (641 cal); 86.2g carbohydrate; 8g protein; 3.5g fibre

---

Coconut cake

PREPARATION TIME 25 MINUTES **COOKING TIME** 40 MINUTES **SERVES** 20

125g butter, softened
½ teaspoon coconut essence
1 cup (220g) caster sugar
2 eggs
½ cup (40g) desiccated coconut
1 ½ cups (225g) self-raising flour
1 ¼ cups (300g) sour cream
⅓ cup (80ml) milk

COCONUT ICE FROSTING
2 cups (320g) icing sugar
1 ⅓ cups (100g) desiccated coconut
2 egg whites, beaten lightly
pink food colouring

1 Preheat oven to 180°C/160°C fan-forced. Grease deep 23cm-square cake pan; line with baking paper.

2 Beat butter, essence and sugar in small bowl with electric mixer until light and fluffy. Add eggs, one at a time, beating until just combined between additions. Transfer mixture to large bowl; stir in coconut, sifted flour, sour cream and milk, in two batches.

3 Spread mixture into pan; bake about 40 minutes. Stand cake 5 minutes; turn, top-side up, onto wire rack to cool.

4 Meanwhile, make coconut ice frosting. Drop alternate spoonfuls of white and pink frosting onto cake; marble over top of cake.

COCONUT ICE FROSTING Sift icing sugar into medium bowl; stir in coconut and egg white. Place half the mixture in small bowl; tint with pink colouring.

☐ **PER SERVING** 17g total fat (11.8g saturated fat); 1317kJ (315 cal); 36.1g carbohydrate; 3.8g protein; 1.5g fibre

This decadent cake is all about the ratio of fat to flour: the extremes are pushed to the limit here. The most important thing to remember when making this cake is not to overbeat the butter and sugar mixture after the eggs are added. If you do, you'll succeed in breaking the butter down too much and the result will be a heavy band at the bottom of the cake.

Basic butter cake

PREPARATION TIME 30 MINUTES **COOKING TIME** 1 HOUR **SERVES** 27

250g butter, softened

1 teaspoon vanilla extract

1 ¼ cups (275g) caster sugar

3 eggs

2 ¼ cups (335g) self-raising flour

¾ cup (180ml) milk

1 Preheat oven to 180°C/160°C fan-forced. Grease deep 22cm-round or 19cm-square cake pan; line with baking paper.

2 Beat butter, extract and sugar in medium bowl with electric mixer until light and fluffy. Beat in eggs, one at a time, beating until just combined between additions. Stir in sifted flour and milk, in two batches. Spread mixture into pan.

3 Bake about 1 hour. Stand cake 5 minutes; turn, top-side up, onto wire rack to cool.

□ **PER SERVING** 8.6g total fat (5.4g saturated fat); 686kJ (164 cal); 19.3g carbohydrate; 2.2g protein; 0.5g fibre

---

Orange cake

PREPARATION TIME 10 MINUTES **COOKING TIME** 40 MINUTES **SERVES** 12

150g butter, softened

1 tablespoon finely grated orange rind

⅔ cup (150g) caster sugar

3 eggs

1 ½ cups (225g) self-raising flour

¼ cup (60ml) milk

¾ cup (120g) icing sugar

1 ½ tablespoons orange juice

1 Preheat oven to 180°C/160°C fan-forced. Grease deep 20cm-round cake pan.

2 Beat butter, rind, caster sugar, eggs, flour and milk in medium bowl with electric mixer at low speed until just combined. Increase speed to medium, beat about 3 minutes or until mixture is smooth.

3 Spread mixture into pan; bake about 40 minutes. Stand cake 5 minutes; turn, top-side up, onto wire rack to cool.

4 Combine sifted icing sugar and juice in small bowl; spread over cake.

□ **PER SERVING** 12g total fat (7.3g saturated fat); 1127kJ (270 cal); 36.3g carbohydrate; 3.8g protein; 0.7g fibre

**1 BASIC BUTTER CAKE 2 ORANGE CAKE
3 WHITE CHOCOLATE ROCKY ROAD [P 524] 4 LAMINGTONS [P 524]**

1

2

3

4

White chocolate rocky road

PREPARATION TIME 20 MINUTES (PLUS REFRIGERATION TIME) **MAKES** 36

300g toasted marshmallow with coconut, chopped coarsely

400g turkish delight, chopped coarsely

¼ cup (40g) roasted almonds, chopped coarsely

½ cup (75g) roasted shelled pistachios

450g white eating chocolate, melted

1 Grease two 8cm x 26cm bar cake pans; line base and sides with baking paper, extending paper 5cm above long sides.

2 Combine marshmallow, turkish delight and nuts in large bowl; working quickly, stir in chocolate. Spread mixture into pans; pressing down firmly to flatten.

3 Refrigerate until set before slicing.

□ **PER SLICE** 6.6g total fat (3.3g saturated fat); 631kJ (151 cal); 20.7g carbohydrate; 2g protein; 0.4g fibre

Lamingtons

PREPARATION TIME 25 MINUTES **COOKING TIME** 35 MINUTES **MAKES** 16

6 eggs

⅔ cup (150g) caster sugar

⅓ cup (50g) cornflour

½ cup (75g) plain flour

⅓ cup (50g) self-raising flour

2 cups (160g) desiccated coconut

ICING

4 cups (640g) icing sugar

½ cup (50g) cocoa powder

15g butter

1 cup (250ml) milk

1 Preheat oven to 180°C/160°C fan-forced. Grease 20cm x 30cm lamington pan; line with baking paper, extending paper 5cm over long sides.

2 Beat eggs in medium bowl with electric mixer about 10 minutes or until thick and creamy; gradually beat in sugar, dissolving between additions. Fold in triple-sifted flours.

3 Spread mixture into pan; bake about 35 minutes. Turn cake immediately onto a baking-paper-covered wire rack to cool.

4 Meanwhile, make icing.

5 Cut cake into 16 pieces; dip each square in icing, drain off excess. Toss squares in coconut. Place lamingtons onto wire rack to set.

ICING Sift icing sugar and cocoa into medium heatproof bowl; stir in butter and milk. Set bowl over medium saucepan of simmering water; stir until icing is of a coating consistency.

□ **PER LAMINGTON** 10.4g total fat (1.8g saturated fat); 1501kJ (359 cal); 59.6g carbohydrate; 5.1g protein; 1.9g fibre

Mandarin, polenta and macadamia cake

PREPARATION TIME 20 MINUTES (PLUS COOLING TIME) **COOKING TIME** 2 HOURS (PLUS STANDING TIME)
SERVES 10

4 small mandarins (400g), unpeeled

2 cups (280g) macadamias

250g butter, softened

1 teaspoon vanilla extract

1 cup (220g) caster sugar

3 eggs

1 cup (170g) polenta

1 teaspoon baking powder

1 tablespoon icing sugar

Polenta is finely ground corn meal, and is an excellent ingredient for those who can't tolerate wheat. To make this cake gluten-free, use gluten-free baking powder and pure icing sugar.

1 Cover whole mandarins in medium saucepan with cold water; bring to a boil. Drain then repeat process two more times. Cool mandarins to room temperature.

2 Preheat oven to 170°C/150°C fan-forced. Grease deep 22cm-round cake pan; line base with baking paper.

3 Blend or process nuts until mixture forms a coarse meal. Halve mandarins; discard seeds. Blend or process mandarins until pulpy.

4 Beat butter, extract and caster sugar in small bowl with electric mixer until light and fluffy. Add eggs, one at a time, beating until just combined between additions; transfer to large bowl. Stir in polenta, baking powder, nut meal and mandarin pulp.

5 Spread mixture into pan; bake about 1 hour. Stand cake 15 minutes; turn, top-side up, onto wire rack to cool. Serve cake dusted with sifted icing sugar.

☐ **PER SERVING** 43.8g total fat (16.9g saturated fat); 2420kJ (579 cal); 39.6g carbohydrate; 6g protein; 3g fibre

Wholemeal yogurt fruit loaf

PREPARATION TIME 20 MINUTES **COOKING TIME** 1 HOUR 30 MINUTES **SERVES** 8

100g butter, softened

2 teaspoons finely grated orange rind

¾ cup (165g) caster sugar

2 eggs

2 cups (320g) wholemeal self-raising flour

1 cup (280g) yogurt

⅓ cup (80ml) orange juice

1 cup (200g) finely chopped dried figs

1 cup (150g) coarsely chopped raisins

Baking a firm textured cake like this one, covered with foil, will result in the cake being moist. The foil cover "steams" the cake during the initial baking, and the pleat in the foil is to allow for the cake's expansion. This loaf will develop a crust during the last 15 minutes of cooking time.

1 Preheat oven to 180°C/160°C fan-forced. Grease 14cm x 21cm loaf pan.

2 Beat butter, rind, sugar, eggs, flour, yogurt and juice in medium bowl with electric mixer, on low speed, until just combined. Stir in fruit.

3 Pour mixture into pan; cover with a piece of pleated foil. Bake 1 hour 15 minutes; remove foil, bake further 15 minutes. Stand loaf 10 minutes; turn, top-side up, onto wire rack to cool. Serve at room temperature or toasted, with butter.

☐ **PER SERVING** 13.9g total fat (8.1g saturated fat); 2023kJ (484 cal); 74.8g carbohydrate; 9.6g protein; 9g fibre

What happened to my cake?

Just so you know that you're not alone, here's some comfort for the pain when you turn out a less-than-perfect cake.

CREAMED MIXTURE CURDLES

Can mean eggs and butter were too cold or the eggs added too slowly: beat only until egg is just combined before adding the next. If eggs were over 60g, omit one or use its yolk.

BUTTER CAKE CRUMBLES

Usually a result of over-creaming (beating butter and sugar together). Don't blend or process unless recipe specifies. Beat with electric mixer until pale and fluffy, however, the sugar does not have to be dissolved.

BUTTER CAKE STICKS TO PAN

Can happen if there is too much sugar, honey or golden syrup in the mixture. It is a good precaution to line with baking paper as well as to grease it to hold the paper in place.

FRUIT CAKE: FRUIT SINKS

Could be that the mixture was too soft to support the fruit (usually caused by over-creaming). Could be because fruit was wet, or not chopped small enough or, too much raising agent was used.

FRUIT CAKE: BOTTOM IS BURNT

Can happen because pan was not lined with enough layers of paper, see Paper & Foil page 549 (see also Preparing Cake Pans pages 572 & 573). Oven temperature could have been too high, or pan in wrong oven position.

SPONGE CAKE: SPECKLED TOP

Caused by sugar that wasn't dissolved when beaten with the eggs. Beat eggs until thick and creamy, then add sugar a little at a time, beating each addition until completely dissolved before adding more.

BUTTER CAKE RISES AND CRACKS

This can mean the oven was too hot or the pan too small. However, cakes baked in loaf, ring or bar pans normally crack slightly because of the confined space of the pan.

BUTTER CAKE FORMS A "COLLAR"

A "collar" around the top outside edge usually means the cake was baked at too high a temperature. Check the accuracy of your oven with an oven thermometer, and adjust the thermostat accordingly.

FRUIT CAKE: SINKS IN MIDDLE

Happens if self-raising flour was used instead of plain flour or too much bicarbonate of soda was added. Cake may not be cooked enough: test with a pointed knife for best results.

SPONGE CAKE IS FLAT AND TOUGH

Flour and liquid weren't folded in correctly. Sift flour twice first and sift over mixture again when adding. Folding means cutting down with the edge of a large metal spoon and lifting some bottom mixture up to the top.

SPONGE CAKE IS CRUSTY

Can come from baking at too high a temperature, or pan being too small or in the wrong oven position – the top of the cooked caked should be in the centre of the oven. Using high-sided pans protects the mixture and helps prevent crustiness.

SPONGE CAKE HAS SUNK

Can be caused by too high an oven temperature, too much sugar, not enough flour, too much liquid, eggs too large, too much raising agent, or, most commonly, insufficient baking.

Apple pecan cake with maple frosting

PREPARATION TIME 30 MINUTES **COOKING TIME** 50 MINUTES **SERVES** 12

Maple-flavoured syrup is just that – a pancake syrup made with sugar, glucose and caramel colouring. Use the more expensive pure maple syrup (distilled from the sap of the maple tree) for a stronger flavour in this recipe.

90g butter, softened

½ cup (80g) wholemeal self-raising flour

1 cup (150g) white self-raising flour

1 teaspoon ground cinnamon

¾ cup (150g) firmly packed brown sugar

¼ cup (60ml) maple-flavoured syrup

3 eggs

1 cup (125g) coarsely chopped pecans

½ cup (85g) coarsely chopped raisins

1 cup (170g) coarsely grated apple

½ cup (60g) pecans, roasted, extra

MAPLE FROSTING

90g butter, softened

1 cup (160g) icing sugar

1 teaspoon maple-flavoured syrup

1 Preheat oven to 180°C/160°C fan-forced. Grease 20cm ring pan; line base and sides with baking paper.

2 Beat butter, flours, cinnamon, sugar, syrup and eggs in medium bowl on low speed with electric mixer until ingredients are combined. Beat on medium speed until mixture is smooth and changed in colour.

3 Stir in nuts, raisins and apple. Spread mixture into pan.

4 Bake about 50 minutes. Stand cake 5 minutes then turn onto wire rack; turn cake top-side up to cool.

5 Make maple frosting; spread on cake, top with extra nuts.

MAPLE FROSTING Beat ingredients in small bowl with electric mixer until light and fluffy.

☐ **PER SERVING** 25.1g total fat (9.3g saturated fat); 1902kJ (455 cal); 50.4g carbohydrate; 5.5g protein; 3.1g fibre

Quince and blackberry crumble cake

PREPARATION TIME 30 MINUTES **COOKING TIME** 2 HOURS 15 MINUTES (PLUS COOLING TIME) **SERVES** 16

Quinces are an ancient fruit that went out of fashion for a while, but they're back on top these days and we love them. It's hard to choose what's the best quality of a quince – its flavour, texture or rosy colour (we take all three!).

185g unsalted butter, softened

¾ cup (165g) caster sugar

2 eggs

2¼ cups (335g) self-raising flour

¾ cup (180ml) milk

2 cups (300g) frozen blackberries

2 teaspoons cornflour

POACHED QUINCE

3 cups (750ml) water

¾ cup (165g) caster sugar

1 cinnamon stick

1 tablespoon lemon juice

3 medium quinces (1kg), each cut into 8 wedges

CINNAMON CRUMBLE

¾ cup (110g) plain flour

2 tablespoons caster sugar

½ cup (110g) firmly packed brown sugar

100g cold unsalted butter, chopped

1 teaspoon ground cinnamon

1 Make poached quince.

2 Preheat oven to 180°C/160°C fan-forced. Grease deep 23cm-square cake pan; line base and sides with baking paper.

3 Beat butter and sugar in small bowl with electric mixer until light and fluffy. Add eggs, one at a time, beating until just combined between additions; transfer to large bowl. Stir in sifted flour and milk, in two batches.

4 Spread mixture into pan; bake 25 minutes.

5 Meanwhile, blend or process ingredients for cinnamon crumble, pulsing until ingredients just come together.

6 Remove cake from oven. Working quickly, toss frozen blackberries in cornflour to coat. Top cake with drained quince then blackberries; sprinkle cinnamon crumble over fruit. Return to oven; bake 20 minutes. Stand cake 5 minutes; turn, top-side up, onto wire rack. Serve cake warm or cold with reserved quince syrup.

POACHED QUINCE Stir the water, sugar, cinnamon stick and juice in medium saucepan over low heat until sugar dissolves. Add quince; bring to a boil. Reduce heat, simmer, covered, about 1 hour 30 minutes or until quince is tender and rosy in colour. Cool quince in syrup to room temperature; strain quince over medium bowl. Reserve quince and syrup separately.

PER SERVING 16.4g total fat (10.1g saturated fat); 1685kJ (403 cal); 56.4g carbohydrate; 4.6g protein; 5.4g fibre

Gluten-free carrot cake with orange frosting

PREPARATION TIME 25 MINUTES **COOKING TIME** 1 HOUR (PLUS COOLING TIME) **SERVES** 6

1 cup (125g) soy flour or besan

¾ cup (110g) 100% maize cornflour

2 teaspoons gluten-free baking powder

1 teaspoon bicarbonate of soda

2 teaspoons mixed spice

1 cup (220g) firmly packed brown sugar

1½ cups (360g) coarsely grated carrot

1 cup (120g) coarsely chopped walnuts

½ cup (125ml) olive oil

½ cup (120g) sour cream

3 eggs

ORANGE FROSTING

125g cream cheese, softened

1 teaspoon finely grated orange rind

1½ cups (240g) pure icing sugar

Besan is flour made from chickpeas and can often be used instead of wheat flour. Pure icing sugar doesn't contain wheaten cornflour, so it must be used for this frosting to avoid gluten. You need about 3 medium carrots for this recipe.

1 Preheat oven to 160°C/140°C fan-forced. Grease deep 20cm-round cake pan; line base and side with baking paper.

2 Sift flours, baking powder, soda and spice into large bowl; stir in sugar, carrot and nuts. Stir in combined oil, sour cream and eggs until smooth. Pour mixture into pan.

3 Bake about 1 hour. Stand cake in pan 5 minutes; turn onto wire rack to cool.

4 Make orange frosting; spread on top of cake.

ORANGE FROSTING Beat cream cheese and rind in small bowl with electric mixer until light and fluffy. Gradually beat in sifted icing sugar until smooth.

PER SERVING 51.9g total fat (14.2g saturated fat); 4000kJ (957 cal); 107.7g carbohydrate; 13.6g protein; 5.4g fibre

Brown sugar sponge

Use the darkest brown sugar you can find; if it looks lumpy, push it through a sieve before using it as the small clumps can retain their shape during baking, and the result will be little puddles of syrup in the cake.

PREPARATION TIME 30 MINUTES **COOKING TIME** 20 MINUTES (PLUS COOLING TIME) **SERVES** 10

4 eggs

¾ cup (165g) firmly packed dark brown sugar

1 cup (150g) wheaten cornflour

1 teaspoon cream of tartar

½ teaspoon bicarbonate of soda

300ml thickened cream

PRALINE

⅓ cup (75g) white sugar

¼ cup (60ml) water

⅓ cup (45g) roasted hazelnuts

1 Preheat oven to 180°C/160°C fan-forced. Grease two deep 22cm-round cake pans.
2 Beat eggs and brown sugar in small bowl with electric mixer about 10 minutes or until thick and creamy; transfer to large bowl.
3 Sift cornflour, cream of tartar and soda twice onto paper then sift over egg mixture; gently fold dry ingredients into egg mixture. Divide mixture between pans; bake about 18 minutes. Turn sponges immediately onto baking-paper-covered wire racks to cool.
4 Meanwhile, make praline.
5 Beat cream in small bowl with electric mixer until firm peaks form; fold in praline. Place one sponge on serving plate; spread with half of the cream mixture. Top with remaining sponge; spread with remaining cream mixture.

PRALINE Stir sugar and the water in small saucepan over heat, without boiling, until sugar dissolves; bring to a boil. Reduce heat, simmer, uncovered, without stirring, about 10 minutes or until syrup is golden brown. Add hazelnuts; pour praline mixture onto baking-paper-covered tray. Cool about 15 minutes or until set. Break praline into pieces then blend or process until mixture is as fine (or coarse) as desired.

PER SERVING 16.1g total fat (8.1g saturated fat); 1300kJ (311 cal); 37.2g carbohydrate; 4g protein; 0.6g fibre

Hot cross buns

Working with yeast is interesting and rewarding. Hot cross buns are not difficult to make, but you do need to allow enough time between each stage. If you want to bake the buns in advance and freeze them, don't glaze them until after they're thawed and reheated.

PREPARATION TIME 1 HOUR (PLUS STANDING TIME) **COOKING TIME** 25 MINUTES (PLUS COOLING TIME) **MAKES** 16

2 x 7g sachets granulated yeast

¼ cup (55g) caster sugar

1½ cups (375ml) warm milk

4 cups (600g) plain flour

1 teaspoon mixed spice

½ teaspoon ground cinnamon

60g butter

1 egg

¾ cup (120g) sultanas

FLOUR PASTE FOR CROSSES

½ cup (75g) plain flour

2 teaspoons caster sugar

⅓ cup (80ml) water, approximately

GLAZE

1 tablespoon caster sugar

1 teaspoon gelatine

1 tablespoon water

1 Combine yeast, sugar and milk in small bowl or jug; cover, stand in warm place about 10 minutes or until mixture is frothy.

2 Sift flour and spices into large bowl, rub in butter. Stir in yeast mixture, egg and sultanas; mix to form a soft sticky dough. Cover; stand in warm place about 45 minutes or until dough has doubled in size.

3 Grease 23cm-square slab cake pan.

4 Turn dough onto floured surface, knead about 5 minutes or until smooth. Divide dough into 16 pieces, knead into balls. Place balls into pan; cover, stand in warm place 10 minutes or until buns have risen to top of pan.

5 Meanwhile, preheat oven to 220°C/200°C fan-forced.

6 Make flour paste for crosses; place in piping bag fitted with small plain tube, pipe crosses on buns.

7 Bake buns about 20 minutes or until well browned. Turn buns onto wire rack.

8 Make glaze; brush top of hot buns with hot glaze. Cool on wire rack.

FLOUR PASTE FOR CROSSES Combine flour and sugar in bowl. Gradually blend in enough of the water to form a smooth paste.

GLAZE Stir ingredients in small saucepan over heat, without boiling, until sugar and gelatine are dissolved.

▭ **PER SERVING** 4.9g total fat (2.8g saturated fat); 1024kJ (245 cal); 42.2g carbohydrate; 6.5g protein; 2.2g fibre

Kumara and pecan loaf

PREPARATION TIME 20 MINUTES **COOKING TIME** 1 HOUR 40 MINUTES **SERVES** 8

200g butter, softened

¾ cup (165g) firmly packed brown sugar

2 eggs

¾ cup (90g) coarsely chopped pecans

½ cup (40g) desiccated coconut

1 cup (400g) mashed kumara

1½ cups (225g) self-raising flour

½ cup (125ml) milk

1 Preheat oven to 170°C/150°C fan-forced. Grease 14cm x 21cm loaf pan; line base and long sides with baking paper, extending paper 2cm over sides.

2 Beat butter, sugar and eggs in small bowl with electric mixer until just combined; transfer mixture to large bowl. Stir in nuts, coconut and kumara. Stir in sifted flour and milk, in two batches.

3 Spread mixture into pan; bake about 1 hour 40 minutes. Stand loaf 10 minutes; turn, top-side up, onto wire rack to cool.

▭ **PER SERVING** 34.2g total fat (17.7g saturated fat); 1940kJ (464 cal); 30.7g carbohydrate; 7.5g protein; 3.9g fibre

Pumpkin can be substituted for kumara if you like but whichever vegetable you choose, since they both have a high water content, drain it well before mashing. Do not add any liquid or butter to the mash.

Festive fruit and nut cake

PREPARATION TIME 20 MINUTES **COOKING TIME** 1 HOUR 45 MINUTES (PLUS STANDING TIME) **SERVES** 12

½ cup (115g) coarsely chopped glacé pineapple

½ cup (125g) coarsely chopped glacé apricots

1½ cups (250g) seeded dried dates

½ cup (110g) red glacé cherries

½ cup (110g) green glacé cherries

1 cup (170g) brazil nuts

½ cup (75g) macadamia nuts

2 eggs

½ cup (110g) firmly packed brown sugar

1 tablespoon dark rum

100g butter, melted

⅓ cup (50g) plain flour

¼ cup (35g) self-raising flour

FRUIT AND NUT TOPPING

⅓ cup (75g) coarsely chopped glacé pineapple

¼ cup (55g) red glacé cherries, halved

¼ cup (55g) green glacé cherries, halved

¼ cup (40g) brazil nuts

¼ cup (35g) macadamia nuts

TOFFEE TOPPING

½ cup (110g) caster sugar

¼ cup (60ml) water

Stained glass, jewel, American, Canadian cake: all different names for what's evolved as one of our favourite cakes for the festive season. Mix and match the glacé fruit and nuts to suit your taste.

1 Preheat oven to 150°C/130°C fan-forced. Grease 20cm-ring pan; line base and side with baking paper, extending paper 5cm above side.

2 Combine fruit and nuts in large bowl.

3 Beat eggs and sugar in small bowl with electric mixer until thick. Add rum, butter and sifted flours; beat until just combined. Stir egg mixture into fruit mixture. Press mixture firmly into pan.

4 Make fruit and nut topping; gently press topping evenly over cake mixture.

5 Bake, covered, 1 hour. Uncover; bake further 45 minutes. Stand cake in pan 10 minutes.

6 Meanwhile, make toffee topping. Turn cake, top-side up, onto wire rack; drizzle with toffee topping.

FRUIT AND NUT TOPPING Combine ingredients in medium bowl.

TOFFEE TOPPING Stir ingredients in small saucepan over heat without boiling until sugar dissolves; bring to a boil. Reduce heat, simmer, uncovered, without stirring, about 10 minutes or until mixture is golden. Remove from heat; stand until bubbles subside before using.

▭ **PER SERVING** 26.9g total fat (8.3g saturated fat); 2495kJ (597 cal); 79.1g carbohydrate; 5.9g protein; 5.5g fibre

Spiced fig and orange cheesecake

PREPARATION TIME 20 MINUTES **COOKING TIME** 1 HOUR 15 MINUTES (PLUS REFRIGERATION TIME)
SERVES 12

Mascarpone, a fresh soft cream cheese of Italian origin, is made with cultured cow milk, a bit like yogurt. It's mostly served with fruit or used in dessert-making, but a spoon of it stirred into a risotto just before serving adds a wonderful rich depth. It doesn't tolerate too much beating.

½ cup (80g) brazil nuts

125g plain sweet biscuits

80g butter, melted

1 cup (250ml) orange juice

1¼ cups (250g) finely chopped dried figs

1 cinnamon stick

pinch ground clove

250g cream cheese, softened

1 tablespoon finely grated orange rind

¾ cup (165g) caster sugar

1 cup (250g) mascarpone cheese

2 eggs, separated

1 Grease 22cm springform tin.

2 Process nuts and biscuits until fine. Add butter; process until combined. Press mixture over base of tin. Place tin on oven tray; refrigerate 30 minutes.

3 Preheat oven to 160°C/140°C fan-forced.

4 Combine juice, figs, cinnamon and clove in small saucepan; simmer, uncovered, 10 minutes or until most of the juice has been absorbed. Discard cinnamon stick. Spread fig mixture over crumb base in tin.

5 Beat cheese, rind and sugar in medium bowl with electric mixer until smooth. Add mascarpone and yolks; beat only until combined.

6 Beat egg whites in small bowl with electric mixer until soft peaks form; fold into cheese mixture. Pour over fig mixture.

7 Bake about 1¼ hours. Cool in oven with door ajar. Refrigerate 3 hours or overnight. Serve dusted with sifted icing sugar, if desired.

▭ **PER SERVING** 29.5g total fat (16.9g saturated fat); 1840kJ (440 cal); 35.8g carbohydrate; 6.4g protein; 3.8g fibre

---

New york cheesecake

PREPARATION TIME 20 MINUTES (PLUS REFRIGERATION TIME)
COOKING TIME 1 HOUR 35 MINUTES (PLUS REFRIGERATION TIME) **SERVES** 12

In America, they use graham crackers for this cheesecake's crust. Blend 125g shredded wheatmeal biscuits and 125g marie biscuits, processed until fine, and you'll have a crust that's close to the equivalent flavour and texture of graham crackers.

250g plain sweet biscuits

125g butter, melted

750g cream cheese, softened

2 teaspoons finely grated orange rind

1 teaspoon finely grated lemon rind

1 cup (220g) caster sugar

3 eggs

¾ cup (180g) sour cream

¼ cup (60ml) lemon juice

SOUR CREAM TOPPING

1 cup (240g) sour cream

2 tablespoons caster sugar

2 teaspoons lemon juice

534 **KITCHEN** | THE CAKE PAN

1 Grease 24cm springform tin. Process biscuits until fine. Add butter, process until combined. Press mixture over base and side of tin. Place tin on oven tray. Refrigerate 30 minutes.

2 Preheat oven to 180°C/160°C fan-forced.

3 Beat cheese, rinds and sugar in medium bowl with electric mixer until smooth. Beat in eggs, one at a time, beating until just combined between additions. Beat in cream and juice.

4 Pour filling into tin; bake 1¼ hours. Remove from oven; cool 15 minutes.

5 Make sour cream topping; spread over cheesecake. Bake 20 minutes; cool in oven with door ajar. Refrigerate cheesecake 3 hours or overnight.

SOUR CREAM TOPPING Combine ingredients in small bowl.

☐ **PER SERVING** 35.9g total fat (22.8g saturated fat); 1873kJ (448 cal); 24.2g carbohydrate; 7.8g protein; 0g fibre

Double chocolate mousse cheesecake

PREPARATION TIME 20 MINUTES (PLUS REFRIGERATION TIME)
COOKING TIME 5 MINUTES (PLUS REFRIGERATION TIME) **SERVES** 12

We used un-iced biscuits for this recipe. Make sure the gelatine mixture and melted dark chocolate are at about the same temperature – cool, but not set – before adding them to the cream cheese mixture.

125g plain chocolate biscuits

75g butter, melted

3 teaspoons gelatine

¼ cup (60ml) water

500g cream cheese, softened

½ cup (110g) caster sugar

2 eggs, separated

1 cup (250ml) cream

150g dark eating chocolate, melted

100g white eating chocolate, melted

2 tablespoons cream, extra

150g dark eating chocolate, melted, extra

1 Line 22cm springform tin with plastic wrap.

2 Process biscuits until fine. Add butter; process until combined. Press mixture over base of tin. Refrigerate 30 minutes.

3 Sprinkle gelatine over the water in small heatproof jug; stand jug in small saucepan of simmering water. Stir until gelatine dissolves; cool 5 minutes.

4 Beat cheese, sugar and egg yolks in medium bowl with electric mixer until smooth; beat in cream. Stir in dark chocolate and gelatine mixture.

5 Beat egg whites in small bowl with electric mixer until soft peaks form; fold into cheese mixture. Pour filling into tin.

6 Combine white chocolate and extra cream in small jug. Swirl white chocolate mixture through cheesecake mixture. Refrigerate overnight.

7 Spread dark chocolate over baking paper to a 20cm square. When set, break chocolate into small pieces.

8 Remove cheesecake from tin to serving plate. Press chocolate pieces around side of cheesecake.

☐ **PER SERVING** 41.9g total fat (26.2g saturated fat); 2341kJ (560 cal); 38g carbohydrate; 8.4g protein; 0.5g fibre

Celebration fruit cake

PREPARATION TIME 20 MINUTES (PLUS STANDING TIME)

COOKING TIME 3 HOURS 30 MINUTES (PLUS COOLING TIME) **SERVES** 36

3 cups (500g) sultanas

1¾ cups (300g) raisins, halved

1¾ cups (300g) seeded dried dates, chopped finely

1 cup (150g) dried currants

⅔ cup (110g) mixed peel

⅔ cup (150g) glacé cherries, halved

¼ cup (55g) coarsely chopped glacé pineapple

¼ cup (60g) coarsely chopped glacé apricots

½ cup (125ml) dark rum

250g butter, softened

1 cup (220g) firmly packed brown sugar

5 eggs

1½ cups (225g) plain flour

⅓ cup (50g) self-raising flour

1 teaspoon mixed spice

2 tablespoons dark rum, extra

1 Combine fruit and rum in large bowl; mix well; cover tightly with plastic wrap. Store mixture in cool, dark place overnight or up to a week, stirring every day.

2 Preheat oven to 150°C/130°C fan-forced. Line deep 22cm-round or deep 19cm-square cake pan with three thicknesses of baking paper, extending paper 5cm above side.

3 Beat butter and sugar in small bowl with electric mixer until just combined. Add eggs, one at a time, beating only until combined between additions.

4 Add butter mixture to fruit mixture; mix well. Mix in sifted dry ingredients; spread mixture evenly into pan. Bake about 3½ hours.

5 Brush cake with extra rum. Cover hot cake, in pan, tightly with foil; cool overnight.

⬜ **PER SERVING** 6.7g total fat (4g saturated fat); 1083kJ (258 cal); 42.9g carbohydrate; 2.7g protein; 2.5g fibre

Chocolate caramel slice

PREPARATION TIME 20 MINUTES (PLUS COOLING AND REFRIGERATION TIME) **COOKING TIME** 25 MINUTES

MAKES 16

½ cup (75g) self-raising flour

½ cup (75g) plain flour

1 cup (80g) desiccated coconut

125g butter, melted

1 cup (220g) firmly packed brown sugar

30g butter, extra

395g can sweetened condensed milk

2 tablespoons golden syrup

200g dark eating chocolate, chopped coarsely

2 teaspoons vegetable oil

1 Preheat oven to 180°C/160°C fan-forced. Grease 20cm x 30cm lamington pan; line with baking paper, extending paper 5cm over long sides.

2 Combine sifted flours, coconut, butter and sugar in medium bowl; press mixture evenly over base of pan. Bake about 15 minutes or until browned lightly.

3 Meanwhile, stir extra butter, condensed milk and syrup in small saucepan over medium heat 15 minutes or until caramel mixture is golden brown; pour over hot base. Bake 10 minutes; cool.

4 Stir chocolate and oil in small saucepan over low heat until smooth; pour over caramel. Refrigerate 3 hours or overnight.

⬚ **PER PIECE** 17.7g total fat (11.8g saturated fat); 1492kJ (357 cal); 44.6g carbohydrate; 4.1g protein; 1.2g fibre

Raspberry coconut slice

PREPARATION TIME 25 MINUTES (PLUS COOLING TIME) **COOKING TIME** 40 MINUTES **MAKES** 16

90g butter

½ cup (110g) caster sugar

1 egg

¼ cup (35g) self-raising flour

⅔ cup (100g) plain flour

1 tablespoon custard powder

⅔ cup (220g) raspberry jam

COCONUT TOPPING

2 cups (160g) desiccated coconut

¼ cup (55g) caster sugar

2 eggs, beaten lightly

1 Preheat oven to 180°C/160°C fan-forced. Grease 20cm x 30cm lamington pan; line base with baking paper, extending paper 5cm over long sides.

2 Beat butter, sugar and egg in small bowl with electric mixer until light and fluffy. Transfer to medium bowl; stir in sifted flours and custard powder. Spread into pan; spread with jam.

3 Make coconut topping; sprinkle over jam. Bake about 40 minutes; cool in pan.

COCONUT TOPPING Combine ingredients in small bowl.

⬚ **PER PIECE** 12.2g total fat (9.1g saturated fat); 970kJ (232 cal); 26.7g carbohydrate; 2.8g protein; 2g fibre

Craisin and pistachio muesli slice

PREPARATION TIME 20 MINUTES **COOKING TIME** 20 MINUTES **MAKES** 30

125g butter

⅓ cup (75g) firmly packed brown sugar

2 tablespoons honey

1½ cups (135g) rolled oats

½ cup (75g) self-raising flour

1 cup (130g) craisins

1 cup (140g) roasted pistachios, chopped coarsely

Kids will love this slice, plus it's quick and easy to make – all the mixing is done in one saucepan. Craisins are dehydrated cranberries; you can replace them with sultanas or chopped raisins, if you prefer.

1 Preheat oven to 180°C/160°C fan-forced. Grease 20cm x 30cm lamington pan; line base and two long sides with baking paper, extending paper 2cm above long sides.

2 Melt butter with sugar and honey in medium saucepan over medium heat; stir, without boiling, until sugar is dissolved. Stir in remaining ingredients.

3 Press mixture firmly into pan; bake about 20 minutes. Cool in pan before cutting.

☐ **PER PIECE** 6.2g total fat (2.6g saturated fat); 431kJ (103 cal); 9.7g carbohydrate; 1.7g protein; 6.2g fibre

Date slice

PREPARATION TIME 1 HOUR (PLUS REFRIGERATION TIME) **COOKING TIME** 25 MINUTES **MAKES** 24

1½ cups (225g) plain flour

1¼ cups (185g) self-raising flour

150g cold butter, chopped

1 tablespoon honey

1 egg

⅓ cup (80ml) milk, approximately

2 teaspoons milk, extra

1 tablespoon white sugar

DATE FILLING

3½ cups (500g) dried dates, chopped coarsely

¾ cup (180ml) water

2 tablespoons finely grated lemon rind

2 tablespoons lemon juice

The pastry for this slice is slightly cakey, due to the use of self-raising flour. It's also a good pastry for any type of fruit pie, providing the filling is not too wet.

1 Grease 20cm x 30cm lamington pan; line base with baking paper, extending paper 5cm over long sides.

2 Sift flours into large bowl; rub in butter. Stir in combined honey and egg and enough milk to make a firm dough. Knead on floured surface until smooth. Cover; refrigerate 30 minutes.

3 Meanwhile, make date filling.

4 Preheat oven to 200°C/180°C fan-forced.

5 Divide dough in half. Roll one half large enough to cover base of pan; press into pan, spread filling over dough. Roll remaining dough large enough to cover filling. Brush with extra milk; sprinkle with sugar. Bake about 20 minutes; cool in pan.

DATE FILLING Cook ingredients in medium saucepan, stirring, about 10 minutes or until thick and smooth. Cool to room temperature.

☐ **PER PIECE** 5.7g total fat (3.6g saturated fat); 757kJ (181 cal); 28.2g carbohydrate; 2.6g protein; 2.7g fibre

THE
SOUFFLE DISH

The Soufflé Dish

There are practical reasons behind the design of the classic soufflé dish. The straight, rather deep side allows the soufflé mixture to rise freely and supports it as it does so, and the indented rim allows the traditional paper collar to be tied securely. The classic dish is made from porcelain, which is thinner than ordinary ovenware so that heat can penetrate readily. The dish may also be made from ovenproof glass. Soufflés got their reputation for being difficult and temperamental in the days before thermostatically controlled ovens. Today, anyone with a reliable oven can provide the correct, steady heat needed, and a soufflé is no harder to make than a cake.

TYPES OF SOUFFLE

Traditional soufflés are based on a thick, flavoured sauce – like an ordinary white sauce only thicker – enriched with egg yolks. The egg whites, beaten to a soft peak with a droopy top, are folded in, and when the mixture is baked, the air trapped in the beaten whites expands and the soufflé puffs. This type of soufflé is gossamer-light with a silken richness. Another style is made by folding the egg whites directly into a fruit or vegetable puree; this type of soufflé is very airy and fragile.

MAKING A SOUFFLE

There are three stages in making a soufflé: preparing the dish, making the base, and adding the beaten egg whites followed immediately by baking. If it suits you, you can space these stages as much as a day apart. Making a soufflé doesn't call for any special skill, but it is helpful to understand the procedure in detail before you start.

PREPARING THE SOUFFLE DISH

Generously butter or oil the soufflé dish (or dishes). For a savoury soufflé, you can also coat the base and side with fine dry breadcrumbs, finely grated parmesan cheese, or a mixture of the two. For a sweet soufflé, coat with caster sugar. Remove excess crumbs or sugar. If you are preparing a dish for a sweet soufflé ahead of time, don't coat with sugar until shortly before baking as the sugar may weep if left to stand.

Traditionally, a paper collar is tied round the dish standing 5cm above the rim; this prevents the soufflé from toppling over as it rises. Cut a doubled strip of baking paper about 8cm wide and long enough to go round the dish with a 7 to 8cm overlap; butter or oil it then tie it securely under the rim with kitchen string, making a single bow for quick removal. If coating the dish with crumbs or sugar, do collar and dish together. If using a collar, you can fill the dish right to the top with the soufflé mixture.

You don't have to use a collar: in this case, fill the dish a good three-quarters full so the side of the dish supports the soufflé as it begins to rise. The top then puffs into a shape like a billowing cloud, as opposed to the higher straight sides and puffy top of a collared soufflé.

PREPARING THE MIXTURE AND BAKING

The following instructions are given as though you are going to make and bake the soufflé in one operation. As mentioned above, you may choose to make the base up to a day ahead, in which case, you will not, of course, preheat the oven until needed and should cover and refrigerate the base until required. Remove from the refrigerator an hour ahead of time and stand it in a bowl of warm water to warm it.

Place the oven rack in the lower half of the oven, making sure you've allowed enough room for the soufflé to rise (remove any shelves above the soufflé) and to allow for quick and easy removal. Place a flat oven tray on the shelf; preheat the oven as directed.

Ensure that all utensils to be used for separating and beating the eggs are completely dry and grease-free as any grease will prevent the egg whites from beating up properly. Use a copper, china or glass bowl for beating egg whites as plastic can hold hidden grease. You can use a wire balloon whisk or electric beaters.

Separate the eggs, ensuring no speck of yolk gets into the whites as this will prevent their beating up.

Make the soufflé base and, if the recipe directs, beat in the egg yolks. Transfer the mixture into a large, wide bowl. Have a large metal spoon and a rubber spatula on hand.

In another large bowl, beat the egg whites as directed in the recipe, turning the bowl and reaching into all parts of the mixture, until the whites form soft peaks. They are beaten to the right consistency when, if you gather a little of the mixture on the whisk, it stands in a soft peak with a droopy top. Don't beat past this stage, as the whites will start to lose their elasticity, which enables them to expand without breaking.

Stir a big spoonful of beaten egg whites into the base mixture to loosen it and then, with the spatula, scrape the rest of the whites onto the surface of the base mixture. Fold in the egg whites by cutting down with the edge of the spoon and lifting some of the mixture up and over, turning the bowl a little each time. This should take only a minute or so. Don't be too thorough – it's all right to have small pockets of egg white remaining, as the mixture will blend a little more as you turn it into the soufflé dish.

Pour mixture into the prepared dish, tap the dish a couple of times on the work surface to expel any large air pockets, then smooth the top. Place on the heated oven tray and close the oven door gently (reduce oven temperature if recipe states).

Bake until soufflé is well puffed up, golden-brown on top and just firm. Place on a warmed serving plate, remove the collar if used, and take immediately to the table. If making individual soufflés, for any but a formal meal, you can take them to the table on warmed serving plates with their collars on, and let the diners remove them. Have a basket ready for the papers and string. To serve a large soufflé, have a warmed serving spoon and fork ready, hold vertically and spread top of soufflé apart; give each diner some of the crust and some of the creamy centre.

Make the crêpes ahead of time – up to weeks ahead since they freeze well, wrapped with a piece of waxed or freezer paper between each, sealed airtight in a zip lock bag. This makes their presentation quick, easy – and even more impressive.

Cheese and crêpe soufflés

PREPARATION TIME 20 MINUTES (PLUS STANDING TIME) **COOKING TIME** 50 MINUTES **SERVES** 6

⅓ cup (50g) plain flour

1 egg

1 egg yolk

20g butter, melted

½ cup (125ml) milk

1 tablespoon finely chopped fresh garlic chives

1 large red capsicum (350g)

1 clove garlic, crushed

½ cup (125ml) cream

CHEESE SOUFFLE

30g butter

2 tablespoons plain flour

1 cup (250ml) milk

4 eggs, separated

¼ cup (30g) finely grated gruyère cheese

¼ cup (20g) finely grated parmesan cheese

¼ teaspoon cayenne pepper

1 Sift flour into small bowl; make well in centre. Gradually whisk in combined egg and egg yolk, butter and milk; strain batter into small jug. Stir in chives. Cover; stand crêpe batter 30 minutes.

2 Meanwhile, quarter capsicum, remove and discard seeds and membranes. Roast under preheated grill or in very hot oven, skin-side up, until skin blisters and blackens. Cover capsicum pieces with plastic or paper for 5 minutes, peel away skin; chop coarsely. Blend capsicum with garlic and cream until mixture is smooth. Pour into small saucepan; stand at room temperature while making soufflés.

3 Heat oiled crêpe pan or 20cm heavy-based frying pan; pour about 2 tablespoons of the batter into pan, tilting pan so batter coats base evenly. Cook over low heat, loosening edge with spatula until crêpe is browned lightly. Turn crêpe; cook until browned on other side. Turn crêpe onto wire rack; repeat process with remaining batter to make six crêpes.

4 Preheat oven to 220°C/200°C fan-forced. Make cheese soufflé.

5 Oil six ¾-cup (180ml) soufflé dishes; place on oven tray. Gently push one crêpe into each of the soufflé dishes to line base and side. Divide soufflé mixture among crêpe "cases"; bake, uncovered, about 20 minutes or until browned lightly. Working quickly, carefully turn soufflés onto serving plates; turn top-side up, drizzle with reheated capsicum sauce. Serve immediately.

CHEESE SOUFFLE Melt butter in small saucepan, add flour; cook, stirring, until mixture thickens and bubbles. Gradually stir in milk; cook, stirring until sauce boils and thickens. Transfer mixture to large bowl, stir in egg yolks, cheeses and pepper; cool 5 minutes. Meanwhile, beat egg whites in small bowl with electric mixer until soft peaks form. Fold egg whites into cheese mixture, in two batches.

▭ **PER SERVING** 26.4g total fat (15.4g saturated fat); 1459kJ (349 cal); 14.4g carbohydrate; 13.5g protein; 1.1g fibre

Potato soufflés

PREPARATION TIME 15 MINUTES **COOKING TIME** 40 MINUTES **SERVES** 4

350g medium potatoes, peeled, chopped coarsely

2 tablespoons packaged breadcrumbs

60g butter

2 tablespoons plain flour

¾ cup (180ml) milk

3 eggs, separated

⅓ cup (90g) coarsely grated cheddar cheese

1 teaspoon fresh thyme leaves

1 Boil, steam or microwave potato until tender; drain. Mash potato in large bowl.

2 Preheat oven to 220°C/200°C fan-forced. Oil four ¾-cup (180ml) soufflé dishes; sprinkle bases and sides with breadcrumbs, shake out excess. Place dishes on oven tray.

3 Melt butter in medium saucepan, add flour; cook, stirring, until mixture thickens and bubbles. Gradually add milk, stirring until mixture boils and thickens; remove from heat. Stir in egg yolks, cheese, thyme and potato, until smooth. Return potato mixture to same large bowl.

4 Beat egg whites in small bowl with electric mixer until soft peaks form. Fold whites into potato mixture, in two batches. Spoon mixture into dishes; bake about 20 minutes or until browned lightly and puffed.

◻ **PER SERVING** 25.9g total fat (15.3g saturated fat); 1542kJ (369 cal); 18.6g carbohydrate; 15.2g protein; 1.6g fibre

---

Gruyère soufflé

PREPARATION TIME 15 MINUTES **COOKING TIME** 40 MINUTES **SERVES** 4

⅓ cup (50g) plain flour

1⅔ cups (410ml) milk

20g butter

6 eggs, separated

1⅓ cups (165g) coarsely grated gruyère cheese

100g sliced smoked salmon

1½ teaspoons baby capers, rinsed, drained

1 tablespoon finely chopped fresh chervil

1 Preheat oven to 220°C/200°C fan-forced. Oil 2-litre (8-cup) soufflé dish; place on oven tray.

2 Place flour in small saucepan, gradually whisk in milk until smooth. Whisk over heat, until mixture boils and thickens. Remove from heat. Stir in butter, then egg yolks and cheese. Transfer to large bowl.

3 Beat egg whites in medium bowl with electric mixer until soft peaks form. Fold whites into cheese mixture, in two batches. Pour into dish; bake about 35 minutes or until soufflé is browned and puffed.

4 Serve soufflé immediately, accompanied with salmon topped with capers and chervil.

◻ **PER SERVING** 33.5g total fat (18.5g saturated fat); 2048kJ (490 cal); 14.5g carbohydrate; 32.4g protein; 0.5g fibre

Goat cheese soufflé with creamed spinach sauce

PREPARATION TIME 15 MINUTES **COOKING TIME** 25 MINUTES (PLUS COOLING TIME) **SERVES** 6

¼ cup (25g) packaged breadcrumbs

30g butter

2 tablespoons plain flour

1 cup (250ml) milk

4 eggs, separated

¼ teaspoon cayenne pepper

150g firm goat cheese, crumbled

CREAMED SPINACH SAUCE

180g baby spinach leaves

⅔ cup (160ml) cream, warmed

It's important to use a crumbly, fairly dry goat cheese here because a really creamy one will upset the fat content of the recipe.

1 Preheat oven to 220°C/200°C fan-forced. Oil six 1-cup (250ml) soufflé dishes, sprinkle with breadcrumbs; shake out excess. Place dishes on oven tray.

2 Melt butter in small saucepan, add flour; cook, stirring, until mixture bubbles and thickens. Gradually add milk; stir until mixture boils and thickens. Transfer to large bowl; stir in egg yolks, pepper and cheese; cool 5 minutes.

3 Beat egg whites in small bowl with electric mixer until soft peaks form; fold whites into cheese mixture, in two batches. Divide mixture among dishes.

4 Bake about 15 minutes or until soufflés are puffed and browned lightly.

5 Meanwhile, make creamed spinach sauce.

6 Serve soufflés immediately with spinach sauce.

CREAMED SPINACH SAUCE Boil, steam or microwave spinach until wilted; drain. Squeeze out excess liquid. Blend or process spinach until almost smooth. With motor operating, gradually add cream; process until smooth.

▭ **PER SERVING** 26g total fat (15.2g saturated fat); 1313kJ (314 cal); 8.8g carbohydrate; 11.4g protein; 1.1g fibre

Paper & foil

Two things that you always have in the pantry, paper and foil, transform into helpful cooking tools in a flash.

MAKING A SOUFFLE COLLAR
Cut a strip of baking paper wide and long enough to go around outside of dish with an overlap. Fold in half lengthways, grease it and tie under dish rim with string.

KEEPING CASSEROLES MOIST
Baking paper, cut to the shape of the pan or dish and laid over the surface of the food, such as a casserole will help keep the food moist and reduce evaporation. This is called a cartouche.

MAKING AN EN PAPILLOTE CASE
Fold baking paper in half, cut a half-heart shape big enough to enclose food; place food inside near fold. Secure parcel by making overlapping folds all round; twist end to close.

WRAPPING VEGETABLES
To cook potatoes and other vegetables in a covered barbecue, oven or campfire, scrub or prepare as you wish, brush all over with oil or melted butter, season, wrap in doubled aluminium foil and cook over high heat until soft.

SHIELDING FOODS FROM HEAT WITH FOIL
To shield food from excess browning or drying out (such as the end of chicken drumsticks), cover with aluminium foil. Shiny-side out, it will reflect heat away from the food; dull-side out, it will gently absorb heat to cook without burning.

USING FOIL IN HEAT
Foil will stand high temperatures, so it is useful for such jobs as baking vegetables or lining an oven rack to catch any spills from a casserole. However, when frozen it sticks to food, so use freezer bags or plastic wrap instead.

LINING A FRUIT CAKE PAN
Cut two pieces of brown paper and one piece of baking paper to line the base of pan, then cut two pieces of brown paper and one of baking paper to line side(s).

USING EDIBLE RICE PAPER
Used for treats such as macaroons – they can be baked on this paper – or to enclose nougat. It's available in specialty cookware shops. Not to be confused with rice paper for wrapping (see Using rice paper for wrapping).

USING RICE PAPER FOR WRAPPING
Dip edible rice paper, one at a time, into warm water until pliable. Place on a board, pat dry with absorbent paper or a clean tea towel; place filling across corner, fold in sides and roll up tightly.

MAKING A PAPER CONE FOR PIPING (1)
Cut a square of baking or greaseproof paper, fold in half diagonally to form a triangle. Bring one sharp point of the triangle over to meet the right-angle, making a cone shape, then roll the other side round it to make a tight cone.

MAKING A PAPER CONE FOR PIPING (2)
Fold in points at top, making a firm crease to hold the cone in shape, secure with a paperclip, or staple (sticky tape if using greaseproof paper) half-fill bag and snip off point for piping.

MAKING CHOCOLATE DECORATIONS
For chocolate decorations that are to be placed on a dessert, pipe melted chocolate, or trail it from a pointed spoon, on to baking paper in spirals, trellis, squiggles or other designs, refrigerate until needed then peel paper off and position decoration.

Frozen citrus yogurt cheesecakes

PREPARATION TIME 20 MINUTES (PLUS FREEZING TIME) **SERVES** 6

500g cream cheese, softened

1 cup (220g) caster sugar

3 cups (800g) vanilla yogurt

1 tablespoon finely grated lemon rind

1 tablespoon finely grated lime rind

½ cup (120ml) orange juice

⅓ cup (80ml) lemon juice

2 tablespoons lime juice

orange food colouring

⅓ cup (25g) shredded coconut, toasted

Toast coconut by stirring constantly over low to medium heat in a heavy-based frying pan until it is just an even golden colour. Remove the coconut from the pan immediately or it will continue to toast and darken unattractively.

1 Place a collar of foil around six ¾-cup (180ml) soufflé dishes; secure with string.

2 Beat cheese and sugar in medium bowl with electric mixer until smooth. Gradually add yogurt; beat until smooth. Stir in rinds, juices and enough food colouring to tint mixture pale orange.

3 Divide mixture among dishes. Cover loosely with plastic wrap; freeze overnight.

4 Remove cheesecakes from freezer; stand 5 minutes. Remove collars; press coconut around sides of cheesecakes. Freeze 5 minutes before serving.

PER SERVING 34.9g total fat (23g saturated fat); 2458kJ (588 cal); 54.3g carbohydrate; 14.2g protein; 0.8g fibre

Passionfruit soufflés

PREPARATION TIME 10 MINUTES **COOKING TIME** 15 MINUTES **SERVES** 4

1 tablespoon caster sugar

2 egg yolks

⅓ cup (80ml) fresh passionfruit pulp

2 tablespoons orange-flavoured liqueur

½ cup (80g) icing sugar

4 egg whites

2 teaspoons icing sugar, extra

It's important to use fresh – not canned – passionfruit. If you don't like the texture of the seeds, strain the pulp into a small bowl, pushing it with the back of a spoon to extract as much juice as possible. You will have to use a few more passionfruits – six or seven should do it – to obtain the required amount but you'll still have all the flavour and colour.

1 Preheat oven to 200°C/180°C fan-forced. Grease four 1-cup (250ml) soufflé dishes; sprinkle bases and sides with caster sugar, shake away excess. Place dishes on oven tray.

2 Whisk yolks, passionfruit pulp, liqueur and 2 tablespoons of the icing sugar in large bowl until mixture is combined.

3 Beat egg whites in small bowl with electric mixer until soft peaks form. Gradually add remaining icing sugar; beat until firm peaks form. Fold egg white mixture into passionfruit mixture, in two batches; divide mixture among dishes.

4 Bake about 12 minutes or until puffed and browned lightly. Serve immediately, dusted with extra sifted icing sugar.

PER SERVING 2.9g total fat (0.9g saturated fat); 794kJ (190 cal); 29.7g carbohydrate; 5.8g protein; 2.8g fibre

Chilled caramel soufflés with walnut praline

PREPARATION TIME 25 MINUTES (PLUS REFRIGERATION TIME) **SERVES** 4

3 eggs, separated

½ cup (110g) firmly packed brown sugar

1 tablespoon gelatine

¼ cup (60ml) water

⅓ cup (115g) golden syrup

300ml thickened cream, whipped

WALNUT PRALINE

¼ cup (55g) caster sugar

¼ cup (25g) walnut pieces

1 Place a collar of foil around four ½-cup (125ml) soufflé dishes, secure with string. Brush inside of foil lightly with oil.

2 Beat egg yolks and sugar in heatproof bowl over simmering water until thick and creamy.

3 Sprinkle gelatine over the water in small jug; stand in small saucepan of simmering water, stir until dissolved. Stir gelatine mixture into egg mixture with golden syrup, stir over simmering water until combined. Remove mixture from heat, transfer to large bowl. Cover; cool.

4 Fold cream into caramel mixture. Beat egg whites in small bowl with electric mixer until soft peaks form; fold into caramel mixture. Pour mixture into dishes; refrigerate until set.

5 Meanwhile, make walnut praline. Remove collars, roll sides of soufflés in praline.

WALNUT PRALINE Melt sugar in small heavy-based frying pan over heat; do not stir. When sugar starts to brown, stir gently to dissolve. Place nuts on greased oven tray, pour hot toffee evenly over nuts. When set, break into pieces; blend or process until finely ground.

▭ **PER SERVING** 37.3g total fat (19.9g saturated fat); 2521kJ (603 cal); 56.3g carbohydrate; 10.6g protein; 0.5g fibre

Making a toffee or caramel relies on evaporating the water. This method, where no water is added, is easy – just move the sugar around by tilting the pan as the sugar melts and browns. Remember that the heat from the pan will continue to caramelise the sugar so take it off the heat a little before the sugar is as dark as you want it.

Tangy lemon soufflé

PREPARATION TIME 15 MINUTES **COOKING TIME** 40 MINUTES **SERVES** 4

90g butter, softened

1 tablespoon finely grated lemon rind

⅓ cup (75g) caster sugar

1 tablespoon plain flour

1 tablespoon cornflour

2 tablespoons lemon juice

1 cup (250ml) warm milk

4 eggs, separated

2 egg whites

1 tablespoon icing sugar

1 Preheat oven to 180°C/160°C fan-forced. Grease 1 litre (4-cup) soufflé dish; place on oven tray.

2 Beat butter, rind and caster sugar in small bowl with electric mixer until light and fluffy. Beat in sifted flours and juice; stir in milk. Transfer mixture to medium saucepan, stir over heat until mixture boils and thickens. Transfer mixture to large bowl; stir in egg yolks.

3 Beat all egg whites in medium bowl with electric mixer until soft peaks form; fold into lemon mixture in two batches. Pour into dish; bake about 35 minutes or until puffed and browned. Serve immediately dusted with sifted icing sugar.

▭ **PER SERVING** 17.5g total fat (10.3g saturated fat); 1074kJ (257 cal); 17.9g carbohydrate; 7.4g protein; 0.2g fibre

Try using orange, tangelo, mandarin or grapefruit instead of the lemon flavours. Lime will work, too, but it is best when mixed with equal parts lemon.

Chocolate soufflés

PREPARATION TIME 15 MINUTES **COOKING TIME** 20 MINUTES **SERVES** 4

⅓ cup (75g) caster sugar

50g butter

1 tablespoon plain flour

200g dark eating chocolate, melted

2 eggs, separated

2 egg whites

1 tablespoon cocoa powder

1 Preheat oven to 180°C/160°C fan-forced. Grease four ¾-cup (180ml) soufflé dishes. Sprinkle inside of dishes with a little of the sugar; shake away excess. Place dishes on oven tray.

2 Melt butter in small saucepan, add flour; cook, stirring, about 2 minutes or until mixture thickens and bubbles. Remove from heat; stir in chocolate and egg yolks. Transfer to large bowl.

3 Beat all egg whites in small bowl with electric mixer until soft peaks form. Gradually add remaining sugar, beating until sugar dissolves. Fold egg white mixture into chocolate mixture, in two batches.

4 Divide soufflé mixture among dishes; bake 15 minutes. Serve immediately, dusted with sifted cocoa powder.

▭ **PER SERVING** 27.1g total fat (16.1g saturated fat); 2040kJ (488 cal); 52.3g carbohydrate; 8.1g protein; 0.7g fibre

Cocoa powders vary greatly in quality with, generally, the more expensive cocoas being richer and smoother to the taste. Aromatic dutch (or continental) processed cocoa is very dark and gives results with a deep colour and rich flavour.

Apricot and honey soufflés

PREPARATION TIME 15 MINUTES **COOKING TIME** 30 MINUTES **SERVES** 6

¼ cup (55g) caster sugar

4 fresh medium apricots (200g)

¼ cup (60ml) water

2 tablespoons honey

4 egg whites

1 tablespoon icing sugar

1 Preheat oven to 180°C/160°C fan-forced. Grease six ¾-cup (180ml) soufflé dishes. Sprinkle inside of dishes with a little of the caster sugar; shake away excess. Place dishes on oven tray.

2 Place apricots in small heatproof bowl, cover with boiling water; stand 2 minutes. Drain; cool 5 minutes. Peel and seed apricots; chop flesh finely.

3 Combine apricot in small saucepan with remaining caster sugar, the water and honey; bring to a boil. Reduce heat, simmer, uncovered, about 10 minutes or until apricots soften to a jam-like consistency.

4 Beat egg whites in small bowl with electric mixer until soft peaks form. With motor operating, gradually add hot apricot mixture, beating until just combined.

5 Divide soufflé mixture among dishes; bake about 15 minutes. Serve immediately, dusted with sifted icing sugar.

▭ **PER SERVING** 0.1g total fat (0g saturated fat); 372kJ (89 cal); 19g carbohydrate; 2.6g protein; 0.6g fibre

Fresh apricots have only a short season, so if you want or need to use dried apricots, use eight, soaking them in boiling water for 30 minutes before proceeding with the recipe.

1 CHOCOLATE SOUFFLES **2** APRICOT AND HONEY SOUFFLES
3 HOT RASPBERRY SOUFFLES [P 554] **4** PINK GRAPEFRUIT SOUFFLES [P 554]

Hot raspberry soufflés

PREPARATION TIME 15 MINUTES **COOKING TIME** 25 MINUTES **SERVES** 4

300g frozen raspberries, thawed

1 tablespoon water

½ cup (110g) caster sugar

4 egg whites

300ml thickened cream

2 teaspoons caster sugar, extra

1 Preheat oven to 180°C/160°C fan-forced. Grease four 1-cup (250ml) soufflé dishes; place on oven tray.

2 Place 250g of the raspberries and the water in small saucepan; bring to a boil. Reduce heat, simmer, uncovered, until raspberries soften. Add sugar, stir over heat, without boiling, until sugar dissolves; bring to a boil. Reduce heat, simmer about 5 minutes or until mixture is thick and pulpy. Remove from heat; push mixture through fine sieve over small bowl, discard seeds.

3 Beat egg whites in small bowl with electric mixer until soft peaks form. With motor operating, gradually add hot raspberry mixture; beat until combined.

4 Divide soufflé mixture among dishes; bake about 15 minutes or until puffed and browned.

5 Meanwhile, beat remaining raspberries, cream and extra sugar in small bowl with electric mixer until thickened slightly. Serve soufflés immediately with raspberry cream.

▭ **PER SERVING** 28.2g total fat (18.3g saturated fat); 1802kJ (431 cal); 36.7g carbohydrate; 6.1g protein; 4.1g fibre

Pink grapefruit soufflés

PREPARATION TIME 30 MINUTES **COOKING TIME** 25 MINUTES **SERVES** 6

⅓ cup (75g) caster sugar

⅓ cup (50g) plain flour

¾ cup (180ml) skim milk

1 tablespoon finely grated pink grapefruit rind

¼ cup (60ml) pink grapefruit juice

1 teaspoon grenadine

20g butter

3 egg yolks

5 egg whites

1 tablepoon icing sugar

1 Preheat oven to 220°C/200°C fan-forced. Grease six ¾-cup (180ml) dishes. Sprinkle inside of dishes with a little of the caster sugar; shake away excess. Place dishes on oven tray.

2 Place remaining caster sugar with flour in medium saucepan, gradually whisk in milk; cook, stirring, until mixture boils and thickens. Whisk in rind, juice, grenadine and butter; remove from heat. Transfer mixture to large bowl; whisk in egg yolks.

3 Beat egg whites in medium bowl with electric mixer until soft peaks form. Fold into grapefruit mixture, in two batches.

4 Divide soufflé mixture among dishes; bake about 15 minutes or until puffed and browned. Serve immediately dusted with sifted icing sugar.

▭ **PER SERVING** 5.8g total fat (2.7g saturated fat); 769kJ (184 cal); 24.6g carbohydrate; 8.1g protein; 0.4g fibre

Coffee soufflés with pecan praline cream

PREPARATION TIME 15 MINUTES **COOKING TIME** 20 MINUTES **SERVES** 6

30g butter

1 tablespoon plain flour

¾ cup (180ml) hot milk

2 teaspoons instant coffee granules

2 egg yolks

¼ cup (55g) caster sugar

3 egg whites

PECAN PRALINE CREAM

¼ cup (30g) pecans

¼ cup (60ml) water

2 tablespoons caster sugar

⅔ cup (160ml) thickened cream, whipped

This method is slightly different from other recipes but works like a charm. A tablespoon of any coffee-flavoured liqueur added to the cream marries with the flavour of the soufflé.

1 Preheat oven to 200°C/180°C fan-forced. Grease six ¾-cup (180ml) soufflé dishes; place on oven tray.

2 Melt butter in medium saucepan, add flour; cook, stirring, over heat until mixture bubbles and thickens. Remove from heat, gradually stir in combined milk and coffee, stir over heat until mixture boils and thickens.

3 Meanwhile, beat egg yolks and sugar in small bowl with electric mixer until thick and creamy; gradually beat in coffee mixture. Transfer mixture to large bowl.

4 Beat egg whites in small bowl with electric mixer until soft peaks form; fold into coffee mixture, in two batches.

5 Pour soufflé mixture into dishes; bake about 15 minutes or until puffed and browned.

6 Meanwhile, make pecan praline cream. Serve soufflés immediately with praline cream.

PECAN PRALINE CREAM Place nuts on greased oven tray. Stir water and sugar in small saucepan over heat, without boiling, until sugar dissolves. Bring to boil, boil, uncovered, without stirring, about 3 minutes or until mixture turns golden brown. Quickly pour evenly over nuts; cool. When set, break into pieces; blend or process until finely ground. Combine praline and cream in small bowl.

☐ **PER SERVING** 21.2g total fat (11g saturated fat); 1150kJ (275 cal); 15.6g carbohydrate; 5.4g protein; 0.7g fibre

THE OVEN TRAY

The Oven Tray

An oven tray is one of your most obliging kitchen helpers. Aside from its main job of holding biscuits, scones, meringues, rolls and buns, focaccia, pizza and pastries for baking, it can also be used to help roast nuts and brown croûtons, freeze bacon slices, meat balls, sausages and cake slices so they won't stick together when packed in a bag, to return biscuits to the oven that have gone soft, to crispness, underpin a flan ring, give a soufflé the instant boost of heat from underneath that starts it rising, and reheat the party savouries, Christmas mince pies and any treats, from croissants to meat pies, that you bring home from the bakery.

CHOOSING AN OVEN TRAY

It is practical to buy oven trays in pairs so you can make a second batch of biscuits or pastries while the first batch bakes. To make best use of the oven, buy the largest trays that fit in it with 5cm or so to spare on all sides. You may also want a smaller tray that will go into your freezer.

For biscuits, our Test Kitchen team uses either oven trays or shallow-sided pans (swiss-roll pans) so that the heat "skims" over the top, ensuring proper circulation and browning. Oven trays with rims are best because cooked items won't slide off. For slices, we mostly use slice or lamington pans (a rectangular pan with sides about 2.5cm high).

MATERIALS

ALUMINIUM is excellent so long as it is good quality: flimsy trays can warp. Aluminium trays with non-stick coatings release baked items perfectly, but don't brown food as readily as the plain metal, and their non-stick performance will deteriorate if they become scratched or worn (read more about non-stick coatings under Finish in *The Frying Pan*, page 23).

STEEL is long-lasting, doesn't warp and performs well, especially if it is black-finished (dark surfaces absorb heat more readily than light ones). You may find that, when using a black steel oven tray, you need to lower the cooking temperature by about 10°C from that given in the recipe, or shorten the cooking time to prevent scorching or overcooking.

A steel oven tray must be dried promptly and thoroughly after washing, as otherwise it may rust. By the time you've emptied and washed your tray, the turned-off oven will be cooled down enough to dry the tray, upside-down, in it.

BAKING TECHNIQUES

MIXING BISCUIT DOUGH Have butter and eggs at room temperature so they mix together readily. When beating the butter and sugar, stop as soon as they are well combined but while the mixture is still firm, so the finished dough will not be too soft and liable to spread. If the finished dough seems a little soft, place the tray of unbaked biscuits in the fridge or freezer for a few minutes before baking.

POSITION IN OVEN Biscuits, scones, breads and pastries are usually cooked in the hottest part of the oven – usually the top half in a gas oven and the bottom half in an electric oven. Fan-forced ovens should bake and brown everything in the oven, but sometimes ovens have hot spots. Get to know your oven and don't be nervous about moving thins around. Follow recipe directions for temperatures and baking times.

You can cook two trays on separate shelves at the same time, as long as there is a gap of at least 3cm between the upper shelf and the top of the food on the lower shelf, to allow proper heat circulation. For even baking, turn trays front to back and swap their positions halfway through the baking time. Fan-forced ovens are designed to maintain the same conditions throughout the oven so that you should not have to turn or change the trays around, but check once or twice to be sure.

SPRAYING BREAD Spraying bread lightly with water two or three times during the first 10 minutes of baking helps make it crusty and minimises cracking. Open the oven door, pull tray forward quickly, spray, push tray back and close door promptly.

PIZZA Heating the oven tray or pizza pan before placing pizza on, it helps crisp the base.

CHECKING FOR DONENESS

BISCUITS are cooked when, if pushed gently with a finger, they will move on the tray without breaking. They will feel soft when first removed from the oven, but will become firm on cooling.

BREAD is cooked when it is browned and when rapped underneath with your knuckles sounds hollow. Pastries are done when they are golden.

COOLING

BISCUITS may be cooled on the tray or on wire racks: follow recipe directions.

BREADS AND PASTRIES are usually cooled on wire racks.

STORING

Leave biscuits until they come to room temperature before storing them in screw-top glass jars or tins with tight-fitting lids; these are better than plastic storage boxes, which don't keep biscuits crisp for long. If biscuits become soft, they can be refreshed: place on an oven tray and heat in a 160°C/140°C fan-forced oven for about 5 minutes; check often, as they overbrown quickly, and cool on wire racks before storing again.

FREEZING AND THAWING

While breads, scones and pastries are best eaten on the day of baking, they can be frozen. For convenience, you may like to slice bread first so that you can take it out slice by slice. Thaw breads, scones and pastries at room temperature. Pastries or scones can then be placed on an oven tray and heated for 5 minutes in a 160°C/140°C fan-forced oven.

Potato wedges

PREPARATION TIME 10 MINUTES **COOKING TIME** 40 MINUTES **SERVES** 4

1kg kipfler potatoes, unpeeled

2 tablespoons olive oil

1 Preheat oven to 200°C/180°C fan-forced. Oil two oven trays.

2 Cut each potato into wedges; toss potato wedges and oil in large bowl. Place wedges, in single layer, on trays.

3 Roast potatoes, turning occasionally, about 40 minutes or until potatoes are crisp and cooked through.

▭ **PER SERVING** 9.4g total fat (1.3g saturated fat); 1041kJ (249 cal); 32.8g carbohydrate; 6g protein; 5g fibre

SPICE VARIATIONS

LEMON PEPPER Combine 1 tablespoon finely grated lemon rind, 1 tablespoon lemon juice and ½ teaspoon freshly ground black pepper in small bowl.

CAJUN Combine ½ teaspoon ground oregano, 2 teaspoons ground cumin, 1 teaspoon hot paprika, ½ teaspoon ground black pepper, 1 teaspoon ground turmeric, 1 teaspoon ground coriander and ¼ teaspoon chilli powder in small bowl.

SUN-DRIED TOMATO Combine 1 tablespoon sun-dried tomato pesto, 2 teaspoons tomato sauce and 1 teaspoon sambal oelek in small bowl.

Beef pasties

PREPARATION TIME 30 MINUTES **COOKING TIME** 45 MINUTES **MAKES** 16

500g coliban potatoes, peeled, chopped coarsely

1 tablespoon olive oil

1 small brown onion (80g), chopped finely

2 cloves garlic, crushed

1 medium carrot (120g), chopped finely

1 trimmed celery stalk (100g), chopped finely

350g beef mince

⅓ cup (80ml) dry red wine

1 cup (250ml) beef stock

¼ cup (70g) tomato paste

½ cup (60g) frozen peas

8 sheets ready-rolled puff pastry, thawed

1 egg, beaten lightly

1 Boil, steam or microwave potato until tender; drain. Mash in medium bowl.

2 Meanwhile, heat oil in medium saucepan; cook onion and garlic, stirring, until onion softens. Add carrot and celery; cook, stirring, until vegetables are tender. Add beef; cook, stirring, until changed in colour.

3 Stir in wine, stock, paste and peas; cook, uncovered, about 5 minutes or until mixture thickens slightly. Stir in mashed potato; cool 10 minutes.

4 Preheat oven to 180°C/160°C fan-forced. Oil two oven trays.

5 Cut two 14cm-rounds from each pastry sheet. Divide filling among rounds, placing mixture in centre of each round. Brush edge of pastry with egg; fold over to enclose filling, pressing around edge with fork to seal. Place on trays.

6 Bake pasties, uncovered, about 30 minutes or until browned lightly.

▭ **PER PASTY** 22g total fat (11.1g saturated fat); 1626kJ (389 cal); 34.9g carbohydrate; 10.9g protein; 2.3g fibre

Napoletana pizza

PREPARATION TIME 30 MINUTES (PLUS STANDING TIME) **COOKING TIME** 30 MINUTES **SERVES** 6

300g mozzarella cheese, sliced thinly

¼ cup roughly torn fresh basil

PIZZA DOUGH

2 teaspoons (7g) dried yeast

½ teaspoon salt

2½ cups (375g) plain flour

1 cup (250ml) warm water

1 tablespoon olive oil

TOMATO PIZZA SAUCE

1 tablespoon olive oil

1 small white onion (80g), chopped finely

2 cloves garlic, crushed

425g can crushed tomatoes

¼ cup (70g) tomato paste

1 teaspoon sugar

1 tablespoon fresh oregano leaves

Pizza dough can be successfully frozen; once it has risen, punch it down and freeze it in a zip lock plastic bag. Remove it from the freezer the morning of the day you want to make the pizza so that it is thawed and no longer ice-cold when you go to roll it out.

1 Make pizza dough.

2 Meanwhile, make tomato pizza sauce.

3 Preheat oven to 220°C/200°C fan-forced. Oil two oven trays.

4 Halve pizza dough; roll out each half on lightly floured surface to 30cm rounds. Place on trays. Spread each with half of the tomato pizza sauce; top with cheese.

5 Bake about 15 minutes or until bases are crisp. Sprinkle each with basil before serving.

PIZZA DOUGH Combine yeast, salt and sifted flour in large bowl. Gradually stir in the water and oil. Knead on floured surface about 10 minutes or until smooth and elastic. Place dough in large oiled bowl; stand in warm place about 30 minutes or until dough doubles in size. Knead dough on floured surface until smooth.

TOMATO PIZZA SAUCE Heat oil in medium frying pan; cook onion, stirring occasionally, over low heat until soft. Stir in garlic, undrained tomatoes, tomato paste, sugar and oregano. Simmer, uncovered, about 15 minutes or until mixture thickens.

▭ **PER SERVING** 18.1g total fat (8g saturated fat); 1919kJ (459 cal); 50.2g carbohydrate; 21.4g protein; 4.4g fibre

Make individual pizzas by using pocket pittas or even wholemeal english muffins or plain bagels. Canned baby beetroots won't work as well as roasted fresh ones but you can substitute goat cheese for the fetta with great results.

Roasted beetroot and fetta pizza

PREPARATION TIME 10 MINUTES **COOKING TIME** 35 MINUTES **SERVES** 4

2 tablespoons olive oil

1kg raw baby beetroots, trimmed, peeled, quartered

4 cloves garlic, crushed

2 teaspoons fresh thyme leaves

4 large pitta breads (320g)

1 cup (260g) bottled tomato pasta sauce

200g fetta cheese, crumbled

20g baby rocket leaves

1 Preheat oven to 200°C/180°C fan-forced.

2 Combine oil, beetroot, garlic and thyme in medium shallow baking dish. Roast uncovered, about 20 minutes or until beetroot is tender.

3 Place pitta on oven trays; spread with pasta sauce. Divide beetroot mixture among pitta; sprinkle with cheese. Cook, uncovered, about 10 minutes or until pitta bases are crisp. Serve, sprinkled with rocket.

▭ **PER SERVING** 23.5g total fat (9.3g saturated fat); 2516kJ (602 cal); 70.4g carbohydrate; 22.5g protein; 12g fibre

When using other cookbooks published overseas and you're instructed to use a cookie sheet or baking sheet, the recipe is simply calling for an oven tray. To guarantee the pizza bases remain crisp in this recipe, sprinkle half of the cheese onto the base before the sauce and other topping. It acts as a barrier between the two, and stops the bases becoming soggy.

Meatlover's pizza

PREPARATION TIME 10 MINUTES **COOKING TIME** 25 MINUTES **SERVES** 4

2 teaspoons olive oil

1 small brown onion (80g), chopped finely

1 clove garlic, crushed

250g lean beef mince

1 teaspoon hot paprika

⅓ cup (80ml) barbecue sauce

2 x 335g pizza bases

2 tablespoons tomato paste

2 cups (200g) pizza cheese

1 stick cabanossi (100g), sliced coarsely

50g sliced spicy salami, chopped coarsely

1 Preheat oven to 220°C/200°C fan-forced. Grease two oven trays.

2 Heat oil in frying pan; cook onion and garlic, stirring, until soft. Add beef; cook, stirring, until well browned. Stir in paprika and 1 tablespoon of the barbecue sauce. Remove pan from heat.

3 Meanwhile, place pizza bases on trays. Combine tomato paste with remaining barbecue sauce; spread evenly over bases. Sprinkle pizzas with half of the cheese. Top with beef mixture, cabanossi, salami and remaining cheese.

4 Cook pizzas about 15 minutes or until bases are crisp.

▭ **PER SERVING** 45.6g total fat (16g saturated fat); 3883kJ (929 cal); 81.6g carbohydrate; 45.4g protein; 5.5g fibre

ROASTED BEETROOT AND FETTA PIZZA

To keep the tandoori oven theme going, buy a packet of naan and use it for these pizzas instead of pre-made bases. Naan, available in supermarkets, delicatessens and Indian food shops, is an Indian leavened bread, made with yogurt and cooked in a tandoor (clay oven). You can also use chicken thighs instead of lamb, if you prefer.

Tandoori lamb pizza

PREPARATION TIME 10 MINUTES **COOKING TIME** 30 MINUTES **SERVES** 4

¼ cup (70g) yogurt

¼ cup (75g) tandoori paste

600g lamb backstraps

30g butter

2 medium red onions (300g), sliced thickly

1 clove garlic, crushed

2 x 335g pizza bases

½ cup (160g) mango chutney

⅓ cup (50g) coarsely chopped raisins

¼ cup (70g) yogurt, extra

⅓ cup loosely packed fresh coriander leaves

1 Preheat oven to 220°C/200°C fan-forced.

2 Combine yogurt, paste and lamb in medium bowl.

3 Heat butter in medium saucepan; cook onion and garlic, stirring, about 15 minutes or until onion is caramelised.

4 Place pizza bases on oven trays; spread each with chutney then top with onion and raisins. Cook about 15 minutes or until bases are crisp.

5 Meanwhile, cook lamb on heated oiled grill plate (or grill or barbecue) until cooked as desired. Cover; stand 5 minutes then slice thinly.

6 Top pizzas with lamb, extra yogurt and coriander.

▭ **PER SERVING** 25.2g total fat (8.7g saturated fat); 3954kJ (946 cal); 112.7g carbohydrate; 50.3g protein; 10.9g fibre

Perhaps the most delicious of all the many wonderful street foods to be sampled in Istanbul, lahmacun or lahm biajn ("meat with dough", what we know simply as Turkish pizza) is often drizzled with lemon juice and eaten, rolled, in the hand instead of being sliced and topped with yogurt. Try it both ways to determine your preference.

Turkish herbed lamb pizza

PREPARATION TIME 45 MINUTES (PLUS STANDING TIME) **COOKING TIME** 35 MINUTES **SERVES** 4

¾ teaspoon dried yeast

1 teaspoon white sugar

¾ cup (180ml) warm water

2 cups (300g) plain flour

1 teaspoon salt

cooking-oil spray

600g lamb mince

1 tablespoon olive oil

1 small brown onion (80g), chopped finely

1 clove garlic, crushed

½ teaspoon ground cinnamon

1½ teaspoons ground allspice

¼ cup (40g) pine nuts, chopped coarsely

¼ cup (70g) tomato paste

2 medium tomatoes (300g), seeded, chopped finely

1 cup (250ml) chicken stock

2 tablespoons lemon juice

¼ cup finely chopped fresh flat-leaf parsley

¼ cup finely chopped fresh mint

½ cup (140g) greek-style yogurt

2 tablespoons cold water

1 Whisk yeast, sugar and the warm water in small bowl; cover, stand in warm place about 15 minutes or until mixture is frothy.

2 Combine flour and salt in large bowl; stir in yeast mixture, mix to a soft dough. Knead on lightly floured surface about 10 minutes or until smooth and elastic. Place in large oiled bowl, turning dough once to coat in oil. Cover dough; stand in warm place about 1 hour or until dough is doubled in size.

3 Halve dough; knead each portion until smooth then roll out to oval shape measuring about 12cm x 35cm. Place each oval on an oiled oven tray; coat lightly with oil spray. Cover; stand in warm place 30 minutes.

4 Preheat oven to 240°C/220°C fan-forced.

5 Cook mince in heated large frying pan, stirring, until cooked through. Transfer to medium bowl.

6 Heat oil in same pan; cook onion and garlic, stirring, until onion softens. Add spices and nuts; cook, stirring, about 5 minutes or until nuts are just toasted. Return mince to pan with tomato paste, tomato, stock and juice; cook, stirring, about 5 minutes or until liquid is almost evaporated. Remove pan from heat; stir in herbs.

7 Spoon mince mixture over pizza bases; cook about 15 minutes or until bases are crisp. Serve drizzled with combined yogurt and the cold water.

▭ **PER SERVING** 26.5g total fat (7.7g saturated fat); 2805kJ (671 cal); 63g carbohydrate; 44.2g protein; 5.3g fibre

Satay chicken pizza

PREPARATION TIME 20 MINUTES **COOKING TIME** 15 MINUTES **SERVES** 4

½ cup (140g) crunchy peanut butter

½ cup (125ml) sweet chilli sauce

4 x 15cm pizza bases

3 cups (480g) shredded barbecued chicken

200g provolone cheese, grated coarsely

50g baby rocket leaves

RAITA

1 lebanese cucumber (130g), chopped finely

1 small brown onion (80g), chopped finely

½ cup (140g) yogurt

2 tablespoons finely chopped fresh mint

1 long green chilli, chopped finely

The perfect after-work meal – little effort and even less time. Just pick up a barbecued chicken on your way home from work and you can get these pizzas in the oven before you can ring home delivery. The raita can be made by substituting a finely chopped tablespoon of rinsed preserved lemon for the cucumber.

1 Preheat oven to 200°C/180°C fan-forced.

2 Combine peanut butter and chilli sauce in small bowl.

3 Place pizza bases on oven trays; spread sauce mixture evenly over each base. Divide chicken and cheese among bases; cook about 15 minutes or until bases are crisp.

4 Meanwhile, combine raita ingredients in small bowl.

5 Serve pizza topped with raita and rocket.

▭ **PER SERVING** 48.1g total fat (16.3g saturated fat); 4301kJ (1029 cal); 73.1g carbohydrate; 70.5g protein; 10.6g fibre

Potato, garlic and oregano pizza

PREPARATION TIME 25 MINUTES (PLUS STANDING TIME) **COOKING TIME** 20 MINUTES **SERVES** 4

2 teaspoons dried yeast

½ teaspoon caster sugar

¾ cup (180ml) warm water

2 cups (300g) plain flour

1 teaspoon salt

2 tablespoons olive oil

2 tablespoons polenta

⅓ cup loosely packed fresh oregano leaves

6 small potatoes (720g), sliced thinly

3 cloves garlic, crushed

2 tablespoons olive oil, extra

½ teaspoon sea salt flakes

1 tablespoon fresh oregano leaves, extra

1 Combine yeast, sugar and the water in small bowl, cover; stand in warm place about 10 minutes or until mixture is frothy.

2 Sift flour and salt into large bowl; stir in yeast mixture and oil. Mix to a soft dough. Bring dough together with hands, adding extra water if necessary.

3 Knead dough on floured surface about 10 minutes or until smooth and elastic. Place in oiled bowl, cover; stand in warm place about 1 hour or until doubled in size.

4 Preheat oven to 240°C/220°C fan-forced. Oil two oven trays.

5 Punch dough down with fist; knead on floured surface until smooth. Divide dough in half, roll halves to 20cm x 30cm rectangle; place on trays. Sprinkle dough with polenta; prick all over with a fork.

6 Divide oregano leaves between bases then layer with potato, overlapping slightly. Brush combined garlic and extra oil over potato.

7 Bake about 20 minutes or until potato is tender and bases are crisp. Sprinkle pizzas with sea salt and extra oregano before serving.

▭ **PER SERVING** 19.5g total fat (2.8g saturated fat); 2328kJ (557 cal); 79.1g carbohydrate; 12.8g protein; 6.1g fibre

Pissaladière

PREPARATION TIME 25 MINUTES **COOKING TIME** 1 HOUR 10 MINUTES **SERVES** 6

50g butter

1 tablespoon olive oil

3 large brown onions (600g), sliced thinly

2 cloves garlic, crushed

1 bay leaf

1 sprig fresh thyme

1 tablespoon baby capers, rinsed, drained

¾ cup (110g) self-raising flour

¾ cup (110g) plain flour

30g butter, extra

¾ cup (180ml) buttermilk

20 drained anchovy fillets, halved lengthways

½ cup (90g) small seeded black olives

1 Heat butter and oil in large saucepan; cook onion, garlic, bay leaf and thyme, covered, stirring occasionally, over low heat about 30 minutes or until onion is very soft but not browned. Cook, uncovered, 10 minutes. Remove bay leaf and thyme sprig; stir in capers.

2 Preheat oven to 220°C/200°C fan-forced. Oil oven tray.

3 Meanwhile, sift flours into large bowl. Rub in extra butter; stir in buttermilk to form a soft dough. Turn dough onto lightly floured surface; knead until smooth.

4 Roll out dough to form a rough rectangular shape, about 25cm x 35cm. Place on tray.

5 Spread onion mixture over dough, spreading it to edges. Top with anchovy and olives in a diamond pattern. Bake about 30 minutes or until base is crisp.

☐ **PER SERVING** 18.2g total fat (9g saturated fat); 1685kJ (403 cal); 36.3g carbohydrate; 22g protein; 3g fibre

Vegetable and fetta freeform tarts

PREPARATION TIME 30 MINUTES (PLUS STANDING TIME) **COOKING TIME** 50 MINUTES **SERVES** 4

1 small eggplant (230g), chopped coarsely

1 tablespoon coarse cooking salt

1 tablespoon olive oil

1 medium brown onion (150g), sliced thinly

2 medium zucchini (240g), sliced thinly

4 sheets ready-rolled shortcrust pastry

¼ cup (65g) bottled pesto

120g fetta cheese, crumbled

8 cherry tomatoes, halved

1 tablespoon finely chopped fresh basil

1 egg, beaten lightly

1 Place eggplant in sieve or colander; sprinkle all over with salt, then stand sieve over sink or large bowl for 15 minutes. Rinse eggplant well under cold running water, drain; pat dry with absorbent paper.

2 Preheat oven to 200°C/180°C fan-forced. Oil two oven trays.

3 Heat oil in large frying pan; cook onion, stirring, until softened. Add eggplant and zucchini; cook, stirring, until vegetables are softened.

4 Cut a 20cm round from each pastry sheet; place rounds on trays. Spread equal amounts of pesto in centre of each round, leaving a 4cm border around the outside edge.

5 Divide vegetables among rounds over pesto; top each with equal amounts of cheese, tomato and basil. Using hands, turn the 4cm edge on each round over filling; brush around pastry edge with egg. Bake about 40 minutes or until pastry is browned lightly.

☐ **PER SERVING** 65.5g total fat (31.2g saturated fat); 4176kJ (999 cal); 79.1g carbohydrate; 21.2g protein; 6.6g fibre

Have you ever eaten eggplant and recoiled from its bitter taste? To prevent this, follow the process described in the method in step 1 which is known as disgorging (see also page 647). Chop the eggplant as required, salt and drain it (weighted with a heavy can if you like) then stand it at least 15 minutes. The salt will turn slightly brown as it absorbs the bitter liquid responsible for the unpleasant taste. This process also helps reduce the amount of oil eggplant absorbs when it is fried.

Beef samosas with peach and raisin chutney

PREPARATION TIME 50 MINUTES **COOKING TIME** 1 HOUR 25 MINUTES (PLUS REFRIGERATION TIME)
MAKES 36

Samosas, can be filled with meat or with a typically Indian potato, coriander and pea mixture, to make perfect finger food. They can be made the day before you want to serve them and refrigerated, covered on a tray in a single layer, until you want to bake them – they should always be served warm.

2 teaspoons vegetable oil

1 small brown onion (80g), chopped finely

2 cloves garlic, crushed

2cm piece fresh ginger (10g), grated

1 tablespoon ground cumin

1 tablespoon ground coriander

1 fresh small red thai chilli, chopped finely

250g beef mince

1 small kumara (250g), chopped finely

⅓ cup (80ml) water

4 sheets ready-rolled shortcrust pastry

1 egg, beaten lightly

PEACH AND RAISIN CHUTNEY

3 medium peaches (450g)

⅓ cup (110g) finely chopped raisins

½ cup (125ml) cider vinegar

2 tablespoons lemon juice

1 small brown onion (80g), chopped finely

¼ teaspoon ground cinnamon

½ teaspoon ground allspice

1 cup (220g) white sugar

1 Make peach and raisin chutney.

2 Heat oil in large frying pan; cook onion, garlic, ginger and spices, stirring, until onion softens. Add chilli and mince; cook, stirring, until mince browns. Add kumara and the water; bring to a boil. Reduce heat, simmer, uncovered, stirring occasionally, until kumara softens. Stir in ⅓ cup of the chutney. Cool 10 minutes then refrigerate until cold.

3 Preheat oven to 200°C/180°C fan-forced. Oil three oven trays.

4 Using 7.5cm cutter, cut nine rounds from each pastry sheet. Place rounded teaspoons of the beef filling in centre of each round; brush edge of rounds with egg, press edges together to enclose filling. Repeat process with remaining rounds and filling.

5 Place samosas on trays; brush tops with egg. Bake about 20 minutes or until browned lightly. Serve samosas with remaining chutney.

PEACH AND RAISIN CHUTNEY Cover peaches with boiling water in medium heatproof bowl for about 30 seconds. Peel, seed, then chop peaches finely. Place in medium saucepan with remaining ingredients; bring to a boil. Reduce heat, simmer, uncovered, stirring occasionally, about 45 minutes or until chutney thickens.

☐ **PER SAMOSA** 5.7g total fat (2.8g saturated fat); 560kJ (134 cal); 17.8g carbohydrate; 3.1g protein; 0.8g fibre

Preparing cake pans

It's worth taking the care to prepare pans properly so your cakes end up with a lovely smooth surface.

GREASING WITH OIL SPRAY

To spray a pan, hold it up with the base vertical and spray lightly and evenly over base and sides. Ideally, do this by an outside door to avoid spray falling onto kitchen fittings.

GREASING WITH BUTTER

Melt butter and, with a pastry brush, brush it evenly over base and sides of pan. If butter collects in corners or where sides meet base, go back and dab with brush to even it out, or use your fingers.

FLOURING A PAN (1)

First grease the pan with oil spray or butter, as described previously, then sprinkle lightly but evenly with a little flour, tilting pan to flour side evenly too.

LINING A ROUND PAN (1)

Place round cake pan on baking paper (close to the edge to minimise waste) and trace around it with a pencil.

LINING A ROUND PAN (2)

Cut out the circle you have traced, cutting just inside the pencil line to allow for the thickness of the pan so it will fit the inside base exactly.

LINING A ROUND PAN (3)

Cut a strip of baking (or greaseproof) paper so that it's long enough to go round the pan with a little overlap, is wide enough to allow for a 2cm turn-up, and extends 5cm above the rim of the pan.

FLOURING A PAN (2)

After flouring, hold pan upside down and tap firmly to shake out excess flour This ensures that the cake browns evenly and there is no flour 'band' around the base of cake after baking.

LINING A RECTANGULAR OR SQUARE PAN

Mark width of pan on baking paper, and cut a strip of this width, long enough to line pan end-to-end with overhang. Mark length and cut another strip to line side-to-side with some overhang. Place strips in pan, overlapping.

LINING A LAMINGTON OR BAR PAN

Mark pan width on baking paper, and cut a strip of this width, long enough to line pan end-to-end and extend over. Place in pan with equal overhang at each end, smoothing to fit.

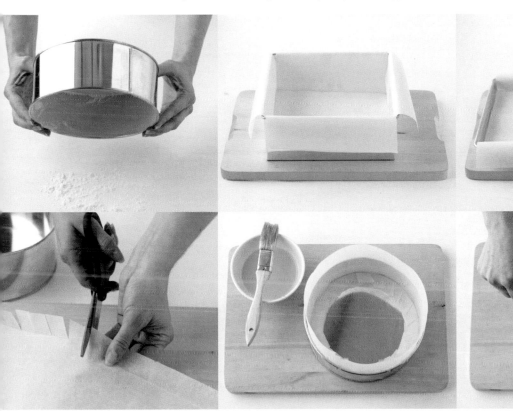

LINING A ROUND PAN (4)

Fold over long side of paper about 2cm from the edge, run a finger along to make a crease; open out and use scissors to make diagonal cuts, about 2cm apart, across the folded strip from edge to crease.

LINING A ROUND PAN (5)

Place paper around inside of pan, with the snipped edge flat on the base, securing it to the side or base, as needed, by greasing with cooking-oil spray or melted butter.

LINING A ROUND PAN (6)

Place the cut-out circle of paper into the pan and smooth it out, covering the snipped edges of the side lining, to fit neatly.

Basic scones

PREPARATION TIME 20 MINUTES **COOKING TIME** 25 MINUTES **MAKES** 20

4 cups (600g) self-raising flour
2 tablespoons icing sugar
60g butter
1 ½ cups (375ml) milk
¾ cup (180ml) water, approximately

1 Preheat oven to 220°C/ 200°C fan-forced. Grease oven tray.
2 Sift flour and sugar into large bowl; rub in butter with fingertips.
3 Make a well in centre of flour mixture; add milk and almost all the water. Use knife to "cut" the milk and water through the flour mixture, mixing to a soft, sticky dough. Knead dough on floured surface until smooth.
4 Press dough out to 2cm thickness. Dip 4.5cm round cutter in flour; cut as many rounds as you can from piece of dough. Place scones, side by side, just touching, on tray.
5 Gently knead scraps of dough together; repeat pressing and cutting of dough, place on same tray. Brush tops with a little extra milk; bake about 15 minutes or until scones are just browned and sound hollow when tapped firmly on the top with fingers.

☐ **PER SCONE** 7.3g total fat (3.1g saturated fat); 464kJ (111 cal); 9.3g carbohydrate; 1.8g protein; 0.6g fibre

Almond macaroons

PREPARATION TIME 15 MINUTES **COOKING TIME** 20 MINUTES **MAKES** 22

2 egg whites
½ cup (110g) caster sugar
1 ¼ cups (150g) almond meal
½ teaspoon almond essence
2 tablespoons plain flour
¼ cup (40g) blanched almonds

1 Preheat oven to 150°C/130°C fan-forced. Grease two oven trays.
2 Beat egg whites in small bowl with electric mixer until soft peaks form. Gradually add sugar, beating until dissolved between additions. Fold in meal, essence and sifted flour, in two batches.
3 Drop level tablespoons of mixture about 5cm apart on trays; press one nut onto each macaroon. Bake about 20 minutes or until firm and dry; cool on trays.

☐ **PER MACAROON** 4.8g total fat (0.3g saturated fat); 326kJ (78 cal); 6.1g carbohydrate; 2.2g protein; 0.8g fibre

1 BASIC SCONES **2** ALMOND MACAROONS
3 FRANGIPANE JAM DROPS [P 576] **4** ORANGE HAZELNUT BUTTER YOYO BITES [P 576]

You should always use real butter when making cookies like these: light margarines and whipped butters have a high water content and will result in a disaster. Made with almond meal, these are a slight departure from the traditional jam drops we all remember grandma making. Best eaten fresh, these are super easy to make.

Frangipane jam drops

PREPARATION TIME 30 MINUTES **COOKING TIME** 15 MINUTES **MAKES** 24

125g butter, softened

½ teaspoon vanilla extract

½ cup (110g) caster sugar

1 cup (120g) almond meal

1 egg

⅔ cup (100g) plain flour

2 tablespoons raspberry jam

1 Preheat oven to 180°C/160°C fan forced. Grease oven trays; line with baking paper.

2 Beat butter, extract, sugar and meal in small bowl with electric mixer until light and fluffy. Add egg, beating until just combined. Stir in sifted flour.

3 Drop level tablespoons of mixture on trays 5cm apart. Use handle of wooden spoon to make small hole (about 1cm deep) in top of each biscuit; fill each hole with ¼ teaspoon jam. Bake about 15 minutes; cool jam drops on trays.

⬜ **PER JAM DROP** 7.3g total fat (3.1g saturated fat); 464kJ (111 cal); 9.3g carbohydrate; 1.8g protein; 0.6g fibre

---

Use almond meal in the sandwiching butter if you don't have hazelnut meal on hand. You can also blend or process a heaped tablespoon of roasted and skinned hazelnuts to obtain the amount required. Lemon rind can also be substituted for the orange, if you prefer.

Orange hazelnut butter yoyo bites

PREPARATION TIME 15 MINUTES **COOKING TIME** 15 MINUTES **MAKES** 20

250g unsalted butter, softened

1 teaspoon vanilla extract

½ cup (80g) icing sugar

1½ cups (225g) plain flour

½ cup (75g) cornflour

ORANGE HAZELNUT BUTTER

80g unsalted butter, softened

2 teaspoons finely grated orange rind

⅔ cup (110g) icing sugar

1 tablespoon hazelnut meal

1 Preheat oven to 160°C/140°C fan-forced. Grease two oven trays; line with baking paper.

2 Beat butter, extract and sifted icing sugar in small bowl with electric mixer until light and fluffy; stir in sifted dry ingredients, in two batches.

3 Roll rounded teaspoons of mixture into balls; place about 3cm apart on trays. Using fork dusted with flour, press tines gently onto each biscuit to flatten slightly. Bake about 15 minutes; cool on trays.

4 Meanwhile, make orange hazelnut butter.

5 Sandwich biscuits with orange hazelnut butter. Serve dusted with extra sifted icing sugar, if desired.

ORANGE HAZELNUT BUTTER Beat butter, rind and sifted icing sugar in small bowl with electric mixer until light and fluffy. Stir in meal.

⬜ **PER YOYO BITE** 14.1g total fat (9.1g saturated fat); 903kJ (216 cal); 20.9g carbohydrate; 1.4g protein; 0.5g fibre

Wholemeal date scones

PREPARATION TIME 15 MINUTES **COOKING TIME** 15 MINUTES **MAKES** 15

1 cup (150g) self-raising flour

1 cup (150g) wholemeal self-raising flour

1 cup (60g) unprocessed bran

¼ cup (25g) full cream milk powder

60g butter

1 cup (140g) finely chopped dried dates

1 cup (250ml) water, approximately

1 Preheat oven to 200°C/180°C fan-forced. Grease oven tray.

2 Sift flours into medium bowl; mix in bran and milk powder. Rub in butter with fingertips, then add dates. Make a well in centre of dry ingredients and stir in enough water to give a soft, sticky dough. Knead dough on a floured surface until smooth.

3 Press dough out to 1cm thickness and cut into rounds with 5cm cutter; place on tray.

4 Bake about 15 minutes or until scones are just browned and sound hollow when tapped firmly on the top with fingers.

☐ **PER SCONE** 4.2g total fat (2.5g saturated fat); 602kJ (144 cal); 20.6g carbohydrate; 3.5g protein; 4.2g fibre

Scones don't keep particularly well (should there be any left over in the first place!), so seal them airtight in plastic and freeze. When you're ready to eat them, thaw unwrapped on a plate then reheat, one at a time, wrapped in a piece of absorbent paper, on HIGH (100%) for 30 seconds in your microwave oven.

Spicy fruit scones

PREPARATION TIME 20 MINUTES (PLUS STANDING TIME) **COOKING TIME** 15 MINUTES **MAKES** 16

1¼ cups (310ml) hot strong strained black tea

¾ cup (135g) mixed dried fruit

3 cups (450g) self-raising flour

1 teaspoon ground cinnamon

1 teaspoon mixed spice

2 tablespoons caster sugar

20g butter

½ cup (120g) sour cream, approximately

1 Preheat oven to 220°C/200°C fan-forced. Grease oven tray.

2 Combine tea and fruit in small heatproof bowl. Cover; stand 20 minutes.

3 Sift dry ingredients into large bowl, rub in butter with fingertips. Stir in fruit mixture and enough sour cream to mix to a soft, sticky dough. Knead dough on floured surface until smooth.

4 Press dough out to 2cm thickness and cut into rounds with 5.5cm cutter; place on tray.

5 Bake about 15 minutes or until scones are just browned and sound hollow when tapped firmly on the top with fingers.

☐ **PER SCONE** 4.6g total fat (2.8g saturated fat); 710kJ (170 cal); 27.9g carbohydrate; 3.1g protein; 1.6g fibre

To say that your kitchen will smell fantastic while these are baking is an understatement. They're best eaten warm, but you can certainly serve them at room temperature. Making scones with dried rather than fresh fruit will provide a more consistent result as seasonal fresh fruit varies in its moisture content. As a rule, the firmer the fruit, the better the scone. Apples work fairly well and, as far as stone fruits go, nectarines aren't too bad, either.

To help overcome butter cookies overspreading, sit the oven tray with unbaked cookies on it in the refrigerator for about 10 minutes. The butter in the mixture will harden slightly and the cookie will retain its shape better.

Wholemeal rosemary butter cookies

PREPARATION TIME 15 MINUTES **COOKING TIME** 15 MINUTES **MAKES** 28

125g butter, softened

2 teaspoons finely grated orange rind

1 cup (220g) firmly packed brown sugar

1⅓ cups (200g) wholemeal self-raising flour

1 cup (100g) coarsely chopped roasted walnuts

⅔ cup (100g) halved raisins

2 teaspoons dried rosemary

⅓ cup (80ml) orange juice

⅔ cup (50g) desiccated coconut

⅔ cup (60g) rolled oats

1 Preheat oven to 180°C/160°C fan-forced. Grease two oven trays; line with baking paper.

2 Beat butter, rind and sugar in small bowl with electric mixer until combined. Transfer to medium bowl; stir in flour then remaining ingredients.

3 Roll rounded tablespoons of mixture into balls, place about 5cm apart on oven trays; flatten slightly. Bake about 15 minutes. Cool on trays.

☐ **PER COOKIE** 7.7g total fat (3.7g saturated fat); 594kJ (142 cal); 15.7g carbohydrate; 1.9g protein; 1.6g fibre

For a simpler version of these scrolls, change the filling to make a sticky sweet breakfast scroll. After you've completed step 2, just sprinkle the rectangles first with dark brown sugar with a little cinnamon stirred into it then a few tablespoons of coarsely chopped roasted pecans and complete the recipe from step 4. Delicious!

Date and walnut scrolls

PREPARATION TIME 20 MINUTES (PLUS REFRIGERATION TIME) **COOKING TIME** 30 MINUTES **MAKES** 28

125g butter, softened

⅓ cup (75g) caster sugar

1 teaspoon ground cardamom

1 egg

1½ cups (225g) plain flour

1 cup (100g) finely ground roasted walnuts

2 cups (280g) coarsely chopped dried dates

¼ cup (55g) caster sugar, extra

2 teaspoons finely grated lemon rind

⅓ cup (80ml) lemon juice

¼ teaspoon ground cardamom, extra

½ cup (125ml) water

1 Beat butter, sugar, cardamom and egg in small bowl with electric mixer until combined. Stir in sifted flour and walnuts.

2 Knead dough on floured surface until smooth; divide into two portions. Roll each portion between sheets of baking paper to 15cm x 30cm rectangles; refrigerate 20 minutes.

3 Meanwhile, stir dates and remaining ingredients in medium saucepan over heat, without boiling, until sugar dissolves; bring to a boil. Reduce heat, simmer, stirring occasionally, 5 minutes or until mixture is thick and pulpy. Transfer to large bowl; refrigerate 10 minutes.

4 Spread filling evenly over dough rectangles, leaving 1cm border. Using paper as a guide, roll tightly from short side to enclose filling. Wrap in baking paper; refrigerate 30 minutes.

5 Preheat oven to 190°C/170°C fan-forced. Grease oven trays; line with baking paper.

6 Trim edges of roll; cut each roll into 1cm slices. Place slices cut-side up on oven trays; bake about 20 minutes.

☐ **PER SCROLL** 6.4g total fat (2.6g saturated fat); 577kJ (138 cal); 17.4g carbohydrate; 1.9g protein; 1.5g fibre

Tropical florentines

PREPARATION TIME 15 MINUTES (PLUS STANDING TIME) **COOKING TIME** 12 MINUTES **MAKES** 25

⅔ cup (160ml) passionfruit pulp

¼ cup (55g) finely chopped glacé ginger

½ cup (55g) finely chopped glacé pineapple

½ cup (90g) finely chopped dried papaya

1 cup (75g) shredded coconut

1 cup (60g) coarsely crushed cornflakes

½ cup (70g) finely chopped macadamia nuts

¾ cup (180ml) condensed milk

1 cup (150g) white chocolate Melts

1 Preheat oven to 180°C/160°C fan-forced. Grease two oven trays; line with baking paper.

2 Strain passionfruit pulp; you need ⅓ cup (80ml) juice. Discard seeds.

3 Combine ginger, pineapple, papaya, coconut, cornflakes, nuts, milk and 2 tablespoons of the passionfruit juice in medium bowl.

4 Drop rounded tablespoonfuls of mixture about 5cm apart onto oven trays; press down slightly. Bake about 12 minutes. Cool on trays.

5 Stir chocolate with remaining passionfruit juice in small heatproof bowl over small saucepan of simmering water until smooth. Spread chocolate over flat side of each florentine; mark with a fork. Set at room temperature.

▭ **PER FLORENTINE** 6.7g total fat (3.2g saturated fat); 518kJ (124 cal); 13.3g carbohydrate; 1.7g protein; 1.7g fibre

Be sure the florentines cool completely on the oven trays before removing them; if they haven't "set" properly when you start to remove them from the trays, they could fall apart. These make a spectacular gift, particularly at Christmas time.

Double choc-chip chilli cookies

PREPARATION TIME 15 MINUTES **COOKING TIME** 15 MINUTES **MAKES** 48

250g butter, softened

1 teaspoon vanilla extract

¾ cup (165g) caster sugar

¾ cup (165g) firmly packed brown sugar

1 egg

2 cups (300g) plain flour

¼ cup (25g) cocoa powder

1 teaspoon bicarbonate of soda

400g dark eating chocolate, chopped coarsely

CANDIED CHILLIES

¼ cup (55g) caster sugar

¼ cup (60ml) water

3 fresh small red thai chillies, chopped finely

1 Preheat oven to 180°C/160°C fan-forced. Grease three oven trays; line with baking paper.

2 Make candied chillies.

3 Beat butter, extract, sugars and egg in small bowl with electric mixer until light and fluffy; transfer to large bowl. Stir in sifted flour, cocoa and soda, in two batches. Stir in candied chillies and chocolate.

4 Roll level tablespoons of dough into balls; place about 5cm apart on oven trays. Bake about 12 minutes. Cool on trays.

CANDIED CHILLIES Stir sugar and the water in small saucepan over heat until sugar dissolves. Add chilli, boil, 2 minutes; cool. Strain, discard syrup.

▭ **PER COOKIE** 6.9g total fat (4.3g saturated fat); 585kJ (140 cal); 17.8g carbohydrate; 1.4g protein; 0.4g fibre

An oven tray should either be cool or at room temperature when the cookie dough is placed on it; otherwise, the dough will start to melt, ruining the cookies' shape and texture. Be sure that your trays fit in the oven with at least 5cm space around the edges for the proper heat circulation.

Honey jumbles

PREPARATION TIME 10 MINUTES (PLUS REFRIGERATION TIME) **COOKING TIME** 15 MINUTES **MAKES** 40

60g butter

½ cup (110g) firmly packed brown sugar

¾ cup (270g) golden syrup

1 egg, beaten lightly

2½ cups (375g) plain flour

½ cup (75g) self-raising flour

½ teaspoon bicarbonate of soda

1 teaspoon ground cinnamon

½ teaspoon ground clove

2 teaspoons ground ginger

1 teaspoon mixed spice

ICING

1 egg white

1½ cups (240g) icing sugar

2 teaspoons plain flour

1 tablespoon lemon juice, approximately

pink food colouring

1 Preheat oven to 160°C/140°C fan-forced. Grease three oven trays.

2 Stir butter, sugar and syrup in small saucepan over low heat until sugar dissolves. Cool 10 minutes. Transfer to large bowl; stir in egg, then sifted dry ingredients, in two batches. Knead dough on floured surface until dough loses stickiness. Cover; refrigerate 30 minutes.

3 Divide dough into eight portions. Roll each portion into 2cm-thick sausage; cut each sausage into five 6cm lengths. Place about 3cm apart on oven trays; round ends with lightly floured fingers, flatten slightly.

4 Bake about 15 minutes; cool on trays.

5 Meanwhile, make icing.

6 Spread jumbles with pink and white icing.

ICING Beat egg white lightly in small bowl; gradually stir in sifted icing sugar and flour, then enough juice to make icing spreadable. Place half the mixture in another small bowl; tint with colouring.

▭ **PER JUMBLE** 1.5g total fat (0.9g saturated fat); 456kJ (109 cal); 21.9g carbohydrate; 1.5g protein; 0.4g fibre

Using buttermilk instead of full-cream milk or cream in this recipe give the scones a buttery richness without all of the fat. Which of course you add back when you serve these light and luscious treats with lashings of whipped cream. Two important things to remember when scone-making: add wet ingredients to dry, and mix the dough as briefly as possible with as light a touch as possible.

Buttermilk scones

PREPARATION TIME 15 MINUTES **COOKING TIME** 15 MINUTES **MAKES** 16

3 cups (450g) self-raising flour

1 teaspoon icing sugar

60g butter

1 ¾ cups (430ml) buttermilk, approximately

1 Preheat oven to 220°C/200°C fan-forced. Grease oven tray.

2 Sift dry ingredients into large bowl; rub in butter with fingertips. Stir in enough buttermilk to mix to a soft, sticky dough.

3 Turn dough onto floured surface, knead until smooth. Press dough out to 2cm thickness, cut into 5.5cm rounds; place scones on tray, just touching.

4 Bake about 15 minutes or until scones are just browned and sound hollow when tapped firmly on the top with fingers.

☐ **PER SCONE** 4g total fat (2.4g saturated fat); 589kJ (141 cal); 21.5g carbohydrate; 4g protein; 1.1g fibre

---

The banana and the brown sugar add a lovely caramel flavour to this scone. Nutmeg goes well with both carrot and banana, making a more-than-acceptable substitute for the ground cardamom.

Carrot banana scones

PREPARATION TIME 30 MINUTES **COOKING TIME** 20 MINUTES **MAKES** 12

2 cups (300g) white self-raising flour

½ cup (80g) wholemeal self-raising flour

½ teaspoon ground cardamom

40g butter

⅓ cup (65g) firmly packed brown sugar

½ cup mashed banana

⅓ cup finely grated carrot

¼ cup (30g) finely chopped walnuts

¼ cup (40g) finely chopped raisins

¾ cup (180ml) milk, approximately

ORANGE CREAM

50g cream cheese, softened

50g butter, softened

½ teaspoon finely grated orange rind

½ cup (80g) icing sugar

1 Preheat oven to 220°C/200°C fan-forced. Grease oven tray.

2 Sift flours and cardamom into large bowl; rub in butter with fingers. Add sugar, banana, carrot, nuts and raisins; stir in enough milk to mix to a soft, sticky dough. Knead on floured surface until smooth.

3 Press out to 2cm thickness, cut into 5.5cm rounds; place on tray. Bake 20 minutes or until scones are just browned and sound hollow when tapped firmly on the top with fingers.

4 Meanwhile, make orange cream.

5 Serve scones with orange cream

ORANGE CREAM Beat cheese, butter and rind in small bowl with electric mixer until as white as possible. Gradually beat in sifted icing sugar.

☐ **PER SCONE** 10.3g total fat (5.5g saturated fat); 1145kJ (274 cal); 39.1g carbohydrate; 4.8g protein; 2.3g fibre

Cinnamon brandy snaps with orange liqueur cream

PREPARATION TIME 25 MINUTES **COOKING TIME** 10 MINUTES **MAKES** 18

60g butter

⅓ cup (75g) firmly packed brown sugar

2 tablespoons golden syrup

⅓ cup (50g) plain flour

2 teaspoons ground cinnamon

1 teaspoon ground ginger

300ml thickened cream

1 tablespoon icing sugar

2 teaspoons orange-flavoured liqueur

1 Preheat oven to 180°C/160°C fan-forced. Grease two oven trays; line with baking paper.

2 Stir butter, brown sugar and syrup in small saucepan over low heat until smooth. Remove from heat; stir in sifted flour and spices.

3 Drop four rounded teaspoons of mixture about 5cm apart on trays. Bake 7 minutes or until snaps bubble.

4 Slide spatula under each snap to loosen; working quickly, wrap one snap around handle of a wooden spoon. Remove handle; place snap on wire rack to cool. Repeat with the remaining snaps.

5 Beat cream, sifted icing sugar and liqueur in small bowl with electric mixer until firm peaks form. Just before serving, fill snaps with cream.

PER BRANDY SNAP 9g total fat (5.9g saturated fat); 510kJ (122 cal); 9.7g carbohydrate; 0.7g protein; 0.1g fibre

For such a straight-forward piece of kitchen equipment, oven trays can present no end of problems: over- or under-browning, overly dry biscuits, too big for the oven, warping, sticking, non-uniform cooking. Most professionals and serious home-bakers agree that light-coloured, non-stick oven trays with a matte surface lined with baking paper produce relatively trouble-free results.

Macadamia anzac biscuits

PREPARATION TIME 15 MINUTES **COOKING TIME** 15 MINUTES **MAKES** 32

125g butter, chopped

2 tablespoons golden syrup

½ teaspoon bicarbonate of soda

2 tablespoons boiling water

1 cup (90g) rolled oats

1 cup (150g) plain flour

1 cup (220g) firmly packed brown sugar

¾ cup (60g) desiccated coconut

½ cup (65g) finely chopped macadamia nuts

¼ cup (45g) finely chopped glacé ginger

1 Preheat oven to 180°C/160°C fan-forced. Grease oven trays; line with baking paper.

2 Stir butter and golden syrup in medium saucepan over low heat until smooth.

3 Stir in combined soda and the water; stir in remaining ingredients.

4 Roll level tablespoons of mixture into balls. Place about 5cm apart on oven trays; flatten slightly. Bake about 15 minutes. Cool on trays.

PER BISCUIT 6.3g total fat (3.5g saturated fat); 422kJ (101 cal); 9.4g carbohydrate; 1.3g protein; 0.9g fibre

As if anzac biscuits weren't already obviously antipodean adding macadamias gives no doubt as to their nationality. Their history dates back to World War I, when mothers and wives of Australian soldiers in Europe came up with the idea for a nutritional sweet biscuit that would survive weeks of sea transport en route to the front. Based on a Scottish recipe using rolled oats, the biscuits' other ingredients were chosen on the basis that they were not likely to spoil. Originally called soldiers biscuits, the anzac got its new name to commemorate Gallipoli.

THE MUFFIN PAN
& THE PATTY PAN

The Muffin Pan & The Patty Pan

Delightful as they are, muffins and cupcakes are just the beginning of the treats you can produce with the aid of the muffin and patty pan family of small moulds .Think of lining those little shapes with something that will bake into a case to hold some delicious filling, and you have a great range of inspirations for party food, stylish entrées and satisfying, easy-to-eat snacks to take to a sporting event, or on a picnic or boat. There are endless variations, too, within the usual idea of filling each cup with a batter to be baked.

CHOOSING PANS

Muffin pans are organised in convenient sets, and come in at least five sizes from mini, with a capacity of just 1 tablespoon, to Texas, with a capacity of ¾ cup – these are the amounts they will hold when full to the top, but muffin or cake mixture, as a general rule, should only fill three-quarters of the muffin hole.

Patty pans vary in depth; avoid the shallower ones as cakes made in them will tend to be dry. Choose sturdy pans with seamless individual cups bonded to the frame, which will give clean-edged shapes, rather than pans with just indents stamped in a metal sheet.

Pans may be finished with a non-stick coating; these vary greatly in quality and are effective only until they become scratched and worn (read more about non-stick coatings under the Finish section in *The Frying Pan*, page 23).

Two new materials coming onto the market for baking ware are hard-anodised aluminium and silicone ware – read more about these under the Material section in *The Cake Pan*, page 513).

BAKING TECHNIQUES

Have the pans prepared, oven shelves in position and the oven heating before you start to mix the muffins or cakes. You may choose to bake them in fluted paper cases, though this means they won't have smooth, browned sides; they will retain their shape better if the cases are placed in muffin or deep patty pan paper cups before filling with batter.

If baking without paper cases, grease the muffin holes or patty pans well, whether or not they have a non-stick finish. It can be difficult to persuade these small cups to release their contents cleanly, so unless you know from experience that yours behave well in this regard, you may want to take out insurance by cutting a stack of small circles, sized to fit, from folded baking paper and slipping one into the base of each cup before filling with mixture. For notes on baking techniques for cakes, please see *The Cake Pan*, page 513.

For muffins, the main point is to mix in a way that will disturb the flour as little as possible because muffins will become tough if overhandled. Pour all the liquid at once over the dry ingredients, then use the edge of a large metal spoon or fork to "cut" ingredients together in as few strokes as possible – the mixture should still look lumpy. Spoon the mixture into each pan, pushing the mixture off with a rubber spatula.

MAKING CRISP CASES IN MUFFIN PANS

You can make crisp cases from bread, wonton or spring roll wrappers, fillo, shortcrust or puff pastry. Cut rounds or squares from pastry, press into prepared pan holes and bake until golden. Squares will make "flower" shapes with the corners as the petals, while rounds will make round cups. You can also make pies by filling uncooked pastry cases and adding pastry lids, as described in Shortcrust and Puff Pastry, below.

Muffin pans work best for deep cases because they can hold the bread, wrappers or pastry in place until it sets into shape. For shallow tartlet cases, use patty or tartlet pans.

BREAD CASES Remove crusts from sliced, day-old white or wholemeal bread and roll with a rolling pin to a thickness of about 2mm. Cut into rounds for shallow pans; leave square or cut into rounds for deep pans. Brush both sides of bread with melted butter and press into pan holes. Place shallow cases in freezer for 15 minutes before baking, to set the shape. Bake deep or shallow cases at 200°C/180°C fan-forced for 15 minutes or until golden, watching carefully to ensure they don't darken too much. Cool 5 minutes in pans, then turn out and cool completely on a wire rack. Store in an airtight container for up to three days or freeze for up to a month

WONTON OR SPRING ROLL WRAPPERS Brush with oil and press into mini muffin pans for wonton wrappers or larger ones for spring roll wrappers. Bake at 180°C/160°C fan-forced for about 7 minutes or until golden. Cool and store as for bread cases.

FILLO PASTRY Brush a sheet of fillo pastry with melted butter or spray with olive oil; repeat twice. Layer sheets, cut into shapes, press into muffin pan holes and bake at 200°C/180°C fan-forced for 15 to 20 minutes or until golden. Cool and store as for bread cases.

SHORTCRUST AND PUFF PASTRY Cut rounds or squares and press into deep or shallow prepared pan holes. Prick all over with a fork and bake at 220°C/200°C fan-forced for 15 minutes or until golden brown, checking once or twice and pushing down any parts that are puffing up. Cool and store as for bread cases.

FOR PIES Fill pastry-lined pan holes with cooked cold fillings; cover with pastry lids cut to fit. Moisten the edge of the bottom crust, pinch edges together to seal then glaze with egg; cut a slit in the top to allow steam to escape and bake at 220°C/200°C fan-forced for 15 minutes or until golden brown. Stand 5 minutes in pan before serving, or cool on wire rack. Freeze or refrigerate until requried.

FILLINGS

WONTON & SPRING ROLL WRAPPERS OR FILLO PASTRY Fill these cases with room temperature mixtures such as chicken or seafood salad; roasted vegetables; hummus with grilled capsicum and black olives. They can be filled with warm mixtures described below.

BREAD OR PASTRY CASES Fill these with warm mixtures such as scrambled egg with chunks of hot-smoked trout and chopped chives; hot white sauce mixed with asparagus, seafood, corn and bacon, hard-boiled egg and bacon; spinach and cheese, etc.

Cheese, corn and bacon muffins

PREPARATION TIME 20 MINUTES (PLUS STANDING TIME) **COOKING TIME** 25 MINUTES **MAKES** 12

½ cup (85g) polenta

½ cup (125ml) milk

3 rindless bacon rashers (195g), chopped finely

4 green onions, chopped finely

1½ cups (225g) self-raising flour

1 tablespoon caster sugar

310g can corn kernels, drained

125g can creamed corn

100g butter, melted

2 eggs, beaten lightly

50g piece cheddar cheese

¼ cup (30g) coarsely grated cheddar cheese

1 Preheat oven to 200°C/180°C fan-forced. Oil 12-hole (⅓-cup/80ml) muffin pan.

2 Combine polenta and milk in small bowl, cover; stand 20 minutes.

3 Meanwhile, cook bacon in heated small frying pan, stirring, 2 minutes. Add onion; cook, stirring, another 2 minutes. Remove pan from heat; cool 5 minutes.

4 Sift flour and sugar into large bowl; stir in corn kernels, creamed corn and bacon mixture. Add butter, eggs and polenta mixture; mix muffin batter until just combined.

5 Spoon 1 tablespoon of the batter into each pan hole. Cut piece of cheese into 12 equal pieces; place one piece in the centre of each muffin pan hole. Divide remaining batter among muffin pan holes; sprinkle grated cheese over each.

6 Bake about 20 minutes. Stand muffins in pan 5 minutes; turn onto wire rack to cool.

▭ **PER MUFFIN** 12.5g total fat (7.1g saturated fat); 1087kJ (260 cal); 25.7g carbohydrate; 10g protein; 1.9g fibre

Chocolate, rum and raisin muffins

PREPARATION TIME 20 MINUTES (PLUS STANDING TIME) **COOKING TIME** 25 MINUTES **MAKES** 6

1 cup (170g) coarsely chopped raisins

¼ cup (60ml) dark rum

1⅔ cups (250g) self-raising flour

⅓ cup (35g) cocoa powder

½ cup (110g) caster sugar

1 cup (190g) Choc Bits

60g butter, melted

¾ cup (180ml) milk

1 egg, beaten lightly

1 Combine raisins and rum in small bowl. Cover; stand 1 hour.

2 Preheat oven to 200°C/180°C fan-forced. Grease 6-hole (¾-cup/180ml) texas muffin pan.

3 Sift dry ingredients into large bowl, stir in raisin mixture and remaining ingredients. Divide mixture among pan holes.

4 Bake about 25 minutes. Stand muffins in pan 5 minutes; turn onto wire rack to cool.

▭ **PER MUFFIN** 20.8g total fat (12.4g saturated fat); 2579kJ (617 cal); 90.6g carbohydrate; 9.7g protein; 3.6g fibre

Banana and cinnamon muffins

PREPARATION TIME 20 MINUTES **COOKING TIME** 20 MINUTES **MAKES** 12

2 cups (300g) self-raising flour

⅓ cup (50g) plain flour

1 teaspoon ground cinnamon

½ teaspoon bicarbonate of soda

½ cup (110g) firmly packed brown sugar

1 cup mashed banana

2 eggs

¾ cup (180ml) buttermilk

⅓ cup (80ml) vegetable oil

½ teaspoon ground cinnamon, extra

CREAM CHEESE TOPPING

125g cream cheese, softened

¼ cup (40g) icing sugar

Make sure the bananas you use are over-ripe, they contain natural sugars, which are an important part of this recipe. When you have some bananas becoming over-ripe, toss them, as they are, into the freezer until you are ready to use them. It doesn't matter if they're black.

1 Preheat oven to 200°C/180°C fan-forced. Grease 12-hole (⅓-cup/80ml) muffin pan.

2 Sift flours, cinnamon, soda and sugar into large bowl; stir in banana then combined eggs, buttermilk and oil. Divide mixture among pan holes.

3 Bake about 20 minutes. Stand muffins in pan 5 minutes; turn onto wire rack to cool.

4 Make cream cheese topping. Spread cold muffins with topping; serve sprinkled with extra cinnamon.

CREAM CHEESE TOPPING Beat ingredients in small bowl with electric mixer until smooth.

☐ **PER MUFFIN** 10.3g total fat (3.2g saturated fat); 1133kJ (271 cal); 37.9g carbohydrate; 5.8g protein; 1.5g fibre

Raspberry and coconut muffins

PREPARATION TIME 10 MINUTES **COOKING TIME** 20 MINUTES **MAKES** 12

2½ cups (375g) self-raising flour

90g butter, chopped

1 cup (220g) caster sugar

1¼ cups (310ml) buttermilk

1 egg, beaten lightly

⅓ cup (30g) desiccated coconut

150g fresh or frozen raspberries

2 tablespoons shredded coconut

Use fresh berries if they're in season, but if they're not, use frozen berries while they're still in their frozen state. If they're thawed, they'll "bleed" into the mixture and will make the texture of the muffin look a little blurred.

1 Preheat oven to 200°C/180°C fan-forced. Grease 12-hole (⅓-cup/80ml) muffin pan.

2 Sift flour into large bowl; rub in butter with fingers. Add sugar, buttermilk, egg, desiccated coconut and raspberries; mix until just combined. Spoon mixture into pan holes; sprinkle with shredded coconut.

3 Bake about 20 minutes. Stand muffins in pan 5 minutes; turn, top-side up, onto wire rack to cool.

☐ **PER MUFFIN** 9.8g total fat (6.6g saturated fat); 1195kJ (286 cal); 42.9g carbohydrate; 5.2g protein; 2.4g fibre

Berry muffins

PREPARATION TIME 10 MINUTES **COOKING TIME** 20 MINUTES **MAKES** 12

2½ cups (375g) self-raising flour

90g butter, chopped

1 cup (220g) caster sugar

1¼ cups (310ml) buttermilk

1 egg, beaten lightly

200g fresh or frozen mixed berries

1 Preheat oven to 180°C/160°C fan-forced. Grease 12-hole (⅓-cup/80ml) muffin pan.

2 Sift flour into large bowl; rub in butter with fingers. Stir in sugar, buttermilk and egg. Do not over-mix; mixture should be lumpy. Add berries; stir through gently. Spoon mixture into pan holes.

3 Bake about 20 minutes. Stand muffins in pan 5 minutes; turn, top-side up, onto wire rack to cool.

☐ **PER MUFFIN** 7.5g total fat (4.6g saturated fat); 1095kJ (262 cal); 42.4g carbohydrate; 5.1g protein; 1.6g fibre

Marmalade almond muffins

PREPARATION TIME 15 MINUTES **COOKING TIME** 20 MINUTES **MAKES** 12

2 cups (300g) self-raising flour

125g butter, chopped

1 cup (80g) flaked almonds

⅔ cup (150g) caster sugar

1 tablespoon finely grated orange rind

½ cup (170g) orange marmalade

2 eggs, beaten lightly

½ cup (125ml) milk

¼ cup (20g) flaked almonds, extra

ORANGE SYRUP

¼ cup (85g) orange marmalade

2 tablespoons hot water

1 Preheat oven to 200°C/180°C fan-forced. Grease 12-hole (⅓-cup/80ml) muffin pan.

2 Sift flour into large bowl; rub in butter with fingers. Stir in nuts, sugar and rind, then marmalade, egg and milk. Spoon mixture into pan holes; sprinkle with extra nuts.

3 Bake about 20 minutes. Stand muffins in pan 5 minutes; turn, top-side up, onto wire rack.

4 Make orange syrup; drizzle over warm muffins.

ORANGE SYRUP Combine ingredients in small bowl.

☐ **PER MUFFIN** 14.7g total fat (6.5g saturated fat); 1421kJ (340 cal); 45g carbohydrate; 5.7g protein; 1.9g fibre

1 BERRY MUFFINS **2** MARMALADE ALMOND MUFFINS
3 VANILLA PATTY CAKES WITH GLACE ICING [P 592] **4** BANANA BLUEBERRY CAKES [P 592]

3   4

1   2

Vanilla patty cakes with glacé icing

PREPARATION TIME 15 MINUTES **COOKING TIME** 25 MINUTES **MAKES** 24

125g butter, softened

1 teaspoon vanilla extract

⅔ cup (150g) caster sugar

3 eggs

1½ cups (225g) self-raising flour

¼ cup (60ml) milk

GLACE ICING

1½ cups (240g) icing sugar

½ teaspoon butter

2 tablespoons milk,
approximately

1 Preheat oven to 180°C/160°C fan-forced. Line two deep 12-hole patty pans with paper cases.

2 Beat butter, extract, sugar, eggs, flour and milk in medium bowl with electric mixer on low speed until ingredients are combined. Increase speed to medium; beat about 3 minutes or until mixture is smooth and paler in colour. Drop slightly rounded tablespoons of mixture into paper cases.

3 Bake about 20 minutes. Turn patty cakes, top-side up, onto wire rack to cool.

4 Make glacé icing. Top patty cakes with icing.

GLACE ICING Sift icing sugar into small heatproof bowl; stir in butter and enough milk to give a firm paste. Stir icing over small saucepan of simmering water until spreadable.

▭ **PER PATTY CAKE** 5.4g total fat (3.2g saturated fat); 627kJ (150 cal); 23.1g carbohydrate; 1.9g protein; 0.4g fibre

---

Banana blueberry cakes

PREPARATION TIME 20 MINUTES **COOKING TIME** 30 MINUTES (PLUS COOLING TIME) **MAKES** 18

125g butter

½ cup (125ml) milk

2 eggs

1 cup (220g) caster sugar

½ cup mashed banana

1½ cups (225g) self-raising flour

½ cup (75g) frozen blueberries

1 Preheat oven to 180°C/160°C fan-forced. Line 18 patty-pan holes with paper cases.

2 Stir butter and milk in small saucepan over low heat until butter melts; cool.

3 Beat eggs in small bowl with electric mixer until thick and creamy. Gradually add sugar, beating until dissolved between additions; stir in banana. Fold in sifted flour and butter mixture, in two batches. Divide mixture among pan holes.

4 Bake 10 minutes. Remove pan from oven; press frozen blueberries into tops of cakes. Bake further 15 minutes. Turn cakes onto wire racks to cool.

▭ **PER CAKE** 6.7g total fat (4.1g saturated fat); 690kJ (165 cal); 23.2g carbohydrate; 2.4g protein; 0.7g fibre

Mini choc chip almond cakes

PREPARATION TIME 20 MINUTES **COOKING TIME** 20 MINUTES **MAKES** 18

3 egg whites
90g butter, melted
½ cup (60g) almond meal
¾ cup (120g) icing sugar
¼ cup (35g) plain flour

100g dark eating chocolate, chopped finely
¼ cup (60ml) cream
100g dark eating chocolate, extra

1 Preheat oven to 180°C/160°C fan-forced. Grease 18 holes of two 12-hole mini (1 tablespoon/20ml) muffin pans.

2 Whisk egg whites lightly in medium bowl with a fork until combined. Add butter, meal, sifted icing sugar and flour; using a wooden spoon, stir until just combined. Stir in chopped chocolate. Drop tablespoons of mixture into pan holes.

3 Bake about 15 minutes; turn onto wire racks to cool.

4 Stir cream and extra chocolate in medium heatproof bowl over pan of simmering water until just melted; stand until thickened. Spoon chocolate mixture over cakes.

PER CAKE 10.6g total fat (5.7g saturated fat); 690kJ (165 cal); 15.3g carbohydrate; 2.1g protein; 0.5g fibre

Try substituting hazelnut meal for almond meal in this recipe. Also, the mixture of these little cakes easily hold air bubbles because it is so dense and heavy. So, don't whisk the egg whites too much, and, if you have time, let the uncooked mixture sit in the pan for about 30 minutes before baking.

Butterfly cakes

PREPARATION TIME 30 MINUTES **COOKING TIME** 20 MINUTES **MAKES** 24

125g butter, softened
1 teaspoon vanilla extract
¾ cup (165g) caster sugar
2 eggs

1½ cups (225g) self-raising flour
⅓ cup (80ml) milk
½ cup (160g) jam
300ml thickened cream, whipped

1 Preheat oven to 180°C/160°C fan-forced. Line two deep 12-hole patty pans with paper cases.

2 Beat butter, extract and sugar in small bowl with electric mixer until light and fluffy. Beat in eggs one at a time, beating well after each addition. Transfer mixture to medium bowl; stir in sifted flour and milk, in two batches.

3 Drop slightly rounded tablespoons of mixture into paper cases; bake about 20 minutes. Turn cakes onto wire racks; turn top-side up to cool.

4 Using a small, sharp-pointed knife, cut a circle from the top of each cake; cut the circle in half to make two 'wings'. Fill cake cavities with jam and cream. Place wings in position on top of cakes; top with strawberry pieces and dust with a little sifted icing sugar, if desired.

PER CAKE 9.8g total fat (6.2g saturated fat); 702kJ (168 cal); 17.2g carbohydrate; 2.2g protein; 0.4g fibre

You'll notice, almost always, the extract, essence or rind is added to the butter. The reason for this, is, fat will hold flavours, so, why not get the most out of the flavours you're adding to cakes, biscuits, cheesecakes, etc.

Baking pans

Sweet and savoury morsels can be produced from a wide array of baking pans.

FRIAND
Traditional friand pans have oval- or rectangular-shaped holes; available separately or, in frames of various sizes. They are made in various materials with different finishes.

MUFFIN AND TEXAS MUFFIN
Regular/medium size muffin pans have a capacity of ⅓-cup/80ml; available in 6-hole, 12-hole and 24-hole frames. A Texas muffin pan holds ¾-cup/180ml and only comes in 6-hole frames.

SMALL AND MINI MUFFIN
Small muffin pans have a capacity of 2 tablespoons/40ml and come in 12-hole frames. Mini muffin pans hold 1 tablespoon/20ml and are available in 12-hole and 24-hole frames.

LAMINGTON
This pan is straight-sided and measures 20cm x 30cm and 3cm deep. It's used for making cake which is then made into lamingtons; it's also used for slices.

DEEP ROUND AND SANDWICH
Deep cake pans come in various sizes and proportions, the most usual being 22cm or 20cm in diameter and about 6cm deep. Sandwich pans (for a two-layer, filled cake) also vary, the most usual being 22cm or 20cm in diameter and 4.5cm deep.

SLICE AND SWISS ROLL
A slice pan is usually 19cm x 29cm and 2cm deep with slightly angled sides. A swiss roll pan is about 25cm x 30cm and 1cm deep.

LOAF

Loaf pans come in slightly different sizes and depths, also in different materials and finishes. The most common size is 14cm x 21cm inside-top measurement and about 5cm deep.

BAR

Bar pans vary slightly in size and shape, but the usual measurements are 8cm x 26cm inside-top measurement and about 4cm deep. They come in various materials and finishes. Bar cakes easily cut into small, neat slices.

PATTY

Patty pans come in round-based and flat-based shapes, mostly in 12 1-cup frames. They come in various materials and finishes. These pans are often "lined" with paper cases to eliminate greasing.

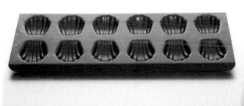

DEEP SQUARE

Usually used for fruit cakes, square pans come in many sizes and proportions. The benefit of the square shape is that it can be cut into the traditional small squares for guests to take home. They come in various materials and finishes.

MADELEINE

Madeleines are traditional, French, individual sponge cakes, usually plain (vanilla) or flavoured with lemon rind. They are baked in small moulds shaped like scallop-shells.

BABA AND BUNDT

A baba is a fluted ring pan about 20cm in diameter. Bundt pans come in various sizes and depths; they are more ornate than the baba pan. Grease both pans well regardless of their finish.

Apple custard tea cakes

PREPARATION TIME 25 MINUTES **COOKING TIME** 40 MINUTES **MAKES** 12

Cake, custard and apple are a winning combination. Make sure the custard does boil to eliminate any floury taste, and slice the apples finely so they tenderise in the brief baking time. These cakes are at their best served warm.

90g butter

½ teaspoon vanilla extract

½ cup (110g) caster sugar

2 eggs

¾ cup (110g) self-raising flour

¼ cup (30g) custard powder

2 tablespoons milk

1 large unpeeled apple (200g), cored, sliced finely

30g butter, melted, extra

1 tablespoon caster sugar, extra

½ teaspoon ground cinnamon

CUSTARD

1 tablespoon custard powder

1 tablespoon caster sugar

½ cup (125ml) milk

¼ teaspoon vanilla extract

1 Make custard.

2 Preheat oven to 180°C/160°C fan-forced. Line 12-hole (⅓-cup/80ml) muffin pan with paper cases.

3 Beat butter, extract, sugar, eggs, flour, custard powder and milk in small bowl with electric mixer on low speed until ingredients are just combined. Increase speed to medium, beat until mixture is changed to a paler colour.

4 Divide half the mixture among cases. Top with custard, then remaining cake mixture; spread mixture to cover custard. Top with apple slices, pressing slightly into cake.

5 Bake about 30 minutes. Brush hot cakes with extra butter, then sprinkle with combined extra sugar and cinnamon. Turn cakes onto wire rack. Serve warm or cold.

CUSTARD Blend custard powder and sugar with milk and extract in small saucepan; stir over heat until mixture boils and thickens. Remove from heat; cover surface with plastic wrap; cool.

⬭ **PER CAKE** 9.8g total fat (6g saturated fat); 815kJ (195 cal); 23.8g carbohydrate; 2.6g protein; 0.6g fibre

---

Black forest cakes

PREPARATION TIME 25 MINUTES (PLUS COOLING TIME) **COOKING TIME** 50 MINUTES **MAKES** 12

If you don't like or don't have cherry brandy, just use regular brandy. Or, if you don't want any alcohol in this cake, use milk instead of the brandy in the cake, and use 2 teaspoons icing sugar instead of the brandy in the cream topping.

425g can pitted cherries in syrup

165g butter, chopped coarsely

100g dark eating chocolate, chopped coarsely

1⅓ cups (295g) caster sugar

¼ cup (60ml) cherry brandy

1 cup (150g) plain flour

2 tablespoons self-raising flour

2 tablespoons cocoa powder

1 egg

⅔ cup (160ml) thickened cream, whipped

2 teaspoons cherry brandy

100g dark eating chocolate

1 Preheat oven to 170°C/150°C fan-forced. Line 12-hole (⅓-cup/80ml) muffin pan with paper cases.

2 Drain cherries; reserve syrup. Process ½ cup (110g) cherries with ½ cup (125ml) of the syrup until smooth. Halve remaining cherries; reserve for decorating cakes. Discard remaining syrup.

3 Stir butter, chocolate, sugar, brandy and cherry puree in small saucepan over low heat until chocolate is melted. Transfer mixture to medium bowl; cool 15 minutes.

4 Whisk in sifted flours and cocoa, then egg. Divide mixture among cases; smooth surface.

5 Bake about 45 minutes. Turn cakes onto wire rack to cool.

6 Top cakes with remaining cherry halves and combined cream and cherry brandy. Using a vegetable peeler, grate chocolate; sprinkle over cakes.

▭ **PER CAKE** 21.8g total fat (13.8g saturated fat); 1785kJ (427 cal); 50.6g carbohydrate; 3.8g protein; 1.1g fibre

---

Banana caramel cakes

PREPARATION TIME 25 MINUTES **COOKING TIME** 25 MINUTES **MAKES** 12

90g butter, softened

½ cup (110g) firmly packed brown sugar

2 eggs

½ cup (75g) self-raising flour

½ cup (75g) plain flour

½ teaspoon bicarbonate of soda

½ teaspoon mixed spice

⅔ cup mashed overripe banana

⅓ cup (80g) sour cream

2 tablespoons milk

380g can Top 'n' Fill caramel

½ cup (125ml) thickened cream, whipped

2 medium bananas (400g), sliced thinly

100g dark eating chocolate

1 Preheat oven to 180°C/160°C fan-forced. Line 12-hole (⅓-cup/80ml) muffin pan with paper cases.

2 Beat butter, sugar and eggs in small bowl with electric mixer until light and fluffy. Mixture will curdle at this stage, but will reconstitute later.

3 Stir in sifted dry ingredients, banana, sour cream and milk. Divide mixture among cases; smooth surface.

4 Bake about 25 minutes; turn cakes onto wire rack to cool.

5 Remove cases from cakes. Fold 2 tablespoons of the caramel into cream. Cut cakes horizontally into three slices. Re-assemble cakes with remaining caramel and banana. Top cakes with caramel-flavoured cream.

6 Using a vegetable peeler, grate chocolate; sprinkle over cakes.

▭ **PER CAKE** 18.5g total fat (11.7g saturated fat); 1576kJ (377 cal); 46g carbohydrate; 6g protein; 1.4g fibre

Top 'n' Fill is simply canned caramelised condensed milk. We don't recommend the old-fashioned method of caramelising condensed milk by boiling the can in water for an hour or so. It can be dangerous. You can caramelise condensed milk by patiently stirring it in a heavy-based saucepan for a long time. A commercial or home made thick caramel sauce could be substituted for Top 'n' Fill at a pinch.

Lemon meringue cakes

PREPARATION TIME 45 MINUTES **COOKING TIME** 35 MINUTES **MAKES** 12

125g butter, softened

2 teaspoons finely grated lemon rind

²⁄₃ cup (150g) caster sugar

2 eggs

¹⁄₃ cup (80ml) milk

¾ cup (60g) desiccated coconut

1¼ cups (185g) self-raising flour

LEMON CURD

4 egg yolks

¹⁄₃ cup (75g) caster sugar

2 teaspoons finely grated lemon rind

¼ cup (60ml) lemon juice

40g butter

COCONUT MERINGUE

4 egg whites

1 cup (220g) caster sugar

1¹⁄₃ cups (100g) shredded coconut, chopped finely

1 Make lemon curd.

2 Preheat oven to 180°C/160°C fan-forced. Line 12-hole (⅓-cup/80ml) muffin pan with paper cases.

3 Beat butter, rind, sugar and eggs in small bowl with electric mixer until light and fluffy. Stir in milk and coconut, then sifted flour. Divide mixture among cases; smooth surface.

4 Bake about 25 minutes. Turn cakes onto wire rack to cool. Increase oven temperature to 220°C/200°C fan-forced.

5 Cut a 2cm deep hole in the centre of each cake, fill with curd; discard cake tops.

6 Make coconut meringue; spoon into a piping bag fitted with a 1cm plain tube.

7 Pipe meringue on top of each cake; place cakes on oven tray. Bake 5 minutes or until meringue is browned lightly.

LEMON CURD Combine ingredients in small heatproof bowl over small saucepan of simmering water, stirring constantly, until mixture thickens slightly and coats the back of a spoon. Remove from heat. Cover tightly; refrigerate curd until cold.

COCONUT MERINGUE Beat egg whites in small bowl with electric mixer until soft peaks form; gradually add sugar, beating until sugar dissolves. Fold in coconut.

☐ **PER CAKE** 22.9g total fat (15.9g saturated fat); 1810kJ (433 cal); 49.5g carbohydrate; 6g protein; 2.5g fibre

Lemon curd is made by stirring the ingredients over a pan of simmering water. The water shouldn't touch the bottom of the bowl and the bowl should be made from glass or china.

If you have a heavy-based saucepan and an easily and quickly controlled heat source, you can by-pass this method and stir the curd directly over the heat until it's thick. The second this happens, pour the curd out of the pan into a bowl to stop the cooking. This method will work, providing you don't overheat the curd – if you do, it will split (curdle) and will have to be thrown out.

Lemon cheesecakes

PREPARATION TIME 25 MINUTES (PLUS REFRIGERATION TIME)
COOKING TIME 25 MINUTES (PLUS REFRIGERATION TIME) **MAKES** 12

100g plain sweet biscuits

50g butter, melted

2 x 250g packets cream cheese, softened

2 teaspoons finely grated lemon rind

½ cup (110g) caster sugar

2 eggs

GLAZE

⅔ cup (220g) apricot jam

2 tablespoons brandy

1 Preheat oven to slow 150°C/ 130°C fan-forced. Line 12-hole (⅓-cup/80ml) muffin pan with paper cases.

2 Blend or process biscuits until fine. Add butter; process until just combined. Divide mixture among cases; press firmly. Refrigerate 30 minutes.

3 Beat cheese, rind and sugar in small bowl with electric mixer until smooth. Beat in eggs. Pour mixture into cases. Bake about 25 minutes. Cool.

4 Make glaze.

5 Pour glaze evenly over tops of cheesecakes; refrigerate 2 hours or until glaze is set.

GLAZE Heat jam and brandy in small saucepan over low heat; strain.

☐ **PER CHEESECAKE** 19.4g total fat (12g saturated fat); 1321kJ (316 cal); 28.3g carbohydrate; 5.3g protein; 0.4g fibre

Caramel mud cakes

PREPARATION TIME 25 MINUTES **COOKING TIME** 35 MINUTES (PLUS COOLING TIME) **MAKES** 12

125g butter, chopped coarsely

100g white eating chocolate, chopped coarsely

⅔ cup (150g) firmly packed brown sugar

¼ cup (90g) golden syrup

⅔ cup (160ml) milk

1 cup (150g) plain flour

⅓ cup (50g) self-raising flour

1 egg

2 tablespoons icing sugar

1 Preheat oven to 170°C/150°C fan-forced. Line 12-hole (⅓-cup/80ml) muffin pan with paper cases.

2 Stir butter, chocolate, sugar, syrup and milk in small saucepan over low heat, until smooth. Transfer mixture to medium bowl; cool 15 minutes.

3 Whisk sifted flours into chocolate mixture, then egg. Divide mixture among cases.

4 Bake about 30 minutes. Turn cakes onto wire rack to cool.

5 Serve, dusted with sifted icing sugar.

☐ **PER CAKE** 12.5g total fat (7.9g saturated fat); 1233kJ (295 cal); 41.6g carbohydrate; 3.5g protein; 0.6g fibre

No-bake chocolate cakes

PREPARATION TIME 15 MINUTES **COOKING TIME** 5 MINUTES (PLUS REFRIGERATION TIME) **MAKES** 18

5 x 60g Mars Bars

50g butter

3½ cups (120g) Rice Bubbles

200g milk eating chocolate, melted

1 Line 18 deep patty pan holes with paper cases.

2 Chop four of the Mars Bars coarsely; cut remaining bar into slices.

3 Place chopped bars in medium saucepan with butter; stir over low heat until smooth. Stir in Rice Bubbles. Press mixture into cases, spread with chocolate; top with sliced bar.

4 Refrigerate about 30 minutes or until set.

☐ **PER CAKE** 8.3g total fat (5.1g saturated fat); 736kJ (176 cal); 22.8g carbohydrate; 2.2g protein; 0.5g fibre

This recipe is rich and decadent. It does well as a slice too. Press the mixture into a greased 19cm x 29cm slice pan and keep it covered in the fridge.

Little moist almond cakes

PREPARATION TIME 30 MINUTES **COOKING TIME** 15 MINUTES **MAKES** 36

6 egg whites

185g butter, melted

1½ cups (240g) icing sugar

1 cup (125g) almond meal

½ cup (75g) plain flour

2 teaspoons finely grated orange rind

ORANGE GLACE ICING

1 cup (160g) icing sugar

1 teaspoon butter

1 tablespoon orange juice, approximately

1 Preheat oven to 180°C/160°C fan forced. Grease three 12-hole mini (1 tablespoon/20ml) muffin pans.

2 Whisk egg whites in medium bowl with a fork until combined. Add butter, sifted icing sugar, meal, sifted flour and rind; whisk until combined. Divide among pan holes.

3 Bake about 15 minutes. Turn cakes onto wire racks, top-side up, to cool.

4 Meanwhile, make orange glacé icing; spread icing over cakes.

ORANGE GLACE ICING Sift icing sugar in small heatproof bowl; add butter and enough juice to make a firm paste. Stir over a small saucepan of simmering water until a spreadable.

☐ **PER CAKE** 6.3g total fat (2.8g saturated fat); 481kJ (115 cal); 12.8g carbohydrate; 1.6g protein; 0.4g fibre

The secret to making good glacé icing is in the under heating. That's why we've suggested you stir the icing over a pan of simmering water. But if you're quick and careful, you can heat the icing directly over the heat, but keep touching the bottom of the saucepan between stirrings. If the pan's bottom becomes too hot to touch, you've gone too far, the icing will almost certainly crystallise. Remember, the other name for glacé icing is warm icing.

Coffee caramel cakes

PREPARATION TIME 15 MINUTES **COOKING TIME** 20 MINUTES (PLUS COOLING TIME) **MAKES** 18

125g butter, softened

⅔ cup (150g) firmly packed brown sugar

2 tablespoons instant coffee granules

1 tablespoon boiling water

2 eggs

2 cups (300g) self-raising flour

½ cup (125ml) milk

18 jersey caramels (130g), halved

1 Preheat oven to 180°C/160°C fan-forced. Line 18 patty pan holes with paper cases.

2 Beat butter and sugar in small bowl with electric mixer until light and fluffy. Add combined coffee and the water, then beat in eggs, one at a time, beating until just combined between additions. Transfer mixture to large bowl. Stir in sifted flour and milk

3 Divide half of the mixture among pan holes. Press 3 caramel halves into the centre of each cake; cover with remaining cake mixture.

4 Bake about 20 minutes. Cool in pan 5 minutes; turn cakes onto wire racks to cool.

▭ **PER CAKE** 7.6g total fat (4.8g saturated fat); 769kJ (184 cal); 25.6g carbohydrate; 2.9g protein; 0.8g fibre

Currant cakes with orange glaze

PREPARATION TIME 20 MINUTES (PLUS STANDING TIME) **COOKING TIME** 15 MINUTES **MAKES** 24

Most cakes which have syrup poured over them require the syrup to be heated before it's poured or drizzled over the hot cake. In this case the syrup is used cold and brushed over the hot cakes to make a glaze.

¼ cup (55g) caster sugar

¼ cup (35g) dried currants

2 teaspoons finely grated orange rind

½ cup (125g) orange juice

125g butter, softened

2 teaspoons finely grated orange rind, extra

½ cup (110g) caster sugar, extra

2 eggs

1½ cups (225g) self-raising flour

⅓ cup (80ml) milk

1 Preheat oven to 180°C/160°C fan-forced. Grease two deep 12-hole patty pans.

2 Stir sugar, currants, rind and juice in small saucepan over heat, without boiling, until sugar dissolves; bring to a boil. Reduce heat, simmer, uncovered, without stirring, 2 minutes. Remove from heat; stand 30 minutes. Strain mixture into jug; reserve currants and syrup.

3 Beat butter, extra rind and extra sugar in medium bowl with electric mixer until light and fluffy. Add eggs, one at a time, beating until just combined after each addition. Stir in reserved currants, then flour and milk, in two batches. Divide mixture among pan holes.

4 Bake about 15 minutes. Turn cakes onto a wire rack over a tray; brush tops of hot cakes with reserved syrup.

▭ **PER CAKE** 5g total fat (3.1g saturated fat); 472kJ (113 cal); 15g carbohydrate; 1.7g protein; 0.5g fibre

Mushrooms

PREPARATION TIME 30 MINUTES (PLUS REFRIGERATION TIME)   **COOKING TIME** 12 MINUTES   **MAKES** 30

90g unsalted butter

1 teaspoon vanilla extract

⅓ cup (75g) caster sugar

1 egg

1⅔ cups (250g) plain flour

⅓ cup (110g) raspberry jam

⅓ cup (45g) crushed mixed nuts

2 teaspoons cocoa powder

FILLING

90g unsalted butter, softened

½ teaspoon vanilla extract

⅓ cup (75g) caster sugar

⅓ cup (80ml) milk

⅓ cup (80ml) water

1   Beat butter, extract and sugar in small bowl with electric mixer until smooth and creamy. Add egg, beat until just combined. Stir in sifted flour, in two batches. Turn pastry onto floured surface, knead gently until smooth. Cover; refrigerate 30 minutes.

2   Preheat oven to 200°C/180°C fan-forced. Grease 30 shallow patty-pan holes. Grease oven tray.

3   Roll pastry on floured surface until 2mm thick, cut 6.5cm rounds from pastry; gently press rounds into pan holes.

4   To make stalks, roll pastry scraps to 8mm-diameter sausage; cut 30 x 1.5cm-long stalks. Place on oven tray.

5   Bake cases and stalks about 12 minutes or until lightly browned. Flatten pastry cases with back of spoon halfway through cooking to remove air bubbles. Cool on wire racks.

6   Meanwhile, make filling.

7   Spoon ½ teaspoon jam into each pastry case; sprinkle with ½ teaspoon nuts. Spread rounded teaspoons filling into each case, sprinkle with a little sifted cocoa pwder. Press stalks into filling.

FILLING Beat butter, extract and sugar in small bowl with electric mixer until as white as possible. Gradually beat in milk and water a teaspoon at a time.

▭ **PER MUSHROOM** 6.1g total fat (3.5g saturated fat); 489kJ (117 cal); 13.7g carbohydrate; 1.6g protein; 0.5g fibre

The first five ingredients of this recipe will give you a crisp biscuit pastry. It's important not to over beat the butter, extract, sugar and egg mixture – over beating would make the pastry too soft, which makes it hard to handle. Once all the flour has been added, handle the pastry as little as possible for good results.

The filling for mushrooms is a lovely soft butter cream. The butter and milk should be at room temperature for best results.

Cream cheese frosting is a favourite on carrot cakes and it's also good on banana cakes – but in this berry-rich cupcake the flavour of it blends superbly. It's important to beat the butter and cream cheese really well with an electric mixer – it must be fluffy for the best results.

Berry cupcakes

PREPARATION TIME 30 MINUTES   **COOKING TIME** 45 MINUTES   **MAKES** 12

125g butter, softened

½ teaspoon vanilla extract

⅔ cup (150g) caster sugar

2 eggs

1 cup (150g) dried mixed berries

½ cup (70g) slivered almonds

⅔ cup (100g) plain flour

⅓ cup (50g) self-raising flour

¼ cup (60ml) milk

SUGARED FRUIT

150g fresh blueberries

120g fresh raspberries

1 egg white, beaten lightly

2 tablespoons vanilla sugar

CREAM CHEESE FROSTING

30g butter, softened

80g cream cheese, softened

1½ cups (240g) icing sugar

1   Make sugared fruit.

2   Preheat oven to 170°C/150°C fan-forced. Line 12-hole (⅓-cup/80ml) muffin pan with paper cases.

3   Beat butter, extract, sugar and eggs in small bowl with electric mixer until light and fluffy. Stir in fruit and nuts, then sifted flours and milk. Divide mixture among cases; smooth surface.

4   Bake about 45 minutes. Turn cakes onto wire rack to cool.

5   Meanwhile, make cream cheese frosting.

6   Spread cakes with frosting. Decorate with sugared fruit.

SUGARED FRUIT Brush each berry lightly with egg white; roll fruit in sugar. Place fruit on baking-paper-lined tray. Leave about 1 hour or until sugar is dry.

CREAM CHEESE FROSTING Beat butter and cheese in small bowl with electric mixer until light and fluffy; gradually beat in sifted icing sugar.

☐ **PER CUPCAKE** 17.4g total fat (9.1g saturated fat); 1689kJ (404 cal); 55.3g carbohydrate, 5.1g protein; 2.5g fibre

Strawberries and cream powder puffs

PREPARATION TIME 25 MINUTES **COOKING TIME** 10 MINUTES **MAKES** 12

Powder puffs are only little sponge cakes, so handle this mixture lightly. Make sure the egg and sugar mixture is thick, creamy and the sugar dissolved. The rest is easy – just fold the triple-sifted dry ingredients in gently.

2 eggs

⅓ cup (75g) caster sugar

2 tablespoons cornflour

2 tablespoons plain flour

2 tablespoons self-raising flour

⅔ cup (160ml) thickened cream

⅓ cup (55g) icing sugar

250g strawberries, chopped coarsely

1 Preheat oven to 180°C/160°C fan-forced. Grease and flour two 12-hole shallow patty pans.

2 Beat eggs in small bowl with electric mixer until thick and creamy. Gradually add caster sugar, 1 tablespoon at a time, beating until sugar dissolves between additions. Sift flours together three times; fold into egg mixture. Divide mixture among pan holes.

3 Bake about 8 minutes. Turn immediately onto wire rack to cool.

4 Beat cream and half of the sifted icing sugar in small bowl with electric mixer until soft peaks form; fold in strawberries. Divide cream mixture among half of the sponges; top with remaining sponges. Serve powder puffs dusted with remaining icing sugar.

▭ **PER POWDER PUFF** 6.7g total fat (4.1g saturated fat); 560kJ (134 cal); 15.9g carbohydrate; 2.1g protein; 0.6g fibre

Pear and hazelnut friands

PREPARATION TIME 15 MINUTES **COOKING TIME** 20 MINUTES **MAKES** 12

Friands, French for "little cakes", are one of the easiest cakes to make: they need very little mixing and can be made in one bowl. If you prefer an almond flavour with pear, then use almond meal and roasted flaked almonds instead of the hazelnut meal and roasted hazelnuts.

6 egg whites

185g butter, melted

1 cup (100g) hazelnut meal

1½ cups (240g) icing sugar

½ cup (75g) plain flour

1 small corella pear (100g)

12 roasted hazelnuts (10g), halved

1 Preheat oven to 200°C/180°C fan-forced. Grease 12 oval friand pans; place on oven tray.

2 Whisk egg whites in medium bowl with fork until combined. Add butter, meal, and sifted sugar and flour; using wooden spoon, stir until just combined.

3 Core pear; cut pear lengthways into 12 even slices.

4 Divide mixture among pans; top each with 1 slice pear and 2 nut halves. Bake about 20 minutes. Stand friands in pans 5 minutes; turn, top-side up, onto wire rack to cool.

▭ **PER FRIAND** 18.4g total fat (8.6g saturated fat); 1166kJ (279 cal); 26g carbohydrate; 3.9g protein; 1.4g fibre

Neenish tarts

PREPARATION TIME 25 MINUTES (PLUS REFRIGERATION TIME)   **COOKING TIME** 15 MINUTES   **MAKES** 24

1 ½ cups (225g) plain flour

100g butter

1 egg yolk

2 tablespoons lemon juice, approximately

MOCK CREAM

1 ½ tablespoons milk

¾ cup (165g) sugar

¼ cup (60ml) water

½ teaspoon gelatine

1 ½ tablespoons water, extra

185g unsalted butter

1 teaspoon vanilla extract

GLACE ICING

1 ½ cups (240g) icing sugar

2 tablespoons milk

½ teaspoon vanilla extract

1 ½ tablespoons cocoa powder

1 ½ teaspoons milk, extra

There are many mock cream recipes, but this one, which is stabilised with a little gelatine is rich, smooth and creamy. Make sure that the butter and extract are beaten with an electric mixer until the butter mixture is light, fluffy and as white as possible.

1 Sift flour into medium bowl; rub in butter with fingers. Stir in yolk and enough juice to make ingredients cling together. Press dough into a ball; knead gently on floured surface until smooth. Cover; refrigerate 30 minutes.

2 Preheat oven to 180°C/160°C fan-forced. Grease two 12-hole shallow patty pans.

3 Roll dough on floured surface to 3mm thick; cut into 7cm rounds. Place rounds in pans; prick all over with fork.

4 Bake pastry cases about 12 minutes or until golden brown. Lift onto wire racks to cool.

5 Meanwhile, make mock cream. Make glacé icing.

6 Fill pastry cases with mock cream, level tops with spatula. Spread a teaspoon of vanilla glacé icing over half of each tart; allow to set. Cover remaining half of each tart with chocolate glacé icing.

MOCK CREAM Stir milk, sugar and water in small saucepan over heat, without boiling, until sugar is dissolved. Sprinkle gelatine over extra water, stir into milk mixture, stir until dissolved; cool. Beat butter and extract in small bowl with electric mixer until as white as possible, gradually add cold milk mixture; beat until light and fluffy. Mixture will thicken on standing.

GLACE ICING Sift icing sugar into small bowl, stir in milk and extract; beat until smooth. Divide icing into two small heatproof bowls. Stir sifted cocoa and extra milk into one bowl. Stir both icings over hot water until icing is smooth and spreadable.

▭ **PER TART** 10.1g total fat (6.5g saturated fat); 811kJ (194 cal); 24g carbohydrate; 1.5g protein; 0.4g fibre

Fluffy frosting is one of those recipes that once you've mastered it, you'll find that you'll use it over and over. It's not vital to have a candy thermometer to make this frosting, but, it's important that the syrup be boiled until it's really thick, but it must not be coloured at all.

It's easy to colour sugar – regular white or caster – put the sugar in a small plastic bag, add a little colouring, then massage the colouring through the sugar – from the outside of the bag. Or rub the colouring into the sugar using disposable gloves on your hands.

Strawberry swirl cupcakes with fluffy frosting

PREPARATION TIME 20 MINUTES **COOKING TIME** 30 MINUTES **MAKES** 12

90g butter, softened
½ teaspoon vanilla extract
½ cup (110g) caster sugar
2 eggs
1 cup (150g) self-raising flour
2 tablespoons milk
2 tablespoons strawberry jam
pink coloured sugar

FLUFFY FROSTING
1 cup (220g) caster sugar
⅓ cup (80ml) water
2 egg whites

1 Preheat oven to 180°C/160°C fan-forced. Line 12-hole (⅓-cup/80ml) muffin pan with paper cases.
2 Beat butter, extract, sugar, eggs, flour and milk in small bowl with electric mixer on low speed until ingredients are just combined. Increase speed to medium, beat until mixture is changed to a paler colour.
3 Divide mixture among cases; smooth surface. Divide jam over tops of cakes; using a skewer swirl jam into cakes.
4 Bake about 30 minutes. Turn cakes onto wire rack to cool.
5 Make fluffy frosting. Spread cakes with frosting; sprinkle with coloured sugar.

FLUFFY FROSTING Stir sugar and the water in small saucepan over heat, without boiling, until sugar is dissolved. Boil, uncovered, without stirring about 5 minutes or until syrup reaches 116°C on a candy thermometer. Syrup should be thick but not coloured. Remove from heat, allow bubbles to subside. Beat egg whites in small bowl with electric mixer until soft peaks form. With mixer operating, add hot syrup in thin stream; beat on high speed about 10 minutes or until mixture is thick and cool.

    PER CUPCAKE 7.3g total fat (4.4g saturated fat); 1024kJ (245 cal); 41g carbohydrate; 3.1g protein; 0.5g fibre

Quick-mix methods for cakes makes things easy, but, there are a few things to know. All the ingredients mix well when they're at room temperature, particularly butter and eggs. From there, make sure the ingredients are combined with an electric mixer, on low speed, before increasing the speed to medium. Beat the mixture until paler in colour.

Lamington angel cupcakes

PREPARATION TIME 30 MINUTES **COOKING TIME** 25 MINUTES **MAKES** 12

90g butter, softened
½ teaspoon vanilla extract
½ cup (110g) caster sugar
2 eggs
1 cup (150g) self-raising flour
2 tablespoons milk
1 cup (80g) desiccated coconut
¼ cup (80g) raspberry jam
½ cup (125ml) thickened cream, whipped

CHOCOLATE ICING
10g butter
⅓ cup (80ml) milk
2 cups (320g) icing sugar
¼ cup (25g) cocoa powder

1 Preheat oven to 180°C/160°C fan-forced. Line 12-hole (⅓-cup/80ml) muffin pan with paper cases.

2 Beat butter, extract, sugar, eggs, flour and milk in small bowl with electric mixer on low speed until ingredients are just combined. Increase speed to medium, beat until mixture is changed to a paler colour. Divide mixture among cases; smooth surface.

3 Bake about 20 minutes. Turn cakes onto wire rack to cool.

4 Make chocolate icing.

5 Remove cases from cakes. Dip cakes in icing, drain off excess; toss cakes in coconut. Place cakes on wire rack to set.

6 Cut cakes as desired; fill with jam and cream.

CHOCOLATE ICING Melt butter in medium heatproof bowl over medium saucepan of simmering water. Stir in milk and sifted icing sugar and cocoa until spreadable.

⬜ **PER CUPCAKE** 16.8g total fat (11.6g saturated fat); 1576kJ (377 cal); 51.9g carbohydrate; 3.8g protein; 1.7g fibre

These lamington cupcakes can each be split in two, then re-joined with jam and cream. Or, cut a circle from the centre of each cake, making a small cavity in the cake. Fill with jam and cream, then top with the circle of cake.

White chocolate and cranberry cheesecakes

PREPARATION TIME 20 MINUTES **COOKING TIME** 55 MINUTES (PLUS COOLING AND REFRIGERATION TIME)
MAKES 6

100g plain sweet biscuits
50g butter, melted
150g frozen cranberries

FILLING
¼ cup (60ml) thickened cream
180g white eating chocolate, chopped coarsely

375g cream cheese, softened
1 teaspoon finely grated orange rind
½ cup (110g) caster sugar
1 egg

The combination of white chocolate, orange and cranberries is sublime. If you like, make this recipe in a 22cm springform tin, it will take about 1 hour to cook.

1 Preheat oven to 150°C/130°C fan-forced. Line 6-hole texas (¾-cup/180ml) muffin pan with paper cases.

2 Process biscuits until fine. Add butter, process until combined. Divide mixture among paper cases; press firmly over base of cases. Refrigerate 30 minutes.

3 Make filling by combining cream and 130g of the chocolate in small saucepan; stir over low heat until smooth. Beat cheese, rind, sugar and egg in small bowl with electric mixer until smooth. Stir in cooled chocolate mixture.

4 Divide mixture among cases, sprinkle with cranberries. Bake about 30 minutes. Cool in oven with door ajar.

5 Refrigerate cheesecakes 3 hours.

6 Just before serving, melt remaining chocolate; drizzle over cheesecakes.

⬜ **PER CHEESECAKE** 44.8g total fat (28.1g saturated fat); 2671kJ (139 cal); 49.5g carbohydrate; 10g protein; 0.8g fibre

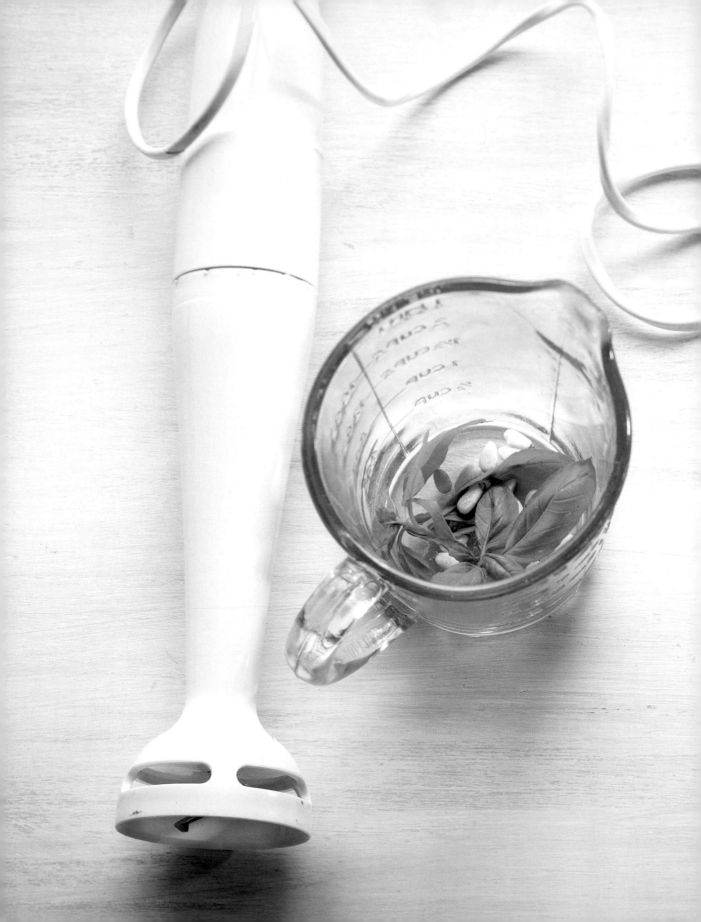

THE SMALL APPLIANCE

The Small Appliance

If you use an appliance a lot, it's one of your best friends; if not, it's an expensive space-grabber. An electrical appliance, such as a mixer or blender, can save you time and effort; a juicer or ice-cream churn can actually do its job so well you can hardly do without it. As you survey the temptations of a big electrical store, try to be realistic about how often you would really use those wonder machines. Look critically at their construction with an eye to flimsy versus solid, and compare them for wattage: more power means a more efficient performance and, usually, a longer life.

ELECTRIC FRYING PAN Electrically-controlled frying pans were popular years ago, but fell out of favour because they never quite reached the fierce heat needed for some operations and were slow to respond to changes in temperature. However, they are still available and are good for cooking at a steady heat (and are also handy if you have limited cooktop space). If buying an electric frying pan, choose one with detachable heat controls so that it can be washed like any other pan.

ICE-CREAM CHURN This appliance goes into the freezer and is powered by a flex thin enough to pass in from an electric socket through the crack of the closed door. The churn, filled with the ice-cream mixture, continually rotates a paddle so that the ice crystals that form as the mixture freezes are broken up so small that they are undetectable to the tongue and the ice-cream feels creamily smooth. The churning also incorporates air, though not as much as in commercial ice-cream, which is the reason why homemade is more dense. There are also stand-alone ice-cream makers available.

JUICER The delicious natural flavours and nutritious value of freshly-made juices are wonderful, yet juice extractors rank high among the appliances that end up at the back of the cupboard. The reasons are that people overestimate their long-term willingness to add another daily task to their lives, and cleaning-the-juicer fatigue sets in. If you buy one, try to improve the odds of regular use by keeping it out, ready to go, rather than in a cupboard. Make it an unbreakable rule that the juicer is always cleaned soon after using, before the pulp, etc., has had time to dry. If you're not sure about your dedication to juicing, settle for an electric citrus squeezer, which is inexpensive, speedy and simple to use and clean, and won't make you feel guilty if you haven't used it for a while.

BLENDERS come in two quite different types. A blender can mean the classic, tall container with blades in the base, on its own stand or attached to a stand mixer. We used these more before the food processor came along, yet the stand blender still reigns supreme for pureeing ingredients to absolute, velvety smoothness for a fine soup or sauce, and is still better than the food processor for making mayonnaise or hollandaise in modest quantities, since a couple of egg yolks get lost under the blades of a food processor.

The other kind of blender is the hand-held stick blender. Variously known as a stab-mixer, stick mixer, mixing wand or hand-blender (the name changes among manufacturers and countries of origin), this blender consists of a stem with blades at the bottom, attached to a handle containing the motor, which can go into any bowl to puree ingredients, whiz up a frothy drink or the hot milk for a cappuccino, or turn a chunky soup into a smooth one right in the saucepan.

SANDWICH PRESS has hinged top and bottom hotplates to toast a sandwich or other food on both sides at the same time. One or both plates may be ridged to give attractive char-grilled markings, and both plates are usually finished with a non-stick coating that needs no more than a wipe with a damp cloth to clean.

Models with simple hinges squash the food fairly flat; models with expandible or "floating" hinges claim not to squash it, although the weight of the top plate does compress it. This is often desirable, making a sandwich crunchy or changing soft Turkish bread or focaccia into an appetising grilled snack for dipping or topping with savoury mixtures.

As supplied, a sandwich press is not suitable for melts, but there are some new more multi-purpose products coming onto the market which will allow you to use the top of the press to generate heat downwards for making melts.

WAFFLE IRON cooks batter into crisp waffles at just the right, thermostatically-controlled temperature, and for just the right length of time, without any effort on your part. Its cooking surfaces usually have a non-stick coating, but as all those little pockets can be reluctant to release their contents cleanly, it is wise to grease them before use, at least to start with until you find out how good your particular waffle iron is in this respect.

ELECTRIC MIXERS are made in two styles: a stand-alone one with a bowl that sits on a stand under the beaters, or a hand held one. Each has its virtues. If you make cakes or anything else that involves heavy mixtures or extended beating, you will be better served by a stand mixer as it is more powerful and can beat the mixture while you do something else. The hand-held model is ideal for beating small quantities, can be used in any bowl or saucepan and can be moved more freely through the mixture as it is beating, to ensure the beaters reach into every corner. Most serious cooks eventually acquire one of each. In both cases, make your choice with a bias towards power.

FOOD PROCESSOR This is the appliance-of-all-work, able to chop, puree, liquidise, grind, reduce meat to mince or a smooth paste, make pastry or breadcrumbs and, with its extra discs, slice paper thin (or thicker), and grate even the hardest and driest of cheese. It does have its limitations – it can't whisk cream or egg whites, it turns potatoes to glue if you try to puree them, and it produces untidy, torn-looking chopped vegetables. And you must be conscious of the fact that a sharp blade is revolving very fast. Unlatching the cover shuts off the motor, but it takes some moments for the whirling blade to stop, so don't whip the cover off and reach in for any reason.

A traditional sukiyaki pan can be purchased from Japanese homeware shops but, unless you plan to make this traditional beef hotpot more than once a month or so, it's just as good made in your electric frying pan. The main issue is that sukiyaki is cooked at the table and shared, with diners helping themselves from the same pan – so an electric frying pan with a long lead is absolutely acceptable.

Sukiyaki *electric frying pan*

PREPARATION TIME 20 MINUTES **COOKING TIME** 10 MINUTES **SERVES** 4

400g fresh gelatinous noodles (shirataki), drained

8 fresh shiitake mushrooms

600g beef rump steak

4 green onions, sliced thinly

300g spinach, trimmed, chopped coarsely

125g can bamboo shoots, drained

200g firm tofu, cut into 2cm cubes

4 eggs

BROTH

1 cup (250ml) japanese soy sauce

½ cup (125ml) sake

½ cup (125ml) mirin

½ cup (125ml) water

½ cup (110g) caster sugar

1 Rinse noodles under hot water; drain. Cut noodles into 15cm lengths.

2 Remove and discard mushroom stems; cut a cross in top of caps.

3 Trim beef of all fat; slice thinly. Retain a small piece of beef fat to grease the pan. Arrange ingredients on platters or in bowls. Break eggs into individual bowls; beat lightly.

4 Make broth; place in medium bowl.

5 Heat greased electric frying pan (or sukiyaki pan on a portable gas cooker) at the table; add a quarter of the beef, stir-fry until partly cooked. Add a quarter of each of the vegetables, tofu, noodles and broth. Dip piping hot cooked ingredients in egg before eating.

6 As ingredients and broth are eaten, add remaining ingredients and broth to pan, in batches.

BROTH Stir ingredients in medium saucepan over medium heat, until sugar dissolves.

☐ **PER SERVING** 33.5g total fat (13.7g saturated fat); 4092kJ (979 cal); 87.6g carbohydrate; 63.8g protein; 13.5g fibre

---

Here's an energy saver: steaming the puddings in a water-filled electric frying pan sure beats using the oven. It also keeps your kitchen cool.

Use the liqueur of your choosing in the anglaise sauce instead of kahlua: try amaretto if you like the taste of almonds, frangelico for a hazelnut flavour, framboise if you like raspberries or Grand Marnier for the hint of orange: each goes well with chocolate.

Steamed chocolate puddings with kahlua anglaise

electric frying pan

PREPARATION TIME 30 MINUTES **COOKING TIME** 35 MINUTES **SERVES** 6

125g butter, softened

1 cup (220g) caster sugar

1 teaspoon vanilla extract

2 eggs

½ cup (35g) fine stale breadcrumbs

¾ cup (110g) self-raising flour

⅓ cup (35g) cocoa powder

⅓ cup (80ml) milk

⅓ cup (60g) finely chopped dark eating chocolate

KAHLUA ANGLAISE

2 cups (500ml) milk

¼ cup (55g) caster sugar

6 egg yolks

2 teaspoons plain flour

2 tablespoons Kahlua

1   Make kahlua anglaise.

2   Grease six ¾-cup (180ml) ovenproof dishes or tea cups. Line bases with baking paper.

3   Beat butter, sugar and extract in small bowl with electric mixer until just combined. Add eggs, one at a time, beating until combined between additions. Stir in breadcrumbs, sifted flour and cocoa, milk and chocolate. Spoon mixture into dishes. Top with a piece of baking paper and foil; secure with rubber bands or string.

4   Place dishes in electric frying pan; add enough boiling water to come halfway up sides of dishes. Cover pan with a tight-fitting lid; boil about 25 minutes or until puddings are cooked when tested with a skewer. Replenish with boiling water as necessary. Remove puddings from the water; stand 5 minutes before turning out.

5   Serve puddings with kahlua anglaise.

KAHLUA ANGLAISE   Place milk in small saucepan; bring almost to a boil. Whisk sugar and egg yolks in medium bowl until creamy; whisk in flour, then slowly whisk in hot milk. Return mixture to pan. Stir over heat until thickened slightly. Stir in liqueur; cover, refrigerate.

▭ **PER SERVING**   50.2g total fat (28.4g saturated fat); 4230kJ (1012 cal); 116.2g carbohydrate; 20g protein; 2g fibre

Chocolate hazelnut gelato *ice-cream churn*

PREPARATION TIME 20 MINUTES (PLUS COOLING AND FREEZING TIME) **COOKING** 20 MINUTES **SERVES** 8

1 cup (125g) hazelnuts

1⅔ cups (400ml) milk

2½ cups (600ml) cream

6 egg yolks

⅓ cup (75g) caster sugar

¾ cup (215g) chocolate hazelnut spread

1   Preheat oven to 180°C/160°C fan-forced. Roast hazelnuts in shallow baking dish about 8 minutes or until skins begin to split. Place nuts in clean tea towel and rub vigorously to remove skins. Chop nuts coarsely. Place nuts in medium saucepan with milk and cream; bring to a boil. Cover, remove from heat.

2   Whisk egg yolks and sugar in medium bowl until creamy; gradually whisk hot milk mixture into egg mixture. Return to pan, stir over low heat, without boiling, until mixture thickens slightly and coats the back of a spoon. Whisk in chocolate hazelnut spread.

3   Transfer mixture to large jug or bowl, cover surface with plastic wrap; refrigerate 2 hours.

4   Strain mixture into jug to remove nuts. Pour mixture into ice-cream churn; churn according to manufacturer's instructions. Pour into deep cake pan, cover with foil; freeze 3 hours or overnight.

▭ **PER SERVING**   57.1g total fat (27.2g saturated fat); 2796kJ (669 cal); 30.2g carbohydrate; 9.5g protein; 1.9g fibre

Ice cream shops are everywhere these days and so is confusion about the differences between the various types. Gelati is Italian for ice-creams, but within that term are several different categories, one of which is gelato, the group most similar in taste and make-up to what we call ice-cream, its main ingredients being cream or milk, egg yolks and sugar. Gelato, however, incorporates lower ratios of butterfat and less "overrun" (aeration) into its making than does ice-cream, which is what makes it more intensely flavoured and richly textured.

Vanilla bean ice-cream *ice-cream churn*

PREPARATION TIME 15 MINUTES (PLUS REFRIGERATION, CHURNING AND FREEZING TIME)
COOKING TIME 10 MINUTES **SERVES** 8

2 vanilla beans
1⅔ cups (410ml) milk
600ml cream
8 egg yolks
¾ cup (165g) caster sugar

1 Split vanilla beans lengthways; scrape out seeds into medium saucepan. Add pods, milk and cream; bring to a boil.

2 Meanwhile, whisk egg yolks and sugar in medium bowl until creamy; gradually whisk into hot milk mixture. Stir over low heat, without boiling, until mixture thickens slightly.

3 Strain mixture into medium heatproof bowl; discard pods. Cover surface of custard with plastic wrap; refrigerate about 1 hour or until cold.

4 Pour custard into ice-cream churn; churn according to manufacturer's instructions. Pour into deep cake pan, cover with foil; freeze until firm.

▭ **PER SERVING** 35.5g total fat (21.4g saturated fat); 1843kJ (441 cal); 24.8g carbohydrate; 6.5g protein; 0g fibre

When you want to finish freezing ice-cream in a hurry, remove it from your ice-cream churn when it's only partially frozen, spread it into a thin layer over the bottom of a lamington pan, cover it well with foil and put it in your freezer. It will become solidly frozen in about an hour.

Peach, apple and strawberry juice *juicer*

PREPARATION TIME 5 MINUTES **SERVES** 1

1 medium apple (150g), cut into wedges
1 medium peach (150g), cut into wedges
2 strawberries (40g)

1 Push ingredients through juice extractor into glass; stir to combine.

▭ **PER SERVING** 0.3g total fat (0g saturated fat); 451kJ (108 cal); 24.3g carbohydrate; 2.2g protein; 5.1g fibre

When juicing, keep in mind that the nutrients in fresh juice are delicate and will dissipate the longer the juice stands. Get the most from your juicing efforts by drinking your mixture straightaway.

Remember to remove the stones, and as many seeds and pits as possible, from your fruits and vegetables just prior to juicing to avoid damaging the juicer's mechanism. Berry and grape seeds are fine to leave in.

VANILLA BEAN ICE-CREAM

Lamb and pesto focaccia *sandwich press*

PREPARATION TIME 10 MINUTES **COOKING TIME** 10 MINUTES **SERVES** 2

400g lamb fillets

20cm-square piece focaccia

¼ cup (65g) basil pesto

½ cup (50g) shaved parmesan cheese

¼ cup (35g) drained sliced sun-dried tomatoes

1 Cook lamb in heated oiled grill pan until browned all over and cooked as desired. Stand lamb, covered, 5 minutes before slicing thickly.

2 Preheat sandwich press. Cut focaccia in half crossways, then in half horizontally. Spread pesto over bases of focaccia, then top with equal amounts of lamb, cheese and tomato. Top with remaining focaccia.

3 Cook in sandwich press about 5 minutes or until cheese melts and focaccia is heated through. Slice focaccia diagonally to serve.

☐ **PER SERVING** 31.5g total fat (11.6g saturated fat); 2943kJ (704 cal); 40.1g carbohydrate; 62.3g protein; 5.3g fibre

---

The sandwich press is a very versatile kitchen tool, as seen here with our pizza recipe. You can cook pancakes and eggs on it too, if it's the hinged, two-sided version. One of our favourite sandwiches is "fried" egg and tomato: cut out a 4cm hole in the centre of a slice of bread; crisp the bread on a heated sandwich press then carefully break an egg in the hole. Allow it to cook about a minute then top the egg with a slice of tomato, salt, pepper and a second piece of bread. Close the press and cook until bread is as browned as you like.

Pizza supreme jaffle *sandwich press*

PREPARATION TIME 10 MINUTES **COOKING TIME** 10 MINUTES **SERVES** 4

1 tablespoon olive oil

2 cloves garlic, crushed

1 small red onion (100g), sliced thinly

1 small green capsicum (150g), sliced thinly

50g swiss brown mushrooms, sliced thinly

1 long loaf turkish bread

¼ cup (70g) tomato paste

120g thinly sliced hot salami

80g marinated artichoke hearts, drained, sliced thinly

100g bocconcini cheese, sliced thickly

1 Heat oil in large frying pan; cook garlic and onion, stirring, until onion softens. Add capsicum and mushrooms; cook, stirring, until mushrooms soften.

2 Preheat sandwich press. Cut bread crossways into four pieces; split each piece horizontally. Spread tomato paste evenly over four pieces of bread, then top with equal amounts of vegetable mixture, salami, artichoke and cheese. Top with remaining bread.

3 Cook jaffle in sandwich press until browned lightly.

☐ **PER SERVING** 23.4g total fat (7.4g saturated fat); 2186kJ (523 cal); 52.7g carbohydrate; 22.6g protein; 5.2g fibre

1 LAMB AND PESTO FOCACCIA **2** PIZZA SUPREME JAFFLE
3 PORK AND CHEESE QUESADILLAS [P 622] **4** REUBEN SANDWICH [P 622]

Waffles can be made savoury or sweet by adding various different ingredients to the batter such as fried crumbled bacon, finely chopped herbs or nuts, grated cheese or finely sliced fresh fruit.

Waffles with caramel sauce *waffle iron*

PREPARATION TIME 15 MINUTES **COOKING TIME** 10 MINUTES **SERVES** 6

1¾ cups (265g) plain flour

¼ cup (35g) self-raising flour

¼ cup (55g) caster sugar

2 eggs, separated

1½ cups (375ml) milk

60g butter, melted

2 tablespoons water

CARAMEL SAUCE

125g butter

1 cup (220g) firmly packed brown sugar

300ml cream

1 Make caramel sauce.

2 Sift flours and sugar into medium bowl. Make well in centre, gradually stir in combined egg yolks and milk, then butter and water; stir until smooth.

3 Beat egg whites in small bowl with electric mixer until soft peaks form; fold into batter, in two batches.

4 Preheat waffle iron. Drop about ⅓ cup of mixture onto heated oiled waffle iron. Close iron; cook about 2 minutes or until golden brown. Repeat with remaining batter.

5 Serve waffles with caramel sauce and ice-cream, if desired.

CARAMEL SAUCE Melt butter in medium saucepan, add sugar; stir over heat, without boiling, until sugar is dissolved. Bring to a boil; simmer, without stirring, 2 minutes. Remove from heat, allow bubbles to subside, stir in cream.

☐ **PER SERVING** 48.7g total fat (31.1g saturated fat); 3453kJ (826 cal); 85.4g carbohydrate; 11g protein; 1.9g fibre

Use dry, grease-free utensils to beat room-temperature egg whites, watching carefully for the forming of "soft" peaks, those that literally fall over when the beaters are lifted. Beating the mixture any longer is likely to make it so dry that the sugar won't dissolve.

Chocolate and almond meringues *electric mixer*

PREPARATION TIME 20 MINUTES **COOKING TIME** 55 MINUTES **MAKES** 20

6 egg whites

1½ cups (330g) caster sugar

2 teaspoons cornflour

1 cup (130g) finely chopped seeded dried dates

150g dark eating chocolate, chopped finely

1 cup (160g) whole almonds, roasted, chopped coarsely

125g dark eating chocolate, melted, extra

24 whole almonds, toasted, extra

1 Preheat oven to 140°C/120°C fan-forced. Line 20 muffin pan holes (⅓-cup/80ml) with paper cases.

2 Beat egg whites in large bowl with electric mixer until soft peaks form; gradually add sugar, beat until dissolved between additions. Gently fold in cornflour, dates, chocolate and chopped almonds.

3 Divide mixture among muffin cases. Bake about 50 minutes. Turn oven off; cool meringues in oven with door ajar.

4 Spread tops with extra melted chocolate, top with whole almonds; stand until set.

▭ **PER MERINGUE** 9.2g total fat (2.7g saturated fat); 928kJ (222 cal); 30.2g carbohydrate; 3.8g protein; 1.6g fibre

Rainbow marshmallows *electric mixer*

PREPARATION TIME 25 MINUTES (PLUS STANDING TIME) **COOKING TIME** 25 MINUTES **MAKES** ABOUT 40

4 tablespoons (56g) gelatine
1 cup (250ml) cold water
4 cups (880g) caster sugar
2 cups (500ml) hot water
2 teaspoons lemon juice
flavouring and food colouring (see variations below)
1 cup (90g) desiccated coconut

1 Sprinkle gelatine over the cold water in small bowl; stand 5 minutes.

2 Stir sugar and the hot water in large saucepan over low heat until sugar is dissolved; bring to a boil. Add gelatine mixture; boil steadily, uncovered, 20 minutes. Cool to lukewarm.

3 Transfer sugar mixture to large bowl of electric mixer; add juice to bowl with flavouring and colouring variation of your choice. Beat on low speed gradually working up to high speed for about 5 minutes or until mixture is very thick and holds its shape.

4 Meanwhile, rinse 20cm x 30cm lamington pan with cold water; do not dry. Spread marshmallow mixture into pan. Sprinkle surface with a little of the coconut to cover Allow to set at room temperature for 2 hours or until firm.

5 Cut marshmallow into 40 squares using a wet knife; toss squares in remaining coconut.

FLAVOUR VARIATIONS

ROSE Add 1 teaspoon rosewater and rose food colouring.

ORANGE Add 1 teaspoon orange blossom or flower water and orange food colouring.

PEPPERMINT Add ½ teaspoon peppermint essence and green food colouring.

▭ **PER MARSHMALLOW** 1.5g total fat (1.3g saturated fat); 456kJ (106 cal); 22.2g carbohydrate; 1.3g protein; 0.3g fibre

Marshmallow making is one exercise when an electric mixer is really a necessity: trying to beat a mixture as thick as this by hand for the right length of time would take super-human effort. And without the right mixing, the mixture will never hold its shape or achieve the right degree of "fluff".

A traditional pavlova calls only for egg whites, a lot of egg whites. It's criminal to waste the yolks, especially when you can freeze them for another day. Drop a single yolk into each section of an ice block tray; cover the tray and freeze, popping out yolks as your needs dictate. Some recipes that call for lots of egg yolks are hollandaise, aïoli, pots de crème and zabaglione.

Allow the whites to come to room temperature before beating them, because it's then that their protein has relaxed and expanded.

Marshmallow pavlova *electric mixer*

PREPARATION TIME 25 MINUTES (PLUS COOLING TIME)
COOKING TIME 1 HOUR 30 MINUTES **SERVES** 8

4 egg whites
1 cup (220g) caster sugar
½ teaspoon vanilla extract
¾ teaspoon white vinegar
300ml thickened cream, whipped
250g strawberries, halved

1 Preheat oven to 120°C/100°C fan-forced. Line oven tray with foil; grease foil, dust with cornflour, shake away excess. Mark 18cm-circle on foil.

2 Beat egg whites in small bowl with electric mixer until soft peaks form; gradually add sugar, beating until sugar dissolves. Add extract and vinegar; beat until combined.

3 Spread meringue into circle on foil, building up at the side to 8cm in height.

4 Smooth side and top of pavlova gently. Using spatula blade, mark decorative grooves around side of pavlova; smooth top again.

5 Bake pavlova about 1½ hours. Turn oven off; cool in oven with door ajar.

6 When pavlova is cold, cut around top edge (the crisp meringue top will fall slightly on top of the marshmallow).

7 Serve pavlova topped with cream and strawberries; dust lightly with sifted icing sugar, if desired.

▭ **PER SERVING** 14g total fat (9.2g saturated fat); 1078kJ (258 cal); 29.6g carbohydrate; 3.1g protein; 0.7g fibre

Serve the dips with raw or lightly steamed vegetables, bread sticks or crackers.

These three dips combine a variety of the best flavours from the warm Mediterranean coast. Hailing from the south of France, pistou, with its high basil content is very similar to Italian pesto, and is traditionally stirred into hot vegetable soup at the table. Thick, black tapenade can be used as an ingredient in dressings and sauces, or eaten on its own as a spread or dip. Anchovy dip is known in Italy as bagna cauda, a "hot bath" of oil, anchovies and garlic that's so good you'll sop up every last skerrick with your bread pieces.

Pistou (basil dip) *food processor*

PREPARATION TIME 5 MINUTES **MAKES** 1 CUP

3 cups (100g) firmly packed fresh basil leaves
⅔ cup (160ml) olive oil
1 clove garlic, quartered
2 teaspoons finely grated lemon rind
2 tablespoons finely grated parmesan cheese

1 Process ingredients until smooth.

▭ **PER 100G** 56.6g total fat (8.8g saturated fat); 2165kJ (518 cal); 0.8g carbohydrate; 2.8g protein; 1.8g fibre

Tapenade (olive dip) *food processor*

PREPARATION TIME 10 MINUTES **MAKES** 1½ CUPS

300g large seeded black olives
2 tablespoons drained capers, rinsed
1 clove garlic, quartered
2 tablespoons lemon juice
1 tablespoon fresh flat-leaf parsley leaves
⅓ cup (80ml) olive oil

1 Process ingredients until smooth.

▭ **PER 100G** 16.9g total fat (2.4g saturated fat); 907kJ (217 cal); 15.7g carbohydrate; 0.6g protein; 1.1g fibre

Anchovy dip *food processor*

PREPARATION TIME 5 MINUTES **MAKES** 1 CUP

40 drained anchovy fillets
1 tablespoon lemon juice
2 cloves garlic, quartered
3 teaspoons fresh lemon thyme leaves
⅓ cup (80ml) olive oil
2 tablespoons hot water

1 Process anchovies, juice, garlic and thyme until smooth.
2 With motor operating, add oil in a thin, steady stream until mixture thickens.
3 Transfer mixture to small bowl; stir in the water.

▭ **PER 100G** 41.7g total fat (6g saturated fat); 1655kJ (396 cal); 0.6g carbohydrate; 5.9g protein; 0.6g fibre

FROM TOP: PISTOU, TAPENADE AND ANCHOVY DIP

Coffees

For those who worship it, it will come as no surprise that coffee is one of the world's greatest commodities.

ESPRESSO (SHORT BLACK)
A standard espresso is 30ml of coffee, made with 7g of ground beans. A doppio is double strength, made with 14g of ground beans. Both should have a 5mm crema.

RISTRETTO
An intense, more concentrated espresso, made with the same amount of ground beans as a standard espresso, but only about 15ml of water. The ristretto is considered the choice of dedicated espresso lovers.

LONG BLACK
Use 14g of ground beans to make a doppio (see left) in a 180ml cup and top with boiling water. For those who want the caffeine hit but not the added milk.

CAPPUCCINO
An espresso (short black) with densely frothed steamed milk mounded above the rim of a short, wide, 180ml cappuccino cup. The top of a cappuccino is usually dusted with chocolate powder.

AFFOGATO
Affogato is a coffee-lovers' dessert made by pouring a hot espresso over top-quality vanilla ice-cream. This must be done at the table so the diner can enjoy it before all the ice-cream melts. They are usually served in separate vessels in cafes.

IRISH COFFEE
Sweetened black coffee is laced with warmed Irish whiskey and topped with lightly whipped cream. It may be served in an Irish coffee (tall, footed) glass cup, or in a stemmed glass to resemble a glass of Guinness.

MACCHIATO

Meaning "marked" or "stained" in Italian, it refers to the dash of steamed milk or dense froth that is added to an espresso. A macchiato can be short (single espresso) or long (double espresso).

FLAT WHITE

An espresso (short black) with a slightly larger quantity of steamed milk than a cappuccino. The milk should be poured so no foam is added and the finished cup of coffee is topped with a very shallow crema.

CAFFE LATTE

Served in a glass, a caffè latte is an espresso (short black) with steamed milk added to fill the glass – more milk than a flat white. A caffè latte should have a head of foam about 1 cm thick.

JAMAICAN COFFEE

For Jamaican coffee, black coffee made from Jamaican beans is laced with white rum and, sometimes, Tia Maria. Topped with lightly whipped cream, it is served in a brandy balloon.

ROMAN COFFEE

Roman coffee is a long black laced with Galliano. Some recipes say to top with cream, some don't. It can be served in a cappuccino cup or, if cream-topped, in a tall handled glass cup, similar to an Irish coffee cup.

MOCHA

For those who can't decide between a hot chocolate and a cappuccino, then a mocha is for you. Combine cocoa powder in a standard espresso and top with frothed steamed milk. Can be served in a glass or cappuccino cup.

Pesto crème fraîche *food processor*

PREPARATION TIME 5 MINUTES (PLUS REFRIGERATION TIME) **MAKES** 1 CUP

½ cup firmly packed fresh basil leaves

1 clove garlic, quartered

2 tablespoons roasted pine nuts

2 tablespoons finely grated parmesan cheese

1 tablespoon olive oil

¾ cup (200g) crème fraîche

1 Process basil, garlic, nuts, cheese and oil until smooth.

2 Tranfers to small bowl; stir in crème fraîche. Cover; refrigerate until cold.

▭ **PER TABLESPOON** 10.3g total fat (4.9g saturated fat); 414kJ (99 cal); 0.6g carbohydrate; 1.2g protein; 0.2g fibre

Crème fraîche, a fermented cream having a slightly tangy, nutty flavour and velvety texture, can be used in both sweet and savoury dishes, much the same way as sour cream.

Goes well with: kipfler potato wedges, grilled chicken breasts; roasted vegetables; as a potato salad dressing.

Rocket and mint pesto *food processor*

PREPARATION TIME 10 MINUTES **MAKES** 1 CUP

½ cup firmly packed fresh mint leaves

40g baby rocket leaves

½ cup (70g) roasted pistachios

¼ cup (20g) finely grated parmesan cheese

2 cloves garlic, quartered

1 tablespoon lemon juice

2 tablespoons water

½ cup (125ml) olive oil

1 Process mint, rocket, nuts, cheese, garlic, juice and the water until combined.

2 With motor operating, gradually add oil in thin, steady stream; process until smooth.

▭ **PER TABLESPOON** 13g total fat (2g saturated fat); 539kJ (129 cal); 1.1g carbohydrate; 2g protein; 0.8g fibre

Pesto is easily made from other herbs or greens and nuts – one of our favourites is baby rocket and pistachio (great with chicken). Try fresh coriander leaves with chilli instead of nuts, and sun-dried tomatoes processed with olives and walnuts.

Goes well with: grilled steaks, grilled lamb cutlets, baked potatoes.

Cranberry and raspberry vinaigrette *food processor*

PREPARATION TIME 5 MINUTES **MAKES** 1 CUP

¼ cup (60ml) red wine vinegar

½ cup (125ml) olive oil

150g fresh raspberries

¼ cup (80g) whole-berry cranberry sauce

1 Process ingredients until smooth.

2 Push dressing through fine sieve into small bowl.

▭ **PER TABLESPOON** 9.5g total fat (1.3g saturated fat); 418kJ (100 cal); 3.4g carbohydrate; 0.2g protein; 0.7g fibre

This dressing suits pan-fried crumbed camembert cheese or a hazelnut and radicchio salad.

PESTO CREME FRAICHE

A quick "cheat's way" of making this dressing is to use a small can of drained sliced beetroot instead of fresh. Russian dressing is good served with roast beef or veal, or in a cold pasta salad with cucumber, capers and red onion.

Russian dressing *food processor*

PREPARATION TIME 10 MINUTES **COOKING TIME** 15 MINUTES **MAKES** 1 ½ CUPS

1 large beetroot (200g), trimmed

2 tablespoons coarsely chopped pickled onions

1 tablespoon capers, rinsed, drained

½ cup (120g) sour cream

1 Boil or steam unpeeled beetroot until tender; drain, reserving ¼ cup of the cooking liquid. When cool enough to handle, peel, then chop beetroot coarsely.

2 Process beetroot with remaining ingredients and reserved liquid until smooth.

🔲 **PER TABLESPOON** 14g total fat (9.2g saturated fat); 681kJ (163 cal); 7g carbohydrate; 1.8g protein; 1.8g fibre

---

Skordalia is a classic Greek sauce or dip, served as part of a mezze or as an accompaniment to grilled meat or seafood. It can be based on either potato or bread.

Goes well with: grilled lamb kebabs, fried zucchini and eggplant strips; battered fish; grilled chicken breasts.

Skordalia *food processor*

PREPARATION TIME 5 MINUTES (PLUS STANDING TIME) **COOKING TIME** 15 MINUTES **MAKES** 1 CUP

1 medium potato (200g), quartered

3 cloves garlic, quartered

2 tablespoons water

1 tablespoon lemon juice

1 tablespoon white wine vinegar

⅓ cup (80ml) olive oil

1 Boil, steam or microwave potato until tender; drain. Cool 10 minutes.

2 Process potato, garlic, the water, juice and vinegar until mixture is pureed. With motor operating, gradually add oil in thin, steady stream; process until mixture thickens.

🔲 **PER TABLESPOON** 6.1g total fat (0.9g saturated fat); 280kJ (67 cal); 2.3g carbohydrate; 0.5g protein; 0.4g fibre

---

Nam jim is the generic term for a Thai dipping sauce; most versions include fish sauce and chillies, but the remaining ingredients are up to the individual cook's discretion. Like most Thai sauces and dressings, nam jim is extremely hot. Deseed the chillies to lessen the heat, if you prefer.

Goes well with: grilled chicken cutlets, grilled fish, stir-fried rice noodles.

Red nam jim *food processor*

PREPARATION TIME 15 MINUTES **MAKES** 1 CUP

3 fresh long red chillies, chopped coarsely

3 fresh small red thai chillies, chopped coarsely

1 shallot (25g), chopped coarsely

2 cloves garlic, crushed

2cm piece fresh ginger (10g), chopped coarsely

⅓ cup (80ml) lime juice

2 tablespoons fish sauce

1 tablespoon grated palm sugar

¼ cup (35g) finely chopped roasted unsalted peanuts

1 Blend or process chillies, shallot, garlic, ginger, juice, sauce and sugar until smooth.

2 Transfer mixture to small bowl; stir in nuts.

🔲 **PER TABLESPOON** 1.4g total fat (1.2g saturated fat); 109kJ (26 cal); 1.8g carbohydrate; 1.1g protein; 0.5g fibre

Passionfruit gems *food processor*

PREPARATION TIME 20 MINUTES (PLUS REFRIGERATION TIME) **COOKING TIME** 10 MINUTES **MAKES** 50

1 cup (150g) plain flour

½ cup (75g) self-raising flour

2 tablespoons custard powder

⅔ cup (110g) icing sugar

90g cold butter, chopped

1 egg yolk

¼ cup (60ml) passionfruit pulp

2 tablespoons icing sugar, extra

Don't over-process the dough, or it will become too soft and hard to handle. Rolling the dough out to cut-out stage, then refrigerating it, makes the handling of these gems really simple.

1 Process flours, custard powder, sugar and butter together until crumbly; add egg yolk and passionfruit pulp, pulse until ingredients come together.

2 Knead dough on floured surface until smooth. Divide into three, roll each third between sheets of baking paper until 5mm thick; refrigerate 30 minutes.

3 Preheat oven to 180°C/160°C fan-forced. Grease two oven trays; line with baking paper.

4 Using 6cm round cutter, cut rounds from dough. Place about 3cm apart on oven trays.

5 Bake 10 minutes. Cool on wire racks. Dust with extra sifted icing sugar before serving.

⬜ **PER GEM** 1.6g total fat (1g saturated fat); 178kJ (43 cal); 6.3g carbohydrate; 0.6g protein; 0.3g fibre

Cream-filled date roll *food processor*

PREPARATION TIME 30 MINUTES (PLUS REFRIGERATION TIME) **COOKING TIME** 15 MINUTES **SERVES** 12

2 tablespoons white sugar

1 cup (140g) seeded dried dates

¾ cup (180ml) boiling water

1 teaspoon bicarbonate of soda

50g butter, chopped

⅔ cup (165g) firmly packed brown sugar

2 eggs

¾ cup (110g) self-raising flour

300ml thickened cream, whipped

This is a really quick dessert, thanks to the food processor. It will keep in the refrigerator for about three days – the lifetime of cream.

1 Preheat oven to 180°C/160°C fan-forced. Grease 25cm x 30cm swiss roll pan; line base with baking paper, extending paper 5cm over long sides. Place a piece of baking paper cut the same size as swiss roll pan on bench, sprinkle evenly with white sugar.

2 Combine dates, the water and soda in bowl of food processor, cover with lid; stand 5 minutes. Add butter and brown sugar; process until almost smooth. Add eggs and flour; pulse until combined.

3 Pour mixture into pan; bake about 15 minutes.

4 Turn cake onto sugared paper, peel baking paper away; cut away crisp edges from all sides of cake. Gently roll cake loosely, using paper as a guide, from a long side; hold for 30 seconds, then unroll. Cover flat cake with tea towel; cool.

5 Spread cake with cream. Roll cake from long side, using paper as a guide. Refrigerate several hours before serving.

⬜ **PER SERVING** 13.7g total fat (8.6g saturated fat); 1095kJ (262 cal); 31.2g carbohydrate; 2.8g protein; 1.5g fibre

Conversion Charts

One Australian metric measuring cup or jug holds approximately 250ml; one Australian metric tablespoon holds 20ml; one Australian metric teaspoon holds 5ml.

The difference between one country's measuring cups and another's is within a two- or three-teaspoon variance, which is only 10 or 15ml and will not affect your cooking results. Most countries, including the US, the UK and New Zealand, use a 15ml tablespoon.

All cup and spoon measurements are level. The most accurate way of measuring dry ingredients is to weigh them. When measuring liquids, use a clear glass or plastic jug with metric markings at eye level.

In this book we used large eggs with an average weight of 60g each. Please note that those who might be at risk from the effects of salmonella poisoning (such as pregnant women, the elderly or young children) should consult their doctor before eating raw eggs.

OVEN TEMPERATURES

These oven temperatures are only a guide for conventional ovens. For fan-forced ovens, check the manufacturer's manual.

	°C (CELSIUS)	°F (FAHRENHEIT)	GAS MARK
Very slow	120	250	½
Slow	150	275-300	1-2
Moderately slow	160	325	3
Moderate	180	350-375	4-5
Moderately hot	200	400	6
Hot	220	425-450	7-8
Very hot	240	475	9

DRY MEASURES

METRIC	IMPERIAL
15g	½oz
30g	1oz
60g	2oz
90g	3oz
125g	4oz (¼lb)
155g	5oz
185g	6oz
220g	7oz
250g	8oz (½lb)
280g	9oz
315g	10oz
345g	11oz
375g	12oz (¾lb)
410g	13oz
440g	14oz
470g	15oz
500g	16oz (1lb)
750g	24oz (1½lb)
1kg	32oz (2lb)

LIQUID MEASURES

METRIC	IMPERIAL
30ml	1 fluid oz
60ml	2 fluid oz
100ml	3 fluid oz
125ml	4 fluid oz
150ml	5 fluid oz (¼ pint/1 gill)
190ml	6 fluid oz
250ml	8 fluid oz
300ml	10 fluid oz (½ pint)
500ml	16 fluid oz
600ml	20 fluid oz (1 pint)
1000ml (1 litre)	1¾ pints

LENGTH MEASURES

METRIC	IMPERIAL
3mm	⅛in
6mm	¼in
1cm	½in
2cm	¾in
2.5cm	1in
5cm	2in
6cm	2½in
8cm	3in
10cm	4in
13cm	5in
15cm	6in
18cm	7in
20cm	8in
23cm	9in
25cm	10in
28cm	11in
30cm	12in (1ft)

Glossary

AIOLI home-made garlic mayonnaise from the south of France served traditionally with seafood stews, like bouillabaisse, or crudités. Aïoli is a love-it or hate-it food, and has inflamed the passions of so many people around the world that they hold annual aïoli festivals at garlic harvest time.

ALLSPICE also known as pimento or jamaican pepper; so-named because it tastes like a combination of nutmeg, cumin, clove and cinnamon. Available whole (a dark-brown berry the size of a pea) or ground, and used in both sweet and savoury dishes.

ALMONDS flat, pointy-tipped nuts having a pitted brown shell enclosing a creamy white kernel which is covered by a brown skin.

blanched brown skins removed.

essence made with almond oil and alcohol or another agent. *see essence/extract*

flaked paper-thin slices.

meal also known as ground almonds; nuts are powdered to a coarse flour texture for use in baking or as a thickening agent.

slivered small pieces cut lengthways.

vienna toffee-coated almonds.

APPLE CIDER, SPARKLING unfermented non-alcoholic type of apple juice with sugar added to make it effervesce.

APPLE-SLICER *see page 140*

ARTICHOKES

globe large flower-bud of a member of the thistle family; it has tough petal-like leaves, and is edible in part when cooked.

hearts tender centre of the globe artichoke; can be harvested from the plant after the prickly choke is removed. Cooked hearts can be bought from delicatessens or canned in brine.

jerusalem neither from Jerusalem nor an artichoke, this crunchy brown-skinned tuber tastes a bit like a water chestnut and belongs to the sunflower family. Eat raw in salads or cooked like potatoes.

ASIAN STEAMBOAT *see page 251*

BABA PAN *see page 595*

BACON RASHERS also known as bacon slices, made from cured and smoked pork side. *Middle rashers* are thin strips of belly pork having a lean, rather round piece of loin at one end; *streaky bacon* is the same cut minus the round loin section.

BAGEL *see page 487*

BAGUETTE *see page 486*

BAKE BLIND a cooking term to describe baking a pie shell or pastry case before filling is added. If a filling does not need to be baked or is very wet, you may need to "blind-bake" the unfilled shell. To bake blind, ease the pastry into a pan or dish, place on an oven tray; line the pastry with baking paper then fill with dried beans, uncooked rice or "baking beans" (also called pie weights). Bake according to recipe's directions then cool before adding the filling. *see also page 440*

BAKING PAPER also known as parchment, silicon paper or non-stick baking paper; not to be confused with greaseproof or waxed paper. Used to line pans before cooking and baking; also to make piping bags. *see also pages 548 & 549*

BAKING POWDER a raising agent consisting mainly of two parts cream of tartar to one part bicarbonate of soda (baking soda). The acid and alkaline combination, when moistened and heated, gives off carbon dioxide which aerates and lightens a mixture during baking.

BAMBOO SHOOTS tender, pale yellow, edible first-growth of the bamboo plant; add crunch and fibre as well as a certain distinctive sweetness to a dish. Available fresh in Asian greengrocers, in season, but usually purchased canned; these must be drained and rinsed before use. There are many different types and sizes of bamboo shoots but the largest is most commonly canned, sliced and used in stir-fries.

BAMBOO SKEWERS used for cocktail food and satay instead of metal skewers, should be soaked in water for 1 hour before use to help prevent splintering or scorching during cooking. Available in several different lengths. *see also pages 279 & 349*

BAMBOO STEAMERS lattice-woven, multi-layered steamers with tight-fitting lids. Inexpensive and available in various sizes from Asian and specialty cookware shops, they can be used for steaming anything from dim sum and vegetables to elaborate fish and meat dishes. *see also pages 233 & 250*

BANANA LEAVES used to line steamers and cook food "en papillote" (enclosed, wrapped); sold in bundles in Asian food shops, greengrocers and supermarkets. Leaves are cut, on both sides of the centre stem, into the required sized pieces then immersed in hot water or held over a flame until pliable enough to wrap around or fold over food; they are secured with kitchen string, toothpicks or bamboo skewers before barbecuing or steaming. *see also en papillote*

BAR TIN *see page 595*

BARBECUE SAUCE spicy, tomato-based sauce used to marinate, baste or as an accompaniment.

BARLEY a nutritious grain used in soups and stews. Hulled barley, the least processed form of barley, is high in fibre. Pearl barley has had the husk removed then been steamed and polished so that only the "pearl" of the original grain remains, much the same as white rice.

BASIL

holy also known as kra pao or hot basil; different from thai and sweet basil, having an almost hot, spicy flavour similar to clove. Used in many Thai dishes, especially curries; distinguished from thai basil by tiny "hairs" on its leaves and stems.

opal has large purple leaves and a sweet, almost gingery flavour. Can replace thai but not holy basil in recipes.

sweet the most common type of basil; used extensively in Italian dishes and one of the main ingredients in pesto.

thai also known as horapa; different from holy basil and sweet basil in both look and taste, having smaller leaves and purplish stems. It has a slight aniseed taste and is one of the identifying flavours of Thai food.

BAY LEAVES aromatic leaves from the bay tree available fresh or dried; used to add a strong, slightly peppery flavour to soups, stocks and casseroles.

BEAN SPROUTS also known as bean shoots; tender new growths of assorted beans and seeds germinated for consumption as sprouts. The most readily available are mung bean, soybean, alfalfa and snow pea sprouts. Sprout mixtures or tendrils are also available.

BEANS

black also known as turtle beans or black kidney beans; an earthy-flavoured dried bean completely different from the better-known Chinese black beans (which are fermented soybeans). Used mostly in Mexican, South American and Caribbean cooking, especially soups and stews.

black-eyed also known as black-eyed peas or cowpea; the dried seed of a variant of the snake or yard-long bean. Not too dissimilar to white beans in flavour; good cooked and used cold in salads.

borlotti also known as roman beans or pink beans, can be eaten fresh or dried. Interchangeable with pinto beans because of the similarity in appearance – pale pink or beige with dark red streaks. The bean of choice for frijoles refritos (refried beans).

broad also known as fava, windsor and horse beans; available dried, fresh, canned and frozen. Fresh should be peeled twice (discarding both the outer long green pod and the beige-green tough inner shell); the frozen beans have had their pods removed but the beige shell still needs removal. Good eaten raw or cooked in salads, tossed through pasta or pureed; often used in Mediterranean soups and dips.

butter also known as lima beans; large, flat, kidney-shaped bean, off-white in colour, with a mealy texture and mild taste. Available canned and dried; best used in soups or salads.

cannellini small white bean similar in appearance and flavour to other *phaseolus vulgaris* varieties (great northern, navy or haricot). Available dried or canned; used in baked beans and traditional ham and bean soup.

green also known as french or string beans (although the tough string they once had has generally been bred out of them), this long thin fresh bean is consumed in its entirety once cooked.

kidney medium-size red bean, slightly floury in texture yet sweet in flavour; sold dried or canned, it's found in bean mixes and is the bean used in chile con carne.

pinto similar to borlotti, a plump, kidney-shaped, pinky-beige bean speckled with brown to red streaks; available canned or dried and used in Mexican cooking.

refried pinto or borlotti beans, cooked twice: first soaked and boiled, then mashed and fried (traditionally in lard). A Mexican staple, frijoles refritos (refried beans) are sold canned in supermarkets.

snake long (about 40cm), thin, round, fresh green beans, Asian in origin, with a taste similar to green or french beans. Used most frequently in stir-fries, they are also known as yard-long beans because of their (pre-metric) length.

soy the most nutritious of all legumes; only recently embraced by the West but a staple in Asia for centuries. High in protein and low in carbohydrates, and the source of products such as tofu, soy milk, soy sauce, tamari and miso. Sometimes sold fresh as edamame; also available dried and canned.

white in this book, some recipes may simply call for "white beans", a generic term we use for canned or dried cannellini, haricot, navy or great northern beans which are all of the same family, *phaseolus vulgaris*.

BEEF

baby back ribs shorter and wider than spareribs; quite lean and meaty.

cheeks boneless inexpensive cut that benefits from slow cooking.

chuck inexpensive cut from the neck and shoulder area; good minced and slow-cooked.

corned beef also known as corned silverside; little fat, cut from the upper leg and cured. Sold cryovac-packed in brine.

eye-fillet tenderloin, fillet; fine texture, most expensive and extremely tender.

gravy boneless stewing beef cut from shin; slow-cooked, imbues stocks, soups and casseroles with a gelatine richness. Cut crossways, with bone in, is osso buco.

minced also known as ground beef.

new-york cut boneless striploin steak.

oxtail a flavourful cut originally from the ox but today more likely to be from any beef cattle; requires long, slow cooking so it is perfect for curries and stews.

porterhouse striploin steak, bone in.

round steak boneless cut from the tender muscle running from rump to ankle; used for stir-fries, minute steaks and pot-roasts.

rump boneless tender cut taken from the upper part of the round (hindquarter). Cut into steaks, good for barbecuing; in the piece, great as a roast.

scotch fillet cut from the muscle running behind the shoulder along the spine. Also known as cube roll, cuts include standing rib roast and rib-eye.

silverside also known as topside roast; this is the actual cut used for making corned beef.

skirt steak lean, flavourful coarse-grained cut from the inner thigh. Needs slow-cooking; good for stews or casseroles.

T-bone sirloin steak with bone in and fillet eye attached; good barbecued or grilled.

BEETROOT also known as red beets; firm, round root vegetable. Can be grated or finely chopped; boiled or steamed then diced or sliced; or roasted then mashed.

BELGIAN-STYLE WAFFLES true belgian waffles are made from a yeast dough; each waffle is sprinkled with sugar, resulting in a crisp, rich product with a slightly caramelised flavour. Available from large supermarket or delicatessens.

BESAN *see flour*

BICARBONATE OF SODA also known as baking soda; a mild alkali used as a leavening agent in baking.

BISCUITS also known as cookies; almost always an "eat-in-your-hand"-sized soft or crisp sweet cake.

BLACK BEAN SAUCE an Asian cooking sauce made from salted and fermented soybeans, spices and wheat flour; used most often in stir-fries.

BLANCHING a cooking term to describe the act of plunging an ingredient, usually vegetable, briefly into boiling water, draining then placing it into a bowl of iced water, or rinsing under cold water, to immediately halt the cooking process. Blanching is used when the cooking time is to be minimal; when it is to precede another cooking process, as with certain hard vegetables before stir-frying; or to loosen the skin on fruit before peeling.

BLOOD ORANGE a virtually seedless citrus fruit with blood-red-streaked rind and flesh, sweet, non-acidic, salmon-coloured pulp and juice having slight strawberry or raspberry overtones. Thought to have occurred in nature by accident in 17th-century Sicily. The juice can be drunk straight or used in cocktails, sauces, sorbets and jellies; can be frozen for use in cooking when the growing season finishes. The rind is not as bitter as that of an ordinary orange; grated or finely sliced, it can be strewn over salads, puddings or cakes.

BRAISING a cooking term to describe the method of slow-cooking food with fat in a covered saucepan or casserole dish over low heat. This process helps tenderise and bring out the flavour in many meats with little added moisture.

BRAN the outer casing (the husk of various cereal grains such as wheat or oats) made up of several layers to protect the inner kernel; rich in vitamin B and carbohydrates and a valuable source of fibre. Usually removed when a grain is milled for flour, but is added to many breakfast cereals or eaten sprinkled over food as a dietary supplement.

BRANDY short for brandywine, the translation of the Dutch "brandwijn", burnt wine. A general term for a liqueur distilled from wine grapes (usually white), it is used as the basis for many sweet-to-dry spirits made with fruits. Cognac and Armagnac are two of the finest aged brandies available.

BRAZIL NUT native to South America, a triangular-shelled oily nut with an unusually tender white flesh and a mild, rich flavour. Good for eating as well as cooking, the nuts can be eaten raw or cooked, or can be ground into meal for baking.

BREADCRUMBS

fresh bread, usually white, processed into crumbs; good for poultry stuffings and as a thickening agent in some soups and cold sauces.

packaged prepared fine textured but crunchy white breadcrumbs; good for coating or crumbing foods that are to be fried.

stale crumbs made by grating, blending or processing 1- or 2-day-old bread.

BRIOCHE French in origin; a rich, yeast-leavened, cake-like bread made with butter and eggs. Most common form is the *brioche à tête*, a round fluted roll topped with a much smaller ball of dough. Eaten freshly baked or toasted; available from cake or specialty bread shops.

BROCCOLINI a cross between broccoli and Chinese kale; long asparagus-like stems with a long loose floret, both completely edible. Resembles broccoli in look but is milder and sweeter in taste.

BRUISE a cooking term to describe the slight crushing given to aromatic ingredients, particularly herbs, with the flat side of a heavy knife or cleaver to release flavour and aroma.

BRUSCHETTA pronounced broo-skeh-tah, this traditional Italian snack is fresh white bread, usually ciabatta, rubbed with garlic-infused olive oil, toasted and served with various toppings such as tomato and basil.

BUBBLE TEA *see page 425*

BUCKWHEAT a herb in the same plant family as rhubarb; not a cereal so it is gluten-free. Available as flour (used for blini, pancakes and soba); ground (cracked) into coarse, medium or fine granules which are called *kasha* and used similarly to polenta; or groats, the whole kernel sold roasted as a cereal product which, like rice or couscous, forms the basis for a grain-and-vegetable main dish.

BUK CHOY also known as bok choy, pak choi, Chinese white cabbage or Chinese chard, has a fresh, mild mustard taste. Use both stems and leaves, stir-fried or braised. Baby buk choy, also known as pak kat farang or shanghai bok choy, is much smaller and more tender than buk choy. Its mildly acrid, distinctively appealing taste has made it one of the most commonly used Asian greens.

BUNDT PAN *see page 595*

BURGHUL also known as bulghur wheat, hulled steamed wheat kernels that, once dried, are crushed into various sized grains. Used in Middle Eastern dishes such as felafel, kibbeh and tabbouleh. Burghul is not the same thing as cracked wheat the untreated whole wheat berry broken during milling into a cereal product of varying degrees of coarseness used in bread making.

BUTTER this book uses salted butter unless stated otherwise; 125g is equal to 1 stick (4 ounces) in other recipes. Butter is basically churned pasteurised cream with salted being the most popular one sold in supermarkets. Unsalted or "sweet" butter has no salt added to the churned cream and is perhaps the most popular butter among pastry-chefs.

BUTTERMILK see milk

CACHOUS also called dragées in some countries; minuscule (3mm to 5mm) metallic-looking-but-edible confectionery balls used in cake decorating; available in silver, gold or various colours.

CANELLE KNIFE see page 140

CAPERBERRIES olive-sized fruit formed after the buds of the caper bush have flowered; they are usually sold pickled in a vinegar brine with stalks intact.

CAPERS the grey-green buds of a warm climate (usually Mediterranean) shrub, sold either dried and salted or pickled in a vinegar brine; tiny young ones, called baby capers, are also available both in brine or dried in salt. Their pungent taste adds piquancy to a classic steak tartare, tapenade, sauces and condiments.

CAPSICUM also known as pepper or bell pepper. Native to central and South America; found in red, green, yellow, orange or purplish-black varieties. Discard seeds and membranes before use.

CARAWAY SEEDS the small, half-moon-shaped dried seed from a member of the parsley family; adds a sharp anise flavour when used in both sweet and savoury dishes. Used widely, in such different foods as rye bread, harissa and the classic Hungarian fresh cheese, liptauer.

CARDAMOM a spice native to India and used extensively in its cuisine; can be purchased in pod, seed or ground form. Has a distinctive aromatic, sweetly rich flavour and is one of the world's most expensive spices. Used to flavour curries, rice dishes, sweet desserts and cakes.

CASHEWS plump, kidney-shaped, golden-brown nuts having a distinctive sweet, buttery flavour and containing about 48 per cent fat. Because of this high fat content, they should be kept, sealed tightly, under refrigeration to avoid becoming rancid. We use roasted unsalted cashews in this book, unless otherwise stated; they're available from health-food stores and most supermarkets. Roasting cashews brings out their intense nutty flavour.

CAYENNE PEPPER see chilli

CELERIAC tuberous root with knobbly brown skin, white flesh and a celery-like flavour. Keep peeled celeriac in acidulated water to stop it from discolouring. It can be grated and eaten raw in remoulade or salads; used in soups and stews; boiled and mashed like potatoes; or sliced thinly and deep-fried as chips.

CHAI TEA see page 424

CHALLAH see page 487

CHAPATI a popular unleavened Indian bread, similar in appearance to pitta, chapati accompany saucy curries, often serving as cutlery to scoop up the food. Made from whole-wheat flour, salt and water, and dry-fried on a "tawa" (a cast-iron griddle). Available from Indian food shops and on the bread shelf in most supermarkets.

CHAR SIU also called Chinese barbecue sauce; a paste-like ingredient dark-red-brown in colour with a sharp sweet and spicy flavour. Made with fermented soybeans, honey and various spices, char siu can be diluted and used as a marinade or brushed directly onto grilling meat.

CHEESE

blue mould-treated cheeses mottled with blue veining. Varieties include firm and crumbly stilton types and mild, creamy brie-like cheeses.

bocconcini from the diminutive of "boccone", meaning mouthful in Italian; walnut-sized, baby mozzarella, a delicate, semi-soft, white cheese traditionally made from buffalo milk. Sold fresh, it spoils rapidly so will only keep, refrigerated in brine, for 1 or 2 days at the most.

brie often referred in France as the queen of cheeses; soft-ripened cow-milk cheese with a delicate, creamy texture and a rich, sweet taste that varies from buttery to mushroomy. Best served at room temperature after a brief period of ageing, brie should have a bloomy white rind and creamy, voluptuous centre which becomes runny with ripening.

cheddar the most common cow-milk tasty cheese; should be aged, hard and have a pronounced bite. We use a version having no more than 20 per cent fat when calling for low-fat cheese.

cottage fresh, white, unripened curd cheese with a lumpy consistency and mild, sweet flavour. Fat content ranges between 15 per cent to 55 per cent, determined by whether it is made from whole, low-fat or fat-free cow milk.

cream commonly known as philadelphia or philly; a soft cow-milk cheese with a fat content ranging from 14 per cent to 33 per cent.

fetta Greek in origin; a crumbly textured goat- or sheep-milk cheese having a sharp, salty taste. Ripened and stored in salted whey; particularly good cubed and tossed into salads. We use a version having no more than 15 per cent fat when calling for low-fat cheese.

fontina a smooth, firm Italian cow-milk cheese with a creamy, nutty taste and brown or red rind; an ideal melting or grilling cheese.

goat made from goat milk, has an earthy, strong taste. Available in soft, crumbly and firm textures, in various shapes and sizes, and sometimes rolled in ash or herbs.

gorgonzola a creamy Italian blue cheese having a mild, sweet taste; good as an accompaniment to fruit or used to flavour sauces (especially pasta).

gruyère a hard-rind Swiss cheese with small holes and a nutty, slightly salty flavour. A popular cheese for soufflés.

haloumi a Greek Cypriot cheese having a semi-firm, spongy texture and very salty yet sweet flavour. Ripened and stored in salted whey; it's best grilled or fried, and holds its shape well on being heated. Should be eaten while still warm as it becomes tough and rubbery on cooling.

jarlsberg brand-name of a popular Norwegian cheese made from cow milk; has large holes and a mild, nutty taste.

mascarpone an Italian fresh cultured-cream product made in much the same way as yogurt. Whiteish to creamy yellow in colour, with a buttery-rich, luscious texture. Soft, creamy and spreadable, it is used in many Italian desserts and as an accompaniment to a dessert of fresh fruit.

mozzarella soft, spun-curd cheese; originating in southern Italy where it was traditionally made from water-buffalo milk. Now generally manufactured from cow milk, it is the most popular pizza cheese because of its low melting point and elasticity when heated (used for texture rather than flavour). We use a version having no more than 17.5 per cent fat when calling for low-fat cheese.

paneer a simple, delicate fresh cheese used as a major source of protein in the Indian diet. Available in cryovac-packs in some supermarkets or loose, in brine, in Indian food shops. Replace it with ricotta if difficult to find in your area.

parmesan also known as parmigiano, parmesan is a hard, grainy cow milk cheese which originated in the Parma region of Italy. The curd for this cheese is salted in brine for a month before being aged for up to 2 years, preferably in humid conditions. Parmesan is grated or flaked and used for pasta, salads and soups; it is also eaten on its own with fruit. Reggiano is the best parmesan, aged for a minimum 2 years and made only in the Italian region of Emilia-Romagna.

pecorino the Italian generic name for cheeses made from sheep milk. This family of hard, white to pale-yellow cheeses, traditionally made in the Italian winter and spring when sheep graze on natural pastures, have been matured for 8 to 12 months. They are classified according to the area in which they were produced – romano from Rome, sardo from Sardinia, siciliano from Sicily and toscano from Tuscany. If you can't find it, use parmesan.

pizza cheese a commercial blend of varying proportions of processed grated mozzarella, cheddar and parmesan.

provolone a mild stretched-curd cheese similar to mozzarella when young, becoming hard, spicy and grainy the longer it's aged. Golden yellow in colour, with a smooth waxy rind, provolone is a good all-purpose cheese used in cooking, for dessert with cheese, and shredded or flaked.

raclette a Swiss cow-milk cheese with a hard, rosy-brown rind and semi-soft interior dotted with small holes. Used in Switzerland and Alsace to make a dish of the same name: the cheese is melted on a special raclette grill and poured over steamed or boiled baby potatoes. Heating releases the cheese's unique fruity and nutty flavour and intensifies its aroma. It can be used to replace gruyère in a recipe.

ricotta a soft, sweet, moist, white cow-milk cheese with a low fat content (about 8.5 per cent) and a slightly grainy texture. The name roughly translates as "cooked again" and refers to ricotta's manufacture from a whey that is itself a by-product of other cheese making.

roquefort considered the "king of cheeses", this is a blue cheese with a singularly pungent taste; made only from the milk of specially bred sheep and ripened in the damp limestone caves found under the village of Roquefort-sur-Soulzon in France. Has a sticky, bone-coloured rind and, when ripe, the sharp, almost metallic-tasting interior is creamy and almost shiny. It is one of the world's best eating cheeses and is most famously used in the self-named salad dressing.

soft blue vein also known as a light blue cheese because it has the creamy, moist texture of a brie but is veined and mildly acidic like typical blues. A double-cream blue cheese; blue castello is an example.

swiss generic name for a variety of slightly firm to hard Swiss cheeses, among them emmentaler and gruyère.

tasty generic name for a variety of processed and naturally made cheddar-like table cheeses.

CHERMOULLA a Moroccan blend of fresh herbs, spices and condiments traditionally used for preserving or seasoning meat and fish, for flavouring stews and tagines, or for use as a baste or marinade. You can keep freshly made chermoulla in the fridge, covered with a thin layer of olive oil to help preserve it, for up to a month. Available ready-made in Middle Eastern food shops, delicatessens and specialty food stores.

CHERRY small, soft stone fruit varying in colour from yellow to dark red. Sweet cherries are eaten whole and in desserts while sour cherries such as the morello variety are used for jams, preserves, pies and savoury dishes (particularly good with game birds and meats).

glacé also known as candied cherries; boiled in heavy sugar syrup and then dried. Used in cakes, breads and sweets.

maraschino pronounced mahr-uh-skee-no. Any variety of cherry can be used; maraschino are macerated in a flavoured and coloured sugar syrup then preserved. Originally an Italian confection, these are most often found in cocktails or as a colourful garnish, but they can be used in baked items and fruit salads.

CHERRY STONER see page 141

CHERVIL also known as cicily; mildly fennel-flavoured member of the parsley family with curly dark-green leaves. Available both fresh and dried but, like all herbs, is best used fresh; like coriander and parsley, its delicate flavour diminishes the longer it is cooked. It's one of the herbs usually included in the French staple *fines herbes* (along with chives, parsley and tarragon) used in the seasoning of omelettes and poached fish dishes.

CHICKEN For tips on preparing a chicken, see pages 326 & 327.

barbecued we use already-cooked whole barbecued chickens weighing about 900g apiece in our recipes. Skin discarded and bones removed, this size chicken provides 4 cups (400g) shredded meat or about 3 cups (400g) coarsely chopped meat.

breast fillet breast halved, skinned and boned.

drumette small fleshy part of the wing between shoulder and elbow, trimmed to resemble a drumstick.

drumstick leg with skin and bone intact.

maryland leg and thigh still connected in a single piece; bones and skin intact.

smoked chicken ready-to-eat, available as whole small bird or breasts sold cryovac-packed in supermarkets.

tenderloin thin strip of meat lying just under the breast, especially good for stir-frying.

thigh skin and bone intact.

thigh cutlet thigh with skin and centre bone intact; sometimes found skinned with bone intact.

thigh fillet thigh with skin and centre bone removed; makes flavoursome mince.

wing the whole wing, bone and skin intact.

CHICKPEAS also called garbanzos, hummus or channa; an irregularly round, sandy-coloured legume used extensively in Mediterranean, Indian and Hispanic cooking. Firm texture even after cooking, a floury mouth-feel and robust nutty flavour; available canned or dried (the latter need several hours reconstituting in cold water before being used).

CHILLI always use rubber gloves when seeding and chopping fresh chillies as they can burn your skin. We use unseeded chillies in our recipes because the seeds contain the heat; use fewer chillies rather than seeding the lot. Excess chillies are easily kept, submerged in oil or vinegar, in clean glass containers with tight-fitting lids in the fridge for up to 3 months. Whole chillies freeze well: wrap 2 or 3 together in plastic bundles and keep in the freezer until required. Chillies can also be dried: for hundred of years, Mexicans have been stringing them into "ristras", long garlands hung at room temperature in a dry spot that make an interesting kitchen decoration as well as an excellent drying method. Dried chillies can be ground and stored in airtight glass bottles.

cayenne also known as cayenne pepper; a thin-fleshed, long, extremely hot, dried red chilli native to South America, usually purchased ground.

chipotle pronounced cheh-pote-lay. The name used for jalapeño chillies once they've been dried and smoked. Having a deep, intensely smokey flavour, rather than a searing heat, chipotles are dark brown, almost black in colour and wrinkled in appearance.

flakes also sold as crushed chilli; dehydrated deep-red extremely fine slices and whole seeds; good in cooking or for sprinkling over a dish as one does with salt and pepper.

green any unripened chilli; also some particular varieties that are ripe when green, such as jalapeño, habanero, poblano or serrano.

hot sauce we use a hot Asian variety made from bird's-eye chillies, salt and vinegar. Use sparingly, increasing the quantity to suit your taste.

jalapeño pronounced hah-lah-pain-yo. Fairly hot, medium-sized, plump, dark green chilli; available pickled, sold canned or bottled, and fresh, from greengrocers.

long red available both fresh and dried; a generic term used for any moderately hot, long, thin chilli (about 6cm to 8cm long).

pasilla pronounced pah-see-yah. Also known as "chile negro" because of its almost black skin; medium-hot, smokey and pungent dried chilli measuring about 15cm to 20cm in length. Many commercial chilli powders are made with pasillas and can replace this chilli in some instances: use sparingly until you discover the right amount for your palate.

paste every Asian cuisine has its own chilli paste, and each is different from the next: Vietnamese chilli paste is quite hot; Indonesian sambal oelek (chilli with ginger, oil and garlic) has medium heat; for more sweetness than fire, use mild sweet thai chilli sauce, made with vinegar and sugar.

powder the Asian variety is the hottest, made from dried ground thai chillies; can be used instead of fresh chillies in the proportion of ½ teaspoon chilli powder to 1 medium chopped fresh red chilli.

sauce, sweet comparatively mild, fairly sticky and runny bottled sauce made from red chillies, sugar, garlic and white vinegar; used in Thai cooking and as a condiment.

thai also known as "scuds"; tiny, very hot and bright red in colour.

CHINESE BARBECUED DUCK *see duck*

CHINESE BARBECUED PORK *see pork*

CHINESE BROCCOLI *see gai lan*

CHINESE CABBAGE *see wombok*

CHINESE COOKING WINE also known as hao hsing or chinese rice wine; made from fermented rice, wheat, sugar and salt with a 13.5 per cent alcohol content. Inexpensive and found in Asian food shops; if you can't find it, replace with mirin or sherry.

CHIVES related to the onion and leek; has a subtle onion flavour. Used more for flavour than as an ingredient; chopped finely, they're good in sauces, dressings, omelettes or as a garnish. Chinese (or garlic) chives have rougher, flatter leaves than simple chives, and possess a pink-tinged teardrop-shaped flowering bud at the end; used as a salad green, or steamed and eaten as a vegetable.

CHOCOLATE

cherry ripe dark chocolate bar made with coconut and cherries; standard size bar weighs 55g.

Choc Bits also known as chocolate chips or chocolate morsels; available in milk, white and dark chocolate. Made of cocoa liquor, cocoa butter, sugar and an emulsifier, these hold their shape in baking and are ideal for decorating.

chocolate Melts small discs of compounded milk, white or dark chocolate ideal for melting and moulding.

cocoa *see cocoa powder*

couverture a term used to describe a fine quality, very rich chocolate high in both cocoa butter and cocoa liquor. Requires tempering when used to coat but not if used in baking, mousses or fillings.

dark cooking also known as compounded chocolate; good for cooking as it doesn't require tempering and sets at room temperature. Made with vegetable fat instead of cocoa butter so it lacks the rich, buttery flavour of eating chocolate. Cocoa butter is the most expensive component in chocolate, so the substitution of a vegetable fat means that compounded chocolate is much cheaper to produce.

dark eating also known as semi-sweet or luxury chocolate; made of a high percentage of cocoa liquor and cocoa butter, and little added sugar. Unless stated otherwise, we use dark eating chocolate in this book as it's ideal for use in desserts and cakes.

milk most popular eating chocolate, mild and very sweet; similar in make-up to dark with the difference being the addition of milk solids.

white contains no cocoa solids but derives its sweet flavour from cocoa butter. Very sensitive to heat.

CHORIZO sausage of Spanish origin, made of coarsely ground pork and highly seasoned with garlic and chilli.

CHOY SUM also known as pakaukeo or flowering cabbage, a member of the buk choy family, easy to identify with its long stems, light green leaves and yellow flowers. Stems and leaves are both edible, steamed or stir-fried.

CIABATTA in Italian, the word means slipper, the traditional shape of this popular crisp-crusted, open-textured white sourdough bread. A good bread to use for bruschetta. *see also page 487*

CINNAMON available both in the piece (called sticks or quills) and ground into powder; one of the world's most common spices, used universally as a sweet, fragrant flavouring for both sweet and savoury foods. The dried inner bark of the shoots of the Sri Lankan native cinnamon tree, much of what is sold as the real thing is in fact cassia, Chinese cinnamon, from the bark of the cassia tree. Less expensive to process than true cinnamon, it is often blended with Sri Lankan cinnamon to produce the type of "cinnamon" most commonly found in supermarkets.

CITRIC ACID commonly found in most fruits, especially limes and lemons. Commercial citric acid helps to accentuate the acid flavour of fruit; it does not act as a preservative.

CLAY POT *see page 250*

CLOVES dried flower buds of a tropical tree; can be used whole or in ground form. They have a strong scent and taste so should be used sparingly.

COCOA POWDER also known as unsweetened cocoa; cocoa beans (cacao seeds) that have been fermented, roasted, shelled, ground into powder then cleared of most of the fat content. Unsweetened cocoa is used in hot chocolate drink mixtures; milk powder and sugar are added to the ground product.

COCONUT

cream obtained commercially from the first pressing of the coconut flesh alone, without the addition of water; the second pressing (less rich) is sold as coconut milk. Available in cans and cartons at most supermarkets.

desiccated concentrated, dried, unsweetened and finely shredded coconut flesh.

essence synthetically produced from flavouring, oil and alcohol. *see essence/extract*

flaked dried flaked coconut flesh.

milk not the liquid found inside the fruit, which is called coconut water, but the diluted liquid from the second pressing of the white flesh of a mature coconut (the first pressing produces coconut cream). Available in cans and cartons at most supermarkets.

shredded unsweetened thin strips of dried coconut flesh.

CONICAL STRAINER *see page 41*

COOKING-OIL SPRAY we use a cholesterol-free cooking spray made from canola oil.

CORIANDER also known as cilantro, pak chee or chinese parsley; bright-green-leafed herb having both pungent aroma and taste. Used as an ingredient in a wide variety of cuisines from Mexican to South-East Asian. Often stirred into or sprinkled over a dish just before serving for maximum impact as, like other leafy herbs, its characteristics diminish with cooking. Both the stems and roots of coriander are used in Thai cooking: wash well before chopping. Coriander seeds are dried and sold either whole or ground, and neither form tastes remotely like the fresh leaf but rather like an acrid combination of sage and caraway. Seeds and ground are both used in garam masala, mixed spice, Indian and Thai curry pastes and sauces, sausages, and some breads and desserts.

CORN FLAKES commercially manufactured cereal made of dehydrated then baked crisp flakes of corn. Also available is a prepared finely ground mixture used for coating or crumbing food before frying or baking, sold as "crushed corn flakes" in 300g packages in most supermarkets.

CORN SYRUP *see page 507*

CORNFLOUR also known as cornstarch. Available made from corn or wheat (wheaten cornflour, gluten-free, gives a lighter texture in cakes); used as a thickening agent in cooking.

CORNICHON French for gherkin, a very small variety of cucumber. Pickled, they are a traditional accompaniment to pâté; the Swiss always serve them with fondue (or raclette).

COUSCOUS a fine, grain-like cereal product made from semolina; from the countries of North Africa. A semolina flour and water dough is sieved then dehydrated to produce minuscule even-sized pellets of couscous; it is rehydrated by steaming or with the addition of a warm liquid and swells to three or four times its original size; eaten like rice with a tagine, as a side dish or salad ingredient.

CRAISINS dried sweetened cranberries, used in cooking sweet or savoury dishes. Can usually be substituted for or with other dried fruit in most recipes

CRANBERRY SAUCE a manufactured product made of cranberries cooked in sugar syrup; the astringent flavour goes beautifully with roast poultry and barbecued meats.

CREAM OF TARTAR the acid ingredient in baking powder; added to confectionery mixtures to help prevent sugar from crystallising. Keeps frostings creamy and improves volume when beating egg whites.

CREME FRAICHE a mature, naturally fermented cream (minimum fat content 35 per cent) having a velvety texture and slightly tangy, nutty flavour. Crème fraîche, a French variation of sour cream, can boil without curdling and can be used in both sweet and savoury dishes.

CUCUMBER one of the oldest and most universally cultivated vegetables; about a third of the world's crop is pickled, with the rest consumed raw. Most are cylindrical in shape and green-skinned, have an extremely high water content, crisp texture, and mildly acidic flavour.

apple round, with pale-green thick skin and very large seeds; very mild and juicy. Must be peeled before use.

gherkin short and broad with a rough, thick skin; most used variety for pickling. . A mini version is pickled and sold as the French cornichon.

lebanese short, slender and thin-skinned. Probably the most popular variety because of its tender, edible skin, tiny, yielding seeds, and sweet, fresh and flavoursome taste.

telegraph also known as the european or burpless cucumber; slender and long (35cm and more), its thin dark-green skin has shallow ridges running down its length.

CUMIN also known as zeera or comino; resembling caraway in size, cumin is the dried seed of a plant related to the parsley family. Its spicy, almost curry-like flavour is essential to the traditional foods of Mexico, India, North Africa and the Middle East. Available dried as seeds or ground. Black cumin seeds are smaller than standard cumin, and dark brown rather than true black; they are mistakenly confused with kalonji.

CURLY ENDIVE also known as frisée; a prickly-looking, curly-leafed green vegetable with an edible white heart. Fairly bitter in flavour (like chicory, with which it is often confused), it is used mainly in salads.

CURRANTS dried tiny, almost black raisins so named from the grape type native to Corinth, Greece; most often used in jams, jellies and sauces (the best-known of which is the English cumberland sauce). These are not the same as fresh currants, which are the fruit of a plant in the gooseberry family.

CURRY PASTES make your own with the recipes found in this book or purchase the ready-made pastes from the supermarket.

balti taking its name from Baltistan, a mountainous region in northern Pakistan, and sharing it with the wok-shaped pot the curry is cooked in (similarly to tagine); a medium-hot, aromatic paste containing coriander, fenugreek and mint, which gives it its distinctive mild "green" flavour.

green hottest of the traditional thai pastes; particularly good in chicken and vegetable curries, and a great addition to stir-fry and noodle dishes.

korma a classic north Indian sauce with a rich yet delicate coconut flavour and hints of garlic, ginger and coriander.

massaman rich, spicy flavour reminiscent of Middle Eastern cooking; favoured by southern Thai cooks for use in hot and sour stew-like curries and satay sauces.

panang based on the curries of Penang, an island off the north-west coast of Malaysia, close to the Thai border. A complex, sweet and milder variation of red curry paste; good with seafood and for adding to soups and salad dressings.

red probably the most popular thai curry paste; a hot blend of different flavours that complements the richness of pork, duck and seafood. Also works well stirred into marinades and sauces.

rogan josh a paste of medium heat, from the Kashmir region of India, made from fresh chillies or paprika, tomato and spices, especially cardamom. It sometimes has beetroot added to make it a dark red.

tikka in Indian cooking, the word "masala" loosely translates as paste and the word "tikka" means a bite-sized piece of meat, poultry or fish, or sometimes a cutlet. Tikka paste is any maker's choice of spices and oils, mixed into a mild paste, frequently coloured red. Used for marinating or for brushing over meat, seafood or poultry, before or during cooking instead of as an ingredient.

vindaloo a Goan combination of vinegar, tomatoes, pepper and other spices that exemplifies the Portuguese influence on this part of India's west coast.

yellow one of the mildest thai pastes; similar in appearance to Indian curries as they both include yellow chilli and fresh turmeric. Good blended with coconut in vegetable, rice and noodle dishes.

CURRY POWDER a blend of ground spices used for making Indian and some South-East Asian dishes. Consists of some of the following spices: dried chilli, cinnamon, coriander, cumin, fennel, fenugreek, mace, cardamom and turmeric. Available in mild or hot varieties.

CUSTARD POWDER instant mixture used to make pouring custard; similar to North American instant pudding mixes.

DAIKON also known as white radish; an everyday fixture at the Japanese table, this long, white horseradish has a wonderful, sweet flavour. After peeling, eat it raw in salads or shredded as a garnish; also great when sliced or cubed and cooked in stir-fries and casseroles. The flesh is white but the skin can be either white or black; buy those that are firm and unwrinkled from Asian food shops.

DARIOLE see page 368

DASHI the basic fish and seaweed stock that accounts for the distinctive flavour of many Japanese dishes, such as soups and various casserole dishes. Made from dried bonito (a type of tuna) flakes and kombu (kelp); instant dashi (dashi-no-moto) is available in powder, granules and liquid concentrate from Asian food shops.

DATES fruit of the date palm tree, eaten fresh or dried, on their own or in prepared dishes. About 4cm to 6cm in length, oval and plump, thin-skinned, with a honey-sweet flavour and sticky texture. Best known, perhaps, for their inclusion in sticky toffee pudding; also found in muesli; muffins, scones and cakes; compotes and stewed fruit desserts.

DEGLAZE a cooking term to describe making the base for a sauce by heating a small amount of wine, stock or water in a pan in which meat or poultry has been cooked (with most of the excess fat removed) then stirring to loosen the browned bits of food adhering to the bottom. After a pan has been "deglazed", the mixture is used as part of the sauce accompanying that food cooked earlier in the pan.

DHAL an Indian food term used to describe both a whole spectrum of lentils, dried peas and beans, and the range of spicy stew-like dishes containing them.

DIJONNAISE a commercial blend of mayonnaise and dijon mustard, available in most supermarkets; used in sauces and salad dressings, and as a sandwich spread or condiment.

DILL also known as dill weed; used fresh or dried, in seed form or ground. Its anise/celery sweetness flavours the food of the Scandinavian countries, and Germany and Greece. Distinctive feathery, frond-like fresh leaves are grassier and more subtle than the dried version or the seeds (which slightly resemble caraway in flavour). Use dill leaves with smoked salmon and sour cream, poached fish or roast chicken; use the seeds with simply cooked vegetables, or home-baked dark breads.

DISGORGING (or degorging) describes how to rid an uncooked eggplant of its bitter juices. Slice or chop the eggplant as required, place the pieces in a colander or on a sloping surface and sprinkle them, both sides, with enough salt to cover the surface of each piece. Stand for at least half an hour; the salt will turn slightly brown as it absorbs the bitter liquid. Rinse the eggplant well under cold running water then pat dry with absorbent paper before using. This process also helps reduce the amount of oil eggplant will absorb when being fried.

DOCKING PASTRY *see page 441*

DRIED MIXED HERBS a commercial blend of dried crushed thyme, rosemary, marjoram, basil, oregano and sage; available in supermarkets.

DRIED PEAS also known as blue boilers, cowpeas or field peas; the classic pea for a pie floater. Hard, round, blueish-green pea grown specifically for drying; once dried, they are split along a natural seam. Whole and split boilers are available packaged in supermarkets and in bulk in health-food stores, and are great, among other things, for soup making.

DUCK we use whole ducks in some recipes; available from specialty chicken shops, open-air markets and some supermarkets.

breast fillets boneless whole breasts, with the skin on.

chinese barbecued traditionally cooked in special ovens in China; dipped into and brushed during roasting with a sticky sweet coating made from soy sauce, sherry, ginger, five-spice, star anise and hoisin sauce. Available from Asian food shops as well as dedicated Chinese barbecued meat shops.

maryland thigh and drumstick still connected, skin on.

DUMPLING PRESS *see page 233*

DUTCH OVEN *see page 368*

EGGPLANT also called aubergine; often thought of as a vegetable but actually a fruit and belongs to the same family as the tomato, chilli and potato. Ranging in size from tiny to very large and in colour from pale green to deep purple. Can be purchased char-grilled, packed in oil, in jars.

baby also known as finger or japanese eggplant; very small and slender so can be used without disgorging.

pea tiny, about the size of peas; sometimes known by their thai name, "makeua puang". Sold in clusters of 10 to 15 eggplants, similar to vine ripened cherry tomatoes; very bitter in flavour, a quality suited to balance rich, sweet coconut-sauced Thai curries. Available in Asian greengrocers and food shops, fresh or pickled.

thai found in a variety of different sizes and colours, from a long, thin, purplish-green one to a hard, round, golf-ball size having a white-streaked pale-green skin. This last looks like a small unripe tomato and is the most popular eggplant used in Thai and Vietnamese curries and stir-fries.

EGGS we use large chicken eggs having an average weigh of 60g in our recipes unless stated otherwise. Shell colour is determined by the breed of hen and what it has been fed on; it has nothing to do with quality. As far as the differences between cage, barn-laid and free-range eggs is concerned, nutrient content, value

for money and taste have all got to be factored into the equation; in the end, the decision is left to individual preference. Store eggs, in the carton they come in, under refrigeration as soon as you bring them home to slow down deterioration. This helps reduce water loss and protects them from absorbing flavour from other fridge items. Most eggs can be kept, in their carton, in the fridge, for up to 4 weeks. Some recipes in this book call for raw or barely cooked eggs; exercise caution if there is a salmonella problem in your community, particularly in food eaten by children and pregnant women.

EGGWASH beaten egg (white, yolk or both) and milk or water; often brushed over pastry or bread to impart colour or gloss.

ELECTRIC RICE COOKER *see page 250*

EN PAPILLOTE *see page 251*

ENGLISH MUFFIN a round teacake made from yeast, flour, milk, some semolina and salt; often confused with crumpets. Pre-baked and sold packaged in supermarkets, muffins should be split open and toasted before eating.

ESSENCE/EXTRACT an essence is either a distilled concentration of a food quality or an artificial creation of it. Coconut and almond essences are synthetically produced substances used in small amounts to impart their respective flavours to foods. An extract is made by actually extracting the flavour from a food product. In the case of vanilla, pods are soaked, usually in alcohol, to capture the authentic flavour. Both extracts and essences will keep indefinitely if stored in a cool dark place.

ESCHALOTS *see onion*

FENNEL also known as finocchio or anise; a crunchy green vegetable slightly resembling celery that's eaten raw in salads; fried as an accompaniment; or used as an ingredient in soups and sauces. Also the name given to the dried seeds of the plant which have a stronger licorice flavour.

FENUGREEK hard, dried seed usually sold ground as an astringent spice powder. Good with seafood and in chutneys, fenugreek helps mask unpleasant odours.

FIGS originally from the countries that border the eastern Mediterranean; are best eaten in peak season, at the height of summer. Vary in skin and flesh colour according to type not ripeness: the purple-black mission or black mission fig, with pink flesh, is a rich-flavoured, good all-rounder; the thick-skinned, pale green kadota, another all-purpose fruit, is good canned or dried as well as fresh; the yellow smyrna has nutty-tasting flesh; and the pale olive, golden-skinned adriatic has honey-sweet, light pink flesh. When ripe, figs should be unblemished and bursting with flesh; nectar beads at the base indicate when a fig is at its best. Figs are also glacéd (candied), dried or canned in sugar syrup; these are usually sold at health-food stores, Middle Eastern food shops or specialty cheese counters.

FISH SAUCE called naam pla on the label if Thai-made, nuoc naam if Vietnamese; the two are almost identical. Made from pulverised salted fermented fish (most often anchovies); has a pungent smell and strong taste. Available in varying degrees of intensity, so use according to your taste.

FISH SLICE *see page 40*

FIVE-SPICE although the ingredients vary from country to country, five-spice is usually a fragrant mixture of ground cinnamon, cloves, star anise, sichuan pepper and fennel seeds. Used in Chinese and other Asian cooking; available from most supermarkets or Asian food shops.

FLORET the small flower that tops the stalks of a much larger composite cauliflower or broccoli head; good eaten raw or lightly steamed.

FLOUR

besan also known as chickpea flour or gram; made from ground chickpeas so is gluten-free and high in protein. Used in Indian cooking to make dumplings, noodles and chapati; for a batter coating for deep-frying; and as a sauce thickener.

buckwheat *see buckwheat*

cornflour *see cornflour*

maize milled from maize (corn); finely ground polenta (cornmeal) can be substituted in some instances.

plain also known as all-purpose; unbleached wheat flour is the best for baking: the gluten content ensures a strong dough, which produces a light result. Also used as a thickening agent in sauces and gravies.

rice very fine, almost powdery, gluten-free flour; made from ground white rice. Used in baking, as a thickener, and in some Asian noodles and desserts. Another variety, made from glutinous sweet rice, is used for chinese dumplings and rice paper.

rye milled from the cereal grain rye; contains less gluten than plain or wholemeal flour. Produces a dense, heavy bread.

self-raising all-purpose plain or wholemeal flour with baking powder and salt added; can be made at home with plain or wholemeal flour sifted with baking powder in the proportion of 1 cup flour to 2 teaspoons baking powder.

semolina coarsely ground flour milled from durum wheat; the flour used in making gnocchi, pasta and couscous.

strong also known as gluten-enriched, baker's or bread-mix flour. Produced from a variety of wheat that has a high gluten (protein) content and is best suited for pizza and bread making: the expansion caused by the yeast and the stretchiness imposed by kneading require a flour that is "strong" enough to handle these stresses. Since domestic breadmakers entered the marketplace, it has become easier to find strong flour; look for it at your supermarket or a health-food store.

wholemeal also known as wholewheat flour; milled with the wheat germ so is higher in fibre and more nutritional than plain flour.

FOCACCIA *see page 486*

FRIAND PAN *see page 594*

FRUIT MINCE also known as mincemeat. A mixture of dried fruits such as raisins, sultanas and candied peel, nuts, spices, apple, brandy or rum. Is used as a filling for cakes, puddings and fruit mince pies.

FRUIT TEA *see page 424*

GAI LAN also known as gai larn, chinese broccoli and chinese kale; green vegetable appreciated more for its stems than its coarse leaves. Can be served steamed and stir-fried, in soups and noodle dishes. One of the most popular Asian greens, best known for its appearance on a yum cha trolley, where it's steamed then sprinkled with a mixture of oyster sauce and sesame oil.

GALANGAL also known as ka or lengkaus if fresh and laos if dried and powdered; a root, similar to ginger in its use. It has a hot-sour ginger-citrusy flavour; used in fish curries and soups.

GANACHE pronounced gah-nash, a creamy chocolate filling or frosting for cakes. Depending on its intended use, it is made from varying proportions of good-quality chocolate and pouring cream. Other ingredients can be added for flavour, or to increase its richness or gloss. Ganache can be whipped, piped or poured like a glaze, and can be frozen for up to 3 months.

GARAM MASALA literally meaning blended spices in its northern Indian place of origin; based on varying proportions of cardamom, cinnamon, cloves, coriander, fennel and cumin, roasted and ground together. Black pepper and chilli can be added for a hotter version.

GARLIC like onion, a member of the lily family with the edible bulb growning underground. Each bulb is made up of many cloves which, uncooked, can be crushed, sliced, chopped, or used whole, peeled or unpeeled. Garlic powder is the ground product made from dehydrated garlic flakes and is used mostly for convenience purposes.

GELATI Italian for ice-cream but within that name are several different types. One, gelato, is most similar in taste and make-up to what we call ice-cream. Two more types, granita (ice) and sorbetto (sorbet in French or sherbet in English), are similar with the essential distinction being that a sorbet is usually more solidly frozen and made only with fruit or fruit juice and egg whites, while granita is an icy slush made from sugar syrup and one of a myriad flavourings, from fruit to coffee to liqueur. Two other frozen sweets that relate to this entry are semifreddo (loosely translated, "a bit cold"), a partially frozen custard-like mixture made of cream and eggs poured directly into a mould without the use of an ice-cream maker, and cassata, two or more flavours of gelati frozen solid in a mould around a candied-fruit and ricotta or whipped-cream centre.

GELATINE we use dried (powdered) gelatine in the recipes in this book; it's also available in sheet form known as leaf gelatine. A thickening agent made from either collagen, a protein found in animal connective tissue and bones, or certain algae (agar-agar). Three teaspoons of dried gelatine (8g or one sachet) is roughly equivalent to four gelatine leaves. Professionals use leaf gelatine because it generally results in a smoother, clearer consistency, it is also most commonly used throughout Europe. The two types are interchangable but leaf gelatine gives a much clearer mixture than dried gelatine; it's perfect in dishes where appearance really counts.

GHEE clarified butter; with the milk solids removed, this fat has a high smoking point so can be heated to a high temperature without burning. Used as a cooking medium in most Indian recipes.

GINGER

fresh also known as green or root ginger; the thick gnarled root of a tropical plant. Can be kept, peeled, covered with dry sherry in a jar and refrigerated, or frozen in an airtight container.

glacé fresh ginger root preserved in sugar syrup; crystallised ginger (sweetened with cane sugar) can be substituted if rinsed with warm water and dried before using.

ground also known as powdered ginger; used as a flavouring in baking but cannot be substituted for fresh ginger.

pickled pink or red coloured; available, packaged, from Asian food shops. Pickled paper-thin shavings of ginger in a mixture of vinegar, sugar and natural colouring; mostly used in Japanese cooking.

GLUCOSE SYRUP also known as liquid glucose, made from wheat starch; used in jam and confectionery making. Available at health-food stores and supermarkets. *see also page 507*

GLUTEN one of the proteins in wheat and most other cereal flours that helps act as a levening agent. *see also flour*

GLUTEN-FREE BAKING POWDER used as a leavening agent in bread, cake, pastry or pudding mixtures. Suitable for people having an allergic response to glutens or seeking an alternative to everyday baking powder. *see also baking powder*

GOLDEN SYRUP a by-product of refined sugarcane; pure maple syrup or honey can be substituted. Golden syrup and treacle (a thicker, darker syrup not unlike molasses), also known as flavour syrups, are similar sugar products made by partly breaking down sugar into its component parts and adding water. Treacle is more viscous, and has a stronger flavour and aroma than golden syrup (which has been refined further and contains fewer impurities, so is lighter in colour and more fluid). Both can be use in baking and for making certain confectionery items.

GOW GEE PASTRY *see wonton wrappers*

GRAND MARNIER orange liqueur based on cognac-brandy.

GRAPEFRUIT one of the largest citrus fruits, grapefruit is available both seedless or with seeds; the seeded variety has more flavour. There are pink seedless and ruby or ruby red varieties in addition to the ordinary yellow fruit. Eat on its own or in salads, sorbets and granitas.

GRAPEVINE LEAVES from early spring, fresh grapevine leaves can be found in most specialist greengrocers. Alternatively, cryovac-packages containing about 60 leaves in brine can be found in Middle Eastern food shops and some delicatessens; these must be well rinsed and dried before using. Used as wrappers for a large of number of savoury fillings in Mediterranean cuisines.

GREEN TEA *see page 425*

GREASING PANS use butter, margarine, oil or cooking-oil spray to grease baking pans; over-greasing pans can cause food to overbrown. Use absorbent paper or a pastry brush to spread the oil or butter over the pan. Try covering your hand with a small plastic bag then swiping it into the butter or margarine. *see also page 572*

GREMOLATA an aromatic garnish usually made of minced parsley, lemon peel and garlic, but can also include breadcrumbs. Can be sprinkled over dishes just before serving (the classic finish to osso buco) or used as a coating for meat.

HARISSA a North African paste made from dried red chillies, garlic, olive oil and caraway seeds; can be used as a rub for meat, an ingredient in sauces and dressings, or eaten as a condiment. It is available from Middle Eastern food shops and some supermarkets.

HAZELNUTS also known as filberts; plump, grape sized, rich, sweet nut having a brown skin that is removed by rubbing heated nuts together vigorously in a tea-towel. Hazelnut meal is made by grounding the hazelnuts to a coarse flour texture for use in baking or as a thickening agent.

oil a mono-unsaturated oil, made in France, extracted from crushed hazelnuts.

HEAT-SPREADING MAT *see page 40*

HERBAL TEA *see page 425*

HERBS we specify when to use fresh or dried herbs in this book. Dried (not ground) herbs can be used in the proportion of one to four, ie, use 1 teaspoon dried herbs instead of 4 teaspoons (1 tablespoon) chopped fresh herbs.

HOISIN a thick, sweet and spicy Chinese barbecue sauce made from salted fermented soybeans, onions and garlic; used as a marinade or baste, or to accent stir-fries and barbecued or roasted foods. From Asian food shops and supermarkets.

HOLLANDAISE a classic sauce, made with butter and egg yolks, usually with the addition of a little lemon juice or vinegar. Goes well with salmon and asparagus.

HONEY the variety sold in a squeezable container is not suitable for the recipes in this book.

HONEYDEW MELON a heavy oval fruit with a pale-green to yellow skin, delicate taste and pale green flesh.

HORSERADISH a vegetable having edible green leaves but mainly grown for its long, pungent white root. Occasionally found fresh in specialty greengrocers and some Asian food shops, but commonly purchased in bottles at the supermarket in two forms: prepared horseradish and horseradish cream. These cannot be substituted one for the other in cooking but both can be used as table condiments. Horseradish cream is a commercially prepared creamy paste consisting of grated horseradish, vinegar, oil and sugar, while prepared horseradish is the preserved grated root.

HUMMUS a Middle Eastern salad or dip made from softened dried chickpeas, garlic, lemon juice and tahini; can be purchased ready-made from most delicatessens and supermarkets. Also the Arabic word for chickpeas.

ICE-CREAM we use a good quality ice-cream having 5g of fat per 100ml for the recipes in this book.

ICING SUGAR see sugar

JAM also known as preserve or conserve; a thickened mixture of a fruit (and occasionally, a vegetable) and sugar. Usually eaten on toast for breakfast, it's also used as a filling or icing for sweet biscuits and cakes.

KAFFIR LIME also known as magrood, leech lime or jeruk purut. The wrinkled, bumpy-skinned green fruit of a small citrus tree originally grown in South Africa and South-East Asia. As a rule, only the rind and leaves are used.

KAFFIR LIME LEAVES also known as bai magrood and looks like two glossy dark green leaves joined end to end, forming a rounded hourglass shape. Used fresh or dried in many South-East Asian dishes, they are used like bay leaves or curry leaves, especially in Thai cooking. Sold fresh, dried or frozen, the dried leaves are less potent so double the number if using them as a substitute for fresh; a strip of fresh lime peel may be substituted for each kaffir lime leaf.

KALONJI also known as nigella or black onion seeds. Tiny, angular seeds, black on the outside and creamy within, with a sharp nutty flavour that can be enhanced by frying briefly in a dry hot pan before use. Typically sprinkled over Turkish bread immediately after baking or as an important spice in Indian cooking, kalonji can be found in most Asian and Middle Eastern food shops. Often erroneously called black cumin seeds.

KASHA see buckwheat

KECAP MANIS a dark, thick sweet soy sauce used in most South-East Asian cuisines. Depending on the manufacturer, the sauces's sweetness is derived from the addition of either molasses or palm sugar when brewed. Use as a condiment, dipping sauce, ingredient or marinade.

KITCHEN STRING made from a natural product such as cotton or hemp that will neither melt nor affect the flavour of the food during cooking as would a string made from synthetic materials.

KIWIFRUIT also known as Chinese gooseberry; having a brown, somewhat hairy skin and bright-green flesh with a unique sweet-tart flavour. Used in fruit salads, desserts and eaten (peeled) as is.

KNIVES see pages 74–77

KUMARA the polynesian name of an orange-fleshed sweet potato often confused with yam; good baked, boiled, mashed or fried similarly to other potatoes.

LAMB

backstrap also known as eye of loin; the larger fillet from a row of loin chops or cutlets. Tender, best cooked rapidly: barbecued or pan-fried.

chump cut from just above the hind legs to the mid-loin section; can be used as a piece for roasting or cut into chops.

cutlet small, tender rib chop; sometimes sold french-trimmed, with all the fat and gristle at the narrow end of the bone removed.

diced cubed lean meat.

fillets fine texture, most expensive and extremely tender.

leg cut from the hindquarter; can be boned, butterflied, rolled and tied, or cut into dice.

minced ground lamb.

rack row of 4, 6 or 8 cutlets still attached.

rolled shoulder boneless section of the forequarter, rolled and secured with string or netting.

shank forequarter leg; sometimes sold as drumsticks or frenched shanks if the gristle and narrow end of the bone are discarded and the remaining meat trimmed.

shoulder large, tasty piece having much connective tissue so is best pot-roasted or braised. Makes the best mince.

LAMINGTON PAN see page 594

LAVASH flat, unleavened bread of Mediterranean origin; good used as a wrapper or torn and used for dips. see also page 487

LEEKS a member of the onion family, the leek resembles a green onion but is much larger and more subtle in flavour. Tender baby or pencil leeks can be eaten whole with minimal cooking but adult leeks are usually trimmed of most of the green tops then chopped or sliced and cooked as an ingredient in stews, casseroles and soups.

LEMON GRASS also known as takrai, serai or serah. A tall, clumping, lemon-smelling and tasting, sharp-edged aromatic tropical grass; the white lower part of the stem is used, finely chopped, in much of the cooking of South-East Asia. Can be found, fresh, dried, powdered and frozen, in supermarkets and greengrocers as well as Asian food shops.

LEMON PEPPER SEASONING a commercially made blend of crushed black pepper, lemon, herbs and spices; found on supermarket shelves.

LEMON THYME see thyme

LENTILS (red, brown, yellow) dried pulses often identified by and named after their colour. Eaten by cultures all over the world, most famously perhaps in the dhals of India, lentils have high food value.

french green lentils are a local cousin to the famous (and very expensive) French lentils du puy; green-blue, tiny lentils with a nutty, earthy flavour and a hardy nature that allows them to be rapidly cooked without disintegrating.

LETTUCE

butter small, round, loosely formed heads with a sweet flavour; soft, buttery-textured leaves range from pale green on the outer leaves to pale yellow-green inner leaves.

coral very curly and tightly furled leaves that do look like coral; comes in distinctive tasting red and green leaves.

cos also known as romaine lettuce; the traditional caesar salad lettuce. Long, with leaves ranging from dark green on the outside to almost white near the core; the leaves have a stiff centre rib giving a slight cupping effect to the leaf on either side.

iceberg a heavy, firm round lettuce with tightly packed leaves and crisp texture; the most common "family" lettuce used on sandwiches and in salads.

mesclun pronounced mess-kluhn; also known as mixed greens or spring salad mix. A commercial blend of assorted young lettuce and other green leaves, including baby spinach leaves, mizuna and curly endive.

mixed baby lettuce leaves very similar to mesclun with the exception that only the very youngest, smallest leaves are used in the mix.

mizuna Japanese in origin; the frizzy green salad leaves have a delicate mustard flavour.

oakleaf also known as feuille de chene; curly-leafed but not as frizzy as the coral lettuce. Found in both red and green varieties.

radicchio Italian in origin; a member of the chicory family. The dark burgundy leaves and strong, bitter flavour can be cooked or eaten raw in salads.

LINING A FRUIT CAKE PAN *see page 549*

LOAF TIN *see page 595*

LYCHEES a small fruit from China with a hard shell and sweet, juicy flesh. The white flesh has a gelatinous texture and musky, perfumed taste. Discard the rough skin and seed before using in salads or as a dessert fruit. Also available canned in a sugar syrup.

MACADAMIAS native to Australia; fairly large, slightly soft, buttery rich nut. Used to make oil and macadamia butter; equally good in salads or cakes and pastries; delicious eaten on their own. Should always be stored in the fridge to prevent their high oil content turning them rancid.

MADELEINE PAN *see page 595*

MANDARIN also known as tangerine; a small, loose-skinned, easy-to-peel, sweet and juicy citrus fruit, prized for its eating qualities more than for juicing. Segments in a light syrup are available canned.

MANDOLINE *see page 349*

MANGO tropical fruit originally from India and South-East Asia. With skin colour ranging from green to yellow and deep red; fragrant, deep yellow flesh surrounds a large flat seed. Slicing off the cheeks, cross-hatching them with a knife then turning them inside out shows the sweet, juicy flesh at its best. Mangoes can also be used in curries and salsas, or pureed for ice-cream, smoothies or mousse. Mango cheeks in light syrup are available canned. Sour and crunchy, green mangoes are just the immature fruit that is used as a vegetable in salads, salsas and curries.

MAPLE-FLAVOURED SYRUP is made from sugar cane and is also known as golden or pancake syrup. It is not a substitute for pure maple syrup.

MAPLE SYRUP distilled from the sap of sugar maple trees found only in Canada and about ten states in the USA. Most often eaten with pancakes or waffles, but also used as an ingredient in baking or in preparing desserts. Maple-flavoured syrup or pancake syrup is not an adequate substitute for the real thing. *see also page 507*

MARINADE a mixture of ingredients blended together in which food (usually meat, poultry or seafood) is immersed for a minimum 3 hours in order to impart as much flavour as possible into the marinating food. It is also used as a method of tenderising food, usually meat.

MARINARA MIX a mixture of uncooked, chopped seafood available from fishmarkets and fishmongers.

MARJORAM an aromatic herb that is a member of the mint family; has long, thin, oval-shaped, pale-green leaves and a sweet taste similar to oregano. Used fresh or dried with lamb, seafood, vegetables and eggs. Usually added at the end of cooking so as not to lose its mild and delicate flavour.

MARMALADE a preserve, usually based on citrus fruit and its rind, cooked with sugar until the mixture has an intense flavour and thick consistency. Orange, lemon and lime are some of the commercially prepared varieties available.

MARSALA a fortified Italian wine produced in the region surrounding the Sicilian city of Marsala; recognisable by its intense amber colour and complex aroma. Often used in cooking, especially in sauces, risottos and desserts.

MARZIPAN a paste made from ground almonds, sugar and water. Similar to almond paste but sweeter, more pliable and finer in texture. Easily coloured and rolled into thin sheets to cover cakes, or sculpted into shapes for confectionery.

MAYONNAISE we use whole-egg mayonnaise. *see whole-egg mayonnaise*

MELON BALLER *see page 141*

MERGUEZ a small, spicy sausage believed to have originated in Tunisia but eaten throughout North Africa, France and Spain; is traditionally made with lamb meat and is easily recognised because of its chilli-red colour. Can be fried, grilled or roasted; available from many butchers, delicatessens and specialty sausage stores.

MEZZALUNA *see page 349*

MILK we use full-cream homogenised milk unless otherwise specified.

buttermilk in spite of its name, buttermilk is actually low in fat, varying between 0.6 per cent and 2.0 per cent per 100 ml. Originally the term given to the slightly sour liquid left after butter was churned from cream, today it is intentionally made from no-fat or low-fat milk to which specific bacterial cultures have been added during the manufacturing process. It is readily available from the dairy department in supermarkets. Because it is low in fat, it's a good substitute for dairy products such as cream or sour cream in some baking and salad dressings.

evaporated unsweetened canned milk from which water has been extracted by evaporation. Evaporated skim or low-fat milk has 0.3 per cent fat content.

full-cream powder instant powdered milk made from whole cow milk with liquid removed and emulsifiers added.

skim sometimes labelled *no-fat*; both have 0.1 per cent fat content.

skim-milk powder dried milk powder with 1 per cent fat content when dry and 0.1 per cent when reconstituted with water.

sweetened condensed a canned milk product consisting of milk with more than half the water content removed and sugar added to the remaining milk.

MINCED MEAT also known as ground meat, as in beef, pork, lamb and veal.

MINT

spearmint the most commonly used variety of mint; has pointed, bright green leaves and a fresh flavour. Common garden mint has rounder, coarser leaves.

thai (saranae) also known as marsh mint; similar to spearmint. Its somewhat thick, round leaves are usually used raw, as a flavouring sprinkled over soups and salads before serving.

vietnamese not a mint at all, but a pungent and peppery narrow-leafed member of the buckwheat family. Not confined to Vietnam, it is also known as Cambodian mint, pak pai (Thailand), laksa leaf (Indonesia), daun kesom (Singapore) and rau ram in Vietnam. It is a common ingredient in Thai foods, particularly soups, salads and stir-fries.

MIRIN a Japanese champagne-coloured cooking wine, made of glutinous rice and alcohol. It is used expressly for cooking and should not be confused with sake. A

seasoned sweet mirin, manjo mirin, made of water, rice, corn syrup and alcohol, is used in various Japanese dipping sauces.

MISO fermented soybean paste. There are many types of miso, each with its own aroma, flavour, colour and texture; it can be kept, airtight, for up to a year in the fridge. Generally, the darker the miso, the saltier the taste and denser the texture. Salt-reduced miso is available. Buy in tubs or plastic packs.

MIXED DRIED FRUIT a combination of sultanas, raisins, currants, mixed peel and cherries.

MIXED PEEL candied citrus peel.

MIXED SPICE a classic mixture generally containing caraway, allspice, coriander, cumin, nutmeg and ginger, although cinnamon and other spices can be added. It is used with fruit and in cakes.

MOLASSES a thick, dark brown syrup, the residue from the refining of sugar; available in light, dark and blackstrap varieties. Its slightly bitter taste is an essential ingredient in American cooking, found in foods such as gingerbread, shoofly pie and boston baked beans.

MORTAR AND PESTLE *see page 348*

MUESLI also known as granola; a combination of grains (mainly oats), nuts and dried fruits. Some manufacturers toast their product in oil and honey, adding crispness and kilojoules.

MUFFIN PANS *see page 594*

MUSCAT also known as muscatel; refers to both the grape variety and the sweet dessert wine made from them. The grape is superb eaten fresh; when dried, its distinctively musty flavour goes well with cheese, chocolate, pork and game. In winemaking, the grape is used for Italian Asti Spumante, a range of Australian fortifieds, Metaxa from Greece and so on.

MUSHROOMS

button small, cultivated white mushrooms with a mild flavour. When a recipe in this book calls for an unspecified type of mushroom, use button.

dried porcini the richest-flavoured mushrooms, also known as cèpes. Expensive but, because they are so strongly flavoured, only a small amount is required for any particular dish. Use in risottos and stews.

dried shiitake also called donko or dried Chinese mushrooms; have a unique meaty flavour. Sold dried; rehydrate before use.

flat large, flat mushrooms with a rich earthy flavour, ideal for filling and barbecuing. They are sometimes misnamed field mushrooms which are wild mushrooms.

oyster also known as abalone; grey-white mushrooms shaped like a fan. Prized for their smooth texture and subtle, oyster-like flavour.

shiitake fresh, are also known as Chinese black, forest or golden oak mushrooms. Although cultivated, they have the earthiness and taste of wild mushrooms. Large and meaty, they can be used as a substitute for meat in some Asian vegetarian dishes. *see dried shiitake*

swiss brown also known as roman or cremini. Light to dark brown mushrooms with full-bodied flavour; suited for use in casseroles or being stuffed and baked.

MUSLIN inexpensive, undyed, finely woven cotton fabric called for in cooking to strain stocks and sauces; if unavailable, use disposable coffee filter papers.

MUSTARD

american-style bright yellow in colour, a sweet mustard containing mustard seeds, sugar, salt, spices and garlic. Serve with hot dogs and hamburgers.

dijon also known as french. Pale brown, creamy, distinctively flavoured, fairly mild French mustard.

english the traditional hot, pungent, deep yellow mustard. Serve with roast beef and ham; wonderful with hard cheeses.

wholegrain also known as seeded. A French-style coarse-grain mustard made from crushed mustard seeds and dijon-style french mustard. Works well with cold meats and sausages.

MUSTARD SEEDS

black also known as brown mustard seeds; more pungent than the white variety; used frequently in curries.

white also known as yellow mustard seeds; used ground for mustard powder and in most prepared mustards.

NAAN the rather thick, leavened bread associated with the tandoori dishes of northern India, where it is baked pressed against the inside wall of a heated tandoor (clay oven). Now available prepared by commercial bakeries and sold in most supermarkets. *see also page 48/*

NAM JIM generic term for a Thai dipping sauce; most versions include fish sauce and chillies, but the remaining ingredients are up to the individual cook's discretion. Used as a dressing and dipping sauce.

NASHI a member of the pear family but resembling an apple with its pale-yellow-green, tennis-ball-sized appearance; more commonly known as the Asian pear to much of the world. The nashi is different from other pears in that it is crisp, juicy and ready to eat as soon as it is picked and for several months thereafter, unlike its European cousins. These very qualities are more apple- than pear-like, which probably accounts for the widespread misconception that the nashi is a cross between an apple and a pear. Its distinctive texture and mildly sweet taste make it perfect for use raw in salads, or as part of a cheese platter.

NECTAR thick, undiluted fruit juice or a mixture of fruit juices (most commonly apricot, peaches and pears); found in cans in supermarkets.

NECTARINES smooth-skinned, slightly smaller cousin to the peach; juicy, with a rich and rather spicy flavour. Good for desserts peeled and sliced with a little cinnamon sugar and lemon.

NOODLES

dried rice noodles also known as rice stick noodles. Made from rice flour and water, available flat and wide or very thin (vermicelli). Must be soaked in boiling water to soften.

fresh egg also known as ba mee or yellow noodles; made from wheat flour and eggs, sold fresh or dried. Range in size from very fine strands to wide, spaghetti-like pieces as thick as a shoelace.

fresh rice also known as ho fun, khao pun, sen yau, pho or kway tiau, depending on the country of manufacture; the most common form of noodle used in Thailand. Can be purchased in strands of various widths or large sheets weighing about 500g which are to be cut into the desired noodle size. Chewy and pure white, they do not need pre-cooking before use.

fried crispy egg noodles that have been deep-fried then packaged for sale on supermarket shelves.

hokkien also known as stir-fry noodles; fresh wheat noodles resembling thick, yellow-brown spaghetti needing no pre-cooking before use.

rice stick also known as assen lek, ho fun or kway teow; especially popular South-East Asian dried rice noodles. They come in different widths (thin used in soups, wide in stir-fries), but all should be soaked in hot water to soften. The traditional noodle used in pad thai which, before soaking, measures about 5mm in width.

rice vermicelli also known as sen mee, mei fun or bee hoon. Used throughout Asia in spring rolls and cold salads; similar to bean threads, only longer and made with rice flour instead of mung bean starch. Before using, soak the dried noodles in hot water until softened, boil them briefly then rinse with hot water. Vermicelli can also be deep-fried until crunchy and then used in Chinese chicken salad, or as a garnish or bed for sauces.

singapore pre-cooked wheat noodles best described as a thinner version of hokkien; sold, packaged, in the refrigerated section of supermarkets.

soba thin, pale-brown noodle originally from Japan; made from buckwheat and varying proportions of wheat flour. Available dried and fresh, and in flavoured (for instance, green tea) varieties; eaten in soups, stir-fries and, chilled, on their own.

udon available fresh and dried, these broad, white, wheat Japanese noodles are similar to the ones in home-made chicken noodle soup.

NORI a type of dried seaweed used in Japanese cooking as a flavouring, garnish or for sushi. Sold in thin sheets, plain or toasted (yaki-nori).

NUTMEG a strong and pungent spice ground from the dried nut of an evergreen tree native to Indonesia. Usually found ground but the flavour is more intense from a whole nut, available from spice shops, so it's best to grate your own. Used most often in baking and milk-based desserts, but also works nicely in savoury dishes. Found in mixed spice mixtures.

OIL

cooking spray we use a cholesterol-free cooking spray made from canola oil.

hazelnut oil *see hazelnuts*

macadamia oil *see macadamias*

olive made from ripened olives. Extra virgin and virgin are the first and second press, respectively, of the olives and are therefore considered the best; the "extra light" or "light" name on other types refers to taste not fat levels.

peanut pressed from ground peanuts; the most commonly used oil in Asian cooking because of its high smoke point (capacity to handle high heat without burning).

sesame made from roasted, crushed, white sesame seeds; a flavouring rather than a cooking medium.

vegetable any of a number of oils sourced from plant rather than animal fats.

OKRA also known as bamia or lady fingers. A green, ridged, oblong pod with a furry skin. Native to Africa, this vegetable is used in Indian, Middle Eastern and South American cooking. Can be eaten on its own; as part of a casserole, curry or gumbo; used to thicken stews or gravies.

ONIONS

baby also known as cocktail or pickling onions. These small brown onions have an average weight of 25g. Pickled in a vinegar brine or cooked whole in stews and casseroles.

flakes packaged (usually in 55g packets) chopped and dehydrated white onion pieces; used more often for garnish than as an ingredient.

fried onion/shallot served as a condiment on Asian tables to be sprinkled over just-cooked food. Found in cellophane bags or jars at all Asian grocery shops; once opened, they will keep for months if stored tightly seeled. Make your own by frying thinly sliced peeled shallots or baby onions until golden brown and crisp.

green also known as scallion or (incorrectly) shallot; an immature onion picked before the bulb has formed, having a long, bright-green edible stalk.

leek *see leek*

purple shallots also known as Asian shallots; related to the onion but resembling garlic (they grow in bulbs of multiple cloves). Thin-layered and intensely flavoured, they are used in cooking throughout South-East Asia.

red also known as spanish, red spanish or bermuda onion; a sweet-flavoured, large, purple-red onion.

shallots also called french shallots, golden shallots or eschalots. Small and elongated, with a brown-skin, they grow in tight clusters similar to garlic.

spring crisp, narrow green-leafed tops and a round sweet white bulb larger than green onions.

ORANGE-FLAVOURED LIQUEUR brandy-based liqueur such as Grand Marnier or Cointreau.

ORANGE FLOWER WATER concentrated flavouring made from orange blossoms.

OXTAIL *see beef*

OYSTER SAUCE Asian in origin, this thick, richly flavoured brown sauce is made from oysters and their brine, cooked with salt and soy sauce, and thickened with starches. Use as a condiment.

PAELLA PAN *see page 171*

PANCETTA an Italian unsmoked bacon, pork belly cured in salt and spices then rolled into a sausage shape and dried for several weeks. Used, sliced or chopped, as an ingredient rather than eaten on its own; can also be used to add taste and moisture to tough or dry cuts of meat. Hot pancetta is lean pork belly first salted and cured then spiced and rolled into a

fat loaf; used in pasta sauces and meat dishes except in its place of origin, Corsica, where it is eaten on its own.

PAPPADUMS dried cracker-like wafers made from a combination of lentil and rice flours, oil and spices. Pappadums need to be reconstituted to make them edible: they are usually deep-fried briefly until they puff and double in size, but they can also be cooked in a low-fat manner in a microwave oven. Unless otherwise stated, we use large plain pappadums in our recipes, however, there are many different size and flavouring combinations.

PAPRIKA ground dried sweet red capsicum (bell pepper); there are many grades and types available, including sweet, hot, mild and smoked.

PARSLEY a versatile herb with a fresh, earthy flavour. There are about 30 varieties of curly parsley; the flat-leaf variety (also called continental or Italian parsley) is stronger in flavour and darker in colour.

PASTA

ditali, or ditalini, are tiny, very short tubes of macaroni, often used in minestrone.

farfalle bow-tie shaped short pasta; sometimes known as butterfly pasta.

fettuccine ribbon pasta made from durum wheat, semolina and egg. Available fresh or dried, plain or flavoured.

fresh lasagne sheets thinly rolled wide sheets of plain or flavoured pasta; they do not requiring par-boiling prior to being used in cooking.

gnocchi Italian 'dumplings' made of potatoes, semolina or flour; can be cooked in boiling water or baked with sauce.

macaroni tube-shaped pasta available in various sizes; made from semolina and water, and does not contain eggs.

orecchiette small disc-shaped pasta, translates literally as "little ears".

risoni small rice-shape pasta; very similar to another small pasta, orzo.

shell pasta shell-shaped pasta ranging from tiny to very large in size.

spaghetti long, thin solid strands of pasta.

spiral pasta corkscrew-shaped pasta available in various flavours and sizes.

tagliatelle long, flat strips of wheat pasta, slightly narrower and thinner than fettuccine.

tortellini circles of fresh plain pasta that are stuffed with a meat or cheese filling, and then folded into little hats.

PASTA SAUCE a prepared tomato-based sauce (sometimes called ragu or sugo on the label); comes in varying degrees of thickness and with different flavourings.

PASTRY For steps on handling pastry see pages 440 & 441.

PASTRY WHEEL *see page 141*

PATTY PAN *see page 595*

PATTY-PAN SQUASH also known as crookneck or custard marrow pumpkins; a round, slightly flat summer squash being yellow to pale green in colour and having a scalloped edge. Harvested young, it has firm white flesh and a distinct flavour.

PEANUTS, also known as groundnut, not in fact a nut but the pod of a legume. We mainly use raw (unroasted) or unsalted roasted peanuts.

PEARL BARLEY *see barley*

PECANS native to the US and now grown locally; pecans are golden brown, buttery and rich. Good in savoury as well as sweet dishes; walnuts are a good substitute.

PECTIN is a carbohydrate present in certain fruits and vegetables which, when combined with sugar, helps a jam, jelly or marmalade to set or jell. Commercial pectin can be bought from health-food stores; it can be used to set jams and jellies made with fruit low in pectin.

PEPITAS are the pale green kernels of dried pumpkin seeds; they can be bought plain or salted.

PESTO a classic uncooked sauce made from basil, garlic, pine nuts, parmesan and olive oil; often served over pasta.

PIDE *see Turkish bread*

PINE NUTS also known as pignoli; not in fact a nut but a small, cream-coloured kernel from pine cones. They are best roasted before use to bring out the flavour.

PIRI PIRI PASTE a Portuguese chilli paste made from red chillies, ginger, garlic, oil and various herbs.

PISTACHIO green, delicately flavoured nuts inside hard off-white shells. Available salted or unsalted in their shells; you can also get them shelled.

PITTA also known as lebanese bread; wheat-flour pocket bread sold in large, flat pieces that separate into two thin rounds. Also available in small thick pieces called pocket pitta.

PLUM SAUCE a thick, sweet and sour dipping sauce made from plums, vinegar, sugar, chillies and spices.

POACH a cooking term to describe gentle simmering of food in liquid (generally water or stock); spices or herbs can be added to impart their flavour.

POLENTA also known as cornmeal; a flour-like cereal made of dried corn (maize). also the name of the dish made from it.

POMEGRANATE dark red, leathery skinned fresh fruit about the size of an orange filled with hundreds of seeds, each wrapped in an edible lucent-crimson pulp having a unique tangy sweet-sour flavour.

POMEGRANATE MOLASSES not to be confused with pomegranate syrup or grenadine (used in cocktails); pomegranate molasses is thicker, browner, and more concentrated in flavour tart and sharp, slightly sweet and fruity. Brush over grilling or roasting meat, seafood or poultry, add to salad dressings or sauces. Buy from Middle Eastern food stores or specialty food shops.

POMELO similar to grapefruit but sweeter, somewhat more conical in shape and slightly larger, about the size of a small coconut. The firm rind peels away easily and neatly, like a mandarin, and the segments are easy to separate.

POPPY SEEDS

black small, dried, bluish-grey seeds of the poppy plant, with a crunchy texture and a nutty flavour. Can be purchased whole or ground in delicatessens and most supermarkets.

white also known as kas kas. Quite dissimilar to the black variety, these seeds from the white poppy are used, ground, as a thickening agent in sauces. Toasted, they take on a nutty flavour so are also used as a substitute for ground almonds.

PORK

american-style spareribs well-trimmed mid-loin ribs.

belly fatty cut sold in rashers or in a piece, with or without rind or bone.

butterfly skinless, boneless mid-loin chop, split in half and flattened.

chinese barbecued roasted pork fillet with a sweet, sticky coating. Available from Asian food shops or specialty stores.

cutlets cut from ribs.

fat selvedge fat from pork loin.

fillet skinless, boneless eye-fillet cut from the loin.

minced ground lean pork.

neck sometimes called pork scotch, boneless cut from the foreloin.

pancetta see pancetta

prosciutto see prosciutto

rack of pork joined row of trimmed cutlets.

shoulder joint sold with bone in or out.

steak schnitzel is usually cut from the leg or rump.

POTATOES

bintje oval, creamy skin, yellow flesh; good all-purpose potato, great baked and fried, good in salads.

collban round, smooth white skin and flesh; good for baking and mashing.

congo purple flesh, small, elongated, sweet, mealy; good boiled and in salads.

desiree oval, smooth and pink-skinned, waxy yellow flesh; good in salads, boiled and roasted.

idaho also known as russet burbank; russet in colour, fabulous baked.

king edward slightly plump and rosy; great mashed.

kipfler small, finger-shaped, nutty flavour; great baked and in salads.

lasoda round, red skin with deep eyes, white flesh; good for mashing or roasting.

new potatoes also known as chats; not a separate variety but an early harvest with very thin skin. Good unpeeled steamed, eaten hot or cold in salads.

nicola medium-sized, oval, beige skin, yellow flesh; good for mashing.

pink-eye small, off-white skin, purple eyes; good steamed and boiled, great baked.

pink fir apple elongated, rosy skin, waxy; good boiled, baked and in salads.

pontiac large, red skin, deep eyes, white flesh; good grated, boiled and baked.

russet burbank long and oval, rough white skin with shallow eyes, white flesh; good for baking and frying.

sebago white skin, oval; good fried, mashed and baked.

spunta large, long, yellow flesh, floury; great mashed and fried.

PRESERVED LEMON an indispensable ingredient in Moroccan cooking and used as a flavouring by many modern chefs; has a silken texture and distinctive flavour. Preserved in salt, oil or lemon juice and occasionally spices such as cinnamon, clove and coriander for about 30 days, the lemon must be rinsed well before being either chopped and stirred into yogurt or a salad dressing without being cooked, or added to a casserole or tagine to add salty-sour piquancy to the finished dish.

PRESERVED TURNIP also known as hua chai po or cu cai muoi, or dried radish because of its similarity to daikon. Sold packaged whole or sliced, it is very salty and must be rinsed and dried before use.

PROSCIUTTO a kind of unsmoked Italian ham; salted, air-cured and aged, it is usually eaten uncooked. There are many styles of prosciutto, one of the best being Parma ham, from Italy's Emilia Romagna region, traditionally lightly salted, dried then eaten raw.

PRUNES commercially or sun-dried plums; store in the fridge.

PU-ERH TEA *see page 425*

PUMPERNICKEL BREAD *see page 486*

PUMPKIN often used interchangeably with the word squash, the pumpkin is a member of the gourd family and comes in a variety of sizes, shapes and colours. Used in sweet and savoury dishes, pumpkin can be boiled, steamed, mashed or roasted.

QUAIL related to the pheasant and partridge; a small, delicate-flavoured farmed game bird ranging in weight from 250g to 300g.

QUINCE yellow-skinned fruit with hard texture and astringent, tart taste; eaten cooked or as a preserve. Long, slow cooking makes the flesh a deep rose pink.

QUINOA pronounced keen-wa. The seed of a leafy plant similar to spinach. Like corn, rice, buckwheat and millet, quinoa is gluten-free and thought to be safe for consumption by people with coeliac disease. Its cooking qualities are similar to rice, and its delicate, slightly nutty taste and chewy texture make it a good partner for rich or spicy foods. You can buy it in most health-food stores and some delicatessens; keep quinoa sealed in a glass jar under refrigeration because, like nuts and nut oils, it spoils easily.

RAISINS dried sweet grapes (traditionally muscatel grapes).

RADICCHIO *see lettuce*

RAITA yogurt that is whipped and seasoned with salt, pepper and one or two piquant spices; often has mint stirred in. Served as a condiment, it possesses cooling properties to help temper the heat of a curry.

RAMEKIN *see page 369*

READY-ROLLED PUFF PASTRY packaged sheets of frozen puff pastry, available from supermarkets.

REDCURRANT JELLY a preserve made from redcurrants used as a glaze for desserts and meats or in sauces.

REMOULADE a French mayonnaise-like mixture traditionally containing capers, dijon mustard and parsley.

RICE

arborio small, round grain rice well-suited to absorb a large amount of liquid; the high level of starch makes it especially suitable for risottos, giving the dish its classic creaminess.

basmati a white, fragrant long-grained rice; the grains fluff up beautifully when cooked. It should be washed several times before cooking.

black also known as purple rice because, although a deep charcoal in colour when raw, after cooking it turns a purplish-black colour. A medium-grain unmilled rice, with a white kernel under the black bran, it has a nutty, whole-grain flavour and is crunchy to the bite like wild rice.

calrose a medium-grain rice that is extremely versatile; can be substituted for short- or long-grain rices if necessary.

glutinous also known as sweet rice or sticky rice; a short, fat grain having a chalky white centre. When cooked it becomes soft and sticky, hence the name; requires long soaking and steaming.

jasmine or Thai jasmine, is a long-grained white rice recognised around the world as having a perfumed aromatic quality; moist in texture, it clings together after cooking. Sometimes substituted for basmati rice.

koshihikari small, round-grain white rice. Substitute white short-grain rice and cook by the absorption method.

long-grain elongated grains that remain separate when cooked; this is the most popular steaming rice in Asia.

medium-grain *see calrose*

short-grain fat, almost round grain with a high starch content; tends to clump together when cooked.

white is hulled and polished rice, can be short-or long-grained.

wild not a true member of the rice family but a very dark brown seed of a North American aquatic grass having a distinctively nutty flavour and crunchy, resilient texture. Sold on its own or in a blend with basmati or long-grain white rice.

RICE PAPER there are two products sold as rice paper. Banh trang is made from rice flour and water then stamped into rounds; is quite brittle and breaks easily. Dipped briefly in water, they become pliable wrappers for food. The other, edible, translucent glossy rice paper is made from a dough made of water combined with the pith of an Asian shrub called the rice-paper plant (or rice-paper tree). Resembling a grainy sheet of paper and whiter than banh trang, it is imported from Holland. Use in confectionery making and baking; never eat it uncooked. *see also page 549*

RICER *see page 348*

RIGANI also known as greek oregano; a stronger, sharper version of the familiar herb used in Italian cooking.

RISONI *see pasta*

ROASTING nuts and dried coconut can be roasted in the oven to restore their fresh flavour and release their aromatic essential oils. Spread them evenly onto an oven tray then roast in a moderate oven for about 5 minutes. Desiccated coconut, pine nuts and sesame seeds roast more evenly if stirred over low heat in a heavy-based frying pan; their natural oils will help turn them golden brown.

ROCKET also known as arugula, rugula and rucola; peppery green leaf eaten raw in salads or used in cooking. Baby rocket leaves are smaller and less peppery.

ROLLED OATS flattened oat grain rolled into flakes and traditionally used for porridge. Instant oats are also available, but use traditional oats for baking.

ROLLED RICE flattened rice grain rolled into flakes; looks similar to rolled oats.

ROLLED RYE flattened rye grain rolled into flakes and similar in appearance to rolled oats.

ROOIBOS TEA *see page 425*

ROSEMARY pungent herb with long, thin pointy leaves; use large and small sprigs, and the leaves are usually chopped finely.

ROSEWATER extract made from crushed rose petals, called gulab in India; used for its aromatic quality in many sweetmeats and desserts.

ROUILLE French for rust; is a capsicum and chilli-flavoured mayonnaise-like sauce used to garnish seafood stews, particularly the French classic, bouillabaisse.

ROUND CAKE PANS *see page 594*

ROTI *see page 486*

RUM we use a dark underproof rum (not overproof) for a more subtle flavour in cooking. White rum is almost colourless, sweet and used mostly in mixed drinks.

RYE BREAD *see page 486*

SAFFRON stigma of a member of the crocus family, available ground or in strands; imparts a yellow-orange colour to food once infused. The quality can vary greatly; the best is the most expensive spice in the world.

SAGE pungent herb with narrow, grey-green leaves; slightly bitter with a slightly musty mint aroma. Dried sage comes whole, crumbled or ground.

SAKE Japan's favourite wine, made from fermented rice, is used for marinating, cooking and as part of dipping sauces. If sake is unavailable, dry sherry, vermouth or brandy can be substituted. If drinking sake, stand it first in a container in hot water for 20 minutes to warm it through.

SALSA the Spanish word for sauce but generally used in cooking to describe any raw or cooked Mexican sauce served also as a salad or dip. Raw, it is called "salsa cruda" or "salsa fresca"; there are a myriad cooked salsas and most are named after their colour or content.

SALSA VERDE while we generally associate the word "salsa" with Mexican salads, sauces or dips, this zesty fresh herb sauce is in fact an Italian classic that adds tang to poached or steamed fish dishes and is a part of a traditional bollito misto, the famous Piedmontese version of a boiled dinner. The herbs used in salsa verde can vary with the single common denominator being parsley.

SALT unless specified otherwise, we use normal iodised table salt. Because we believe cooks salt as they like or not at all, the vast majority of our recipes do not list it as one of the ingredients.

SAMBAL OELEK also ulek or olek; Indonesian in origin, this is a salty paste made from ground chillies and vinegar.

SAVOIARDI also known as savoy biscuits, lady's fingers or sponge fingers, they are Italian-style crisp fingers made from sponge cake mixture.

SCORE a cooking term to describe making shallow cuts, usually in criss-cross pattern, over meat, vegetables or seafood; often used on squid.

SEAFOOD

balmain bug also known as slipper or shovelnose lobster, or southern bay lobster; crustacean, a type of crayfish. Substitute with moreton bay bugs, king prawns or scampi.

barramundi an Aboriginal word, barramundi means "river fish with large scales". Wild barramundi, found in both coastal and fresh waters in the tropical northern half of Australia, weigh an average 4kg; farmed barramundi are an average 400g in weight. "Baby" barramundi (often referred to as "plate-size"), also farmed commercially, are a firm, moist white fish best served whole. Substitute with nile perch.

blue swimmer crab also known as sand crab, blue manna crab, bluey, sand crab or sandy. Substitute with lobster, balmain or moreton bay bugs.

blue-eye also known as deep sea trevalla or trevally and blue-eye cod; thick, moist white-fleshed fish.

bream (yellowfin) also known as silver or black bream, seabream or surf bream; soft, moist white flesh. Substitute with snapper or ocean perch.

calamari a mollusc, a type of squid; substitute with baby octopus.

clams also called vongole; we use a small ridge-shelled variety of this bivalve mollusc. For steps on preparing clams, see page 297.

cod, smoked substitute with smoked haddock.

crab meat flesh of fresh crabs; frozen uncooked flesh is also available. Use canned if neither is available. For steps on preparing crab, see page 296.

dhufish also known as WA pearl perch and jewfish; caught off the West Australian coast, popular with recreational fisherman. Substitute with snapper or bream.

dried shrimp also known as goong hang, salted sun-dried prawns ranging in size from not much larger than a rice seed to big ones measuring about 1cm in length. They are sold packaged, shelled as a rule, in all Asian grocery stores.

fish fillet use your favourite firm-fleshed white fish fillet. For steps on preparing fish, see pages 110 & 111.

flathead many varieties, most commonly dusky flathead, which is also the largest. Mostly fished from river mouths and estuaries; substitute with whiting or your favourite white fish.

kingfish (yellowtail) also known as southern yellowfish, kingie, Tasmanian yellowtail. Substitute with jewfish.

lobster (rock lobster) also known as cray, spiny lobster, eastern, southern or western lobster. Substitute with balmain or moreton bay bugs. For steps on preparing lobster, see pages 296 & 297.

mahi mahi also known as dolphin fish, dorado. Substitute with swordfish, mako shark or striped marlin.

marinara mix *see marinara mix*

mud crab also known as mangrove crab, green or black. Native to the tropical regions of the Bay of Bengal and the Pacific and Indian oceans. Substitute with scampi, lobster or balmain bugs.

mussels should only be bought from a reliable fish market: they must be tightly closed when bought, indicating they are alive. Before cooking, scrub shells with a strong brush and remove the beards; do not eat any that do not open after cooking. Varieties include black and green-lip. For steps on preparing mussels, see page 297.

ocean perch also known as coral, red or sea perch, or coral cod; white flesh with a delicate flavour. Substitute with snapper.

ocean trout a farmed fish with pink, soft flesh. It is from the same family as the atlantic salmon; one can be substituted for the other.

octopus usually tenderised before you buy them; both octopus and squid require either long slow cooking (usually for the large molluscs) or quick cooking over high heat (usually for the small molluscs) — anything in between will make the octopus tough and rubbery. For steps on preparing octopus, see page 110.

oysters available in many varieties, including pacific, bay/blacklip, and Sydney or New Zealand rock oyster. For steps on preparing oysters, see page 297.

pipis small smooth-shelled triangular shaped bivalve mollusc; substitute with clams or vongole. For steps on preparing pipis, see page 297.

prawns also known as shrimp. Varieties include, school, king, royal red, Sydney harbour, tiger. Can be bought uncooked (green) or cooked, with or without shells. For steps on buying and preparing prawns, see page 296.

roe *see page 111*

salmon red-pink firm flesh with few bones; moist delicate flavour.

sardines also known as pilchards; small silvery fish with soft, oily flesh. Substitute with garfish.

sashimi *see page 110*

scallops a bivalve mollusc with fluted shell valve; we use scallops that have the coral (roe) attached. For steps on preparing scallops, see page 297.

squid also known as calamari; a type of mollusc. Buy squid hoods to make preparation and cooking faster. For steps on preparing squid, see page 111.

swordfish also known as broadbill. Substitute with yellowfin or bluefin tuna or mahi mahi.

tuna reddish, firm flesh; slightly dry. Varieties include bluefin, yellowfin, skipjack or albacore; substitute with swordfish.

white fish means non-oily fish. This category includes bream, flathead, whiting, snapper, dhufish, redfish and ling.

whiting (sand whiting), also called silver whiting, summer whiting, king george whiting or trumpeter. Substitute with bream.

SEAWEED, SHEET (yaki-nori) *see nori*

SEGMENTING a cooking term to describe cutting citrus fruits in such a way that the pieces contain no pith, seed or membrane. The peeled fruit is cut towards the centre inside each membrane, forming wedges.

SESAME SEEDS black and white are the most common of this small oval seed, however there are also red and brown varieties. The seeds are used in cuisines the world over as an ingredient and as a condiment. Roast the seeds in a heavy-based frying pan over low heat.

SEVEN-SPICE MIX (shichimi togarashi) a Japanese blend of seven ground spices, seeds and seaweed. The mixture varies but will include some hot and aromatic flavours. Used as a seasoning with noodles and cooked meats and fish.

SHERRY fortified wine consumed as an aperitif or used in cooking. Sherries differ in colour and flavour; sold as fino (light, dry), amontillado (medium sweet, dark) and oloroso (full-bodied, very dark).

SHRIMP PASTE also known as kapi, trasi and blanchan; a strong-scented, very firm preserved paste made of salted dried shrimp. Used sparingly as a pungent flavouring in many South-East Asian soups, sauces and rice dishes. It should be chopped or sliced thinly then wrapped in foil and roasted before use.

SICHUAN PEPPERCORNS also known as szechuan or Chinese pepper, native to the Sichuan province of China. A mildly hot spice that comes from the prickly ash tree. Although it is not related to the peppercorn family, small, red-brown aromatic sichuan berries look like black

peppercorns and have a distinctive peppery-lemon flavour and aroma.

SILVER BEET also known as Swiss chard and incorrectly, spinach; has fleshy stalks and large leaves, both of which can be prepared as for spinach.

SKEWERS metal or bamboo skewers can be used. Rub oil onto metal skewers to stop meat sticking; soak bamboo skewers in water for at least 1 hour or overnight to stop them burning.

SLICE PAN *see page 594*

SNOW PEAS also called mangetout; a variety of garden pea, eaten pod and all (although you may need to string them). Used in stir-fries or eaten raw in salads. Snow pea sprouts are available from supermarkets or greengrocers and are usually eaten raw in salads or sandwiches.

SOURDOUGH BREAD *see page 486*

SOY SAUCE also known as sieu; made from fermented soybeans. Several variations are available in supermarkets and Asian food stores; we use Japanese soy sauce unless indicated otherwise.

dark deep brown, almost black in colour; rich, with a thicker consistency than other types. Pungent but not particularly salty, it is good for marinating.

japanese an all-purpose low-sodium soy sauce made with more wheat content than its Chinese counterparts; fermented in barrels and aged. Possibly the best table soy and the one to choose if you only want one variety.

light fairly thin in consistency and, while paler than the others, the saltiest tasting; used in dishes in which the natural colour of the ingredients is to be maintained. Not to be confused with salt-reduced or low-sodium soy sauces.

tamari similar to but thicker than japanese soy; very dark in colour with a distinctively mellow flavour. Good used as a dipping sauce or for basting.

SPATCHCOCK a small chicken (poussin), no more than 6 weeks old, weighing a maximum of 500g. Also, a cooking term to describe splitting a small chicken open, then flattening and grilling.

SPATTER MAT *see page 41*

SPECK smoked pork.

SPINACH also known as english spinach and incorrectly, silver beet. Baby spinach leaves are best eaten raw in salads; the larger leaves should be added last to soups, stews and stir-fries, and should be cooked until barely wilted.

SPRING ROLL WRAPPERS also known as egg roll wrappers; they come in various sizes and can be purchased fresh or frozen. Made from a delicate wheat-based pastry, they can be used for making gow gee and samosas as well as spring rolls.

SPRINGFORM TIN *see page 460*

SQUARE CAKE PANS *see page 595*

SQUASH *see patty-pan squash*

STAR ANISE a dried star-shaped pod whose seeds have an astringent aniseed flavour; commonly used to flavour stocks and marinades.

STARFRUIT also known as carambola, five-corner fruit or Chinese star fruit; pale green or yellow colour, it has a clean, crisp texture. Flavour may be either sweet or sour, depending on the variety and when it was picked. There is no need to peel or seed it and they're slow to discolour.

STOCK cubes, powder or concentrated liquid can be used. As a guide, 1 small stock cube or 1 teaspoon of stock powder or 1 portion of stock concentrate mixed with 1 cup (250ml) water will give a fairly strong stock. Also available in ready-to-use bottles, cans or tetra packs. If you prefer to make your own stock see recipes on pages 192 & 193 – these can be made up to 4 days ahead and kept, covered, in the refrigerator. Remove any fat from the surface after the stock has been refrigerated overnight.

SUGAR we use coarse, granulated table sugar, also known as crystal sugar, unless otherwise specified. *see also page 507*

brown an extremely soft, fine granulated sugar retaining molasses for its characteristic colour and flavour. *see also page 507*

caster also known as superfine or finely granulated table sugar. The fine crystals dissolve easily so it is perfect for cakes, meringues and desserts. *see also page 506*

cinnamon combination of ground cinnamon and caster sugar. Most commonly sprinkled over buttered toast.

cubes *see page 506*

demerara small-grained golden-coloured crystal sugar. *see also page 506*

icing also known as confectioners' sugar or powdered sugar; pulverised granulated sugar crushed together with a small amount (about 3 per cent) of cornflour. *see also page 507*

palm also known as nam tan pip, jaggery, jawa or gula melaka; made from the sap of the sugar palm tree. Light brown to black in colour and usually sold in rock-hard cakes; substitute with brown sugar if unavailable. *see also page 506*

pure icing also known as confectioners' sugar or powdered sugar.

muscovado *see page 506*

raw natural brown granulated sugar. *see also page 506*

SUGAR SNAP PEAS also known as honey snap peas; fresh small pea which can be eaten whole, pod and all.

SUMAC a purple-red, astringent spice ground from berries growing on shrubs that flourish wild around the Mediterranean; adds a tart, lemony flavour to dips and dressings and goes well with barbecued meat. Can be found in Middle Eastern food stores.

SUN TEA *see page 424*

SUNFLOWER SEED KERNELS grey-green, slightly soft, oily kernels; a nutritious snack.

SWEET CHILLI SAUCE *see chilli*

SWISS ROLL PAN *see page 594*

TABASCO brand-name of an extremely fiery sauce made from vinegar, hot red peppers and salt.

TACO SEASONING MIX a packaged seasoning meant to duplicate the Mexican sauce made from oregano, cumin, chillies and other spices.

TAGINE a stew of Moroccan origin; also the name of the dish in which the stew is cooked.

TAHINI sesame seed paste available from Middle Eastern food stores; most often used in hummus and baba ghanoush.

TAMARIND the tamarind tree produces clusters of hairy brown pods, each of which is filled with seeds and a viscous pulp, that are dried and pressed into the blocks of tamarind found in Asian food shops. Gives a sweet-sour, slightly astringent taste to marinades, pastes, sauces and dressings.

TAMARIND CONCENTRATE (or paste) the commercial result of the distillation of tamarind juice into a condensed, compacted paste.

TAPENADE a thick paste made from black or green olives, capers, anchovies, olive oil and lemon juice.

TARRAGON often called the king of herbs by the French, it is used as the essential flavouring for many of their classic sauces (béarnaise, tartare, etc) It is one of the herbs blended with parsley, chives and chervil to make *fines herbes*, and is the unique taste giving singularity to so many French egg, fish and chicken dishes.

TARTLET PANS *see page 460*

TAT SOI also known as pak choy, rosette and chinese flat cabbage; a member of the same family as buk choy, it has the same mild flavour. Its dark-green leaves are usually eaten in salads, but are also good in soups, curries and stir-fries.

TEMPERING the process by which chocolate is melted at a specific temperature that enables it to set with a glossy finish.

TEQUILA colourless alcoholic liquor of Mexican origin made from the fermented sap of the agave, a succulent desert plant.

TERIYAKI either home-made or commercially bottled, this Japanese sauce, made from soy sauce, mirin, sugar, ginger and other spices, imparts a distinctive glaze when brushed over grilled meat or poultry.

THYME a member of the mint family; there are many types of this herb but two that we use most. The "household" variety, simply called thyme in most shops, is French thyme; it has tiny grey-green leaves that give off a pungent minty, light-lemon aroma. Dried thyme comes in both leaf and powdered form. Lemon thyme's scent is due to the high level of citral in its leaves, an oil also found in lemon, orange, verbena and lemon grass. The citrus scent is enhanced by crushing the leaves in your hands before using the herb.

TIMBALE *see page 368*

TOFU also known as soybean curd or bean curd; an off-white, custard-like product made from the "milk" of crushed soybeans. Comes fresh as soft or firm, and processed as fried or pressed dried sheets. Fresh tofu can be refrigerated in water (changed daily) for up to 4 days.

firm made by compressing bean curd to remove most of the water. Good used in stir-fries as it can be tossed without disintegrating. Can also be flavoured, preserved in rice wine or brine.

fried packaged pieces of deep-fried soft bean curd; the surface is brown and crunchy and the inside quite dry. Add to soups and stir-fries at the last minute so they don't soak up too much liquid.

sheets also known as dried bean curd skins or yuba. Manufactured product made from the sweet, stiffened skin that forms on warm soybean liquid as it cools. Must be reconstituted before being used as a wrapper. Also good, cut into strips, as a garnish.

silken not a type of tofu but reference to the manufacturing process of straining soybean liquid through silk; this denotes best quality.

soft delicate texture; does not hold its shape when overhandled. Can also be used as a dairy substitute in ice-cream or cheesecakes.

TOMATOES

canned whole peeled tomatoes in natural juices; available crushed, chopped or diced, sometimes unsalted or reduced salt. Use in recipes undrained.

cherry also known as tiny tim or tom thumb tomatoes; small and round.

egg also called plum or roma, these are smallish, oval-shaped tomatoes much used in Italian cooking or salads.

grape small, long oval-shaped tomatoes with a good tomato flavour.

green simply, underripe tomatoes.

paste triple-concentrated tomato puree used to flavour soups, stews, sauces and casseroles.

puree canned pureed tomatoes (not tomato paste); substitute with fresh peeled and pureed tomatoes.

semi-dried partially dried tomato pieces in olive oil; softer and juicier than sun-dried, these are not a preserve thus do not keep as long as sun-dried.

sun-dried tomato pieces that have been dried with salt; this dehydrates the tomato and concentrates the flavour. We use sun-dried tomatoes packaged in oil, unless otherwise specified. Also available in flavoured oil, such as chilli or herbs.

truss small vine-ripened tomatoes with vine still attached.

TOMATO SAUCE also known as ketchup or catsup; a flavoured condiment made from tomatoes, vinegar and spices.

TORTILLA thin, round unleavened bread originating in Mexico; can be made at home or purchased frozen, fresh or vacuum-packed. Wheat and corn flour varieties are available.

TREACLE thick, dark syrup not unlike molasses. *see golden syrup*

TURKISH BREAD also known as pide. Sold in long (about 45cm) flat loaves as well as individual rounds; made from wheat flour and sprinkled with black onion seeds. *see also page 487*

TURMERIC also known as kamin; is a rhizome related to galangal and ginger. Must be grated or pounded to release its somewhat acrid aroma and pungent flavour. Known for the golden colour it imparts, fresh turmeric can be substituted with the more commonly found dried powder.

V-SLICER *see page 348*

VANILLA

bean dried, long, thin pod from a tropical golden orchid grown in central and South America and Tahiti; the minuscule black seeds inside the bean are used to impart a luscious vanilla flavour in baking and desserts. Place a whole bean in a jar of sugar to make the vanilla sugar often called for in recipes; a bean can be used three or four times.

essence obtained from vanilla beans infused in alcohol and water.

extract obtained from vanilla beans infused in water; a non-alcoholic version of essence.

VEAL

osso buco another name butchers use for veal shin, usually cut into 3cm to 5cm thick slices and used in the famous Italian slow-cooked casserole of the same name.

rack row of small chops or cutlets.

scaloppine a piece of lean steak hammered with a meat mallet until almost see-through; should be cooked over high heat for as little time as possible.

schnitzel thinly sliced steak.

VERMOUTH a wine flavoured with a number of different herbs, mostly used as an aperitif and for cocktails.

VINEGAR

balsamic originally from Modena, Italy, there are now many balsamic vinegars on the market ranging in pungency and quality depending on how, and for how long, they have been aged. Quality can be determined up to a point by price; use the most expensive sparingly.

brown malt made from fermented malt and beech shavings.

cider made from fermented apples.

raspberry made from fresh raspberries steeped in a white wine vinegar.

red wine made from red wine.

rice a colourless vinegar made from fermented rice and flavoured with sugar and salt. Also known as seasoned rice vinegar; sherry can be substituted.

sherry natural vinegar aged in oak according to the traditional Spanish system; a mellow wine vinegar named for its colour.

white made from distilled grain alcohol.

white wine made from white wine.

WALNUTS as well as being a good source of fibre and healthy oils, nuts contain a range of vitamins, minerals and other beneficial plant components called phytochemicals. Each type of nut has a special make-up and walnuts contain the beneficial omega-3 fatty acids, which is terrific news for people who dislike the taste of fish.

WASABI also known as wasabe; an Asian horseradish used to make the pungent, green-coloured sauce traditionally served with Japanese raw fish dishes; sold in powdered or paste form.

WATER CHESTNUTS resemble true chestnuts in appearance, hence the English name. Small brown tubers with a crisp, white, nutty-tasting flesh. Their crunchy texture is best experienced fresh, however, canned water chestnuts are more easily obtained and can be kept for about a month in the fridge, once opened. Used, rinsed and drained, in salads and stir-fries.

WATERCRESS one of the cress family, a large group of peppery greens used raw in salads, dips and sandwiches, or cooked in soups. Highly perishable, so it must be used as soon as possible after purchase.

WHEAT BRAN *see bran*

WHITE RADISH *see daikon*

WHITE TEA *see page 424*

WHOLE-EGG MAYONNAISE commercial mayonnaise of high quality made with whole eggs and labelled as such; some prepared mayonnaises substitute emulsifiers such as food starch, cellulose gel or other thickeners to achieve the same thick and creamy consistency but never achieve the same rich flavour. Must be refrigerated once opened.

WILD RICE *see rice*

WINE the adage that you should never cook with wine you wouldn't drink holds true in this book; unless specified otherwise, we use good-quality dry white and red wines in our recipes.

WITLOF also known as belgian endive; related to and confused with chicory. A versatile vegetable, it tastes as good cooked as it does eaten raw. Grown in darkness like white asparagus to prevent it becoming green; looks somewhat like a tightly furled, cream to very light-green cigar. The leaves can be removed and used to hold a canapé filling; the whole vegetable can be opened up, stuffed then baked or casseroled; and the leaves can be tossed in a salad with other vegetables.

WOK *see page 232*

chan *see page 233*

deep-frying basket *see page 232*

draining rack *see page 232*

ladle *see page 232*

lid/cover *see page 233*

ring *see page 232*

wire mesh skimmer *see page 232*

WOMBOK also known as Chinese cabbage, peking or napa cabbage; elongated in shape with pale green, crinkly leaves, this is the most common cabbage in South East Asia, forming the basis of the pickled Korean condiment, kim chi. Can be shredded or chopped and eaten raw or braised, steamed or stir fried.

WONTON small parcels of a filling encased in a thin noodle or pastry wrapper then steamed or fried.

WONTON WRAPPERS and gow gee or spring roll pastry sheets, made of flour, egg and water, are found in the refrigerated or freezer section of Asian food shops and many supermarkets. These come in different thicknesses and shapes. Thin wrappers work best in soups, while the thicker ones are best for frying; and the choice of round or square, small or large is dependent on the recipe.

WORCESTERSHIRE SAUCE thin, dark-brown spicy sauce developed by the British when in India; used as a seasoning for meat, gravies and cocktails, and as a condiment.

YAKI-NORI *see nori*

YEAST (dried and fresh), a raising agent used in dough making. A microscopic living organism that grows best in warm, moist conditions; over-hot conditions or dissolving liquid will kill yeast and keep the dough from rising. Granular (7g sachets) and fresh compressed (20g blocks) yeast can almost always be substituted one for the other when yeast is called for.

YERBA MATE (TEA) *see page 424*

YOGURT we use plain full-cream yogurt in our recipes unless specifically noted otherwise. If a recipe in this book calls for low-fat yogurt, we use one with a fat content of less than 0.2 per cent.

ZA'ATAR a blend of whole roasted sesame seeds, sumac and crushed dried herbs such as wild marjoram and thyme, its content is largely determined by the individual maker. Used to flavour many familiar Middle Eastern dishes, pizza and savoury pastries; available in delicatessens and specialty food stores.

ZESTER *see page 140*

ZUCCHINI also known as courgette; small, pale- or dark-green, yellow or white vegetable belonging to the squash family. Good cored and stuffed with various meat or rice fillings; in Italian vegetable dishes and pasta sauces; and as one of the vegetables that make ratatouille. Harvested when young, its edible flowers can be stuffed with a mild cheese or other similarly delicate ingredients then deep-fried or oven-baked to make a delicious appetiser.

Index

A

General manager *Christine Whiston*
Editorial director *Susan Tomnay*
Creative director and designer *Hieu Chi Nguyen*
Senior editor *Stephanie Kistner*
Feature writers *Meg Thomason, Karen Hammial, Sarah Schwikkard*
Food director *Pamela Clark*
Food editor *Cathie Lonnie*
Nutritional information *Belinda Farlow*

Director of sales *Brian Cearnes*
Marketing manager *Bridget Cody*
Business analyst *Ashley Davies*
Operations manager *David Scotto*
International rights enquires *Laura Bamford*
lbamford@acpuk.com

ACP Books are published by ACP Magazines
a division of PBL Media Pty Limited
Group publisher, Women's lifestyle *Pat Ingram*
Director of sales, Women's lifestyle *Lynette Phillips*
Commercial manager, Women's lifestyle *Seymour Cohen*
Marketing director, Women's lifestyle *Matthew Dominello*
Public relations manager, Women's lifestyle *Hannah Deveraux*
Creative director, Events, Women's lifestyle *Luke Bonnano*
Research Director, Women's lifestyle *Justin Stone*
ACP Magazines, Chief Executive officer *Scott Lorson*
PBL Media, Chief Executive officer *Ian Law*

The publishers would like to thank the following for props used in
photography *Barbeques Galore; The Essential Ingredient; Leung
Tim Choppers Co.; Panasonic; Plenty Kitchen & Tableware; SMEG;
Sunbeam; Top 3 by Design.*

Photographers *Alan Benson, Steve Brown, Luke Burgess, Joshua
Dasey, Ben Dearnley, Louise Lister, Andre Martin, Rob Palmer,
Stuart Scott, Brett Stevens, Rob Taylor, John Paul Urizar,
Ian Wallace, Andrew Young, Tanya Zouev.*
Stylists *Wendy Berecry, Julz Beresford, Janelle Bloom, Margot
Braddon, Kate Brown, Marie-Helene Clauzon, Yael Grinham,
Jane Hann, Trish Heagerty, Amber Keller, Michaela le Compte,
Vicki Liley, David Morgan, Kate Murdoch, Sarah O'Brien, Louise
Pickford, Christine Rouka, Stephanie Souvlis.*

Chapter openers
Photographer *Louise Lister*
Stylist *Margot Braddon*

Special features
Photographer *John Bader*
Stylist *Vicki Liley*
Food preparation *Louise Patniotis*

Produced by ACP Books, Sydney. Published by ACP Books, a division of ACP Magazines Ltd.
54 Park St, Sydney NSW Australia 2000. GPO Box 4088, Sydney, NSW 2001.
Phone +61 2 9282 8618 Fax +61 2 9267 9438
acpbooks@acpmagazines.com.au www.acpbooks.com.au
Printed by C&C Offset Printing in China.

Australia Distributed by Network Services, GPO Box 4088, Sydney, NSW 2001.
Phone +61 2 9282 8777 Fax +61 2 9264 3278 networkweb@networkservicescompany.com.au
United Kingdom Distributed by Australian Consolidated Press (UK),
10 Scirocco Close, Moulton Park Office Village, Northampton, NN3 6AP.
Phone +44 1604 642 200 Fax +44 1604 642 300
books@acpuk.com www.acpuk.com
New Zealand Distributed by Netlink Distribution Company, ACP Media Centre, Cnr Fanshawe
and Beaumont Streets, Westhaven, Auckland. PO Box 47906, Ponsonby, Auckland, NZ.
Phone +64 9 366 9966 Fax 0800 277 412 ask@ndc.co.nz
South Africa Distributed by PSD Promotions, 30 Diesel Road Isando, Gauteng Johannesburg.
PO Box 1175, Isando 1600, Gauteng Johannesburg.
Phone +27 11 392 6065/6/7 Fax +27 11 392 6079/80 orders@psdprom.co.za

Clark, Pamela.
Kitchen: the Australian women's weekly.
Includes index.
ISBN 978-1-86396-709-9
1. Cookery. 2. Recipes.
I. Title. II. Title: Australian women's weekly.
641.5
© ACP Magazines Ltd 2007
ABN 18 053 273 546

To order books, phone 136 116 (within Australia).
Send recipe enquiries to: recipeenquiries@acpmagazines.com.au